☆ ☆ ☆ ☆ ☆ ☆ ☆ ☆

STRANDED
AT THE
DRIVE-IN

☆ ☆ ☆ ☆ ☆ ☆ ☆ ☆

By the same author

This is Uncool: The 500 Greatest Singles Since Punk and Disco
Fear of Music: The 261 Greatest Albums Since Punk and Disco
Popcorn: Fifty Years of Rock 'n' Roll Movies

☆ ☆ ☆ ☆ ☆ ☆ ☆ ☆

STRANDED AT THE DRIVE-IN

THE 100 BEST TEEN MOVIES

☆ ☆ ☆ ☆ ☆ ☆ ☆ ☆

Garry Mulholland

Copyright © Garry Mulholland 2011

The right of Garry Mulholland to be identified as the
author of this work has been asserted by him in accordance
with the Copyright, Designs and Patents Act 1988.

This edition first published in Great Britain in 2011 by
Orion Books
an imprint of the Orion Publishing Group Ltd
Orion House, 5 Upper St Martin's Lane,
London WC2H 9EA
An Hachette Livre UK Company

10 9 8 7 6 5 4 3 2 1

A CIP catalogue record for this book
is available from the British Library.

ISBN: 978 1 4091 2250 0

Typeset by Input Data Services Ltd, Bridgwater, Somerset

Printed and bound by CPI Group (UK) Ltd, Croydon CR0 4YY

The Orion Publishing Group's policy is to use papers
that are natural, renewable and recyclable and made
from wood grown in sustainable forests. The logging and
manufacturing processes are expected to conform to the
environmental regulations of the country of origin.

Every effort has been made to fulfil requirements with regard
to reproducing copyright material. The author and publisher
will be glad to rectify any omissions at the earliest opportunity.

www.orionbooks.co.uk

To Matt

CONTENTS

ACKNOWLEDGEMENTS

The main source of information for *Stranded At The Drive-In* – as well as the original source book from which I made my list of movies to watch and write about – is *The Radio Times Guide To Films*, published by BBC Worldwide. Updated annually, it's the epitome of the comprehensive and informed movie reference book.

As constant fact-check sources, the online resources at Wikipedia (wikipedia.org), All Movie Guide (allrovi.com), Entertainment Weekly: The 50 All-Time Best High School Movies (www.ew.com) and the Internet Movie Database (imdb.com) were invaluable.

Other books used for background on specific films, historical context or examples of how to interpret film were:

Seeing Is Believing – Peter Biskind (Bloomsbury)
Easy Riders Raging Bulls – Peter Biskind (Bloomsbury)
Down And Dirty Pictures – Peter Biskind (Bloomsbury)
Yipee Ki-Yay Moviegoer: Writings On Bruce Willis, Badass Cinema and Other Important Topics – Vern (Titan)
Scenes From A Revolution – Mark Harris (Canongate)
Rebels & Chicks: A History Of The Hollywood Teen Movie – Stephen Tropiano (Back Stage)
1001 Movies You Must See Before You Die – Edited by Steven Jay Schneider
Where The Girls Are – Susan J. Douglas (Times Books)
From Reverence To Rape: The Treatment Of Women In The Movies – Molly Haskell (Penguin)
The New Biographical Dictionary Of Film – David Thomson (Little Brown)

Thanks as always to Ian Preece. Ian has been the editor for all four of my books and deserves some kind of medal for patience and calm, as well as my heartfelt gratitude for keeping my writing on track and believing in me. Similar could be said of Julie Burchill, with the addition of friendship way above and beyond the call of duty.

As always, the biggest shout-out goes to my wife and best friend

Linsay McCulloch. Still a young savage after all these years. Finally
... I've dedicated this book to my son Matthew Stevens who, apart
from helping me write the *Footloose* entry, got me back in touch with
my adolescent self when he was being the coolest teenage son a guy
could hope for. Love ya, Kid.

If you have any comments or observations on, or corrections or
criticisms of *Stranded At The Drive-In*, you can reach the author at
garrymul@aol.com and at Twitter on @GarryMulholland.

INTRODUCTION

> *Stranded at the drive-in*
> *Branded a fool*
> *What will they say*
> *Monday at school?*

The above lyric, taken from the song 'Sandy' as sung by John Travolta in the film version of *Grease*, lends this book an appropriate title. Not only do we get a cinema reference, but a neat summing-up of a few of the key elements of teen fiction: thwarted romance, peer pressure, school, the quest for night-time pleasure, fear of humiliation.

Grease's perennial popularity lies in its inter-generational under-standing of the pain of being a teenager, and its ability to see those growing pains from both sides of the gender divide. The fact that the songs are catchy and the jokes are dirty and sweet doesn't hurt either. But *Grease* is just one of many films about being a teenager that resonate with future generations of movie audiences long after their initial release. So I figured it was high time someone took a long, hard look at the reasons why. Ergo *Stranded At The Drive-In*, an attempt to choose the 100 best teen movies since the 1950s and search out the meanings and messages that have made the teen movie the most vibrant sub-genre in modern film.

An outrageous claim? I don't think so. Here's a quick list of great movies of the last few years: *Juno*, *Twilight*, *Napoleon Dynamite*, *The Class*, *Superbad*, *Kidulthood*, *Donnie Darko*, *Teeth*, *Hard Candy* ... yep – all teen movies. Now let me have it with a list of recent non-teen movies that are as good as that bunch. *The Lives Of Others?* OK, I'll definitely give you that one. *Wal-E* and *Toy Story 3* and *Waltz With Bashir?* You're right ... works of genius. Anything else that *isn't* a cartoon? *Slumdog Millionaire?* Well, actually ... that would be a teen film *and* a cartoon to all intents and purposes. And not included in this book. But we'll get back to that later ...

The point I'm trying to make is that film – and especially Holly-wood film – is going through a moribund phase. The thrillers, dramas, action movies and adult comedies that make up the central seam of mainstream film seem to have been in perennial decline since the Golden Age of the '30s and '40s ... with a brief pick-up in the New Hollywood late '60s/early '70s. Horror and sci-fi have lost their souls to cynical gore and comic book CGI flash respectively. And while I obviously admire the sophisticated wit of, say, *Sideways* ... it's neither as funny, nor as universally relevant, nor as 'real' as *American Pie*.

The one topic that continues to provoke screenwriters and directors into their best work and persuades studios to fund innovation and substance over piledriver special effects overload is the infinite well of deep and difficult emotions that is Teenage. Sadly, the piece of classic screen fiction that forced me to really sit up and take notice of this phenomenon is something I can't write about in *Stranded At The Drive-In*. And that is, of course, the greatest television series ever made: *Buffy The Vampire Slayer*.

Joss Whedon's massively influential horror-comedy-soap about a 15-year-old girl (played by Sarah Michelle Gellar) who is forced to protect the world from a constantly encroaching horde of evil demons was given a total of 144 43-minute episodes to explore every dimension of its real subject – the agonies of a young girl's journey from 15-year-old *ingénue* to parentified 21-year-old woman. Every vampire, demon, beast, God and monster evoked over the series' six-year run was a metaphor for another facet of the nightmare of adolescence. Hell – the girl even died (twice!) to save the world, yet still endured her worst moments at the hands of three dashing but emotionally stunted boyfriends who either tried to kill her (Angel), smother her (Riley) or rape her (Spike) in their efforts to take away the power she acquires, not just as The Slayer, but as a woman. In the mythical Californian suburb of Sunnydale, the high school is literally built on top of the mouth of hell, and Whedon and his ridiculously talented cast and crew make merry with that universally understood metaphor until you understand that there is no possibility of freedom for Buffy and her equally charming and funny pals except razing the school to the ground. Again ... twice.

Some readers, at this point, will be doing the equivalent of thrusting one hand in the air and hissing, 'Miss! Miss!' under their breaths at the back of the class in their impatient attempts to point out that there *is* a *Buffy The Vampire Slayer* feature film. But, lest we forget,

Stranded At The Drive-In is an attempt to locate the 100 *best* teen movies – and the movie version of *Buffy* is an almost unwatchable dog. Indeed, it was the mess made of a brilliant idea that forced Joss Whedon to take it to television where he could keep tighter overall control of the project.

But enough about *Buffy* ... for now, at least. The point is that my love of the show led me to look at teen fiction in a completely different way, and to notice how many teen movies are based on very adult metaphors for very adult themes. The monster as male sexual predator. The school as symbol of repression and psychic imprisonment. The quest for sexual satisfaction as arm-wrestle between innocence and experience. The teen obsession with popularity as vacuous desire to conform. And, most powerfully perhaps, the adult's mourning of teenage friendships, when bonding with one's peers meant everything, before career, marriage, mortgage, kids and the very adult fear of appearing needy get in the way and reduce the intensity of our youthful friendships to dinner parties planned months in advance and cards swapped at Christmas. We all miss the spontaneity and passion of our teen friendships, but have no idea how to regain those bonds as adults. Many of the best teen films are driven by that sense of loss.

Yet, when most adults are asked whether they would go through their teenage years again if given the chance, we shudder involuntarily at the torments and embarrassments that never entirely leave us, and say never again. Another reason, perhaps, why good teen movies resonate far beyond the youth demographic they are generally aimed at. Adults get to relive both the infinite possibilities of youth, and the humiliations and terrors that come with those infinite possibilities, at something like a safe distance.

But one thing that I do think unites all good teen movies is that they make you remember what it was like to be young without leaving you too full of disappointment and regret at the dreams that you didn't follow. That's best left to talky adult dramas, Radiohead records and the whole middle-youth culture of resigned disappointment. And you're welcome to it, frankly.

Once Orion had very generously agreed to publish the latest indulgence of my cultural passions, I still found myself in need of another inspiration, aside from the movies themselves, concerning exactly how to write about things that are theoretically designed for people a third of my age. This is where I want to pause to thank a man called Vern.

My wife bought me one of Vern's books. It's called *Yipee Ki-Yay Moviegoer: Writings on Bruce Willis, Badass Cinema and Other Important Topics*. Vern has no surname and writes for the *Ain't It Cool News* website at www.aintitcool.com. He is an American fan of action movies and writes about them in a conversational, iconoclastic, wildly digressive and bloomin' hilarious style. Just as I was embarking upon *Stranded* and feeling a little intimidated and lost for words, reading *Yipee Ki-Yay* … reminded me what kind of anti-academic cultural criticism I love, and helped me relocate my own voice and stop feeling self-conscious about trying to match up to all those learned film critics that have gone before. So I feel I at least owe him a big-up and a book plug. *Yipee Ki-Yay Moviegoer: Writings on Bruce Willis, Badass Cinema and Other Important Topics* is published by Titan Books and it is very, very good indeed. Back to the matter in hand.

Before Marlon Brando wrapped himself in leather and mounted his boss hog in 1953, teenagers in films were children who just happened to be 13 or over, or adults that just happened to be under 20. *The Wild One* exists because 1950s America was more frightened of the juvenile delinquent – the enemy within – than it was of The Bomb, race riots, or reds under the bed. At exactly the same time as sensational headlines and learned studies about criminal kids became an American obsession, big business was identifying the newly affluent post-pubescent as the most significant new market to be exploited. Wild youth had money, and it needed its own dress codes, its own music … and its own movies. Every peer group wants to see itself and its preoccupations onscreen. And now that the labour of school-leavers was needed to help rebuild post-war economies, and middle-class college-goers were getting bigger allowances from their newly affluent and more indulgent parents, Hollywood had to respond to their spending power – and could do so while also exploiting the older generation's fear of spoiled and rampant youth. Producer Stanley Kramer, who had already made himself the new king of 'message movies' with the post-war angst of *The Men* (also starring Brando) and the thinly veiled anti-McCarthy western allegory *High Noon*, saw his cake-and-eat-it opportunity when he happened upon a short story called *The Cyclist's Raid* in a 1951 magazine. The tale of a takeover of a small town by a violent biker gang was based loosely on a real-life incident in 1947, when a Fourth Of July holiday in Holister, California was invaded by rioting leather boys. Perfect. For the kids, sexy rebels doing naughty stuff to petrified fuddy-duddies. For the adults, a salutary tale about what might happen if we don't give our kids the tough love and discipline they all secretly crave. All you needed to add was the hottest young actor of his generation, a leather jumpsuit, a jaunty peaked cap and a whole bunch of roaring motorbikes.

The Wild One is a film about the one thing that concerns a teenager more than anything. Nope, not sex. Nor 'rites of passage' nor 'coming of age' . . . none of us know that that's what we're experiencing until long after the fact. Not money, nor love, nor school, nor bad parents, nor rebellion against authority. Not even freedom. The one thing that defines teenage life more than any other one thing is . . . boredom. The fear of it. The battle against it. The drive to do anything, no matter how stupid or ill-advised, that will keep the hideous monster at bay. When a young person is bored, they have only two choices: get into trouble or give in and have nothing to do except *think*; about sex, coming of age, school, parents, money, rebellion, authority and the terrifying prospect of being an adult, and working for a living, and accepting responsibility. Add the 'too adult for toys, too childish to be trusted with beer' thing that defines tweenage, and every moment that a teenage head and body isn't fully occupied brings terror of the dark unknown that is our future, and of all the appalling things that have already happened to us but we refuse to acknowledge and deal with until we're ready for our midlife crisis. Boredom is the shadowy nemesis of all teenagers, no matter how good or easy their life appears on the surface. And *The Wild One* is about the sort of thing that post-war youth were increasingly driven to do to beat that shadowy nemesis down, at least for a short while.

So the teen movie began as an exploitation genre with two specific strands: the message movie made by esteemed directors on moderately large budgets and exemplified by *The Wild One*, *Rebel Without A Cause* and *The Blackboard Jungle*; and semi-ironic poverty row B-movie 'trash' in the shape of teen sci-fi (*The Blob*), horror (*I Was A Teenage Werewolf*), frothy romance with music (a hundred largely forgotten beach party movies and cutie-pie cautionary tales for girls like the Sandra Dee vehicle *Gidget*) and hysterical satirical sideswipes at adult fears of juvenile delinquency like *The Cool And The Crazy*, made by fly-by-night independent production companies like the legendary American International Pictures.

But the teenage phenomenon also came along at roughly the same time as film-making's equivalent of rock 'n' roll. The iconoclasts of the French and British versions of the 'New Wave' made movies that looked like real life and took teen angst seriously. Inspired by François Truffaut's accusatory borstal boy masterpiece *The 400 Blows*, a trail of Angry Young British Directors including Tony Richardson, Lindsay Anderson, Ken Loach, Mike Leigh and Alan Clarke set about inventing and establishing the anti-establishment teen docu-drama, a tradition which has continued and inspired a host of directors from around the globe.

But teen movies are inclined to reflect the mood of the times. So, while even the most bleak '60s teen movies seethed with the possibility of youth revolution, images of '70s adolescence reflected the disillusion and more hardened stances of failed revolutionaries and post-Watergate/Vietnam despair. Teen sci-fi movies like *A Clockwork Orange* and *A Boy And His Dog* didn't just present ultra-violent dystopias caused by nuclear war or totalitarian regimes, but seemed determined to take their anger out on women with almost manic levels of misogyny.

Which is probably why few noticed a modest but profitable game-changer from Canada, in which a gaggle of girls of various levels of sexual awareness are trapped in a house, stalked and murdered by an irrational psycho, leaving one Final Girl to survive against all the odds, which also featured a devilishly sequel-friendly open ending. *Black Christmas 2* never did get made, but the 1974 original invented the setting, style and rules of the teen slasher genre, which were further established by John Carpenter's *Halloween* (1978) and went on to such universal popularity that the most commercially successful teen slasher movie of all-time was essentially one long, self-referential piss-take of its endlessly repeated formulas (that would be 1996's *Scream*, of course).

The other '70s teen horror notable was *Carrie*, Brian De Palma's sub-Hitchcockian adaptation of Stephen King's debut novel, which now looks increasingly like one mad-as-hell-and-not-going-to-take-it-anymore girl taking symbolically menstrual revenge on the relentless misogyny of '70s Hollywood. But what it certainly did was establish a place in teen movies for young women to be central protagonist *and* scary monster, and dramatise specifically feminine kinds of teenage angst.

Meanwhile, 1972's *American Graffiti* was a giant hit on a tiny budget, identifying the perennial popularity of pre-'60s nostalgia, setting the tone for *Grease* and *Back To The Future*, and allowing its director to sell some fool his dodgy pitch about a semi-Oedipal space opera where one of the heroes is a bear and the pretty boy wants to shag his sister and kill his dad. I didn't see it but I'm sure it wasn't very good.

Teen movies were changed for ever by a bloke with a mullet from Michigan called John Hughes. The writer-director's much-loved run of 1984–7 teen comedy-dramas rewrote the rules of the genre by taking teen angst seriously while making light work of contemporary slang, fashion and music, and highlighting the hierarchies, status anxieties and class conflicts that made school feel like hell for its teen viewers. It was like the teen movie equivalent of political 'triangulation', whereby extremes are rendered redundant by a centre party that just co-opts all their most popular ideas. From this point on, the semi-ironic teen B-movie only worked in the horror genre, and even the slightest teen drama or comedy was expected to deal with some of the issues explored in all those bleak and angry docudramas. The by-product was Hughes's establishment of a set of teen archetypes – jock, mean girl, nerd, rebel, loner, outsider, bully – that continue to pervade every corner of teen fiction and strongly imply that the teenager's only real concern in life is popularity, which is a polite word for conformity.

But one teen genre that never died or truly wavered was the juvenile delinquent drama, which became increasingly played out through exploiting our fear of teenage gangsters. The stylised gangs of *The Warriors*, *The Outsiders* and *Rumble Fish* in the late 1970s, early 1980s gradually mutated into the fact-based *vérité* threat of the protagonists in *La Haine*, *City Of God* and *Kidulthood*; just the kind of feral kids in hoods who have recently become Public Enemy No. 1 in Britain. These movies tell you why far more convincingly than the agenda-ridden soundbites of political talking heads from either the Left or Right.

The teen movie finally came of age at 40, rather than 21. Young, smart, film-buff directors, who had all grown up with the Hughes movies and either adored or despised them, saw that their best way into film was to make low-budget movies about teenagers – because teens are the only audience that are 100 per cent guaranteed as they always want to escape their parents, either by going to the cinema or watching DVDs in their bedroom on the TVs or computers that all kids now owned.

When Richard Linklater's *Dazed And Confused* remixed *American Graffiti* for the grunge generation in 1993 it signalled the beginning of teen cinema's Imperial Phase, as 'indie' directors as eclectic and accomplished as Larry Clark, Wes Anderson, Alexander Payne, David O. Russell, Sophia Coppola, Kinji Fukasaku, Matthieu Kassovitz and Fernando Meirelles produced a series of complex, multi-dimensional teen dramas and comedies that treated teens – both on- and off-screen – like adults. If I knew the plural of *annus mirabilis* I'd apply it like gangbusters to the run of millennial teen classics in this book, beginning with 1998's *Pleasantville* through to 2002's *City Of God*.

But this doesn't mean that things have sharply declined since, in a period that includes the likes of *Juno, Superbad, The Class, Dogtooth* and *The Social Network*. Simply that the classics that transcend the teensploitation genre are not coming quite as thick and fast as they were ten years ago, as disappointments like *Kick Ass* and *Submarine* prove.

Another curious and long overdue thing happens to the teen movie around the turn of the century. A genre dominated by lead protagonists in the James Dean mould suddenly becomes, through the auspices of movies like *Election, The Virgin Suicides, Ginger Snaps, Bring It On* and *Ghost World*, a far more female-friendly place, populated not just by strong presences onscreen, but increasing numbers of female writers and directors.

So – let's get down to definitions. What, for the purposes of this book, is a 'teen movie'? Actually, it's pretty simple. It's a movie made about, or from the viewpoint of, protagonist(s) aged between 13 and 19, and where the story is set in the post-1950s period after teenage became a named and shamed phenomenon.

This, sadly, forces me to leave out spectacularly creepy Swedish vampire movie *Let The Right One In* and Penny Marshall's superb *Big* because the central male protagonists are actually supposed to be 12 years old. Guess that means that pre-pubescent sex is a pretty rich source of metaphor, too. But teen says teen, so 12-year-olds have got to go.

No place either for *The Graduate*, *Diner* or *Scott Pilgrim Vs The World*, because the protagonists, despite still experiencing growing pains, are in their early twenties. Rules is rules.

I've also left out films where the teens just happen to be the most interesting characters among a cast of all ages (there goes *The Addams Family*, *The Brady Bunch* and *Apt Pupil*) or where the fact that the main characters *might* be teenagers doesn't really make any difference to the main thrust of the movie (bye-bye *The Blair Witch Project*). A teen movie concerns itself with teenage life first and foremost, and takes its plot and explores its other themes from a teen perspective. I decided to concentrate on screen fiction, so no *Hoop Dreams* or other teen-orientated documentaries.

After that, it's all down to personal opinion – mine. Like my previous three books, the list presented to you here is a purely personal choice of what constitutes quality, irrespective of box-office figures or critical reputation. The wide variety of styles within teen movies reflects the equally wide variety of teen experience, and it's perfectly fitting that a book that wants to look at heavyweight critical faves like *The 400 Blows*, *If . . .* , *Rebel Without A Cause* and *Badlands* from a fresh perspective, also attempts to unpick the subtleties and nuances in presumed trash such as *Dirty Dancing*, *I Was A Teenage Werewolf*, *Bring It On* and *Final Destination*. The teen movie, like all the great film sub-genres, is a place where the high- and lowbrow talk to each other, across generations, and against the grain of received notions of good or bad taste.

Which brings me neatly to *Slumdog Millionaire*, and why one of the most popular and praised films of this weird generation is not in this book. It's a movie that seemingly depicts every adult Indian as a psycho Nazi and suggests that the only way to make that better is to escape it by winning a million pounds on *the game show that helped financed the film*. Oddly, the adults who celebrated *Slumdog . . .* as if it was some kind of feelgood political rebel movie are the very adults who love to portray teens as consumerist sheep blindly buying into the product placement culture of rap videos and *The X Factor*.

The excellence of the best recent teen flicks puts this kind of hypocrisy into perspective. Teen movies get better and better because each generation of kids is smarter, more culturally informed and less willing to accept being patronised than the last. Film-makers have constantly risen to that challenge and ensured that any list of great teen movies operates as a shadow list of the finest, funniest and most thought-provoking movies ever made.

Stranded At The Drive-In is an attempt to tell a part of that story, from Brando in 1953 to Pattinson in 2008, and with a couple of dozen proto-Buffys slyly emancipating young women in between. And if watching these 100 gems has told me anything, it's that teen movies are always concerned with power: the spending power of youth in the post-war years that invented the phenomenon of the teen; and the perennial struggle of these teen movie characters to exercise adult power in a world that insists that they are still children. The horror, comedy, drama, rebellion, sexual anticipation and panic that buoys these 100 movies often leaves their characters stranded, and feeling like fools. But we love them for it, because we felt exactly the same.

So invite the girls round, break out the pyjamas and popcorn, and let's bitch and braid each other's hair while we enjoy the best that screen teen fiction has to offer. But behave. 'Cos you know what they'll say, Monday at school.

1950s

THE WILD ONE

1953

Starring: Marlon Brando, Mary Murphy, Robert Keith, Lee Marvin
Dir.: László Benedek

Plot: Just wrap your legs 'round his velvet rims and strap your hands 'cross his engines.
Key line(s): *Girl*: **'Hey Johnny – what are you rebelling against?'**
Johnny: **'Whaddya got?'**

The biggest cheat in this book is Entry One. There's nothing in *The Wild One*, nor the literature surrounding it, to confirm or deny whether its young protagonists are teenagers, or not. It doesn't take place in a high school or a college or a readily recognisable teen milieu. Its lead actor was 29 by the time it was released, but this doesn't confirm things one way or the other because Hollywood was reluctant to use actual teens in teen roles until the 1980s. The actors playing the gangs and their girls all look well into their thirties, but largely act like children ... but if that was allowed to define the parameters of the teen movie then the entire *oeuvre* of Adam Sandler would have to be considered.

But *The Wild One* is here because it has to be. Its look, attitude, storyline and target audience, coupled with its commercial success and notoriety, is plainly the beginning of the teen movie as an identifiable sub-genre.

The plot is a neat example of tight, taut and slightly nuts screen-writing, as John Paxton manages to squeeze incident after incident into 75 minutes of screen-time, a soundstage that looks like its been left over from a B-western, and the passage of one day.

Johnny Strabler (Brando) leads his band of merry bikers The Black Rebels Motorcycle Club into a small Californian town that is playing host to a motorcycle race meet. After some perfunctory attempts to cause aimless chaos, they are faced down by the local police chief who orders them out of town. They leave – but not before stealing one of the trophies. It's only a trophy for second place, which serves as a neat metaphor throughout for Johnny's inability to get exactly what he wants, and his potential destiny as both fake winner and eternal loser.

The BRMC (or, as one of the minor gang members calls it, the 'Black Rebels Motor-sickle Club.' Sickle! Like Hammer and Sickle! This truly was communist subversion the whole time!) then ride into the even smaller town called Wrightsville which largely consists of one main drag. It has one café that serves as a saloon and one tiny hotel, and a bunch of fearful busybodies as a population, reinforcing the influences *The Wild One* takes from traditional westerns. But here, instead of talking authentic frontier gibberish, the rough types who invade the peaceful and boring Wrightsville discourse in thrilling mutant beatnik.

Jive Talk is always a good temporary boredom buster. The bartending goober gets the full bebop era gobbledegook assault from two of Johnny's gang, who slide gracefully into a scat-jazz rhythm that sounds suspiciously like that rock 'n' roll music various southerners were cooking up even as the movie was being shot.

The aforementioned goober Jim, played by 80-year-old William Vedder, is occasionally our narrator, speaking almost into camera and defining the terms of all coming rebellions. 'Where's he going anyway? Always going someplace . . . crazy . . . excited. Taking a lot of vitamin pills, drinking . . . over-stimulated!' Heh. *Vitamin pills.* 'I listen to the radio. Music, that is. The news is no good. It excites people.' And: 'Everything these days is pictures. Pictures and a lotta noise.' Yes it is . . . or soon will be. Jim is doomed, of course, for the crime of being the harbinger of doom.

Anyway, we're getting ahead of ourselves. The BRMC cause an accident. Johnny clocks pretty waitress Kathie (Murphy) and decides that there may be more interesting ways to beat the boredom. We also meet her father Harry Bleeker (Keith), the local police chief. He is one of the first and best examples of a key teen movie trope, The Weak Father, who, according to '50s movies like *Rebel Without A Cause* (see p. 28), is the cause of just as much youth carnage as an abusive or authoritarian Bad Dad.

Much art and literature of the 1950s is absorbed by a crisis of masculinity, brought about by a shortage of live and physically and mentally healthy men after the Second World War, and the need for women to enter the workplace during the war and their refusal to end their careers when men returned. So the constant theme in the first flurry of teen movies is the emasculated middle-aged father, who, being someone who probably avoided the war for one reason or another, believes in talking and being reasonable, rather than bullying his progeny into line. This – for Johnny in *The Wild One* and Jim Stark in *Rebel Without A Cause* – is an apocalyptic disaster, for these troubled but basically decent boys would have been happy and fully integrated future factory fodder if Daddy had just given 'em a swift backhander once in a while.

So, unlike the previous proper copper from the motorbike race, Harry can't bring himself to face down Johnny and throw the gang out of town. He quibbles and quakes and pleads with everybody to be reasonable. Bad move.

The barely kept peace is finally destroyed when The Beetles (yep, this is where they got their name), a BRMC splinter gang led by Lee Marvin's wonderfully unhinged Chino, join the fun. Is Chino, with his dirty, stripy shirt, beret-like hat, straggly beard and aviator goggles, supposed to represent the cowardly French? He even hollers, 'Storm The Bastille!' at one point, apropos of absolutely nothing. Director Benedek can't go as far as dressing Johnny in white and Chino in black, so he symbolises their respective potentials for redemption – their underlying characters – with personal hygiene. You can almost smell Lee Marvin when he oozes malevolently into the picture, and it ain't the fragrance of gardenias. Brando is, in the Miles Davis vernacular, as clean as a motherfucker – that is, he dresses well and looks like he washes regularly.

There's a Brando–Marvin fist-fight, much brilliant booze-driven revelry and flirting, a riot caused by Chino being thrown in jail, an ad hoc lynch-mob, a false rape accusation, one of the most sado-masochistic beatings in movie history, and an inevitable death-by-motorbike. When Johnny is arrested for manslaughter by a proper State copper, Kathie, her father and a remorseful lynch-mob leader get him off scot-free by telling the truth about the accidental death. Laconic, defiant Johnny refuses to thank his benefactors or learn a valuable lesson. But he does return to the town to give a delighted Kathie his stolen trophy, before riding off into the sunset – presumably to cause sex-and-violence-induced mayhem somewhere else. Or not. Whether the basic decency inside Johnny has been brought to his brooding surface by the day's events is left entirely up to the viewer.

But the prophecies of future teen rebellion play themselves out in iconic imagery and dialogue, rather than plot machinations. The hilarious mockumentary hypocrisy of the opening caption: 'This is a shocking story . . . a public challenge not to ever let it happen again.' Yeah, right. And as it fades, the delicious long-shot of motor-sickles riding right at you, one skidding skilfully inches away from camera. The even funnier, cheap-as-chips back projection of Brando heading the gang, leaning a little occasionally to try and convince us that he's not sitting on a stationary motorbike in a studio, but so utterly beautiful in peaked cap and shades. Throughout the film his lips are as obscene and indecent as Presley's would be two years later, a promise of freaky sex much more convincing than the graphic stuff he'd treat us to two decades on in *Last Tango In Paris*.

But *The Wild One is* a lurid, trashy melodrama; so much so that Brando appears to be laughing sourly at the whole thing from time to time. See Brando's camp, sighing 'Oh my' when stopping two biker underlings from taking the piss out of his newly beloved. The tale goes that Brando didn't want to do the movie at all, but felt he owed Stanley Kramer for making him the lead in his very first screen role as paralysed war vet Ken in *The Men*.

But back to that crazy beatnik jive, Daddio – still the only English patois that is even more entertaining than post-hip hop ebonics. And perfect for extemporising on the perennial theme of teenage boredom and adding urgency to courtship rituals, at one and the same time. Johnny: 'If you're gonna stay cool you've got to wail. You've got to put sumthin' down. You've got to make some jive. Don'tcha know what I'm talkin' about?' Um . . . nope, Marlon, not really. But I'm doing exactly what Kathie's doing – watching your mouth, fascinated, delighted. Kathie: 'My father was going to take me on a fishing trip to Canada once . . . We didn't go.' A perfect, deadpan Brando pause. 'Crazy', he mumbles, with repressed exasperation.

This is immediately followed by possibly the best-ever way of asking a girl to dance: 'Wanna struggle?' one of the BRMC cats asks a chick. That – so sharp, funny and politically charged – would've been the key line in any other movie.

But just a few minutes later, as the bikers revel in the bar, we get THE greatest two lines in this whole damn book, a sucker-punch-to-the-yarbles humdinger that has since come to encapsulate all forms of non-politicised rebellion. The possibly apocryphal story is that real-life biker gang members were hired as extras, and that one of the film crew asked one of them the question, and got the answer, and that Paxton and Benedek just hastily stole it. A beautiful accident, for sure. But would this line be so immortal if not delivered exactly as Brando dispatches it here?

It's delivered as a dry comic quip – and accepted as such as by the two characters that hear it. And the way that Brando pouts, camply, just before he delivers, shows as much contempt for the answer as it does for the question. One suspects that if any other of our male '50s teen stars had said the line – even James Dean – they would've oversold it, gone all deliberately wide-eyed and evil in an attempt to convey the threat of violent revolt. But Brando ... Man, Brando is *not interested* in rebellion. He's interested in nihilism. The idea that life has nothing at all to recommend it. The 'What have you got?', *not* the 'rebelling'. And the only sure way to convey true, black, futility is with ironic distance ... a conscious lack of interest in living. For one second, Brando *is* the greatest actor of all time. Because conveying a blank absence of ambition, love or future – The Abyss we all fear – and making it sexy, funny and inspiring enough to be one of the most quoted and admired lines in popular culture ... this – not rubbing your bald pate in Vietnam nor stuffing your mouth with cotton wool to sound Sicilian – is genius. When I watch this scene I feel 50-plus years of youthquake shoot from my head right through to my shaky knees, and can barely laugh to keep from crying. Everything great about the latter part of the 20th century and beyond begins with those two words spoken by this strange, curmudgeonly man. It's the entire 'destroy to create' imperative in two seconds of screen-time.

There are good reasons why the question has to be asked by a girl. Because when trouble starts, Kathie is advised by a man to 'go home and stay there'. This is what 1950s men wanted women to do, and this is exactly what Kathie doesn't do. She roams the streets, looking for Johnny, looking for trouble, looking for risk over safety. When Johnny threatens to slap her around, an entirely un-scared Kathie taunts him about his fear of women. She's the only person in the movie who isn't either shoved into violence or entirely intimidated by Johnny. The only trustworthy agent of control. And the only person, aside from Johnny, who makes individual decisions. Johnny's male gang are his bitches. Like most soldiers, they really would jump over a cliff if the man in charge told them to. The men of the town can only stand up to Johnny when they've organised themselves into a lynch-mob, accusing him of rape without bothering to give the girl herself a voice. Johnny aside, men are useless in this movie. And even he's a mumbling emotional cripple.

I'm not going to go so far as to call *The Wild One* a feminist movie. But the nihilism that swirls around it is created and sustained entirely by men, and its only leading female character is a non-conformist possessed of both courage and optimism. This *is* somewhat undercut, though, by The Bad Girl, who begs Johnny for sex (OK ... she doesn't say 'sex', but we get the picture if we get the picture) with such an ugly absence of dignity you suddenly see why the more misogynist strain of gay man saw something in the movie for them. And there's the sado-masochistic gleam in the eyes of the lynch-mob as they beat sexy Johnny to a bloody pulp. Can't forget that.

No, but really, some of the sexual imagery in *The Wild One* is outrageous. My favourite none-too-subtle hint is when Johnny finally asserts himself with Kathie, threatening to trash her bar if she doesn't stop 'needling' him. He makes the fateful decision not to leave town as he promised her father, sits down at the bar, grabs a beer, swigs, and bashes it down. Cut to the phallic bottle, gushing over with a fountain of white spray. It's a seminal moment.

Almost as good is the aftermath of Johnny and Kathy's long bike journey into the woods at night. When Kathy ... erm ... dismounts, fondly fondling Johnny's formerly throbbing engine, she wears the unmistakable, mussed but dreamily serene look of a girl who has just felt the Earth move. The biggest blow to the motorcycle manufacturing business came when the first woman sat on her tumble dryer.

Critics have always been sniffy about *The Wild One*, particularly in comparison to supposedly heavyweight early Brando flicks like the wildly overrated *On The Waterfront* and *A Streetcar Named Desire*. Here, Johnny ignores the bad girl and falls for the nice, homemaker type ... the civilising, emasculating influence. He is then dependent on her love to get him out of trouble. The biker riot – despite the intimations of potential rape – is about as scary as a Sunday School picnic. Johnny ain't no anarchist – he's just misunderstood! So retrospective reviews of *The Wild One* often write it off as typically sentimental, liberal Hollywood fudge. But you can't judge a pre-'60s American movie by its ending, any more than you can expect a Soviet-era director to have devoted his life to anti-communist movies. There was a code in place, and in the 1950s great movie people's careers were ended if they even got close to trespassing against the self-appointed guardians of American morals. If you wanted to say something interesting in Hollywood between 1934 and 1968, the years governed by the paranoid self-censorship of The Hays Code, then you went ahead and said it . . . but made damn sure that the plot – and particularly the ending – said something entirely opposite. As long as subversive characters either conformed or got their just desserts – prison sometimes, death mostly – you could give the people exactly what they wanted in the bits of the film that really mattered . . . the images and the dialogue.

But the ending of *The Wild One* has a few more dimensions than the surface would suggest. Because the key character – the one who represents what the target audience really feel – is obviously Kathie. We learn gradually, every time she speaks, that her attraction to Johnny is not down to the irresistible lure of the heathen he-man. He's simply a symbol of freedom. As she finally fingers the neighbourhood bullies who she's presumably expected to live the rest of her life with and protests Johnny's innocence, Kathy puts the film's real theme most eloquently. 'I wasn't trying to get away from him. I was trying to get away.'

The other key scene develops beautifully as a cop delivers the '50s cliché 'conform and be grateful' speech to Johnny as he deigns to let him go. In the majority of '50s delinquency movies, the Bad Boy dies or sees the error of his ways and pleads to be allowed into society. But Johnny is apparently unchanged by the liberal generosity of the cop and Kathie. He refuses to be grateful or conform. He won't even look at Kathy, not even when she talks about him like he's an errant dog. The potential humiliation of being patronised by an alliance of cops and sex object washes right over him.

He and the gang appear to leave, but Johnny does return. He still can't thank Kathy. And he sure as hell ain't asking her for dinner and a movie and suburban marriage. He gives her the bike trophy – which Lee Marvin's Chino slyly labels as a 'beautiful object, signifying absolutely nothing' – and smiles, and leaves for his wild, wild life, away from society. Because the beautiful object does signify something. It's a universally recognised symbol of achievement . . . and is therefore useless to somebody who still doesn't acknowledge the worth of society's approval. He leaves it and he leaves the girl who might civilise him. I reckon this is pretty cool for a movie made for a newly recognised audience in the most repressive years of the 20th century.

The Wild One gave a generation of youth who were finally becoming conscious of their own power – spending and otherwise – exactly what they wanted: sex, rebellion, and a celebration of violent action and rebels that boys wanted to be and girls wanted to fuck. Considering how quickly Brando's dress was adopted as the ultimate in universally identifiable gay male iconography, it's a crying shame that a generation of women didn't go on to a life of riding big motor-sickles and beating up Lee Marvin.

The rest of the pleasure is purely aesthetic – Leith Stevens's sleazy jazz score, pumped full of deliberate jungle juice. The gorgeous monochrome. Brando's clothes. The Triumph sickles. The queasy slant of the camera angle on Brando's face when the gangs signal riot with the ceremonial beeping of horns, as the world prepares to tip into chaos. It's a great-looking, great-sounding movie which can be taken as trash and laughed at, or just as easily seen as the film that invented the modern world. What I can say with certainty is that it's the film that invented this book and all who sail in it, and that's plenty good enough for me.

★ ★

THE BLACKBOARD JUNGLE

1955
Starring: Glenn Ford, Sidney Poitier, Vic Morrow
Dir.: Richard Brooks

Plot: The inner-city classroom as Theatre Of War.
Key line: 'Take it easy, Chief. He's crazy. He's high. He's floatin' on Sneaky Pete wine!'

Famously, this movie started a riot in a cinema in south London. The British teen was apparently such a hormonal explosion waiting to happen that, in a picture-house in rough old Elephant And Castle, an unruly horde of Teddy Boy types heard the opening blend of hep cat jazz drum solo and military tattoo segue into Bill Haley's 'Rock Around The Clock', and went bug-eyed mental, dancing frenziedly in the aisles and slashing the seats with flick-knives, the '50s juvenile delinquent equivalent of a mobile phone with Bluetooth. The same sort of thing reputedly happened in America and, once the controversy and hand-wringing had calmed down, a new genre was born. No self-respecting capitalist could turn down the kind of free publicity generated by teenage film.

I wonder if these crazy kids even bothered to look at the words of warning that roll across the screen at the outset of *The Blackboard Jungle*. To assure the censors and adults generally that the movie's makers had America's best interests at heart, the captions assure us that *The Blackboard Jungle* is 'concerned with juvenile delinquency' and performs a necessary social function because 'Public awareness is a first step towards a remedy.' For a few weird years in the 1950s, juvenile delinquency was an American obsession and rivalled communism as the No. 1 source of dread under the bed. Blame rock 'n' roll, or post-war affluence, or working mothers, or a decline in the practice of respecting your elders, but a series of lurid headlines and learned academic reports insisted that America's kids were out of control and coming for your daughters. In the end, it was the US military coming for your sons that gave this apparently causeless rebellion a sense of purpose and genuine anti-establishment threat.

But right now, in 1955, at New York's North Manual High School, those rough boys have something less noble on their minds.

In the opening scenes of this wonderful black and white orgy of hysteria, these thugs' idea of communicating with the laydees involves becoming literally animal – rattling and gurning through the bars of the school fence, topped off by much post-*The Wild One* (see p. 13) bottle play. Vic Morrow's Artie West, the villain of this piece, goes as far as holding the bottle of pop at his groin like a phallus before dispatching the foamy contents roughly in the direction of a sophisticated blonde.

This is one of the things I love most about pre-'60s movies. Nowadays, if a kid in a teen film – or a guy in a grown-up one, for that matter – pulled the bottle-as-cumming-penis gag, the character would know exactly what he was doing, and would shake it all about with knowing irony. In movies like *The Blackboard Jungle*, the male aggressor doesn't appear to know anything about symbolism. He is shoving his dick in our faces in deadly earnest, which is both scarier and funnier.

But as well as being a movie about juvenile delinquency, *The Blackboard Jungle* is also about male humiliation. Or, to be precise, the potential humiliations men suffer at the hands of a society that had changed radically since the Second World War. As we know, men risked their lives to fight fascism between 1939 and 1945 and, if they made it back whole, soon realised that no place had been found for them in civic life. Women had entered the job market while they were away and many had no intention of returning to domestic drudgery. The US economy needed to rebuild. So vets like Rick Dadier (Glenn Ford) found themselves pleading for work.

In the opening scenes we see that Dadier – who only seems to get this unlikely French name so the kids can call him Daddy-O – is among a large group of teachers looking for a job at Hooligan High. Most are men. When Dadier enters the office for his interview he is greeted by a cold, pompous, authoritarian Principal. This Dadier is nervous and cringing. It turns out that he earned his teaching degree at a girls' school that made a place for ex-military. His interviewer barks at him about his quiet voice and forces him to recite Shakespeare at top volume. Staff and rival interviewees smirk at the sound of his desperation. Dadier is being humiliated at every turn.

So *The Blackboard Jungle* is, on one major level, about an emasculated man who must quest to find his testicles. Instead of traversing across dangerous terrain, he has to locate his bollocks by taking on a bunch of children whose entire demeanour is a threat to the authority of the adult male. And he's not going to get any help. After getting the job, Dadier asks about 'the discipline problem'. He is brusquely and aggressively informed that it doesn't exist. Principal Halloran is King of Denial.

This school is a war. The Principal is the aloof general, cosseted away from the action. The teachers are the foot-soldiers on the frontline. The men, led by über-cynic Murdoch, immediately hit Dadier with war stories and call the school 'The garbage can of the educational system,' while making wisecracks about the sentences for statutory rape that would apparently be inevitable if they worked at a girls' school. The one female teacher who wanders into view is gawked at like a stripper on a building site. 'Uplifting' ending aside, *The Blackboard Jungle* is a bitter and angry movie that implies that the education of children can only be improved by an individual – a strong leader – who is prepared to meet violence with violence. And that men of any age are unable to control their primal desires when confronted with any female under the age of 40. We're not in William McKinley High any more, Toto.

But enough about Daddy-O and the wrinklies. This is a book about cinematic teens, right? And the best thing about *The Blackboard Jungle* is the best schoolroom bad boys this side of a *Daily Mail* editorial. Immaculate in their rockabilly rags, greasy of hair and sneery of lip, these multi-ethnic Bad Bwoys are exactly the juvenile delinquents you've always wanted to hang out with. They talk in high-pitched Beastie Boy whines and yelps. They read the *Racing News* at school assembly. They drive stolen wheels so fast that they knock parked cars a-rolling and a-tumbling into shop windows, 'cos being stationary is strictly Squaresville. And they snap their fingers and bebop to Bill Haley, all day and all night. OK, that last bit might get wearing after 15 minutes or so, but otherwise, this is the gang of your wildest rock 'n' roll dreams. What's more, the fantastic Morrow (who famously and tragically died in a stunt-gone-wrong on the set of *The Twilight Zone* movie in 1982) and his partners-in-grime actually look like boys you would prefer not to meet in an alley no matter what the lighting situation was, unlike your usual podgy whitebread '50s hood-from-Central Casting. Morrow's West, in particular, looks like he lives on speed and raw roadkill.

Poitier's Gregory Miller is from some other planet entirely. Luminously beautiful, he looms over teacher and pupil alike, dwarfing anyone else's attempts to attract viewer attention, no matter how wildly they overact. He is, of course, the redeemable Bad Lad. But it is still fascinating and bravely progressive that Brooks chose a young black actor to be the movie's pop idol and moral compass while much of America was still living under pre-civil rights apartheid. How the hell did he convince the studio to risk alienating half of *The Blackboard Jungle*'s potential audience? Or was everybody involved aware, perhaps prompted by the young's love of mutant rhythm 'n' blues, that racism was already the older generation's problem, and that the coming decade's politics, art and entertainment would sweep away the last vestiges of Klanism? I know – it's a lot to project onto a dumb old movie. But someone took the decision, and, although Poitier was already 27 years old and a veteran of six previous movies, it was his impact as Gregory Miller that set him on the road to being Hollywood's first black Best Actor Oscar winner (in 1963 for *Lilies Of The Field*) and, in 1967, America's No. 1 box office leading man.

We soon suss out the eternal triangle being drawn here. Dadier and West are locked in a battle for the souls of the class, who, like most humble infantry, are little more than easily led by the toughest tough guy in close proximity. But, in order to win, they have to win over Miller, who, apart from being the coolest and hand-somest – and, because he is black, the most authentic – dude in the theatre of war, is tough ... but reasonable. If he has been a bad boy up to now, it's not his fault. He's a strong and intelligent young man – which means he knows when to conform and when not to. Nope, he's a victim of society, poverty, bad environment and, until Daddy-O comes along, untrustworthy authority figures. It being the 1950s, the best role model for a misguided black boy is a white soldier.

But Daddy-O's blend of military experience and Psych 101 is a little too blatant at first. After the first fractious class meeting he pulls Miller aside, flatters him with a bunch of shuck and jive about being 'a natural born leader', and basically asks him to control the animals for him. Miller seems to agree. But nothing comes that easy.

By the time hierarchy and order are inevitably restored, we've had an attempted rape (including an awesome fight scene where the foiled teen rapist attempts to escape Daddy-O by diving headfirst through a window!), a neat exercise in civil disobedience as the boys deliberately get a blackboard exercise wrong, a kid who just grins who's creepier than all the scowlers combined, teachers sadistically clobbered in a back alley, the symbolic destruction of briefcases and swing-era record collections, a visit to a 'good' school where the kids appear to hail from Stepford, the constant backdrop of unbearable train and workshop noise, showing rather than telling us about the distractions and pressures of the big bad city, a racism debate featuring more 'niggers' and 'spics' than the average episode of Oz, Miller successfully finding that Dadier isn't quite the anti-racist crusader he wants to be, a violent truck-jacking, and West reasoning that jail time is better than the draft, his blank glare when the rest of the class are watching a cartoon Daddy-O brings into class proving that he's the kinda guy who even sees laughter as compromise, with his insistence that the real meaning of Jack And The Beanstalk is 'crime always pays'.

The tiresome sub-plot of Miss Hammond – a single woman of child-bearing age who doesn't seem eager to be a mom and therefore is A Monster – chucking herself at the completely asexual Glenn Ford does serve a plot purpose. Since Dadier has kept most of his cool even after a savage beating, it has to be something real bad to force the inevitable showdown with West. Writing notes and making calls about Daddy-O's alleged infidelity to his pregnant wife, until she gets so freaked out she gives birth prematurely and almost loses it ... that does the trick nicely. West finally forces Dadier to make their conflict physical, daring him to back down in front of the class. West is also happy to disobey Dadier's corporal Miller and break their uneasy alliance with his own racist abuse. Even the most enthusiastic teen rebel would, by this time, want grey, earnest Daddy-O to discover his inner animal and put West down. Miller makes the right choice, and, with the liberal tough guys now aligned, the rest of the class fall, somewhat pathetically but entertainingly, into line. The last bad guy gets overpowered by ... an American flag!!!

Does that mean West is some kind of symbol of communism? Erm ... no. It means that Brooks was kind of worried that all this bullish anti-racism might be construed as anti-Americanism by what was left of the McCarthyite witch hunters, and thought he'd pre-empt with hilariously overstated patriotism.

We close on Miller and Dadier agreeing a 'pact' that feels more like a political reconciling of black and white, of youth and manhood, than anything to do with teacher and pupil. You almost feel they should turn to camera, warmly shake hands, and walk into the White House. Instead, Brooks just gives the kids 'Rock Around The Clock' again. And very nice it is, too.

But my very favourite thing about *The Blackboard Jungle* is ... no matter how many times I watch it, I can't exactly tell whose side it's on. Brooks was seriously ingenious at the cake-and-eat-it attitude you needed to make funky films before the last vestiges of the paranoid Hays Code was finally swept away in the late '60s.

The scene that best exemplifies this is the one that features a familiar character ... the 1950s teen movie Therapy Cop. Therapy Cop has different cop names and is always played by a different actor. He sometimes takes the pure Freud route, and at others veers more towards cracker barrel sociology. But he's the same Therapy Cop, setting the audience straight every time.

This time he's an oldish feller in a detective hat and trench coat. He's supposed to be at the school to find out who beat up Daddy-O and poor wimpy teacher Josh Edwards, but is somewhat distracted by a desire to sum up ten years of weighty newspaper theories about the juvenile delinquency problem. 'They were five or six years old in the last war,' he drones. 'Father in the army, mother in a defence plant. No home life. No church life. No place to go. They formed street gangs ...'

This is obviously designed for the grown-ups in the cinema (or the critics who'll tell the parents what to think about the film), who want to know that little Janet and Johnny with their wild music and flipped-out hair aren't going to see a gratuitous orgy of teen violence. You could make these films, and even occasionally get mainstream affirmation, as long as they had A Message that reaffirmed the status quo.

But, as Therapy Cop drones on, we see Daddy-O's Class of 55 Flick-knives file past him, giving him a sidelong glance and sneering. Last of these, the only boy allowed to walk across the screen behind Therapy Cop, is Poitier's Miller, looking, literally, too cool for school. Every boy looks fucking brilliant, and you can't help suspecting that, while the parents nod contentedly at just how comforting it is that such wise older men will keep the heathens in line, Brooks is simultaneously saying to the teen viewers: I know. They really do talk bollocks, don't they? Let them think you're listening and I'll give you the altogether sexier future to look at. Deal?

This goes as far as something very weird, which I only noticed on this viewing. Dadier and Miller are at the garage where Miller works after school as a mechanic. He is explaining, in case we hadn't got it, that there is no point in a poor black boy taking school seriously, because he's 'coloured', and therefore barred from social mobility. He explains that he worked hard at first, 'but what's the use? Nobody gives a ...'

What you hear is the word 'hoot'. But it is slightly louder than the rest of the talk track. It's also doubled, almost comically, by the double hoot of a car-horn. But I swear you can hear the beginning of an 'F—' sound, and that Poitier is mouthing the word 'fuck'.

This couldn't have been in the original script, for obvious reasons. So . . . maybe Poitier got so into his part that he said the offending word, and Brooks decided to keep that take and drop in the hoots. But this is not an intense scene. Miller is being amiable and matter-of-fact as he lays down the facts of black life for his white mentor. It just doesn't add up that he'd need to curse to make the scene work. Was Brooks trying to give his teen audience a swear word subliminally?

One of the great pleasures of *The Blackboard Jungle* is unavoid-able. Its view of everything is so outdated that none of us hip modern things can resist the belly laughs. One of the ironies that became apparent while doing this book is that the terribly serious and 'concerned' likes of *The Blackboard Jungle* are generally more laugh-out-loud funny than the knowingly daft likes of *The Blob* (see p. 44). Like the bit where Dadier plies his pregnant wife with champagne (and how thrilled she is that she's getting ravioli, too!). The bit where Dadier is recounting the tale of a teacher's sexual assault to the missus and just gets a response that the teacher 'provoked it' by being too sexy, before she rejects female solidarity completely and gives him the third degree about whether he'd like to take Miss Hammond roughly up the refectory as well. Or the scene where the Principal accuses Daddy-O of being a racist . . . and then asks him to direct the school Christmas show! Or the well-meaning but misguided inverse racism of the scene where the black boys prove what fine men they are by singing a negro spiritual round the old Joanna.

Watching *The Blackboard Jungle* is like taking a holiday in the pre-enlightenment world that the brilliant *Mad Men* TV show mocks, at a point where it was still utterly convinced of its moral and ethical rectitude. As such, its overload of messages, subtexts, contradictions and unintentional laughs makes it a far richer text than the majority of the wiser, politically correct teen movies of later years. It's Tradio, Daddy-O, and all the better for it.

* *

REBEL WITHOUT A CAUSE

1956

Starring: James Dean, Natalie Wood, Sal Mineo, Jim Backus, Dennis Hopper
Dir.: Nicholas Ray

Plot: Beautiful, doomed boy transforms spoiled-brat teen angst into The Meaning Of Life, The Universe And Everything.
Key line: 'I don't know what to do any more. Except maybe die.'

If you were one of the millions of kids who went to see *Rebel Without A Cause* within the opening months of its release, you were paying your money to watch a dead man. Famously, just four weeks before James Dean's second starring role hit the streets, he died while speeding in a car, giving a face to the 'Too fast to live, too young to die' myths of the rock 'n' roll generation. He was just 24 years old. And because of this, it becomes impossible to judge how much of Dean's impact was down to his talent and charisma, and how much was down to the poignancy death lent to his work here. What we perhaps can venture is that Dean's shrugging, mumbling, slouching, swaggering, weeping and hysterical 'method' performance had the same impact on acting style as The Beatles and Dylan had upon rockers and doo-wop singers around seven years later. He made Hollywood's actors look ancient and ludicrously stagey with little more than the way he pulled up the collars of the many jackets that form crucial parts of this oddest of movies.

The iconic imagery forged by the partnership between Dean and legendary director Nicholas Ray is all laid out in the opening scene. As the credits roll over him, Dean's drunk Jim Stark falls to the floor in the middle of a deserted road and plays with a cymbal-clapping toy monkey. He grins at in delight, picks at it like a toddler torturing an insect, examines it like a scientist. He covers the toy with its wrapping paper like a pet – or a child – watching it lie there inanimate, as an enraptured parent watches their baby sleep. Not a word of dialogue nor a sniff of plot, yet we already know that this is a mannish boy caught between two warring impulses: the desire to stay a child and the yearning to be a father.

The new trend for psychotherapy was big in American popular culture in the mid '50s, and the psychobabble comes, thick, fast and early. The first action takes place in a police station which appears to be full of troubled teens. Judy (Wood) has been picked up for walking the streets at 1 a.m., the implication being that she's a teen *streetwalker*, rather than a child walking the streets. She's escaping from a father who thinks she's 'a dirty tramp' because she wears lipstick and therefore likes to manhandle and humiliate her in front of the rest of her family. But the nice-but-tough cop at the nick is a self-appointed shrink, listening to Judy's complaints about her Bad Dad with a gently furrowed brow, and suggesting ... nah, insisting ... that Judy walks the streets at night to attract Daddy's attention.

If this guy reacts to his daughter's affections by grabbing her roughly and violently rubbing the red from her lips I reckon he's paying her rather too much attention already. But I'm not a part of the police–teacher–social-worker–authority-figure consensus, so what the fuck would I know? In *Rebel*, the only people who are capable of fixing the most complex of messes are confident, wise, strong but ultimately good-hearted public servants, who are qualified to judge the uselessness of parents – that is, everybody who isn't a public servant – and entirely within their rights to intervene whenever they deem it appropriate. They are The System, and, in *Rebel*'s world, The System is a fine thing. So fine that, if these confused kids and rubbish parents had just stopped reacting emotionally and done what they were told from the off, the entire film would never have happened.

But within eight melodramatic, sourly funny and beautifully shot and acted minutes, we know all we need to know about exactly what's wrong with this picture. This bit of Los Angeles is full of gorgeous children who have been royally screwed up by ... Bad Dad.

Judy's dad is too domineering, but also, apparently, too distant. When the cop tells Judy that Mom is picking her up, the girl lets out a shriek of pure pain. Turns out the cop was right about that attention stuff. Whooda thunk it?

Meanwhile, Jim has the opposite problem. When his parents come to pick him up, all togged out for some function or other, we know poor old Pa Stark is a disaster. Memorably played by Jim Backus, in a thankless role where he has to be the quivering fall guy foil for a boy so gorgeous and talented he was changing the entire face of acting in every scene the pair shared, Jim's Dad's badness derives from being too weak to stand up to either Jim or stereotypical Mom. Jim mocks Dad for his clothes, Dad goes along with it, laughing, and gets a proto-Joe Pesci, 'You think I'm funny?' for his pains. The right thing, the thing that Jim craves, is for Dad to walk in, smack Jim around a bit, and then, presumably, smack Mom around just to be on the safe side. Men are so disappointing.

If you're thinking that *Rebel* inhabits a world where fathers can't win, well, award yourself a clapping-cymbal toy monkey, 'cos you've got it. At one point, Jim actually advocates the benefits of Dad punching Mom unconscious, an idea treated with gently amused agreement by Therapy Cop, who promptly starts a local self-help group where troubled couples can attend together and Dad can be encouraged to give Her Indoors the full pummelling she deserves in a safe, nurturing environment.

Nah, just kidding about that last part. But the Stark home is an especially enduring middle-class nightmare, where Dad talks entirely in Jolly Nice Chap homilies, Mom bullies him, and Gran bullies Mom in order to show Jim that she was a much better mother than her own daughter. It's a mother-in-law joke without a punchline, and you can start to see why they have to keep moving town because Jim rips apart other boys with his bare hands every time someone calls him 'chicken'.

So let's get this straight: *Rebel Without A Cause* is a massively dated melodrama where cops are better than parents, and where middle-class kids with all the advantages of money, status and education whinge constantly about how appalling their lives are because Daddy is too butch/not butch enough/both, using this an excuse to beat each other up. It advocates domestic violence and insists the world is being destroyed by the rise of strong women. It has a ludicrous orchestral soundtrack that screams every passing emotion at us like Celine Dion after being shown 24 hours of films about dead kittens. And it's entirely dominated by an over-acting stud-muffin whose obvious agenda is forcing every viewer to look at him and only him, all of the time. The only rational reaction to its overblown pretensions is so-bad-it's-good laughter, especially in the first cop shop scene when gay symbol Plato (Mineo) is cringing heroically under various chidings from a stereotype black mammy (who is still wearing her apron!), and another cop therapist asks him: 'So . . . do you have *any* idea why you shot those puppies?'

So . . . do we have *any* idea why *Rebel Without A Cause* is still one of the best teen movies ever?

Well, for a start . . . it does make some good points. Our parents do fuck us up . . . I think someone pointed out once that they do not mean to, but they do. Strong male role models are key and, although I think most of us have moved on from the idea that male strength is best represented by slapping the old ball and chain around, there are still too many absent fathers in the world, and many of them are absent even when their big fat arses are glued to the living-room sofa.

And, of course, teenage emotions are more melodramatic, pretentious and self-absorbed than either pre-adolescent or adult emotions, so *Rebel*'s hysteria and Dean's attention-grabbing is thematically immaculate. And, in essence, the cod therapy that *Rebel*'s authority figures bandy about with sanctimonious certainty is exactly the kind of half-formed shite that has forged a billion-dollar industry of quacks, gurus, self-help books and TV soap-Oprah, and that me and you spout to each other every single day when faced with anything too complicated to fix with money, a shag or an Elastoplast. So when we laugh at *Rebel* we laugh at what we've become and wonder if this wonderful movie was symptom or . . . ahem . . . cause.

And then there's the dialogue. *Rebel*'s kids – and Natalie Wood's Judy actually uses the term 'The Kids' – use this uniquely entertaining vernacular which is part beatnik post-jazz wiggerism, part sixth-form poetry, and part post-Sartre existentialist nitwittery. It is bloody marvellous. *Par exemple*, these edited highlights from the first exchange between Judy and Jim, as he tries to give her a lift to school in his flash motor.

Jim: Hi. I've seen you before.

Judy: Well. Stop the world.

Jim: You don't have to be unfriendly.

Judy: True. But life is crushing in on me.

Jim: Life can be beautiful . . . You live here, don't you?

Judy: Who lives?

Jim: I got my car. You wanna go with me?

Judy: I go with The Kids.

Jim: Yeah. I'll bet.

Judy: You know . . . I'll bet you're a real yo-yo.

Jim: I love you, too.

One Of The Kids (nodding at a departing Jim): What's that?

Judy: Oh – that's a new disease.

That's *a new disease*?! Man, I don't know about you. But looking at that written down almost makes me want to cry. When you've got James Dean and Natalie Wood actually bringing this stuff to sneery, sexy life, it damn near makes you melt into a muddy puddle.

And then there is the stunning run of iconic set-pieces. Toy Monkey and Cop Shop Therapy ('*YOU'RE TEARING ME APART!!!*') we've already mentioned. But the planetarium scene is visionary, with Jim's humiliating attempts to ingratiate himself with his new classmates, and he and Plato's gently homoerotic bonding given a magical realist feel by a man's voice poetically describing the stars, and the darkness, and the twinkling of the heavens, and the final, explosive flashes and roars of the Big Bang, presenting the suddenly freaked-out tough kids with an imminent future where 'we will disappear into the blackness of the space from which we came, destroyed, as we began, in a burst of gas and fire!', and where 'the problems of man seem trivial and naive indeed'. A tale of juvenile delinquents and petty complaints becomes transcendent, cosmic and bathed with a kind of luminous apocalyptic glow that never quite leaves the film.

This leads quickly – after a knife-fight between Jim and chief hood Buzz (Corey Allen) where a watching Observatory security guard would rather give us a meta-movie quip ('Look . . . there's your audience') than intervene – to *Rebel*'s most famous scene, the Chickie Run.

Neatly parodied in the likes of *Beat Girl* (see p. 66) and *Footloose* (see p. 251), the Chickie Run involves Jim and Buzz driving at high speed towards the edge of a cliff in stolen cars. First one to jump out is 'chicken'. We already know that 'chicken' has the same effect on Jim as the words 'cleaning woman' have on Steve Martin in *Dead Men Don't Wear Plaid*, so we suspect this won't go well. It does give Wood's Judy (currently Buzz's girl, inconveniently) the opportunity to be a kind of Master Of Ceremonies, bathing in the sexual thrill of men in danger, giving future orgasmic frenzy acting tips for Nancy Allen to pick up on 20 years later in *Carrie* (see p. 150). And shows off Ray's skill with action scenes, of course, in a display of fast edits and kill thrills that made *Rebel* teen film's first true work of art.

When Buzz inevitably gets his leather jacket snagged on the car door and cops it – bomber jackets do a lot of work here as symbols of doomed rebellion – his abandoned thugs get real mad at Jim's attempts to join The Machine by reporting it all to those nice Therapy Cops. So Jim, Judy and Plato end up on the run.

But the clincher is what Ray and co-writers Irving Shulman and Stewart Stern choose to do with the alienation of their three mis-understood heroes. Jim expresses to Therapy Cop his desperation to belong somewhere, and, in most teen movies, this usually means joining a gang or tribe, conforming, fitting in. But Jim, Judy and Plato can't fit in, no matter how hard they try. And besides, what they all crave is a family, not social acceptance . . . the extremity of their angst places them way beyond the current teen obsession with being 'popular'. And who can blame them, when the hoods are now so out of society's control that they become real criminals, invading the adult world by harassing Jim and Judy's hapless parents.

So, in a gorgeous, almost celestial abandoned Hollywood mansion that Plato takes them to, the three make their own nuclear family unit, with Jim as the strong, mumbly but attentive Dream Dad, Judy as the loose, non-judgemental Dream Mom and Plato as the damaged, needy, but affectionate child they all are, in reality.

I mean, these kids really are in need of some non-toxic examples of traditional parenting. Because, in my rush to get from planetarium to Chickie Run, I almost forgot the Freudian orgy that is Jim and Judy's typical evening at home.

In preparation for his meeting with a fast car and a sharp fall, Jim heads back to base. He reaches into the fridge and drinks milk from the bottle like this was, well, milk from somewhere else entirely. We hear a crash . . . and soon we see just how bad a Dad Mr Stark really is.

The crash was Mom's dinner tray hitting the floor. We now see El Castrato crawling around the floor trying to salvage the food . . . and he's wearing an apron! A frilly yellow apron! Over his suit!!! This big girl's blouse cooks food for his woman, instead of the other way round! Man, no wonder Jim has chicken issues. 'Mom?' a puzzled Jim enquires up the stairs, so confused about gender now that we almost expect to see Mrs Stark wearing a greasy wife-beater, scratching her balls and reading the racing pages. When Frilly Apron Dad can't tell Jim everything it means to be A Man in 30 seconds, Jim dons the macho Red Bomber Jacket Of Destiny and bolts for the Chickie Run, pausing only to steal cake.

This is small potatoes compared to the patriarchal minefield at Judy's place, though. She keeps kissing her very handsome and young-looking Dad. He's so freaked out by his inability to separate her love and her sexuality that he responds to a kiss with a right-hander. The man is so much more comfortable with her little baby brother . . . and you have some sympathy, frankly, 'cos something real unhealthy is going on with this girl. Can *you* imagine having a cute little girl, and then you come home one day . . . and she's Natalie Wood in a push-up bra, and she keeps sort of coming on to you? Plus your wife looks like your spinster aunt? Tough spot.

Still, he really doesn't handle it well. Judy runs away and cues up another big '50s theme, as Mom says, 'She'll outgrow it, Dear. It's just the age,' and little brother, wielding a ray gun, chips in: 'The atomic age!' You can see why everyone's so distracted from the emotional needs of their loved ones, what with the four horsemen of the apocalypse repeatedly shaking dust off their spurs and saddling up their gee-gees just over the not-too-distant horizon.

An apocalypse does indeed come. But not for everyone. When the hoods track down our trio of dreamers, and Plato produces a gun that he's stolen from his absent mother, Jim and Judy realise that he, like the hoods, is beyond the social pale. So when Plato hides in the Observatory and is besieged by coppers, Jim steps up and does The Machine's dirty work. He persuades Plato to let him look at the gun and then disarms it while Plato isn't looking, reinforcing the liberal consensus theme that dishonesty is entirely justified when it benefits the greater good . . . a stance that he rejects out of hand when his father suggests it, in a scene in the Stark home which Ray directs like a seasick voyeur and Dean acts with an intensity of feeling and need that completely obscures the fact that Jim Stark is, in essence, a complete fuckwit. ('You want to kill your own father!' Mom Stark screams as Jim chucks Dad around and chokes him. Duh! Please don't ask what he wants to do to you!) Inevitably, when Jim leads Plato out of the Observatory, Plato freaks and waves the empty gun around, provoking a volley of gunshots from cops who've got way beyond the therapeutic stage. He is wearing Jim's red bomber, so

Pop Stark thinks Jim's a goner. When he realises he isn't, both parents are so relieved that their damaged darling's OK that they immediately become what Jim wants them to be: authoritarian Dad and sub-missive Mom. 'You did everything a man could,' Dad Stark insists, as Jim regresses to babyhood ... 'Trust me.' Jim leaves the Red Jacket Of Rebellion with the dead weirdo. Everyone's so happy that the centre now holds that everyone forgets the dead weirdo. The outsider is only truly mourned by another outsider: his black nanny, the only black face in the entire movie, who is conspicuously not invited into the newly reborn white middle-class consensus. And ...

... And I really am making this sound despicable. It kind of is, politically, morally. But what a fantastic melodrama, lurid and confident enough to end the short period of teen film, and begin the never-ending genre of teen cinema. It makes opera and Greek tragedy out of the pettiest adolescent problems and social concerns of the day, and gives us an acting performance from Jimmy Dean that all male teen performances since have had to attempt to take on board and match up to. They come close sometimes. They never quite make it.

★ ★

I WAS A TEENAGE WEREWOLF

1957
Starring: Michael Landon, Yvonne Lime, Whit Bissell
Dir.: Gene Fowler Jr

Plot: Hairy moments from the days before anger management classes.
Key line: 'Hugo! Prepare the scopolamine!'

AIP favoured a hard-hitting style. And nowhere more than here, where, around ten seconds in, you get punched in the face.

Of all American International Pictures' teen exploitation films, *I Was A Teenage Werewolf* was the most profitable, influential and notorious. The movie grossed $2 million on a production budget of $82,000. It spawned three further '50s hit AIP movies – *I Was A Teenage Frankenstein*, *Blood Of Dracula* and *How To Make A Monster* –

which weren't strictly sequels, but used elements of the same daft plot and many of the same actors. It was remade (kind of) in 1985 as *Teen Wolf*, a terrible but popular film starring Michael J. Fox. Its trash title has been referenced in so many movies, books, records and TV shows that it's become part of the language of irony ... in fact, an alternative title mooted for *Clueless* (see p. 332) was *I Was A Teenage Teenager*, which someone thankfully concluded was irony gone mad. In the 21st century it's a film that almost everyone in the Western World has heard of but few have seen, and it isn't even available on DVD in Europe any more. This is a scandal. Because ... *Teenage Werewolf* is a teensploitation classic: funny, strange and more wiseass subversive each time you see it.

But first, a word about our sponsor. American International Pictures was a poverty row production company set up by movie salesman James H. Nicholson and brilliantly named lawyer Samuel Z. Arkoff. They aimed their movies squarely at teenage boys, producing a stream of flicks about beach parties, rock 'n' roll, aliens and monsters, and later branching out into Roger Corman's much-admired adaptations of Edgar Allan Poe novels and '60s hippy exploitation films, including *The Wild Angels* starring Peter Fonda and *The Trip* starring Jack Nicholson.

The garish titles of AIP movies were key to Nicholson and Arkoff's business plan. Rather than buy or commission scripts, they would raise the money to make a film on the basis of nothing but the title ... exploitation at its purest. Shoving together the buzzword 'teenage' and a popular movie monster was a perfect money-raiser in the 1950s. But the story that co-writers Herman Cohen and Aben Kandel wove around the concept was both insane and ingenious.

Michael Landon – who went on to a hugely successful TV career playing leads in western perennial *Bonanza* and period weepie *The Little House On The Prairie* – is Tony Rivers, a teenage rebel with a violent temper. After yet another fight at (here comes another perfect name) Rockdale High School, he is persuaded to go into therapy. Problem is, our shrink Dr Brandon (Bissell) is actually a mad scientist in the Dr Frankenstein mode, who wants to use troubled kids to prove his crackpot theory that Man can only be saved from Armageddon by reverting to a pre-evolutionary state. He hypnotises Tony, and it turns out that Darwin was lying after all, because pre-evolutionary man was, you know, a werewolf.

When Tony kills a couple of fellow teens he returns to Dr Brandon to get cured. Instead, the doc turns him back into a werewolf. Mayhem ensues and, as transgressors in AIP movies were always harshly punished, it doesn't end well for Tony *or* the evil scientist.

The reasons why this preposterous scenario works here are entirely down to director Fowler and stars Landon and Bissell, who instinctively understand that the only way to make something stupid stick is to play it straight.

The central idea is simple; adults are so bewildered by teenage behaviour that they refer to adolescents as monsters ... so what if they actually were? While the script plays fast and loose with contemporary obsessions – juvenile delinquency, therapy, fear of The Bomb, crazy beat music – Fowler shoots the movie in a gritty monochrome, throwing in expressionist angles and great gimmicks like the punch into the camera. And Landon plays Tony with genuine pathos and rage, and creates one of the big screen's most sympathetic (and cute) victims of anger issues.

In the opening fight scene we see that Tony is a lousy and dirty fighter, at one point wielding a shovel that could easily kill his opponent. When the cops – who obviously favour a 'Why can't we all just get along?' approach to law enforcement – break it up and begin a dialogue, we realise that Tony is nuts, too, starting the fight because the other guy – a friend – slapped him on the shoulder. 'I don't like to be touched!' Tony rages, weirdly. Detective Donovan (Barney Phillips) decides to be the Therapy Cop to end all Therapy Cops, suggesting that Tony go see a radical modern doctor who hypnotises bad kids until they're fit to be a part of society. As Tony's surprisingly not-Bad Dad says, 'Sometimes you just have to do things the way people want 'em done. That way they're happy and they leave you alone.' It's a steal from *Rebel Without A Cause* (see p. 28) ... Jim Stark's emasculated father says something similar. But here, from an older man who seems entirely masculine, it seems even more depressing, and exactly what any self-respecting teenager doesn't want to hear. This little scene in the Rivers' home is packed full of info: Mom is absent, Dad is always out working but is loving enough to prepare Tony's food the way he likes it before he leaves ... and Tony already has the peculiar habit of eating raw hamburger. *Teenage Werewolf* is full of little winks at its audience, rejecting the sledgehammer moral approach of movies like *Rebel* and *Blackboard Jungle*, treating the teen viewer as a smart friend who is far too slick to be manipulated by condescending adults. And the scene also tells us that whatever is ailing Tony isn't, for once, the fault of the parent.

The dance party scene is rich with top dance action, crazy jive talk, a bongo-playing teen crooner who has a real gone fusion of rock and jazz going on, and an incredibly keen appreciation of who the audience are. One young couple have a good old sneer at adult-approved entertainment, and, in tribute to all the boys who've taken their girl to the drive-in hoping to take advantage of the scary bits, the big party laughs are provided by Halloween-style pranks played by the boys on the girls, who scream with pleasure. But Tony ruins it all by responding to one prank with those uncontrollable fists of fury. He accidentally knocks his simpering blonde girlfriend Arlene (Lime) to the ground, and hangs his head in shame as all the other kids at the party glare at him in mute disapproval. Suddenly, we're accompanying Tony to the evil shrink's surgery. Because Tony is, again, a typical teen: the cop can't make him do anything. Neither can his Dad or Arlene's parents. Arlene herself got short shrift when she sided with Therapy Cop. But peer pressure . . . that'll do it.

Dr Brandon unveils his evil plan, and even encourages poor Tony to see his drug-induced hypno experience as 'a trip'. By the time we get to Tony's first onscreen transformation into a hairy head in a jock jacket – cheap, cheerful, wonderful – he is being praised for improved conduct at school. But those primal urges are all man . . . his second victim is a girl being lithe and gymnastic in the school sports hall.

The scenes of Landon running around the woods in wolfie head make-up are hilarious. And, as with all good trash movies, you can't tell whether it's deliberate comedy or accidental ineptitude. But everything else is played resolutely straight, with Malcolm Atterbury, as Tony's Dad, especially heart-rending as the helpless father, wondering if he should have remarried after Tony's Mom died (or left – it's not made entirely plain), as if lack of mother love routinely leads to young men growing fangs and baying at the moon.

I Was A Teenage Werewolf has a message, and, as was the tradition in AIP pictures, it's delivered to us through the film's last line of dialogue: 'It is not for man to interfere in the ways of God.' Critics have attempted to interpret the film as a repudiation of science, and The Big Society of 1950s America. I personally read it as a big, dumb bunch of meaningless hokum which becomes subversive entertainment precisely because of its sneering contempt for '50s message movies. It's a satire at the expense of the three movies we've already looked at, and was a huge hit because these new teenage creatures were already smart enough to get the joke.

★ ★

THE COOL AND THE CRAZY

1958
Starring: Scott Marlowe, Richard Bakalyan, Dick Jones, Gigi Perreau
Dir.: William Witney

Plot: The teenage *Reefer Madness*.
Key line: 'Quit the clowning. I need some more M. I need some more M now!'

The beautiful opening image: a camera simply placed on the grass of a school playing-field, and an in-your-face shot of a teenage girl ... tying her shoelaces. In 1950s teensploitation classics, you can often feel this joyful mutual pact between director and target audience; a sense of amazement that the styles and settings of '50s teen life are actually up there on the big screen. The shot is quick; it doesn't linger and there's no leering at the girl in question. It isn't about sex. It's a shot that says, 'Here *you* are. And we, the grateful adults who are allowed to tell your stories, are looking *up* at you, as we put you on the pedestal you deserve.'

As the standard big-band sleaze-jazz blares away, promising cheap thrills like a plump stripper in a burlesque show, we find ourselves following a hot curly-headed boy who actually looks something close to teenage. The *Radio Times Guide To Film* describes Scott Marlowe as a 'James Dean wannabe', and that sums it up neatly, as his doomed Bennie Saul character slouches, leers and twitches constantly in a mesmerising attempt to bring The Method to *The Cool And The Crazy*'s reefer madness. Sadly, Marlowe never got to die tragically and iconically after a couple of movies, nor play Evil Buddha in Coppola war movies, nor found his own successful range of spaghetti sauces. But he is truly fabulous here as the sexy but doomed drug dealer. Can't act, exactly. But when you have this whole piercing eyes/curly hair/cat-like swagger thing going on, thespian short-comings are moot. He's a great smug, sexy, psycho punk. And the film suffers a little every time he's not on screen.

When we first meet Bennie, in a post-*Blackboard Jungle*, JD-disrupted classroom scenario, we immediately understand that he is cool, but imagine he might get over the crazy and be redeemed. Then we remember that this is an AIP picture (see *I Was A Teenage Werewolf*, p. 35) where the lead kid is exactly the same as a AIP sci-fi alien and therefore never gets a chance at a happy ending.

Bennie is the New Kid In School at a campus somewhere in America. Don't ask me where ... sometimes it looks like a leafy middle-class suburb. Other times it resembles South Central LA if all the black people were moved to Beverly Hills. When Bennie takes a beating from the greasy class Bad Boys, and then pulls a knife, yet still wants to be their friend, it all seems a bit weird. It turns out that he's an enthusiastic apprentice for the neighbourhood dope-peddling Mr Big, who lives in a seedy hotel, smokes cigars and never smiles. When Bennie suddenly beats up head Bad Boy Stu, and therefore becomes Head Of The Pride, he then feeds the boys evil, evil dope: you know ... grass, Mary Jane, spliff, Ganja ... seen, Dread? One puff and the entire gang are Jonesing like crack ho's in a hip hop flick, suddenly acquiring shooters and planning stick-ups to feed the habit they got, erm, two days ago. From there, the plot becomes utterly ridiculous. All you need to know is that enthusiastic B-movie actors do an hour's-worth of barely feasible stuff, and it ends with an exploding car and a cop insisting that we all learn a valuable lesson before dramatically chucking away his strictly non-jazz cigarette. Forget all that mimsy shit about how weed leads to harder stuff. The truth is that marijuana itself is so addictive and brain-addling that if you let your kids even look at a joint they won't live long enough to discover the good things in life ... like, for example, smack, angel dust and amphetamine sulphate.

But part of the pleasure in watching inspired trash like *The Cool And The Crazy* lies in the sheer unpredictability of hastily contrived plot. In the first five minutes, you think you're in a classroom-based drama about the reform school bad boy who may or not be redeemed by/get off with the strait-laced, authoritarian teacher. Then, when Bennie gets slapped around in the playground by Stu, it could turn out to be a drama about a misunderstood victim of bullying. Then a hard-bitten LA *noir*. Then a *Wild One*-style orgy of teen jukebox coffee-bar riot shenanigans. Then, when gang clown and human punchbag Jackie falls for good-girl Amy, a dull-bird-tames-the-savages romance. You wouldn't be entirely surprised if a Bacofoil alien suddenly arrived to introduce The Kids to Venusian acid.

Parents barely exist here and the only adulthood that truly engages with these kids are cops, and that engagement's limited to threatening 'em with severe beatings and death by poisoning. Amy's parents are really calm and liberal though, not even batting an eyelid when their little darling tells them she brought home Jackie, aka Dick Bakalyan, who has a face so unlovable that he's spent the rest of his life playing loser thugs on TV and in B pictures. So the real message is there somewhere ... if parents just scrubbed up nicely and then let teens do pretty much what they liked, they wouldn't get into drugs, fighting and Brylcreem. Shagging funny-looking boys *is* just a phase we all go through. So I hear.

The heathen working classes seem to be the problem here in Crazyville. When Jackie visits Amy, he's blown away by how clean her house is. He tells colourful lies to make his failures and unemployed Dad seem more interesting. He assumes that this nice girl's parents will despise him on sight, so makes a bolt for it when he hears them coming. He's ashamed about being a boy from the wrong side of the tracks ... if Crazyville has tracks. Or trains. It's difficult to tell. *The next day* he's going to church with the prospective in-laws and wearing tank tops. Suggestible boy.

But then, so is Bennie, in a different sort of way. Bennie's real problems are not class crisis nor his moral choices about making money. First, his Dad is a broke, bone-idle drunk who can barely stand up, and definitely not to his own son. 'I'm a product of a complex society,' a smirking Bennie says to teacher early doors, signalling how quickly teens had become self-conscious about their perceived neuroses after all those headlines and government reports about juvenile delinquency, not to mention the birth of therapy culture.

But Bennie's big mistake is that he's getting high on his own supply ... always a disaster for drug dealers in Movie World. The boy's so spaced that he thinks a car's headlights are two motorcycle cops, and tries to drive right in between 'em. That might be the big clue to his downfall right there, I reckon. Every time he says he knows the score the audience are increasingly aware that he doesn't, and that his inevitable punishment for hubris and stoner-dom is going to be as out of proportion as the gang's reaction to a quick toke.

It would be fascinating, though, to know how many kids who went to see *The Cool And The Crazy* at the time actually knew anything about dope, and knew that they were being lied to. How many took the film's apocalyptic warnings seriously and how many knew enough to react to the gang's instant bad trip traumas as the comedy we all see it as today? Perhaps the oddest scene in the movie comes when the thuggish Stu and his hapless school gang ask Bennie to do 'something big' to serve as a sort of gang initiation. What Bennie chooses to do is drive to the nearest police station and sort of ... flounce around. That really is the only way to describe it. He does that round-shouldered stagger-slouch thing that young post-Dean actors did, switches genders on his back-story for no good reason (Dad's dead, Mom's an alcoholic), vaguely tempts the cops to arrest him ... and then leaves. It's obviously a shoddy tribute to the cop shop scenes in *Rebel Without A Cause* (see p. 28), but with so little point or aim that it actually does look like the most surreal thing that cool, crazy Bennie could've done to impress a bunch of tools. 'Hey Lieutenant! Another delinquent,' the desk sergeant calls, jadedly. They're all too used to being flounced at by pretty boys in ... erm ... wherever the fuck this place is.

One thing I am curious about is why, if AIP wanted to aggressively exploit teens, their '50s movies resolutely refused to acknowledge the existence of the Hot New Thing that teens were most obsessed with *en masse*. Even the band in *The Cool And The Crazy*'s obligatory dance hall scene is a proper jazz group ... black guys in black suits, playing horns. Three theories. One – AIP's teen movies needed to get the right ratings with a minimum of fuss, and rock 'n' roll was still too controversial, especially in the wake of the seat-slashing riots that had apparently been inspired by Bill Haley songs in *Blackboard Jungle* (see p. 20) and *Rock Around The Clock*. Or, two – many of AIP's juvenile leads favoured clothes and language that derived from beatniks rather than rockers, so a jazz soundtrack was their movies' one stab at authenticity. Or – and I think three is most likely – Arkoff,

Nicholson and co. just hated rock 'n' roll and, like most adults of the 1950s, saw it as a white trash fad that would eventually be crushed by proper cutting-edge music … that is, jazz, which the collegiate middle classes had a big old wigger Jones for. Whichever way, the theme song played for the jiving kids at the disco has just enough rhythm 'n' blues in it to qualify as jump-jive, which is almost, kind of, rock 'n' roll.

Once reefer madness sets in at the disco, it's Stu, played by Dickie Jones, who gets all the fun stuff to do … chain-smoking, sweats, stealing a bus-stop and thinking it's a girl, falling acrobatically down stairs, ranting like a looney fella and stoving his friend's head in with said bus-stop. This is some Grade A shit, Homes.

As I mentioned in the entry for *I Was A Teenage Werewolf* (see p. 35), Arkoff and Nicholson discovered superstars, including Jack Nicholson, Peter Fonda and Roger Corman. But most of their directors were probably like William Witney; no great *auteur*'s vision, perhaps, but a really stylish shot-maker. You recall the opening shot of the teen tying her shoes? Girls' legs are obviously Witney's pet metaphor. At one point we cut to nasty Mr Big's hotel room – the real villain in an AIP teen movie is always an adult – and again, we're at a dramatically low angle, staring, from the floor, up at a woman's perfect legs, dangling from a bed, skirt pulled up to the thigh. The angles are almost identical, and we immediately contrast the innocence of the opening leg shot with the seaminess of the gangster's girl's legs, when taken in tandem with the right on-cue hoochie music. The girl has no face, just one of those gangster's moll voices, dismissing Mr Big's concerns about kids getting 'into the needle'. Innocence and experience expertly contrasted, and, with mean old Mr Big hovering behind the woman's legs, experience manages to be both sexier and uglier at one and the same time. As coded messages to kids go, it's one of the truer ones.

The key scene comes towards the end, when Bennie stands up in class, and with great linguistic *élan*, defines the 'subjunctive mood' our freaked-out teacher seems obsessed with … an obsession shared, oddly, by the teacher in the far weightier *The 400 Blows* (see p. 47) a year later. Bennie, you see, is possibly a genius. But no one at home has focused that intelligence into anything worthwhile, so … all is gangsters, 'M' and a literal trip to the fires of hell.

Crazyville may not be a recognisable American town, but it does have a real feel … one of confusion and chaos and a great deal of beauty, particularly in its period cars and bleached monochrome look. *The Cool And The Crazy* cost less to make than an Iggy Pop insurance ad and is one of the best, funniest and strangest examples of no-budget film-making you'll ever see. Just don't smoke while you watch it. You'll burn the sofa.

★ ★

THE BLOB

1958

Starring: Steven McQueen, Aneta Corseaut, Earl Rowe
Dir.: Irvin S. Yeaworth Jr

**Plot: Teens save the world from amorphous mass hysteria.
Key line: 'It's the most horrible thing I've ever seen in my life!'**

This may be the only movie in this book where the best thing is the theme song.

So, imagine a less raucous version of 'Tequila' by The Champs. Acoustic guitar, cheesy sax, MOR male harmonies, over a discreet Latin rhythm with a built-in cha-cha-cha. As the opening credits roll – decorated by nothing more than a pulsating confusion of vaguely circular red lines – the wordless harmonies finally coalesce into a song. It goes:

> Beware of The Blob it creeps
> And leaps
> And glides
> And slides across the floor
> Right through
> The door
> And all across the floor
> A splotch
> A blotch
> Be careful of The Blob . . . .
> BEWARE OF THE BLOB!

This masterpiece of kitsch was written by Mack David and none other than Burt Bacharach. I doubt if it rates as a proud moment for the foremost easy-pop composer of his day. But I'll take it over 'Raindrops Keep Fallin' On My Head' or that tragically pretentious album he made with Elvis Costello because it makes me happy. And it sets the perfect tone for the teen sci-fi B-movie that proves that cheapo '50s exploitation gems were knowingly funny, rather than unwittingly so.

And yes, Steven McQueen is Steve McQueen. His first leading man role ran simultaneously to hit US TV show *Wanted: Dead Or Alive*, a bounty hunter western series which allegedly had more impact upon his journey to becoming America's favourite leading man than this lurid mass of wobbly horror. I dunno. I'm thinking that any Hollywood producer who watched McQueen navigate this hokum with dignity and some degree of method naturalism intact would figure that the guy's a star. McQueen rejected a percentage deal and went for $3,000 upfront, figuring that something this stupid was bound to bomb. It made $4 million.

The Blob's premise is direct and to the point. A small town called Phoenixville in Pennsylvania is invaded by aliens. Or maybe alien singular, it's hard to tell. Because this hostile visitor is an amorphous mass of goo that must be jelly 'cos jam don't shake like that. It doesn't do too much leaping (unless you count the jerk-edit special effects), but it's very good at sliding across the floor, killing puny humans by absorbing them. Steve McQueen is Steve is the boy who leads a group of teens who foil its evil plan to turn Earth into a giant trifle.

Like all '50s teen movies, it has A Message designed to tell its target audience what it wanted to hear. The adults of Phoenixville, including cops and doctors who can usually be relied upon to make The System run smoothly and tend to the needs and desires of dumbass civilians, don't believe The Kids when they tell 'em that a killer mousse is on the loose. They think that all teens are juvenile delinquents, and are therefore fucking with the townsfolk for kicks and shit. And the fact that *The Blob* cleans up after itself doesn't help.

But The Kids are right and The System is wrong. So wouldn't the world be a better place if adults stopped labelling kids juvies (or hooligans or hoodies or chavs or gangstas) and just *listened* to them, because we believe the children are our future and they could maybe save us all from bad stuff like The Bomb and The Commies, if we only gave 'em a chance. How very '60s. Indeed, the the-older-they-are-the-dumber-they-be theme is punched home from the very get-go, when The Blob's first victim and incubator of Blobular destruction is an old man who decides that the best way to examine a meteor-type object that fell from the Heavens and emits weird noises is to poke it with a big stick. By the end of the movie, brave young Steve hasn't just taught the town toughs the value of united action against a common enemy, but is effectively marshalling a military operation.

But hey ... subtext schmubtext. The pleasure of watching *The Blob* lies in ingeniously cheap special effects plus hysterical over-acting in the face of the least scary serial killer in movie history. The Blob itself is a silicone ... well ... blob with added red vegetable dye. The crew shook it about a bit and pushed it through holes and the film was run at high speed to make it like it was going somewhere. This reaches a peak of low-budget hilarity when The Blob becomes ginormous enough to cover an entire diner where Steve, his simpering girl Jane (Corsaut) and her pesky kid brother are trapped. This was apparently done by placing the silicone gunk on a table next to a photograph of the diner, then shaking the table until The Blob rolled off, and then running the film backwards. CGI has ruined everything.

The day is finally saved when our puny humans accidentally dis-cover that The Blob doesn't like the cold. The townspeople freeze it with fire extinguishers, and then an Air Force plane parachutes the defeated alien into the Arctic Circle. (Does this explain Blobal Warming? *Blobal Warming!* Blimey. Tough crowd.) With tongues firmly in cheeks and eyes firmly on potential sequels, the words 'The End' fill the screen ... and then morph into a question mark.

Critics have pondered the hidden meaning of The Blob's chilly demise. Many sci-fi movies of the time were interpreted as thinly veiled comments upon America's struggle with the Soviet Union. This struggle was called the *Cold* War. As The Blob absorbs more solid American citizens and grows in size, it becomes increasingly *red*. Get it? Good. I suspect that this is wishful thinking. But it's a very enjoyable pastime, projecting big political metaphors onto dumb B-movies. *The Blob*'s most famous moment does make for a nice comment about the power of cinema and its grip on teenagers, though.

Steve and teen-friendly Police Lieutenant Dave (he doesn't appear to have a surname – he's very informal) call a mass night-time meeting outside the supermarket where The Blob is holed up to warn the good townsfolk about the ever-growing, pulsating threat within their midst. Their reaction is half-panic, half kid-fearing scepticism. Meanwhile, most of the town's teens are at the cinema's midnight 'spook show', watching an old classic called *Daughter Of Horror*. Guess where The Blob's heading?

While the teens laugh hysterically at the old movie's camp horror, a far camper horror is oozing through the cinema air-vents. The poor old projectionist becomes the filling in a big doughnut. Soon, in a set of genuinely convincing, funny and beautifully composed shots, screaming kids are trampling each other to death in their desperation to escape the treacly terror. The increasingly jammy-looking Blob squirms magnificently through the cinema doors, contrasted with a sign over the diner that flashes 'Home Baking'. Priceless.

★ ★

THE 400 BLOWS

1959
Starring: Jean-Pierre Léaud, Claire Maurier, Albert Rémy, Patrick Auffay, Guy Decomble
Dir.: François Truffaut

**Plot: Why it's big and clever to be a juvenile delinquent.
Key line: 'He's beyond all limits.'**

The French title of this movie is *Les Quatre Cents Coups*. It is the debut film of François Truffaut and, along with *Les Cousins* by Claude Chabrol, *Hiroshima Mon Amour* by Alain Resnais and *A Bout De Souffle* by Jean-Luc Godard, launched the movie thing we've come to know as the *nouvelle vague*, or the French new wave. It's also, far more importantly, the genesis of this book and my previous book on film, *Popcorn*. Because, to my eternal shame, I only saw it for the first time in 2006, at the Duke Of York's Playhouse in Brighton, just five years ago. But I went into the cinema a film fan, and came out a movie geek, with all my previous fears of foreign and 'art' film banished for ever. No piece of art has had such a profound effect on me since I first heard Public Enemy's 'Rebel Without A Cause' single sometime in 1988. It didn't just make me want to write about film. It made me able to.

The 400 Blows is the semi-autobiographical tale of Antoine Doinel, a 13-year-old Parisian boy who falls foul of parents, school and the French justice system, played by the extraordinary Jean-Pierre Léaud. Léaud, a real-life wild boy who went on to star as Doinel in four further Truffaut movies, is the key element here. The young actor was just 14, and, just as *The 400 Blows* argues that children's ideas and desires are more important and interesting than those of the uncomprehending adults around them, Léaud's performance proves that children are better at playing children than adults. Doinel is the first fully rounded and utterly believable adolescent youth ever put onscreen. Without Truffaut and Léaud, no Mick Travis (see p. 97), Billy Casper (see p. 101) nor Jimmy The Mod (see p. 180). But also, no John Hughes. When Truffaut situates his camera at the back of the classroom during the school scenes, forcing us to watch like one of the naughty pupils at the back, he forever changes the viewpoint in teen movies from 'them' to 'us'. *The 400 Blows* is a monochrome dress rehearsal for *The Breakfast Club* (see p. 263).

If Antoine is Truffaut, his best friend René Bigoy is based upon Robert Lachenay, Truffaut's school friend and this movie's assistant director. Although both insisted that the events are a mixture of things that happened to them and people they know, Truffaut *was* a school dunce, lost and found himself in books and films, played truant in the streets of Montmartre, lied constantly and was sent to a juvenile detention centre. What he chooses to do with this is cinema's first visual poem on the subject of adolescence.

The 400 Blows begins in a classroom, with bored boys handing around a girlie calendar, and Antoine getting caught. The grainy, dirty detail of schoolroom and playground is quickly established, and it's vital to keep in mind that movies simply didn't look like documentaries in 1959. These scenes are the beginning of *cinéma vérité*. You can see just how much of this was shot guerrilla-style by the various street scenes, where passers-by will suddenly notice the camera and catch our eye in an unselfconscious way that no actor could pull off so naturally. Truffaut literally filmed the pulse of his city's life while saving a lot of money on getting streets closed down and hiring hundreds of extras to do what people do quite naturally.

The movie's comedy lies in the it's-funny-'cos-it's-true detail. The curly-headed boy trying to copy a literary passage being recited by the crabby, authoritarian teacher, repeatedly making mistakes, and tearing more and more pages from his exercise book until there's nothing left. The kid is cute, his ineptitude funny; but the teaching is inept and pointless, too. This is a revenge movie; the vindictive masterpiece of a boy told by monsters in bleak classrooms that he'd amount to nothing, now able to look down on lowly, loser teachers from his lofty perch as doyen of a new cultural *demi-monde*.

In a later comic scene, cheekily 'borrowed' from Jean Vigo's *Zéro De Conduite*, a bizarre PE class involves jogging through the streets in civilian clothes while a teacher in shorts blows a whistle. Kids keep breaking off to hide in doorways until the teacher is blithely leading no one at all, which all reminds me that, at my secondary school in London, 'cross-country running' actually involved tramping around Muswell Hill, with the more rebellious kids taking it as an opportunity to lag behind and have a fag. We were 12. Not a lot really changed between the '50s and the '70s.

But the detail mounts up until it becomes something far bigger than Truffaut's revenge. It's tempting to view every early *nouvelle vague* classic as a prophecy of the 1968 student-led Paris uprisings … the closest any western European country came to revolution in the 20th century. Every rebellious and subversive move these movies make seems charged with pre-revolutionary fervour lent by hindsight. But, in this case, the feeling is unavoidable. In the early classroom scenes the boys take the piss out of the sexy bits in the teacher's recitation, provoking him to threaten them ('Confess or I'll punish anybody!'), call them 'morons' and, in a scene filmed in 1958, actually utter the exasperated line: 'What will France be like in ten years time?' Truffaut knew that something was brewing in the apparently moronic mischief of French students. As Teach (whom Antoine refers to as Sourpuss) also rants, 'I've known morons but at least they didn't let it show. They hid in their corner.' *The 400 Blows* itself is a key example of France's young morons refusing to hide in corners any longer, invading centre-stage and looking for trouble.

Paris looks amazing here … even more like one giant film set than Hollywood's New York. Sure … Paris is a good-looking town anyway. But through Truffaut and Jean-Luc Godard's eyes it's so beautiful and tough and smoky and stylish and dirty and claustrophobic and effortlessly charismatic it just makes you want to hug it, and kiss it and never let it go. It's a city where impossibly glamorous women accost boys at night to help them look for a lost dog they've never named, and where impossibly glamorous men emerge, Harry Lime-like, from shadowy doorways to 'help', and where none of this seems filmy.

But Truffaut takes, and gives, just as much pleasure from looking at the mesmerised faces of children at a puppet show. The opening credits, where we are in a car looking up the buildings of Paris, with the Eiffel Tower dominating the sky from every angle, playing peek-a-boo with us, are suffused with love. Truffaut was so obsessed with the Eiffel Tower that he collected models of it throughout his life.

But I digress. Antoine lives in a rabbit hutch apartment with his parents. He sleeps in a sleeping-bag in the floor of the hall. We meet the fun and apparently loving Dad and the Bad Mom who does nothing but bark orders and admire herself in the mirror, wondering, you imagine, how a woman so chic ended up with a poor man and a chaotic teen in a poky apartment. She takes money meant to make Antoine's life better and spends it on mysterious things; perhaps the afternoon 'dates' her husband teases her about. Dad may be The Nice Parent, but he's as keen as Mom to pack Antoine off to a summer camp, just to get rid of him. We eventually learn that Dad is actually Stepdad.

There is an interesting side-theme whereby various women talk about how disgusting childbirth is. A prophecy of the impact con-traception would have on the lives of Western women? Or another sign that France despised its young?

Having pissed off Sourpuss with the girlie calendar, then written a rude poem about Sourpuss on the classroom wall, and then failed to do his extra homework, the definitively alienated Antoine decides to play truant with René. This inspires a particularly memorable scene where Antoine is taken for a ride by a fairground contraption, a giant circular drum which spins so quickly that the centrifugal force pins the punter to the wall. Truffaut switches quickly from shots of the boy, out of control, throwing shapes, lost in the ecstasy and pain of the moment, and of the faces of people watching above, laughing, even at blinding speed, at Antoine's struggle to cope. In a few seconds of screen-time a perfect metaphor for society's sickening chaos and gleeful contempt for youth. But who needs metaphors when you walk around the corner and catch your mother making out in the street with a handsome Arab?

Antoine may look pretty cool without the aid of nice clothes, but he is also as daft as a brush. When asked why he wasn't in school he panics and says that his mother is dead. Soon his parents are in school and Nice Stepdad is slapping him around in front of his class. Afraid to go home, he spends a night at René's uncle's old print shop, and roaming the streets. A contrite mother welcomes him back and tries to show him some love. He responds by making a candle-lit shrine to Balzac and accidentally starting a fire. He then submits an essay which cribs word-for-word from Balzac's *A Sinister Affair*. He's humiliated and expelled by the Prof and, again afraid to go home, secretly hides at René's house.

The pair settle all too easily into a life of scams and petty theft. You know where it's going: if Doinel really is Truffaut, then Truffaut was a self-deprecating man, happy to paint himself as painfully incompetent when it came to rebellion. His theft of a typewriter from his father's office is probably the most useless caper in movie history. But it's still a shock when Nice Dad takes Antoine to the police and pleads with them to take the boy away. The copper recommends an 'Observation Centre' for juvenile delinquents. Antoine is now a borstal boy for doing little more than trying to escape the cruel intentions of various uncaring adults. While waiting to go to court, he is thrown in a tiny cage with adult criminals. He cries silently as the van takes him away through the beautiful streets of night-time Paris, his real parent.

But Antoine takes to being brutalised by the system with the same sanguine adaptability as he takes to every situation. He reclines in his holding cell smoking newspaper roll-ups and takes on the demeanour of the hard-bitten con. The Observation Centre is leafy and rural, and replaces the military academy that his father has previously threatened him with. The boys are in uniform and march up and down, aimlessly, obediently. The idea that French boys of the period are merely marking time until they are drafted haunts the film at a time when Vietnam was more a French problem than an American one.

But assessment by The System gets Antoine one privilege. He gets to explain himself to someone who is actually listening. The assessment officer is off-camera so Antoine tells his back-story to us;

a shrugging, articulate account of his lying and stealing, and of a mother who was only persuaded not to have him aborted by his now-dead grandmother. Léaud twitches and fiddles as he talks, utterly natural, tragic but refusing to act the victim, and it hits you just how small and young he is. His rude smirk when asked if he's a virgin is a true and adorable thing. But the story he tells of hanging out on Rue St Denis with a north African pimp paints a quietly frightening picture of how much his parents have neglected him.

It turns out that Antoine has written a letter to Dad telling him about his mother's affair. It's another gambit that just makes things worse. Mlle Doinel visits Antoine, tells him that Dad believes her lies over his truth, and that neither parent wants him back. René also tries to visit but is refused entry and the boys wave uselessly at each other.

The ending is a mystery, and a joy, and the most famous *j'accuse!* in movie history. Faced with the prospects of trade school at a foundry, Antoine makes a bolt for it during a borstal football match. We watch him run and run through the French countryside, expecting him to be caught at any moment. But Truffaut found a Third Way to end one of the best teen movies ever made, and one far more resonant than the triumph of escape or the tragedy of capture.

As another gorgeous Jean Constantin waltz swells gaily (the light, bright lyricism of the music ensures that *The 400 Blows* never becomes grim), Antoine reaches a bleak beach. He trots towards the sea. The beach is huge, and the jog seems to take for ever, as we long to know what he's heading for.

But Antoine is not heading for anything. He reaches the sea and . . . that's it. He looks briefly around him and – suddenly looking old and adult and tough and immeasurably cool in his borstal boiler-suit, as if he has instantly aged 20 years – begins to swagger back. For the one and only time in the movie, he breaks down the fourth wall. He makes straight for the camera – for us – and finds a look of infinite dimensions for us to juggle. There is anger. Some exhaustion. No fear, but perhaps a little bemusement. But, mainly, there is cold, hard accusation. His eyes are asking what we are going to do about this, and how we can live with the world we've created. The camera zooms tight into that look, and freezes. And the legend 'FIN' – The End, of course – is superimposed upon Antoine's face in white, cartoonish font as the music dies slowly on a plucked violin.

The first time I saw it I swear my heart stopped for a second. I don't understand where this kid found this expression, and I didn't know what to do with it. But I've not been exactly the same person since.

1960s

WHERE THE BOYS ARE

1960

Starring: Dolores Hart, Yvette Mimieux, Paula Prentiss, Connie Francis, George Hamilton, Jim Hutton, Frank Gorshin
Dir.: Henry Levin

Plot: Why first love and first shag are rarely the same thing. Key line: 'So why don't we get down to the giant jackpot issue? Like should a girl, or should she not, under any circumstances, play house before marriage?'

Where The Boys Are is one of the movies that sowed the seeds of this book. I remember first seeing it on daytime TV around six years ago, and being amazed that a film so rich in feminist subtext had been made at the arse-end of the early rock 'n' roll era. The point was hit home when I found a superb book by Susan J. Douglas about 'Growing Up Female with the Mass Media' that took its title from the movie and devoted a short chapter to its impact upon the writer as an adolescent. *Where The Girls Are* mixes academia with memoir in order to analyse the sweeping changes in '60s youth culture that led to women like Douglas becoming feminists. The acknowledgement that this fizzy, cute but strangely dark picture was key to those youthquakes made me realise that I hadn't been nuts to feel so moved and intrigued by a film that, on the surface, appears both lightweight and old-fashioned.

Where The Boys Are is a classic subversive pop artefact, weaving its big theme – when should a girl lose her virginity, and why? – into a frothy beach party musical format. And, even after fifty years of 'sexual liberation', its discourse about adolescent female sexuality still feels relevant and thought-provoking.

The premise upon which this exploration of 'the giant jackpot issue' is based is that peculiar American phenomenon, Spring Break, when thousands of well-to-do teens descend upon Stateside beach resorts during spring school and college holidays to have one last party hearty before the last term and exams descend upon them. We follow four girls from the frozen Midwest as they decamp to Fort

Lauderdale, Florida to find fun, which means romance ... and, possibly, something less hygienic.

Each of the four symbolises a different aspect of the teenage girl's attitude to men, love and sex. The gangly, deep-voiced Tuggle (Prentiss) is an old-fashioned girl who is already looking for the boy she will eventually marry. Melanie (Mimieux) is the insecure hot chick who is on a mission to pop her cherry. Angie ('50s pop megastar Francis, in her first film role) is the jokey tomboy who strikes out with the boys. And Merritt (the excellent Hart) is the smart, assertive and intelligent audience representative, who seems to have already sussed out that sex is a feminist issue. Their essential characters lead them down four differing paths with four separate boys, and all end up somewhere unexpected and life-changing.

The film sets out as a comedy, full of pithy witticisms and a wry sense of exaggeration. The opening voiceover, delivered by a male newsreader type over travelogue shots of beautiful, empty Fort Lauderdale beaches, is drenched in irony as it insists that thousands of teens will turn this sea of tranquility into 'bedlam', and that, while the girls are there for the boys, the boys are there for the beer. The apparent sexism is tempered by the underlying truth, which is that girls are always a few years ahead of boys in terms of maturity, and that, even though the male characters are given plenty of life by the engaging male leads, *Where The Boys Are* is a movie about girls for girls. Of course, the very presence of a beach and the implication of sex ensures that boys will be watching, too, what with the promise of all that Hollywood cheesecake in swimsuits.

Boys must have liked the early classroom scene as much as girls, too. An elderly teacher in the kind of twinset that makes an argument for celibacy in itself is delivering a lecture on a sociology book which appears to be a thinly veiled warning against the 'dangers of random dating', that is, promiscuity and pre-marital sex, using language like 'interpersonal relationships' to intellectualise basic prudishness. Merritt is ostentatiously bored. Picked out to be humiliated by Teach, she is having none of it, and engages with the dry, lofty text from a position of frustration and knowledge, bringing the name of Dr Kinsey – author of the Kinsey Reports, the two infamous books about male and female sexual desire published in 1948 and 1953 that helped sow the seeds of 'the sexual revolution' – into the exchange to make her teacher seem ridiculously out of touch, delivering our key lines above in a way that is more political speech at a feminist rally than pupil–teacher discussion. At this stage, Merritt seems well up for it, and fully engaged with the idea that this is a political matter as well as a personal one.

But, once the film takes its extraordinary turn towards the abyss, we're forced to look back to this speech and see that the implications of 'promiscuity' *can* be dangerous for young women. Blonde bombshell Melanie is sitting next to Merritt in class and is so impressed by her friend's sexual militancy that she makes a decision that leads her into a kind of hell. This, obviously, could be seen as a deeply conservative message. But it's what happens to the characters around Melanie that defuses that message somewhat. We'll get back to it.

Right now, we're seeing just how hostile American power is to women who have the temerity to treat their minds and bodies as their own. Teach packs Merritt off to the Dean, who promptly threatens her with expulsion in a deeply condescending manner, making Merritt understand that her continued academic career is dependent upon the girl 'see[ing] things more clearly' after Spring Break. And she will, but perhaps not in the way that arbitrary power would approve of. The Dean goes so far as to ask Merritt if she is 'overly concerned with the problem of sex'. Merritt's anxious demeanour might be because she has a cold and she's now freaked out about flunking, but there is an implication, deftly delivered by scriptwriter George Wells and director Henry Levin, that her palpable sense of panic and physical discomfort comes from somewhere else entirely.

But sex on the brain doesn't stop it from working. Merritt, composure regained, simply remarks that there are half a million college kids in America who are overly concerned with sex. 'I guess that makes me fairly normal,' she smiles. The Dean shifts uncomfortably in her seat, as adults constantly do in this movie as they are confronted with the new sexual frankness of these baby-boomer brats.

Wells's script is so loaded with subterfuge and winks to a hip new teen audience that any one of a couple of dozen lines could have been chosen as key. At one point plain Jane Angie explains not having to lie to parents about her outdoor activities thus: 'That's the nice part about being captain of the girl's hockey team – your parents know you're safe.' Is that as obvious a coded lesbian reference as it seems these days? Probably not – just a perennial truth about girls who do rough sports being seen as unfeminine by their male peers. But maybe not. It's interesting in itself that Francis – the biggest female pop idol of her day – was so boyish and unglamorous.

The film is also fond of playing with gender stereotypes. The first guy we meet, TV Thompson (Hutton), is a goofy, penniless hitchhiker who talks too much about nothing and drives really badly. He is the powerless irritant in this situation, constantly mocked by the girl he ends up with. Tuggle seems only to choose him because he's one of the few readily available men who is taller than she is. What's more, he is a New Man, of sorts, an easy-going chap secure enough in his manhood to be unthreatened by the apparent emasculation.

In contrast, adults are mocked for their terror of teenage. One of the funniest scenes takes place outside Fort Lauderdale police station, where a set of suited and booted coppers are being assembled like an army repelling an invasion, which is exactly what they are. The grizzled police chief addresses his troops like a general giving a last pep talk to doomed Civil War volunteers. 'Gentlemen ... the city of Fort Lauderdale is once again under fire from the North. We've survived it before and I reckon we're gonna survive it again. To you newly installed officers who've never seen action in the war against higher education ...' – you get the idea. The cops laugh, because in this movie, even adult squares do understand irony. And the speech becomes more interesting when it moves away from its comic metaphor, as the police chief reminds his stormtroopers that The Kids have 'a right' to have some fun, that they are 'future citizens and future voters' of the good old USA, and that he wants his cops to control their antics 'without arresting anyone'. It's like some liberal paradise!

But even here, a discourse about class joins the one about age, with the blue-collar cops from the South doing battle with college kids from the North, in a neat little comic prophecy of what was coming over the next decade in the protests for civil rights and against the Vietnam War.

Because *Where The Boys Are* is a film that sees 'The Sixties' coming, far more so than even *The Wild One* (see p. 13) or *Rebel Without A Cause* (see p. 28). Wells and Levin appear to have had an early grip on the issues that would really drive what movie critic Peter Biskind calls 'The children's crusade' of the '60s, which was for freedom of expression for the young and an end to the sexual repression that their parents had accepted as necessary, largely brought about by the invention of the contraceptive pill. Drugs, music, race awareness and anti-war agitation were simply the lifestyle choices added to the imperative – an end to eternal hormonal frustration – and the resulting explosion of new possibilities once one saw clearly that the personal is political. Whereas *The Wild One* provided blatant sexual imagery without having the nerve to address the S word directly, and *Rebel* ... ignored teen sex completely because we all apparently wanted to fuck either Mom or Pop, *Where The Boys Are* addresses the burning issue of its day head on, and repeatedly reminds you that sex is the most important obsession of the hormonal adolescent.

It's a brave, sophisticated piece of writing which would have been as good if not better than a *Rebel* ... or *The 400 Blows* (see p. 47) if it had been directed with their iconoclastic flair. As it is – and probably to make sure it got through the layers of censorship and media watchdog-ery as much as anything else – it looks and sounds like a dodgy Elvis movie, all fluffy holiday colour, corny music and lack of cutting edges that might hurt a child when handled incorrectly. But, again, that is what makes *Where The Boys Are* more genuinely subversive than the *auteur* classics I mention.

The presentation of a liberal paradise for kids is entirely connected to what would have made the film entertaining for teens of the time. The movie is full of the seaside shenanigans that kids find amusing and adults find annoying (it occasionally resembles a template for 50 per cent of MTV's future programming) with every adult bullied by sheer weight of numbers. But, most of all – parents are absent. Every kid travels alone or with their friends and temporarily gets to 'play house' in a more wholesome way than Merritt is alluding to. This also makes for another unusual element that differentiates most teen films of any era from *Where The Boys Are* – nothing that happens here is the fault of the parents. They aren't just absent from Fort Lauderdale, but from the picture. So the good and bad decisions of our heroines are their own, and nothing is blamed on Bad Dads or Moms. These are late teens who are preparing for adult life and are not presented as victims of their childhoods. This must have been a refreshing change for kids who were at the cinema precisely to escape their parents. But it also suggests that, by the time we're old enough to think about sex, we're also old enough to make decisions about it that aren't based on whether Mom is a shrew or Dad is a bully. And that not everyone doing things that the older generation disapproved of was doing those things for that reason primarily. The movie gives kids a tantalising glimpse of what it must be like to be free of parental control and able to make independent decisions, while accepting that totally fucking up those decisions from time to time is part of what being adult is.

There is also an interestingly cynical view of love – or, at least, the word 'love'. In one scene, Merritt points out that Melanie is insisting that she's in love with one boy when, just a few days previously, she was insisting she was in love with his friend. The thing the two boys have in common is that they've slept with her, and Melanie is obviously using the word as a justification for having gone from virgin to ho without passing Go. We cut to a scene where Merritt has dragged Melanie along on a trip on her man's boat to save her from herself. As Merritt and her man talk, he remarks that he really 'likes' Merritt, and then pauses, adding that that was the first time he had ever said that to a girl. Merritt scoffs. 'Oh . . . I've told plenty of girls I love them. But not *like*,' he explains. The couple exchange a look and a smile. They both understand that, in the game of seduction, 'like' stands for respect and is worth a hundred 'love's, which is just a sexual justification for young men, too.

So how else do these laydees learn and grow? The charismatic Paula Prentiss's Tuggle fends off TV's sexual advances until his eye roves towards older woman and comedy 'mermaid dancer' Lola Fandango, played by Barbara Nichols. Tug simply learns that a choice to remain celibate until marriage will probably chase away the kind of freewheeling maverick she seems to be attracted to. TV is so slippery that he confesses to being 'tricky' and 'a fake', and then bullies Tuggle with what becomes the movie's most loaded question: 'Are you a good girl?'

It's Tuggle (*I know* – I have no idea!) that gets the movie's most notorious lines, when she declaims, 'Girls like me weren't built to be educated. We were made to have children. That's my ambition – to be a walking, talking baby factory.' Nice. But although Tuggle is a likeable character, the language of the willing victim of conservative values is so extreme you can almost hear the thousands of *ingénue* viewers shuddering with horror all the way from 1960.

Even a girl who really doesn't want to do anything except be a mother would not want to think of herself as a mindless breeding machine. Tuggle's view of herself is a comment on her mother's generation, and what conservatives wanted women to be. She eventually gets the guy without popping her cherry, but you suspect that she isn't a willing baby factory any more.

And actually, I said all four learn and grow, but that's not true. Having been cast as the 'ugly girl', Connie Francis has the thankless role of comic relief. Angie cops off with 'dialectic jazz' bassist Basil, played by impressionist Frank Gorshin, whose famously googly eyes get lent an added air of slapstick laffs by a pair of fishbowl specs. He is a pretentious pseud – one of his post-Miles Davis excursions is called 'A Meeting Between Shakespeare And Satchel Paige On Hampstead Heath'. Angie is, predictably, Basil's last resort, at first. Then, at a gig, she – well, Connie Francis – transforms his shapeless jazz tune into a gospel-tinged pop hit. He ends up calling her 'beautiful' because he loses his glasses. There is no lesson learned. So, OK . . . it's not *all* feminist subterfuge.

Merritt pulls suave trainee lounge lizard Ryder, played by George Hamilton, who is so greasy here he leaves a trail of slime on the beach. He is rich, older – 22 – and woos 19-year-old Merritt in swanky cocktail bars rather than crowded student pubs. He can take her smartarse mocking and his IQ is even higher than hers, the equivalent (this is essentially the late '50s, lest we forget) of TV having to be just that few inches taller than the 5 foot 10 inch Tuggle. Ryder even risks his neck to rescue the damsel in distress. He is every girl's dream Spring Break catch . . . if you don't mind following behind him with a mop and bucket.

But the film takes its dark turn with Melanie. For her, sexual experience has not been a passport to maturity, but terror. It's as if someone unplugged a pipe that was holding back a flood of insecurities. Those insecurities split her off from the safety of the group and take her into self-imposed isolation. She is raped by misogynist posh boy Dill in a motel, and appears to have been drugged. Except that there is no mention of drugs, any more than anyone says the word 'rape'. Whichever way, her experience has made her a suicidal zombie, and she wanders into the middle of a busy road, almost dies, and does end up hospitalised. 'I feel so old,' she wails, mourning the end of her childhood and the slaying of her innocence.

So the simple interpretation is that the only girl to lose her virginity is brutally punished for her 'crime', a fine tradition later taken up by the makers of teen slasher movies. But is it *that* simple? Or does Melanie suffer because she shows terrible judgement about men, pandering to their whims (she even starts smoking because her man does) because they are students from Yale and have high social status? Even this is a con, and the sinister nature of her eventual attacker is cleverly foreshadowed by Levin: while the other three male leads get plenty of quality screen-time and dialogue – we get to know them and therefore trust them – Melanie's seducer Dill is constantly shot with his back to camera or in profile, as if hiding from us. In fact, the first time we meet him he has his back to us; he is with an even more anonymous jock mate, and they are flipping a coin. The script doesn't have to make it clear that the pair are flipping for who gets to bed Melanie.

So Melanie betrays the sisterhood by immediately bailing on her friends to chase after these guys – their holiday apartment is increasingly full of strange girls given a temporary home through female solidarity, yet Melanie is rarely present – and she betrays herself by doing what the guys want and not making independent decisions based upon her own desires ... and, for that matter, refusing to listen to Merritt's sisterly advice. One can interpret the morality tale by inferring that Melanie is raped for being too easy. But you could make an equally compelling case for inferring that Melanie is punished for being easily led, a social climber and a bad feminist ... and as dumb as a box of rocks. Weirdly, the way Melanie behaves when she's drunk is a very thinly veiled parody of Marilyn Monroe, and Melanie's fate here feels like a prophecy of the star's death two years later. There is something here about the insecure good-time gal as helpless victim of male power that has continued to resonate down the years.

By contrast, smart, sensible and *loyal* Merritt is given an ending as clever as she deserves – an unresolved one. She agrees to a long-distance relationship with Ryder. She may meet up with him, and, if she does, she might sleep with him. But it will be her choice, and one that will depend entirely on her desires and whether she feels she is ready.

The film does the biggest service to its viewers by not presenting an entirely happy ending at the expense of Melanie. Nothing that includes a sexual assault can end happily. Melanie's experience has simply given Merritt food for thought, and therefore the girls in its audience the same food for thought about one of the most profound experiences that everyone on this planet faces. Or, as Merritt puts it, when Ryder calls her strong: 'No girl is when it comes to love – or what she thinks is love. How do you know the difference?' Notice careful use of the word 'girl', *not* woman. *Where The Boys Are* is not an attempt to stop girls growing up. It is a warning about not trying to grow up too soon. As potentially happy couple Merritt and Ryder step from the dark of the shade into the light of the ocean, Connie Francis's theme tune swells and hits home the final point: 'Where the boys are ... someone *waits for me*.' Consider any boys in the audience duly chastised.

The female loss-of-virginity theme of *Where The Boys Are* has been played out in more recent quality teen movies, notably *Grease* (see p. 165), *Little Darlings* (see p. 191), *But I'm A Cheerleader* (see p. 367) and *Twilight* (see p. 468). *Grease* even rights the wronging of Melanie, and gives its sexually experienced woman Rizzo a happy ending of sorts. But none of these movies talks about the issues with as much honesty, wit and courage as *Where The Boys Are*, when taken in the context of how little film-makers could get away with when discussing adolescent sexuality in the 1950s. You've got to remember ... the '60s, as we think we know it, didn't even begin until 1963.

At times, *Where The Boys Are* feels like a public information film for young women injected with songs, gags, a plot and Hollywood production values. I hope that doesn't put you off. Because, rape and plain girl storylines notwithstanding, it is more thoughtful and less glib about sex than any of the hundreds of cynical campus comedies that have come in its fifty-year wake. And, if it's not the best teen movie of all time, it might just be the most prophetic about a woman's right to choose.

★ ★

BEAT GIRL

1960

Starring: Gillian Hills, David Farrar, Noelle Adam, Christopher Lee, Adam Faith, Shirley Anne Field, Peter McEnery, Oliver Reed
Dir.: Edmond T. Gréville

Plot: The modern city eats its young.
Key line: 'Next week . . . VOOM! Up goes in the world in smoke. And what's the score? Zero! So now, while it's now, we live it up. Do everything. *Feel* everything. Strictly for kicks!'

This incredibly strange cult movie is such a hotch-potch of great and awful film-making that it's impossible to make sense of it all at first viewing. But the more you watch, the more richly rewarding *Beat Girl* becomes, existing as a relatively believable document of the British teen underground as it stood on the cusp of becoming the planet's mainstream youth culture. Because, once you get past plot, main themes and acting that veers between the sublime and the utterly fucking useless, the film's great pleasures lie in crazy scenes of gone teens in caves, cellars and other thrillingly sleazy places.

There's the bit where you suddenly see a junkie playing drums. Except he's not actually a junkie, but a boy called Pinky Ross who is trying to break the world drumming record, which currently stands, according to *Beat Girl*, at 57 hours, 22 minutes and 14 seconds. He is close to collapse, haphazardly thumping a tom-tom as a rock 'n' roll tune thunders on, ignoring him. The kids in the café ignore him too, apart from one pretty blonde girl in regulation tomboy drag, who watches him dreamily while distractedly sucking on an ice lolly. Finally, Pinky just keels over, face-first, onto his drum kit. She rolls her eyes. 'Oh well – not this time,' she sighs, with an air of futility, and minces away up the stairs, leaving Pinky to face his percussion pains alone.

There's the bit where a black stripper called Pascaline does a proto-rap-video-ho routine in a Soho sex joint, and the face of our titular heroine Jenny (Hills) does so many subtly suggestive things that, if *Beat Girl* were a cartoon, you'd get a visual of steam coming out of her. Except it wouldn't be coming out of her ears.

And there's all the best bits which involve implausibly sexy Brit teens frugging wildly in cellar clubs and Chislehurst Caves either to pop idol Adam Faith's surreal-abilly Eddie Cochran tributes or the John Barry Seven's unique blends of rock 'n' roll and film *noir* jazz. There is something wildly enjoyable about watching the young Oliver Reed get so gone, Man, that his eyes roll around his head like he's getting a world-class BJ. But not as wild or enjoyable as the dance floor action of Ms Hills, the feral offspring of Marlene Dietrich and an alien sex rodent, as she twists and writhes and narrows her cat eyes and stares you down with the kind of sexual arrogance that is every parent's worst nightmare writ large. Gillian Hills would prob-ably win the unofficial Best Teen Star In This Book award if someone hadn't invented talking pictures thirty years before. When you look at her, the world is full of sordid action. But then the poor girl opens her mouth . . .

Beat Girl's seriously weird plot goes like this: Paul Linden (Farrar), a middle-aged posho architect, goes to Paris for a few months to get over his divorce and comes back with a French dolly-bird wife Nichole (Adam), who's only eight years older than his 16-year-old daughter. Said daughter Jenny (Hills), who is already being turned into a Bad Lot by art school and hanging round Soho coffee bars listening to cool jazz and hot rock with other rich brats and token authentic working-class existentialist Adam Faith, gets really hostile. Meanwhile, Jenny's chance meeting with Soho stripper Greta reveals that Stepmum has a sordid past. Jenny is handed a chance to expose the hypocrisy of Bad Dad while watching strippers in a sleazy club with just a little too much interest. Club owner Kenny (Lee) sees *his* chance to lure the disco dolly to a life of vice. It all ends in blood and chaos.

This would all be entertainingly exploitative enough. But *Beat Girl* also has Big Ideas that transform a cheap rock movie into purest (s)existentialism, as you might expect from a French director who is obviously influenced by both *film noir* and his homeland's *nouvelle vague*.

Beat Girl's subtexts emerge in two scenes. When Linden first takes Nichole home – if you can call this space-age office space home – to meet Jenny, the daughter quickly shows the Stepmother what she's up against in the war for Daddy's attentions. Linden's obsession is 'City 2000', a proposed 'fresh start' for humanity which is currently a large circular model of identical high-rise blocks he finds so thrilling that poor Nichole finds her herself wrestling him away from its cubist Lego charms in order to get laid. Linden is such a post-Ayn Rand modernist that he literally wants to demolish human history and put us all in dystopian environments where 'a man can be as alone as if he was 10,000 miles from anywhere'.

This fear of modernism and the urban finds its echo in a scene where Jenny's gang of friends go raving in Chislehurst Caves, where we find out that Adam Faith's Dave is so virulently anti-booze, fighting and everything else that might be considered fun by teen boys (he's very fond of declaring that all decadent pleasures are 'for squares, Man') that anyone would think he was only there to assure censors and shocked parents that the film is actually a very serious warning to kids not to do all the thrilling things that it's putting onscreen. Once he's told everyone off, the gang sit and talk about why they're so gorgeously, nihilistically unimpressed by the world. It turns out that neither Mater, Pater, nor school or the government are the problem. The problem is that they were born in the Second World War, huddled in underground bunkers, hiding from death by doodlebug, expected to keep a stiff upper lip when Mummy got blitzed. 'We're like rats in a hole, that's us,' sneers Dave, the only street kid among these students from St Martin's College, later the site of the first Sex Pistols show and where Jarvis Cocker had his fateful meeting with a posh bird who wanted to shag him 'cos he was common.

A cave that could be '10,000 miles from anywhere' appears to be the only place these kids feel safe enough to reveal the source of their angst. Soon, on their way back to Jenny's for a parent-baiting party, they will be playing a game in which they rest their necks on rail tracks and wait for oncoming trains. Post-war progress, in the shape of cities, speed and more deadly potential wars, is coming to kill these kids. And none of them seems to mind too much.

The anti-city theme is punched home at the movie's end. Jenny is rescued from Soho's sex trade and The Abyss by Dad and Step-_mère_. But as the music swells and the credits roll, the three are not being whisked away on happy-ever-afters. The three walk into Soho, and the shadows and neon and darkness and threat of London's sleaziest square mile swallows them, making them look insignificant and doomed, just like rats in a hole.

If you're wondering why a film this wild, woolly and exciting isn't routinely touted as a classic of British and teen cinema, the answer mainly lies in dodgy film-making. While Gréville is fantastic with music set-pieces, set design and *chiaroscuro* light, he seems deeply uninterested in basic editing techniques or, indeed, actors. And one has some sympathy when the support players – particularly Faith, McEnery and Lee – are superb, but *Beat Girl*'s leads are memorably, laughably awful. Hills gets away with it through sheer presence, but Farrar and Adam ... well, David Farrar had been one of the great Michael Powell's leading men, and he looks deeply embarrassed that he is now in movies that are aimed at geezers in dirty macs as much as rebellious teens. And while you can make excuses for the very French Ms Adam based upon her struggling with a second language, that really doesn't explain the blank, bewildered look on her face throughout, as if the casting director bumped into her at a bus-stop, kidnapped her and pushed her in front of the camera when Farrar or Hills needed a moving prop.

The bad acting does have some fringe benefits, though. In one early scene, Jenny taunts her dad's new fancy piece by undressing for bed in front of her, flirting outrageously. If Adam was capable of any other expression except startled rabbit on drugs, then we would be told what to think about this scene. Does Jenny want to shag a woman she met ten minutes ago? Is she competing with her for her father's incestuous favours? Or is she on commission at the local bra shop? We're left to laugh and ponder the polymorphous perversity of it all and make up our own dirty minds.

★ ★

A TASTE OF HONEY

1961
Starring: Rita Tushingham, Dora Bryan, Murray Melvin, Robert Stephens, Paul Danquah
Dir.: Tony Richardson

Plot: A very English lament for the unwanted child.
Key line: 'A bit of love, a bit of lust and there you are. We don't ask for life. We have it thrust upon us.'

Tony Richardson and Shelagh Delaney's seminal snapshot of life in a '60s northern town deserves its place as one of the best of all British films. It was adapted from Delaney's hit play, which was also directed by Richardson. It stars the wonderful Rita Tushingham in her debut role as the quintessential mousy teenage Goddess and the equally wonderful Dora Bryan as the world's worst mother. And the kind of ribald and poetic dialogue that befits a tale set in Manchester, home of the sharpest tongues in England. *A Taste Of Honey* is a key example of what came to be known as 'kitchen sink drama' and the British new wave. Oh . . . and the song of the same name, which The Beatles covered in 1963 and was initially written as a recurring instrumental motif for the American version of the play, doesn't appear here at all.

Tushingham is Jo, a 15-year-old about to leave school, parentified by her slutty and neglectful mother who has never hidden the fact that she never wanted a child. When Lovely Rita dreams, you dream right along with her. Her eyes – huge, slightly off-centre, blank yet full of vim and vigour – express something quintessential about longing to be anywhere but where you are. Broad hips and chubby legs aside, there's a startling resemblance between Tushingham and Malcolm McDowell, star of *If* . . . (see p. 97) and *A Clockwork Orange* (see p. 111). His slight femininity and her edge of butch make them equally unnerving. There is some special knowledge in their eyes and voices, a feeling that they represent not just threatening youth but the rise of a New North. More than occasionally, Richardson just puts a close-up camera on Tushingham here, knowing that her thousand-yard stare says more about frustration and imminent change than any amount of self-conscious speechifying. In a different age that fierce androgyny would have made her a superstar. But the '60s and '70s offered worse parts for subversive actresses than any other period of screen-time, and this was not a face to play vapid romantic lead, nor victim, nor whore.

The opening credits – which occur after scenes of Jo playing netball at school and explaining to a friend that she can't go out because she has no clothes and 'we might be moving home again' – show the influence of *The 400 Blows*, as does the brutal, documentary-style monochrome and relentless authenticity of light and location. Jo and her ma Helen (Bryan) have had to do a 'flit' – that is, leave their flat in secret owing rent – and take their worldly belongings on a bus to who knows where, giving us a tour of Manchester as the credits roll and a kiddie choir sing the children's song 'The Good Ship Sails'. Richardson's camera is rightly obsessed with Tushingham's face, an unforgettable mix of big-eyed soulfulness, startled rabbit and sulky pout, topped off with androgynous pudding-bowl haircut. This is the stuff of Smiths' record sleeves and working-class beauty amidst damp northern grit and poverty. Like Truffaut, Richardson chooses a lyrical orchestral soundtrack that lightens the mood, reflecting the optimism of the young and their ability to endure the worst possible starts in life.

Because *A Taste Of Honey* is a love letter to mordant pessimism, the life-blood of the British northern working class. Barely a conversation passes without a mention of death, and an implication that it would be a blessed relief. A definitive exchange between daughter and mother occurs early when Jo remarks that the new bed is like a coffin and Mother replies, 'Well, that's where we all end up, in the end.'

I find this strangely comforting. I'm a born and bred Londoner but my mother's family all hailed from Hebburn, a tiny town near Jarrow in the north-east of England. Their entire narrative was drenched in mortality and miserabilism, and their favourite reading matter was *The Spiritualist News*, as if they'd all been waiting to die since they'd been born. Considering they'd all been born into service, raised as children to know their place, wait on the rich and never move on, they all had a fair point. The constant sighing resignation to life-stinks-and-then-you-die can and did suck the joy out of a young 'un. But ... they all meant well. And, in hindsight, it was both funny and true, and militated against the kind of five-a-day, salad-munching, hair-shirt, no fun today lest we suffer tomorrow, Western middle-class delusion that if one behaves and does what one's told, one will never, ever die.

By this time we've met Helen's beau, Peter (Stephens), who, with his too-bright suit and bow tie, rakish moustache and used car business, is the very essence of slippery spivery, a wolf in wolf's clothing. We've also seen how uncomfortable he looks when Helen entertains the boozers with a mildly bawdy song in the pub. This surely won't end well.

It turns out that Jo wants to get a job after leaving school, and leave her mother as quickly as possible, and that she is an artist ... something she's never bothered to share with Mother. But a far more controversial Jo secret becomes the meat of *A Taste Of Honey*. She begins a relationship with a sailor who happens to be black. Or rather, coloured. Brits of that generation still think 'coloured' is the enlightened term, what with it being less abusive than most of the terms used at the time. These were times when a white girl could say to a black man, 'There's still a bit of jungle in you somewhere', and he would, apparently, think it was a funny joke. No black people were involved in the writing of this film.

Oddly, the age difference ... he looks at least 25, Jo can be no more than 15 ... is not raised as an issue, whereas the eight-year difference between Helen and Peter is, repeatedly. But have things changed that much in this regard? Isn't older man–younger woman still seen as more 'natural' than older woman–younger man?

By now we know that Jo is condemned to repeat the unwanted pregnancy mistakes of her mother. But who can blame her? There's a shot of Jo and her beau standing beneath a street light, shot from below, framing them in shadow against the windows, walls and fences of a dark street, that captures every thrill of young night-time romance. Besides, the boy's hot, kind, attentive and represents exoticism and escape.

Despite the snotty insults to mother – 'You don't look 40. More a well-preserved 60' – and professed desire for independence, Jo is more vulnerable and childlike than she wants to admit. She insists on joining Helen and Peter on a day-trip to Blackpool when, theoretically, she could have had Jimmy The Sailor-Man and the flat all to herself. She may be an outsider, but she is still lonely.

The day-trip, which also includes a couple we haven't met until now, is a small and beautiful nightmare, and one that can only be dreamt in cramped, grey England. Peter, who we learn has a glass eye, sees Jo as both an impediment to sex and a terrifying bringer of home-truths. He reveals that he's already bought a house for his impending marriage to Helen ... a bungalow with bay windows, every working-class Brit's paradise.

But the childish seaside japes that delight the adults leave the child cold. She's a fabulously disapproving onlooker, a study in blank, bored insolence. By now, Richardson has unleashed the trashy British rock 'n' roll and the shaky hand-held camera, and, like many a middle-class Brit director of the '50s and '60s, he is not a fan of the working class at play, as they laugh manically at things that aren't funny, eat junk and chase cheap thrills. Still, can't really knock him for that. I love my background but largely hated its idea of fun. That's why we peasants needed all these working-class bohemian art-schoolers – The Beatles and The Who and Bowie and the Sex Pistols – to make intellectual noise and allow us to believe we could find better things to do, to *be*. The Swinging '60s hasn't really hit this Blackpool yet. It needs Jo to grow up, put that disgruntlement to good use and become the Shelagh Delaney she obviously is. Of course, the day turns to disaster when Peter loses patience with Jo's taunting and gives Helen the me-or-her ultimatum. And of course, it rains. And of course, Jimmy is waiting for Jo when she gets off the bus, injecting life and love and the old I-sail-away-tomorrow spiel into her bleak world at a time when she's far too vulnerable to say no. Uh-oh.

The film is haunted by the biggest English obsession of the 1960s – the unmarried mother. Helen's offhand description of Jo's absent-presumed-dead father as 'a bit simple' is cruel and exactly the kind of thing ashamed working-class single mothers tell their children. Again, I know, from experience. No matter what happens at the end of *A Taste Of Honey*, Jo will live her life convinced that she has inherited an unimaginable madness. Helen tells her she has her father's eyes. It is not a compliment. The Pill may have turned out to have side-effects, medically, emotionally. But it was, briefly, the salvation of the woman who refused to be a virgin until marriage. This was all such a short time ago, really. It feels like another millennium.

Dora Bryan is quite brilliant in these scenes. As she explains that

Jo was conceived in her first sexual encounter, she makes something that seems initially kind and romantic – that our first time is something we always remember – into something frightening and charged with dread, using little more than a wayward glance, a thoughtful pause, a wrinkle of her angry mouth. She then goes off to get married, having never considered inviting her own daughter, utterly uninterested in the fact that her only child left school yesterday and enters the world of work in two days' time. The pessimism of *A Taste Of Honey* touches everything, but nothing is tainted quite as firmly and finally as love and sex, the working-class woman's killer drug of choice. 'I hate love,' Jo whimpers, in a cave, which is fitting.

With Helen and Jimmy gone, the film moves from superior soap to something altogether more extraordinary. It becomes a kind of travelogue through the life of a precocious teenager's first taste of independent adult life in atmospheric Manchester, made yet more non-conformist by the introduction of Geoff, Jo's gay best friend, charismatically played by Murray Melvin. One of the first fully rounded and utterly believable gay characters in mainstream cinema, Geoff is a gaunt and sallow student of 'textile design' who understands, at first glance, that Jo is not like everybody else. With him, a night at the fair is pleasure not trauma. He introduces Jo – and the young female viewer of the time, one imagines – to the delights of male friendship without sexual agenda. Although the bullying way she demands information about 'you people' proves that Jo is her mother's daughter, when all is said and done. He becomes her flatmate – and domestic Goddess – anyway.

Inevitably, Jo's one night of comfort and joy has left her in the family way. Geoff tries to make himself straight for her, 'for the baby's sake', but this is one stroppy modern girl who isn't marrying anyone for anything's sake. 'I'd rather be dead than away from you,' he confesses, and, again, the summoning of The Void feels unavoidable. Jo is soon looking ruefully at a boy with Down's Syndrome, her pessimism an engulfing shroud.

Helen's attempts to reconcile with Jo are undermined by drunk lunk Peter in a scene of rich and tragi-comic character acting. When Helen inevitably gets dumped and moves herself into their brilliant bohemian loft, you just know that poor Geoff's days are numbered.

But the best scenes belong to Tushingham and Melvin, playing out their strange kinda love by the dirty side of the Manchester Ship

Canal, where Jo's lover seduced her and sailed from her. They are often surrounded by urchin children and they say things like: 'You need someone to love yer while you're looking for someone to love.'

'Have you been unhappy with me?'

'Who's happy?'

Bloody marvellous. The pair fittingly won Best Actor and Actress awards at 1962's Cannes Film Festival.

The movie's other great supporting actor is Manchester itself, shot in all its dank, sinister, post-industrial glory. There are no dark satanic mills, but plenty of dark satanic factories, looming over the drama, impervious except for providing physical proof that there's no point cheering up, because it probably will happen.

If all this sounds like one long Smiths' song, you are not wrong. Morrissey fans will already know that he pinched one of his most famous lines – 'I dreamt about you last night/And I fell out of bed twice', from 'Reel Around The Fountain' on The Smiths' debut album – straight from the mouth of Jimmy The Sailor-Man. The Smiths' love of pretty-ugly working-class glamour, and view of Manchester as a beautiful but dangerous place with 'so much to answer for', finds its absolute definition in these 96 minutes, right alongside Moz's identification with the young outsider, too clever to conform but too fatalistic to ever escape a chronic loneliness. All this, and its smart placing of black, gay and working-class woman as equally excluded outsiders whose time is fast approaching makes *A Taste Of Honey* prophetic and inspiring.

And, for me, *A Taste Of Honey* holds a special place. I look at it as being as close as I can get to story of my mother, before I was born. OK . . . my mum was in London. Her mother was depressed puritan rather than strumpet extrovert. And she was 23 when she had me, not 16. But . . . she had an accidental child in the early '60s with a black man called Jimmy who quickly disappeared. She painted. She had friendships with men who volunteered to be stepdads, but chose her mother, for better and for worse. And, like Jo, she was something new in her family, modern and angry and doomed to never marry. I don't know that Jo would never have married, but I suspect that, like my mother, by the time she'd devoted every last second to her child in order to avoid making the mistakes of her own mother, she wouldn't have had anything left to give a man, especially trust. So I watch *A Taste Of Honey* and feel both illuminated and somewhat uncomfortable, as if I've watched something I was never supposed to have seen.

It's got to be a pretty great movie to do that to someone who wasn't even born when it was made. The best British teen film bar none, and far more besides.

★ ★

WEST SIDE STORY

1961

Starring: Natalie Wood, Richard Beymer, Russ Tamblyn, George Chakiris, Rita Moreno
Dir.: Jerome Robbins and Robert Wise

Plot: The jazz hands *Romeo And Juliet*.
Key line: 'Life can be bright in America/If you can fight in America/Life is all right in America/If you are white in America.'

How different would the greatest teen musical of all time have been if one of the many other actors considered for Tony had got the part? Let us consider, for a moment … Anthony Perkins? Nah … too psycho. Burt Reynolds? Too moustachy. Warren Beatty? Too vain. Bobby Darin? Too vapid. Richard Chamberlain? Too smooth. Dennis Hopper???!!! Really, I don't know where to start *or* finish with that level of weirdness.

But here's one to think on. At one point it was a real possibility that the tragic Romeo in this New York gangland/hoofer orgy could have been … Elvis Presley.

No, really. The producers of this movie version of an already huge Broadway hit dearly wanted Elvis to be their juvenile lead. Apart from his looks, voice, popularity and all-round Elvisness, he had form: he'd played a knife-wielding punk with a heart of gold in *King Creole* (see *Popcorn*) and been great. How perfect: the biggest pop star of the day in the biggest pop musical of the times?

But Hollywood didn't reckon with Presley's huckster manager Colonel Tom Parker. Once Elvis had done his patriotic stint in the US Army, Parker wanted Elvis to make the smooth transition to family-friendly MOR entertainer. Despite having already made millions out of rock 'n' roll, Parker believed this jungle music was a teenage fad and that his protégé had to move away from it as quickly as possible. Of course, *West Side Story* doesn't have a note of rock in it; it is based around the immaculate jazz-classical compositions of Leonard Bernstein (music) and Stephen Sondheim (lyrics). But it had rock 'n' roll attitude, with its jive-talkin' juvenile delinquents and themes of inner-city poverty and racial tension. So Parker kept his boy well away from the project.

Picture poor old Elvis, kicking back with his Memphis Mafia at one of the private screenings he would demand at his local cinema, watching a movie that won Ten Academy Awards, including Best Picture – more than any other musical in history – and spawned the biggest-selling soundtrack album of its times, while he pondered making a fool of himself in one of the musicals Parker preferred; maybe *Fun In Acapulco*, *Tickle Me* or *Clambake*. What a sap.

But, while it's fun to imagine him uh-huh-huhing his way through 'Something's Coming', Elvis couldn't have starred in *West Side Story*. What would they have done about the singing? There's no way Presley could've performed these arty melodramas without making it sound like he was taking the piss. And would they really have gone as far as having the hottest singing star on the planet lip-syncing to the operatic tenor of Jimmy Bryant, who provides the vocals for the guy who did get to play Tony, one Richard Beymer? It's all a non-starter, even within the world of pleasure provided by Elvis Presley 'What ifs?'

So let's stick with Richard Beymer. Even at the time, even in light of the Oscars and the millions of box office dollars, many were bemused by how poor a lead Beymer was. With his pleading eyes, weak chin, tombstone teeth, and pouty top lip, it's like someone dumped Cliff Richard into the middle of *Cabaret*. So much so that *West Side Story* became the end of a conventional film career for Beymer, rather than a beginning.

After *WSS*, Beymer scored a minor success among a star-studded cast in 1962 war epic *The Longest Day*, before sidelining acting for a career as an activist. He decamped to Mississippi for the great civil rights voter registration drives of 1964, and directed a documentary, *A Regular Bouquet: Mississippi Summer*, based upon his experiences. He directed an avant-garde movie called *The Innerview* in 1974. And then virtually disappeared from sight until being cast in the role of Ben Horne in David Lynch's seminal cult TV show *Twin Peaks* in the 1990s.

As a creepy postscript to all this, Beymer began a relationship around the time of *West Side Story* with a girl called Sharon Tate. He encouraged her to go into acting, a decision that ended with her violent slaughter by Charles Manson and his 'Family' at Roman Polanski's Hollywood mansion in 1969. Careers adviser not a job option, then.

So . . . interesting guy, all told. But a genuine contender for a non-Academy award for Worst Actor In A Lead Role In A Movie That Turned Out Great Despite His Presence. I suspect Beymer is the major reason why a film so famous and successful doesn't inspire the same level of acclaim and affection in the 21st century as the likes of *Cabaret*, *Singin' In The Rain*, *The Sound Of Music* or *Grease*. You just can't get past the guy.

But I really do adore *West Side Story*. And my love remains true purely because of three of its musical set-pieces, two of which prominently feature Beymer. Don't get me wrong: I love the gritty (for a musical) New York locations and lurid colours, and the way Wise (despite his co-director credit, Robbins, the *WSS* stage director who was essentially there to choreograph the dance sequences, was fired during the production) makes squalor look so beautiful. I love the toe-tappin', finger-snappin' presentation of the violence and posing of young working-class men. I love Wood and Moreno and Tamblyn. I love the bizarrely gymnastic way Tamblyn – as Jets leader Riff – dismounts from a high rail early in the movie; a death-defying move that would now form the entire centre-piece of some amateur film on YouTube, here dispensed with in a couple of seconds. And I especially love the ingenious basis of the whole enterprise, courtesy of Bernstein, Sondheim and Arthur Laurents's original 1957 stage musical . . . Shakespeare's saga of warring families the Montagues and Capulets recast in the image of teen gangs the Puerto Rican Sharks and the Caucasian Jets indulging in America's favourite pastime: race war.

But it's *West Side Story*'s three best songs that have taken up permanent residence in my psyche and which, for me anyways, represent the high watermark of non-rock-based American Song.

The first is 'Maria'. This is, visuals-wise, a Beymer solo. But I don't care that he's rubbish because it's all about the song; a melody so romantic that it entirely defines that unforgettable moment when one is first smitten by someone, usually some time in your teens. You remember: time stood still, your heart pounded and your stomach and legs did things you that you couldn't understand, invisible birds chirp merrily and all that talk of paradise and heaven which you'd just learned to be cynical about suddenly made perfect sense because you realised that it had nothing to do with God. An orchestra swirls in your ears and it's definitely a waltz, but one where the rhythm is replaced by the rush of your own blood.

If you don't recall, 'Maria' – original cast recording, sung by Jimmy Bryant – will bring it all flooding back. Make you sad that love and lust can never feel that new and shocking again. Make you happy that someone or something designed human beings to feel it at all. Make you remember that the pain of everything that happened at the time made you feel as alive as the pleasure, if you were lucky enough to get any, particularly the part where loud music backdrops the line, 'Say it loud and there's music playing', and then soft music frames the whisper, 'Say it soft and it's almost like praying.'

And then there's the raucous satire that is 'America'. After Maria's (Wood) patrician Big Brother Bernardo forbids her to see Tony, as earthy heroine Anita (future Oz star Rita Moreno), turns *feminista*. 'Girls here are free to have fun. She is in America now!' But Bernardo has the anti-multicultural answer to that. 'Puerto Rico is in America now.' The scene and the following song and dance are played for laughs, but sometimes one needs to sugar the bitter pill. 'America' and its surrounding dialogue hits the nails of economic migration and the gap between the realities and fantasies of integration squarely on the head. And the song, from its mutant Latin sound and the cartoonish joy of the Hispanic accents, through to the cruel irony of Sondheim's lyrics, still stands as the truest, funniest art statement on the lie of The American Dream, while its ebullience says something significant about the genuine freedom that America does offer. Its good-natured anger defines the coming civil rights crusades as perfectly as Sam Cooke's 'A Change Is Gonna Come', the cultural miscegenation of rock 'n' roll and the speeches of Martin Luther King. It is ten minutes of pure pleasure which gives anyone a crash course on the conflict between the liberal desire to assimilate and the conservative qualities of cleaving to one's own culture, and then punches the point home that none of this is about race. It's about class. It's about money. *It's always about money*.

And finally . . . possibly my favourite song in the world, and a song very powerfully connected to the previous couple of masterpieces. A duet that comes very close to illuminating the core element of The Human Condition. A melody so beautiful I can't listen to it, not even in company and when I'm feeling at my most butch and stoic, without gushing tears like a likkle girlie girl who has just watched Justin Bieber, her teddy bear and a kennelful of puppies being run over by a tank. It is called 'Somewhere', and . . . and . . . sorry . . . wait a minute . . . No, I'm fine, just something in my eye . . .

That's better. Where was I? Oh yeah, possibly the greatest song ever written, and I say that in an entry that mentions 'A Change Is Gonna Come' so don't you dare write this off as hyperbole. 'Somewhere' is about a vision of heaven. Of peace of mind, and escaping the traps that most of us live in, again, largely due to money. It's about hope, and our extraordinary ability to keep looking at the stars, even when the gutter is about to engulf us. It is astonishingly short here, which only goes to show how little time you need to transcend, when you have the right means at your disposal. There's a fantastic cover version by Tom Waits on his *Blue Valentine* album, which, by way of his rusty drain of a voice, makes the point that it's not just the young who need hope and poetry to carry on living.

So, there you go. *West Side Story* is one of those pieces of art that does make you feel somewhat in awe of what human beings can achieve, so deftly does it shuffle complex themes and then find the ideal pictures and music to bring them home. But I think this lofty excellence might be the other reason why *WSS* is not loved like, say, *Grease*, which is, in comparison, a tacky piece of am dram.

There's this gag in Seth McFarlane's scabrous cartoon show *Family Guy* – bear with me – where the Griffin family are locked in a panic room and are forced to make conversation. They find themselves talking about films, and *The Godfather* in particular. Peter Griffin doesn't like Coppola's masterwork because, he says, 'It insists upon itself.'

West Side Story insists upon itself. It knows just how clever and classy it is. And that's why it's 145 minutes long instead of a comfortable 90, and why, though it's an easy film to respect, it's a hard film to love. You can't imagine anyone turning up to a late-night screening in Jets or Sharks gear, or getting the girls round to watch it and laugh and bond nostalgically. It has a superior air, an arrogant distance from its audience that is only closed when the best songs swell and make you swoon.

Which is also why, when I've talked to various friends about this book, and they've started to reel off a list of what they feel are quintessential teen movies, not one person has mentioned *West Side Story*. It's an extraordinary film, and deserves its place here. But it's not an extraordinary film about teenagers. It isn't really interested in them, except as ciphers on which to project an intellectual-philosophical Big Statement about class, race, young love, Shakespeare, jazz and the true meaning of America. Maybe Elvis would have mocked the enterprise enough to prick some of the pretensions and make *West Side Story* less admirable, and more lovable.

★ ★

THE YOUNG SAVAGES

1961
Starring: Burt Lancaster, Shelley Winters, Telly Savalas, Stanley Kristien, John Davis Chandler
Dir.: John Frankenheimer

Plot: Former trapeze artist provides safety net for crazy, mixed-up kids.
Key line: 'He was 15 or 16 years old. And I was trying with all my heart to kill him.'

Savages, 'cos, you know, it's a jungle out there. Out There being 1961 Spanish Harlem (just Harlem in the film, but there is nary a black person to be seen). Instead, three Italian-American teen hoodlums race through the streets to a dissonant jazz soundtrack. We know they're hoodlums because they wear leather, kick over a child's doll's pram and don't stop to pick up their five-a-day from the fruit market. They almost knock over a little girl too, but the camera has no time to stop and take this in, being busy, busy, busy following the boys' date with destiny – to the stoop of Puerto Rican teen Roberto

Escalante. There is a rush and a push, knives are pulled and the camera falls back to show us what those gangland jazz riffs were telling us all along – somebody's going to get their head kicked in tonight. Roberto dies in front of his sister Louisa (played by Pilar Suerat).

Can't stop to mourn though, because that camera's getting busy again, following the boys' attempted escape through building sites, dodging wrecking balls where the old world is being demolished to make room for a New World Order of youth gangs and tribal divisions. Director John Frankenheimer, maybe best known for bonkers masterpiece *The Manchurian Candidate*, lets his camera run wild in every imaginable way – views from above, low-screen angles including a child's-eye view, deep focus a go-go, a rotational view that beckons the main character through a door and then swivels to follow him up a flight of stairs. Oh … and Steadicam-type shots apparently from the vantage point of the Coney Island rollercoaster. Throughout the film, this camera ain't playing second fiddle to no puny story.

Back to Harlem. Picked up by the fuzz, the boys soon find themselves in a police station being questioned by Burt Lancaster, helped by chronically smirking cop Telly Savalas, who, before he gets a full Telly Savalas like his real-life niece Jennifer Aniston in *The Break-Up*, makes do with two fashion-forward Brazilians over his ears.

The boys are members of the Italian-American Thunderbirds gang: Arthur Reardon, the brains of the outfit, who wants to be a psycho when he grows up (played by John Davis Chandler); Anthony Aposto, nicknamed Batman and intellectually 'backward' (Neil Nephew); and Danny DiPace (Stanley Kristien).

Burt is the assistant District Attorney Hank Bell, his anglicised name tolling the death knell of his immigrant identity and birth name Bellini. For Burt is Italian, he's from the streets, and it turns out he also knows one of the boys, DiPace – he used to date DiPace's mother Mary, played by perennial Queen Victim in the gender- and class-war films of the '50s and '60s, Shelley Winters.

But that was back in the day, and Burt has now set his sights a bit higher. He's married to Karin (Merrill) who could not be more WASP if her girdle was black-and-yellow striped. They live in a modern apartment block, and have a perky 14-year-old daughter

Jenny. But Burt's not home as often as he might be, and Jenny's growing up. She wears a bra, and Burt's not noticed she needs one (though that's probably a good thing for a father not to notice, or is that just me?). She's also dating a boy called Lonnie. 'I thought it was Greg,' says Burt to his missus, who confirms it used to be. 'Did I ever meet Lonnie?' 'You didn't meet Greg,' snaps Mrs Wasp. Could it be that Burt is – gasp – a Bad Dad himself? Could Jenny be heading for a troubled life and tragedy on the stoop? No, because luckily they don't have a stoop, they have an elevator. Burt's got out of the ghetto, remember?

Burt interviews the boys, Reardon and Batman Aposto in jail, Danny in juvie as he's only 15. Reardon is the ringleader, absolutely without remorse. Batman is ... well, he's variously described as retarded, stupid, insane – terms apparently interchangeable in this film. To illustrate this, Reardon has him bang his head on the jail wall, which Batman does without hesitation. You get the feeling he's maybe the teensiest bit suggestible. Meanwhile, Danny says he don't need no stinking help, not from his mum and not from proxy-dad Burt neither.

The three boys are claiming self-defence, saying that Roberto pulled a knife first, apparently witnessed by a neighbourhood girl. But Burt's investigation finds that Roberto was blind (just like justice herself, in one of the clunkier juxtapositions), and that shiny knife the girl saw glinting in the sun was a harmonica. Did the T-Birds commit the premeditated murder of a blind defenceless harmonica player, just because he's a member of the rival Puerto Rican gang The Horsemen? Burt thinks so, and if they're guilty, that's Murder One and a one-way trip to the plug-in deterrent of the electric chair. You don't kill Stevie Wonder on Burt's watch and get away with it.

Who's going to argue? Not Burt's boss, being mentioned as a possible state governor, because nothing spells votes in an American election like the possibility of executing juvenile delinquents. Not the boys themselves, with their misguided view of manhood. Not Roberto's mourning-clad mother, looking like an Old Country fury from a Universal '30s horror film, and charging Burt with exacting revenge on her son's murderers – she wants an eye for an eye for her dead, blind son.

But there's another mother involved. Two actually. First, Mrs

Wasp gets drunk at the boss's fundraiser for his election campaign, and expresses some liberal doubts about murdering teenagers for votes. After all, this is a gubernatorial race in New York, not a presidential election in Texas. Cue some more cinematricks and distracting camera-work, as Burt and the missus glower at each other front-of-frame, while there's some deep-focus speechifying in the background. (Interestingly she doesn't recant these views, even when threatened by The Horseman herself. If this was a less liberal movie, she'd have had a day-long recant-athon, taking breaks every hour to admit that hubby always knows best and ladies is rubbish.)

The second mother is Shelley Winters/Mary DiPace, Burt's ex (kind of hard to believe in the film, but, as we'll see below, truth may have been stranger than fiction). She doesn't want her boy to fry – she believes he may be good-bad, but not evil. After all, he saved a young Puerto Rican from being drowned by his fellow gang members. Despite Danny's absent father (Mary found out on the wedding night that said father was a Petty Racketeer, and now he's gone, either to the big racket in the sky, or maybe prison, or maybe spraying racketeer seed elsewhere in Harlem, it's not important, he's just absent, OK?), Mary's loved him and tried to bring him up well. But they don't have an elevator, so the siren call of the streets has proved too strong.

It all ends, as it has to, in a sweaty, hysterical court room. There's a bit of business around who wielded which knife, Louisa the murdered boy's sister reveals her own Mommy-implicating secret, and Burt's boss starts to realise he can't count on executing ethnic and mentally disabled children for political gain. Trainee psycho Reardon goes gloriously nutazoid and is gagged … but there are no super-injunctions here, this is an actual hanky gagging his mouth. Ah, the literal '60s. Danny comes back into the family fold and accepts some proxy-dad advice – 'Tears are for men too.'

The boys are found guilty, but today nobody dies. There's no way back to society for Reardon, who gets 20-to-life in the big house. But there's a nice padded therapeutic Batcave waiting for insane/stupid/retarded Aposto, and Shelley's boy Danny, who did no actual stabbing, gets a year in juvie for rehabilitation. Judging by Shelley's relieved reaction, you'd think his sentence was being sent to bed with no dinner. But then she hasn't seen *The Wire* and doesn't know that a year in juvenile custody, while on paper better than the chair, will inevitably make your nice son a sociopathic badass.

A Hollywood ending? Well, yes, but there's a scene in court that jolts and jars you just as you're dropping off to liberal certainty. And it's that nosy hyperactive camera to blame, for once not moving, just looking. Shelley's in the courtroom of course, but she's not the mother that counts today. In an astonishing shot, Mrs Wasp and Jenny, in all their fragrant Nordic Western middle-class prettiness and pastel clothes, are sitting directly in front of Roberto's mother and sister. Ostensibly from Puerto Rico, these women, still in almost niqab-like mourning, stare unmoving like Mittel European agents of vengeance. Whatever happens in that courtroom, this class/race war shit ain't over.

Visually and thematically, the film brings to mind Orson Welles' *Touch of Evil*, though it's a New York to Mexico distance behind that stone classic. So if it's no masterpiece, why is *The Young Savages* in here? Well, there are some great scenes and set-pieces – the on-location funeral, a never-mentioned passed-out drunk in a neighbourhood bar, a metaphor-laden scene involving billiard balls between Burt and Pretty Boy (Chris Robinson), leader of The Thunderbirds. Burt gets a beautifully shot, young and savage teen kicking on the subway to boot. Unusually, some of the teen characters are more than just symbols, including (the admittedly pretty symbolic-sounding) Pretty Boy and Zorro (Luis Arroyo), leader of The Horsemen. Roberto and his sister turn out to be not-so-innocent bystanders in Harlem gang and criminal life, so it's not all black and white. And it has one of the most memorable – and memorably ugly – teen thugs in Chandler's Arthur Reardon, a genuinely disturbing mess of drunk, swimming eyes and slobbering chops.

But in the end, the clincher is Burt Lancaster. From his brilliant debut in *The Killers* through to this in 1961, Burt Lancaster was a titanic talent in *From Here to Eternity*, *The Leopard*, *Sweet Smell of Success* and the previous year's *Elmer Gantry*, for which he won the Oscar. Astounding performances in future cult favourite *The Swimmer* and for European maestros Louis Malle and Bernardo Bertolucci were still to come. He also wielded power behind the camera as part of the über-successful Hecht-Hill-Lancaster production company.

So what was he doing slumming it in this overwrought (albeit imaginatively filmed) teensploitation? This film is like the Knorr stock cube of teen movies, with every teen ingredient carefully concentrated into 90 minutes. Absent fathers? Oh yes. Cops and psychiatrists? Fo' sho'. Gangs as surrogate families? Uh huh. Anxious mothers trying their best but defenceless in the face of youth-powered change? You betcha. (By the way, the source novel was written by Evan Hunter, aka Ed McBain, birth name Salvatore Albert Lombino. Hank Bell isn't the only one to realise that changing your name changes the game.)

Maybe it was because Lancaster was a long-term and vocal liberal, raised in East Harlem himself, who could afford to promote his beliefs through a race and class message movie. Maybe it was another chance to work with long-time colleagues and friends – Harold Hecht, his long-time business partner, was producer on this film and Lancaster knew co-star Shelley Winters well too; in fact Winters' autobiography maintained they had an affair lasting many years. Maybe he had a hunch it was the start of another beautiful friendship – *The Young Savages* was the first of five collaborations between Lancaster and Frankenheimer, including the following year's megaacclaimed *Birdman of Alcatraz* for which Lancaster was also Oscarnominated.

Whatever his reasons, he's head and shoulders above everybody else in the film. He elevates the movie and gives it a grace and grandeur it wouldn't have without him. 'Cos he could do that. Chuck Heston is good enough in *Touch of Evil* – actually brilliant, for him – but imagine Burt Lancaster in that kohl moustache facing off with Orson Welles and Marlene Dietrich, and dream. He was some kind of a man, even in a weird, trashy movie like this one.

★ ★

THE LONELINESS OF THE LONG-DISTANCE RUNNER

1962

Starring: Tom Courtenay, Michael Redgrave, Avis Bunnage, Alec McCowan, James Bolam, Topsy Jane, Julia Foster, John Thaw, James Fox
Dir.: Tony Richardson

Plot: Baby, we were born to run.
Key line: 'I'd get all the coppers, governors, posh whores, army officers and members of parliament, and I'd stick 'em up against this wall and let them have it. Because that's what they'd like to do to blokes like us.'

Tony Richardson's second great teen movie has all the elements you would expect from Britain's late '50s/early '60s Free Cinema movement. Like *A Taste Of Honey* (see p. 70), it is interested in The Grim Up North (well, actually, Nottingham in the Midlands – but the Midlands counts as Up North in movies of this era), disadvantaged youth, class conflict, documentary monochrome and a lead performance by an English EveryYouth of such charisma that all possibilities of bleak worthiness are cast aside. Unlike *A Taste Of Honey*, it's also about The System . . . the greatest bogeyman of Angry Young Man cinema. Adapted by Alan Sillitoe from his own, equally essential short story, *Loneliness* . . . is based around the simplest of metaphors: in a society where freedom and social mobility is impossible to achieve for most of its members, the rebellious boy runs, and runs, and runs some more . . . and never moves anywhere.

Tom Courtenay plays Colin Smith, a bright but troubled boy who has been sentenced to reform school for robbing a bakery. The scandalously posh governor (Redgrave) of the borstal has a bug up his arse for athletics and learns that Colin is a prodigiously talented cross-country runner. He awards Colin privileged status in return for him running in a sports event against a nearby public school, an event the governor dearly wants to win. As Colin trains for and runs in the race, we see flashbacks to exactly how he got to this lonely, exhausting place. Friend Mike (Bolam) questions Colin's willingness to sell out, and the public school boys – in preparation for *If . . .* (see p. 97) presumably – appear to have more in common with the borstal boys than one might imagine. By the time Colin gets to the finishing line, he has sifted the harsh details of his life, the empty promises of material success, and the hypocrisies of the governor, the ruling-class and everyone else over the age of 25. So he rebels in the only way left to him. He stops running.

Or, to put it another way, this is a pioneering English class war template for all those American high school movies about dumb or sensitive jocks who are awarded King Of School status because they're good with various types of ball. Colin is given privileged status because he's good at sport, and his reaction to that determines whether he's hero or villain. American high school movies are full of jocks given privileged status because they're good at sport, and, in films like *The Breakfast Club* (see p. 263) and *Dazed And Confused* (see p. 307), and a TV show like *Glee*, their reaction to that determines whether they're hero or villain. The governor spots Colin's talent for running during a football match, and ignores the new, new-fangled liberal idealist member of staff, Mr Brown (McCowan), when he suggests that life might be more complicated than a game of football.

It's also a feast for Brit telly nostalgists. The late John Thaw of *The Sweeney* and *Inspector Morse* fame is one of Colin's fellow inmates, playing a Scouser and sporting a very fetching Teddy Boy DA cut. And pug-nosed cockney comic stooge Arthur Mullard – the most appropriately named man in TV history – is one of the governor's henchmen. Future *Likely Lad* Bolam gets a bigger part as Colin's mate and partner-in-petty crime, while future *Performance* star Fox is the star public school boy Colin races against.

Loneliness . . . is not as great a film as *A Taste Of Honey*. There are too many dodgy acting performances. Too many sledgehammer political speeches. Too many ironic uses of William Blake's 'Jerusalem' in the annoyingly busy score. So much class anger that you wonder if the whole movie doth protest too much. There is one reason why the film is here, and its name is Tom Courtenay.

Those who know Courtenay from a later and much-admired career of playing comic dreamers, fey aesthetes and wimpy nice guys will barely recognise him in his second film role. In sharp contrast to his next role in the brilliant *Billy Liar*, Courtenay is a flint-eyed threat, wiry and gaunt, mouth drawn into a constant hard and baleful glower. His pale and skinny body in vest and shorts, running and running, legs so thin you fear they'll snap in two if he treads on a bug, is the image you take away from *Loneliness* . . . Because he is small and thin, the threat Courtenay carries isn't of the punch-you-out variety. It's more about an absence of fear and an infinite capacity for pain. He feels like a rock 'n' roll northerner, a Mark E. Smith or a Liam Gallagher, a mixture of impenetrable insolence and smartarse street smarts. Courtenay *is* the movie.

We know Colin is brighter than the other boys. Partly because he's the only one who doesn't have a greasy rocker cut, but mainly because he is as unimpressed by Brown's intrusive reformism as he is by the aloof authoritarianism of the governor and his thugs. He accepts his life of dead dad and miserable mum, downbeat romance, days out at Skegness (in European new wave movies, there is always a beach), borstal riots, and the wonders of poverty row television and consumerism with a weary stoicism. He's a study in pessimism and a mix of Antoine from *The 400 Blows* (see p. 47) and Trevor from *Made In Britain* (see p. 210). He could go on to become a thoroughly bad lot or Poet Laureate, and would probably insist that there wasn't any difference, when it came right down to it. Colin is a practical existentialist, which is probably what will save him from flirting with fascism like Trevor.

Existentialism actually gets a mention, oddly. At one point Colin and Mike watch a party political broadcast on TV, mocking the empty platitudes. The PM then goes into a very weird rant about 'continental existentialists' before calling America 'our cousins in affluence'. This cosying up to the Yanks and rejecting the influence of Jean-Paul Sartre is presumably, according to Sillitoe, A Very Bad Thing.

And this is the meaning of the unforgettable, inspiring, sobering ending. America is where winning means everything. The British Left hate America. So losing becomes an anti-capitalist, anti-American act. Which, apart from explaining much about British sport, carries a unique political sting. Colin's refusal to play the game doesn't give him revolutionary glory. We leave him among the other boys, privileges long gone, being hollered at in the borstal workshop.

They are making gas-masks; slave labour in preparation for war. *Jerusalem* plays us out.

Top stuff. I miss The Old Left. Sometimes.

★ ★

TO SIR, WITH LOVE

1967

Starring: Sidney Poitier, Judy Geeson, Christian Roberts, Suzy Kendall, Lulu, Geoffrey Bayldon
Dir.: James Clavell

Plot: The Swinging '60s *Blackboard Jungle*.
Key line: 'Unless you can work up a little black magic, these little bastards have a multitude of tricks.'

No film makes an exiled Londoner more nostalgic for the old Route-master double-decker London buses. You're not entirely sure at first which western suburb Sidney Poitier's Mark Thackeray is travelling from (it turns out to be Brentwood), but the opening credits take you on a journey through London at its bustling best, through the West End and past Tower Bridge and the Tower Of London and right on through to the wild East End, where everyone suddenly becomes louder, friendlier and scarier, which they do. I get all over-come with removed nostalgia by a glimpse of a No. 15 to Ladbroke Grove, which, in 1967, would be taking you right into the middle of plans for the early Carnivals, the first Pink Floyd and Soft Machine shows, the ever-growing rebellion against evil landlord Peter Rachman, black power leader Michael X, Marc Bolan living in a squat, and the beginnings of the underground press. Sigh. Born too late.

Thackeray is a rookie teacher thrown into the lion's den at a tough secondary modern school in, we think, East Ham. The credulity-stretching question as to why a dazzling African-American intel-lectual stud-muffin has ended up in London to educate the poor – apart from persuading American bums onto cinema seats, of course – is taken care of by the early explanation that he's an immigrant from British Guiana who 'spent some time in California'. He's only become a teacher because he can't get work in racist England as an engineer, despite his splendid qualifications.

Suzy Kendall is the fellow-teacher love interest, which is funny, because Kendall was kind of a poor man's Julie Christie – all blonde hair and blow-job lips – but is made into a teacher here by – you guessed it – an elastic band round the do and a pair of black horn-rim glasses. As soon as she walks onscreen you're on standby alert for the bit where she shyly shakes her hair free and Sidney removes the glasses and declares, 'But, why, Miss Blanchard . . . you're beautiful!'

Far better is the presence of a young Patricia Routledge, the future Hyacinth Bucket from the *Keeping Up Appearances* sitcom. Not only is she quite shockingly hot, but she has the cut-glass upper-class accent Hyacinth would've killed for, and her character is called Clinty Clintridge. Clinty Clintridge! A couple of 'N's away from a career in porn. Where did it all go wrong, Patricia? But while the rest of the teachers talk in tired platitudes, Clinty – hur! – is the Voice Of Reason.

The ostensible villain is cynical veteran teacher Weston, played by Geoffrey Bayldon, who made a '70s career out of eccentric goobers, most notably in Marc Bolan's Ringo-directed *Born To Boogie* movie and much-loved kids' time-travelling wizard telly show *Catweazle*. Weston parades his loathing of both youth and the working classes with jaded sneers, and everything he says to Thackeray has some kind of jauntily racist undercurrent. Just in case Poitier's presence isn't courting the American audience enough, one of Weston's rants proves he hates Yanks as much as everyone else, so he's obviously an English middle-class loser.

If you've already read the entry for *The Blackboard Jungle* (see p. 20), then your head is probably spinning by now. *To Sir, With Love* really does play like Gregory Miller grows up to be a teacher and finds himself having to deal with kids like him . . . in England! And they're mostly white, and he's all black, which therefore shows off how much we white liberals have grown in the last ten years of the civil rights struggle! This really should be a confused, contrived and condescending wet liberal disaster. But it isn't. Director and screenwriter James Clavell, an Australian former prisoner of war who made magic from his experiences by writing the script for *The Great Escape*, has too much heart to let that happen.

This school – which remains unnamed, oddly – is one of these new-fangled '60s experiments in liberal education. Teachers are not allowed to punish the kids. Not just physically . . . I mean, not *at all*. And, apropos of nothing, in the middle of the school day, the kids have discos. Real discos, in a big hall, with crazy beat music which just happens to be sung by Lulu, who, as killer bee-hived pupil Barbara, is dancing right upfront. None of the kids asks her about how the pop career's going. They're all too cool for that. But this cool doesn't stretch as far as the dancing which is triumphantly bad. Teen movies may have got better, all things considered. But the genre lost something crucial when it started to employ actors who could dance and gave them proper choreography. Every film ever made would be substantially improved by a bad-freaky-dancing at-a-disco-scene. *The King's Speech. Inception.* Everything by Woody Allen. It's just laziness, is what it is.

Anyway, the pupils at this paradise – sorry – deeply troubled school are rejects from other schools and this place is essentially just baby-sitting them until they are old enough to become grunt soldiers in the ever-growing reserve army of labour. This is easy to suss because they all have Dick Van Dyke, 'ave-a-banana-I-should-coco-guv cock-er-knee accents, rather than talking like normal London urchins, who, by the time this Londoner was four, were already starting to sound like Dizzee Rascal.

In terms of the standard classroom war zone, these kids go in more for the drip-drip-drip of low-level disruption, rather than flick-knives or assault with a deadly chair. But after a couple of days, the frustrated and rather distant Mark is circling local paper ads for engineers. His food for thought moment is, perhaps, the moment that makes the movie seem personal to me, leading me to forgive much of its soft-soap sentiment and the mockney over-acting of one Christian Roberts as head Bad Boy Denham.

Mark has a conversation after school with his class's token mixed-race boy, Seales. The boy's angry and miserable because his white mother is ill and his black father is absent. I, too, grew up with an absent black father and a white mum who physically and psy-chologically buckled under the strain of raising me on benefits and low-paid jobs. The scene is nicely under-played . . . teacher doesn't take Seales under his wing and provide a black male role model to make everything all right for the boy. It just reminds him that these kids have been fucked up and have a right to be hostile, and that their teachers have little idea of how bad things are at home, aside from Clinty's sweeping assumption that they're slapped around by Bad Dads.

Because America is a gun culture, the vision of juvenile delinquency in American film is always apocalyptic, on some level. But this is a school I recognise, where the pain of being a 'disadvantaged' child doesn't play itself out in shoot-outs, gang-fights or death, but the drawn-out nightmare of a hellish home life and a school system that, largely, doesn't give a shit how you turn out as long as you turn up. *To Sir, With Love* captures a British cultural cringe, in the '60s and '70s, around the 'problem' of working-class youth, unmarried mothers and 'half-caste' children, a constant implication, dressed up in liberal hand-wringing, that there was something naturally *wrong* with our start in life, and that the emphasis should be on teaching us to be obedient rather than how to achieve our intellectual potential.

I'm not saying that a bright working-class kid – of any colour – might not have identical grievances in 2011. Simply that there isn't another movie, that I've seen anyway, that talks about *my* '60s/'70s London childhood with any degree of honesty while coming to the conclusion that being working class in England isn't inevitably a dead end. And that is why I love *To Sir, With Love*.

The tension in the early part of the film revolves entirely around Poitier's USP – the proud and beautiful black man, attempting to keep his dignity intact under assault from lesser beings. In this case, unlike most of his best-known roles, Poitier is caught up in generational war, rather than race war. We are simply waiting for him to lose his temper and tame the beasts. And the incident that creates the tipping-point is a weird, creepy one that must have seemed fairly daring back in 1967.

After being narrowly missed by a water-bomb, Thackeray strides into his classroom to find something burning. Nobody says it out loud, but, from his horrified reaction and targeting of the girls, we infer that one of the little madams has set fire to her used sanitary towel in the classroom bin. In truth, the story needs this huge upping of the ante, because water-bombs and slammed desktops aren't really getting over the idea that these kids are, as Mark now declares, 'Devils incarnate'. But burning bloody sanitary towels is the kind of nastiness that stands the test of teenage time.

It provokes Thackeray's eureka moment, one that would be

familiar to the writers of Season Four of *The Wire*. These kids are in their last term of being in school before being spat out into a life of soldiering or shopwork or far, far worse. There's no curriculum – at least, not one that anyone in authority gives a shit about. So ... treat these children like adults ... up to a point. Spend class time allowing them to talk about their lives, and pay them the courtesy of listening. If you can't send them out into the world with reading skills and times-tables intact, at least try and encourage them to have social skills, and to treat others – and each other – with respect. Soon, Mark is very smartly diverting a Denham wind-up question about black women in Africa always being naked into a discourse about teen style and The Beatles, which smoothly becomes a plug for a simply must-see new exhibition at the Victoria & Albert Museum. Genius, really. And, with the exception of a few bravura scenes of conflict and tearjerking feelgoodery, that's your movie.

Admittedly, this is still the 1960s, so the sexual politics lags a little behind the race and class consciousness. Hence the Mark Thackeray/James Clavell Charter For The Education Of Young Women: 'Soon boyfriends and marriage will concern you. No man likes a slut for long ... and the competition for men on the outside is rough.' It's a war out there, ladies. And one doesn't win the right to drop sprogs and wash his streak-marked undies by wearing mini-skirts and waving your sanitary towels around. It's like a red rag to a bull.

Nevertheless, we have a proto-feminist in the movie. Judy Geeson's Pamela Dare – daring by name and by nature – is the one character other than Thackeray who is prepared to take stands about race and other principles, and, after her mother has begged Thackeray to speak to Pamela about her daughter staying out all hours, the maker of a sexual liberation speech inspired by The Pill: 'We're the luckiest bunch of kids, the luckiest generation. ... We're the first to be really free to enjoy ...' – a neat pause – '*life*, if we want. Without fear.' Oh, the naivety.

The best scenes are often as much down to Clavell's willingness to innovate and a love of pop as they are good writing. The museum visit is rendered as a montage of photos – fresh-faced kids looking happily awestruck as a new, old world is unveiled to them through the exhibits – while the wonderful theme song plays. This is where I declare another unusual fetish: for me, Lulu's 'To Sir, With Love' is the best teen movie theme song ever, ever, ever. Music by Marc London, lyrics by Don Black and arrangement by one of the great unsung geniuses of British pop, Mike Leander, 'To Sir, With Love' is a blue-eyed soul ballad about being (platonically) in love with one's teacher which includes the graceful, gorgeous question: 'How do you thank someone/Who's taken you from crayons to perfume?'

An American No. 1 in 1967, the song busts right through the potential for inappropriate child–adult romance, which was never going to be easy. The film, incidentally, pulls the same trick, making the crush that Judy Geeson's Pamela eventually has on Thackeray into something pure and heartfelt about the gratitude you really do feel, as a kid, when an adult shows you kindness and understanding above and beyond the call of duty. We all need mentors beyond our parents, and 'To Sir, With Love', the song, is a fitting tribute to memories of adults who helped you when you needed it.

The opening scene on a bus is a stand-out too, despite its absence of teens. It brings me thudding back to my own childhood, and memories of shrinking with embarrassment as loud middle-aged geezerettes you'd never met made ribald jokes about sex that you didn't entirely understand but knew, instinctively, were about the fact that you were just the new version of the never-ending sexual disappointment that was men. The loud and proudly hideous woman here is Rita Webb, another '70s TV comedy stalwart who always played the same happy but ball-shrinking cockney harpy, made for a life of working in launderettes or on fruit and veg stalls, and long immune to insults about her looks or weight . . . a force of nature and living testament to working-class Blitz spirit and mustn't grumble attitude.

The tale's flashpoint comes in a nicely unexpected way. You know all this sweetness and light can't last, and you're expecting Pamela to lure Mark into something compromising, or grumpy old Weston to find some way to stop the new boy making him look bad. But actually, the cause of ill-feeling comes down to two letters than can still cause many grown-men to regress into foetal positions and relive all their worst adolescent nightmares . . . PE.

Admittedly, we haven't met either a kid called Fats or the bullying PE teacher before now. But the scene of a fat kid being forced to jump a gym horse the teacher knows full well he can't negotiate is horribly familiar. Problem is, all this Thackeray talk about his class being adults is making these boys feel responsible for each other. When Fats breaks the horse and hurts himself, instead of having a good laugh at his expense, they rise up against the pointless humiliation. Cheeky chappie and Denham sidekick Potts goes for Teach with a bit of wood. Thackeray stops him before blood is spilled, but our hero now has to make them understand why standing up to a bully is very, very wrong . . . Hey! Wait a minute! It isn't, is it?

But such are the inequities of the education system – you can't beat up teachers, even when they've really been asking for it. And the perceived reverting to type of Thackeray forces a confrontation between him and Denham for control of the group. Right back in *Blackboard Jungle* territory again, then.

Meanwhile, Seales's mother dies and Thackeray finds out that the kids can't take a wreath round because their reputations will suffer if they enter a 'coloured' person's home. There's a great close-up of Poitier, trying to process the news that, despite being so much better and brighter than these kids and their parents, he is still seen as a blight, an inferior to be tolerated at arm's length. It's a look Poitier had to pull a great deal in his career, but he really was the master of the form.

Thackeray's attempts to form a society of consensus among the savages are being undermined by outside forces. In the end, he can only reassert his leadership of the herd with a right uppercut. Typical American. Once order is restored, it's feelgood all round, courtesy of a funeral, another disco, a wonderfully camp Poitier/Geeson dance-off . . . and Mark's pondering of whether to run off to make engines in the Midlands or continue with his missionary work in darkest Plaistow.

It's only at movie's end you realise that Ms Kendall is a complete red herring . . . there is no love interest. There is no shakes-her-head-and-removes-glasses, duckling-to-swan moment. No nasty Lolita threat from Pam. But, sadly, this isn't down to subversive screenwriting. It's because the price that Sidney Poitier paid for being the first mainstream African-American leading man was that he was never allowed to display his sexuality. An America which was still shaking itself loose of segregation could deal with one black star if he didn't pose a sexual threat, and especially not with white women. And to be honest, Britain wasn't any more comfortable with black sexuality in 1967. It was Poitier's typecasting as the noble, desexualised black 'role model' that eventually turned the star away from acting and into directing and producing.

But, to be fair to *To Sir, With Love*, it didn't offer any pat solutions to the fact that most of the kids are leaving school for unemployment and being unpaid skivvies for their parents. No judgement, either way, as to whether this liberal schooling is a good or bad idea. And Thackeray is never given a single preachifying speech. In short, all the clichés that you expect at the beginning of the film never emerge. Just a heartbreaking theme song, a London with the strange beauty it had in the 1960s, and a genuinely uplifting film about the importance of being respected and making the best of a bad lot. Very British, then, and all the better for it.

★ ★

IF . . .

1968
Starring: Malcolm McDowell, David Wood, Richard Warwick, Hugh Thomas, Peter Jeffery, Arthur Lowe, Robert Swann, Christine Noonan
Dir.: Lindsay Anderson

**Plot: Portrait of the English schoolboy as a young guerrilla.
Key line: 'Don't push us, Stephans. The day is coming.'**

Released in a year of counter-cultural insurrections largely led by youth, *If . . .* remains the teen film that most perfectly captures the fantasy of teenage revolution. It does so by presenting a satirical and surreal view of a very specific reality: life in an English post-war Home Counties public school. The school remains nameless, but its blackly comic blend of arcane rituals, militaristic hierarchies, religious hypocrisies, physical humiliations and teenage homosexual affairs was based upon the experiences of screenwriter David Sherwin at Tonbridge School in Kent in the 1950s. The film was, intriguingly and bizarrely, first offered to American director Nicholas Ray of *Rebel Without A Cause* (see p. 28) fame, a hero to new wave film-makers of the time, who had to let it go because he was having some kind of breakdown. Ray was also approached to make a Rolling Stones movie at roughly the same time.

Instead, the job went to Lindsay Anderson, who was already one of the British new wave's most acclaimed directors through his work on his 1963 debut adaptation of Angry Young Man novel *This Sporting Life*. Anderson was the perfect choice: a product of an upper-class British army family stationed in India whose own rebel anger stemmed from his experiences at Cheltenham College in Gloucestershire, where he somehow managed to shoot most of *If . . .* (two other colleges had turned down the opportunity as soon as they got wind of the movie's themes).

Like the French new wave directors, Anderson had begun his movie life as a radical critic and worshipped at the altar of Jean Vigo, a French film-maker whose surreal schoolboy comedy short *Zéro de conduite* was the major influence upon Francois Truffaut's teen new wave classic *The 400 Blows* (see p. 47). For *If . . .*, Anderson took the revolutionary implications of Vigo and Truffaut and made them explicit: society is sick and corrupt, and, as schools are both literal and metaphorical breeding-grounds for this corruption, the best thing for all concerned would be a children's uprising, in the form of an armed revolution. Being a French-inspired film that hit screens to great critical acclaim and commercial success as France reeled from a dramatic insurrection led by Paris students, *If . . .* became the film that symbolised the imperial wobbles of 1968.

The (gunpowder) plot is minimal. Three students, led by Michael 'Mick' Travis (McDowell), rebel against the strictures of a brutal public school in various mocking, mischievous ways. Mick swishes into school in a black hat with a scarf covering his face, and gets compared to Guy Fawkes, that most infamous of failed English revolutionaries, and the boys clip photos of big angry black men toting machine-guns out of magazines, experiment with asphyxiation by plastic bag and occasionally spout epigrams like, 'War is the last possible creative act.'

The school is a petri-dish for the development of brutality, as the most sycophantic older students are given *carte blanche* to repress their peers, language is mangled into abusive labels like 'scum', 'shag' and 'bumf', and teachers smack or grope pupils without fear of censure. It's all working a treat on the kids who, when left unsupervised for the odd moment, have nothing else left in their interaction locker but callous bullying and chaotic violence.

Boys must be locked up in the school by 5 p.m. and are not allowed to mix with the peasants of the town, reinforcing both the prison feel of the institution and its symbolic value as a micro-society. And, as they re-register for this winter term, the boys must line up and have their genitals inspected by the Matron. This involves dropping their trousers while she peers at their bits with a torch. *If* . . . was, apparently, entirely accurate about the details of public school in the 1950s and '60s.

After Mick and Johnny (Wood) escape the school grounds for an afternoon of sex and motorbiking, and Wallace (Warwick) gets caught in an after-hours smoking session with pretty first-year Bobby Phillips (Webster), our heroes must be punished. This involves Head Boy Rowntree (Swann) taking a long run-up and caning the boys' arses until they bleed. The most important part of this debasement ritual is that the victim must politely and respectfully thank his spanker, as boys throughout the school must always thank whoever is torturing them currently, and as we, in turn, must always thank those above us for allowing us to be exploited and humiliated by them.

After a surreal sequence of events involving war games and apologising to a dead priest who is sleeping in a drawer (watch it – it will all make sense, honest), the boys and Mick's girl (Noonan) stumble upon a cellarful of heavy artillery. They clamber aboard the school roof and proceed to take out the faculty and assembled dignitaries with extreme prejudice. A visiting military general organises a fightback and the public school becomes a theatre of war. The head appeals for calm and Mick's girl shoots him in the head. The film ends with an outnumbered and outgunned Mick manically firing his weapon, and the screen fades to the unresolved, titular question.

But none of this makes *If* . . . a classic movie. After all, left-wing movies are notoriously dull and worthy. The bad guys and good guys here are ciphers, rather than fully imagined characters. And *If* . . . is rooted in '60s notions of radical chic; almost the only music on the soundtrack is the 'Sanctus' theme from 'Missa Luba', a once-popular version of the Latin Mass based on Congolese folk songs and sung by African children, which beats you over the head with its dated and racist views of all blacks as nobly savage revolutionaries. 'Sanctus' even gets to soundtrack the movie's memorably surreal and savage sexual dream sequence in a deserted monochrome café. Oh yeah . . . there are also the bits where colour suddenly turns to black and white, that most pseudish of art cinema short-cuts to symbolism.

Yet, *If* . . . really doesn't date. It has something timeless, you see. It has Malcolm McDowell.

Just as he gave focus and heart to the scattershot violence of *A Clockwork Orange* (see p. 111), the Yorkshire-born actor, already 25 by the time Anderson cast him in his screen debut, makes Mick Travis into the idealised EveryYouth. His every gesture and expression mocks power, yet his pain and humiliation is poignantly rendered in the caning scene. He is funny, sexy, hard, vulnerable and his eyes seem to pierce through to the truth at the core of every lie. He is as iconic in the formal dress of the public schoolboy as he is as leather-jacketed revolutionary assassin. He is shot through with life and ironic loathing, and the dual innocence and cynicism needed to survive any indignity. As symbolic revolutionaries go . . . he's pretty fucking good. And although Anderson's directorial style is full of gorgeous compositions, energy and stark comedy, and Sherwin's dazzling script refuses to sacrifice entertainment for propaganda, it's McDowell who does the hard work of both making privileged children sympathetic, and making their insurrection feel like the fulfilment of the dreams of anyone who has suffered at the hands of the arbitrary wielding of power and allowed themselves to dream of murderous revenge as an act of human liberation. Which, I suspect, is absolutely everyone in a world that can't yet shake its addiction to hierarchy and a fundamental belief that human beings are too sick and selfish to allow themselves to be truly free.

There is also a treatment of adolescent homosexuality which was entirely ahead of its time for a film made only a year after homosexuality had been decriminalised in England. The gay theme forms a kind of parallel story to Mick's rebellion, centred around Bobby Phillips.

Phillips is passed around by the whips (the head prefects) as both their 'scum' (slave) and desired object of unseen sexual abuse. His blank acceptance of this miserable situation is brought to an end when he watches Mick's friend Wallace (Warwick) giving an impromptu display of parallel bar gymnastics, and falls dreamily in love. The scene switches between Wallace's slow-motion swoops through the air of the gym to the young boy's captivated stare, also shot in slow motion, in what is a pretty blatant celebration of homoeroticism. Wallace and Phillips bond in a room full of phallic rifles. Anderson attempted to keep his homosexuality a secret until his death in 1994, and, if Phillips's extremes of experience have any bearing on Anderson's coming of age, this may give some insight into his complex relationship with his own sexuality.

No work of art questions the morals of using the words 'thank you' so relentlessly as *If . . . .* But I've given a lot of heartfelt thanks down the years to Messrs Anderson, Sherwin and McDowell for giving me the only fictional images of English revolution that I can believe in. There's nothing else in cinema like this film, and no teen movie has ever come close to emulating its fervour. But then, no one since has had a social context to work in like 1968, or found a young actor as extraordinary as Malcolm McDowell.

★ ★

KES

1969
Starring: David Bradley, Colin Welland, Freddie Fletcher, Lynne Perrie, Brian Glover
Dir.: Kenneth Loach

Plot: We wish we could fly. Like a bird in the sky. But we can't. Key line: 'Go back to sleep, yer pig. Hog. Sow. Yer drunken bastard. Bastard, bastard, drunken pig!'

Shot on location in the Yorkshire mining town of Barnsley, this adaptation of Barry Hines's coming-of-age novel *A Kestrel For A Knave* is one of British cinema's most admired and influential films. It is shot in documentary-style with actors who don't act like actors, and concerns the hard-knock life of Billy Casper, a working-class teen from a '60s sink council estate whose only pleasure in his grim and hopeless existence is the training of a wild bird. Its star, David Bradley, gave a performance so rich and believable that the film still makes perfect sense to children, even though the world it depicts seems distant enough to be almost Dickensian. It's a performance summed up by the film's iconic promo poster: a grainy, over-exposed shot of a scruffy urchin giving a defiant two-finger salute to the whole fucking world.

Billy's life is defined by the relentless disapproval of every adult he is forced to share air with. His every idea and blunt utterance is insulted and dismissed by Mother, teachers, the bloke who owns the shop from which Billy does his paper round, and, especially his grown-up big brother Jud (Fletcher), a contemptuous mutton-chopped thug who works down the local coal mine and with whom Billy is forced to share a bed. Jud seems satisfied enough with his birds, beer and mod suits, but his major aim in life is ensuring that no one around him is happy. Especially Billy.

But Billy is a tough little shit. He has to be. And somewhere beneath the hard, mouthy shell this tiny boy has to shield himself with in order to survive, is a poetic soul. His saving grace is the surrounding Yorkshire countryside (we know this because fluttery flute music plays every time we see it), and the specific saving grace for Billy is his fascination for the birds of prey that swoop around the moors. All of the uplifting moments of this movie are based around a scruffy urchin training a kestrel he names Kes to swoop, dive and return on command. All shot on shaky camera, in a mucky, grainy colour, backed by fluttery flute music. It should be the dullest thing on Earth. It is, in fact, painfully beautiful. But context is all, and the context is the contrast between the entirely-in-the-moment pleasure of Billy's outdoor life, and the ugly hopelessness of home and school.

Finally, amidst Billy's daily indignities, one teacher at school, Mr Farthing (Welland), spots Billy's potential and encourages his birdy enthusiasms. But Mr Farthing is no match for Jud, and *Kes* ends with an inevitable tragedy that has made generations of viewers weep angry tears for the small, pale boy who exists only to have his dreams choked and slung in a dustbin.

A scene in a public library, as Billy tries to borrow a book about falconry, is played for gentle laughs, but says huge things about the urgency of children and how a world silently conspires to keep the underclass from civilisation. Billy needs the book *now*, because he's excited *now*, and because he's a child, and because gratification deferred is no gratification at all. He can't take a book out because he's not a member. He can't become a member without a parent's signature. His dad has left the family home and his mother's at work. And, even though we haven't met Mum yet, we've seen enough of

Big Brother to know that she isn't going to be encouraging her child's interests in anything. Blocked from access to useful and inspiring education by bureaucracy and adult lack of interest, Billy does the only thing a determined autodidact can do. He goes to a shop and steals the book. His immediate reward at home is not concern at his criminality, but monstrous Jud mocking his attempts to better himself. And that, in a nutshell, is the history of the working class.

But Billy's Mam – played by Lynne Perrie, who later went on to a great career as *Coronation Street*'s Ivy Tilsey and a proto-Kerry Katona celebrity fuck-up – is actually a decent, articulate woman who means well. In the scene in the local working-men's club, where a band of greasy pre-hippy throwbacks play curdled Merseybeat versions of the hits of the day and a gurning comic sings a smutty song about a big marrow, Mrs Casper, in conversation with friends, gives us a handy summing-up of young Billy's situation: 'Perhaps if he had been brought up in a different environment, and had a better education, he would have made more than he has done.' Billy, at the age of 15, has been written off by the only person who loves him. The film's major theme, the self-assembled traps of the working class, is punched home when we cut immediately to handsome but dunder-headed Jud, a man facing a life working in a hole (well ... until Thatcher came along, at least), whose only leisure activity is going to the same club with the same people and shagging the same girls twice a week, announcing proudly, to his mates, to us: 'I'm happy as I am. I doubt if I could be any happier.'

The schizophrenic way that British society looks at its working class is always fascinating to observe. On the one hand, the middle class label us 'chavs', characterise us as ASBO-bearing, brat-breeding slags and scallies and spend most of their lives and money ensuring that little Josh and Jocasta don't have their childhoods polluted by our foul odours by moving as far away from where we live as is possible on such a tiny island. On the other, they glorify us, stealing our culture and worshipping at the altar of our authenticity, trying to emulate our vernacular to look cool and forever apologising for not having our gruelling set of childhood 'we had it tough' tales, which, of course, we exaggerate completely in order to keep the suckers entertained and fearful.

So our current government's recent revival of the phrase 'social mobility' is interesting. *Kes* is a vivid reminder of a time, not so long ago, when the British working class truly knew their place, and happily stayed right there. And while it's difficult to judge whether things changed because of or in spite of the likes of Thatcher and Blair, they have changed, and for the better. My mother was pushed into a sweatshop at the age of 15. Her mother was born into service and her male peers were wiped out in a war fought for the empires of the ruling classes. Now my son gets to choose what he wants to do, within the boundaries of profit-driven capitalism, of course, and has already travelled, worked, lazed around, been to university and seen and done things my mother could only have dreamt of. At his age now, she was a single mother faced with a future of factory work and cleaning jobs to keep us alive. Watching *Kes* reminds me how much better life is for my tribe than it used to be, which is an important wake-up call when you live in a country whose default position is whinging.

There was never anything that glorious about the traditional British working class. Most of them were exactly like Jud. That's why so many of us got socially mobile and are truly fucking relieved to have escaped.

Digress, digress, digress. Where were we? Of course . . . the Brian Glover football scene. Legend.

Routinely cited as the greatest piece of football-related cinema ever filmed – admittedly, a winner in a field of one – this ten minutes of magic is essentially a tragicomic farce two-hander between Bradley and character actor/screen villain/professional wrestler Brian Glover. Glover plays Mr Sugden, a school PE teacher who uses football lessons as an excuse to play out his pathetic fantasies of being a star professional footballer. Yorkshire viewers will immediately note he's a wrong 'un because Sugden pretends he plays for Manchester United, a club so hated by fans of nearby Leeds United that they still regularly taunt Man. U fans at games by spreading their arms and making a noise like a plane crashing, in reference to the Munich Air Disaster of 1958 in which the majority of Manchester United's excellent young 'Busby Babes' team died on a German runway while returning from a European Cup match.

One of the survivors of Munich was Bobby Charlton and, in the year after Charlton had captained a new Man. U side to become the first English team to win the European Cup, that is who Sugden decides he really is. The resulting scene is a perfect amalgam of every bad memory of every humiliating games lesson that every Englishman has ever endured, as small boys are trampled into freezing mud by the kind of egomaniacal bully that always seems to choose a career in physical education.

The comic contrast is provided by Bradley's Billy, encased in giant shorts that reach up to his armpits, legs and arms like icy toothpicks. Billy, to the general derision of the other boys, is stuck in the giant goal because he's weedy and crap and, while Sugden indulges his fantasy up-field, refereeing the game so he can't help but win, our hero occupies himself by swinging on the crossbar like a plucked monkey and diving dramatically *away* from any ball that goes near him.

Part of the reason why the scene is so memorable, apart from its surgically accurate depiction of what passes for English sporting education and the lifelong humiliation men never quite recover from when kids and teachers pick teams and they find themselves picked last (actually, Billy is picked second-last; there's a fat kid – there's *always* a fat kid), is that Glover, Bradley and the real pupils of St Helen's school are enjoying themselves so much that they keep having to stop themselves giggling. Loach hits home the joke by using the old theme from BBC sport show *Grandstand* to introduce the hilarious Glover, and flashing score updates ('Manchester United 0: Spurs 1') onscreen. For reasons unknown, Loach never came close to being so funny again.

Sugden's Manchester United, incidentally, don't win. This man is such a loser he can't even fix a game of schoolboy football. Still, the job has its perks. He can still take it out on tiny Casper, slapping him around in the dressing-room, forcing him to take a cold shower as a form of naked humiliation. We're not laughing any more.

And as a PS, in regards to the key theme of the discouragement of working-class potential, Sugden is entirely uninterested in the gymnastic talent Billy shows off while swinging on the crossbar and climbing out of the shower.

The black comedy hits its high and low point in a scene where an angelic pupil heads to the headmaster's office with a message from a teacher and finds himself getting caned because the head, like every adult, feels children only exist to be ignored or beaten. Besides, he's busy ranting about the wonderful estate that's replaced the slums, and how old pupils stop him in the street and laugh with him about 'the thrashings I gave them', and how children don't deserve the marvellous things his generation have given to them. It's dated stuff, especially since *Monty Python* took the piss out of it on their 'Four Yorkshiremen' sketch. But I was nowhere near Yorkshire as a nipper, and old cunts really did talk drivel like this to me, so I figure they did to everyone else in England.

It's an extraordinary scene; the head's fury that young people can now afford cars, the hysterical, silent laughter of the boys when he turns his back, the bewildering logic of a man beating children while admitting that it doesn't make those children behave as he wants. 'You are the generation who don't listen!' he rages, while refusing to listen to the protests of our angelic message-bringer. And the caning, when it comes, is obviously real, and the angelic boy's shocked reaction is genuinely upsetting, and still makes me angry about all the violent assaults I watched supposedly responsible public servants hand out to defenceless kids at my London junior school.

Kes is about the imminent death of traditional working-class culture. And while I understand people looking in horror at town centres dominated by shopping malls and working-class kids all glued to separate mobile phones and far more obsessed with celebrity gossip than organised labour and community ... I suspect those people were those lucky enough to never live in a lousy estate and go to a poor person's school, or be around members of your 'community' whose favourite topic was how you'd never amount to anything, so fuck off to the nearest manual labour and be grateful. There are few things more beautiful in cinema than Billy Casper's face as he blithely ignores everything the careers officer says about his inevitable future down t'pit. He's a hero; a natural refusenik with higher things on his mind than the machinations of those who feel they control him. You can't control someone who isn't there. But it never occurs to Billy to mention that, yes, he does have a hobby. He tames things that can't be tamed. And we know it's a missed opportunity, even if the essentially decent careers officer probably can't produce a bird-trainer job out of his back pocket. No adult has helped Billy before. Why should this one?

It's no surprise when Jud kills Kes. The man is a bringer of misery, a human dementor whose only real pleasure in life is making sure others get no more out of life than him, a symbol of what Hines and Loach appear to think about the sadistic and proudly ignorant bottom-feeder male. But it is a shock when the film just ends with Billy burying the bird. No punchline. No coda. No hope. No future.

Bradley's performance remains one of the most singular and believable in movies. But an overdue shout-out needs to go to Freddie Fletcher as Jud. It's a thankless role – most movie villains are at least given some kind of devilish charm – yet Fletcher nails it with memorable power. His dead eyes and brutal slang capture the essence of the soul-less bully, giving *Kes* its very own Bill Sikes. He went on to a good bit-part career in British TV, but, on this evidence, deserved more.

For Ken Loach, *Kes* was the film that launched a career as the directorial byword for socially concerned cinematic authenticity that lasts to this day. But no Loach movie since has contained either the life or the truth of *Kes*, which captures a shameful side of Englishness with great energy, humour and anger. Nevertheless, it's telling that the only great recent British teen film is *Fish Tank* (see p. 482), a film for which the label 'Loachian' could have been invented. I'm sure no one is more surprised than Loach that the style he forged has become – courtesy of Shane Meadows, Lynne Ramsey and *Fish Tank*'s Andrea Arnold – the only kind of film Britain's any good at making any more.

This Is England ain't no *Kes*, though.

1970s

★ ★

A CLOCKWORK ORANGE

1971

Starring: Malcolm McDowell, Warren Clarke, Patrick Magee,
Anthony Sharp
Dir.: Stanley Kubrick

**Plot: Horrorshow droogie tolchocks society in the gulliver.
Key line: 'Yarbles!'**

A Clockwork Orange was and remains the most controversial teen
movie of all time. Famously, it prompted such hysteria about incidents of copycat violence that its director, Stanley Kubrick, in fear
of both legal action and death threats, effectively banned his own
film from being shown until his death in 1999. It's 'Nadsat' language,
invented by the highly original novelist Anthony Burgess, named
bands (including Heaven 17 and Moloko) and introduced the words
'droog' (friend/gang member), 'horrorshow' (great), 'yarbles'
(testicles) and 'ultra-violence' (you get that one) to the English
language. And when any band or arty type wants to nick an image
resonant of teen gang violence, they will break out the bowler hats,
white boiler suits, boots, braces and mascara around one eye sported
by chief protagonist Alex (McDowell) and his nasty posse of
droogs.

So it remains difficult to cut through *ACO*'s notoriety and influence
and see it purely as a movie. To talk about it as something that gives
pleasure immediately implies that you are the kind of person who
thinks that, say, raping a woman while crooning 'Singing In The
Rain' is a bit of a laugh, and also quite cool and rebellious. But there
are great scenes in *A Clockwork Orange* that are not sick.

My favourite bit of *ACO* takes place in a futuristic record shop: an
endlessly spiralling phantasmagoria of mirrors and multi-coloured
neon chart rundowns, containing '70s glam-rock kids who all nicely
set off Alex's Edwardian frock-coat. One day I will be rich, and I will
open this record shop, even if you soul-less bastards do still insist on
load-sharing your MPFrees off your crappy laptops, and I will prance
proudly around it, in a purple Edwardian frock-coat/yellow Harry

Hill shirt ensemble, making myself poor but happy, surrounded by obscure pre-punk electronic vinyl at exorbitant prices. Sigh. And one day, an American girl with an extravagant mullet will wander in sucking on an ice lolly and say to her friend, 'What you getting, Bratty? Goggly Gogol? Johnny Zhivago? The Heaven 17?' And I will die, right there and then, of excessive wish-fulfilment. See? It's not all gratuitous violence and wild over-acting.

I'm not going to take up too much space with outlining the plot here. It's very famous, you can Google the detail. In a dystopian future England that looks like the 1970s viewed through a lava-lamp, a schoolboy thug called Alex and his three friends go out every night, drink milk laced with drugs and commit violent crime. Alex murders a woman and is caught and imprisoned when betrayed by his droogs. After pretending to be a model prisoner for a couple of years, he is thought the perfect guinea-pig for a law-and-order government's new crime prevention idea, the Ludovico Technique. This involves forcing the unrepentant teen psycho to watch films of the planet's vilest horrors while pumping him full of nausea-inducing drugs and playing him Beethoven. Now 'cured' – that is, unable even to contemplate sex or violence without being physically disabled – Alex is released from prison unable to protect himself from a world out to get him. When he attempts suicide, the press backlash against the government forces them to reverse the treatment.

In Burgess's original version of the novel, Alex goes on to grow up and realise the error of his ways. The American publishers insisted on omitting this final chapter, and it's this shorter, bleaker version that Kubrick's screenplay is based on. The nihilist satire he intended to shoot had absolutely no place for learning and growing.

Whatever you may think of the content of Kubrick's films, *ACO* proves that the England-based American was the King Of Composition. Almost every damn shot of his career looks like a 3-D painting with almost fathomless depth. And perhaps the biggest problem with this movie is that it made terrible things look too good.

Let's take, for example, the cool shapes the thugs throw – forget all this stuff about the guys in suits walking in slo-mo in *Reservoir Dogs* and how its choreographed cool is a tribute to *film noir* or some obscure Japanese B-movie. It's *A Clockwork Orange*. Except Tarantino can only make cool-looking guys in cool suits look cool. Kubrick made three ugly blokes (and McDowell) in white boiler suits, bovver boots, bowler hats and grotesque off-white codpieces look iconic while walking through some municipal hell-hole. It's image-making on some next level shit, Cuz.

So does it glorify violence? Ha. HAHAHA!!! ... *of course* it bloody does! The couple whose house the droogs invade are so ra-ra posh, particularly when contrasted with McDowell's salt-of-the-earth northern vowels, that we are invited to approve of the rape as a kind of class war gesture. When the husband, a left-wing writer called Mr Alexander, is re-introduced later in the film he is a gibbering lunatic (with what seems to be a muscle-bound gay lover) that no viewer could have any sympathy for. When Alex assaults the couple while performing a comic rendition of 'Singing In The Rain', it is evil, evil comedy. Why else would Kubrick make the victims scream in time to the song if not to make us laugh, in exactly the same way we laugh at *Tom & Jerry* (or *Itchy & Scratchy*)? This is brutal violence as comic entertainment, pure and simple. If it's meant to make us confront our love of violence as movie-goers ... well, yes, I suppose. But I don't think Sam Peckinpah's characters being blown away in slow motion carries this film's sadistic enjoyment of humiliation.

I realise Kubrick isn't around to answer back, but tough, frankly, because I think the director is getting a woody from these scenes, and especially the scenes with female victims (who are all conventionally sexy), and that he's doing his best to give male viewers a woody, too. There are endless pointless tit shots and the sexual assault scenes look like the nastier end of porn, but with better camera angles. In the first home invasion scene, Kubrick actually spares us the rape, preferring to focus on extraordinary fish-eye lens shots of the horrified Alexander looking on. But, by that time, we've already had a good look at the actress's tits and fanny, watched her wriggle amusingly and fruitlessly, seen her rendered utterly powerless ... by the droogs, by Stanley Kubrick. So I think we've gang-raped her anyway.

All this is punched home by a pungent loathing of sex, which is constant in the form of ridiculous imagery – plastic coffee-tables in the shape of open-legged women, snakes crawling towards pictures of open-legged women, giant plastic white sculptured cocks, a sex scene filmed like ultra-fast silent comedy and backed by 'The William

Tell Overture' in which Alex is revealed to have the infinite sexual appetites of 30 porn studs on Bionic Viagra. The giant cock is key in the second home invasion scene, as the woman of the house tries to fight him off and is comically pathetic, missing him by miles, whirling around uselessly – while Alex thrusts the enormous cock at her and laughs before stoving her head in with it. Subtle this isn't. But man ... what happened to poor Stanley to make him so repulsed by women and sex, and so in awe of men who can rape? In fact, the movie's final shot appears to suggest that Alex fantasising about sex – *not* rape – is exactly the same thing as his love of violence. I mean ... that's just weird.

Just to add to this ... the incidental male characters (the only lead is McDowell) are full of the eccentricities and comic touches that Kubrick sprinkled throughout *Dr Strangelove*. Aubrey Morris's vicious social worker P.R. Deltoid is especially funny and repellent. Yet the female characters are all non-characters, mainly there to be raped, killed, or fucked, unless they're cold functionaries or idiot mothers. If you wanted to make one film the symbol of the wave of misogyny that saturated '70s New Hollywood movies, *A Clockwork Orange* would even outstrip Peckinpah's *Straw Dogs*, Eastwood's *Play Misty For Me* and Friedkin's *The Exorcist*. Thing is, they are all great movies, too. So are *Birth Of A Nation* and Riefenstahl's *Triumph Of The Will*. At least, so critics tell me.

What I'm saying here is ... there *is* something palpably sick and wrong about *A Clockwork Orange*, and I think Kubrick realised it. His neuroses are all over this film; but these kinds of neuroses are simply not present in Burgess's novel. And the least you can do, if you unleash a beast, is take responsibility for it, which he didn't. Great film-maker. Bit of a tosser.

You know what supporters of the film are going to say. It's that old 'this film deliberately implicates its audience' defence, beloved of intellectual purveyors of amoral imagery since the dawn of movie time. 'It's funny how the colours of the real world only seem really real when you viddy them on a screen,' Alex intones over a typical crime-thriller image of a chap being beaten bloody red by Alex-type droogs, and, yes, we get it. A film about how we're being desensitised towards violence by our love of movie violence which rubs our noses in gratuitous movie violence ... but ironically.

Not buying it. Why? Because Kubrick takes too much pleasure

in it all, that's why. The first fight between Alex's droogs and a rival gang is circus slapstick – the kind of fun boys have when play-fighting as a child. It implies that violence is a playful letting off of steam, rather than something that kills or maims. And Kubrick has far, far too much empathy with Alex's love of rape, because the violent sexual assault that Alex and co. interrupt looks like jolly good fun.

But, but, but ... there *is* a great deal of irony within *A Clockwork Orange*, which, I would imagine, would be Kubrick's more convincing get-out clause. The teen droogs becoming policemen and behaving no differently, their moronic violence now sanctioned by The Man. There is a large element of farce in Alex chancing upon his every enemy when being released from prison, and Kubrick plays it so, making the scenes look like parodies of sentimental British theatre and knockabout sitcom, encouraging wildly over-the-top performances from the likes of Magee. And that ending *is* a dark, dark laugh, as are ideas like Alex studying The Bible in prison to gain the law's approval – but actually fantasising about being the centurion that whips Jesus as he carries the cross to his own crucifixion (this Bible scene also gives dirty old Stan a chance to show more pert young tits upon women with blank faces, apropos of a superfluous Roman fantasy scene). Alex's manipulations of the old duffers of The System is what *ACO* shares with standard teen comedies, making it a *Ferris Bueller's Day Off* (see p. 270) for sick fucks. Of which I must be one, I guess.

Because I love *A Clockwork Orange*. The things that appal me are almost entirely overwhelmed by Kubrick's compositions and visual designs, Walter Carlos's synthesizer versions of classics, the language, the irreverence, and, especially, Malcolm McDowell, who goes way beyond anything you might label 'acting' here. Once you see him, eyelids pinned back, electronic gizmo upon tousled dome, blue eyes moving from moronic shit-eating grin to scared and sick to mask of horror as he watches films of rapes and Nazi crimes while the aversion drugs take hold and synthetic Beethoven skips merrily ... that shit'll stay with you. It's among the most powerful and unforgettable images ever put on screen.

Alex is the least teen-looking schoolboy in movies (McDowell was 27 at the time, and made no real attempt not to look or act his age). But what a performance! His finest work here is all done in voiceover and, especially, when performing, silently, straight to camera. Alex's boiling, feral face as he masturbates to Beethoven, before Kubrick cuts to a montage of the 'lovely pictures' of stylised violence and destruction flowing through his terrible mind. The cobalt blue eyes lend something seductive to his vicious relish and cruel glee. He is something far more than the standard teen psycho, and nothing like the hard bastards you meet in real life. Alex is a (black) magical symbol of all the failures and confusions and leaps-forward and falls-backward of the liberal 1960s, connected so strongly to *If . . .* 's Mick Travis (see p. 97) that you understand that he is the same character rendered satanic: a bringer of chaos, a lover of pain, a prophecy of the fearless revolt against everything we projected upon Johnny Rotten a few years later ... an anarchist and an antichrist. In these two career-making performances, McDowell's every look, at co-star, at audience, is a dare and a taunt and a massive Fuck You. He goes big, always and brilliantly, and his eyes gleam and sparkle, and his mouth sneers and smirks, and his body coils and struts, and he is an unstoppable force. He makes the simple act of being fed while lying disabled in a hospital bed look like spitting in the eye of the world. Alex is not a revolutionary, nor even a rebel. He's a sociopath. Yet ... there is a charm, and something intensely lovable about him. I don't think *A Clockwork Orange* was a makeable movie without Malcolm McDowell.

So there's McDowell, and the space-age interiors, and the insane pop-art clothes. Kubrick's astounding ability to make the squalor of the council estate and the high-rise look like high art. The way he makes the squirming Alexander look like a bust of Beethoven as he uses Ludwig Van to drive Alex towards suicide. The way that, in one stunning image, Alex reaches down and out to us, his face a manic, blissful invitation to join him in his carnival of debasement and sadism. It all adds up to one inescapable conclusion: *A Clockwork Orange* is an indefensible masterpiece. Once seen, never forgotten, even if it should never have been seen at all.

★ ★

THE LAST PICTURE SHOW

1971

Starring: Timothy Bottoms, Cybill Shepherd, Jeff Bridges, Ben Johnson, Cloris Leachman, Ellen Burstyn, Randy Quaid, Eileen Brennan
Dir.: Peter Bogdanovich

Plot: Teenage wasteland in pre-rock 'n' roll Texas.
Key line: 'Nuthin's really bin right since Sam The Lion died.'

It's about the wind. Whenever I think of Peter Bogdanovich's desolate coming-of-age masterpiece, it's the sound of the wind that dominates. It's a cold and constant thing, whistling through a deserted main street in a tiny Texan town, whipping up dust and blowing tumbleweed through the broken hearts of the inhabitants of Anarene, echoing the way that Jacy Farrow blows through the lives of the men of the town, picking them up and whirling them around without any thought or aim but a love of chaos. The wind doesn't choose victims; it just is. Nothing stops it or breaks it. It rules this desolate place, and never listens to reason, nor shows any mercy. It overwhelms the characters, even though they are given life by some of the best actors in this book. It is the carrier of the cold horror of no escape and roads to nowhere.

But it's no real wonder that, when critics and film buffs discuss *The Last Picture Show*, the sound of the wind barely merits a mention. There's so much else to talk about, most of it chronicled by the ultimate film-buff-as-director-and-self-mythologist Peter Bogdanovich. That Bogdo – we always call him Bogdo round these parts – was better known as a critic and programmer for art cinemas than as a director when selected as the latest *protégé* of BBS, the independent studio that produced *Easy Rider*, promoted Jack Nicholson and Dennis Hopper, and gave birth to the late '60s/early '70s New Hollywood and the movie brat era of American rebel *auteurs*. That Bogdo saw Larry McMurtry's novel *The Last Picture Show* in a drugstore, liked the title, hated the blurb about growing up in Texas, but was given the book a few weeks later by Sal Mineo, one of the stars of *Rebel Without A Cause* (see p. 28). That Cybill Shepherd was cast when Bogdo and then-wife and collaborator Polly Platt saw a picture of her on the front of *Glamour* magazine, and were intrigued by the girl who 'looked like she had a sexual chip on her shoulder'. And the epic consequences of that chance glance, as Shepherd channelled the sexually destructive Jacy so thoroughly that she shagged Jeff Bridges, taunted Timothy Bottoms to distraction and then copped off with the director, managing to destroy Bogdo and Platt's marriage in the six weeks it took to shoot the movie in Archer City, Texas.

Then there was the death of Bogdo's father during the shoot, and the fact that Orson Welles was Bogdo's houseguest at the time and it was Welles's idea to shoot the movie in black and white. And the skinny-dipping scene that showed real pubic hair and got the film briefly banned in Phoenix, Arizona. And the fact that McMurtry's autobiographical novel was based around real characters in Archer City, who were expected to be welcoming to the Hollywood invaders while knowing that their very real dirty linen was being aired to the entire planet. And that McMurtry had changed the name of Archer City to Thalia, but Platt and Bogdo's obsession with legendary director Howard Hawks led them to change it again to Anarene, which sounded a bit like Abilene, which was the cow-town in Hawks's western *Red River*, which is the last picture show when Anarene's cinema shuts down at the end of the movie, and also the name of Anarene's leading stud. Keep up.

Going back to sound ... *American Graffiti* (see p. 135) likes to pretend it invented a soundtrack entirely comprised of hits of the period. Nuh-uh ... that would be *The Last Picture Show*, which plays out its doomy scenario to hits mainly from the voice and pen of Hank Williams, dispensing with incidental music entirely. Who needs music telling you what to feel when you have Hank's lonesome howl and that goddamned wind?

And finally ... the small matter of eight Oscar nominations, with two statuettes going to Cloris Leachman and Ben Johnson for supporting actress and actor. Of the film making stars of its largely unknown cast. And Bogdo and Platt deliberately setting out to mix the look and style of their directorial heroes Hawks and John Ford, and the sexual and verbal honesty of the French New Wave, and succeeding in spectacular fashion. Bogdo was all set to be his generation's greatest director. But, having destroyed Platt's life and

'A hairy head in a jock jacket.' Michael Landon awaits the coming of CGI in *I Was A Teenage Werewolf* (Underwood & Underwood/Corbis).

'Cinema's first visual poem on the subject of adolescence.' Jean-Pierre Léaud as Antoine Doinel in *The 400 Blows* (AF Archive/Alamy).

'A flint-eyed threat, wiry and gaunt, mouth drawn into a constant hard and baleful glower.' Angry Young Tom Courtenay in *The Loneliness of the Long-Distance Runner* (Moviestore Collection Ltd/Alamy).

'Capturing every thrill of young night-time romance.' The interracial kiss from *A Taste of Honey* (British Lion/Woodfall/The Kobal Collection).

'A New World Order of youth gangs and tribal divisions.' Burt Lancaster
points an accusing finger at The Kids in *The Young Savages* (Photos 12/Alamy).

'"How do you thank someone/Who's taken you from crayons to
perfume?"' Sidney Poitier tames the white trash savages in *To Sir,
With Love* (AF Archive/Alamy).

'A scruffy urchin giving a defiant two-finger salute to the whole fucking world.' David Bradley invents Liam Gallagher in *Kes* (Woodfall/Kestrel/ The Kobal Collection).

'"A sexual chip on her shoulder."' Cybill Shepherd sirens it up in *The Last Picture Show* (John Springer Collection/Corbis).

'A happy film about incest and paedophilia. Who else but the French?'
Lea Massari and Benoît Ferreux in Louis Malle's *Le Souffle Au Coeur*
(Photos 12/Alamy).

'Boy-meets-granny, boy-loses-granny.' Ruth Gordon and Bud Cort as odd
couple *Harold and Maude* (AF Archive/Alamy).

'Educating teens about gender hypocrisy since 1978.' The gang's all here in *Grease* (Photos 12/Alamy).

'A nutter in a rubber William Shatner mask with a giant phallic knife.'
Michael Myers plugs *Halloween* (Pictorial Press Ltd/Alamy).

bailed on his kids for the trophy girlfriend, Platt, of course, never worked with him again. And Bogdo never got close to making a film this good again. But then again, neither did Platt.

In short, this is one of those movies where the story of what happened on set would make just as good a movie as the movie. As long as it was shot with the same eerie and uniquely beautiful Robert Surtees *chiaroscuro* monochrome that gives *The Last Picture Show* one of the most stand-out looks in the history of cinema.

This is such a towering work that it's rarely seen as a teen movie. After all, the teen movie genre is about exploitation, designed to be funny, scary, dirty and/or sensationalist enough to keep the attention of the young and restless. Even 'serious' teen classics like *Rebel Without A Cause* (see p. 28), *The 400 Blows* (see p. 47) and *If . . .* (see p. 97) were based around the theme of rebellion, and therefore immediately appealing to the teenage obsession with bucking authority and declaring their parents' generation uncool and embarrassing. *The Last Picture Show* is something completely different. It is slow, arty, novelistic and self-conscious about wanting to be seen as A Classic Movie. Its teen characters' lives are entirely entwined with those of the surrounding adults, and they are no more or less heroic. Rebellion is not uppermost in any of the teens' minds. The major nightmare of all teens – boredom – is more powerfully realised here than in perhaps any other teen movie; but the adults suffer more profoundly in its suffocating grip than the kids, who are still young enough to escape the nightmare of a place where there is no transient population, no stimulation, no culture, no future. In Anarene the only distraction is sex, and the film carries the faint odour of inbreeding and the overpowering stench of children condemned to repeat the mistakes of their imprisoned parents, if they don't get themselves together and get the fuck outta Dodge. The only thing more boring than being outside in Anarene is being inside, gazing at a television that has killed the movie star, watching the urban middle classes doing things you'll never do. Add the wind and the dust and the class conflict, and Anarene is a vision of a kind of hell that argues that hell is, actually, not enough other people.

The plot is narrow, soapy and pinched, reflecting the smallness of a town based entirely on Texas oil. It is 1951, and Sonny (Bottoms) and Duane (Bridges) are the joint captains of the local high school's lousy football team. They are estranged from their parents, and share an apartment, spending most of their time hanging with father-figure Sam The Lion (Johnson), who owns the town's bar, diner and cinema. Duane is going steady with the town's teen rich-bitch vamp Jacy, who is more interested in rich kid Bobby. But Bobby won't go out with a virgin. So Jacy uses Duane for sex, only to find out that Bobby has moved on to another teen sucker. While Sonny and Duane are road-tripping in Mexico, Sam The Lion dies. He has left the pool-room to Sonny.

Meanwhile, Sonny has started sleeping with Ruth Popper (Leachman), the hauntingly depressed wife of the high school football coach, who is far more interested in his boys than in his wife. Jacy seduces the lover of her mother (Burstyn) and then steals Sonny from Ruth. Duane, who has decided to join the army and is preparing to be shipped off to Korea, smashes his friend in the face with a bottle in a jealous rage. An impressed Jacy invites Sonny to elope with her but has, in fact, detailed the pair's plans in a note to her parents, ensuring that the pair are caught. Mrs Farrow confesses to Sonny that Sam was the love of her life and advises him to stay away from her daughter – who is, essentially, her Mini-Me – not for her sake, but his.

Jacy goes off to big city college in Dallas. Duane and Sonny re-bond and go to the final movie in a cinema killed by television. Duane heads off to Korea and Sonny's mute little-brother substitute Billy is run over by a truck. A distraught Sonny goes to Ruth for comfort, only to get a barrage of abuse. But she comforts Sonny anyway, and the unhappy couple fade out as the wind and the dust and the abandoned cinema on the desolate main street overwhelm them.

Admittedly, I've never read the original novel, but . . . this really is potboiler stuff, isn't it? How this gets transformed into high art is entirely down to what those critic types call *mise en scène* and a commitment to the idea that even the most sordid and cowardly human action carries some kind of poetry. Bogdanovich falls in love with these characters – a little too literally, in one case – and gives them a dignity and charisma that transcends the banal betrayals and petty power-plays that drive their actions. And, unlike the vast majority of teen films, *The Last Picture Show* features teen characters who operate as the equals of the adults around them . . . not economically, perhaps, but certainly in terms of how much emotional carnage they can cause, and how willing they are to imitate the worst aspects of their elders while (un)happily having sex with them. It's an uncomfortable, incestuous and semi-paedophiliac look at what coming of age may mean, and, while somehow never feeling remotely tasteless, taps into the kind of Oedipal fantasies we never want to openly discuss. It's kind to the trapped and unhappy, and excuses their sins.

This is done by virtue of scenes of classic cinema, many of which pay homage to classic cinema. Sonny peering over the head of his dowdy, gum-chewing girlfriend while he snogs her, enraptured by the aspirational beauty of Elizabeth Taylor on the big screen in *Father Of The Bride*. Cybill Shepherd's delicious introduction to the world, looking straight at camera, at us sitting in the stalls gazing upon her beauty, amused at our lust and admiration, and purring, in Scarlett O'Hara sing-song southern accent, 'Hi. What y'all doin' back here in the dark?' A lot of bare young breast, which still, perhaps because of the black and white, *Grapes Of Wrath*, look of the movie, carries the shock of such things being allowed in mainstream cinema as the anti-censorship floodgates finally opened in early '70s cinema. A bra draped over the wing-mirror of a pick-up truck. The terrible, terrible sex between Sonny and Ruth, and Duane and Jacy, and between doomed mute kid Billy (played by Sam Bottoms, Timothy's brother) and a fat hooker, and the film's uncompromising refusal to romanticise. There's never been a film so obsessed with sex yet so relentlessly appalled by its ugliness. Perhaps it told us more about Bogdo and Platt than his affair with Shepherd ever could.

The notorious skinny-dipping scene, where Shepherd didn't have to act her embarrassment . . . Bogdo had to shoot her on a closed set, cleverly editing in the rest of the naked cast. Its portrayal of rich kids with completely different moral standards to the poor felt like some kind of barbed dig at the hippy generation, of which the traditionalist Bogdo was proudly not a member.

But – and unusually for a teen movie, and one with three such talented and appealing leads – the star of the film is one of the adults. Cloris Leachman's Ruth Popper is one of the screen's greatest studies of repressed rage. Every smile, grimace and thousand-yard glare speaks of another disappointment, or indignity, or the sheer visceral agony of being starved of sex and intimacy in a life where nothing else good is possible. Her face is often a mask of frozen terror, yet she's somehow even more beautiful and sexy than Shepherd, and her fury at the film's end feels like a feminist call-to-arms ('I haven't done anything wrong! Why can't I quit apologising?') even though preaching is studiously avoided. *The Last Picture Show* was only Leachman's tenth role in 24 years, and her Oscar is one of the few that went to the best rather than the most politically expedient choice.

In 1990 Bogdanovich directed a sequel to his greatest film. It was called *Texasville* and brought together the original cast. Its plot insists that everyone stays where they are, and makes Bridges and Shepherd a proper, adult couple. I'll never watch it, 'cos, in my far superior version, Duane dies in Korea, Sonny and Ruth run away together and become beatniks in the Lower East Side, and Jacy marries a Bush and becomes the first female President. Everywhere she goes, you hear the wind whistling, even on a still day. And everything seems to be in black and white.

★ ★

LE SOUFFLE AU COEUR (MURMUR OF THE HEART)

1971
Starring: Benoît Ferreux, Lea Massari, Daniel Gélin, Marc Winocourt, Fabien Ferraux, Michel Lonsdale
Dir.: Louis Malle

Plot: The only angst-free teen movie ever made. Oh . . . and the hero fucks his mother.
Key line: 'I don't want you to be unhappy, or ashamed, or sorry. We'll remember it as a very beautiful and solemn moment that will never happen again.'

If you haven't seen Louis Malle's celebrated but controversial coming-of-age classic . . . beware. It's a minefield and a mindfuck. No, there are no scenes of rape back-dropped by old musical numbers. No sleazy subterranean peril. No violence, borstals, pregnancies, mad scientists or therapy cops. No nihilistic kids living in the streets, spreading deadly diseases or screaming into the void about the ever-lasting angst caused by terrible parents or a society that doesn't care. No drugs, unless you count booze and cigars. Not even a wobbly alien or a bloody corpse in sight. That's why this is so unsettling.

There is virtually no teen angst whatsoever, despite the fact that its teen male hero is, technically speaking, sexually abused by his parent. *Le Souffle Au Coeur* is a happy film about incest and paedophilia. Who else but the French?

Set in 1954 Dijon against a backdrop of the French war against Indo-China – which would soon become the American war against Vietnam – *Le Souffle Au Coeur* tells the semi-autobiographical tale of 14-year-old Laurent Chevalier (Benoît Ferreux) and his wealthy upper middle-class family. Laurent and his two brothers are right scallywags, nicking jazz records by their beloved Charlie Parker, pinching cash from mom's purse, collecting in the streets for charity and keeping the proceeds to spend on adult proclivities, like the booze and cigars. Dad is a remote rich guy, but Italian Mom Clara (Massari) is a whole different kettle of dangerous fish. Young, beautiful, spoiled, immature and entirely unwilling to discipline her boys, she is a flirtatious sister rather than an authority figure.

Laurent's main preoccupation is losing his virginity. An attempt to do so with a hooker in a brothel is foiled by his annoying older brothers. But the unlikely solution to his problem is found when he is diagnosed with a heart murmur after a dose of scarlet fever, and Clara takes him to a spa to recuperate. He goes there a boy and comes back a man ... or something like that.

Critics are fond of pointing out that prurient types in 1971 paid all the attention to the incest scene, and that *Le Souffle Au Coeur* is about far more than an illicit sexual act. Nevertheless, when you sit down to write a script based upon your own teenage years and then include a scene where 'you' shag your mother, I think you are, at the very least, consciously aware that the shock of incest is going to overwhelm all your subtle *mise en scènes* and deftly written subtexts. The guy knew that the press would howl, and that the scandal would put bums on seats. And it did. *Le Souffle Au Coeur*, unlike most of Malle's films, was a global success that grossed millions of francs.

The special feature on the current UK DVD features an interview with Malle's brother and collaborator Vincent. He reveals that this most mellow and lyrical of the French new wave's directors (Louis Malle died in 1995) really did have a heart murmur in his teens and that their mother did take him to a spa to recuperate. He then assures us, with a dismissive laugh, that they didn't share a bed. Without wishing to speak ill of the dead or the Malle family ... if you had done your mother, would you tell your brother about it? The same goes double if you're the mother, right?

But anyway, I'm getting prurient, so I'll cease and desist. If you really are going to decide to put a teen–mother incest plot point in your movie about a happy childhood, the most crucial and sensitive problem becomes: how do you shoot a positive scene about paedophilia in such a way that you don't get lynched, or, at the very least, banned from making movies ever again?

One key element is the casting of a non-actor in the lead role. Benoît Ferreux went on to have an acting career, most bizarrely in legendary football/prisoner of war curio *Escape To Victory* alongside Sylvester Stallone, Bobby Moore, Michael Caine and Pelé. But, until he was cast in *Le Souffle Au Coeur* at age 14, Ferreux had never acted, and he brings the same level of anti-acting naturalism to Laurent as was pulled off by the cast of Larry Clark's *Kids* (see p. 328) in the mid '90s. The lesson from those two movies seems to be, if you are going to depict children in taboo sexual acts, don't employ actors. As soon as proper actor types start emoting theatrically, the viewer will feel exploited. Keep a straight face and maybe we'll see the scene in context.

The rest is all down to undercutting the potential perviness with elegant virtuosity.

Laurent and Clara have returned to their chintzy room at the spa after a drunken Bastille Day party packed full of soldiers on leave and suffused with class conflict. Clara collapses on the bed, complaining of exhaustion. Laurent offers to undress her, and she lets him. I should point out that the pair have spent the entire film being far more touchy-feely with each other than we would expect 14-year-old boys to be with their mothers. But then, most mothers don't look like Lea Massari.

Clara turns on to her side as if falling asleep. Laurent removes her dress and her bra, without being able to see her breasts. He pauses. He then bends on to the bed, says goodnight, and nuzzles her neck just a little too affectionately. She turns on to her back and holds him to her. He continues to nuzzle. Massari quickly and cleverly purveys a brief moment of benevolent panic, forcing his head down so she's not looking at him. We can't see Laurent's face, but he is squirming. She kisses the top of his head a couple of times. And then, very suddenly, as if she's lost all resistance, she begins to kiss his head harder and faster, and . . .

That's it. A jump-cut to a naked Laurent, lying on his side in bed. Clara, in a white dressing-gown, is also on the bed, watching him as he apparently sleeps. She begins to say the key lines above, and Laurent is not asleep and turns to look at her. He grabs her and hugs her. She swears him to secrecy, like any other paedophile, one supposes, and he agrees. Scene over.

The whole scene last less than four minutes and is a lesson in economy, suggestion and . . . and here's the scary bit – eroticism. Nope, never wanted to shag my mum. Yep, do think both incest and adults having sex with 14-year-olds is disgusting. But, yep . . . the incest scene is *Le Souffle Au Coeur* is sexy. Louis Malle was one evil son of a bitch.

We can't know for sure that Laurent is not traumatised by the experience. But the way Charlie Parker is tootling away on the soundtrack while he sneaks out in his jazzy tweed blazer and powder-blue shirt in order to go to the room of a girl at the Bastille Day party and try to get laid again suggests, very strongly, that this is not an event that he is seeing as abuse. He even pulls it off with Girl 2. The implication is that he is now man enough to get what he wants and know what to do with it. The film ends with the entire family in uproarious laughter, utterly bonded and full of joy, amused at the slapstick comedy that is sex.

Oops . . . I've committed the crime, ain't I? I've made a masterpiece all about the controversial bit, as if that's all Malle's film is. You need to know how well this matches up to other teen dramas about having your cherry popped like *Where The Boys Are* (see p. 57) and *Little Darlings* (see p. 191). Well, rest assured: *Le Souffle Au Coeur* is not some dull art film spiced up by a tacked-on dirty bit. It is a gorgeous, funny, spiky snapshot of what it was like to grow up rich and bourgie bourgie in a France that was still fighting imperial wars, and was all set to bequeath its Asian mistake to America, and then stand back and pretend it was nothing to do with them. Even though it is shot in colour and doesn't feature Jean-Paul Belmondo behaving like a '50s gangster or an accusatory ending on a beach, it is drenched in the French new wave's unique ability to merge drama and documentary while remaining pure cinema. It is light, gay, satirical, sensual, has an instantly evocative jazz soundtrack provided by the likes of Parker, Dizzy Gillespie and Sidney Bechet and is entirely lovely to look at.

It would have been a very, very good movie without the incest scene. But it wouldn't have stood out from any other affectionate childhood memoir. Instead, *Le Souffle Au Coeur* resonates, and leaves you with the discombobulating feeling that you've just witnessed a film that argues, with a mixture of aesthetic rigour and flowery flippancy, that if we could all just lose our virginity to our parents, our sexual rites-of-passage would be so much better. So despite – actually, strike that – *because* of the classy music and sets, the skilled composition and the integrity of the naturalist performances, *Le Souffle Au Coeur* easily beats the likes of *Kids*, *Martin*, *A Clockwork Orange* and *Harold And Maude* to the dubious honour of being the most twisted teen movie of all time. Who else but the French?

★ ★

HAROLD AND MAUDE

1972
Starring: Bud Cort, Ruth Gordon, Vivian Pickles
Dir.: Hal Ashby

Plot: Boy-meets-granny, boy-loses-granny.
Key line: 'It's a very common neurosis, particularly in this society, whereby the male child subconsciously wishes to sleep with his mother. Of course, what puzzles me, Harold, is that you want to sleep with your grandmother.'

Hal Ashby was a world-class editor turned director who made a string of key New Hollywood movies in the 1970s. Despite being nearly 40 by the time hippy culture hit the mainstream, Ashby was the real thing, a bearded long-hair left-winger who loved The Rolling Stones and raged against the Vietnam War. He also, like so many of his generation, got heavily into drugs in the '70s while his personal, idiosyncratic movies fell deeply and quickly out of favour in the post-Lucas/Spielberg '80s. He died, in 1988, aged 59, of liver and colon cancer, an almost-forgotten film-maker despite having directed huge commercial and critical hits *The Last Detail*, *Shampoo*, *Coming Home* and *Being There*. In Peter Biskind's definitive study of the movie brat era, *Easy Riders And Raging Bulls*, the author ends his story with Ashby's painful death, seeing it as the final nail in the coffin of counter-culture idealism in American film.

In hindsight, the trouble with Hal Ashby started right here. What kind of holy fool decides that his second film should be the story of a love affair between two people with a 60-year age gap, written by a pool cleaner as a college assignment? And then reels in shock and horror when the tale is greeted with exactly the same repulsed hostility by critics as its characters are greeted within the film? *Harold And Maude* cost $1.2 million dollars to make and was thrown off cinema screens within one week. It has become a much-loved cult film, which didn't do Ashby much good in his lifetime of battling film studios to keep control of his gently transgressive visions.

Harold Chasen (Bud Cort) is a gangling and translucently pale 19-year-old with the face of a baby and the voice and demeanour of a dour middle-aged man. He always sports formal wear and has a pudding-bowl haircut. His favourite hobby is faking his own grisly death. His mother's favourite hobby is playing the ignore-him-and-he'll-get-over-it game. This is fair enough, except someone young who is screaming for attention usually needs it in some way, even if it is tiresome. So Harold is going slowly more and more insane.

They are very rich and live in a grand but gloomy mansion that looks like a haunted house. He never has any company of his own age, but his mother (Vivian Pickles) and posh friends talk about him as if he's not really there. Despite his painful weirdness, Mater simply dismisses any problems he might have by saying things like, 'Please try and be more vivacious, Dear', while regaling her dinner guests with elegant but dull stories of foreign travel.

Nevertheless, Mother does suggest cures for her son's chronic morbidity, all of which are greeted with a stare of memorably wide-eyed terror. He goes to therapy. He is ordered to get married through a dating agency ('They screen out the fat and the ugly'). She sends him to a psycho military uncle with a missing arm, played by Charles Tyner, a character actor who actually looks like the accidental off-spring of a man and a hawk, who attempts to force Harold into the army. This last element was almost obligatory in all American films made by newish directors from around 1968 until the end of the Vietnam War in 1975. In that sense, Ashby wasn't the most original of movie brat storytellers. The Uncle Victor scenes are straight out of *Dr Strangelove* and *M*A*S*H*, while the hippy singer-songwriter soundtrack and swimming pool scenes are borrowed from *The Graduate*. What made Ashby different from his peers is the gentle, rambling and droll manner with which he paced his counter-cultural satires, eschewing anger or hysteria for a resigned amusement at the stupidity of the human race in the vein of Kurt Vonnegut or John Kennedy O'Toole's peerless *A Confederacy Of Dunces*. He's a master of creating unlikely comedy simply from shots where human beings look unavoidably small and distant; a large object will dominate the frame, dwarfing the characters and their shallow obsessions and values. One especially choice scene involves Harold's mother swimming past his apparently lifeless corpse floating face down, and the offhand way she shoots a distracted glance, rolls her eyes, and gets on with perfecting her breast-stroke.

Ashby's understated surrealism manipulates us into empathising with Harold, even though he's a scary little creep. There's something of the Malcolm McDowell (see *If . . .*, p. 97 and *A Clockwork Orange*, p. 111) about Cort's alien intensity and mad eyes, and, if the story had taken another turn, you can imagine him as a baby-faced killer, like George A. Romero's *Martin* (see p. 156). As it is, when faced with these blind, pretentious adults and the ludicrous world they've created, Harold's chronic death wish seems the only rational response.

While indulging his other favourite hobby – he buys a hearse and gatecrashes funerals – Harold meets Maude aka Dame Marjorie Chardin (Ruth Gordon), an eccentric octogenarian whose energy and fuck-you attitude displays all the lust for life that Harold entirely lacks. She attracts his attention by hissing 'Pssst!', flirting inappropriately and offering him liquorice . . . a black sweet, naturally . . . before stealing a priest's car. She lives in a trailer full of stolen junk and her own left-field art installations, including a sort of giant wooden vagina. The two fall in love and head towards an ending that, for obvious reasons, can neither be happy nor ever after.

Ruth Gordon won a Golden Globe nomination for her role here – as did Cort – and should have received far more for one of cinema's most memorable performances. Thin and birdlike, she's the nightmare embarrassing old broad as bringer of life-affirming chaos; a crazy old bat just as likely to show you her knickers as offer you a cup of oat straw tea. Gordon doesn't so much act in the film as gleefully attack it. Her looks are irrelevant; a sexual energy courses from her regardless of – and entirely separate from – her physicality. Maude is designed to personify positivity born out of struggle and this is exactly what Gordon does, crackling with a rude idealism that makes transgression not just funny, but necessary, and managing to carry off some fairly cringe-inducing hippy-dippy dialogue. She tells Harold (and us) that she is going to die very soon within seconds of her first appearance onscreen, and helpfully explains her role in the film: 'I'm merely acting as a gentle reminder: here today, gone tomorrow. So don't get attached to things.'

Like Stanley Kubrick (see *A Clockwork Orange*, p. 111), Hal Ashby favours painterly composition and as little noise and movement as possible. In Harold's therapy sessions, patient and shrink sit on brown leather armchairs at either ends of the frame. The still, eye-level camera accentuates their distance from each other, the foolishness of the therapy ritual, and the fact that they are both talking to us rather than each other.

All of which sets up the film's highlight comedy scenes nicely. Once you've got a boy who likes staging impossibly real suicides meeting posh young women he has no intention of marrying, the jokes come kinda natural. In the first, a chubby student explains to Mom Chasen that she's only doing agency dates as a dare, while, way in the background, through the window and into the garden, Harold is busy dousing himself with petrol and setting himself on fire. Except, like a magician, Harold walks into the drawing-room door just as the hapless girl spots what she thinks is his grotesque demise. Um ... it's the way I don't tell 'em, honest. It's very funny. And Cort even gets to give the camera an evil grin, before being pulled back into his reality by disapproving Mom.

The main dark joke is that no one could actually survive these fake suicides. Harold floats face down in the pool without a breathing apparatus for far too long. He shoots himself with live rounds but just appears in the next scene. He really did set himself on fire and really couldn't have escaped burning and got into the house without a hair out of place. It's the child's fantasy of death without pain or consequences, when you're still of an age where mortality seems like something that only happens to old people.

Ashby and screenwriter Colin Higgins don't bother us with too much superfluous back-story. We don't know where Harold's father is, nor why the Chasens are so wealthy. We do learn that a school chemistry lab mishap saw Mom Chasen informed that Harold was dead, and that it was her dramatic reaction that has got him so addicted to trying to convince her that he's died again. In other words, Harold is obsessed with how emotional people get over you when you snuff it, as opposed to actually seeing it through. Quite a nice metaphor for death's starring role in public life in the ultra-violent early '70s, as well as a boy's neurotic need to be loved.

What makes *Harold And Maude* so unusual and intriguing is its mix of subtle cinema techniques and brutally unsubtle themes. Maude represents life, Harold represents death. Age equals purpose and youth equals nihilism because Maude's generation fought a necessary war – Maude turns out to be a Nazi concentration camp survivor – and Harold's generation are fighting a useless and futile one, in Vietnam. He takes her to see a demolition while she takes him to see flowers blooming in a greenhouse. Maude's authority-baiting antics are a fantasy of civil disobedience with no nasty consequences. The two maverick protagonists are 'good' because they are outside of conventional society, and the hated and buffoonish authority figures are not the middle classes nor mere 'straights', but the ruling elite: politicos, military, cops, priesthood, doctors. Maude teaches Harold to live by embracing death, and Harold ends the film 'cured' and playing a banjo and dancing and wearing bright clothes, in a trick ending involving a motor vehicle and a cliff that was cribbed by Franc Roddam for *Quadrophenia* (see p. 180). These are classic '60s hippy platitudes and could have been truly awful. But Ashby's Buster Keaton-esque sense of humour and two effortlessly strange stars make the story add up to far more than the sum of its parts, even managing to rise above the ill-advised Cat Stevens songs, another early '70s hangover from the success of *The Graduate* and its huge Simon And Garfunkel soundtrack.

What *Harold And Maude* isn't necessarily saying, in case you were wondering, is that unhappy 19-year-olds should seek out sexual relationships with 79-year-olds, or vice versa. Harold and Maude are symbols, and Cort and Gordon's ability to breathe reality into them is what makes the entire movie hang together as some kind of love story, even if you neither know nor care about Vietnam-era counter-culture, or are as horrified by the thought of gerontophilia as the movie's amusingly bilious priest. The sex, incidentally, is off-screen, and its intimations are immaculately tasteful, and quaintly romantic.

As far as influence on teen movies goes, the *Harold And Maude* effect is probably negligible. There's some of Cort's baleful zombie demeanour in Jake Gyllenhall's turn in *Donnie Darko* (see p. 405), maybe. A deadpan, comic sympathy for oddballs that *Harold And Maude* shares with *Napoleon Dynamite* (see p. 432) and *Lucas* (see p. 279), perhaps. But this cult cinephile favourite's true legacy lies in all those gently quirky American 'indie' comedies: *The Kids Are All Right*, *Little Miss Sunshine*, *Sideways*, all the Wes Anderson movies. Films that charm you rather than move you, but do leave you feeling that you probably take the small but necessary joys of life a little too much for granted, and wouldn't the world be better if we were just a little more optimistic and appreciative of what we have. Which probably wasn't entirely the effect that Ashby was after. But is, in the end, just about as much as you can expect from a hippy who liked Cat bloody Stevens. We're just a little too cynical to see such lovable silliness as agitprop now.

★ ★

THAT'LL BE THE DAY

1973
Starring: David Essex, Ringo Starr, Rosemary Leach, Robert Lindsay
Dir.: Claude Whatham

Plot: The parallel birth of British rock'n' roll and pretty boys who hated women.
Key line: 'Please sir . . . can I leave the womb?'

I've just re-read the review I did of this sorely underrated film for *Popcorn*, my previous book about rock movies. It's really good, if I do say so myself. So good, it leaves me with little else to say. But we believe in value here at Orion, so no cheating by just reprinting the *Popcorn* entry. Nope . . . that would be wrong. Wouldn't it, Ian? Ian, my editor, says it would. He's a stand-up guy. More's the pity.

So, for those few who have neither seen David Essex's first starring role nor read my previous best-selling masterpiece, *That'll Be The Day* is the first of two films about a London boy called Jim McLaine who becomes a rock star and loses it big time in a castle in Spain. The second film, *Stardust*, is mental and disturbing. But the first is a sort of grubby English twin to George Lucas's game-changing teen odyssey *American Graffiti* (see p. 135), which also came out in 1973 and dealt with a similar period in recent history, in this case, the late 1950s–early '60s. *That'll Be The Day* also shares obsessions with rock 'n' roll and sex, a keenness to give kids the adult language and themes which we craved at the time, a soundtrack of '50s classics and an interest in the rites of passage of young men. But *American Graffiti* won hearts and big box office moolah by insisting that life had been better before long hair, politics and songs that weren't about girls came along and spoiled everything by, you know, challenging stuff. Being British and therefore both more realistic and pessimistic, the less feelgood and therefore far less successful *That'll Be The Day* views pre-rock 'n' roll life as a kind of grey, rain-soaked prison camp where even big cities behaved like small towns and The Kids were just waiting for The Beatles and The Pill to come along and turn monochrome to colour.

Fair enough. So far, so liberal-progressive. Except that, according to screenwriter Ray Connolly, England wasn't hell because of the post-war economy, or The Tories, or cultural repression, or music that was just too white and polite. Nope. England was shit because women were shit. It was all Mum's fault. The bitch.

Connolly's tale begins with Bad Dad as a kind of mysterious renegade hero. Mr McLaine (James Booth) comes back from the war when Jim is a nipper, attempts to settle into a life of routine as a husband, father and shopkeeper, and can't stand it, leaving the powerless Ma McLaine (Leach) to stare stoically into the middle-distance, lip a-quivering, in that passive-aggressive way that women have when men do things they don't want them to. It's like father, like son all the way for Jim from that point on, as he inherits Dad's wanderlust and fondness for ruining women's lives.

Because women really are all mothers, whores or victims, and often all three in Jim's world. Within seconds we're watching Jim, now a beautiful teenager who looks like David Essex, being mugged off by a couple of birds at the local café after school, mockingly taking him for Coke and jukebox money before two bigger boys come along and claim ownership, as big boys are wont to do. A few minutes after that, Mummy is sitting in the kitchen planning his future (passing his exams, going to Uni) with a jaunty disinterest in what poor Jim wants, dominating him and his granddad with brisk efficiency.

So Jim's only option is to escape women completely and pull a Dad. He runs away to Brighton and summer fun and freedom. There he is befriended by a real-life Beatle called Ringo, who is actually, for the purposes of this tale, a Teddy Boy called Mike. Mike guides him from deckchair attendant to barman to a dream job at the funfair, where the pair have nothing to do except fiddle the take and attempt to get laid.

Jim's coming of age is less the passing from innocence to experience, and more the transition from shy victim of money-grubbing bitches to studly conqueror of foolish sluts. He seduces the boss's middle-aged wife and humiliates the homely Mike, whose boasts about sexual conquest are pure fraud. But things turn dark. As Jim moves from the friendship's beta to alpha male, a queer undercurrent swirls around the pair; Mike becomes more intimidated and awe-struck by Jim's success with the birds and is beaten up by marauding Teds. And Jim rapes an under-age girl. The boy, without the civilising influence of Mother, has become a monster.

Last straws are reached when his old school-friend Terry invites him to a dance at his college. While Jim has been living the vagabond life as a rock 'n' roll roustabout, Terry has been studying and acquiring a duffle-coat and a beatnik beard, a penchant for trad jazz and a posh totty girlfriend. Jim tries to impress the college gals and hits his head on a class ceiling. They're not impressed by his fairground life and they're far too smart to fall for his lies about writing a novel. He leaves with his horny tail between his skinny legs, humiliated by more worldly women in identical fashion to his earlier experiences at café and fairground.

Then Jim has a nasty tryst with a girl who has her crying baby in the same room while they are trying to shag. Trust a woman to introduce you to the horrors of the consequences of your actions. Chastened, he once again does a Dad. He returns home to Mum. He conforms, working in the family shop. He bumps into an old girlfriend (Jeanette, played by Rosalind Ayres), they get married, she gets pregnant. But just as the drab early '60s threatens to become

THE SWINGING SIXTIES!!!, the old wanderlust grabs a hold. He inevitably bails, leaving Jeanette holding the baby.

He doesn't have a plan, but a shop in the High Street solves that problem. In a final shot that filled me with so much excitement when I was ten that I swear it was crucially responsible for the years I spent being a failed pop star, Jim notices and stares in awe at his Saviour and destiny ... an electric guitar, in all its phallic glory.

Some morality is injected into this tale in the *Stardust* sequel; Jim does get his comeuppance eventually, but not before getting absolutely everything he wants, and more, and especially from women. But the reason why such a misogynist film has now been bigged up by me in two bleedin' books is because ... *That'll Be The Day* is a great movie. And although, in gender enlightenment terms, it makes *Porky's* look like *Thelma And Louise*, it carries a truth. That is, that adolescent boys react very badly to the sudden understanding of how much power Mother and various female objects of desire hold over us. If one reads a few books, comes to terms with parental rebellion, has some great experiences with great girls ... just grows the fuck up, basically, then one stops hating women and unconsciously punishing them for all one's shortcomings. If one doesn't, one becomes a monster like Jim McLaine ... and there's plenty of those to go around, even in these more enlightened times.

On top of this, *That'll Be The Day* is a wonderfully well-made film. Strong performances from all the leads. Immaculate period recreation, not just in the look and sound of the film, but of how well it builds the tensions inherent in post-war England that heralded the coming of a new, youth-oriented culture with an entirely different moral outlook. A wicked, grubby, ribald script by Connolly, who certainly has a flair for misogynist jokes and creating a repressed world where sex is still something infused with homophobic anxiety and a kind of implied violence.

And then there's the director. Claude Whatham didn't quite match the impact of George Lucas. Nobody lauded his directorial excellence on *That'll Be The Day*, nor handed him a sci-fi empire to strike back with. He made a few terribly English and Earthbound mini-hits: *All Creatures Great And Small*, *Swallows And Amazons*, *Buddy's Song*. But *That'll Be The Day* is fabulous work, deftly evoking the period while managing to blend the *vérité* grime of work like *A Taste Of Honey* (see p. 70) and Michael Caine's breakthrough *Alfie* with something altogether pop and glam-rock.

I love the film because it reminds me of my 1973, rather than my Mum's 1959. Which, now I think about it, is very much in keeping with *That'll Be The Day*'s attitude to mothers.

★ ★

AMERICAN GRAFFITI

1973
Starring: Richard Dreyfuss, Ron Howard, Paul Le Mat, Charles Martin Smith, Cindy Williams, Mackenzie Phillips, Harrison Ford
Dir.: George Lucas

Plot: The film that made youth into nostalgia.
Key line: 'Do you wanna end up like John? You just can't stay 17 forever!'

Although *American Graffiti* will never be awarded the seminal status of more celebrated movie-brat-era movies, it is, pound-for-pound, the most important and influential film of its time.

First, it proved that a low-budget American film didn't have to be either experimental art movie or exploitation trash. Mainstream audiences would now accept a lack of spectacle if they could relate to characters and setting. Second, it reinforced the notion that the creatives understood more about what punters wanted than control-freak executives. Lucas was coming off the flop arty sci-fi film *THX 1138* and spent a couple of humiliating years trawling his script about cruising '60s teens around Hollywood, only getting the green light when his friend Francis Ford Coppola, director of *The Godfather*, came on board as producer. Even then, Universal executive Ned Tanen hated *Graffiti* on sight, and Coppola had to fight tooth and nail to get the movie released. When it took an astonishing $55 million at the box office and became the most profitable film ever made, it helped give the New Hollywood *auteurs* enough rope to dominate the decade until hanging themselves with expensive commercial disasters like Michael Cimino's *Heaven's Gate* and William Friedkin's *The Sorceror*.

And third, and crucially, it contained the seeds of the death of the *Easy Riders/Raging Bull* aesthetic, proving that, even as Hollywood's brats bombarded movie-goers with dark, violent themes, explicit sex, bad language and bitter critiques of Nixon's America, what people really wanted was a new version of innocent fun and permission to feel nostalgic about pre-'60s American values. Lucas's next good idea was this Buck Rogers-type space opera affair where the good guys were pretty and wore white, the bad guys were ugly and wore black, and aliens were just funny-looking aliens, not metaphors for queers or foreigners. People liked it so much they made Lucas into a corporation, and he and his similarly ambitious and nostalgic friend Steven Spielberg killed off their movie brat peers by making a spectacular kind of family cinema that dovetailed neatly with Reagan and Thatcher's insistence that the '60s had just been the children being naughty while the responsible adults had been away fighting the Commies.

American Graffiti, for better or for worse, bequeathed the world an American blockbuster entertainment that has defined our cultural codes and expectations for the last 30-plus years and counting. Not bad for a film that cost $750,000 and took 28 days to shoot.

The plot is barely a plot at all. It is 1962 in Modesto, California and two teenage boys, Curt (Dreyfuss) and Steve (Howard) are enjoying a last Saturday night with their friends John (Le Mat) and Toad (Smith) before they head to college. This involves a high school dance, girl troubles, drive-in diners where the waitresses wear roller-skates, a constant soundtrack of '50s rock 'n' roll, and, mainly, cruising the cramped Modesto streets in gorgeous cars.

Each has adventures that help them to learn and grow, defined by two parallel symbolic quests. While middle-class intellectual Curt searches for a perfect blonde beauty he's never spoken to, driven by a vision of transcendent love, the older, working-class John searches for sex, driven by machismo, habit and an existential 'circuit' he's been cruising around for years and will never escape.

But it wouldn't be an American '70s film without an unhealthy dollop of misogyny. Steve begins the film as the nice guy off to college, wanting to explore his '60s sexual freedom by suggesting to girlfriend Laurie (Williams, who joined Howard in the cast of monster hit TV show *Happy Days*, which was pretty much *American Graffiti* for children) that they both date other people while he's away. He ends the film domesticated and tied to Modesto for life, the willing victim of Laurie's manipulations of his macho jealousy. Obviously, when faced with a choice of heady sexual experimentation or hen-pecking some nerd into marrying her, no decent teen girl would pass up the opportunity to house train the potential stud and enter a partnership based on resentment and mutual sexual repression, now would they? Laurie is the film's only deeply horrible character, dressed to look as plain as possible, constantly nagging Steve from a stereotypically female high moral ground, bullying him into staying through a mixture of guilt and convincing the guy that he's a pathetic child without her. The movie brat directors' obsession with women as sexual-maternal prison wardens even touched the monumentally nerdy Lucas, who maybe felt he needed to impress proper men's men like Coppola and Dennis Hopper. Or, maybe, Lucas's film is very good because it sees its own arguments from both sides, fixing Laurie as the representative of soul-sucking '50s morality, reminding us that there were good reasons why the rock 'n' roll years didn't hang around for ever.

At the film's end, only Curt leaves small-town heaven/hell. As his plane departs, onscreen captions tell us of the boys' fates, telling us what we already know: that Curt's escape is the beginning of a fulfilling creative life while his three friends are trapped and doomed. Despite this potentially elitist theory, the feeling that Lucas somehow leaves you with is that the Big Bad 1960s were out to get American manhood, and that if it had just left these ordinary boys alone, they could have driven around the same town with their childhood sweethearts for ever, listening to corny doo wop and leaving that nasty Dylan and Hendrix music to a few beatnik weirdos in the kind of Big City colleges where they wouldn't know a good automobile if it ran 'em over, and let's hope it does, Yessirree, ah tell you what. That feeling is reinforced by Curt's future as a writer ... in Canada. Perhaps he was just dodging the Vietnam draft that kills one of his friends. Or maybe the only way to escape the horror of '60s America is to leave it completely.

You do feel haunted by this now-familiar revelation of characters' futures in caption form. And particularly by the film's biggest victim John Milner, who may have seemed cool but was destined to drive in circles, dogging an ever-shrinking pool of available women, risking his life in drag races no one in the big wide world will ever see, at least for a little while before getting dead drunk. He's the working-class no-hoper who peaked too soon, a boy all of us knew at school.

By the time *American Graffiti* had its way with the teen movie it had irrevocably changed the entire genre. Films about youth went on to mostly avoid the linear beginning–middle–end narrative, properly reflecting the unfocused, hormonal energy that dominates teenage life, as well as noticing that coming of age is the start rather than the end of a tale. All crazy kids will soon become sane adults in an insane world, and *American Graffiti*'s final roll-call of the boys' futures feels like the moment when, in what seems, superficially, like a more shallow film than the likes of *The 400 Blows* (see p. 47) or *If . . .* (see p. 97), the teen movie finally – yup – came of age. Among the gags and car fetishism and nostalgic jukebox soundtrack and dirty talk and sex and romance, there's a poignant melancholy about the inevitability of adulthood, as if a small part of Lucas really wanted to be John Milner, cruising for ever with pack of Camels tucked into sleeve of tight white t-shirt, refusing to accept the inevitability of adulthood, forcing time to stand still.

It's this that drew such huge audiences at a time when the optimism of the '60s had curdled into the anger and pessimism of the '70s, as people wondered whether sex, drugs, rock 'n' roll and protest would have been best left alone and waited for *Star Wars* and Ronald Reagan to close Pandora's Box and offer the simple comforts of good, evil and The American Way.

★ ★

BADLANDS

1973
Starring: Martin Sheen, Sissy Spacek, Warren Oates
Dir.: Terrence Malick

Plot: When they met, it was moider.
Key line: 'He was handsomer than anyone I'd ever met. He looked just like James Dean.'

In November 1958, a young man called Charley Starkweather, who had just turned 20 years old, embarked on a road trip through

Nebraska and Wyoming with his 14-year-old girlfriend, Caril Fugate. It began with Starkweather shooting Caril's father, and ended in late January 1959, with a further ten people dead. Often labelled the first modern American serial killer, Starkweather was executed by electric chair in June '59, and Fugate spent 17 years in jail. She was still in jail in York, Nebraska when she served as an informal consultant on a movie about her crimes. The movie changed the names and moved the action to South Dakota, but made no real attempt to cover up its true-life subject.

The maker of the movie, an Assyrian-American called Terrence Malick, became a sort of myth in himself, partly because he has gone on to make just four further films in the ensuing 38 years, and partly because he has steadfastly refused to be either interviewed or photographed by the media. In fact, just about the only sighting of Malick is in this very movie, where he has a small role as a man who knocks on a door. Martin Sheen reckons that the only reason the scene is there is because Malick was let down by an actor and Sheen refused to reshoot the scene with someone else. So now we know that Malick was a tall, dark-skinned, chubby but handsome guy in 1973. Nice.

This first Malick film, discounting a 1969 student short called *Lanton Mills*, was, in part, a film about celebrity, because Malick's version of Starkweather, Kit Carruthers, played by Martin Sheen, is convinced he is one because he murders people. When he is caught, he doles out souvenirs to the arresting cops and poses self-consciously for imaginary cameras, a kind of rockabilly version of Gloria Swanson at the end of *Sunset Boulevard*, waiting for his imaginary close-up, delighted by the fact that one of the cops thinks he looks like James Dean (see p. 28). It is haunting and chilling and funny 'cos it's true and probably tells us why Terrence Malick ain't gonna be showing us around his beautiful home in the pages of *Hello!* any time soon.

Because Malick has scarcity value he is routinely referred to as a genius. I don't know about that – *The Thin Red Line* was a pretentious mess – but I do know a thing or two about *Badlands* because it has fascinated me ever since I first saw it as an 11-year-old. If Malick's reclusiveness makes him cinema's very own J.D. Salinger, then *Badlands* is his *Catcher In The Rye*: a tale of American youth that seems to both encapsulate the darker impulses of teenager-dom and say something far wider and deeper about America and the world. In many ways, Malick uses incredible shots of the American landscape, a soundtrack of subtle, bucolic optimism (courtesy, mainly, of a gently undulating xylophone instrumental called 'Gassenhauer' by Carl Orff, an insidious repeating motif with an almost Aboriginal feel) and the charisma of Sheen and co-star Sissy Spacek to suggest that serial killers are beautiful things. Not the killings, mind . . . they are nasty, brutish and short. But the young killers, with their worlds of deluded fantasy that protect them from their actions.

The movie is (unreliably) narrated by the skipping southern drawl of Spacek as Holly Sargis, and hers is the voice we hear as the film innocently begins with a girl playing on her bed with a dog. We soon meet Kit, who is a dustman. His entire demeanour, even when dumping garbage, is a knowing take on rock 'n' roll juvenile delinquent, with his slouchy swagger, side-parted quiff, cowboy boots and wiry frame squeezed into white t-shirt and bluest blue jeans. At times Sheen looks so much like his magnificently errant son Charlie that it's just plain weird. Of course, if this was a Charlie Sheen movie he'd just be down the local bar trying to get laid and having a good time succeeding. But Kit has other ideas about love.

While attempting to court Holly after spotting her twirling her baton, Kit gets fired, leaving him with much too much time to devote to hitting on his under-age quarry, despite his next job on a farm, which he of course glamorises as being a cowboy. While Holly regales us with her love-struck narration, words and images clue us in to their incipient madness. Why *does* Kit want Holly when she'd 'never been popular at school and didn't have a lot of personality', especially as 'he could've had any girl in town'? She changes their ages to suit her fantasy, subconsciously reminding us that Kit is, in essence, a paedophile. He plays with dead animals like a naughty child and she throws gasping fish into the garden because they're 'sick', and you can feel the sickness they've spotted in each other, even while the music skips lightly and their picnics in the Montana countryside look like paintings by Manet. Their conversation is stilted to the point of banality. Kit takes Holly's virginity like he'd just performed an annoying chore. Meanwhile, Holly's father, played by the ever excellent Warren Oates, is too busy working on his own paintings to notice that his child is going out with a grown man.

There's 20 minutes of this mesmerising visual poetry before the surreal road movie rampage begins. There is no rhyme or reason to Kit's actions. People just get in his way, in shacks and mansions, amidst stunning landscapes and immaculately designed interiors, and he dispatches them like a man swatting flies. He shoots his friend Cato in the gut, and Holly perches on a seat in front of Cato, mildly interested in his inevitable death, and asks him about a spider he keeps in a bottle. This is madness evoked as something almost innocent, a mere extension of a child's mix of curiosity and low attention span. But even here Sheen and Malick come up with something special. When Kit runs, shoots, moves, he seems almost impossibly kinetic, and lighter than air. As if he was built to kill.

And, all the time, Kit points out which souvenirs people could keep to tell of his coming, revelling in his status as the most wanted man in America. He is the star of his own hit movie, a lurid melodrama that, as Holly explains, makes him dread 'the idea of being shot down alone without a girl to scream his name'.

But when the end comes, Holly abandons Kit anyway. She is not a victim of hopeless love, prepared to risk her life for a daredevil escape. She's just a spoiled girl whose story about being loved by the handsomest man in town got out of hand. She doesn't get to scream his name. But then, he doesn't die a cinematic death. He's just caught, like any other criminal.

The irony is, of course, that the two cops who catch Kit are happy to be cast in his movie. Having caught an outlaw who has been handed mythical status by the media, they are stars now, too. The older one is less impressed, throwing Kit's hat out of the cop car when he begins to patronise them in his brilliantly insane way. But the younger one is awestruck, in the way you would be if you'd met your favourite action movie star. He asks Kit why he did it. 'I always wanted to be a criminal, I guess,' Kit replies, sucking in his cheekbones. 'Just not this big a one. Takes all kinds, though.' The three grin conspiratorially and you don't know whether to laugh or take a shower.

So the cop tells him he looks like Jimmy Dean and we're suddenly in an aircraft hanger watching Kit, strapped to a light plane, holding court. The soldiers and cops surrounding him aren't peace officers any more. They're journalists. They fire questions at him, press conference style.

'Who's your favourite singer?'

'Eddie Fisher. Who's yours?'

'How old are you?'

'Don't you read the papers?'

Kit and Holly have a final inane conversation – 'Too bad about your dad' – and Malick adds some final bleak jokes. A shot of a father holding up his small child and pointing out the famous serial killer is contrasted with a quicker shot of a postman carrying a sack of mail, oblivious to the star in his midst, holding the evidence that life carries on and Kit is now yesterday's news. Holly informs us, in voiceover, that, once Kit got the electric chair, she was set free and married her lawyer. A cop remarks that Kit is 'quite an individual'. Kit gives him a dumb insolent, open-mouthed stare, and sneers, 'Do you think they'll take that into consideration?' Holly grins shyly and we fly into a perfect sunrise. What a fucking ending.

Kit Carruthers is in the Jim Thompson tradition of Southern Gothic psychopaths: men with good manners and bad intentions who are much smarter than they appear, but far less smart than they think. And Malick's debut is a perfect film, utterly complete in its making on a budget of next-to-nowt, but so full of loose ends and unresolved implications that you never get to the bottom of it, no matter how many times you watch. It was showered with acclaim upon release, but bombed at the box office, possibly because, after Arthur Penn's 1967 *Bonnie And Clyde*, the public had had just about enough of sympathetic travelling serial killers who symbolise youth rebellion.

Back in the real world . . . when Caril Folgate was released from prison in 1976, she began a new life as a medical aide. She never married. At the trial, Starkweather had maintained that she had carried out some of the murders. The jury didn't believe him, but they didn't believe Folgate's claims that she was an unwilling hostage either. She has continued to maintain her total innocence to this day.

But the existence and cult popularity of *Badlands* means that the world will always see Folgate as a delusional child, living in a fantasy world where life and death are irrelevant. It seems strange that she was happy to advise on a film that made her look like that. But then, the important thing about celebrity is being famous, not what you happen to be famous for. Kit Carruthers would surely have approved.

★ ★

BLACK CHRISTMAS

1974

Starring: Olivia Hussey, Margot Kidder, Keir Dullea, John Saxon, Andrea Martin, Marion Waldman
Dir.: Bob Clark

Plot: The post-hippy Agatha Christie flick that invented the teen slasher.
Key line: '*Lick it! Lick it! Let me lick your pretty pinky cunt! HEEHEEEHUEUGHHEEHEE!!!*'

When horror geeks discuss the origins of the teen slasher movie, *Black Christmas* never gets a mention. Perhaps it's because it's Canadian. Because all of the basic genre tropes are present and correct, a full four years before *Halloween* (see p. 169) was unleashed upon the world. A suburban setting. A crime scene in a spooky college sorority house. An unhinged, unseen maniac. A politically dodgy connection between adolescent sexuality and grisly demise. Hapless cops. An ending that doesn't end. Even A Final Girl. Unlike the majority of its progeny, there is a large whodunit element and a last twist, rather than a last scare. But otherwise … this could easily be read as the template for any movie which involves nubile young women attempting to survive the irrational violence of an other-worldly male monster. Admittedly, it isn't quite as memorably suspenseful as *Halloween* or cartoonish as *A Nightmare On Elm Street* (see p. 238). But its dark humour, evocative setting and ghastly slayings make *Black Christmas* a peculiar, stylish and prophetic little movie.

There is a good reason why *Black Christmas* didn't become a megahit, though. Writer A. Roy Moore and director Bob Clark thought it would be an interesting idea to make a movie about killing where you *never* saw the killer. This is *Black Christmas*'s cleverest and creepiest innovation, largely involving innovative camera operator Bert Dunk climbing up walls and down stairs with a camera harnessed to his shoulder, and the rare, hugely effective glimpse of the killer's wild eyes peaking through shadows.

But we would all soon learn that money-spinning horror franchises were built out of memorable monsters who were barely off-camera; killers with humanoid bodies but alien faces, who became ironic heroes to horror fans who would happily pay to watch increasingly awful sequels to *Halloween*, *A Nightmare . . .* , *Friday The 13th* et al. In *Black Christmas*, much of the stalking and slashing is done by us – that is, Dunk's subjective camera, prowling the claustrophobic staircases and corridors of the sorority house, forcing us to see this small, dark world through the eyes of the killer rather than the victims.

This means that a great deal of the fright work in *Black Christmas* is done by inspired sound design. Carl Zittrer's rumbling, groaning avant-garde music, made by attaching household objects to the strings of his piano and playing with the music's speed, mingles with the breathing and babbling of the killer. And then there are the phone calls.

Billy – the killer does have a name – is fond of calling the sorority house and freaking out the girls. But this guy is the obscene phone caller to end them all. Wes Craven revives the idea in *Scream* (p. 339) but plays it for arch laughs. Here, the calls are the work of a gibbering lunatic, so schizoid that he can become completely different voices, possessed of knowledge about the girls that only a friend could know, calling them cunts and whores, or, more often than not, just making nightmarish squealing and gurgling sounds.

The first call is a shock to the system. Taken by heroine Jess (Hussey), it begins with the usual heavy breathing, but then grows in volume, intensity and madness, courtesy of director Clark actually employing five different voices – including his own – to mix into one impossible diatribe. The caller sucks and gasps and gurgles and unleashes a series of pig noises before breaking into uncontrollable laughter. Soon we're into liberal use of the 'C' word: he wants to lick it. He wants his 'fat juicy cock' sucked. When hard-living bitch-queen Barb (the ever excellent Kidder) takes over the call he continues his sexual tauntings with increasing hysteria. When Barb taunts back, refusing to be impressed or intimidated by his rapist verbals, Clark pulls his masterstroke. Suddenly, the killer says, in a measured, matter-of-fact and entirely human tone: 'I'm going to kill you,' and hangs up. Barb, like us, knows that he means it, because, when the lunacy is switched off, our caller sounds serious about his work.

The calls are heavily influenced by the bizarre, demonic noises that emerge from the possessed Linda Blair in *The Exorcist*, easily the most successful and influential horror flick of the early '70s. But coming from someone invisible, entering your home from somewhere unknown, the calls are profoundly disturbing. Without them, and the insane interior dialogue Billy continues to maintain while stalking, our killer is nothing more than a camera walking around a dimly lit building.

The plot itself is actually slight. Billy breaks into Toronto sorority house while the girls are having a Christmas party. He makes his calls and begins to bump off the few that haven't gone home for the holidays. We suspect a couple of the boyfriends, especially Peter (Dullea), self-obsessed pianist boyfriend of Jess, who doesn't react well to Jess's decision to abort the couple's unplanned baby.

The cops try to hunt the killer and trace the calls but get nowhere. Finally, after murders by way of plastic clothes-bag and a big hook on a pulley, plus the violent demise of an unfortunate pussycat and the two best characters – alcoholic House Mother Mrs MacHenry (Waldman) and foul-mouthed tough chick Barb, who gets stabbed while angelic children sing 'O Come All Ye Faithful', drowning the sounds of her suffering with their infernal Christian rhyme – we get to the inevitable showdown between killer and Final Girl Jess. Jess wins and everyone thinks the drama is over. But we know different. The movie ends with still-undiscovered corpses in the attic, and the whispers and mumbles of the real killer, as the camera pulls away from the attic window, leaving a house alone with its failure to understand that the enemy was always within, and us with no real idea of who Billy is and why he's killing these women, and the increasingly deafening ring of an unanswered phone.

Aspects of the film have dated badly, especially in the coiffeur department. And, despite having just become a star by playing the female lead in Franco Zeffirelli's hit version of *Romeo And Juliet*, Hussey is a terrible, terrible actress. But Clark's low-budget *mise en scène* is impeccable, the foul-mouthed script a shock even now, and there are genuinely memorable characters played with enormous gusto by Kidder, Waldman, the ever-reliable Saxon as the square-jawed cop, and Dullea, who brings the same dimpled, long-faced, blank-eyed strangeness to Peter as he did to the lead astronaut in *Kubrick's 2001: A Space Odyssey*. The film has a haunting otherness; a gothic quality that later teen slasher movies rejected in favour of splashy pop culture nastiness, as if Italian art-horror maverick Dario

Argento had suddenly decided to make popcorn entertainment for American teens.

There is a great scream-out-loud moment, too. *Black Christmas* was one of the first adult horror movies I managed to sneak into as a nipper, and I still have thrilled memories of the ruckus in the stalls when the killer – face still ingeniously kept out of shot – chases Jess down stairs and manages to shoot out a hand and grab her hair.

And interestingly, the punishing of sexually active women isn't the point here. In fact, the control-freak nastiness of Peter, and his status as main suspect, establishes a clever pro-choice sub-plot. But on the other hand, the uproarious Barb does seem to get punished for her sexual taunting of various square older men with funny scenes involving the sex lives of turtles and improper use of the word 'fellatio'.

Nevertheless, all of the girls appear to have active, permissive-society sex lives, and some live, and some die. Whether the cat got any before meeting its maker remains one of *Black Christmas*'s many mysteries.

★ ★

A BOY AND HIS DOG

1975
Starring: Don Johnson, Tiger, Tim McIntire, Susanne Benton, Jason Robards
Dir.: L.Q. Jones

Plot: After you've had your way with a girl, you should at least make her dinner.
Key line(s): *Boy*: **'I know what you mean! Over the hill where the deer and the antelope play and it's warm and clean and we can relax and have fun and grow food right out of the ground. How do you like that pipedream?'**
Dog: **'It's called farming.'**

Remember how I said, just a few entries ago, that Louis Malle's *Le Souffle Au Coeur* (see p. 122) was the most twisted teen film of all time? Well, I was forgetting this movie and the fact that the 1970s weren't over yet. The incredibly strange *A Boy And His Dog* combines several of the most popular recurring elements of the American 'Movie Brat' era. Post-nuclear apocalypse dystopia. Rampant machismo. Anti-Christian ranting. Relentless pessimism. A cynical loathing for humanity. Male bonding. And extreme misogyny. The only thing it's missing is Charlton Heston and lines about damn dirty apes.

A Boy And His Dog is based upon a celebrated novella by sci-fi mini-legend Harlan Ellison. The year is 2024 and the world has been destroyed by World War IV, which lasted all of five days. In this parallel universe, the money poured into space travel in the '60s was spent on bombs, futuristic technology, building androids and doing crazy experiments on animals. Which is how come an 18-year-old rapist called Vic (played by Don Johnson of *Miami Vice* fame) is wandering around an arid desert wasteland accompanied only by a telepathic dog called Blood.

Slipped the 'R' word right in there, just to see if you were really concentrating. You see, among Earth's few human survivors, women are even scarcer than men, because many of the men were off fighting while the women were all at home waiting in the cities for the bombs to drop. So Vic, as well as every other man, it seems, feels that sex has become a right to take by force. Or, as Buffy Summers once memorably put it when Xander Harris was possessed by a mystical hyena in classic *Buffy* episode 'The Pack', 'His idea of wooing doesn't involve a Yanni CD and a bottle of Chianti.'

The price Blood (played by cute mongrel Tiger and voiced brilliantly by Tim McIntire) has paid for being made super-intelligent and telepathic by some mad scientist is that he's lost his ability to track food. Even though he can track women. Yeah, I don't really get that either. But anyway, the boy and his dog have become mutually dependent to a post-apocalyptic degree. As the boy is dumb and the dog is smart, Blood acts as both teacher and taunter, giving us much of the pre-bomb back-story as impromptu history lessons for Vic while also mocking him for his sexual urges and lack of education. He delights in calling him Albert, which we assume is Vic's real name.

So life for the pair is one long scavenger hunt with added bickering, what with laws, ethics and morals having been rendered redundant by Armageddon. For a start, slavery has also joined random rape and pillage among the survivors' relapse into uncivilised habits. Vic manages to steal some food from a desert slave-master and barters his way into one of the wilderness's rare settlements, where there is company, a movie projector showing scratchy vintage soft porn ... and a woman.

The woman is evil schemer Quilla June (Benton), whom Vic saves from bandits and mutants, and finally gets his oats from as recompense. Blood doesn't like her, but that's always the way in '70s bromances, even when one of the bros has four legs and bad breath. But he has a point, because Quilla June's idea of post-coital intimacy is to knock Vic unconscious and disappear. She also leaves him a card that gets him into 'Downunder', the underground paradise that she's told Vic all about. The injured Blood advises Vic that a violent woman and a mysterious subterranean world might be equally dangerous things to enter. The dog pleads with Vic not to go and leave him, especially as Blood believes in 'the promised land', a magical place running over with rapeworthy women and hot and cold running popcorn (Blood's favourite food) that he insists is just yonder, 'over the hill'. Vic follows the pussy. Bad move.

It turns out that Quilla was just bait for a trap laid by her Bad Dad Lou Craddock (Robards), who has started a crazy fundamentalist Christian utopia enforced by a mighty grinning android called Michael where everyone is forced to wear dungarees and mime make-up while acting out a grotesque parody of small-town American life, pitched somewhere between *Gone With The Wind* and *The Waltons*. But this new start for humanity means breeding, and 'Topeka' doesn't have enough virile young men. This is all starting to sound like an 18-year-old boy's wildest fantasy, except that Craddock doesn't believe in nature taking its course. Vic is strapped to a machine that extracts the semen right out of him and then artificially injects it into young women dressed as brides. And once he's impregnated 35 'wives', Vic buys the farm. Or rather, he gets sent to 'the farm', a place no one comes back from because it basically means Michael crushes your puny human head with his bare robot hands. Cue daring escape.

The meat of the matter comes when Vic and a now contrite Quilla June return to the surface. Poor Blood has been waiting there patiently, as dogs do, and, what with his non-existent food-finding skills, is now one of those tear-jerking dog rescue ads. They can't go back to the settlement to feed him because bandits have taken it over.

Quilla presents Vic with that old, 'If you love me, you'll leave the dog to die' chestnut. The screen fades to black.

We hear the faint sounds of a fire, and then gradually see smoke. We hear Blood do his think-speak thing. As he and Vic walk away into the distant sunrise, nattering, we begin to understand Vic's solution to his thorny problem.

'She said she loved me,' Vic's voice intones. 'Well . . . it's not my fault she picked me to get all wet-brained over.'

A pause. 'Well', answers Blood, 'I'd say she certainly had marvellous judgement, Albert . . . but not particularly good taste.' And the damn dog laughs. And we're asked to laugh right along with the fact that a man has fed his girlfriend to his dog.

Ellison was reportedly angry about the jaunty misogyny of the ending. But the only thing screenwriters Jones, Alvy Moore and Wayne Cruseturner added was the jokey line. The novella still ends with Vic and Blood eating Quilla June.

I know. I should be utterly ashamed of myself for putting this movie in this book. Problem is . . . it's a really great movie. Despite the low budget, the desert dystopia and the genuinely terrifying Topeka are superbly designed. The movie projector settlement scene was surely where George Miller drew inspiration for the dirty dystopian chaos of his *Mad Max* movies. The dog voiceover is outstanding, with McIntire making Blood into a strange sort of misanthropic professor with a love-hate fixation on his master that absolutely fits our ideas about what our dogs might be thinking. McIntire also provided the soundtrack's imaginative mix of folky whimsy and avant-garde electronica, along with Jaime Mendoza-Nava and former Door Ray Manzarek. And the dog's very good, too, especially in the sad bits.

And Johnson, who was actually 26 here and nine years away from his *Miami Vice Zeitgeist* moment, is a revelation. Like John Amblas in *Martin* (see p. 156), he has to carry a film as a protagonist with virtually no redeeming features while also playing a fair few scenes reacting silently to a dog as voiceovers carry the conversation. He gets it wrong, the film becomes unwatchably confusing *and* nasty. But Johnson somehow manages to imbue Vic with enough hick charm to make the film seem like a reasonable tilt at how an ignorant boy might become corrupted under such circumstances, rather than an exercise in sheer loathing for womankind.

Nevertheless, there really isn't any further that teen cinema – or any other kind of cinema – could take feminist backlash misogyny than making women into dog food. *Carrie* and *Halloween* are on their way, and, from that point on, Ms Spacek and Ms Curtis ensure that women start to get a little more respect around here.

★ ★

CARRIE

1976
Starring: Sissy Spacek, Piper Laurie, Nancy Allen, Amy Irving, William Katt, Betty Buckley, John Travolta
Dir.: Brian De Palma

Plot: The last night at The Prom. The *very* last night at The Prom.
Key line: 'After the blood comes the boys, like sniffin' dogs, grinnin' and slobberin' and trying to find out where *that smell* comes from!'

Carrie has a great set of casting stories. Brian De Palma was coming off a minor hit with *grand guignol* rock opera *Phantom Of The Paradise* (see *Popcorn*). But the original casting sessions for *Carrie* were held as a joint effort with another director, to save money and time. The end result was that the whole of young Hollywood turned up to a room to test for De Palma *and* a new science fiction film by the guy who had had a surprise mega-hit with *American Graffiti*. If you came to try out for *Carrie*, you were also auditioning for *Star Wars*. So I guess everyone who bagged *Carrie* is kinda pissed off, in retrospect, even though, in the real world, *Carrie* is a much, *much* better film.

Amy Irving, who went on to be the singing voice of Jessica Rabbit in *Who Framed Roger Rabbit?* after marrying Steven Spielberg and getting a divorce settlement of a reported $100 million, got the part of Sue Snell. Because De Palma had enjoyed working with a mother–daughter team in an earlier movie called *Sisters*, he immediately cast Irving's mom Priscilla Pointer as her onscreen mother.

Piper Laurie had been astonishing alongside Paul Newman in 1961s *The Hustler* but had completely retired from acting when fan

De Palma sent her the *Carrie* script. She read the part of Margaret White and dismissed it as schlocky cliché until her husband pointed out that all De Palma's previous, arty movies had had a satirical edge. She read the script again with that in mind, got it, and took what would be her second and final iconic role.

Before being Chris Hargensen, Nancy Allen was just one of those thousands of wannabes who do a bit of stage-acting and get a few commercials in New York and head to Hollywood with dreams of being a movie star. And, like most of those thousands she'd got absolutely nowhere and, by November 1975, had decided to give up and move back to New York. A few days before leaving she went to the gym and, as she was coming out of the steam room, a woman called her name. She was Harriet Helberg, the casting director for *Carrie*, and she had hunted Allen down to persuade her to take just one more audition. So, in the very last slot in the very last day of casting, Allen tested. Two years later, she married Brian De Palma.

And Sissy Spacek, who made Carrie White into one of cinema's most profoundly believable and sympathetic monsters, was not even on De Palma's radar as casting began. She was married to production designer Jack Fisk, whom she had met on the set of *Badlands* (see p. 138). He gave her a copy of Stephen King's novel and she was desperate to play the title role, but De Palma was not a fan of her previous work, and already had another actress in mind. Spacek, who, bizarrely, had gained little success from her stunning performance in *Badlands*, had an audition for a commercial on the same day as the last casting call for Carrie White. She called De Palma, asking which audition she should go to. He told her to go for the commercial because she had no chance of getting the lead in *Carrie*.

Furious, she went home and re-read the *Carrie* screenplay, obsessing over De Palma and Hollywood's lack of interest in her pale, cold strangeness. She felt abused by the system. She got up the next morning, blew off the commercial, vandalised an old sailor suit her mother had given her as a child, rubbed Vaseline in her hair and turned up at De Palma's casting as dirty, angry and little-girl-lost as she felt. She then proceeded to blow De Palma's unlucky first choice out of the room. The rest is horror history.

Based on Stephen King's first novel – but possibly the only King screen adaptation that is better than the source – *Carrie* is the story of Carrie White, a teenage girl living a repressed, abused life with her maniacally religious mother. Margaret White roams around the neighbourhood trying to convert the hostile natives, eats dinner in front of a giant print of *The Last Supper*, calls breasts 'dirty pillows', and locks her daughter in a closet every time she expresses the vaguest interest in anything worldly. So damaged is Carrie by repressing her hormonal desires, the physical and mental torture at home, and the bullying and humiliation she suffers at school, that she has developed telekinetic powers that are unleashed at moments of unbearable stress. When a group of mean girls are punished by nice gym teacher Miss Collins for attacking and taunting Carrie when she has her first period in a shower after games (her mother has never bothered to warn Carrie about 'the curse'), they take revenge on Carrie by setting her up on a date at the senior prom with school heart-throb Tommy Ross (Katt). When I say 'mean girls' these are Mean Girls Deluxe, led by Chris Hargenson, who gets orgasmic feelings when successfully enlisting her brutish boyfriend Billy Nolan (Travolta) to do her dirty works. So this prom night revenge involves a bucket of pig's blood, dropped from a great height, just at the moment when Carrie thinks she's finally been accepted by her peers. Driven insane by this final cruel humiliation, Carrie kills everyone in school by way of destroying the building with the power of her mind. When she arrives home, her mad mother stabs her so she kills her in a symbolic act of crucifixion which Mad Mom seems to rather enjoy. And then Carrie burns down the house and dies, too. In a famous and much-imitated coda, we see nice-ish girl Sue Snell, prom night's one survivor, take flowers to Carrie's grave. As she kneels to place the flowers, a blood-streaked arm shoots out of the ground and grabs her. We cut to Sue screaming in a hospital bed, hysterical and being held by her horrified mother. Sue may have lived through prom night, but it looks very much like Carrie is driving her insane from beyond the grave, living on through a nightmare that will never fade.

Now this should all be preposterous. Especially when you add the clunky attempts at comedy, the bad rock music, the horribly dated '70s clothes and hair. There's a compelling argument that *Carrie*'s true horror lies not in the supernatural, but in William Katt's super-naturally bad do, an unforgettable mixture of blonde Afro and explosion in a curly perm factory. Then there's De Palma's career-long tendency to smash viewers in the face with his intentions for each scene, using gimmicks like split-screens and something called a split dioptre lens that provides those amazing shots where a character's face is in extreme close-up with a sort of halo effect at one end of the frame, while completely in-focus stuff goes on in the background at the other end.

But this, I think, is *Carrie*'s secret. It's an exercise in hysteria, with the utterly over-the-top performances of Laurie and Spacek (both so good they forced the Oscar dummies to break their traditional loathing of horror and nominate the pair for Academy Awards) matched all the way by De Palma's good taste-rejecting obsession with pastiching Alfred Hitchcock (the school is named after *Psycho* killer Norman Bates, the shrieking violins are pulled wholesale from Bernard Herrmann's *Psycho* score), releasing cathartic baggage about his own Catholic upbringing, and exploring his (and our) fear of and repulsion at menstruation. How many of us knew that teenage girls were so universally feared before we saw *Carrie*? Is a sexually repressed girl the most dangerous creature on Earth? And how many other post-'60s films would have the audacity to have Carrie's mother say the key words, 'The prom?', have a clap of thunder and a flash of lightning provide the punctuation, and play it with a straight face? It was De Palma's unusual post-Russ Meyer blend of cinematic reverence, virtuoso technique and fearless bad taste that ensured that he and *Carrie* belonged together. It was the perfect vehicle for De Palma's bleakly ironic view of manipulating audience emotions, too. You can almost feel his loathing of the viewer in many of his films. The reason you don't feel it in *Carrie* is because he has horrible characters that he can loathe right along with us.

Despite Laurie's wittily unhinged performance providing the essential glue that sticks everything together, it is three scenes without her that define *Carrie*'s place in the communal mind of film fans. The first is the shower scene, where De Palma's Big Themes come together with his mischievous manipulations of audience. At first, the scene is soft porn ... and fairly shocking soft porn for a '70s movie at least partly aimed at under-18s.

Carrie has just done the perennial school outsider thing and fucked up the last point in the volleyball game. We enter the shower and, in graceful slow motion, get every boy (and man's) fantasy of being allowed access to the wonders of the girls' changing-room. Hot girls laugh and play, and Nancy Allen's small pert breasts bounce towards us, and all is voyeuristic thrills and guilt-free perving. We then move gradually towards Carrie in the shower, alone, hiding her body from us and the world. But even she – and we only really realise how pretty Sissy Spacek can be in her moment of prom joy before she unleashes hell – is allowed to turn the viewer on, caressing her legs in slow motion, hands moving inevitably towards crotch. Except – this is not wank fantasy. This is horror. And what greater horror for a girl than realising that blood is gushing out of you for reasons unknown, or for a boy than having that reality rubbed in your face? De Palma gave each and every gawping lad a right slapping here, and the older you get, the more you know you deserve it.

But if boys can be sexually inappropriate, De Palma seems to say, then girls can be downright evil. Now in real-time and with a suddenly shaky camera, he follows Carrie as, thin and hunched and terrified, she runs to her classmates for help, looking for just one who will tell her what is happening to her. Instead, the girls become a bullying, baying mob, laughing, throwing tampons at her, taunting and lashing out until she's a cornered rabbit, in foetal position in the corner of the shower, reeling in shock at how much she is despised. You want to cry. How many horror films make you want to actually cry tears of sympathy?

But even this wonderful scene has to take second place to ... The Prom. Oh my. Where to start. The stunning crane shot that shows you around the gym, allowing every main character to walk into shot, unaware that these will be their last carefree moments? Or how touched you are when Tommy begins to really like this fragile, alien girl, and gives her the dream prom moment for such a cruelly short, crucial moment? Or the dastardly plot, revealed in its hideous glory in fast edits, a stunning parade of ropes and buckets and different views of different characters?

This stuff is all amazing. But I suspect, for anyone who has ever watched this film, we all recall little except the blood from the sky, and the look of unbearable agony, and the strange comedy of the bucket striking Tommy's head, and the way the lights catch Spacek's white, translucent face as she stands, hands tensed into claws, body caked in crimson blood.

And then ... The Eyes. I mean, the ensuing mayhem is as beautifully choreographed as everything else. But nothing that happens to any of the guilty parties is as horrible, as wrong, as shocking and mesmerising as Sissy Spacek's gigantic ghost eyes cutting through her veil of blood and tears. You really believe, for a few stunning minutes, that this girl could kill people just by staring, really, really hard.

You know a movie has got you for life when you refuse to accept that what happens, happens. I've never been able to watch the prom scene in *Carrie* without wanting it to be different this time. Why doesn't Tommy know something's wrong? Why doesn't that nice Miss Collins spot the bucket, or Chris and Billy sneaking around? Why doesn't Sue get onstage and make Carrie move rather than twat about underneath the stage? Why doesn't that nice Miss Collins recognise that Sue is the nice-ish girl and listen to what she's saying? Why can't they just choose someone else to be prom King and Queen, and then Tommy can take Carrie home and give her a first magical goodnight kiss? Then Margaret finally runs naked through Main St and gets carted off to the funny farm, leaving Carrie to move in with Miss Collins, who, through much love and liberal parenting, transforms Carrie into a normal member of society who, eventually, uses her telekinetic powers for good, foiling rabid fundamentalist pro-lifers and maybe preventing Liverpool's domination of European football in the 1980s?

But no, damn you . . . No. That bucket of pig blood falls on Carrie, every time. It's probably just as well, because, if we could really change films, really stop that idiot from checking out the bumping noises in the dark cellar or shagging his wife's sister, we would deny ourselves things as black magical as the terror of Sissy Spacek's face, saucer eyes alien and deathly, drenched in symbolic menstrual blood and fit for crucifying her mother with kitchen implements and grabbing Sue's arm from the depths of her coffin, due to live on in everyone's nightmares. We'd just never let it happen. Because – and this is so key to the achievement of Spacek and De Palma here – we feel so, so sorry for Carrie. Even when she's on a tamponic rampage. Even when she chops that nice Miss Collins in half with a basketball board. We don't blame her for wanting to kill us all. I'd kill me all, too, if I was her.

And, finally, the final scene. A girl walking to a grave, shot at night with fluorescent light and made to walk backwards away from the headstone, so that, when the film was run backwards, it would amp up the unreality of the picture; clue us in that this is just a dream. It didn't help. That hand shot – much more slowly than you recall –

out of the ground, and people in cinemas screamed and wept and had nightmares for weeks, just like poor, mad Sue Snell in her hospital bed. Everyone's copied it – hell, *Buffy* repeated the theft around 50 times – but no one came close to the primal effect it had on audiences, or its implication that trauma never, ever ends, not even when you sleep, and, for all any of us knows, even when you die.

A great movie. Period.

★ ★

MARTIN

1978
Starring: John Amplas, Lincoln Maazel, Christine Forrest
Dir.: George A. Romero

Plot: Does a boy need fangs to be a vampire? Horror legend bites the hand that feeds him.
Key line: 'There's no real magic. Ever.'

Beloved of critics, horror fans and B-movie aficionados, ignored by the general public, *Martin* is Zombiemeister George A. Romero's secret masterpiece. A unique mix of vampire film, serial killer thriller, sombre character study, social critique and *vérité* art movie, it concerns a teenage boy called Martin Mattias who believes he is an 84-year-old vampire. This presents two pressing problems: first, he craves the blood of beautiful young women; second, he has no fangs, no superpowers, he doesn't burst into flame in sunlight, and garlic and crosses have no effect on him. In short, he just appears to be a common-or-garden psychopath. This allows Romero, who also wrote *Martin*, to explore the gap between romantic horror myth and the grim reality of brutal murder. Romero literally attempts to drain the blood right out of the monster movie.

The setting for this disturbing, uncomfortable movie is crucial. Martin (Amplas) is sent from whereabouts unknown to live with his great uncle Tada Cuda (Maazel) and cousin Christina (Forrest) in the crumbling steel town of Braddock, Pennsylvania. The dying, economically deprived suburb provides an appropriately bleak backdrop for a boy whose reality has no connection to his fantasy life.

While Braddock is shot in grainy colour, Martin's sudden visions of olde worlde vampiric seductions of helpless maidens are in mono-chrome, plucked, as they are, from literature and early cinema's images of Dracula's eroticised killings. As the town decays, we see Martin decay right along with it, trapped within a barbed visual comment on the absence of magic in both Martin's life and America's present.

Crazy uncle Tada is part of a heavily Catholic Eastern European family who believe that vampires exist, and that the family is cursed to produce one every now and again. Martin is the latest, and Cuda's self-appointed mission is to save Martin's soul before killing him. Christina, understandably, reckons that the entire family are loonies and that Martin's mute, introspective weirdness is entirely the fault of their religious manias. Both might have a somewhat different opinion of the situation if they knew what Martin had done on the train to Braddock.

Martin, you see, has found ways around the whole no-fang problem. As we watch the opening murder on the train, we imme-diately understand that we are in neither conventional horror movie nor conventional serial killer terrain. The first ten minutes of *Martin* are among the most disconcerting in cinema.

First, we are given no time to get to know either killer or victim. The camera lingers a little upon the extraordinary John Amblas (who has to carry the film on little more than a blank, intense but vulnerable, stare) and we get that he is Martin. He's a relatively typical, almost good-looking teenage boy with a short mullet, t-shirt, bomber jacket and jeans. He chooses his victim almost arbitrarily and instantly. Before we've had time to adjust to Romero's jolting edits and jarring close-ups of syringes and hands flopping from beds, Martin has broken into her cabin. We immediately cut to his fantasy: a monochrome shot of the woman as smiling, willing victim, reaching out to be taken. Crash – we're back in reality. The woman is not there at all. The toilet flushes and we realise where she is. We almost expect him to change his mind and bolt. He doesn't. He positions himself behind the toilet door.

When the woman emerges from the loo, she is not the long-haired glamour-girl in lingerie that he wants. Her frizzy hair is tied up, her face smeared with a clownish mud-pack. Her nightie is green and thermal and she is blowing her nose.

She gets on to the bed, turns, sees Martin in the shadows ... and does something weird. She just ... looks at him. It's not a look of desire, exactly. But it's not the shock and panic that anyone would feel when seeing a strange man in their train cabin with a syringe between his teeth. With so little information to go on, we wonder: do they know each other? Is this all some kind of kinky sex game? Or was she, for some other, more mystical reason, expecting him? Before we can ponder any more, Martin lunges.

What ensues is not a movie murder. And it definitely isn't sexy. It's a fight between determined ineptitude and an unwilling victim fighting back against a 'freak rapist asshole'. He's stuck her with the drugs, but she's taking a long time to go under. As they grapple clumsily, he pleads with her not to fight or scream and seems to lack the requisite skills in physical violence to subdue her. You think she's going to survive this, but the drugs do work and no one is coming to her rescue. He manages to stop her from screaming and she asks if he wants money. She reaches for a shoe to hit him with, but drops it. She finally passes out ... and an exhausted Martin assures her that it won't hurt, although she can't hear him.

We cut to the train's exterior, and then quickly back to the cabin as he carefully positions a razor blade. The woman's face is now clear ... the face-pack was removed in the struggle. In the darkness we see that Martin is now naked. He removes her nightgown. He begins to make love – gently – to her sleeping body, placing her arms in places that enable him to pretend he's being embraced. Finally, after too long a time for the viewer's liking, he reaches for the razor blade. He picks up her wrist and holds it high above their bodies. He slices ... but only draws a blob of blood. He slices again, harder, faster – success! A river of blood flows gracefully down her arm and spurts onto his bare chest. With a look of manic excitement, he presses her wrist to his mouth, and drinks.

He discards the blade. We see a tight close-up of it seeping blood into the carpet. Martin's mouth is ringed with blood and he tenderly kisses the woman. As he does, she seems to wake for a moment ... and the prospect of her waking and seeing and understanding what's been done to her suddenly seems far worse than her death. But ... no. Her eyes are glassy. Martin puts his fingers gently on her eyelids and closes them, and continues to gorge on her wrist.

Another cut to the train's exterior, and then quickly back to the cabin light being switched on. Martin's tryst is over and there is work to be done. We look up at him standing, covered in gore. He is quizzical, arranging the dead woman on the bed like a window-dresser arranging a mannequin. In montage, he cleans up and adds the final touches – more razors, pills – to make it look like a suicide. As he dresses we finally get the opening credits.

This all goes way beyond 'horror' and bathes us in real, true, genuine horror at what we've just watched. The only murder I can compare it to in this book is the killing of the mother at the end of *Heavenly Creatures* (see p. 315). But even though Peter Jackson's film is about a true-life event, he at least gives us 90-plus minutes of character and back-story in order to pack the moment with emotion. Here ... we don't know these people, and the anonymity of the act along with the devilish detail all makes it seem that much worse. If what Romero is trying to say in *Martin* is that all our fantasies about mythical erotic monsters are evidence of a sickness within us, that we find stimulation and glamour in what is, when all is said and done, the violent ending of a person's hopes and dreams and loves and future, even that the horror and thriller genres in themselves are romantic justifications of despicable crimes ... then he's cracked it. Cheers for that, George. *Thanks.*

Much of the success of *Martin* as art comes down to the per-formance of John Amplas. Amplas was actually 28 when he played this teen psycho, and, although Amplas looks no more than 17, it needed an experienced actor to pull off the near-impossible – make you feel sympathetic towards a lead protagonist with no redeeming features. Martin is either lunatic or cold-blooded killer or both. He barely says anything. He has no witty lines, no cool moves and no human warmth. But, as the slayings persist, you find yourself rooting for his redemption. Some of the credit for this goes to Lincoln Maazel, who has a whale of a time playing the old-school creepy cartoon hysteric Cuda, growling 'Nosferatu!!!' at the kid and refusing to accept the possibility that the myths of the old country are just myths. But, in order to keep the movie from sliding towards camp, Amplas can't be a cartoon. There is no eye-rolling, giggling or slavering. Just this cold haunted visage, more frightened than fright-ening, silently absorbing the madness and drowning in it. And because of the vulnerability within Amplas, you root for the idea that nice, sane Cousin Christina is going to provide some sort of redemption for Martin. OK, it would be a redemption involving locking him in a maximum security psych unit and throwing away the key. But the fact that you even find yourself pondering the real-life consequences for Martin speaks volumes for what Romero, Amblas and the sad hulk that is Braddock, Pennsylvania achieve with a story that is potentially ludicrous.

The abrupt, ironic climax of *Martin* ensures its status as a horror movie that lingers and disturbs. Our lost boy has begun fucking with his MO, killing homeless men in nearby Pittsburgh, killing a housewife that he has had a conventional affair with, and confessing his crimes on a local radio phone-in. Of course, anyone calling himself The Count and describing himself as a vampire with deadly earnestness is treated as an entertaining black joke by the DJ, and Martin becomes a cult hit with the listeners.

When Martin only escapes arrest by virtue of some conveniently placed drug dealers – a bizarre diversion which gives Romero the chance to try out some blaxploitation chops – he makes a last call to the radio, explaining to the DJ that, 'in real life, you can't get them [people] to do what you want them to'.

Suddenly Martin is walking through some sort of Mardi Gras-style parade. He seems to quite enjoy himself, marching along, like a child. But normal human pleasures are not part of Martin's world. We suddenly jump to Martin asleep in bed at his great uncle's home. Cuda is ranting at him about breaking a deal about killing the townsfolk of Braddock. He's sussed Martin's crimes, but, of course, still believes they are the crimes of a vampire. He has given up on saving Martin's soul. He hammers a large wooden spike into Martin's chest.

As the credits roll, we see a hand sowing grass seed over a grave in Cuda's front garden and hear the radio phone-in, growing in volume. The DJ and his regular callers want to know what happened to their favourite eccentric The Count. As we watch Cuda wipe Martin's presence from the world in broad daylight, the calls become increasingly ridiculous, with callers writing songs about him and insisting that his cape was paisley, not black. As Cuda crosses himself and places a crucifix upon the grave, we hear a caller say, 'It was a good gimmick.' But the last call is from a man with a soft, creepily gentle voice. He says he has a friend who he thinks is The Count. We suspect there's no friend.

In death, Martin has achieved the mythical status he so desired, enough to inspire followers. He was wrong about there being no magic. It's just that, these days, the spells are woven by the monsters of the mass media.

* *

NATIONAL LAMPOON'S ANIMAL HOUSE

1978

Starring: John Belushi, Tim Matheson, Peter Riegert, John Vernon, Donald Sutherland, Tom Hulce, Stephen Furst, Verna Bloom, Kevin Bacon
Dir.: John Landis

Plot: The dregs of society vs the military-industrial complex. With tit gags.
Key line: 'TO-GA!TO-GA! TO-GA! TO-GA! TO-GA! TO-GA!'

Some idea of the nihilism with which screenwriters Harold Ramis, Douglas Kenney and Chris Miller approached this movie becomes apparent when you know that one of their original script ideas had been called *Charles Manson In High School*. Perhaps they felt the best way to get rid of America's long '60s hangover was to poke fun at the most horrifying product of hippy culture, removing its power by making him just another subject for dumbass gags.

The first and still the best campus 'gross-out' comedy, *Animal House* also introduced non-Yanks to the bizarre, arcane world of American university Fraternity and Sorority houses – especially those that the rich attended – with their sado-masochistic initiation rites, addictions to barbershop quartets, and freemason-style cliques and codes.

And, of course, it made John Belushi a star before the fool ended that just four years later by shooting a 'speedball' cocaine/heroin cocktail and dying in the Chateau Marmont hotel on Sunset Boulevard. Many have tried to emulate his surreal slob as cosmic force of nature performance as Bluto. And all will always fail, as Jack Black is rapidly discovering.

Despite its knockabout, smutty, slapstick humour, *Animal House* produces its satirical credentials early on. As Larry (Hulce) and Ken (Furst) are introduced to the Omega frat house initiation cocktail party by the hideous Neidermeyer (the excellently repellent Mark Metcalf), they are, as 'a wimp and a blimp', shown immediately and repeatedly to the only suitable corner of the soirée. There sit the gathering's only black, Asian and disabled guests, with a boy called Sidney who could be sidelined because of his nerdish image ... or because he looks suspiciously Jewish. If I needed to explain to a small child exactly what social exclusion meant, I'd show them this two-minute scene and go have a cup of tea.

Director Landis, producer Ivan Reitman and future *Ghostbusters* writer and star Ramis are all Jewish. And one suspects that much of the film's depiction of WASPs at an American campus in 1962 is a settling of scores from anti-Semitic bullyings past. The wealthy boys and girls of Omega and its sister house at Faber College are pure Nazi to their Aryan cores, attempting to create an on-campus world – and, by default, a future America – where everyone who isn't pretty, white and from pure upper-middle-class stock is denied access to both power and basic human dignity. They are encouraged in this by the college head Dean Wormer (the craggily self-parodic Vernon) who the writers admitted was based upon Richard Nixon.

The film gets its comic momentum from an increasingly nasty war between the fascists and an ad hoc band of outsiders thrown together by social exclusion. The Delta resistance army's ideas of a good time are entirely based around the '60s ideals of sex, drugs, black music and doing as little work as is humanly possible. After enduring assaults by the Omega jocks that border on the sado-masochistic (and not funny), the impure Delta house gang get revenge in a violent, gleeful climax that resembles a comedy re-enactment of World War II.

And even before this, Landis takes plenty of opportunity to humiliate the Aryans without the help of his liberation army, particularly in a car masturbation scene which is spectacularly rude by late '70s standards and implies that the reason WASP men are so appalling is because – sin of sins! – they can't get erections. The film forces us with relentless ferocity to identify with what the American establishment would deem 'losers', and cheer as every blonde in the film is thoroughly debased.

Animal House may take its year and its affectionate, jukebox nostalgia cue from *American Graffiti*, but there is no nostalgia here for pre '60s values. The more you watch it, in fact, the more it looks like an attack on Lucas's film and its message that small-town white kids were benign innocence embodied before everything got ruined by long hair, drugs, The Beatles and Vietnam. The film's climax mercilessly parodies the 'where are they now?' captions at the end of *American Graffiti*, going as far as to suggest that head Omega Nazi Gregg Marmalard will go on to join the Nixon administration and end up raped in prison as a result. As I said, this apparently silly movie has an undertow of dark anger.

It isn't a hippy movie, though. Sutherland's proto-hippy lecturer is a predatory prick, and Bluto acts for us all when he smashes a smug folk singer's guitar into tiny bits of wood. It's kind of a punk film, but more a precursor to the Blink 182/Offspring brand of '90s frat-house punk than anything to do with the late '70s kind.

Not that any self-respecting punk would own up to the xenophobia depicted in the Dexter Lake Club scene. Four of the Delta boys and their dates go on a road trip, and stumble upon a gig by Otis Day And The Knights, the soul revue band who had played their toga party. Problem is, they've walked blithely into a club full of black people. Cue much hilarity at the white American's terror of black men, reinforced by the kind of malevolent threat that white Americans seem to feel is inevitable when Whitey stumbles innocently into black territory. It's one of the most uncomfortably racist scenes in cinema, a mix of stereotyping and white liberal guilt that I'm inclined to skip over in an effort to pretend it isn't there, making a bad smell in one of my fave films.

Ah well, nobody's perfect. And anyway, the most memorable scenes in *Animal House* will always belong to the late John Belushi, who was instructed to play Bluto as a cross between Harpo Marx and the Cookie Monster and came up with the most subversive slob in screen history. There's the canteen-zit scene, of course, and his brilliant cartoon version of cat-burgling, involving much staccato frog-jumping and moronic staring. But the Belushi scene that has been ripped off and parodied many times is the bit where he climbs a ladder to a window of the sorority house and witnesses a topless pillow-fight, such an enduring male fantasy image that it even gets parodied in an episode of *Buffy*. We get his awestruck reaction as a reflection in the window, before he bounces the ladder, noisily and impossibly, along to the window of Gregg's frustrated girlfriend Mandy, where he watches her strip for bed. Mandy, played by Mary Louise Weller, faces the window, blind to Bluto's presence in a way you only can be in comedy's parallel universe. She begins to give us a dreamy, distracted, pre-masturbation soft-porn show. Before he topples backwards in the inevitable pratfall, Belushi gives us the look that serves as his epitaph. He turns to the camera, side on, grinning without leering somehow, looking directly at all the guys in the audience as if the women aren't there at all ... and flips a simple double-eyebrow twitch that says more about the pervy male's inexhaustible – and conspiratorial – pleasure in voyeurism than a library full of Freud. Genius.

So, *Animal House* is rabidly sexist. And dodgy on race. And puerile. And hugely pleased with itself and it's boys club atmosphere. And it's responsible for hundreds and hundreds of bad films – the four worst movies I endured in researching this book are *Porky's*, *Lemon Popsicle*, *Revenge Of The Nerds* and *National Lampoon's Van Wilder*, which is a truly desperate attempt to revive *Animal House*'s Otter character (played, incidentally, with almost impossible amounts of charm by future *The West Wing* star Tim Matheson), and they are all runty offspring of this movie, and are probably just the tip of an iceberg of misogynist and mirthless campus comedies.

But ... *Animal House* is also hilarious, and the best bit of modern slapstick comedy direction this side of *Airplane!*. Landis got more laughs out of an object whistling past an oblivious Belushi's head, or a horse having a heart attack, than Richard Curtis has got out of his entire career. His use of crashing sound is hooligan genius. His love of his actors' faces and ability to shoot their over-the-top reactions at just the right angle and hold for just the right amount of milliseconds is second-to-none. It's Landis's best work, the world-changing *Thriller* video and 1983s class and race satire *Trading Places* notwithstanding.

Animal House is a movie that does exactly what The Marx Brothers did at their best – it makes you forget about logic and the rational world and frees you from your principles, hang-ups and politically correct baggage for 90 joyful minutes. I can vouch for its safety, having watched it at least a dozen times and never felt the necessity to hit myself on the head with a can, talk to my naked and strikingly handsome best male friend about 'porking' Marlene Desmond yet kid myself that I'm not completely in love with him, leave my wife with a black man while running and screaming in terror, nor describe breasts as 'major league yabboes'. Or maybe it's 'yarboes'. Whichever ... all I'm saying is that it's the funniest male-bonding anti-Nazi movie in existence, and it's given me too much pure pleasure to feel guilty about.

★ ★

GREASE

1978
Starring: John Travolta, Olivia Newton-John, Stockard Channing, Jeff Conaway
Dir.: Randal Kleiser

Plot: Why girls are great and boys are rubbish.
Key lines: 'I could stay home every night/Wait around for Mr Right/Take cold showers every day/And throw my life away/On a dream that won't come true.'
From 'There Are Worse Things I Could Do'

Who the fuck is Randal Kleiser?

For shame, Garry. I've already written about this movie in my previous book *Popcorn*, with the much-needed assistance of my lovely wife Linsay. I've seen the damned thing a million times. And I've only just noticed that the director of the most popular film musical ever is ... some bloke I've never heard of. *Randal Kleiser*. Ring any bells? No? Didn't think so. Best we find out who he is, then, and see if there are any clues as to why the guy remains completely obscure.

Kleiser hails from Philadelphia and was a University of Southern California room-mate of George Lucas, even playing a bit part in Lucas's graduation short. He earned his shot at features by directing for TV, including a couple of episodes of *Starsky And Hutch*. The big break came in 1976 with TV movie *The Boy In The Plastic Bubble*, a cult true-life potboiler about a boy who lived in a plastic bubble, 'cos he was allergic to everything. The star? John Travolta.

Grease was Kleiser's first feature film. And here's where it all goes a bit Orson Welles. He followed it up with *The Blue Lagoon*, a remake of a 1949 hit which was a none-too-subtle attempt to exploit the under-age sexuality of 15-year-old model Brooke Shields. It was an expensive and legendary turkey, and once you make one of those in Hollywood it's tough to come back. Kleiser was typecast as a kids' director, his only minor hit a Disney sequel *Honey, I Blew Up The Kid*. After attempting a remake of Hitchcock's *Shadow Of Doubt* in 1998, he has mostly been teaching and developing the digital technology around film-making. His house was used to shoot scenes in *Scream 3*. It's all a bit ... disappointing, shall we say. Imagine how that feels: your very first film is the biggest musical *ever*, and ... that is basically that.

This has surely got to be a case of bad luck rather than lack of talent. Because *Grease* is extraordinary work for a first-time director, mainly because so much is happening so entertainingly onscreen that you don't notice a director at work. And that, perhaps, was the problem. What would anyone refer to as 'the Kleiser style'?

But Kleiser did make a key decision that has made *Grease* the kind of mega-hit that endures. Warren Casey and Jim Jacobs' musical may have been a hit on stage since 1971. The songs and the all-important '50s nostalgia setting may have been bequeathed to him. And no one can deny how cleverly screenwriters Bronte Woodard and Allan Carr mixed innocent family fun and cynical smut in their screenplay. But somewhere along the line the director chooses the emphasis of any movie. And the emphasis Kleiser chose was the right one, commercially, aesthetically, morally. Because *Grease* went out of its way to be the first mainstream kids' movie to assure teenage girls that wanting sex was healthy. And then punched the point home by giving the female characters a rounded, mature and honest attitude to sex, while the male characters were children so out of their depth about sexuality that their only real agenda, until being civilised by the girls, was impressing each other with lies about shagging. In that sense, Grease completes the work begun by Henry Levin's proto-feminist 1960 gem, *Where The Boys Are* (see p. 57).

Travolta's Danny Zucco may have been the film's big box office draw. And it may feel, to some boys especially, like *Grease* is Danny's story. But his real mirror character isn't Sandy, but Betty Rizzo, made into one of cinema's most subversive teen characters by the wonderful

Stockard Channing. Rizzo is the force of nature and the bringer of truth. While the lyrics of 'Summer Nights' finger Danny as an insecure liar – shown up by the delicious beach-movie-parodying irony of the opening scene – Rizzo's 'There Are Worse Things I Could Do' tells the truth about teenage sexuality and gives a good, hard kicking to the perennial coming-of-age story of boy-who-fucks-is-cool, girl-who-fucks-is-whore. The result is '70s movie gender roles turned upside-down ... Rizzo is the central protagonist and the rounded character. By the end of the film, Danny is nothing more than the pretty dunderhead. The gender reversal is even reflected by names: we know Danny by his first name. We know Rizzo by her surname. Who even recalls that her given name is Betty?

Whether *Grease* improved things for generations of schoolgirls I severely doubt. But it did establish a new attitude to female sexuality in popular entertainment that becomes increasingly obvious as you read this book and see how many more strong and sexualised female characters take centre-stage in teen films from 1979 onwards. So Randal Kleiser didn't just do something very right. He did something brave too, because, if *Grease*, with its celebration of adolescent female sexuality and graphic references to tit, pussy and periods, had fallen foul of paranoid parents and moral guardians and resolutely bombed ... well, he probably wouldn't have got to make *Honey, I Blew Up The Kid*, and then where would we be?

As I'm figuring that anyone who buys a book about 100 teen movies has seen *Grease* more than once, I'm not going to waste your time with the plot, which, after all, is just a knowing parody of cheap '50s teen romances packed with enough holes to drop songs into. I thought, instead, that I'd chew over a few *Grease* factlets that give rise to a few choice 'What ifs?'

Travolta had played minor *Grease* character Doody on Broadway, but was still considered too young to play Danny onstage. Ms Neutron-Bomb had not acted at all since a disastrous 1970 British sci-fi-rock flick called *Toomorrow* (directed by B-movie king Val Guest, who did pull off a classic musical with *Expresso Bongo* in 1959), which was made before her pop career took off. She had so little confidence in her ability that it was she that insisted she do a screen test when the producers had already made their minds up.

Rumours persist that Sandy was initially offered to Marie Osmond who turned it down because she was too virginal to do the bad girl stuff at the end, but this is possibly apocryphal. What does appear to be true is that first choice for Danny was originally Henry Winkler aka The Fonz, who decided that he didn't want to be typecast as a '50s tough teen.

Henry Winkler. In love scenes with Olivia Newton-John. And singing, and dancing. Oh Lord . . . can you imagine? Still, at least he didn't get typecast, eh?

If you notice blurry signs inside the Frosty Palace soda bar, you're right, they do look like Coca-Cola signs. That's because the producers took money for Pepsi product placement and neglected to tell the director. So, to save money reshooting the Frosty Palace scenes, the Coke signs got fuzzied.

The original choice for Coach Calhoun was a porn star called, wait for it, Harry Reems. Someone came to their family movie senses and cast comedy legend Sid Caesar. And . . . *Grease* has a legendary 'cut scene'. Kleiser originally shot a bit involving a row between Rizzo and Kenickie (Conaway) which was so angry and brutal that one of the crew members compared it to Martin Scorsese. It was such a bizarre change of mood for the film that they snipped and chucked it, which presumably means we'll never get to see Stockard Channing say, 'You think I'm funny? What, I amuse you?' before shoving Kenickie's head in a vice.

The drive-in scenes – where an animated hot dog does an outrageous symbolic in-and-out with a bun onscreen behind Travolta as he sings 'Sandy' – were shot at the Burbank Pickwick Drive-In in LA. It's now – you guessed it – a shopping mall.

And the last thing is personal. When *Grease* was released I was a punk rocker, so I wouldn't allow myself to like that clip of Travolta and Newton-John doing 'You're The One That I Want' in black leather at a fairground that was on *Top Of The Pops* for ever as the record stayed at No. 1 for weeks. How Danny Zucco, now I think about it. But I watch it now and I really do get chills, and bugger me if they ain't multiplyin'. A big old delayed reaction, I guess, to a song and piece of film that I share with my entire generation, which is something that is going to happen less and less in the fractured post-internet age.

I'm sorry Randal Kleiser didn't become as big as his swotty classmate George. But I don't feel sorry for anyone who has pulled off a piece of mass entertainment which co-invented everything from *Dirty Dancing* to *Buffy* to *Glee*, and which will be delighting people and educating teens about gender hypocrisy long after me, you and good old Randal Kleiser are long gone. There are worse things he could have done.

★ ★

HALLOWEEN

1978

Starring: Jamie Lee Curtis, Donald Pleasance, Nancy Loomis, P.J. Soles
Dir.: John Carpenter

Plot: The Plato's *Republic* of teen slasher movies.
Key line(s): *Laurie*: 'Was that The Boogeyman?'
***Dr Loomis*: 'As a matter of fact, it was.'**

Halloween is the definition of the movie that punched above its weight. Made for just $320,000, John Carpenter's third film had, by 2010, grossed over $200 million, largely through video and DVD rentals. Beyond the number-crunching, this simple B-movie with its homemade soundtrack and largely unknown actors created enough firsts and influenced so much of what is good and bad about cinema that its legacy is daunting to examine. But let's give it a go.

First, what *Halloween* isn't. *Halloween* isn't the first teen slasher movie. That honour could go to 1974's *Black Christmas* (see p. 143), or maybe Dario Argento's disorienting 1976 bloodfest *Suspiria*, or perhaps even Wes Craven's cheap and nasty 1972 debut *Last House On The Left*, which isn't in this book simply because it's far more interested in its murderers than its two teen girl victims. Likewise, the backwoods psychos of *The Texas Chainsaw Massacre* (1974) may terrorise youngish people rather than teens, but most of the basic rules and recurring stylistic motifs of the teen slasher movie were invented by Tobe Hooper's notorious 'video nasty'.

But what *Halloween* was is the first movie to make serial killers murdering young people into mainstream entertainment. No one tried to ban it because there was relatively little gore. Although it is actually an extraordinary work of art, *Halloween* didn't play like an art movie. It bowled along, tight and simple enough for a child to understand, while containing enough believable peril to keep a cynical adult appropriately spooked. And, while Hooper and Craven were obviously an influence on Carpenter and *Halloween*'s co-writer Debra Hill, this movie took its horror cues from Hitchcock's *Psycho* rather than its more gore-splattered peers or the supernatural monster movies of the past, paying explicit tribute to The Master by casting Jamie Lee Curtis, daughter of *Psycho*'s doomed heroine Janet Leigh, in the lead role. Like Hitchcock, Carpenter believed that insane people were scarier than scary monsters, and his killer Michael Myers is burdened with the same truckloads of psychological baggage as Norman Bates. Even the usual square-jawed hero is replaced by a short bald psychiatrist who seems almost as nuts as the murderer.

The input of Debra Hill perhaps explains what is arguably *Halloween*'s most important influence on popular culture. A year before *Alien* gave us Sigourney Weaver's extraordinary Ripley, *Halloween* introduced the feminist action heroine. That is, the girl in peril who doesn't just freeze and die or scream and wet herself until a man comes to save her. Whoever made the decision that the only teen to survive Myers' irresistible rampage would be what critics now refer to as The Final Girl was some kind of prophetic genius, because, unlikely as it seemed in the feminist backlash '70s, the teen boys who made up the majority of the potential audience for horror movies loved the idea of tough birds. I mean, we *had* had punk, which gave us Pattis, Debbies, Siouxsies and Chrissies who obviously, if unlucky enough to be faced with a nutter in a rubber William Shatner mask with a giant phallic knife, would have pulled a machete out of their knickers while the boys in the band huddled behind them. In short, we'd been prepared and had realised that helpless girlie girls were dull and annoying. Curtis's Laurie Strode was useful in a fight *and* hot as hell. A perfect combination which, after 20 years of Tank Girls and Lara Crofts and more and more Final Girls, finally gave us Buffy Summers. For that alone, Carpenter and Hill are Gods.

Curtis's performance is key. Her role in *Halloween* and lesser teen slasher movies like *Prom Night* saw her dubbed The Scream Queen, and, Boy, can she scream. But what made *Halloween* stick was how convincing Curtis was as someone who was entirely terrified yet brave enough to still think clearly and fight back. There is an inner strength in Curtis's looks and demeanour, and just enough boyish androgyny to make her someone men could empathise with, rather than pity. You wanted to rescue her but knew she didn't need you. Not an easy trick to pull off while screaming hysterically and stabbing masked men with coat-hangers.

And then there is the masked man. Taking a cue from *The Texas Chainsaw Massacre*, in which the maddest murderer wore a flayed victim's visage as a mask and never showed his face, Carpenter gave Myers a cheap William Shatner mask from a toy shop and stumbled upon something crucial. We are, in the end, more scared of a person than a supernatural monster. But we're even more scared of a human who has no facial expressions, and therefore gives us no clues as to what he's going to do to us, or why. This great idea spawned an entire genre of Jasons and Freddys (see *A Nightmare On Elm Street*, p. 238) who looked like monsters while being driven by entirely human neuroses.

But being human, in a modern teen slasher, doesn't necessarily mean that you are mortal . . . another phenomenon we have to thank *Halloween* for, for better or, mainly, worse. When Carpenter allowed his psycho to rise from the apparently dead twice during *Halloween*, he didn't just give clever permission for numerous, profitable and largely awful *Halloween* sequels, but permission for any successful slasher idea to become a never-ending franchise. It works because, even though slashers are human, they are still, metaphorically, monsters of the Id; the bogeymen of our shared childhood nightmares whose unquenchable desire to 'get' you isn't bound by anything as rational as mortality.

This leads to *Halloween*'s two smartest breaks from horror tradition. In trad horror, the victim has to be drawn into a haunted house, or spooky castle, abandoned motel, or mad scientist's lab, or, even post-*Halloween* and repeatedly, a remote cabin in the woods. In the end, even the most gullible enthusiast for celluloid terrors has to conclude that the best way to avoid being sliced into pieces fit for the meat counter at Tescos is . . . don't go to the scary place. All movies set in a scary-looking setting come with a side order of irony.

But *Halloween* is about home invasion. The worst thing imaginable is that the source of all your primal fears is in the one place where you lock your door and feel safe. People are, in the end, more scared of burglars than vampires. Carpenter's insistence that no place is safe from the bogeyman is taken to logical extremes by *A Nightmare On Elm Street* where the bogeyman actually lives in our brains, which is, of course, *exactly* where he lives, and is exactly what horror writers are attempting to exploit. *Halloween* even mocks the haunted house tradition when Laurie walks right up to the door of the creepy old Myers home, and walks cheerily away, unaware that her soon-to-be nemesis is lurking behind the door.

The other great break from tradition is all about what our friend Vern (see introductory chapter, p. 4) calls 'filmatism'. Carpenter does things with cameras and music which only visionaries can pull off. The lo-fi keyboard drones and loops that Carpenter self-composes for his films reach a pinnacle here that match Ennio Morricone's legendary spaghetti western themes. Like the shrieking violins in *Psycho* and the rumbling, accelerating two-note cellos that soundtrack *Jaws*, Carpenter's music makes otherwise entirely innocent images into agonizing suspense or sudden shock, so much so that whenever the gently twitching piano-and-synth motif kicks in, audiences found themselves emitting spontaneous groans of 'please-God-not-again' dread in a kind of Pavlov's Dog reflex acknowledgement of the inevitable horrors to come.

But even greater, perhaps, was Carpenter's revolutionary use of exteriors. In conjuring his imaginary killing field of Haddonfield, Illinois (actually filmed in South Pasadena, California), Carpenter noticed something that others had missed. In suburbs that are almost entirely residential, lack community centres like pubs or shops, and where everyone is wealthy enough to drive ... neighbourhoods become ghost towns. No one walks anywhere. The white middle classes come out of their fortress, get into another moving fortress to go about their business, return just before nightfall, lock their doors, close their curtains and seek to repel all potential invaders to their one private space. By using beautifully composed shots of this pretty, leafy and almost always deserted suburb, with its huge driveways that set the big houses way back from the street, Carpenter finds a perfect visual metaphor for suburban isolation, and illuminates a secret fear we all share: that, in this increasingly privatised modern world, we could be suffering unimaginable horrors in our own homes and no one would even hear us scream. Many of *Halloween*'s creepiest scenes take place in familiar, everyday, *comforting* places in broad daylight. The film is haunted by the absolute lack of community in Haddonfield, established so persuasively that we entirely believe that help would only come from crazy Dr Loomis, an outsider and the only character who appears to care for the welfare of suburban children. Parents and cops are almost entirely absent. *Halloween*'s nightmare is entirely human, and more socio-political big-picture than private fears of psychos in masks.

Which leads neatly to the most enduring criticism of *Halloween*. Famously, all its teen characters have sex and then get brutally slain. The only teen who survives is the virgin. Add the fact that Myers only seems interested in killing adolescents (he has been in the nut-hatch from ages 6 to 21, which perhaps explains why kids free to explore their sexuality piss him off so much), and Carpenter and Hill are obviously and blatantly punishing sexualised teens and warning their impressionable audience to remain abstinent without even knowing what AIDS would do to the sexual mores of Western society over the next decade. This became such a repeated motif in formula teen horror that it became the biggest black joke in that ultimate meta-movie, *Scream* (see p. 339).

Carpenter has constantly refuted any reactionary intent in *Halloween*. And I have no idea what was going on in his and Hill's clever heads. But I do know that no young horror fan, of my generation or later, ever gave up shagging because of the meta-phorical punishments of slasher movies. I also know that Carpenter is such a fan of and expert on Golden Age Hollywood film-making that all of his films are peppered with referential in-jokes for movie buffs, and that he's forged a pretty nifty alternative career as a leading authority on film history. And that *Halloween* belongs firmly within a thriller tradition whereby the loud, arrogant blowhard characters are always cruising for a bruising, while the sensitive, vulnerable and humble character goes on to discover their inner hero and save the day. *Halloween*, again, taps into a shared experience of its target audience: there were always these kids at school who bragged constantly about how much sex, booze and adult action they got, and, whether they were bullshitting or not, we always secretly wanted them to get their comeuppance for making us feel childish and inadequate. We relate to Laurie and not to her friends, not because she's chaste, but because we like to think that we are/were as rounded, admirable and strong as she is. Drunken sex is a useful metaphor for being a bit rubbish, because, even when we were having lots of adolescent sex, none of us wanted to think of ourselves as shallow sluts. And Laurie survives not because she's celibate, but because she takes life more seriously than her friends, and therefore fights harder to keep hold of it. So I suspect Carpenter and Hill stumbled upon their right-wing formula by accident, because, innovative though they were, they believed in the emotional pull of traditional Hollywood storytelling.

Blimey. That really is a lot of baggage for a cheap horror flick to have carried for so many years, isn't it just? But then, that's why it has lasted, been copied relentlessly and parodied mercilessly, and why its director is a cult in himself, through his work here and on *Dark Star*, *Escape From New York*, *The Thing*, *They Live* and, especially, the peerless B-movie masterpiece that is *Assault On Precinct 13*. The best compliment I can pay *Halloween* is that the hundreds of bad versions of its accidental formula have had no impact whatsoever on its power. The terror etched upon Jamie Lee Curtis's face while she's trapped in a wardrobe still hurts. The bit where an out-of-focus, dead Michael suddenly sits up straight and turns towards us still freaks me out. And that glowering, droning, tinkling music always has a welcome place in my most enjoyable nightmares.

★ ★

THE WARRIORS

1979
Starring: Michael Beck, James Remar, David Patrick Kelly,
Deborah Van Valkenburgh, Lynne Thigpen, Roger Hill
Dir.: Walter Hill

**Plot: New York gangs as teen opera. But nobody's singing
'I Feel Pretty'.**
Key line: *'WARRIORS! COME OUT TO PLAAYY-YAAYYY!!!'*

I struggled a while over whether this unique, controversial cult film
qualified as a teen movie. *The Warriors* operates in such an irrational
parallel universe that it's impossible to tell whether its gangstas are
teenagers or not. I plumped for a Yes because even though, like most
teen films of this era, its lead actors are well into their twenties, the
surreal spirit of the movie is teen to its core; a fantasy of inner-city
violence where, even when people die or attempt rape, the images
are just too cartoonish to hurt.

Action director Walter Hill's best and most enduring movie is
based upon Sol Yurick's 1965 novel; a relatively serious, socially
concerned tale of poor kids forced into gangs by poverty and their
environment. What Hill saw was a chase movie with added comic
book possibilities and a connection to the history of ancient Greece.
The Warriors is a retelling of the war between the Athenians and the
Spartans. Specifically, in this case, the tale from Xenophon's *Anabasis*
of a mercenary Greek army, isolated after battle and miles away from
home, struggling to return to the sea. This weighty source was initially
intended to be a big part of the movie as a narrative voiceover read
by none other than Orson Welles, but the studio wouldn't cough up
the bucks.

For the recent director's cut DVD version, Hill couldn't go back
to the now-deceased Welles to right that perceived wrong. But he
could and did restore another idea initially rejected for budgetary
reasons. When Hill and co-writer David Shaber first developed the
script, they put the point that the only realistic way to do New York
teen gangs was to make them black and Latino. Paramount baulked.

So Hill figured that the only way around this was to create an alternative reality, based in a comic book vision of what gangs might look like. Hill produced a list of colourful imaginary gang names, and costume designer Bobbie Mannix, who had no experience of gangs, was allowed to let her imagination run wild, coming up with a set of gang uniforms that remain the most memorable element of *The Warriors*. Especially great are The Baseball Furies, who dress in baseball uniforms (with baseball bats as weapons, naturally) and wear Kiss-style make-up, giving them a look not unlike an American spin on the droogs from *A Clockwork Orange* (see p. 111).

To make this comic vision clear to viewers, Hill wanted actual comic book art to form transitions between scenes. Again, the studio weren't keen on an idea which is now commonplace but had no precedent in 1979. Presumably, Hill was stung by some of the bad reviews at the time, which sneered at the film's lack of realism and stilted dialogue, and has now taken the opportunity to insert the panels and illuminate the cartoon aesthetic.

And the result? An annoying waste of time. The reason why the film has sustained enough of a fanatical cult following to inspire a range of Warrior dolls and a Warriors video game as late as 2005 is because everybody who sees the movie understands that it wasn't meant to be a documentary. Hill's magical realism worked just fine without a need to clump us over the head with it.

But, thankfully, the comic cuts don't have enough impact to spoil a classic. The action revolves around a mixed-race Coney Island gang called The Warriors, who favour hippy-biker leather waistcoats as their 'colours'. When Cyrus (Hill), the leader of Manhattan's most powerful gang The Gramercy Riffs, suggests a summit meeting between all of the gangs, The Warriors send the requested nine unarmed members. But, as Cyrus is making a rousing speech in Riverside Park about united gangs taking over the city, he is shot by Luther (the show-stealing David Patrick Kelly), leader of The Rogues. In the ensuing melee, Luther fingers The Warriors as the shooters and Warriors leader Cleon is caught and beaten to death by The Riffs.

The rest of The Warriors escape and, after a power struggle with mouthy loose cannon Ajax (Remar), chiselled hunk Swan (Beck) is charged with leading his troops back to the safety of Coney Island. Trouble is, The Riffs have a female radio DJ (Thigpen: gorgeous even though you only hear her voice and see her extraordinary mouth) relaying coded orders to every gang in Manhattan to kill The Warriors on sight. On their odyssey through the New York night, the weapon-less Warriors fight off gangs and cops, encounter subway fires and Molotov cocktails, pick up a girl (Van Valkenburgh as Mercy), get fake-seduced by girl gang The Lizzies, get separated, are entrapped into sexual assault, reunite and lose members to death and arrest before their inevitable western-style showdown with The Riffs and The Rogues on the beach at Coney Island.

The Warriors was entirely filmed in its New York location at night in authentically rough areas: The Bronx, Queens, Brooklyn, Coney Island. This entailed liaising with the NYPD over which areas were the least likely to be terrorised by real gangs, which makes the gang rally all the more extraordinary. Shot in Riverside Park, it involved corralling 1,000 extras, most of whom were drawn from around 200 real New York gangs. These were unruly guys with no acting experience, yet they had to be controlled and choreographed in a very specific way to make the riot scene work.

Cyrus, the stunningly handsome mixed-race man who has the charisma to attempt to organise a criminal revolution, is actually played by a real gang member called Roger Hill. The brilliant, boxing-announcer-meets-carnival-barker way he hollers the phrase 'Can you dig it?' was entirely his idea and is one of the most enduring motifs in the movie (it was sampled on a minor 1988 hit single by British indie band Pop Will Eat Itself), even though Hill was a last-minute replacement for another actor who was cast, but disappeared.

Similarly inspired ideas from various crew members established the crucial visual aesthetic. Director of Photography Andrew Laszlo saw one problem before shooting started. The chances of shooting an entire movie on the streets of New York over a number of weeks without encountering rain were pretty slim. So Laszlo suggested that the voyage back to Coney Island be set in a downpour, which then meant that the streets could be washed down for key scenes. Light and colour bouncing off the black, puddled concrete gives *The Warriors* a further element of magical hyper-realism and yet another level of nocturnal atmosphere.

In these times of CGI overload and the sleight-of-hand cheats of over-fast cutting, it's also still great to watch low-budget action sequences where you can actually see what's happening. The fight scenes are rightly legendary: a mix of comic overstatement, Peckinpah-style slow-motion ballet, and Samurai flick-influenced choreography, in tribute to Akira Kurosawa. The score is also crucial. Barry DeVorzon's atmospheric little jazzy soul instrumentals contrasted brilliantly with the main theme, which sounded like Giorgio Moroder jamming with Led Zeppelin. This gem was matched by the film's closing theme, a classic arena rock song by sometime Eagles member Joe Walsh called 'In The City', which has nothing to do with The Jam and everything to do with relocating the blue-collar angst of early Springsteen as cheesy survivalist heavy metal. Pure genius and a score right up there with any by John Carpenter (see *Halloween*, p. 169).

Towards the end of the movie, for just a few minutes, *The Warriors* suddenly, abruptly, taps into novelist Yurick's original, politicised vision, and gets real. These two key scenes involve neither balletic fight sequences, nor explosions, nor crazy made-up gangs.

First, Swann and Mercy have actually made the last stretch of the train journey to Coney Island. As they recline, relieved, three squeaky-clean teen couples, on their way home from the prom, board the train. They sit opposite our Warrior couple and we are suddenly hit by the contrast between middle class and working class, rich and poor, the socially integrated and the social outcast. Swann gives them a hard stare as the prom couples take in his and Mercy's battered appearance and symbols of gangdom. They shift uncomfortably, but not as uncomfortably as Mercy. The rough girl is suddenly acutely aware of how she looks in comparison to the nice girls. She drops her eyes and begins to fiddle with her hair. Swann, while still staring defiantly at the clean teens, simply raises one hand and, gently but firmly, stops her from subconsciously trying to improve herself. Without saying anything, without even looking at his new love, he has told the couples, and Mercy herself, that he chooses her over conventional teen femininity. It's genuinely moving and romantic to a degree that should be impossible in such a deliberately unreal movie.

Swann and Mercy finally reach the end of the line. They disembark the subway as dawn is beginning to rise, and ... we see what they see. Coney Island from above: a set of cramped, dirty and malevolent slum dwellings. The blank, handsome hardness of Swann's stare makes his question all the more resonant: '*This* is what we fought all night to get back to?'

But actually, they fought all night to give us the final showdown, which has to be between evil Luther and heroic Swann, and has to be beside the seaside. Yet again, inspired improvisation plays an enormous part, because it turns out that The Warriors' most quoted lines and image were made up on the spot.

Hill had a first go at shooting the scene where The Rogues arrive on the Coney Island boardwalk in their graffiti-ed Cadillac hearse and call The Warriors out. But he felt that what was in the script simply wasn't enough. He took David Patrick Kelly aside and told him that he had to find a more intense, interesting way of taunting The Warriors, and that he had to come up with it in about five minutes.

Kelly lived in a rough New York neighbourhood and had a neighbour who delighted in trying to freak him out. He did this by singing his name in a high sing-song whine. Kelly used this and a couple of beer bottles that he spotted under the boardwalk, and came up with a taunt which, when coupled with his runty, maniacal, almost Charles Manson-esque features, became the film's catchphrase and this entry's key line, accompanied by the percussive clink of beer bottles jammed onto his fingers, like hooligan castanets. It's so catchy and joyfully malevolent that it's difficult to imagine anyone loving *The Warriors* as much if Kelly had simply shrugged and reminded Hill that he wasn't the screenwriter.

The Warriors was an immediate teen smash and hit No. 1 at the US box office. But there were newspaper reports of gang violence at theatres in California and Boston. Paramount pulled advertising, cinemas hired security staff at screenings, and the studio finally panicked and pulled the film out of American cinemas for a few weeks. The furore died down and *The Warriors* was redistributed, going on to do quite nicely. But crucial momentum was lost and *The Warriors* didn't quite become the mega-hit that it potentially was.

It's extremely hard now to see what the fuss was about. Contemporary critics compared the film's impact on teens to the seat-slashing antics inspired by *The Blackboard Jungle* (see p. 20) and *Rock Around The Clock* in the 1950s, but what seems far more likely is that *The Warriors* was a victim of its own word of mouth: gang members went to see it because it was a gang film, spotted rival gang members and kicked off. The violence in *The Warriors*, with its cartoonish exaggeration and acrobatic dance moves, looks incredibly tame after the buckets of blood unleashed in the last 20 years of action movies.

What does stand up is Hill's understanding of what makes great camp. You have to play it straight and deadpan, and keep just enough meaning behind the mocking to make the characters' nobility or amorality stick, and get you cheering and booing and enjoying the experience. This, and a unique *mise en scène* that presents New York as a more authentic take on Gotham City, keeps *The Warriors* as fresh as a newly hosed sidewalk. Can we dig it? Yes, and for ever.

* *

QUADROPHENIA

1979
Starring: Phil Daniels, Lesley Ash, Mark Wingett, Toyah Willcox, Phil Davis, Sting, Ray Winstone
Dir.: Franc Roddam

Plot: Fix up. Look sharp. Go bonkers.
Key line: 'I can't think straight, that's all. I mean ... nothing seems right apart from Brighton ... I was a mod there, y'know? I mean ... that's *something*, innit? Eh?'

One of the most intriguing factlets about *Quadrophenia* concerns Johnny Rotten. The Sex Pistols singer apparently screen-tested for the role of Jimmy Cooper in this classic mod film based upon The Who's *Quadrophenia* double concept album, and was set to do it. But the aura of violence and infamy that surrounded The Pistols still hung around Rotten aka John Lydon in 1979, despite his departure having effectively split the band early in the previous year. Insuring Lydon for the role proved prohibitively expensive for *Quadrophenia*'s mod-est budget. The lead role went to young cockney thesp Phil Daniels instead.

How weird would it have been if John Rotten had been Jimmy The

Mod? It's not that he wouldn't have been able to pull it off: if you get the chance, track down 1983's *Order Of Death*, a strange, sado-masochistic little *noir* in which Lydon has to share equal billing with none other than Harvey Keitel, and does enough to not get entirely blown off screen. No ... the problem would have been that the Sex Pistols were still so notorious, so adored and reviled in equal measure, that *Quadrophenia* would have immediately become a Sex Pistols film by default. Both critics and punters would have judged the movie based on how much they wanted Lydon to succeed or fail, expecting his every word and glare to start the revolution, or somesuch. Add the 'rock 'n' roll swindle' schtick that Malcolm Mclaren had successfully attached to his former protégés and young audiences at the time would have found themselves second-guessing the entire movie as some kind of smartarse scam. Lydon's presence would have transformed the most admired and popular British teen and rock movie of all time into a post-punk celebrity circus.

Quadrophenia without Phil Daniels? Unthinkable, innit? The wiry urchin channelled Johnny Rotten's wired, furious, thousand-yard stare anyway, particularly in the train scene, which is surely the closest Brit cinema has ever got to a vision of male madness as iconic as Robert De Niro's Travis Bickle in *Taxi Driver*. Daniels' schizoid energy drives *Quadrophenia*, perfectly capturing the manic extremes, futile violence and self-immolating self-pity familiar to any working-class man who went through an adolescent period of feeling so helplessly alienated that each new emotion comes hard and uncontrollable. The more one wants to break down and cry for Mummy, the more one feels trapped by the tribe's demand for unflinching machismo. When you feel like that sex, drugs and rock 'n' roll – even The Who – just don't help.

Quadrophenia's greatest achievement is its success in taking something very specific – British mod culture in 1964 – and making it universal rites-of-passage stuff. Jimmy Cooper is *still* every boy who felt that life was laughing at him, that he shouldn't be here, that The Void may be preferable. No wonder Daniels never got any better. This was Big Magic to make at the tender age of 20.

Key to that magic is Daniels' ability to make us feel so warm towards Jimmy. Because Jimmy is a little shit. A violent, racist gob-shite so lost in his own relatively petty problems that he can't relate to anyone around him. He sees everything – especially women – in terms of status symbols. His values are so screwed that he allows his friend Kevin (Winstone) to get beaten up because he can't bring himself to stand up for anyone outside of his futile tribal allegiances. Kevin and Monkey (Willcox) represent salvation, simply being decent people who offer him love. But he barely notices either, so intent is he on pyrrhic victories and mythologising his aimless life. We ought to be hoping he does throw himself off Beachy Head (incidentally, he doesn't, and there's no mystery about the ending – the opening shot has Jimmy walking away from the cliff, beginning his story at the end) but we don't, because Daniels so successfully makes Jimmy a product of his times, *and* a symbol of whatever bad choices we made when we were teens. He might be dumb, but he's not stupid, and Daniels lets us see, in every frame, that he will inevitably escape the hole he is in. He's better than those around him, full of potential, just as we like to think we were when we were hanging with a bad crowd or treating people like crap when we were kids. We cheer him on because we fondly imagine that we went through the same journey, even if we never swallowed tons of speed, or rode a scooter, or took part in massive tribal battles on Brighton beach.

The ending to Jimmy's tale is important because it illuminates the major differences between *Quadrophenia* the album and *Quadrophenia* the film, and tells us why *Quadrophenia* is not merely a curio of '70s rock excess, like Ken Russell's 1975 film version of The Who's *Tommy*. In Pete Townshend's original tale, the emphasis is on Jimmy's mental illness, whereby he is four entirely separate personalities, hence 'Quadrophenia' instead of schizophrenia. He does live the mod lifestyle, take part in a bank holiday seaside riot, row with his parents, fuck up everything he holds dear and head down to Brighton on a commuter train. But, while seeing that The Ace Face (memorably played, or rather, posed by Sting here) is actually a bellboy in a posh hotel does dash the last of his mod-power dreams, album Jimmy goes further than film Jimmy in escaping his nightmare. He nicks a rowing boat and makes his way to a rock off the Brighton coast (I live in Brighton. There isn't a rock. But poetic licence and all that), where, driven by a storm and huge power ballad 'Love Reign O'er Me', he experiences some sort of cosmic epiphany. What he does with this new info remains a mystery, but, as his boat has smashed and he's being lashed by storm waves, there's every possibility that he just dies and ascends to some kind of higher state of consciousness.

It was all a thinly veiled statement about Townshend's own discovery of the teachings of spiritual guru Meher Baba. And, although it made for a fantastic album – maybe The Who's best – it was always a dodgy post-hippy, prog rock premise, what with the supposedly enlightened Pete being strung out on smack and booze at the time; surely the kind of thing that great enlightenment is supposed to render redundant.

So director Roddam and co-writers Dave Humphries and Martin Stellman made a great decision about the script. In their view the most interesting things about *Quadrophenia* were the references to the mod lifestyle, the bank holiday riot, and the barely sketched characters that surround Jimmy in his Shepherd's Bush rat-trap milieu. Having written a teen drama ripe for shooting in realist style, no good could come from Jimmy ascending to heaven from a mythical rock. So instead, Jimmy smashes the ultimate symbol of the futility of joining tribes, following self-appointed leaders and buying into consumerism. The film's ending is still beautiful, and somewhat mystical. But it's also logical, real and damn good advice to any watching adolescent.

After over 30 years, a sequel to *Quadrophenia* is apparently in the pre-production stage, with an early script written by Martin Stellman. I admit, I'm intrigued. Does Stellman hire the new Phil Daniels and begin with Jimmy walking away from Beachy Head? If so, does he break away from his life entirely or head back to Shepherd's Bush to attempt to mend bridges and conform? Or do we meet Phil as Jimmy 30 years later, fat, lazy and ignorant like his Dad, complaining about his teen son watching hip hop on TV, wondering how they call that noise music?

It's intriguing ... but a big part of me hopes it slips into development hell and never sees the light of day. I like being left with Jimmy, walking away from Beachy Head, heading onwards and upwards to God knows where. The best stories don't have endings. They belong to us and carry on for ever.

★ ★

OVER THE EDGE

1979
Starring: Matt Dillon, Michael Eric Kramer, Pamela Ludwig, Harry Northup, Vincent Spano, Ellen Geer
Dir.: Jonathan Kaplan

Plot: White riot, they wanna riot.
Key line: 'Sometimes I think they're really like a herd of baboons!'

One of the strangest and most prescient curios in the teen movie lexicon, *Over The Edge* is the movie that punked the '50s teen rebel movie, inspired the smell of Kurt Cobain's teen spirit, and discovered Matt Dillon. It was given a limited release and seen by few, but is one of those movies that was destined to be clasped warmly to the bosom of future generations of cult movie aficionados. It's also one of those films that is both fabulous *and* bizarrely flawed, because it throws two opposing cinematic forces together to create a camp update of '60s youth revolt fantasies like *If* ... (see p. 97).

On the one hand, Kaplan's drama of suburban teen alienation in a 'planned community' in the American desert (called 'New Towns' in the UK) did immaculately docu-dramatic things: story based on real events in Foster City, California 1973, cast of real teens who had never acted before; grim location setting, accurate run-through of the problems inherent in environments where kids are given nothing to do. But, on the other, Kaplan melds these *vérité* authenticities to a melodramatic plot and a camp revival of the tropes of '50s and '60s message movies, right down to the teen martyr death of a James Dean figure, cops and parents who comically don't understand, a liberal 'therapist' of the system, a caption of portentous 'facts' over the opening images, cheesy incidental music, and a triumphalist ending designed to make watching kids punch the air and feel suitably rebellious towards The Man.

In short, it's a movie that predicts the true-life tales of no-man's-land council estate environments featured in serious future movies like *La Haine* (see p. 336) and *Fish Tank* (see p. 482), but behaves like *Rebel Without A Cause* (see p. 28) and kitsch parodies of early rock movies like *Rock 'n' Roll High School* (see *Popcorn*) and the original *Hairspray* (see *Popcorn*). It shouldn't work at all, but, somehow, it does. And when you add a culturally accurate contemporary soundtrack – which acknowledged that suburban kids mixed the metal of Van Halen with the punk of the Ramones and the radio-friendly new wave of bands like The Cars and Cheap Trick, because they didn't have the self-conscious fashion snobberies of kids from major cities and college towns – then you can understand exactly why suburban kid Kurt Cobain cheerfully(!) admitted that *Over The Edge* had been a childhood favourite and a major influence on the attitude of Nirvana's breakthrough video for 'Smells Like Teen Spirit'.

The action takes place in New Grenada, a dystopian mix of condominiums and townhouses (filmed in a real planned community in Colorado) surrounded by freeways, arid marshland and a never-ending building-site. New Grenada has a whole bunch of problems: the contrast between the swanky detached homes and the cramped tenements mean that this brave new world has simply replicated the class conflicts that families had fled the city to escape; the relationship between politicians, business leaders and police is a little too cosy; and ... *Goddamn*, it's ugly.

But the biggest problem is that planners built the homes and moved families in before giving a thought to the adolescents of the community and what the hell they are expected to do with themselves after school. There is one community youth centre – a warehouse called The Rec run by youth worker Julia (Geer), the only adult in town who gets these kids – and it shuts at 6 p.m. The response of adults to this problem is curfews, crackdowns and futile attempts to bully The Kids off the streets, because the most important thing to this new venture is money, and the only way to attract investment is to invite businesses to town and assure them that New Grenada is a desert Stepford full of willing workers and law-abiding citizens. When the kids even attempt to explain why they are being so naughty, the grown-ups, including their parents, just put their fingers in their ears and go blahblahblah until they stop. Or make them sit and watch spectacularly bad public service films about why they should all be good girls and boys, which they cheer and applaud every time something smashes.

No surprise, then, that The Kids seek to bust the nightmare of boredom by way of sex, drugs, booze, vandalism, theft and shooting BB guns at cars from the safety of a bridge overlooking the freeway.

The fascinating thing about Kaplan's take on all this is his complete lack of anything approaching a balanced view. Even a knowing exercise in bad taste '50s pastiche like *Class Of 1984* (see p. 205) entertains the viewer with lots of gratuitous teen violence but paints the bad kids as Bad Kids who eventually have to be defeated by adult nice guys, no matter how ironically. Kaplan has no time for this kind of having it both ways. He loves kids on drugs doing dangerous shit. Every shooting, drug deal, winding-up of the cops or stolen car is played out to excellent rock 'n' roll and shot as not only fun, but entirely the right thing to do under the circumstances. There is no movie in existence that loves juvenile delinquency as much as *Over The Edge*.

Things eventually turn properly dark when evil copper Sgt Doberman (Northup) gives high-speed chase to Carl (Kramer) and Ritchie (Dillon) after the latter nicks Carl's Mom's car. Ritchie is tooled-up and Doberman inevitably shoots and kills him.

Dillon dominates the film and you understand why he became the most in-demand teen actor of his generation, despite the fact that *Over The Edge* wasn't a hit. The casting directors found Dillon in a school while searching for their non-actor stars. It was a fairly posh middle school, but Dillon was apparently slouching away around the corridors and acting tough, faking that whole Dee Dee Ramone-meets-The-Fonz dumbass accent and teen rumble demeanour that has pretty much carried him through a 30-year career in movies. They spotted well, because he really does capture, in *Over The Edge*, that good-looking kid you knew who was always in trouble and lived to bait authority, but got all the girls because he was basically a sweetheart hiding behind a macho façade that he'd been raised to adopt as a survival mechanism. But, no matter how much you liked him, you knew he was bound to come to a sticky end. Not because he was nasty, but because he was as thick as two short planks. Dillon fans who've never seen this movie might be surprised at how androgynous the boy looks with long, Farrah Fawcett hair, though.

Now that The Kids of New Grenada have a martyr to the cause of badly needing something to do, they get organized. The movie becomes a wish-fulfilment fantasy for everyone who has ever felt mistreated and ignored as a teenager, as they barricade all the town's most prominent adults into the school – where they are, of course, discussing the teen problem without actually inviting any teens – and riot, setting fire to cars, and generally going mindless and feral. In the midst of this there is a neatly ironic scene where Julia, who had attempted to talk sense about the problem to the assembled adults before being rudely interrupted by stuff blowing up, uses the fact that she's the only adult the kids trust to persuade one of the younger riot boys to go get her a phone. She may be the liberal therapist. But she still snitches the kids out to the cops when it comes to the crunch.

The movie ends with explosive revenge on Doberman, and a blunt refusal on Kaplan's part to teach these kids a valuable lesson. As the riot's ringleaders are taken off to face court and possible prison, they look cool and defiant, and are given a hero's send-off by the resistance fighters – sorry – bored children they leave behind. They look pretty happy. After all, how bad can jail be after New Grenada?

1980s

★ ★

LITTLE DARLINGS

1980

Starring: Kristy McNichol, Tatum O'Neal, Matt Dillon, Armand
Assante, Krista Errickson
Dir.: Ronald F. Maxwell

**Plot: Trailer-trash heroine and snotty rich bitch race to lose
their virginity. Valuable lessons learned.**
Key line: 'Virgins are weird, right?'

The makers of this provocative coming-of-age drama entirely understand what they have in one Kristy McNichol.

The opening shot is of a light blue quilt, presumably hanging on
a washing line. It's simply a nicely colour-coded backdrop for the
entry of McNichol, from stage right. And you swoon, and maybe
gasp, and possibly drool a bit.

She's in half-body close-up, and you take in the shaggy, flick-back
mullet, the black t-shirt, the denim jacket, the wiry body and an
extraordinary face that seems to have been designed to show off the
most beautiful things about both boys and girls. Her eyes are feminine, big, knowing, questioning, amused, vulnerable. But her mouth
is tough, pouting, sneery, macho, set within a strong jaw. As she
watches something we can't see – something that could be worrying,
although she could just be playing up those big eyes because she
knows we're watching her – she slouches a little, pulls a fag from a
pack of Marlboros, sparks up, takes a breath, and begins to strut
towards this worrying place. You see just how thin and androgynous
her body is. A boy wolf-whistles, laughs, and runs up to her to run
his lines. He is spoiling the view, and the film-makers know it. We
just want to watch this cross-gender amalgam of every teen rebel
hero and heroine walk, and want to tell the git to fuck off on her
behalf. No need. 'Slide me somethin' nice,' the asshole demands.
She smiles – I swear, violins play and tweety birds start fluttering
around your head – and kicks him in the balls. I mean Wayne-Rooney-
volley kicks him in the balls. She stands over him like Muhammad Ali
looming over a prone Sonny Liston.

Another couple of lads, who should be natural allies of our hapless victim of feminist justice, laugh uproariously on our behalf. And fair enough. How could you not be on this girl's side?

Little Darlings takes its thematic cue from that other great teen chick flick, *Where The Boys Are* (see p. 57). It's a comedy-drama with a strangely gooberish pop soundtrack (Blondie? Of course. But John Lennon, Rickie Lee Jones and Supertramp?) about how, why and when a girl should lose her virginity, set in a summer camp in Georgia. The version released for US TV was censored to make it appear that our two central protagonists, Ferris (O'Neal) and Angel (McNichol), were engaged in a bet to see which one could make a boy fall in love with them. For once, one can understand the anxiety of broadcasters when dealing with viewing parents in the less liberal corners of America. Because these girls are only 15.

I had absolutely no knowledge of this movie until it was recommended to me for the book by a female friend. Not only did she big it up, but insisted that *Little Darlings* was a vital coming-of-age touchstone for her. My friend, incidentally, is gay, but didn't discover her sexuality until well into her twenties. I watched the movie with that in mind, and, by the time it reached its uplifting conclusion, got precisely what it had said to my friend without being explicit about it, and why it had resonated for her without her fully understanding why.

But the big feminist themes of the movie work despite the world of difference between its two leads. Put simply, Kristy McNichol is stunningly good, and Tatum O'Neal is achingly bad. And it's difficult not to project their real lives on to their *Little Darlings* characters, and imagine that some kind of on-set competition between opposites worked in the movie's favour.

Tatum O'Neal plays spoiled rich princess Ferris. In real life, Ms O'Neal was to the Hollywood manor born. Daughter of Ryan O'Neal, one of the biggest Hollywood box office stars of the early '70s, she won a Best Supporting Actress Oscar in 1974 for her role as a con artist opposite her father in Peter Bogdanovich's (see *The Last Picture Show*, p. 117) depression-era comedy *Paper Moon*. She was 10.

She had further commercial hits with *The Bad News Bears* and *International Velvet*, but *Little Darlings* turned out to be the end of her imperial phase, largely because, at 16, she still acted like an annoying 10-year-old. In 1986 she virtually quit acting to marry temperamental tennis icon John McEnroe. Divorce inevitably followed stormy marriage, and she never regained her place at acting's top table. But in 2011 her public soap opera life was enough to bag her a Oprah Winfrey-sponsored reality TV show, *Ryan And Tatum: The O'Neals*, about the father and daughter's attempts to reconcile after barely speaking for 25 years.

Kristy McNichol plays working-class tough girl Angel. In real life, she and her brother Jimmy had formed a kind of childhood double-act, working their way up through adverts and small TV parts. She got her big break in 1976 when cast as one of the stars of a US TV drama called *Family* alongside the likes of Michael J. Fox and Helen Hunt. But in 1978 she and brother Jimmy made a pop album which was launched at New York's notorious Studio 54 disco. It bombed.

Her career peaked with *Little Darlings*. By the time she was 20 – in 1982 – it was downhill all the way. When she disappeared from the set of a movie called *Just The Way You Are* – which also bombed – rumours circulated around the industry that she was a drug casualty. No one wanted to risk hiring her.

She got another break in 1988 when cast in hit TV sitcom *Empty Nest*, a spin-off from *The Golden Girls*. But, again, she went AWOL on set. In 1992, both she and brother Jimmy were diagnosed with bipolar disorder. By the end of the '90s she had completely retired from show business. She teaches acting and does charity work in LA, and was last spotted as the butt of two jokes on *Family Guy*.

Can't help thinking that telling those two stories as parallel epics about the price of child stardom would make one motherfucker of a great movie. Anyone got Oprah's number?

Anyway . . . what I'm saying is that there is an interesting onscreen contrast between the girl who worked her way up through her talent, and the girl that, well, didn't. And that adds a little more edge to a movie that manages to be great despite some of the lousiest direction this side of Michael Winner.

The tale begins with a bunch of girls boarding a yellow bus to summer camp. Angel already appears to be an outcast, because her mother drove up in a noisy, battered car, and because she looks like working-class trouble. We immediately know that we're not just here for the campfire songs and hymn-singing when we eavesdrop on a conversation about movies between a few of the girls as the bus waits to leave. When one says she's seen *Grease* six times, an unseen voice bigs up, of all things, Jean Cocteau's *Beauty And The Beast*, before a loud brunette trumps them by boasting about her repeated viewings of *Last Tango In Paris*. Michelangelo Antonioni's 1972 Marlon Brando vehicle may have been intended as an intellectual study of loveless sex, but in 1980 it was still viewed as arty, shocking porn, as natural a byword for illicit screen titillation as *Deep Throat* or *Emmanuelle*. These Georgia girls appear to be somewhat mature and obsessed with rumpy-pumpy.

Little rich girl Ferris arrives late and in an extraordinary white pant-suit complete with cap. She is as immediately outcast as Angel because she is ostentatiously rich. Within minutes Angel and Ferris are having full-on class-war fisticuffs, minus girly screaming and hair-pulling, egged on by the other girls, who appear to be as entertained by violence as teenage boys.

The most crucial update that *Little Darlings* makes on the world of *Where The Boys Are* is in the arena of perceived differences in behaviour between teen boys and teen girls. There aren't any. To hammer the point home, there is a scene where the girls watch a bunch of boys skinny-dipping through binoculars, making the same sort of sexist quips as any other group of cinematic peeping Toms. Except Angel, who seems ... *uninterested*. We'll get back to that shortly.

Our little darlings are entertainingly weird. One girl called Sunshine – played by 14-year-old Cynthia Nixon of future *Sex And The City* fame – is a dippy hippy who wears a crown of flowers and feeds everyone drugs ... in the shape of vitamin tablets and ginseng. Another, Penelope, is a pug-faced tomboy in a girl guide uniform who stuffs hankies in her bra to try and appear like she has bazongas so she doesn't have to camp with her fellow pre-teens. And most of them boast about sex like locker-room Lotharios. Having identified Angel and Ferris as different and willing to compete with each other to be accepted, the group proceeds to bully them into admitting that they are virgins and making a bet as to which one can pop their cherry first. Cinder (Krista Errickson), a vain diva who fancies herself as a supermodel and woman of the world, is the requisite Mean Girl who appears to have missed the memo which insists that promiscuous girl equals slut: 'Two little virgins. Quaint! No wonder you're always fighting. It's all that unreleased energy. Probably lezzies.'

Now, I think we're probably all aware, in this day and age, that

15-year-old girls are precocious enough to talk to each other this way. But, in 1980, *on film*, we weren't. What makes the exchange somewhat shocking is that, in spite of the fruity language and earthy eccentricity of the characters, *Little Darlings* is shot like a children's film; all pretty colours, corny montage, clumsy over-emphasis and terrible, bland, incidental muzak. It's like someone suddenly mentioning clitoral orgasms in a Disney movie.

But we didn't really need the 'L' word to read the subtext. We've watched Angel dispatch a male threat with utter confidence. But the camera lingers on McNichol's face as Cinder taunts her, and she's like a rabbit caught in headlights. She doesn't seem scared of Cinder, nor even that intimidated by peer pressure. She seems in awe of her, as if a boy she had a crush on had decided to publicly humiliate her. That, taken with her 'Boys are a pain in the ass' defence, gives *Little Darlings* the feel of a secret gay movie without ever letting its female characters articulate any kind of mutual attraction.

Despite this uncomfortable start, and the bet, life at Camp Little Wolf does settle into female bonding rituals fairly quickly. They muck about on boats, play sports, quote Shakespeare, cheek their elders, have a sexy food fight in the canteen – Ferris makes milk explode over Angel's bejeaned crotch in a manner that might make Brando in *The Wild One* (see p. 13) feel inadequate – and hijack a bus to go into town and steal condoms from a men's toilet. Normal kids' stuff. But it's all padding, really, for the impending Shag-Off. Most of the conversation is clever, funny stuff about the myths around sex among teens who haven't had any yet. And, if the dialogue here is anything to go by, it's illuminating to know that confused but horny girls talk much of the same bollocks as confused but horny boys.

Having already risked a few taboos, screenwriters Kimi Peck and Dalene Young decide to go gung-ho. While Angel hangs her hopes of victory on Matt Dillon's predictable motorbikin' Ramone-alike Randy (not everything's subtle) from the neighbouring boys' camp, Ferris sets her white cap at Mr Callahan, the thirtysomething camp counsellor and moonlighting French teacher. And when your star is Armand Assante, no amount of naming him Gary, dressing him in t-shirts and making him do sporty activities can stop him looking like a Monte Carlo gigolo from Latin Lounge Lizards Inc.

So, we're now being asked to enjoy watching a sullen brat manipulate a sleazy youth worker into paedophilia. Quaint!

The idea that this world is some sort of female conspiracy against men is established in even the smallest scenes. In one, parents visit a couple of the less visible girls. While Dad asks them inane questions, Mom is looking through their drawers. She discovers a pile of condoms and gasps with horror. But, when Dad innocently asks if the girls are being neat, Mom keeps him out of the loop, and the scene moves swiftly on, as if the entire point of the scene's inclusion was to illuminate male naivety and place gender solidarity even before marriage and parenthood.

The question of whether Angel is independent woman or surrogate man also hovers around the movie. When she makes up her mind to get Randy, she rows out alone in a boat to where he and all his skinny-dipping pals are sitting, utterly fearless, and almost whistles him like a dog. I mean, there's confidence and there are things that no 15-year-old girl would have the bottle to actually do. If she was a superhero, Angel would be Men-don't-scare-me Girl; lousy name, great pre-Buffy Summers ball-kicking powers. She chain smokes, drinks beer, can make excellent mating bird noises, has this glittering smile . . . look, I'm not a pervert, OK? I was 17 when this came out, so I'm just . . . projecting backwards. In time. Gimme a break.

So her mix of assertiveness and realistic target looks to have won Angel the bet. But we know pretty quickly that she and Randy's night-time tryst isn't quite right. A storm thunders. The barn they row out to is all abandoned and creepy. She's reluctant to kiss him, and even wants him to turn around while she gets naked. Angel is confident about men. But she's just not ready for sex. At least, not in this perfunctory, functional way, with a guy who is just too dumb to pick up on her reluctance. McNichol is great in this scene, vulnerable without being weak, her suppressed panic a powerful reminder of how awful it feels to feel you have to go through with something painful in order to save face. Her boyishness lends another layer of oddness to the scene, especially when you notice that she and the macho Dillon could almost be brother and sister.

When Angel's attempts to delay the happy event finally exhaust Randy's patience, and he rejects her, she tries to talk him back into it. She's just too young to know what she wants, and this asshole is too young to be a patient seducer, or admit that he has feelings. 'I'm not sexy to you, huh?' she asks. 'All girls are sexy,' he grunts, and her face is a mask of humiliation. Or is it agreement?

Still, it could be worse. Ferris is depressed because her parents are getting divorced, and the object of her lust is singing that terrible folk song about cherries that have no stones or whatever around a campfire in the kind of preppy choirboy voice that makes you want to go completely Bluto (see *National Lampoon's Animal House*, p. 161). Nevertheless, Ferris turns up at Gary's cabin in a nightie. As his chintzy classical soundtrack, white socks and rug-like chest hair don't send her running for the hills of eternal celibacy, we assume that losing her virginity has become some sort of abstract concept now, like a quest, or maybe a cosmic assault course.

Ferris's attempt at seduction is the comic contrast to Angel's bleak barn dance. And it's fine, because none of us want to take the possibility of statutory rape seriously, not even in a film that seems comfortable with its own mixed messages. And so is Ferris. One minute she's assuring Gary she's in love. The next she's asking if she can stay the night, 'just for appearances'. When you're a teen, how you look to your peers is more important than anything, including sex or breaking the law. Which is probably why the overwhelming majority of the 'how I lost my virginity' tales I've been told by friends are anti-climactic at best and tragic at worst. Most of us do it the first time to please everyone else but ourselves.

It turns out Angel and Ferris's choices weren't too bad, though. Gary rejects Ferris in a kind and flattering way, allowing her a romantic fantasy about the night she *could* have, and enough fuel to pretend that she's won her bet.

And Randy works out that tough Angel ain't so tough after all, and shows the girl some love. 'Some guys like to rush,' he mumbles, Stalloneishly. 'But not me.' It's very endearing, but Dillon's speciality was that pre-Joey Tribbiani dumb-hunk-with-a-heart-of-gold thing, and he's essentially the same love thug here as he is in *Over The Edge* (see p. 184), *The Outsiders* (see p. 226) and *Rumble Fish* (see p. 229).

So Angel does lose her virginity but opts to keep it private. Ferris doesn't and makes up a bet-winning fantasy. 'This is better than books,' once of the girls fizzes as they enthusiastically swallow Ferris's Mills & Boon version of shagging. 'The truth always is,' says Sunshine, with neat layers of unintentional irony.

But, for most of us, the truth is the reason why romantic fantasies exist. We don't see Angel and Randy make love, but we do see the post-coital fallout, and Angel seems miserable. When Randy finally wends his weary way through her beautiful layers of self-defence, and asks her what's wrong, she simply says: 'It wasn't what I thought it would be. God ... it was so personal. Like you could see right through me.' Randy's initial wounded hostility gives way when she confesses that it was her first time. He then performs a radical U-turn and tells her he loves her, but our tearful tomboy is not exactly jumping for joy. 'I feel so lonesome,' she whispers, and it's like he isn't there at all.

From there, plot comes thick and fast. Cinder tells Randy that he was just part of a bet so he hits on her out of revenge. Gary is in big trouble for obvious reasons. When Angel confesses all to Randy and sends him packing, she says, 'I'll never forget you. Ever.' And we think about our own first lovers and realise how true that is.

Angel and Ferris confess all to each other and bond, and Ms McNichol is so wracked with shame, loss and delayed trauma in this scene that you see the end of Tatum O'Neal's acting career right there. Cinder gets her comeuppance as the other girls bond against her in a feminist show of all having lied about their sexual experience, which is, now I think about it, a weird thing to be all high moral ground about. Peace-loving Sunshine gets the satisfaction of actually punching the mean girl on our behalf. Ferris tells the truth to the camp authorities so Gary isn't sacked, despite the chest hair. He tells her she's 'quite a woman', which I suspect isn't necessarily what you'd say to someone who'd come close to getting you put on the Sex Offenders Register. When they all leave the camp and get back to the car park full of doting parents – not before Angel and Ferris have flirted outrageously with each other on the bus – Angel informs her slutty Mom and Ferris's cuckolded Dad that Ferris is her best friend. It's corny as all hell ... but you really feel the pair have earned their moment of hands-across-the-classes feel-good.

You also really feel you've just watched a brilliantly written but badly made film, with one stand-out performance, that implies that sex with men is rubbish and that every girl should just hold out for the right girl. I think I get what my friend saw in it.

* *

TAPS

1981

Starring: Timothy Hutton, George C. Scott, Sean Penn, Ronny Cox, Tom Cruise
Dir.: Harold Becker

Plot: Why we're against the war, but for the soldiers.
Key line: 'You go to the movies. You read books. A military leader is *always* portrayed as slightly insane.'

Taps is a fascinating early '80s curio, subverting many teen movie conventions by aligning rebellion with conservatism. It's an allegory – if you're not good at suspending disbelief, then this movie's plot and scenario will drive you nuts – about duty, authority and the chaos of human interaction, which also works as a tragic adventure story about teens under siege. Its also a Vietnam hangover film which asks what place militarism might still hold in American society, and whether we can still admire the courage and self-sacrifice of the soldier, and at what point those apparently selfless attributes might become self-serving and dangerous. It is held together by remarkable acting by a young ensemble cast and one living legend who is asked to revive his most successful character and make him into a modern equivalent of Powell and Pressburger's Colonel Blimp: a man out of time, unable to survive new values that are entirely alien to him.

It begins with the sounds of men singing the hymn 'Onward Christian Soldiers', a song of worship it is impossible to hear without wincing at its militaristic imagery, and the sound of a man's voice lifelessly intoning chapter 13, verse 11 of Corinthians … 'I put away childish things', and so forth. A long tracking shot edges warily down the aisle of a church, taking in the uniformed males filling the pews, the choirboys in white tunics, the visual order of shining floor and humans arranged in straight lines. This is already an unlikely '80s teen film, kicking off with a slow tempo and a set of sounds and images designed to make your average teenager run for hills full of tit gags and rock action. *Taps* is over two hours long and takes its own sweet time to reach the nub of the crux. It is fascinated by what the Bunker Hill Military Academy looks and feels like, and attempts, successfully, to make the viewer understand the intimidating grandeur of this Pennsylvania school for soldiers, and why a set of boys may feel enough loyalty to an institution to put themselves at risk to defend it.

In church we get our first glimpse of George C. Scott and are unavoidably and deliberately reminded of his portrayal of an American military legend in *Patton: Lust For Glory*, for which Scott won an Oscar which he refused to accept. He is addressing a group of young cadets in archaic uniform, and a bugler plays 'Taps', or 'The Last Post' as we call it in Britain, a lone bugle lament for those who have fallen in action, while Scott's General Harlan Bache reads a list of school graduates who never returned from the great wars of the 20th century. This is a film that foreshadows death at every turn.

We meet our three principal boys in the bustle of the school. Brian Moreland (Hutton) is the head boy and star of his class who is set to begin the next graduating year as Cadet Major. A future military career is his life. Sean Penn, in his movie debut, is Alex Dwyer, Brian's best friend. He is academically superior and funny but doesn't take the school's calls to duty as seriously as Brian. We are told, almost in passing, that he is without parents for reasons never explained, so he is therefore closer to adulthood by virtue of forced independence. He is the 'normal' teen with an independent point of view, the voice of reason who becomes the audience representative by taking the sensible stances we hope we would emulate in a similar situation. His mirror image and rival is David Shawn, played by Tom Cruise, a bullish, macho, born sergeant-major type whose severe skinhead crop immediately marks him out as a quasi-fascist.

US critic Roger Ebert, in his review of *Taps* for the *Chicago Sun-Times* (www.webcitation.org), compares the film to William Golding's classic study of boys without adult guidance *Lord Of The Flies*. If that comparison holds, then Brian is Ralph, Alex is Simon and David is Jack. The charismatic leader, the thinker, the thug. *Taps* is as much about the uneasy interaction between these archetypes as it is about militarism under threat or boys attempting to be men, but also suggests that every army – or teen gang – needs all three to function successfully. The trick is finding the balance.

The school's grand look, crusty military attitude and rigid hierarchies also put the viewer in mind of Lindsay Anderson's public school revolution classic *If* ... (see p. 97). But here, the older kids have power but rarely abuse it. Bunker Hill is not dysfunctional. Everyone accepts their roles, and Brian is loved and admired for his privileged position. *Taps* is not concerned with youth rebellion against institution. It's more interested in a sheltered, self-contained society's rebellion against the real world.

Brian's promotion means that he is granted the ultimate end-of-term privilege; dinner and brandy with the outgoing Cadet Major and General Bache. As Bache (pronounced 'Baysh', but if you prefer to think of it as 'Bash' go right ahead) regales the boys with war stories in the gentlemen's club atmosphere of his study, you can imagine Alex, like any normal teenage boy, stifling giggles while watching the clock. But the two boys are rapt, and Brian looks at General Bache with an expression that combines shock, awe, gratitude and undying love. You can't help but wonder, at this point, why Brian is in such dire need of a father figure when his own dad is also a military man.

We are then treated to several minutes of parade-ground pageantry full of boys marching with stiff and bullish pride, images designed to sort viewers immediately into those who admire the discipline and strength of fit young boys in uniform, and those who want to hide behind the sofa until the Hitler Youth go away.

But the show of strength is ironic. Bache, suddenly looking old and weary of battle, takes the mic to announce that Bunker Hill is to be closed in a year's time. The trustees intend to sell it to a real estate company who want to build that ultimate symbol of rootless civilian yuppieness – condominiums.

The school is at such odds with the civilian world that its only meeting with it takes away both adult leadership and the year's grace. A gang of local teens park up outside the Academy's graduation dance and commence with the mocking. These military men do not inspire respect or fear among teens in post-'50s jeans. They're just alien teens, ripe for the same macho, homophobic taunting as any gang of others. A fight breaks out. When Bache rushes out to restore order, he's attacked just like his boys. The kid tries to pull the gun from his pocket (I know.... why has a guy brought a loaded pistol to a formal dance? As I said, suspend that disbelief) and Bache accidentally kills the leader of the gang. He is arrested, and bang goes Bunker Hill's 12-month reprieve.

But the now-absent Bache, who also suffers a stress-related heart attack, commands his boys by proxy. When he waxed defiant and said that he intended to fight to get the school's closure reversed, Brian Moreland had taken the sentiment literally. Brian convinces the boys to occupy the school, arm up and refuse to leave the building until Bunker Hill is saved to provide future generations of cannon fodder. Parents, police and, inevitably, the military itself are called in to talk the battalion of children down and protect the real American way of life ... the relentless march of capitalism. *Taps* becomes a fiendishly provocative subversion of rebellious anti-military students occupying American colleges to protest against the Vietnam War.

But Brian is fighting to prove himself to two very different father figures as much as he is for principle, tradition and loyalty and against what he perceives as a world of gutless and hostile civilians. The cadets, some of whom are as young as 12, move gradually from willing participants in an exciting, adult-baiting game to terrified children who understand that their lives are in danger as Brian digs himself and his 'men' into a deeper and darker trench. He is isolated, old enough to ape Bache's notions of duty and honour, but deprived of the old man himself, and therefore the wise counsel of the only adult he appears to trust. By the time he realises that he is not man enough to understand the complexities of leadership, and that part of a leader's responsibility might lie in knowing when to surrender, it's too late. Tragedy ensues.

Before the inevitably violent climax to the tale, we learn that Brian has issues with Bad Dad over his mother's death. The soldier had ordered the then 12-year-old to cry out his grief for 15 minutes ... and then never cry over her again. The scene where Pop Moreland leads the parents' delegation and attempts to persuade his son to relent is key, and testament to Hutton's excellence. He is the essence of a being trapped between that grieving, frightened 12-year-old and his extreme attempt to prove that he is now more of a man than his father. Dad orders the gaggle of parents around like dumbass privates on parade, neatly suggesting that the world Brian is fighting to preserve is not worth preserving. 'A leader who loses his humanity becomes a tyrant,' Bache has already told Brian, and that was the clue to what Brian loves about Bache and despises about his own father. When Brian refuses to accept his father's authority over him (the son potentially outranks the father, in strict military terms), Dad changes the tone from father to mocking militarist bully, ranting about his son's strategic errors, informing his son that he could 'break his neck' if he felt like it. When Brian evokes the example of his beloved General Bache, Dad is sent into rage, not because he is concerned for Brian or the other cadets, but because Bache and his son are of the officer class, and he isn't. He finally just hits Brian. It is Dad's final defeat, as he loses all control of himself and the situation, while Brian maintains his dignity. Hutton's repressed tears and accusatory stare remind you that, a few years ago, Brian was forbidden to cry by this same monster. From this point on, you just can't stop yourself wanting the boy to somehow obliterate his father's influence and win this thing.

But one of his father's accusations has hit home. The outside world believes that he is holding other cadets hostage. To be a good and just leader – a better man than Bad Dad – Brian has to confront this head on and encourage reluctant recruits to leave. This parade-ground scene is where the film proves its good intentions. Because, in a bad film, every cadet would make one of those weird gung-ho bellows that macho American males are fond of, and conform. They don't. Some stay. Some leave. Brian has made the fair choice, but it has left him weakened. It sows the seeds of future desertion, rather than leaving the remaining cadets more committed.

The movie's last act finally strides confidently into action movie territory, and it does so with the same sure-footed mastery of storytelling with which it leads us through Bunker Hill's insular bunker mentality, its rain-soaked parade-ground scenes and the differing viewpoints of its teen characters and Ronny Cox's military negotiator Colonel Kerby, who is the strong but sympathetic father figure that Brian really needs. When the besieged boys are finally confronted by the full might of the real military-industrial complex, you're immediately reminded of traditional against-all-odds cinematic images, particularly Michael Caine's gritty Brits in *Zulu* and the doomed German trench rats in *All Quiet On The Western Front*. *Taps* becomes a strange kind of war film about an outnumbered and outgunned army fighting a battle they can't win for ultimately futile reasons. Actually, not so strange, now I think about either World War One or Vietnam.

The film earns the right to make its images of dead boys as haunting and emotional as any in conventional war films. Penn is the accomplished naturalist actor we come to know in later years, but shorn of some his more scenery-chewing elements. Cruise is fascinating because he isn't Tom Cruise yet. Cast in a thanklessly ugly role, he is chubby of face and thick of neck, a ball of redneck mindlessness. The one glimpse of his future persona occurs early, when he has to fire a gun into the air and makes it look like he's fucking the entire planet and making us like it. But it does feel inevitable that Penn's Alex is the one character who can bring a sane solution to the problem, and that David should be able to destroy that solution and tip the world into war with one Cruise missile. Cruise can't resist making it kind of gonzo funny, too. You can understand exactly why Paul Brickman's original choice for the lead in *Risky Business* (see p. 215) was Hutton rather than Cruise. There's no evidence here that this ugly skinhead could do anything onscreen other than die like a maniac.

One of the many unusual things about *Taps* is that the film lingers after leaving, but you struggle to decide exactly what it's trying to say. Teen movies usually write their base message large, but *Taps* is neither entirely liberal nor conservative, neither pro-military nor anti-military, neither moral nor amoral. It's a strong story with an insane ending that leaves you feeling that you've been shown something true and disturbing about the military mindset, and about boys' relationship to violence, but without the usual route map to guide you to the makers' intentions. One thing's for sure, though: if the cops, parents and armies of Pennsylvania are truly as hapless as they are in *Taps*, I'd rather take my chances in Beirut.

★ ★

CLASS OF 1984

1982

Starring: Perry King, Timothy Van Patten, Roddy McDowall, Michael J. Fox, Merrie Lynn Ross, Lisa Langlois
Dir.: Mark L. Lester

Plot: The punk rock *Blackboard Jungle*.
Key line(s): *Mr Norris*: **'I think Stegman's actually a brilliant kid.'**
Mr Corrigan: **'So was the Marquis de Sade.'**

Class of 1984 proudly presents its tongue-in-cheek exploitation credentials from the get-go. It begins with a trick pulled straight from the The Blackboard Jungle (see p. 20) box of fake social concern: a caption that informs us that there were 280,000 instances of classroom violence last year, apparently, and, therefore, this movie is based on real events. Where any of these figures and real events come from is anyone's guess.

Then, as we watch beardy, pointy-chinned music teacher Andrew Norris (King) drive to his new job at Abraham Lincoln High School, we hear a song. A truly, spectacularly terrible song, which begins with gnarly John Carpenter synth before flattening into the kind of techno-rock power balladry that could only mean the 1980s. With halting melodrama, over a melody that barely qualifies as melody, the singer sings the words: 'When does a dream/Become a nightmare?/When do we do what must be done?' By this point, Mark L. Lester has lost interest in Mr Norris, and who can blame him? In the urban jungle that lies beyond his four wheels, The Kids are runnin' wild. A teen thief is chased down a busy street by a shopowner. Punky looking types are graffiti-ing on walls. A young couple are snogging enthusiastically outside school gates. A boy hitches a ride to school by jumping on the back of the school bus at high speed and hanging on for grim death. There's a scrap in the school playground. Because Nazi punks informed by the comic-book hyper-realism of *The Warriors* (see p. 175) are on a crazy rampage, Dude, and we're going to watch them and laugh for 90 minutes while going along with the pretence that we're actually sharing the film-makers' *faux*-sincere concern for the future of Western civilisation.

By 1982, the B-movie had become an aesthetic choice rather than a film industry necessity. Gigantic blockbusters like *Jaws* and *Star Wars* had further established that filmgoers were happy to go to the cinema to watch one movie; there was no need any more to fund low-budget films to play as support features. But the tacky look, sly subtexts and exploitative feel of cheap movies had claimed a place in the heart of budding genre directors and a generation of trash-loving movie fans. It would take until the 1990s for smart-acres like Quentin Tarantino to intellectualise the B-movie so completely that self-conscious irony and big budgets overwhelmed the joys of sincerely delivered schlock. A movie like *Class Of 1984* is still perfectly balanced between providing tight and unpretentious slam-bang entertainment, and knowingly winking at an audience who have spent many an hour chortling ironically at bad (and good) high school movies from the '50s and '60s.

So, for the second unofficial remake of *The Blackboard Jungle* that merits a place in this book (see *To Sir, With Love*, p. 90), '50s moralising and '60s liberal optimism are replaced by early '80s nihilism. We still have an idealistic middle-class teacher locked in a classroom power struggle with a working-class gang. But Lester and co-writers Tom Holland and John Saxton take the word 'gang' to its logical conclusion. If a group of kids gain enough power in a school to make the teachers quiver in terror, then surely they would use that power to become actual gangsters. The Bad Kids – which include girls now that we're in the less courtly '80s – deal drugs, pimp and use violence to extort money and protect their position. On top of all that nastiness, the gang are informed by 1982's American juvenile delinquency public scare ... punk.

Ordinary American kids jumped on the punk bandwagon a few years later than us Brits, but made up for lost time by bypassing the arty alternative post-punk phase completely and going straight to the brutal, Sid Vicious-inspired underclass bit, which Brits called Oi! At best, this involved sexless thrash rock, slam dancing, sniffing glue, smelling bad and acting dumb. At worst, it became an extreme right-wing white power subculture which proudly proclaimed itself 'Nazi punk'. So the children of the perfectly named Abraham Lincoln school have moved way beyond random sexual molestation and sneering, and are committed, Swastika-wearing, fascist-saluting scum-buckets ... albeit – because, after all, this is a pop film, not a documentary – scum-buckets who have the best fashionista fetish glam-punk clothes and hair this side of a fight in a vintage clothes shop between Alice Cooper (who provides that brilliantly awful theme song 'I Am The Future') and Billy Idol. Apart from the fat, sweaty, skinhead character. You can't make those guys sexy.

So this might be one hell of an ugly-pretty gang of naughty young scamps. But we're pretty quickly aware that it's going to take something a little more radical than marching them off to the principal's office to restore truth, justice and the liberal consensus to poor old Lincoln High. Guns, maybe. Weapons, certainly. Perhaps a tactical nuke or two. Whatever it takes to 'do what must be done', right? Besides, the principal's busy sitting in his office watching his students on CCTV and wringing his hands pathetically. Surveillance. Big Brother. 1984. It's only two years away and, as the *Class Of 1984* gang are fond of reminding us, 'We are the future!' Scary shit.

Certainly things can't go on like they are at the beginning of the movie. Mr Norris arrives for his trip to hell and bumps straight into the faculty's obligatory jaded cynic, Mr Corrigan, played by the hilarious Roddy McDowall. Within seconds Corrigan is jauntily asking Norris if he knows any martial arts, and introducing us to one of our favourite recurring images of the decline of American civilisation, the airport-style metal detector in the school's lobby. The detector is manned by tough-looking security guys, but their hearts are plainly not in their work ... style-mag toughs are waving knives in their faces and they wave 'em through. Corrigan assures Norris that his survival at Lincoln High will depend on his willingness to follow that example and ignore the horrifying truth. This is a very poor show.

A quick word about Roddy McDowall, a man whose acting career took him to some very odd places, who died in 1998, aged 70. Born in London, he became a child star through his '40s starring roles in *How Green Was My Valley* and *Lassie Come Home*. And, like most child stars, he was never taken seriously as an adult lead. His greatest acting triumph came with his face completely obscured by prosthetics as the nice chimp in the long-running *Planet Of The Apes* movies and spin-off TV show. Although McDowall never officially came out, his sexuality was pretty obvious from his many appearances as all-purpose wit and raconteur on American chat and game shows. Which perhaps explained the mini-scandal he was embroiled in, when his home was raided in 1974 and McDowall arrested for copyright infringement on account of his personal library of movie prints. Considering that this collection included the home movies of notorious hung-stud and sex perv Errol Flynn, and that Rock Hudson was among the customers who hired the films, it was always suspected that the arrest had some form of homophobic intent.

McDowall was also one of the villains (The Bookworm) in the '60s TV version of *Batman*, and it was that kind of camp that this slight, good-natured presence could be relied upon to bring to movies with a self-parodic B-movie aesthetic. In *Class Of 1984* his droll performance is vital to the film's success, because, while everyone else in the cast plays it dead straight, McDowall is telling a sly running joke to the viewer along the lines of: 'Yes, we know this is ridiculous. So do you. Fun, isn't it?', and never allows his nods and winks to tip over into loathing for himself, the movie or the audience.

The other star of the movie is Timothy Van Patten as gang leader Peter Stegman. Stegman has the looks of a Greek god and the winning personality of Vlad the Impaler. He beats up jive-talking black kids called Leroy, before insisting that 'We're the only niggers that sell shit in this school!'

Class Of 1984's major curio factor involves the presence of Michael J. Fox as trumpet-playing nerd Arthur. This Michael J. Fox is a chubby berk with a pudding-bowl haircut who is so clean-cut and annoyingly whingy that he almost makes you feel empathy for his psycho tormentors. He's almost impossible to connect with the impishly lovable Marty McFly of *Back To The Future* (see p. 259), yet the 21-year-old Fox is just three years away from being the most popular 'teen' actor of his generation, and mere months from his Emmy and Golden Globe-winning breakthrough role on sitcom *Family Ties* (a part he only got, incidentally, because Matthew 'Ferris Bueller' Broderick turned it down), where the wry Reaganomics joke revolved around the relationship between

Fox's right-wing yuppie teen and his ex-hippie liberal parents. Here, in only his second film, he is doomed to be stabbed in the school cafeteria for being a suck-up.

The plot is note-for-note *The Blackboard Jungle*, but with an injection of genuine nastiness that makes you feel slightly sick and wrong for enjoying it so much. Remember the 'last straw' in *The Blackboard Jungle*, where Rick Dadier is finally forced into action when Vic Morrow's gang write poison pen letters to his pregnant wife? Well, we still have the pregnant wife. But Van Patten's monsters cut out the men-of-letters routine and just go round to the nice suburban Norris family homestead and commence with the rape and torture. Norris is forced to leave the school concert he's supposed to be directing and become Charles Bronson's prettier vigilante action hero kid brother. And Lester then does the right thing and heads right out of dramatic logic and right into *grand guignol* action/horror/slasher territory involving severed arms and heads crushed by cars, for a final battle showdown between Stegman and Teach, which has an ending so gasp-out-loud ridiculous that Brian De Palma could have happily smuggled it into the end of *Carrie* (see p. 150) without anyone noticing.

The rest is all great scenes, in school corridors covered with disgusting graffiti, in *Warriors*-style gang fights under deserted underpasses, in punk rock clubs with kids cavorting violently to the savage strains of a band called Teenage Head. There's a hilarious parody of the Sidney Poitier-sings-spirituals scene in *The Blackboard Jungle*, when Van Patten's Stegman suddenly stops Norris's class in its tracks with his virtuoso piano skills. There are comically impotent police, a skinned rabbit on a skewer, and the awesome bit in the school toilet when Stegman, blood pouring over his crazy eyes, starts head-butting mirrors and sinks. And, best of all, there's the movie's most admired and darkly funny set-piece, when camp old Corrigan finally loses the plot and forces the gang to listen to his biology lesson at gunpoint. McDowall momentarily beams himself in from another film, where the agony of a middle-aged teacher who has never been allowed to educate anyone might finally boil over and become real despair, real rage. You start watching the scene wanting to laugh, and end it genuinely freaked out. But, as soon as the moment of peril passes, McDowall plays it for camp laughs again, cutting the tension. Corrigan's tantrum doesn't get him a nice lecturing job at Yale.

Class Of 1984 is less about Orwellian paranoia and more about making hysterically explicit what 30 years of juvenile delinquency movies only hinted at: that some children really are plain evil and will grow up to be serial killers unless you hang them. Hang 'em all! It's a minority view in education policy circles. But one worth 93 minutes of serious consideration.

★ ★

MADE IN BRITAIN

1982
Starring: Tim Roth, Eric Richard, Bill Stewart, Terry Richards
Dir.: Alan Clarke

Plot: The Nazi teen as the ultimate anti-hero.
Key line: 'You hate the blacks more than I do only you don't admit it. You hate the blacks more than I do 'cos they frighten you. That's why you lock 'em up. You lock up anything that frightens you.'

Made In Britain is one of only two films in this book that were not made to be shown in cinemas. The two movies have a few things in common: actor Tim Roth, a right-wing skinhead character, the poor end of working-class London shot with unflinching realism. Although they were both made for TV and promoted as 'plays', they are here because there is nothing theatrical about them. They are cinematic experiences given life by the grim streets and very specific interiors in which they are shot. They were both made by legendary British directors who took their cue from the British 'Free Cinema' directors of the late '50s and early '60s. And, from a personal perspective, they were made at a time when I was just exiting my own teen years, and put people onscreen that I'd known and tried my best to avoid – and avoid being – for the previous five or six years. They say something accurate and disturbing about Britain under Thatcherism, and provide much information for historians about why left-liberals of a certain age despise Thatcher so much. They also give the lie to those who are nostalgic about the early '80s because they liked the music, or whatnot. Things were shit at the time. Really, really shit.

Set in east London, *Made In Britain* is a character study of a 16-year-old racist called Trevor. Trevor is played by Tim Roth, making his screen debut at age 21. The film is an extraordinary four-way collaboration between Roth, Liverpudlian shock tactic director Clarke, gritty social realist writer David Leland and innovative cinematographer Chris Menges. They conspire to create the world's worst boy: a fearless, nihilistic, articulate, violent force of nature with a swastika tattooed on his forehead. We follow Trevor over the course of a few days on his journey through a court appearance, his referral to an assessment centre for juvenile offenders, his escapes from the centre, and, finally, into a police holding cell. In 1982 you came away from the 70-minute film feeling like you'd just been beaten up. The years have not dimmed its sickening power. And the power comes from the gamble that Clarke took with the character of Trevor. All right-thinking people thought that young fascist skinheads were ugly, thick and inadequate. This was a comforting thought whenever you considered the possibility of far-right organisations like the National Front or the British Movement progressing from a few scattered thugs exploiting a white working class that felt abandoned to a genuine popular movement with its own paramilitary force. But Trevor is not ugly, thick or inadequate. He is what a great many young men look up to and long to be: a tough, charismatic, free spirit who can look authority figures in the eye and refuse to be intimidated. He is brave, good at fighting, right about a great many things ... and even, to some extent, cool. *Made In Britain* is, on some levels, an attack on liberal apathy and self-satisfaction; the belief among so many of a leftish persuasion that anyone who doesn't share their views is simply doomed to failure because they must be stupid, or easily led, or weak. Trevor is clever, strong and packed full of leadership qualities. Successful monsters generally are.

Roth's performance was so extraordinary that he didn't need David Leland's dialogue to be particularly amazing. Trevor's power comes from the actor's Johnny Rotten eyes, switching between wild fury and dead insolence; his rictus grin full of hatred and sadism; his wiry body, always tensed for war; his taunting voice, again, suffused with Johnny Rotten's withering scorn; and, most of all, his walk. An open-legged, bouncing swagger, fists bunched by sides, body coiled like a spring, a wide, forceful gait that always looks to be going towards you to do you unspeakable damage.

Clarke emphasises Trevor's visceral presence with the deliberate ugliness of everyone around him. Assessment Centre head Peter Clive (Stewart) is perhaps the least attractive man to ever 'grace' the screen. This isn't the kind of ugliness that has a charisma of its own. It's an anonymous mess of greasy hair and skinny-rimmed glasses, small, piggy eyes, Mr Byrite suit with no-brand trainers. A mean but ultimately anonymous face that just doesn't exist to be looked at. In comparison to a man like Peter, Trevor can only leap from the screen, stand out in his environment. He is designed to excite the teenage imagination: all that arrogance and fear-lessness, physical power and bug-eyed threat. He is what teen boys dream of being ... a law unto himself, a dominator of authority, a pure anarchist rejecting the 'real world' utterly by refusing to live in it.

The 'shocking' scenes are not the most memorable scenes. We watch Trevor and his hastily co-opted black sidekick Leroy (Terry Richards) smash a Job Centre window, steal cars, throw bricks through an Asian man's window, sniff glue and urinate and defecate on their Assessment Centre case files. In fact, the least convincing scene in the movie comes when Trevor beats up the Centre's cook, and Clarke's limitations as a director of action – exposed in his ridiculously overrated 1977 borstal drama *Scum* – are obvious.

Clarke is at his best when shaping the way Menges's Steadicam follows and stares in horrified awe at Roth as he produces a per-formance composed of such frightening intensity you find yourself wondering what his upbringing as the son of a left-wing journalist might have to do with it. Is he taking gleeful pleasure in being his father's worst nightmare?

So the scenes you take away are Trevor striding topless through the Blackwall Tunnel at night, so insane with rage that he's willing to fight a passing car. Or him stopping to look at a design of a perfect middle-class family living-room in a shop window complete with mannequins. You're positive that this is about to become the latest victim of Trevor's love of the sound of breaking glass. But he just peruses the scene, curiously, much as one might look at a group of animals in a zoo, fascinated, it seems, by the alien world it depicts.

But the best scene begins with Trevor largely silent. It takes place in an empty room in the Assessment Centre ... a place that looks like a bleak blend of inner-city classroom and police interrogation room. It starts with a mesmerising lecture on the checks and balances of the system with regard to juvenile delinquents delivered by the Centre's nameless Superintendent, played by the excellent Geoffrey Hutchings. The speech treads a perfect line between factual information, mesmerising art and scathing cynicism about a failed system. The Superintendent is northern and has a copper's bearing, right down to the scruffy trench-coat. He doesn't attempt to befriend Trevor ... the other workers' constant use of his first name, like they know him, is a particular Trevor bugbear. But, when faced with this man, Trevor shuts up and listens, even though he is telling him nothing he doesn't already know. Is Trevor responding to the Superintendent's job title, or no-nonsense demeanour, or salt-of-the-earth working-classness? We never know for sure. He is the one person who looks as if he might have some chance of taming the boy whom he repeatedly compares to an 'animal'. We never see him again.

It's then that we get Tim Roth's moment: the few minutes onscreen that made him the star that Trevor, at one point, insists that he is. His verbal slaughter of the hapless and condescending Centre workers Peter and Barry is compelling and terrifying in equal measure, as he convinces us that there is a new generation of young working-class men who believe themselves immune to a system they despise, and that depends for hope on a fascist revolution they see as inevitable.

But don't think *Made In Britain* is a straightforward liberal film. It sneers at the 'caring' aspects of the system like a *Daily Mail* leader column. The more repulsive and uncontrollable Trevor is, the more the system spends on trying to placate him. Apart from giving him the money that enables him to go on his glue-sniffing, car-nicking, Job Centre-trashing rampage, the rant at Peter and Barry simply encourages Peter into giving him yet more. He offers to take the boy banger racing at the state's expense. Hell, he even arranges things so he can compete. A terrible punishment for a car thief. It's not that a film as non-preachy as *Made In Britain* is exactly suggesting that the Trevors of this world should just be given twenty lashes and locked up as a lost cause. But Leland and Clarke laugh darkly at the middle-class managers of a broken system and their futile attempts to make Trevor into a good dog by throwing him bones.

The ending is haunting in its refusal to resolve. Trevor, now out of the youth system and into a grown-up police cell, tries to wind up a couple of coppers the way he has wound up everyone else. One blow with a truncheon to his knee, and everything we've watched for the previous 72 minutes falls away from Trevor. He's a small, shocked boy, trying not to cry or cry out in pain, finally shutting up for fear of more violence.

But he is also the boy in the final freeze-frame . . . a nod to *The 400 Blows* (see p. 47), perhaps. The two cops leave him alone in his cell, and Trevor simply sits and stares, and allows that demented, defiant grin to slowly return. You're reminded of the glee with which the Sex Pistols chanted the words 'No future' at the end of 'God Save The Queen'. Trevor greets violence, no-future in prison, oblivion, with the same determined rejection of everything that our world would define as reason or goodness. He is a terrifying vision. And the film has equally steadfastly refused to provide anything that might qualify as a potential solution to the insoluble problem that is the working-class youth who will not conform to a liberal agenda, no matter how much you hurt him.

Made In Britain isn't perfect. The film could have done with one black character who, in the light of Trevor's vile racism, offers some more intelligence and backbone than the useless Leroy, who can't read and blithely follows the orders of a boy who calls him 'a fucking baboon' to the point of copying his abuse of other non-whites. It's Leroy, rather than Trevor, who forces you to wonder about the politics of Leland and Clarke.

But then, Leland and Clarke patently weren't setting out to make a balanced portrayal of real people. They were deliberately setting out to shock TV viewers out of their passive state and make them frightened and concerned for the future of Britain. Unlike most planned outrage, *Made In Britain* turned out to be both 'water-cooler TV' and art of lasting worth. The major reason for that remains Tim Roth, whose wild eyes, demented sneer and swaggering gait perfectly captured an archetype of '80s Britain for posterity, and gave it a voice that we didn't want to hear.

I have no idea what racist skins thought of Trevor . . . maybe some claimed him as inspirational role model. But I do know that 1982 was roughly the year that one started to notice that the marauding Nazi skin began to disappear from England's streets, gigs and football matches. Pure coincidence, possibly. But I like to think that Trevor broke something that desperately needed breaking.

Got to watch that liberal apathy, though. The young '80s fascists may not have had their race war, but boys like Trevor will always exist, no matter how much we choose to ignore them. Left untended, they occasionally grow up into men who murder children in socialist Norwegian summer camps.

★ ★

RISKY BUSINESS

1983
Starring: Tom Cruise, Rebecca de Mornay, Joe Pantoliano, Richard Masur, Curtis Armstrong
Dir.: Paul Brickman

Plot: Diary of a teenage pimp.
Key line: 'It was great the way her mind worked. No guilt. No doubts. No fear. None of my specialities. Just the shameless pursuit of immediate material gratification. What a capitalist.'

It's hard to pick a favourite scene from a movie entirely composed of great scenes, but I'll go for this one. It's the scene where we meet the teenage hero's parents and it is a small, but perfectly formed, cinematic marvel. The hero becomes the camera becomes us, allowing us to be directly patronised by his archly country-clubbish Mom and Pop, played by Janet Carroll and Nicholas Pryor. As we follow them around their immaculate, soulless home, Mom interrogates us about our test scores, passive-aggressively suggesting that we should take the tests again, before asking if Dad has packed her Mace. Before we can ponder the reasons why Mom needs a spray-weapon to take on holiday, we are following Dad into a room and his voice is being drowned out by the nastiest lift muzak you've ever heard. He asks us if we hear something unpleasant. Well, yeah . . . your fucking terrible music, Gramps. But we hear Joel dutifully answer 'No' on our behalf. Dad opens a cabinet and reveals an expensive stereo. The 'unpleasant' noise is 'the preponderance of bass, perhaps'. The laugh-out-loud comes from the idea that this woolly din actually has any discernible low end. The delayed laugh comes from imagining this git's reaction if you put a King Tubby record on his stereo and ratcheted up his precious graphic equaliser. You're so busy laughing you barely notice that we've swung round to look at a glass egg that is the plot's major *deus ex machina*.

Mom and Pop continue to stare us down and nag us right into the airport while casually revealing the visit from a Princeton college admissions officer that will also become key later in the movie. Whether your parents were wealthy WASPs or not, the scene revives every painful, relentless, 'No shit, Sherlock' lecture you ever received from parents who didn't trust you (and usually had good cause not to). The first time you watch *Risky Business*, you get off on the story, the gags and the satire. The second time, you start to trip on what a scriptwriting masterclass *Risky Business* is, with its carefully arranged foreshadowings and unforced but memorable language – 'The preponderance of bass, perhaps' is just beautiful – and, when you clock that the excellent direction illuminates the screenplay while never distracting from story and character, like a truly great musician serving song before self, you start to wonder why writer and director Paul Brickman never became a superstar film-maker. The guy even directed one of the most-imitated scenes of the 1980s ... a minute or so of punch-above-its-weight imagery that invented the Tom Cruise we know and love to taunt about his sexuality.

When left alone at home, the first thing Cruise's Joel wants to do, naturally, is emphasise the preponderance of bass on that expensive stereo. Cue a scene where Tom Cruise dances and mimes to the unlikely strains of Bob Seger's 'Good Old Rock 'n' Roll', a piece of workingman's bar-room boogie chosen to confront the antiseptic perfection of Joel's suburban home and Joel's repressed urge to be naughty ... but not too naughty. Famously, Cruise slides into frame on socked feet, stops, back to camera, in Elvis pose, and mimes to the song using a candle-stick as mic and wearing just pink shirt, white socks and a tiny pair of white briefs, which initially make him look tantalisingly naked.

I still think the young Cruisemeister in knickers is more likely to turn on an ageing queen who's got a Jones for twinks who look like soldiers than the teen girls of 1983. But something clicked, because these few glorious seconds made Cruise a star. Cruise improvised the performance, flicking his head around in exaggerated musical theatre style, sinking to his knees in phallic metal homage, jumping on the sofa and miming a man attempting to have sex in missionary position while having 30,000 volts shot through his anus. But he didn't come up with the way the cameras circle up, down and around him, being his dance partner, reflecting the director's absolute delight in what his star has managed to produce from the basic script instruction: 'Joel dances to rock song.'

There is something about the scene which seems to sum up the cinema of the 1980s – the return to short-haired manliness, the get-up-and-go desperation, the swaggering narcissism, and I'm making it sound awful, and it did invent awful things, including *Top Gun*, but it's a scene so short, sharp and rousing that you really do always want to be in the room with Joel/Tom, cheering and applauding and trying out your own knee-drops and candle-stick action.

And the song, stodgy though it is, is just the first of Brickman's many revelations of his true agenda. 'Today's music ain't got the same soul,' Seger wails, and you appreciate the delicious irony of Brickman's anti-'80s discourse inventing the 1980s' most stupefyingly shallow icon of white male yuppie triumph even while he was attempting to use all its visual signifiers to damn the whole Reagan era.

The following short scene further illuminates Brickman's point. Joel and his friends are in a diner. They are talking about someone they know who has got into Harvard, and how much money he, and hopefully, they, are likely to be making sooner rather than later. Joel haltingly questions their values. When they ask what he wants to do, he says, 'Serve my fellow mankind.' But before he has even finished the phrase, the shy, serious expression has started to break into the shit-eating smirk we would come to know only too well. His mates laugh approvingly at his self-mockery, and jolly good yuks are had by all. But Cruise has done enough, with a face that moves from flickering fear of exclusion to relieved resignation to the demands of the pack, to let us know that he is severely troubled by the destiny he is expected to fulfil. It isn't just these friends or his teachers or his parents who expect him to be a self-serving prick. It's the whole of

America. What option does he have but cynicism? You feel the weight of the whole Reagan era on the souls of potentially decent American kids in the '80s in this tiny, almost incidental scene. That's how good Cruise and Brickman are in *Risky Business*.

It reaches the point where every scene is a fiendishly clever, dark laugh. The bit where one of Joel's horrible mates brings his girl round to fuck in his bedroom because they know his parents are away is a sly nod to Billy Wilder's *The Apartment*, another great anti-corporate comedy. When Joel and business studies partner Barry (Bronson Pinchot) get tired of listening to the upstairs grunt 'n' groan, we see an automated garage door rise precipitately, a sexy muso-funk lope taken straight from a car ad slams in, and we are staring at the back of a gleaming Porsche. The car backs a little towards us. It stops, and so does the music, abruptly. Joel has stalled the car, and we're reminded that, no, actually, this isn't an ad for a Porsche lifestyle, and the sound design is so exquisitely timed, the wink at us gets another laugh. Genius, really. And we haven't even got to the meat of this matter, so best I stop stalling.

As we've learned from the film's opening scenes, Joel Goodson (geddit?) is a mediocre and well-behaved upper middle-class student who is near-traumatised by failure anxiety and so obsessed with sex that he has weird dreams about naked women in showers. When his parents go away without him, he is encouraged by his cleverer and wilder friend Miles (Armstrong) to invest the money his parents left him in a wild night with a hooker. After a false start with a black transsexual (memorably portrayed by Bruce A. Young), he purchases a night of sin with Lana (the spectacularly good de Mornay), who, as well as possessing all the right moves, also gives a passable impression of a non-sex-industry-employed cute blonde who actually likes him. Being a gauche motherfucker, Joel leaves Lana in the house alone and comes back to find that his mother's fabulously expensive Steuben glass egg has gone. When he tracks Lana down to retrieve it, he soon becomes a junior yuppie-in-peril as Lana's greasy pimp Guido (Pantoliano) chases him with a gun.

Various sneaky plot points – including a growing hands-across-the-classes bond between Joel and Lana, and the accidental dumping of the Porsche into Lake Michigan – lead to the inevitable, when, in order to make enough money to repair the car, Lana and Joel transform his house into a brothel. But even though Lana is giving Joel a crash-course in the sharp end of supply-side economics that his business teachers only theorise about, there is one major crasher at the profitable sex party. Remember that Princeton admissions officer? Joel didn't. Now transformed from nerdish innocent into shades-wearing flash bastard, Joel is forced to conduct a humiliating interview about his future education in the midst of an illegal orgy. While the Princeton man investigates the madness, Joel and Lana disappear and have sex on a train.

When Joel returns, he finds that Guido has burgled the entire house and is holding the contents to ransom. But Joel has made enough money as a pimp to pay the ransom, fix the car and get it all sorted before Mater and Pater return. It turns out that the Princeton man was very impressed by his entrepreneurial skills after all, and grants Joel admission. All's well that ends well. Until Ma notices the tiny crack in her Steuber egg ...

The ending of *Risky Business* is a fascinating story in itself. Brickman originally conceived of an anti-climax where Joel fails to repair the damage and get into Princeton, and he and Lana sit on a roof and talk about the disaster. The studio did one of those director-baiting test screenings and demanded a more upbeat ending. So Brickman delivered the 'triumph', but undercut it all with Tangerine Dream's dreamily mournful electronic soundtrack, Cruise's cynical sneer acknowledging the hollow, ironic victory of getting into Princeton by giving the admissions officer free sex with prostitutes ('Princeton can *use* a guy like Joel. His exact words!' Joel's father pants delightedly), and a final Joel–Lana scene in a restaurant that quietly accepts that the enormous gap between their prospective futures means that they will never see each other again. Clips of the school's Future Enterprises awards, where students are congratulated for making profits of $850 from paper-towel holders, are mocked by Joel's helpless concern for Lana's real-world capitalist concerns of prostitution, violent pimps, daily degradation, all conveyed with almost no dialogue, and no grand-stand emoting.

Still not 'upbeat' enough. Cue a further, short tacked-on bit where we see Lana and Joel walk through a park, behaving like boyfriend and girlfriend, joking merrily about the rules of selling your body for chump change as they stroll off into the Chicago night. It's a travesty. Brickman gets to get half of his way in the 25th anniversary edition of *Risky Business*, presenting the second version as an 'alternate ending' without the entirely phoney park bit.

The first time I saw *Risky Business*, I was surprised that Tom Cruise had ever been so good in anything, and shocked that a film that I'd always thought was a nasty frat-boy sex comedy with added Cruise-in-Ray-Bans appeal was so good. The second time I watched it, the penny dropped and I realised that the movie is a masterpiece. Imagine, perhaps, that some sensible person had wrested *Wall Street* from Oliver Stone's sledgehammer grip and given it to Michael Mann. Or that someone had persuaded Mike Nichols to remake *The Graduate* for sadder, harder, greedier times.

The final irony lies in the ensuing career trajectories of writer/director and star. Tom Cruise went on to become Tom Cruise. And no wonder. The wonderfully adult, complex chemistry with Rebecca de Mornay. The brilliance of his comic reactions in the hilarious Porsche-in-the-lake scene, and the tragic vulnerability he displays when he runs to Lana for comfort. The entire transition from anxious *ingénue* to slick swaggering pimp is really something very special. But Brickman directed just one more obscure movie and wrote little besides. What happened?

Well, obviously, I have no idea whatsoever. But a piece of info included on the *Risky Business* trivia thread at the Internet Movie Database (www.imdb.com) keeps worrying away at me as these kind of things sometimes do. According to this, the failing sunglasses brand that is the Ray-Ban Wayfarer multiplied its sales by 2,000 per cent after *Risky Business* became a hit among teens. In the movie, Brickman uses Cruise's donning of the shades as a signifier of hubris and loss of innocence. But on the successful publicity poster they just look like something that makes a screen stud look even studlier, and that's what Reagan's materialist teens took away from *Risky Business*.

So Hollywood could obviously *use* a guy like Paul Brickman. But, considering the utter loathing for corporate values that power this brilliant movie, perhaps just the once.

* *

MEANTIME

1983

Starring: Phil Daniels, Tim Roth, Gary Oldman, Marion Bailey, Pam Ferris, Alfred Molina, Jeff Robert, Tilly Vosburgh
Dir.: Mike Leigh

Plot: Thatcher's teens, in all our ugly glory.
Key line(s): *Hayley*: 'What you been doin'?'
Colin: 'Nuffin.'
Hayley: 'Ain't you bin out?'
Colin: 'Nah.'
Hayley: 'Just stayed in?'
Colin: 'Yeah.'
Hayley: 'Did ya?'
Colin: 'Yeah.'

Meantime is Mike Leigh's most underrated film, perhaps because it was made for British television rather than cinema. It showcases three iconic young English actors at their peaks. It's a bracingly accurate document of a time and place – Bethnal Green, East London, 1983 – we know as Thatcher's Britain. It is made from the angst of its time – unemployment, generation gap, council estates, demoralised working-class victims, racism, government leaving the youth on the shelf – yet rejects preaching and anger in favour of bitter comedy and Leigh's ability to take our boring, mundane selves and make us worthy of being watched. It's the perfect bookend to the explosive sensationalism of *Made In Britain* (see p. 210), because, while Leland and Clarke's Trevor is a vision of just how bright and bad alienated British youth can get, Leigh's three hopeless losers are what most alienated British youth are ... ugly, awkward, rootless, inarticulate or, in the case of Phil Daniels's Mark, bright enough to occupy the high moral ground but too frightened of failure to make that into anything meaningful.

 Meantime also scribbles a strange footnote into the margins of pop; Graham Coxon of Blur happily admitted that his dress and demeanour during his band's peak years was heavily influenced by

Tim Roth's Colin, an open-mouthed, spittle-flecked semi-autistic kid with learning difficulties, dressed in NHS specs and a green parka more muddy than moddy. And how the hell the boy made that work says something about why Blur were the best thing to happen to British guitar pop since The Smiths, who were, after all, led by a man who made glam style out of a hearing-aid. We Brits are at our best and most subversive when we align ourselves with the damaged and distressed.

Meantime begins with one family visiting another. The boys Colin and Mark are forced to tag along with miserable mum Mavis (Ferris) and dad Frank (Robert) to the suburban home of Mavis's sister Barbara (Bailey) and her successful husband John (Molina). Within minutes we have a complete picture of every major character quirk and every dimension of division between this family rent asunder by social mobility and lack of same. While Mavis and Barbara fight to be in control of the environment, pompous John lords it over the weaselly, sneering Frank with talk of home improvement. Mark is a permed and bespectacled Johnny Rotten with a '70s footballer moustache, saying no to everybody and everything, intent on making everyone as uncomfortable as possible. Colin is a shuffling, confused child who shrinks away from Mavis's offhand physical abuse like a kicked dog. The small, dark, bland interiors seethe with the conflagration of competing economic and family resentments.

And the miracle of this scene? It's funny. Not *American Pie*, snort-beer-out-of-your-nose funny . . . but comically resonant of the swirl of petty jealousy and neutered rebellion that is family life among the working and lower-middle class of England. It's a house you've been to, and people you know, and, if you're very lucky, you're laughing at the fact that you've escaped. Or laughing darkly at the fact that you haven't, not really.

While the Pollocks return to their hellish high-rise, and the boys regale their depressed parents with punk rock, Barbara and John get ready for bed and represent two sides of '80s Toryism. John is Thatcherite self-interest, toadying to his boss and urging that his wife's nephews should stand on their own two feet. But Barbara is a One Nation Tory . . . she believes that they – or at least, she – can fix the broken members of her family with benign condescension. Barbara is lonely, makes mistakes, talks down to people, competes with her sister. But she is the adult heroine of this piece. She believes that things can be changed for the better. She means well, and she means it.

But most of *Meantime* is taken up with scenes of council estate life for the young unwashed and unwanted. Dole queues and their attendant humiliations. Sticky-floored pubs and weak lager. Piss-stinking lifts and bleak launderettes. And a skinhead mate called Coxy who Gary Oldman gets so brilliantly right that special Channel 4 Services To Yoof Oscars should have been invented in his honour.

Unlike *Made In Britain*'s Trevor, Coxy is an idiot. Most skinheads were. They made friendships through bullying. They adopted racist attitudes because that's what people who wore lace-up boots and those hideous ballpoint pen tattoos did. They were never comfortable until someone else was tense, but when anyone finally stepped up to them, and they had no back-up, they were pathetic cowards. They could be a laugh sometimes, because of their energy and mischief. They could relieve your boredom. But if they sucked you in they would immediately make you regret it, mood-swinging, under influence of cider or solvent abuse, towards random violence at the flick of a mysterious mental switch. They always had an abusive father and a pathetic mother, and you tried to pity them. But their answer always seemed to be to play that scenario out again and again, but with themselves in the Daddy role, and they could hone in on someone weaker and needier than them with an unerring eye for the possibility of wielding arbitrary power. They weren't like Trevor, in the end, because Trevor had purpose, even if that purpose was sheer nihilism. They just existed to make someone feel worse than themselves, and made you wonder how you had become masochistic enough to let them into your life.

Gary Oldman, as the gobbing, flobbing, belching and squelching Coxy, is every one of those lost and worthless boys.

Oldman hits his peak in a lift. Coxy and Colin are going to visit Hayley in her high-rise flat, and enter a lift with a young Jamaican man pushing a pram. Coxy begins to goad the man with crap racist jokes. Eventually, when he ventures the word 'coon', he gets the violent reaction we thought he wanted. But ... he's used to people backing down, because of the haircut, the boots, the uniform. This man has called his bluff. Oldman's face ... the terror, the shock, the way that he visibly regresses from young man to small boy, is one of the finest pieces of dialogue-free reaction you'll ever see. Even as you cheer the racist being put in his place, you see, in Oldman's eyes, a full picture of the violence that he's endured and that he is attempting to ape. No back-story needed. Truly stunning. Oh . . . and you should keep an eye on the black guy's pram, too. It isn't just a prop.

Eventually, among the short vignettes about bitching teens and gambling mums, Special Brew and staring at the telly, launderettes and unwanted pregnancies, and jumpers and cardigans so spectacularly ugly that times have come full circle and they're now highly sought-after fashion items on the mean streets of nearby Shoreditch, a story emerges through the fug of mean times.

Colin has a crush on Hayley, played by beautiful, baleful Tilly Vosburgh, (a sort of female James Bolam whose I-hit-bottom-then-things-got-worse demeanour has lit up British TV for years without ever getting the woman her due), but Hayley has an unfortunate, sado-masochistic thing for the bullying Coxy. Meanwhile, Barbara tries to provide employment for Colin by offering him money to paint her and John's semi-detached palace in leafy Chigwell, an attempt at patronage that the anarchistic Mark can't leave unpunished because, despite apparently living to humiliate his damaged brother, Colin is, in truth, the only thing he loves. But Mark and Barbara have an intellectual connection, and he, and we, finally see the full horror of her bored suburban life. And everything comes down, in the end, not to an epiphany, nor money from the sky, nor even coming of age and escape from these two different but connected prisons. But one bespectacled, abused boy screaming the words, 'Shut Up!' In a world where absolutely no one is capable of making themselves understood, the only freedom is the freedom to scream. And shave your head, regret it, and remind the audience that just a few months earlier you were playing the hardest skinhead on Earth.

Leigh's genius lies in his ability to see the natural comedy in the bleakest scenario. At one point, four people who hate each other all trying to use the one toilet in a tiny corridor in a hideous flat becomes a beautifully choreographed parody of bawdy French farce – you know, someone heads out of a door and just misses someone coming out of another door, that sort of thing. You're watching lives that have no hope of improvement, but you're too busy chortling and vibing off the brilliant acting to feel despondent. Daniels and Roth are especially extraordinary, completely subverting their charismatic rebel breakthrough roles in *Quadrophenia* (see p. 180) and *Made In*

Britain (see p. 210). Roth's walk here – a comic, fall-forward stagger – is as powerful and bold a statement as Trevor's malevolent wide-boy swagger.

You come out of Leigh's best work – *Abigail's Party, Nuts In May, Life Is Sweet, Secrets And Lies* – feeling strangely uplifted by grim truths and cramped lives, as if pessimism can be as inspiring as optimism, as long as you adopt that mustn't-grumble, chin-up, never-say-die spirit, and laugh at yourself. A surreal scene in the Pollock flat defines the freewheeling spirit.

Barbara has come round to make her offer to Colin but is interrupted by the sudden arrival of a stranger. He's a good-looking, youngish guy with a college scarf and kind eyes, who says 'Hi' in that submerged posh, Hush Puppie way that says, 'Hello. I'm a hippy elitist. I'm now going to control your life and make you grateful for it.' Richard Branson and Tony Blair took this voice all the way to the top.

Bizarrely, he's the bloke the council have sent round to sort out the flat's broken window. Obviously, he's not going to actually fix the window. But he's not going to just do the paperwork either. He's a Zen council worker.

He crouches in the lounge because he doesn't like chairs. He flirts with Barbara and says things like, 'We're all old. We're all young. Yeah?' He gets into an argument with her about whether economics is money, or power, or both, and seems hugely reluctant to leave. And then, when he's resigned himself to having to concentrate on his job and move on, he treats the assembled to a tortured analogy about single grains of sand eventually becoming anthills. Andrew Dickson's wonderful, dreamy piano motif plays, the Pollocks look bewildered, and I remember why I didn't become a social worker. He finally leaves, and Colin stares at his mother and asks, 'Have we got ants?' Gotta have a punchline.

No one laughs at their own uselessness quite as heartily as The British. I wonder if that's what's happened to the teen gangs who held up England for trainers and cellphones in August 2011. They've forgotten how to laugh at failure.

★ ★

THE OUTSIDERS

1983

Starring: C. Thomas Howell, Ralph Macchio, Diane Lane, Matt Dillon, Patrick Swayze, Rob Lowe, Emilio Estevez, Tom Cruise, Glenn Withrow, Leif Garrett, Tom Waits
Dir.: Francis Ford Coppola

Plot: The Brat Pack as the world's prettiest teen gang.
Key line: 'Stay gold, Ponyboy. Stay gold.'

At the time, what immediately impressed about going to see *The Outsiders* was that it was a Francis Coppola movie. Now, it's hard not to be staggered by the cast. The greatest triumphs of Cruise, Swayze, Lane, Dillon, Lowe, Estevez et al. were largely ahead of them. But so many famous faces in one young ensemble cast pays quite some tribute to Coppola's star-spotting abilities. The fact that *The Outsiders* was made before anyone even coined the The Brat Pack phrase yet ranks high among the best work of any of its stars says a lot for his abilities as an actors' director, too.

The movie exists because of a unique teen fantasy wish-fulfilment. A group of students from the Lone Star Elementary School in Fresno, California wrote to Coppola urging him to make a film of their favourite book. S.E. Hinton's 1967 novel *The Outsiders* is the first of five extraordinary coming-of-age tales the female author based in her hometown of Tulsa, Oklahoma. Coppola read it and fell so heavily in love with its poetic view of class-based teen gang warfare that he shot adaptations of both *The Outsiders* and Hinton's 1975 novel *Rumble Fish* (see p. 229) on location in Tulsa over a few feverish months in 1982. But even though *The Outsiders* was and continues to be a huge bestseller in print, and both films were acclaimed, they flopped commercially, hastening the collapse of Coppola's Zoetrope production company and ending Coppola's imperial phase that was launched by *The Godfather*.

Why *The Outsiders* fared even less well than *Rumble Fish* at the box office remains a mystery. It's a beautiful piece of magical realism that takes our romantic attachment to teen gangs full of sexy, misunderstood boys to its operatic conclusion. But it and *Rumble Fish* are *auteur* films, full of the self-indulgent visual and sonic flourishes that that implies, at a time when Coppola's old friends and protégés Steven Spielberg and George Lucas had re-introduced the world to old-fashioned, bombastic cinematic storytelling. Coppola's under-valued twins were, indeed, outsiders.

Set in a 1960s that still looks like the 1950s, the story concerns the war between working-class gang The Greasers from the northern and wrong side of the tracks, and their preppy rivals The Socs (pronounced 'soashes', as in short for 'socials') from the posh south-side. Imagine *National Lampoon's Animal House* with evocative light-ing and without the zit and tit gags.

Ponyboy Curtis (Howell) and Johnny Cade (Macchio) are junior Greasers, sensitive kids following somewhat reluctantly in the foot-steps of Ponyboy's older brothers Darry (Swayze) and Soda (Lowe), and obnoxious hard nut Dallas 'Dally' Winston (Dillon). Ponyboy's parents are dead and Darry is now Daddy of the house, which makes him the authority figure to be rebelled against. Darry and Sodapop aside, the boys do what movie boys of that era do: hang around, go to the drive-in and the soda bar, hassle small children and girls, wear t-shirts and jeans and leather jackets and grease on their hair and fags behind their ears in order to look cool and mean.

But juvenile delinquency is plumb outta hand in old Tulsa. Johnny's paranoid because a Soc recently slashed his face with a knife, and everywhere you go some group of kids are shoving some poor loner or weedy-looking boy around, or threatening to. So when rich kid Bob Sheldon (Garrett) catches Ponyboy, Johnny and Two-Bit (Estevez) walking his girl Cherry (Lane) home from the *Beach Blanket Bingo/Muscle Beach Party* double-bill, Greaser–Soc tensions are ratcheted up a notch or twenty.

Eventually Ponyboy is set upon by Socs and poor, introverted Johnny stabs Bob and kills him. Johnny and Ponyboy head out on the lam, holing up in an abandoned church, homoerotically bonding over bleaching Ponyboy's hair blonde, *Gone With The Wind* in novel form and Robert Frost poetry. But, while out grabbing a meal with Dally and talking about turning themselves in, a party of school children invade the church and accidentally start a fire. Our three heroes rescue the kids but Johnny suffers severe burns and a broken back.

Despite his injuries and heroism, Johnny is still charged with manslaughter for the killing of Bob. While Johnny lies in hospital, The Greasers and The Socs have a huge rumble which is so balletic, sweaty and rain-soaked it resembles some kind of mud-wrestling soft-porn movie for female Swayze and Cruise fans. The Greasers win, but, by now, even successful violence has been exposed as an exercise in futility.

Johnny dies a saintly death. Dally goes mental and gets shot after robbing a shop. And the movie ends it where it begins: with Johnny writing a school essay about the whole tragic melodrama.

A number of things make *The Outsiders* a magical movie experience. One major one is Coppola's immersion in Americana and rock 'n' roll myth. The tale is played out to a soundtrack of chirping crickets and lonesome train whistles and the sound of Them's 1964 hit 'Gloria' (yep, I know Van Morrison's Irish. But this record is an outsider's view of what being young and American is, and is therefore more American than something American, and absolutely perfect for this movie).

Coppola's prodigiously talented cast look like the embodiment of doomed American youth, captured so poignantly and prettily that, unlike the characters in *American Graffiti* (see p. 135), you can't imagine them ever growing old. The boys' faces are haunted and hunted, but gorgeously. It isn't the pain in the story that moves you. It's the aesthetic qualities of how that pain is made to look.

The whole movie glows and flickers, very much like the deep night would when illuminated by movie lighting. Perhaps the major reason for the film's failure – along with that of *Rumble Fish* and Coppola's love letter to Hollywood romance *One From The Heart* – is that *The Outsider* is a movie about movies. Coppola makes no attempt to make things feel 'real'; instead, *The Outsiders* is a stylised amalgam of and tribute to every angst-ridden American teen film we've already covered, and especially *West Side Story*, *Rebel Without A Cause*, *The Wild One*, *Blackboard Jungle*, *The Last Picture Show*, *American Graffiti* and *The Warriors*. It's the first meta-teen movie. And, as such, it was just too much of an art film to attract an actual audience of real '80s teens and compete with the likes of *Back To The Future* and *A Nightmare On Elm Street*. Those who saw it were adult film buffs. In that sense, the movie it and *Rumble Fish* are closest to – in spirit and commercial fate – is 1981's *The Loveless* (see *Popcorn*), Kathryn

Bigelow's surreal and homoerotic homage to biker movies, which also got some critics excited but died a box office death.

Incidentally, if you watch the film and wonder how Stevie Wonder could have written a theme song as awful as 'Stay Gold', look at the credits and you'll notice that Wonder wrote only the lyrics. The music, like the movie's overwrought score, was written by Coppola's brother Carmine. You've got to hand it to old fat Frank: he's a man who puts family loyalty way beyond the health of his films. You've seen *The Godfather 3*, right?

★ ★

RUMBLE FISH

1983
Starring: Matt Dillon, Mickey Rourke, Nicolas Cage, Diane Lane, Vincent Spano, Chris Penn, Dennis Hopper, William Smith, Laurence Fishburne
Dir.: Francis Ford Coppola

Plot: A nerd's love-letter to cinematic juvenile delinquency. Key line: 'If they can get The Motorcycle Boy, they can get anyone.'

Francis Ford Coppola's second S.E. Hinton adaptation (see *The Outsiders*, p. 226) is a guilty pleasure. It is, in many ways, a laughable movie, and people laughed at it. It cost $10 million to make, and only took $2 million at the box office. It pretty much killed off Coppola's Zoetrope production company. It was booed when first shown at the New York Film Festival. Its visual overload is in direct relation to its lack of genuine emotion.

It's a film packed with directorial gimmicks: high contrast *chiaroscuro* monochrome; sudden gratuitous deep focus; seasick Steadicam; shadows and light plucked from Orson Welles, German expressionist silent cinema, John Ford, *film noir*, French new wave and Bogdanovitch's *The Last Picture Show* (see p. 117); constant rock show smoke that looks like it blew over from the set of *The Warriors* (see p. 175); shots of land and skyscapes composed of *Koyaanisqatsi*-style time-lapse photography, charting the passage of clouds or the journey

of the sun in gorgeous but irrelevant seconds. Its most famous visual
conceit? The Siamese Fighting Fish – the 'Rumble Fish' of the title –
shot in lurid colour as they swim in a pet shop tank surrounded by
nothing but black and white. Add to this, the final, utterly confounding element . . . the ersatz biker soundtrack of rock 'n' roll hits
that the entire movie screams to dance to, replaced by a modern, art
rock-jazz-reggae soundtrack of drums, bass and pianos by Stewart
Copeland of The Police, often mixed so loud that it obscures the
conversation of the characters.

There is no way to be neutral about all this. You either fall helplessly
in love with the bravura visual aesthetic and sheer inappropriateness
of everything – or you write it off, within minutes, as one of the most
soullessly pretentious vanity projects that a major director has ever
indulged himself with.

And, as *Rumble Fish* is here, I guess you know which side I'm on.
There are a few reasons, but only one really good reason. And that
reason would be Mickey Rourke.

Rourke's Motorcycle Boy is one of the coolest ciphers ever put
onscreen and asked to mumble incoherently. *Rumble Fish* is so much
about his charisma that Coppola even places him completely out of
time, visually, from the rest of the movie. While every other character
in this Tulsa, Oklahoma-based melodrama dresses like '60s kids who
never got over the '50s, Rourke's spiky hair, ragged stubble, plaid
shirt and tweed jacket with upturned collar is pure New York punk
scene circa 1977.

He is also a Ninja, if Ninjas were obsessed with Marlon Brando.
He beats up all-comers without getting a hair put of place while
constantly making Zen-like pleas for peace. And he's so skilled with
a motorbike that, if he wants to beat someone up, he just skips off
the hog and lets it hurtle into the intended victim, sending him
somersaulting into the air.

Those who only know Rourke from his recent post-comeback
movies will, I suspect, be genuinely shocked when they get the first
Rumble Fish close-up of the loony New Yorker. You've only seen him
as a monster in *The Wrestler* and *Sin City*, using the face rendered
hideous by his bizarre boxing career and extreme plastic surgery as
a way into *Beauty And The Beast* roles. But at 32 (he was playing a
21-year-old), he was stunningly handsome; the kind of laconic, lazily
amused, gently androgynous face that you just want to look at, even

when its barely doing anything. Coppola announces his arrival off-screen and then slams into a close-up ... and you got, at the time, some idea of what it must have felt like to be young and to see Presley, Brando, Dean or Montgomery Clift for the first time in the 1950s ... to look at a boy who looks like The Future.

Things didn't go too smoothly for any of those four so Rourke ended up in a fine tradition. He made awful films like *9½ Weeks* and *Angel Heart*, he went mental, no one would hire him, he decided to become a (terrible) professional boxer, he destroyed his face in what seemed like a dedicated mission not to be what fans of *Rumble Fish* and the excellent *Diner* wanted him to be. So here is the only place where you really get to see the short-lived myth that was Mickey Rourke: Next Big Thing.

What 'happens' in *Rumble Fish* is that Rusty James (Dillon) and his mates Smokey (Cage) and B.J. (Penn) fight, while his girl Patty (Lane) and his sensitive, intellectual, bespectacled friend Steve (Spano) worry. Rusty James's brother The Motorcycle Boy (no other name present or necessary) used to lead the gang but now heads off to who-knows-where (he says California, all-American symbol of sex, sun and freedom) on his sickle. But he has returned to the hood, much to the chagrin of evil cop Patterson (Smith).

The Motorcycle Boy wants Rusty James to leave the gang life. He is enigmatic, withdrawn, occasionally prone to getting all sweaty and twitchy when no one but a fish-eye lens is looking. So everyone thinks he's gone nuts. They go to visit alcoholic Dad (Hopper, chowing down on innocent scenery like only Hopper can) who posits the theory that The Motorcycle Boy takes after absent Mom ... that is, too mystical, intelligent and ephemeral to hang around with born losers like him and Rusty James. The boys get into more fights.

The Motorcycle Boy is obsessed with those colourful Rumble Fish in the pet shop window, what with them being things born to fight that have been imprisoned and long to be free. One night, he breaks into the pet shop to release the fish and the rest of the animals. Officer Pattinson shoots him, as you do when confronted with pet shop desperadoes. Rusty James frees the fishes in the muddy river.

The final shots are of Rusty James on – and if you've been reading thus far, or have a working knowledge of everything influenced by the French new wave, you're way ahead of me – the beach. He has made it to Cali, albeit without his Zen-thug big Brando bro, who sleeps with the rumble fishes.

The look and sound of the characters ... the wife-beaters and bandanas, the broad working-class accents, the glamorised view of being trapped in Nowheresville with lowlifes with colourful names, always reminded me of the New Jersey boardwalk world conjured by Bruce Springsteen on his first three albums, especially when you compare the lyrics of 'Born To Run' with a doomed rebel known only as The Motorcycle Boy ... although it's actually 'Streets Of Fire' that plays in my head while I watch it. It's also a Boy's Own fantasy of the perfect, heroic big brother.

In truth, Coppola's folly was simply a film made out of time. In the 21st century fans of genre and action movies have got used to both rock video and the heavily stylised, impossibly sexy violence of Asian extreme cinema. An audience raised on *Old Boy* or *Battle Royale* (see p. 389) would get *Rumble Fish*, especially if it ratcheted up the blood and guts. But this movie bears no relation to anything else made in the 1980s, not even its soapier twin *The Outsiders*. It's pure spectacle, but without the colourful explosions and emotional manipulations of Coppola's friends/rivals Lucas and Spielberg. It assaults the senses and bypasses the heart.

You can also understand why it got booed in New York. It rejected American film-making tradition completely and gloried in the aesthetic of Jean-Luc Godard at his most brash and existential. It implies that emotions are weak and sentimental, and that visual panache and iconography are all. Even pure exploitation movies, from *The Blackboard Jungle* (see p. 20) to *The Warriors* (p. 175) acknowledged, on some level, that working-class teen gangs were a real problem. Kids really do rumble and sometimes die in tribal battles. Young people are led into lives of crime and addiction that they can't escape from. Adults who do are left physically and emotionally scarred by their experiences. People who live in areas dominated by gangs live in real fear. Despite the elegiac tone of S.E. Hinton's original teen novels, the sad waste of teen gang violence is most of the point.

Coppola is patently uninterested in any of this. Gangs simply exist to enable Coppola to shoot fights full of hot young boys throwing shapes choreographed by Michael Smuin, a co-director of the San Francisco Ballet. The knives that take children from their parents glint beautifully in the spotlight and sing when they are unsheathed, like swords in Samurai movies. The characters are barely characters ... they exist to look lost and delicious while riding motorcycles, walking down alleys or posing with fags hanging out the corners of their pouty mouths. There is – and I can't believe I'm even writing this in a book where I've tried to find meaningful themes in the likes of *I Was A Teenage Werewolf* and *Dirty Dancing* – absolutely no meaning whatsoever in *Rumble Fish*. So much so that that feels like its USP.

The closest anyone can find to a point to it all is that Coppola meant Rourke's Motorcycle Boy as a loving tribute to his own big brother August. The fact that he has to stamp this onscreen at the end of the end credits is kind of a giveaway ... The Motorcycle Boy is such a stylised amalgam of every mysterious, cool rebel since Dean, Brando, Elvis and Jean-Paul Belmondo that no one could possibly imagine that he was based on a human being.

This really doesn't matter. *Rumble Fish* is a film moulded from our most florid dreams about the sexiness of doomed teenage rebels. What is it rebelling against? The real world, where teens fart, and have zits, and grow up, and Tom Waits isn't the barkeep at the local pool hall. I'm with Coppola.

★ ★

WARGAMES

1983
Starring: Matthew Broderick, Ally Sheedy, Dabney Coleman, John Wood, Barry Corbin
Dir.: John Badham

Plot: Ferris Bueller starts World War 3.
Key line: 'A strange game. The only winning move is not to play. How about a nice game of chess?'

WarGames features the only key line in this book which is uttered by a machine. But the most striking thing, initially, about *WarGames*, is the first two people you see on screen. The two nuclear missile operatives on their way to a personal conflict which leads to America's nuclear artillery being taken out of human hands are Leo McGarry out of *The West Wing* and Mr Blonde out of *Reservoir Dogs*. It isn't just the surprise of seeing Michael Madsen and the late John Spencer playing tiny support roles in a high-concept teen sci-fi movie. More the pleasure of watching The White House Chief Of Staff and a psycho gangster having a natter about Buddhist chanting and growing your own dope. Weird.

This is the only surreal thing about *WarGames*. What distinguished this big commercial and critical hit was how convincingly writers Lawrence Lasker and Walter F. Parkes and director John Badham presented the terrifying idea that a scary new kind of juvenile delinquent called a 'computer hacker' could accidentally trigger a nuclear holocaust. Despite its light, bright, post-Spielberg adventure movie tone, *WarGames* made more people lie awake at night worrying about The Bomb than all those dark nuke movies like *Dr Strangelove* and *The War Game*. It was bad enough when you believed that human life was in the hands of sabre-rattling warmongers. But the idea that humans could be taken out of the equation completely and that annihilation could all be down to one hasty hit of the return button was pretty sobering, particularly when mooted by a film that was largely aimed at children.

The opening non-teen scenes, full of Arctic missile bases, giant computerised maps of the world and the full military might of NORAD (North American Aerospace Defence Command) are key. They present a scenario you are vaguely aware of, but never (want to) think about: that every day of our lives, a couple of ordinary human beings go to a place where they could end the world. They go through their procedures, chatting, perhaps, about growing your own, in denial about what they could, potentially, be asked to do. If you were that person, and, suddenly, the right lights blinked and the correct alarms wailed and you were given the correct codes that confirmed that you were now required, as Mr Spencer says here, to kill 20 million people ... would you do it? Would any halfway sane person simply follow orders and unleash Armageddon? Suddenly, you completely buy the idea that some nutter might decide that this very special job is too important to be given to humans.

After the missile silo scene, we are quickly introduced to *War-Games*' neat twist on Armageddon movie tradition. In earlier films, we generally see the trigger-happy hawkish military man who has to be controlled by the liberal-intellectual man-in-a-suit. Remember that line in *Taps* about the screen's 'insane' military leaders? The speaker of that line, George C. Scott, had played one of the most famous of those military mad men, General Buck Turgidson, in Stanley Kubrick's 1963 satire *Dr Strangelove*.

WarGames turns that familiar schtick on its head and instead goes back to that '50s B-movie favourite, the Mad Scientist. Except that, by 1983, mad scientists aren't loonies in lab coats and they are not yet cuddly Einstein throwbacks like *Back To The Future*'s Doc Brown. They are technocrats. They wear suits. And, in the shape of Dabney Coleman's John McKittrick, they are the extremists who believe that, when it comes to obliterating humanity, humanity should be taken 'out of the loop'.

This is especially clever because, as soon as we meet Barry Corbin's General Beringer, we're sure that he is going to be the Turgidson-style Big Problem. He is fat and dumb-looking. He wears his uniform and puffs out his barrel chest to display his string of medals. He speaks with a southern accent and patronises the well-educated suits around him with down-homeisms like 'we've had men in these silos since before you were watching *Howdy Doody*'. He is the only working-class man in the room and the only one who believes that the fate of the world should, ultimately, be controlled by humans.

Who else can bring this eternal class conflict to a head but a kid? We're soon meeting David Lightman – great name, pointing out his lack of substance while also alluding to the blinking lights of the computers he is obsessed with. David is bright but uninterested in school. He'd much rather use that brain power sitting at home, alienated from real life and healthy pursuits, hacking into his school's computer and making his failed grades into passes. And geniuses who are not at one with society, who spend too much time in fevered isolation ... well, they're a class apart. In no time, his I-can-hack-anything hubris – partly inflamed by his attempts to impress fellow academic refusenik Jennifer (Ally Sheedy) – has wormed its way into the mad scientist's perfect plan and royally fucked it up.

From there, we have a little post-*ET* terror of the military-industrial complex as David is tracked down by the government and accused of being a Soviet spy. We have another, more glamorous, Oppenheimer-esque mad scientist called Professor Falken (Wood), who invented the WOPR (War Operation Plan Response) system, which is programmed to play the war games that have become horribly real. In despair at the realisation of what his invention will inevitably be used for, he is living under the scientist equivalent of witness protection, and has to be shaken out of his resigned nihilism by teen optimism, and brought back to help stop his machine, which he has named after his dead son Joshua, from destroying the world. This computer must have a name because, like cinema's most famous out-of-control computer Hal from Kubrick's *2001: A Space Odyssey*, it has developed a will of its own, but, like many an errant child, without the ability to listen to reason.

And then we have suspense. More suspense than should be possible when you're watching a movie which you know, because of its comedy-thriller feel and David's obvious need to prove himself smarter than the grown-ups *and* be redeemed, is not going to end with the world blowing up. The suspense is built so gradually and expertly by Badham that I feel no guilt at all about giving the end away in the following couple of paragraphs. If you've never seen *WarGames*, trust me, you will still form a deep and lasting attachment to the edge of your seat. But it is a film that can't be written about without reference to its ingenious endgame.

Each attempt to stop Joshua playing the 'game' of a nuclear war between the US and the Soviets has locked it further into a loop where it believes it must finish the game to fulfil its primary objective. Because the misguided McKittrick convinced the President to share his mistrust of human failing, there is now no one in the silos to provide a failsafe. If you just pull Joshua's plug, it assumes that NORAD has been destroyed and launches the missiles anyway. Humanity 'out of the loop' is looking like a seriously flawed idea.

The world is minutes away from buying the farm when David comes up with a bright idea. Joshua is programmed to play games. Perhaps playing one of the games in its system might allow humanity back in.

One of the games is tic-tac-toe, or, as we know it here in Blighty, noughts and crosses. As any school-kid knows, if two people play the game logically, it always ends in a stalemate. What better way to make Joshua understand that some games, like, for example, mutually assured destruction, can't be won?

It's a stunning sequence. As we're carried along by the suspense of Joshua gradually locating launch codes number-by-number, we see, on a giant hi-tech screen, in a room full of soldiers and boffins, a huge game of noughts and crosses that spells out the no-win nature of nuclear war. Finally, Joshua gets the point and, in a spectacular firework display consisting of every possible bomb-dropping strategy that the superpowers could play out, the computer comes to its senses just in the nick of time. Joshua has discovered the essence of futility. And the makers of this smart, thrilling and poignant piece of mainstream entertainment have found a way to explain the utter stupidity of adults in a manner that the smallest child might understand.

The action sequences, largely based around the teen heroes' escape from and then back into NORAD's mountain base, are decent. Broderick and Sheedy are a great deal more charming than your average alienated teen. Badham was not interested in the teen fashion and music of the time, so, ironically, *WarGames* has not dated visually as much as most of its peers. But that is contrasted, amusingly, with unavoidable nostalgia for times when Space Invaders was cutting-edge video game technology and when computer hackers were seen as geniuses rather than annoying bastards that keep forcing you to change your email password. The leads are all solid, fill their archetypes with a little depth, and pull off convincing reactions to imminent disaster quite nicely.

But everything great about *WarGames* is in its initial ideas and the way they are played out in one thrilling room lined with big flashing images. The movie's end leaves you feeling genuinely relieved and a little drained. And it's definitely the only family movie that forces you to wonder who, exactly, has their finger on the button, right now. And, if that finger slipped, whether anyone is still in a position to teach the system the true meaning of noughts and crosses.

★ ★

A NIGHTMARE ON ELM STREET

1984
Starring: Heather Langenkamp, Robert Englund, John Saxon, Ronee Blakley, Johnny Depp, Amanda Weiss
Dir.: Wes Craven

Plot: The bloody birth of Fredward Scissorhands.
Key line: 'I know you too well now, Freddy.'

The first things that strike you about Johnny Depp's film debut are his big '80s hair and his powder-blue tank top. The King Of Cool with a peacock fringe and pastel clothes ... eee-yeww! The second is that, even under those sartorial and tonsorial conditions – the guy looks exactly the same. The guy hasn't aged in 27 years! Is Freddy Kruger *really* more sinister than that?

And the third is that Dorian Depp's first onscreen girlfriend is toothy plain Jane Heather Langenkamp, and within ten minutes ... she's turned down a shag. From Johnny Depp! Forget dream-dwelling serial killers with knives for fingers ... this is where *A Nightmare On Elm Street* really loses credibility.

And the fourth thing is the excellence of the long scene that plays under the opening credits: in an industrial boiler house full of steam, dripping dirty water, filth you can touch ... and a passing lamb. The nursery-rhyme synth music is definitive; the blonde girl in a nightdress a vivid image of innocence and vulnerability. All leading up to the fantastic jump shot, where Fred 'not Freddy yet' Kruger pops up from beneath and behind her. All we know so far is that he has metal attached to his hands and he wears something that is a deep, rich red. How could any of us know that this creep would not just become familiar and famous, but strangely ... cuddly.

Wes Craven, who had already made low-budget cult horror history with *Last House On The Left* and *The Hills Have Eyes*, puts all his cards on the table early. The first act of the film is a breathless scramble of dream sequences, teen dirty talk, blood, guts, teen sex and the subtext about absent fathers, as it's revealed that local tough, handsome cop Lt Thompson (Saxon) is the father of heroine Nancy

(Langenkamp), and that he and Nancy's Mom (Blakley) are divorced and squabbling over whether their adolescent darling is being raised right.

By that time, we've also seen Fred Kruger (Englund), a bogeyman deluxe made of flat hat with brim and filthy red and green-striped sweater, disfigured face, crazy extended arms and metal fingernails that scrape along walls and shred your nerves before he shreds your innards.

And we've also had the first murder . . . and one that immediately raised the bar on teen slasher imagery. That same blonde girl (Amanda Weiss) not just ripped apart by those finger-knives, but lifted by something invisible and thrown around ceiling and walls as she screams in agony and finally expires in a lake of blood. This is the special effects skill and sick imagination of adult horror post-*The Exorcist* applied to a story which rejects the *Black Christmas*/*Halloween* (see pp. 143 and 169) formulas of mysterious stalker and normal killing. Apart from the *grand guignol*, the concept of a hideous monster that can butcher you in your dreams is fiendishly smart because the one thing you can't run away from is your own subconscious. And also, by the end of the movie, you're more frightened by the thought of never being able to sleep again than you are by old Fred.

Oh . . . almost forgot. The girl that gets laid gets killed. The girl that doesn't, doesn't. But, of course, Craven, like every other horror film-maker who has presented this link between female adolescent sexuality and brutal punishment, wasn't trying to push celibacy or abstinence, nor apply any right-wing or anti-feminist morality to his scary movies. Any resemblance to fundamentalist religious nutters, or anyone else who hates the idea of young women feeling free to do what they want with their bodies without guilt or fear, living or dead, is purely coincidental.

This is perhaps the most notorious and curious anomaly of the teen slasher genre, and one that Craven defined here and in the movie that gleefully postmodernised his and every other teen slasher classic, *Scream* (see p. 339). On the one hand, constant sadistic retribution visited on sexually active teen femmes. On the other . . . the monster always finally beaten by The Final Girl. Nowhere does this built-in contradiction play itself out more than *A Nightmare. . .* and especially in the scene where Freddy's finger-knives appear between Nancy's legs while she nods off in the bath. It's scary and funny, but the viewpoint – we watch the scene as if we were right behind Freddy's dangerous digits, poised for soapy cunnilingus – is point-of-view porn before anyone knew what that was.

But perhaps the way to look at A Nightmare... – rather than competitors and inferiors – is to notice how huge a part childhood plays in the texture of the movie. From the recurring 'Freddy's Coming For You' nursery rhyme, to the relentlessly sing-song nature of the soundtrack, to Mommy Thompson's attempts to comfort Nancy with warm milk and toddler talk, to the way that the rooms where the most horrific deaths take place mock the sanctity of a child's earliest private world ... their bedroom. There is something here, in these dreams of experiences the victims aren't ready to face, about mourning the loss of innocence involved in growing up.

Craven had originally envisaged Fred Kruger as an abuser of children. He changed his mind after a series of high-profile child molestation cases in America just before filming began. But perhaps the connection between sex, cynicism and death in A Nightmare... would've have made more sense if his monster had been a paedophile – a man who had stolen the dreams and the innocence of children. There would also have been a little more emotional pull towards the movie's suburbaphobic, anti-right-wing vigilante subtext, what with Fred's somnambulist rampage having been set in motion by the townspeople killing him and keeping it as their own pre-David Lynch dark underbelly secret.

A Nightmare On Elm Street is an average film in many ways. The acting is wooden, the dialogue dull. But none of that matters when Johnny Depp is sucked into a bed and spat out as a geyser of blood. It's a movie about extraordinary special effects, a dark but childlike imagination, deft suspense-and-shock jolts, a wonderfully realised bad guy ... and an unbeatable idea that makes the stuff of nightmares into the stuff of nightmares.

Buffy nicked so much from this movie that it would be fair to call it the bastard daughter of A Nightmare On Elm Street and Heathers (see p. 295) There's no greater compliment I can give. Just don't make me watch any of the Freddy sequels, because therein lies true horror.

★ ★

NIGHT OF THE COMET

1984
Starring: Catherine Mary Stewart, Robert Beltran, Kelli Maroney, Mary Woronov, Geoffrey Lewis
Dir.: Thom Eberhardt

Plot: The only camp post-apocalypse zombie teen feminist comedy sci-fi action thriller – made by film geeks, for film geeks.
Key line: 'Come on, Hector. The Mach-10 sub-machine gun was practically designed for housewives.'

Before the comet changes everything, we are living in a world where teenage girls say to their slutty, cheating stepmothers, 'You were born with an asshole, Doris. You don't need Chuck', and are rewarded with a right-hook that sends them flying, and it's supposed to be funny. And sad. And is. So, as this movie suggests before anything apocalyptic happens … would the end of our world really be so terrible? Especially for kids?

Thom Eberhardt's second feature is one of those classic '80s B-movies about B-movies. One of those movies where, when you see a special effect as awful as the bright red action painting that signals the apocalypse here, you have no idea whether it's due to poverty, ineptitude or ironic homage to the awful special effects that delight us in the '50s sci-fi B-pictures it's so clearly in love with. A movie that jars, but in an entertaining and subversive way, by following, say, a beautifully composed shot of the eeriness of an entirely deserted Los Angeles with a woodenly unfunny one-liner, as if the maker can't make up his mind whether he's Orson Welles or Ed Wood. Because it is, at its roots, a film about films, it is liberally scattered with in-jokes for film buffs, like the vintage poster for Clark Gable and Jean Harlow's *Red Dust* (the comet leaves the sky red and makes us into little piles of red dust), a look and cheesy rock songs stolen from Walter Hill's *The Warriors* (see p. 175), minimalist electronic incidental music filched from John Carpenter (see *Halloween*, p. 169), and entire swathes of its basic scenario from Zombiemeister George

A. Romero (see *Martin*, p. 156). The more nerdy you are about cult movies, the more you feel in on the joke, the more you realise that a movie that looks superficially dodgy is actually very, very good. At times *Night Of The Comet* has nothing more on its mind than playing a cheesy rock instrumental while watching a hot babe ride a motorbike. The gorgeous shots of a completely deserted city pre-date *28 Days Later*. Its all-kicking, all-punching rock 'n' roll teen heroines anticipate Buffy. And there's only one gag-inducing dollop of splattery gore, so it's fun for all the family.

The planet is having a millennium-style street party because Earth is passing through the tail of a comet that last visited us 65 million years ago. No one has noticed that this is precisely the same 65 million years ago when all the dinosaurs disappeared – except the camp and portentous narrator at the beginning of the movie. Los Angeles teen queens Reggie (Stewart) and Samantha (Maroney) survive because both turned down an invite to nasty Stepmom's party; gorgeous, pouting Reggie to have sex with her boyfriend in the projection room of the cinema where they both work, and chubby cheerleader little sis Sam to hide in a shed so she didn't have to watch Stepmom making out with one of the neighbours while their soldier dad is away fighting for truth, justice and The American Way against commie Sandinistas in Honduras. See, Kids ... disobeying your elders could actually save your life!

Before either can get used to the death of everything, they are being attacked by flesh-eating zombies who are still being turned into red dust, but more slowly and hideously. When the sisters hear a music radio show, they head to the radio station to meet the DJ survivor. But there isn't one. It's just a tape (for some reason, the end of the world doesn't stop the electricity working. Who knew?). There they meet Hector (Beltran), a hunky truck driver survivor who, being both hot and working class and therefore naturally decent, is just what a girl needs in a situation like this. Eventually, the trio must save cute defenceless children from a team of scientists who want to harvest the blood of survivors to create a serum that will cure the zombie-dust madness, but only for them, because only geniuses deserve to live.

Scattered in among the scatty plot are the great little digressions that make a dumb action movie into a smart-dumb action movie. For example, there's a poke at the LAPD when Sam has vivid nightmares about being eaten by zombies, but the zombies are always former cops in uniform. And no matter how much comic-book daftness is going on, Eberhardt never neglects the basic ingredients of classic teen angst.

Take the lovely scene in the radio station bunker, where Reggie explains her distant soldier dad's disappointment that she and Sam weren't boys, and the chemical reaction between her and Hector begins to do its slow-burning thing. Hec needs to go back to his native San Diego to see if any of his nearest and dearest have survived. Reggie pleads with him not to go. The sincerity of actors and dialogue is sneakily undercut by the last-dance-at-the-disco lighting and the appallingly cheesy ballad playing on the radio. The scene switches to Sam, sitting alone, watching them, her face full of resentment, and fear, and resignation, and you can feel years of sibling rivalry, and boys that Sam liked only having eyes for her glam big sister. But she then scratches, distractedly, at her shoulder, and we realise that more than her heart might be crumbling to dust.

The scene exemplifies the best of this wee gem of a movie: an uncanny ability to move from monster-movie spoof to coming-of-age tale, from comedy to pathos, from cheap thrills to resonant drama, neatly suggesting, as it does so, that even if the end of the world happened tomorrow, the few survivors would still keep humanity alive by needing, wanting and not getting exactly the same things they craved before the fall.

The army brat back-story also provides deft ballast for the best action heroine moments. We're soon watching Sam, a curly blonde midget in a cheerleader outfit that mocks her every move, handling a machine gun with laconic legs-akimbo aplomb, taking out a car with extreme prejudice. Joss Whedon has never mentioned *Night Of The Comet* among his acknowledgments of where his best *Buffy* ideas came from. But so much of Sam and Reggie survive in the character and look of Buffy Summers that it surely can't be coincidence. Like Buffy, the pair are equally at home kung-fu kicking monster ass or discussing boy trouble, and have the tough-but-vulnerable Buffy ingredients to a tee, including the corny comic-book wisecracks.

The best female bonding moment is also the most explicit nod to Romero's zombie touchstone *Dawn Of The Dead*. Serenaded by a terrible cover version of 'Girls Just Wanna Have Fun', Reggie and Sam play dress-up in a department store where everything is now at a permanent and very generous discount. Sadly, the store's stock boys are now punk rock Bond-villain zombies who can talk, organise, move at normal human speed, handle automatic weapons, and like making arch super-villain announcements over the store intercom. The girls ain't having fun for too long. Eberhardt can't resist mocking Romero too. *Dawn Of The Dead* was famously hailed as a great satire on consumerism because the action was set in a shopping mall. Here, one of the mad scientists just goes right ahead and announces: 'Here's the closest shopping arcade. But the whole area's an absolute monument to consumerism!', thus putting smug critics like me out of work.

Eberhardt also sets himself a little challenge whereby, if you hear a cheesy rock song commenting on the action, well, so do the characters themselves. So much so that, when one perilous action sequence comes to an end, the winning character yells, 'Knock that shit off' and one of his henchmen finally stops the dire shootout music by blowing a radio away with a shotgun.

And a special word about former Warhol and Amazonian and-rogyne Mary Woronov, who plays tragically heroic scientist Dr Audrey White, and is one of my all-time fave under-rated screen presences. She is the kind of deliberately 'bad' acting genius who can let an entire viewing audience into a film-makers' joke just by the way she pronounces the word 'apparently'. Here, she gets her 'And the parallel universe Oscar goes to . . .' moment when she performs the sexiest suicide scene in movie history while wearing shades and a boiler suit.

At the movie's end, Reggie, Hec and the two sprogs they rescue have become a conveniently instant nuclear family. Sam watches them from across the street, contemplating a man-less future and noticing that the four 'look like the Brady Bunch'. The traffic lights are, for some reason, still operational, and Reggie forbids the two children to cross until the proper moment. As Sam questions her sister's sanity, a speeding car screeches around the corner, almost knocking her down. And Sam gets a cute, man-sized present that explains the apparently pointless opening scene involving Reggie, a video arcade game and the letters DMK.

Apart from the agreeably goofy storyline, the wry satirical laughs and the sheer comic-book fun of *Night Of The Comet*, it also cleverly presents a teenager's view of The End Of The World entirely at odds with the bleak vision of *A Boy And His Dog*'s misogynist madhouse (see p. 146). Here, Armageddon is a parent-less anarchist playground where no one owns anything and there are no annoying authority figures to tell you what to do, or control your future. A running joke involves the characters kidding around about giving each other a football stadium or Texas, because there's no military-industrial complex to ensure that anything belongs to anyone any more.

There was no sequel, but in my imaginary *28 Weeks After The Comet*, Reggie, Hec and family provide a non-hierarchical shelter for socialist survivors, while Sam quips away her around America, kicking zombie ass in a cheerleader's outfit she never grows out of. Who says the apocalypse is a bad thing?

★ ★

RED DAWN

1984
Starring: Patrick Swayze, Charlie Sheen, Lea Thompson, C. Thomas Howell, Jennifer Grey, Brad Savage, Harry Dean Stanton, Powers Boothe, Ben Johnson
Dir.: John Milius

Plot: The Brat Pack vs Communism.
Key line(s): 'Who's on our side?'
'Six hundred thousand screaming Chinamen.'
'Last I heard there were a billion screaming Chinamen.'
'There were.'

The incredibly strange *Red Dawn* is a noisy, bad taste essay on resistance fighting. Why resistance is heroic. Who would resist, and why. The actual military details of how to resist a powerful occupying force. It has been compared, with some deliberate mischief, by a conservative writer or two, to the classic 1966 movie *The Battle Of Algiers*, a surgical study of Algerian guerrilla resistance against French occupation which remains a high-point of leftie cinema ... and they have a point. It's a popcorn-trash *Battle Of Algiers*. And it dares to suggest that, if your country is invaded by a totalitarian regime, the hope lies in The Kids.

You've got to appreciate a movie that doesn't fuck around. *Red Dawn* kicks off with four minutes that gives you all the context and back-story you need ... and then gets right on with the killing. We have captions that explain the lead-up to World War III ... the USA isolated by NATO, a failed Soviet wheat harvest, a revolution in Mexico, a Soviet invasion of Poland, the commie armies of Cuba and Nicaragua conquering El Salvador and Honduras. Most amusing of all, the Green Party taking control of the West German parliament and immediately getting rid of all nukes from European soil, because Europe is, as all Americans know, just one single pesky country with different weird accents. And it's always the Germans' fault.

This all begins with a shot of The Rough Riders statue. The Rough Riders were a voluntary cavalry unit set up in 1898 to help Civil War-depleted troops fight the Spanish-American War. Their second-in-command was future President Theodore Roosevelt, and we are given a Roosevelt quote which could serve as a justification for the movie: 'Far better it is to dare mighty things than to take rank with those poor, timid spirits who know neither victory nor defeat.'

We see small-town America waking up on a sunny winter's morning: a paper boy on his rounds, cute kids going to school, empty placid streets that are lent a romantic beauty by the kind of elegiac classical music that often sound-tracked a show like *The West Wing*: a music that oozes a kind of specifically American patriotic pride, offset by a sentimental paternalistic kindness. How America likes to see itself, I guess, when it isn't attaching electrodes to the bollocks of ragheads in Guantanamo.

It then continues with a classroom lecture from a black teacher about the brutal fighting methods of Genghis Khan's Mongol army. He stops talking when he notices that paratroopers are landing on the school playing field, just a few yards away from the window. It is 4 minutes 30 seconds into this mental little movie, and the Soviet invasion of Colorado is already under way.

This is where I sat up and took notice of *Red Dawn*. Like many a lefty, I didn't see the film on release, and never went looking. The critics of 1984 hated this movie, and saw it as evil right-wing propaganda. It was released just as hatred of America was hardening over the militaristic excesses and covert anti-socialist actions of the Reagan administration. The 1983 invasion of Grenada. The 1986 'Contragate' scandal, in which the American military were selling arms to

'Every girl should just hold out for the right girl.' Kristy McNichol learns a valuable lesson from Matt Dillon in *Little Darlings* (Moviestore Collection Ltd/Alamy).

'Tipping the world into war with one Cruise missile.' Tommy boy goes postal in *Taps* (AF Archive/Alamy).

'The world's worst boy: a fearless, nihilistic, articulate, violent force of nature with a Swastika tattooed on his forehead.' Tim Roth in *Made in Britain* (Moviestore Collection Ltd/Alamy).

Gary Oldman as 'the gobbing, flobbing, belching and squelching Coxy'
in Mike Leigh's *Meantime* (Moviestore Collection Ltd/Alamy).

Above: 'The world's prettiest teen gang.' Messrs Estevez, Lowe, Howell, Swayze and Cruise beat up the '80s in *The Outsiders* (Sunset Boulevard/Corbis).

Left: 'The desperate acts of an empty vessel.' Bizarrely awful publicity poster for *Ferris Bueller's Day Off* (Pictorial Press/Alamy).

'The girl that gets laid gets killed. The girl that doesn't, doesn't.'
Bathtime fun with Freddy and Nancy in *A Nightmare On Elm Street*
(AF Archive/Alamy).

'Would the end of our world really be so terrible? Especially for kids?'
Night of the Comet laughs at the zombie apocalypse (Moviestore Collection Ltd/
Alamy).

(CinemaPhoto/Corbis)

(CinemaPhoto/Corbis)

(AF Archive/Alamy)

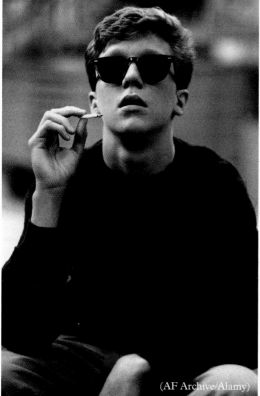
(AF Archive/Alamy)

'Bright, shiny, vibrant playgrounds for the head games of unusually self-analytical, articulate and media-savvy children.' The muse of Hughes reaches its peak in *The Breakfast Club*.

'He's frolicking in the woods with his friend in a cowboy hat, who keeps dropping to his knees and beckoning his penis on.' Kevin Bacon and Chris Penn do a dance called The Brokeback Mountain in *Footloose* (Paramount/The Kobal Collection).

Iran in order to fund Nicaragua's right-wing guerrilla forces. The covert war against Chile's left-wing government. The 'Star Wars' initiative, Cruise missiles and the funding of anti-Soviet fighters in Afghanistan, some of whom went on to be Osama bin Laden. *Red Dawn*'s context for World War III reads like one long, chest-beating justification for American paranoia and the resulting abuses of its power. Add to this its with-a-bullet entry into *The Guinness Book Of Records* as the most violent film ever made (at the time) – 2.23 acts of violence per minute, apparently – and it sounded like *Rambo* as directed by Oliver North. Not a natural cinema choice for a Smiths fan from Brixton.

So I watched it, for this book, for the first time a few months ago. And I was, for no want of a better phrase, blown away. And this scene, where, with the movie barely started, peril falls from the sky while kids sit in a classroom, blithely wondering about what's for lunch and whether Betty Sue will let 'em get to second base this recess, got me on board. *A Nightmare On Elm Street* (see p. 238) might do a pretty convincing job of manifesting the night terrors of the young, but I never had bad dreams about men with black hats and knives for fingers. I did – after learning about the Second World War, Belsen and Auschwitz, Hiroshima and Nagasaki – have childhood nightmares about this: a faceless force, dropping into my world, destroying everything, irrational, unstoppable. I don't think I was alone. Any random listen to pop records made between around 1977 and 1984 betrays a mass cultural fear of World War III. And frankly, when the oblivion begins, does it really matter who started it?

There is something about the invasion in *Red Dawn*, the suddenness and speed, the brutality and surrender, the end-of-life-as-we-know-it-ness of it, that outdoes any alien invasion or war movie you care to name. As soon as those parachutes land, and *Red Dawn* has successfully tapped into a source of primal fear, I'm just not interested in the hysterical pre-Tea Party political views of John Milius and co-writer Kevin Reynolds any more. I don't care. I'm just ... scared.

Besides, no matter your views on right-wing propaganda, *Red Dawn* is, in the end, asking you to believe that the superpowers would simply agree not to fire nukes at each other. That being abandoned by NATO means that the Pentagon would just switch all the radar machines off. And that revolutionary America's toughest guerrilla cell would be led by Patrick Swayze and Charlie Sheen. It's not a documentary.

Milius is pretty interesting in himself. This is the man whose scriptwriting talents provided the world with 'I love the smell of napalm in the morning', 'Do you feel lucky, punk? Well ... do ya?' and 'Go ahead make my day', from the scripts for *Apocalypse Now* and *Dirty Harry*, of course. He also wrote the *USS Indianapolis* bit in *Jaws*. He was the inspiration for the characters of John Milner in *American Graffiti* (see p. 135) and Walter Sobchak in *The Big Lebowski*, has made two films about his hero Theodore Roosevelt ... and invented the cage in Ultimate Fighting Championship (UFC). The man is entirely singular in the American arts – proudly macho, right-wing, pro-war, loves violence – and widely admired by people who aren't. So the fact that his big war film as a director is also a teen movie is both as eccentric and fitting as *Red Dawn*'s inability to decide whether a vision of America being abandoned by the world and left to fight The Axis Of Evil alone (apart from 'England', we're informed, which 'won't last long') is horrifying or the sexiest thing in the world. Perhaps the forthcoming remake (the new invaders are ... North Korea!!! Sadly, it's not being directed by Trey Parker and Matt Stone) will sort out that bit of schizophrenia. Wouldn't bet on it, though. They do love being John Wayne.

Red Dawn occasionally resembles Milius's attempt to remake *Apocalypse Now* in Colorado (actually Las Vegas, location-wise), minus the pretension and the billion-dollar budget. The fact that Milius is nowhere near as accomplished a director as Francis Ford Coppola helps this particular movie. The battle scenes in *Apocalypse Now* looked sexy, remote, exotic. Here, they look like a callous but somewhat flung together army wielding hardware they can barely use, causing chaos in remote fields and streets that look like sets that could be used for *Back To The Future* (see p. 259). It feels like war might feel if it was being waged outside your front door. It's loud and confused. It doesn't lend itself to Doors songs or wry quotes about napalm. It's a weird mix of action movie boys blowing stuff up and what you imagine Beirut or Baghdad might feel like under invasion. It's tasteless. Few directors do the morally right thing and make war look tasteless.

There are so many bombs and explosions that the orchestral soundtrack becomes a 114-minute take on that bit from the 1812 overture where the cannons are firing. Perhaps Ollie North was diverting some of those ill-gotten weapons to Milius. The US military do love him. The operation to capture Saddam Hussein was code-named, you guessed it, Operation Red Dawn. Satire is dead.

But *Red Dawn* is a great film because it's a strange film. And it's strange because it steadfastly refuses to do what it's supposed to. It's supposed to take time introducing you to its teen heroes before the action starts, showing you their teen angst and love interests and making you care about them. The paratroopers take care of that. It's supposed to show you these plucky kids doing *Goonies*-style adventure capers where no one really dies and the peril stays resolutely mild. It doesn't. It gets dark, pessimistic and kills lead characters. And it's surely supposed to end when the great US military machine does its cavalry thing and arrives to save the day and give our heroes a *Star Wars* ceremony moment for having single-handedly scuppered the Russkie Death Star. It really, *really* doesn't do that at all. The Wolverines – so-named after their high school mascot and football team – are overwhelmed by greater power, and have to settle for small, ultimately pointless victories. The cavalry never arrives. The great cities of America are destroyed. The USA remains occupied and enslaved. The end. Damn.

The basic plot is straightforward enough. The Commies take over America. When they hit Calumet, Colorado, a group of teens take to the hills with guns and supplies. When they realise that their families are dead, prisoners or in fear of their lives, they make themselves into organised insurgents. They plan and orchestrate daring raids on the alliance of Soviet and Latin American troops. The only problem is ... they are still kids. Some are braver than others. Some are more stable than others. They are forced to become as ruthless and amoral as the enemy. And, if you're going to be a successful army, those who won't follow orders have to be sacrificed for the greater good ...

The rest is fantastic action scenes and a how-to manual on waging guerrilla war. The pure pleasure of seeing Jennifer Grey (see *Dirty Dancing*, p. 289, and *Ferris Bueller's Day Off*, p. 270) and Lea Thompson (see *Back To The Future*, p. 259), looking as filthy and feral as the boys and wielding sub-machine guns with extreme prejudice, fabulous cameos from Harry Dean Stanton and, especially, Powers Boothe, as every cynical, hard-bitten Viet Vet in movie history rolled into one sneering, doomed ball of existential despair. *Lord Of The Flies*-style meltdowns, traumas, nobilities, betrayals, the initially most scaredy-cat boy becoming the most committed murderer, and one of the most shocking killings anywhere in this book, as befits a group of kids thrown into unbearable circumstances. The film could really have done without one of those scores that insists on telling you how to feel through every scene. But the basic foundation of conservatism is that people are incredibly stupid and must be told how to feel, so big surprise (the most depressing thing about growing into middle-age, for me, was the slowly dawning revelation that the basic foundation of socialism is exactly the same).

Swayze, Thompson and Howell are outstanding, forced to carry a preposterous scenario, and giving it levels of emotional truth that make a potentially dumb film into a compelling, dramatic adventure story. The ending of *Red Dawn* is melodramatic and riddled with clichés about noble deaths and mutual respect between enemy warriors. But it's brave. Foolishly so. Sending American teens out of the cinema feeling that America would inevitably lose if it got invaded? This was a suicidal gambit in the gung-ho '80s. Lea Thompson's closing voiceover says, 'In time this war, like every other war, ended.' But doesn't say who won or lost. The final seconds are a bizarre mix of valediction for all resistance fighters who die rather than collaborate, and immediate camp, as we get closing credits snaps of the cast posing like supermodels doing a military chic magazine spread over pummelling marching band music. Very, very odd.

Yet *Red Dawn* was a reasonable commercial success and has lived on as a cult favourite, gaining the ultimate kudos of warranting affectionate parody by *South Park* and *Family Guy*.

And there is sound battle advice, too. For example, if, after a carefully crafted set-piece raid on an enemy, you find that you have outflanked your shadowy nemesis, and crept up behind him with a gun ... don't pause for a valedictory 'You lose!' Just shoot him. In the back. This is useful survival info for a *Spider Man* and *Buffy* fan, trained to believe that there is always time for a pithy wisecrack before dispatching The Big Bad. In truth, they don't stop to laugh bitterly. They just shoot you.

★ ★

FOOTLOOSE

1984
Starring: Kevin Bacon, Lori Singer, John Lithgow, Christopher Penn, Dianne Wiest, Sarah Jessica Parker
Dir.: Herbert Ross

Plot: Dance missionary Kevin Bacon brings civilisation to Hicktown.
Key line: 'If we let some punk push us around now, before long every standard in the community will be violated!'

When writing *Popcorn*, my book about rock movies, I had a severe mental block about *Grease*. Couldn't think of a damn word to say about it. So I asked my wife Linsay for emergency aid. She's been a lifelong fan of the movie, and kindly agreed to watch it with me and talk about it. I used the resulting conversation as the *Grease* entry. Readers seemed to think that worked pretty well.

So, when I came to a similar impasse with *Footloose*, I went to my family for help again. The problem this time was what I'd already written for *Popcorn* ... an essay which I thought summed up everything about the movie, even if I do say so myself. I had nothing left to say. Enter the cavalry, in the shape of my son Matt Stevens.

Matt knew *Footloose* well. But he read my entry in *Popcorn* and took exception to it. As far as his generation was concerned, he reckoned (he's 24, incidentally), *Footloose* was just '80s kitsch. No subtexts. No themes worth exploring. Just dumb songs and comedy dancing.

So I asked him to watch it with me and allow me to try and persuade him that *Footloose* was more than so-bad-its-good. I failed miserably, I suspect.

> *Me*: I didn't even go to see *Footloose* at the time. I didn't go to see dance movies with silly synth pop songs when I was 21. I took myself far too seriously. I'd just moved to London. It came out in the year I met your mother.
> *Matt*: Well, no wonder you didn't see it! You'd just moved to the big city to find your rhythm and your rock 'n' roll ... The

exact opposite of what Ren McCormack is doing in *Footloose*.
This small town Beaumont is like March. [March is a tiny
town in Cambridgeshire where Matt's mum hails from. It is
Matt's and my shared vision of hell.] Except March hasn't got
those picturesque mountains in the background. But anyway
... that's the point. Everyone's got a concept of what *Footloose*
is without actually watching it.

Me: John Lithgow is brilliant as the Bad Dad, Reverend Shaw
Moore. I'm not sure the film would work without him. Most
actors would just be bug-eyed over the top as the Evil Priest.
But Lithgow's real.

Matt: Would you say Kevin Bacon's good-looking? Was he seen
that way at the time?

Me: He's very good-looking for a man who has a face like a rodent.
He looks like he's constantly gnawing cheese. But I do think
he's charismatic. I will give bad films a chance if Kevin Bacon
is in them.

Matt: With these kind of films, it's always 'small towns' ... but
these towns are fucking huge! Thousands of students and
thousands of young people who all have completely different
likes and dislikes. That's not a small town! [Matt grew up in a
really small town in Suffolk.] This place is like Brighton. If you
can imagine Brighton, right, where all of its young have been
forcibly thrown back to the 1950s. Doesn't Lori Singer look
kinda like Kevin Bacon?

Me: Yeah ... never noticed before, but you're right. The same
strange rat-nose thing going on.

Matt: The stars aren't that beautiful ...

Me: But I think they wanted the audience to relate to the
characters. It's like Jennifer Grey in *Dirty Dancing*; she's not a
conventional pin-up.

*We reach the scene where Ren bumps into aggressive bumpkin
Willard (Chris Penn) and charms him completely with one lame
insult.*

Me: If only it was that easy to turn around the meathead school
bully ...

Matt: You know what I mean? In the real world he would've just
punched him in the face. Is Willard supposed to be a bully?
It's not really made clear ...

Me: No. He looks like one at first glance and then becomes every boy's gay best friend.

Matt: How old are they supposed to be? Bacon and Penn look about 28 . . .

Me: But teens largely weren't cast in teen films until the '90s. The exceptions were the art movies . . . *Kes, The 400 Blows*. But in the mainstream they went for actors in their twenties . . .

Matt: Perhaps that's why they worked so well. The internet has changed things, hasn't it? Back in the '80s you wanted to see these dream worlds. Now we know too much about what's out there, and we need to see kids playing kids' roles because we're addicted to reality. Back then you wanted to believe you could just rebel and dance and everything would just work out, partly because you look older than you actually are. That the world's a better place than it actually is. Today's youth are too cynical for that. Teen films have become bleak. But why do you need films telling us how bleak our lives could be? It's a strange idea.

Me: Sadly, film directors convince themselves that if nobody smiles in a film, it must be deep.

Matt: Ren is like the first Metrosexual, isn't he? He's manly, but understanding. And in touch with his feminine side while doing incredibly gymnastic things on monkey bars.

Me: The chicken race scene is genius. This is such a hick town that they have to race on tractors.

Matt: I dunno. I think a chicken race with tractors is pretty badass.

Me: Badass . . . yes. But not sexy.

Matt: Oh my God . . . they race to 'Holding Out For A Hero' by Bonnie Tyler? I'd completely forgotten about that!

Me: *Footloose* is not lacking in irony.

Matt: But this is also the most homoerotic thing in the movie. Two raging hormonal guys hurtling towards you in tractors to 'Holding Out For A Hero'?

Me: I dunno. I'm not really taking tractors as seriously as you obviously do. It must be all those years living in the country, mate. Tractors just don't have the same sexual connotations to us dashing urban types.

Matt: We were doing it in Suffolk all the time. Fuck sex and Elvis. Break out the scrumpy and drive JCBs at each other. Mind you, if someone had actually suggested that to me at 16 I would've been well up for it ... [There is a very funny long shot which shows just how slowly the tractors are 'hurtling' towards each other] ... OK ... fair enough. They're taking the piss. Tractors go way faster than that, by the way. Also, Ren's tractor is much, much bigger than the other guy's. He's got a huge vehicle ... AHA! Sarah Jessica Parker. The best actress of our time. She was mildly attractive when she was younger, though. Compared to now. When a cartoon calls you a 'transvestite donkey witch', I think that says it all.

Me: That was *South Park*, yeah? But she's a very successful transvestite donkey witch. She's braying all the way to the bank. And she's married to Matthew Broderick.

Matt: Really? And life promised so much for Ferris Bueller.

Me: You're losing focus. Back to *Footloose*. Both Ren and Ariel are completely driven by the need to impress absent fathers ...

Matt: Yeah. But it's a very soft version of adolescence. I mean, Ren's stepfather isn't too bad. The house is quite nice. And no one bullies him at school, despite his Metrosexuality. He's made loads of friends. He's a bit of a wuss.

Me: Ah ... the warehouse scene. The dance routine that shaped a generation. People say that Tom Cruise miming in his pants in *Risky Business* (see p. 215) is the ultimate '80s movie scene. But I think it's Kevin Bacon and his dance stunt-double dancing camply in a warehouse to 'Never' by Moving Pictures. Montage plus bad dance routine plus dodgy synth-rock. It's a triple threat. I mean to say ... at least in *Dirty Dancing* they hired Patrick Swayze because he *could* dance.

Matt: It's not quite *The Black Swan*, is it? But nowadays people expect the commitment and skill that Natalie Portman showed in *The Black Swan*. Any film using a dance double so blatantly now would be laughed out of cinemas.

Me: You say that, but Travolta and Karen Lynn Gorney did their own dancing in *Saturday Night Fever* way back in 1977. *Footloose* is unusual in being a dance movie where none of the leads can actually dance.

Matt: I'm just gonna throw this out there. But ... if I wandered into an abandoned warehouse in the middle of the night and found a guy doing that, I wouldn't be yelling, 'Whooh! Big

Time!' I'd be like, what the fuck? I'm not going anywhere near that guy. And with your whole feminist angle . . . Ariel wouldn't strike me as a feminist icon. She doesn't know who she wants to sleep with. She's in denial. She's naive and scared. That doesn't seem too feminist to me. The opposite.

Me: But in pop movies it's more what you do than what you're driven by. She isn't a girlie girl. She's defiant. She won't be pushed around by men.

Matt: But the men aren't strong enough to push her around. Chuck's a dumb hick, Ren's a girl and Dad's having a mid-life crisis. She's a dominant female in a world of weak men, who doesn't seem to do anything with that power except work out how to fuck someone and get other girls to do her dirty work.

Me: Wow. You're not keen on her, are you? Don't you just love this whole emasculating bit with the train and her ever-present death wish, though?

Matt: I'm more interested in the idea that fun in Beaumont involves just going up to the train tracks and standing there. Whooh! Big time! And that the peril comes from another really slow-moving vehicle.

Me: It's a metaphor for how slowly small-town life moves.

Matt: I see. So she moves to a city, sees a Porsche and just faints dead away. And let's not even think about planes . . . [We reach the scene where Ariel confronts Daddy on the dark sinister staircase in their home] . . . Why is she so scared of him? 'It doesn't get much better' . . . that really is a strange line, isn't it?

Me: That whole scene has a strange sexual undertone I can't quite get to the bottom of.

Matt: I'm gonna put this out there, too: this town doesn't seem too bad. No one has said, at any point, that if you dance you'll be arrested. It seems like the punishment for breaking this law is . . . a really dirty look from an adult.

Me: You're right. At the beginning it promises that the cops are gonna be out there cracking the heads of anyone who taps their foot to a show tune. People are making cracks about the evils of reading and you think Beaumont is going to be a full-on fascist fiefdom. And then . . . mild disapproval is as bad as it gets.

Matt: I'm not really sure what these kids are rebelling against. Religion?

Me: Actually, this scene [Reverend Moore is talking to a group of pensioners about the wonders of living in a small town until you die] is more deliberately scary than anything the law is threatening to do. So many American movies are terrified of small towns. Probably because all the writers live in New York and LA. On the other hand, look at this whole redneck dance bar scene. This is a Utopian vision of what a bar full of drunk country-ass shitkickers in cowboy hats would be like. Except for the total absence of black, brown or yellow faces. That's accurate. What would've happened if Ren had taken them to a rave?

Matt: Their minds would explode. That would be the best comedy scene ever. Bacon and Singer rolling into a hip hop or house club and dancing like that. Personally, I'd be happy in any bar playing *Footloose* by Kenny Loggins. What a song. And I love the idea of a cowboy rock shack where everybody's just dancing and getting along. No bar fights. The floor's clean. Hot girls dancing with fat guys. It's a little vision of heaven. Until Willard starts a fight, of course. Lori Singer grows on you as the film goes on. She might not be conventionally that hot, but she's a good actress playing a character with no inhibitions.

Me: I think John Lithgow and Dianne Wiest are so key as Ariel's parents. They are the big thing this movie has over, say, *Dirty Dancing*. They're so good that they give you this huge sense of back-story: of why their lives have turned out like this, of why Beaumont is like it is. They take corny conservative Mom and Dad and give them dignity and dimensions. They have a tragic air without saying very much.

Matt: Definitely. You buy them. The film really isn't about dancing at all. That's just the sideshow. It's a film about families attempting to grow as people. And someone thought, 'let's have some dancing in it'.

Me: It's an updated '50s teen movie about dysfunctional families and misunderstood teens. At last ... my favourite bit of the movie: Ren teaching Willard how to dance in montage, to the strains of 'Let's Hear It For The Boy' by Deniece Williams. Movie magic.

Matt: You couldn't get more gay if you tried.

Me: See this bit? It's almost like Ren has Willard on a lead . . .

Matt: . . . and Willard is staring at Ren's arse. Bad '80s montages, though: fucking fantastic. Now they're frolicking and gambolling through a field. They're so very much in love. And look at that last Chris Penn gesture . . . 'Take me, Ren! Take me!' How did they get away with this?

Me: Everybody was so hetero in the '80s they just didn't notice. They thought it was innocent macho horseplay. Now, here's the bit where I think they get confused over exactly who The Reverend Moore is. On the one hand, he wants to ban all forms of hedonism, including pop music, dancing and booze. On the other . . . he's a liberal crusader when it comes to book burning and sacking progressive English teachers. I think they needed him to shit or get off the pot at some point, repression-wise. And here's the bit of feminist iconicness from Ariel. Chuck is beating her down but she just keeps getting up and fighting back.

Matt: She does kind of bring it on herself, though. She didn't need to hit him first.

Me: Oh . . . come on. He does call her 'a bitch in heat'!

Matt: Ah! So we should all be beating each other up over words now, eh Dad? 'My, you're a horny dog.' BOOF!!!

Me: You're so literal.

Matt: Whereas, Kevin Bacon's character is very moral. It takes him till almost the end of the movie to even kiss Ariel.

Me: Mate . . . *he's gay*. He may not know it yet. He may not fully understand it. But he's hating every second of that snog. He's picturing Willard.

Matt: I'm not even gonna try to argue. He's frolicking in the woods with his friend in a cowboy hat, who keeps dropping to his knees and beckoning his penis on. Meanwhile, this hot girl is begging him to just kiss her and all he keeps saying is, 'Hey . . . maybe one day.' This is a pity kiss. She's been beaten up by her ex. Her dad hates her. 'Oh . . . let's do her a favour' . . . HAHAHA!!! 'Only fairies dance.' You mentioned that line in *Popcorn*, didn't you? One stray homophobe while everyone else in the school is going, 'Whoo! Dancing!'

Me: I quite like the fact that the big triumphant moment, when they win the right to hold the dance, is quite quiet and muted. Lots of conspiratorial smiling. No whooping and hollering and throwing their hats in the air. Wait a minute . . . where did all The Kids suddenly get motorbikes from?

Matt: So these kids have all got cars, motorbikes . . . and tractors. Is this town really rich?

Me: Beaumont must have been one of those towns that really benefited from farm subsidies.

Matt: And the school is the dream high school. No one's uncool. No one bullies. Everyone just wants to dance. Incidentally, Lori Singer's dress for the dance is *horrible*. Whatever happened to Lori Singer?

Me: This is a recurring theme in this book. Blah Blah is really great in this movie. And then . . . nothing. My theory with Lori Singer is, like a lot of women in Hollywood once they're not kids anymore, she was caught between two stools. She's not a character actress. But she isn't pretty enough to be the romantic lead. The typical thing about lousy, one-dimensional roles for women in Hollywood movies. You're either the sex symbol or Mom. Nothing in-between.

Matt: The beginning of the dance, where they're all too awkward to do anything, is hilarious. The guy who picks his nose and wipes it on his posh trousers. These kids are badly in need of liquor and drugs.

Me: But that gives Ren the opportunity to show them how to have an urban good time . . .

Matt: . . . By clicking his fingers. These kids have never been allowed to dance . . . yet they can break-dance. And body-pop. And do The Robot. Someone's been living a lie.

Me: It's because Kevin Bacon told them they can. The citizens of Beaumont are forever waiting for a strong leader to tell them what to do next. Basically . . . Kevin Bacon or John Lithgow do something and they all fucking do it.

Matt: Perhaps that the true message of *Footloose*. If anyone mildly charismatic comes along . . . follow 'em. To the ends of the Earth. Or until someone else mildly charismatic tells you to do the opposite.

★ ★

BACK TO THE FUTURE

1985
Starring: Michael J. Fox, Christopher Lloyd, Crispin Glover, Lea Thompson, Thomas F. Wilson
Dir.: Robert Zemickis

Plot: Reagan's America turns back the clock.
Key line: 'Yeah, well . . . history is gonna change.'

Back To The Future, like a lot of the most successful ideas, came from a man holding on to a stray, random thought. Co-screenwriter Bob Gale stumbled upon his father's high school yearbook and, as he noticed that Dad had been class president, wondered if he would have been friends with his own father if they had gone to school at the same time. From this weird rumination came the most unit-shiftingest teen movie ever and highest-grossing film of 1985; a phenomenon that spawned two money-spinning sequels, fairground rides, best-selling video games and enough nerdy internet obsession to pull off the *Star Wars* trick and qualify as mainstream heavy-hitter *and* cult.

Of course, that nice little Dad-loving genesis story doesn't flag up Gale's darker thoughts about time travel. Because *BTTF*'s main source of memorable humour runs more along the lines of: what if you copped off with your own mother when she was still young and hot?

But all this – and the brilliant Industrial Light & Magic special effects, the parade of memorable set-pieces, the wish-fulfilment happy-ever-afters – distracts from *BTTF*'s true agenda. Which is providing a visual accompaniment to the Reagan administration's populist desire to wipe the complex web of America's triumphs and disasters of the 1960s and '70s out of history, and turn back the clock to a semi-mythical 1950s, when America was strong, values were small-town, money was abundant, hair was short, men were men and women were grateful. If the future wants to know what America wanted to be in the mid 1980s it could do the hard work of reading old newspapers and writing history books. Or it could just save a lot of time and anti-spirit-of-Reagan intellect and watch *Back To The Future*.

Let's begin with Michael J. Fox's Marty McFly, possibly the only iconic teen character to be so anti-rebellious that he rejects slouching, nicotine, alcohol and sugar . . . the guy's like a skateboarding billboard for Diet Pepsi. We know peppy Marty's a healthy, red-blooded American male because he plays self-indulgent electric guitar, turns the collar up on his denim jacket, dreams of owning flash cars and looks at other girl's arses while his own girlfriend is talking to him. Jennifer, along with Marty's Mom, is one of only two vaguely developed female characters and her and Mom's jobs are to talk to their men about their wants, needs and ambitions, being dutifully supportive, while never acknowledging that they might have any of their own. But Marty is duty-bound to zone out of Jennifer's selfless chatter when he gets a whiff of unconquered pussy, and Jennifer just smiles gently and competes harder for his favours. She is as natural a woman as Marty is a natural man. During the movie, we learn a great deal about what Marty McFly wants. We never learn what any female character wants because it's understood that all they want is a man.

Before Marty changes history according to his own tastes and aspirations, the McFly family are sad and ugly because they are working class. They have a family member in jail, they speak in broad accents and Dad is bullied by the same guy who bullied him in school because his inability to mark his territory with force is a sign of irredeemable weakness. Mom is rubbish simply because she's chubby and homely and insists on talking incessantly. They have no money and are almost presented as criminals for having failed economically.

The new improved McFly family are happily-ever-after wonderful because they are middle class. They are wealthy enough to have acquired nice things, no one is in jail and, most importantly of all, Mom is good because she is slim. Maybe, in another potential sequel, Marty will just give her what she wants and fuck her.

Christopher Lloyd's Doc Brown is allowed to be nuts and Einstein-ugly because he has mastered nuclear technology in the era of Reagan's Soviet-baiting 'Star Wars' space bombs. He is especially heroic because he cons Libyan terrorists out of bomb-making materials.

The movie is littered with Reagan references. Perhaps they were nothing more than entertaining 'in-jokes', but they looks to me like deferential doffs of the cap to their great leader, who responded in kind by loving the movie so much he referenced it in a speech, as did his successor George Bush Senior.

But, in historical revisionism terms, the most astonishing scene is the Chuck Berry bit. Chuck Berry isn't in it, of course ... that's the whole point. You remember ... Marty has to dep on guitar with the black band at the high school dance. He plays 'Johnny B. Goode', complete with trademark, rock guitar-inventing Berry licks and even the famous duck walk. And the bandleader Marvin Berry sneaks off stage to call his cousin Chuck and give him a blast of 'that new sound you were looking for'. So ... a nerdy Caucasian who thinks sugar is the work of the devil actually invented The Devil's Music.

I've never been able to watch this scene without being stunned at the chutzpah. Forget the 'joke' for a second: this is a movie aimed at white teenage boys for whom rock has become the only music that matters, and *BTTF* goes right ahead and grants those boys their dearest secret wish: a rewriting of history where the annoying truth that African-Americans invented everything that they find enjoyable is reduced to dope-smoking negroes grinning with joy as Whitey shows them the future. The evil lies in the fact that the joke is clever, and the scene rousing (Fox, incidentally, was neither singing nor playing the guitar). It makes you nod your head and tap your feet to the racist subtext. It may be the most sinister scene in movie history.

Now, if I had use of a souped up DeLorean and was writing in the rabidly right-wing '80s, I'd be written off as a loony leftie and accused of not having 'balance'. So here is the balance. Gale and Zemickis went all out to make their audience feel good about themselves and did it so well – the Chuck Berry scene is counter-balanced by Goldie Wilson, the black boy who travels from sweeping up in a diner to mayoral candidate by knuckling down, working hard and pursuing that American Dream – they earn the right to slip in a few home truths here and there.

Zemickis presented us with the difference between Hill Valley in the '50s and the '80s by building a pristine '50s town square on a studio backlot and then trashing it for the '80s scenes. This neatly reflects some sadness at the spectacle of an '80s America where town centres are dying and the cinemas are now houses of porn and God-bothering evangelists. There's a clever irony when those images are juxtaposed with Marty's relief at being home: 'Everything looks

great,' he exclaims, and the next shot is of a very modern building
... The Bank Of America.

Ideal Mom is now a sexual liberal, rather than the original prude.
Ideal Dad is not head of a corporation, but a science-fiction writer,
a creative type. But then again ... revenge on bully Biff consists of
middle-class Dad treating him like a blue-collar slave. Marty's final
triumph is having that gleaming 4×4. And, underlying absolutely
everything, is a horror that presumably plays as comfort to a nation
where only one in ten people ever bothers to own a passport. No
matter how Marty or Doc Brown alter history, all of the movie's
characters are destined to remain in the same tiny town, knowing the
same even tinier amount of people for their entire lives. Even Frank
Capra injected some sense of darkness into that model of living in
It's A Wonderful Life.

But *BTTF* works because it is a magnificent piece of film-making.
That's how The Man gets you ... he shows us bright, shiny things
and brainwashes the world into walking over its fellow man to get
them.

There is, for example, genuine screenwriting genius in the *deus
ex machina* whereby a flyer given to Marty by a preservation
campaigner contains the information needed to ensure our boy
can return home. The flyer contains the exact time and date in
1955 when a bolt of lightning hits the town's clock tower, and a
bolt of lightning is the only thing that can generate enough power
to revive the time machine. Not only does this make the plot work,
it also sets up a perfect, suspenseful action set-piece while managing
to say sly things about the exact nature of time, and boys who never
clean their clothes nor empty their pockets, and the importance of
preserving history, and even as I'm writing I am filled with envious
feelings towards the problem-solving talents of really, really good
storytellers.

Because *Back To The Future* is a great teen-sci-fi-comedy-adventure
movie. It sells you Reagan's America with such a light touch you
barely notice that that's what it's doing, at a moment when Reagan
had barely landslided his way to a second term. And the big twist is
that some of what it has to say about what America Corp can offer
is true.

At one point, Doc Brown expresses his desire to travel forward in
time and see who wins the next 25 World Series. But even Robert

Zemeckis and Bob Gale would probably have scoffed if you'd told them that, as that last ball gets pitched in the last of those baseball games, Goldie Wilson has become President. Of course, what Barack Obama didn't tell the American people about, along with the name change, was that his political career was all the idea of a skinny, peppy white kid wearing a life preserver.

* *

THE BREAKFAST CLUB

1985
Starring: Judd Nelson, Molly Ringwald, Emilio Estevez, Anthony Michael Hall, Ally Sheedy
Dir.: John Hughes

Plot: One learns valuable lessons at school. But not from teachers.
Key line: 'When you grow up, your heart dies.'

The death of John Hughes in August 2009 felt significant to the over-35s. The obvious irony of a man so associated with teenagers dying relatively young – of a heart attack, aged 59 – twinned naturally with shared memories of seeing films like *The Breakfast Club*, *Pretty In Pink* (see p. 275) and *Ferris Bueller's Day Off* (see p. 270) for the first time, and gave us one of those short, sharp insights into our own mortality.

Hughes is also entirely associated with the 1980s, which has been the hip decade to reference in pop culture for some years now. He directed his last film in 1991, and although he continued to write and produce through the '90s, nothing made the impact of his '80s movies. He slid into a reclusive semi-retirement in the first decade of the 21st century, unable, perhaps, to really excel at writing adult stories, yet equally unable to relate to The Kids any more.

Home Alone was Hughes's big commercial blockbuster, and he enjoyed some adult comedy success at the end of the '80s with *Planes, Trains And Automobiles* and *Uncle Buck*. But it's the run of mid-'80s teen comedy-dramas that have become enduring cults, defining both the 'Me Decade' and the art of the teen movie for many.

The Breakfast Club remains the key Hughes film because it changed teen movies overnight. Before *The Breakfast Club*, the introspective, self-analytical teenager in film was always an outsider, or rebel, occasionally even a monster; a fledgling intellectual made lonely and driven crazy by insisting on thinking rather than acting. *The Breakfast Club* insisted that even the pretty, popular, athletic teens had 'issues' which could only be made bearable by talking them out, preferably with other teens. This dialogue-heavy, almost-theatrical film made teen movies into therapy. From *The Breakfast Club* onwards, we have expected our screen youths to be hyper-articulate about culture, the social world and, especially, themselves.

It begins with one of the great all-time openings in teen cinema: the ludicrous 'Don't You Forget About Me' by Simple Minds plays, and the credits morph into a delicious 'you grown-ups will never understand!' quote from, of all things, 'Changes' by David Bowie. 'And these children that you spit on . . .' etc., etc.

The black background shatters to the noise of dubwise breaking glass revealing the exterior of Shermer High School. A montage of still shots of key American high school images – the cafeteria, a piece of wood where a bored pupil has scratched 'I'm eating my head', vandalised lockers, 'I don't like Mondays' etched into a wall, classroom, gym – ensues, while a voiceover by the as yet unseen Brian Johnson reads out the beginning of the essay that he has written as part of his Saturday detention punishment for bad deeds unknown.

'You see us as you want to see us, in the simplest terms and most convenient definitions. You see us as a brain, an athlete, a basket case, a princess and a criminal. Correct? That's the way we saw each other at seven o'clock this morning. We were brainwashed.'

In three minutes, we are able to understand not only that this is a high school movie about troubled teens, but that, as far as Hughes is concerned, it's the very stereotypes created and established by teen fiction that are the major reason for the travails of the angst-ridden adolescent. We are then treated to what is essentially an exceedingly talky stage play made cinematic by Hughes's ability to make the most drab and unpromising interiors into bright, shiny, vibrant play-grounds for the head games of unusually self-analytical, articulate and media-savvy children.

In Hughes's world adults are monsters. For a start, this example of American detention involves going into school on a Saturday at 7 a.m. and spending nine hours in one room, theoretically neither speaking nor moving. And we are introduced to our five protagonists by way of them arriving for detention in their parents' cars. The pouting princess (Molly Ringwald as Claire Standish) has been made so by a wealthy father who thinks it's adorable that his precious cut class to go shopping. The brain (the ever-underrated Anthony Michael Hall as Brian Johnson) is ordered to break the rules and study by his hot-housing, shrewish Mom. The athlete (Emilio Estevez as Andrew Clark) is obviously being pushed towards a wrestling scholarship by a macho Dad. The criminal (Judd Nelson as John Bender) ambles towards school in shades and that enduring symbol of existential male cool, the long overcoat, apparently parent-less. And the basket case (Ally Sheedy as Alison Reynolds) is simply dropped off without a consoling or angry word by sinister creatures that we cannot see as they drive away. The scene creates such a feeling of Us vs Them at the outset that you want to see these unfeeling bastards drive straight into trees and over cliffs. Hughes was a master of short, punchy manipulations of audience emotions, of taking well-worn storytelling clichés and breathing new, post-modern life into them. You know he's setting you up. He knows you know. And we can't help but join his crusade for youth over adulthood because we all want to be innocent.

From there, *The Breakfast Club* is simplicity itself. Virtually the entire film is shot on one set, the school library, as the five fight, talk about their feelings, rebel, acquiesce, smoke dope, flirt, bully, confess, dance, fall in love and learn that none of them are what they initially seem, or, more pertinently, that none of them want to fulfil the destinies and embody the stereotypes that their parents and teachers have projected upon them. It's both a great ensemble acting piece, and a cunning statement about teen fiction itself, and how its exploitation of teenagers has led to the young being labelled and dehumanised by the simplistic fantasies of popular culture. The library is like a jail, and so, Hughes argues, is American teen culture.

Of course, even a prison that big needs a warden. And that unfortunate role goes to Paul Gleason as Dick Vernon, one of the most evil representatives of the teaching profession ever created for the screen. While our students are given so many dimensions over the next 90 minutes you almost want to make them cease and desist being so goddamn complex, Vernon has but one. He hates kids. He loves punishing them. He is almost sexually aroused by the wielding of arbitrary power. He uses the phrase 'monkey business' without irony. He is a fascist buffoon for no reason other than the fact that he is over 21 and terminally disappointed with his lot in life. He exists only to be broken, and we immediately know that it won't take much. Like the adults in *Home Alone* and *Ferris Bueller's Day Off*, Dick is a John Hughes grown-up, which means he's a deluded bully and no match for the cheek, intelligence and resourcefulness of The Kids. Although you can't help having a sneaking empathy for Dick when he calls our famous five 'smug little pricks' under his breath.

We also pick up quickly that two into five won't go. And, despite Hughes's confounding of the most obvious couplings being much of the point of the movie, we know early on that the skinny, plain, nerdy boy ain't getting one of the girls. Hughes may have had subversive qualities, but the film was a benchmark of the Reagan 1980s, and intelligence wasn't going through one of its more popular phases. No matter how misunderstood and complex Claire and Alison are, it's always the Jock and the Bad Boy who pull in these situations, and poor Brian will probably have to settle for being a girl's *quasi*-gay best friend for the rest of his days in high school hell.

It's Nelson's tough-but-vulnerable-deep-down rebel who gets all the best clothes and all the best lines, mainly at the expense of the all-American wrestler, Andrew: 'I wanna be just like you. I figure all I need is a lobotomy and some tights'; 'You're an idiot anyway. But if you say you get along with your parents – you're a liar, too.'

Hughes also gives Bender lines which attempt to invent a brand new '80s hipster slang: 'Face it – you're a neo-maxi-zoom dweebie' (translation: 'You are a nerd') and 'So, Ahab – kybo my doobage?' ('Sir – do you still have the marijuana that I gave you for safe-keeping?'). As you can probably gather, this gambit failed to create thrilling new catchphrases among the planet's youth, although *Break-fast Club* fans are still intrigued by one specific insult Bender throws at Dick Vernon: 'That guy's a Brownie Hound.' This, we BC nerds suppose, can only mean one of two things: a homophobic insult in the vein of 'shit-stabber' or 'fudge-packer'. Or an accusation of paedophilia; i.e. this man chases after Girl Guides and Brownies. Whichever way, it didn't catch on either.

Nevertheless, a film this talky wouldn't work unless the dialogue sparkled, and Hughes locates many incisive epithets about the eternal struggles of being a tweener, the best of which include: 'Everyone's home life is unsatisfying. If it wasn't people would live with their parents for ever' and 'If you say you haven't – you're a prude. If you say you have – you're a slut. It's a trap.'

Bender is undoubtedly a Brando throwback with dangerous '60s and punk tendencies, singing Cream songs under his breath, rocking the plaid shirt look, refusing to lose the battle of wills with Vernon, no matter what the cost. But the important battle of wills is fought between Bender and Ringwald's 'pristine' Claire.

Both are immediately attracted to each other, both are trapped by their personas, and Bender's initial solution to this is typical of all young men ... verbal sexual bullying. Bender seeks to degrade her into submission with 'jokes' about gang rape and virginity. But Claire's winning response isn't verbal, where she mostly can't compete. It's all in the Ringwald face – The Pout Of Steel. Her glare is a beautiful symbol of the woman who refuses to be broken by male cruelty, even though she suffers. She takes Bender's childish misogyny apart with that pale and sallow stare, tames him and leaves him potentially house-broken and ready for domestication. No wonder Ringwald became a teen girl icon of the time, with her ability, in *The Breakfast Club* and as Andie Walsh in *Pretty In Pink*, to physically manifest feminism without having to say the word that '80s girls were being brainwashed into believing meant nothing except looking butch and lacking a sense of humour.

Hughes's take on class is interesting, too. At one point, a janitor makes an entrance and responds to a Bender insult with a knowing humour that forces a respect from the kids that Vernon is incapable of commanding. And Bender's verbal supremacy and courage in the face of authority is unmistakable – the working-class social outcast dominates the film. His mirror is Sheedy's near-invisible Alison who barely says anything at all, yet effortlessly disturbs everyone with her witchy ways and almost joyful embrace of apparent madness. She is entirely classless, of course – but she reinforces the theme that it's the three middle-class kids-most-likely-to who seem out of their intellectual depth and in desperate need of permission to rebel.

The scene where Vernon locks Bender in a classroom and threatens him with a beating is still shocking in what, up until this moment, has largely been a comedy. And it's because the violence is reinforced by Vernon's loathing for Bender's working-class background and the sadistic pleasure he takes in predicting the boy's hopeless, ugly future. To call *The Breakfast Club* an anti-Reagan movie is perhaps over-egging the pudding a little. But it does display a loathing for middle-class values and the bourgeois obsession with money and status that reaches a peak of genuinely disturbing intensity in this scene.

Nevertheless, affection for *The Breakfast Club* does come with a healthy dollop of kitsch appreciation. This is because Hughes occasionally loses faith in his audience and allows scenes that over-state the case to an embarrassing degree. The moments when our heroes do their crazy dance bit, and when Nelson starts acting out Bender's violent home life and ends up chewing the scenery over a pointless splurge of synth music, are the kind of scenes which force you to laugh to keep from squirming. They mark the film for ever as typical, dated '80s Hollywood, when a desperation for nostalgic values led directors to encourage inappropriate pre-'60s melodrama without the old-school production values (or acting talent) to back it up. Nelson's a good enough rebel without a cause to carry much of *The Breakfast Club*, but he ain't no James Dean ... or Gene Kelly, for that matter.

And it's a big disappointment, in terms of the movie's sexual politics, when Alison gets her guy because Claire gives her a cutesy-pie makeover. I suspect I am just one of many who boo that scene, and not simply because it reinforces the idea that girls must conform to male standards of femininity before a man will deign to fuck them, and that that, in the end, is all any woman wants. It's also because Ally Sheedy looks far hotter in all the 'black shit'. It's one of the most sexist and aggravating 'ugly duckling' rip-offs in screen history. Like I say, Reagan '80s.

But Hughes does pull off most of the stuff that matters. For example, the vast majority of '80s youth films date horribly because the fashions are so bad, and quite obviously have been chosen by people who only see kids when they're in other films. The clothes and hairstyles in *The Breakfast Club* have barely dated at all, and everything about the film exudes a genuine knowledge of and fascination with the detail of being a teenager – not just circa 1985, but from any era you care to name. At one point, Hughes makes superb silent comedy out of nothing more than the kids' packed lunches and the perennial food fads of the young. Hughes's best movies were made out of spot-on observation, and I suspect the concerns of *The Breakfast Club*'s five protagonists will make as much sense and provide as much pleasure to 21st-century teens as they did to the 1985 model. Hell – even the gloriously shallow, trebly 'new wave' synth-pop has come back into fashion.

This is among the many reasons why I love *The Breakfast Club*, and why its faults – or rather, the bits I don't personally agree with – are part of its excellence. I've watched it many times, and no amount of familiarity with the text renders the film mere entertainment. It's a work of art, to argue against and agree with. It makes you shout at the screen as much as laugh or cry with recognition. It is provocative and dissuades the viewer from being passive. Its key scene is not the typically gung ho '80s, much-parodied and copied, air-punching ending. It is the part where, for a full 20 minutes of screen-time, five actors sit in a semi-circle and bond and break over the agonies of parental and peer pressure. The scene is a masterpiece of movie dialogue, and one of the finest ensemble acting scenes on celluloid – one that none of the actors came close to again – because it dares to risk both boring its audience and being seen as pretentious. But, if you watch the scene – and if you have, watch it again! – you'll see that it explores every single one of the key themes that the movies in this book are concerned with.

That's an extraordinary achievement for one 92-minute movie set in one featureless building. *The Breakfast Club* is, in its tacky, plastic, manipulative, hugging and learning way, an absolute bloody masterpiece. Now excuse me, won't you, while I watch it all over again.

★ ★

FERRIS BUELLER'S DAY OFF

1986
Starring: Matthew Broderick, Alan Ruck, Mia Sara, Jennifer Grey, Jeffery Jones, Edie McClurg, Charlie Sheen
Dir.: John Hughes

Plot: Spoiled brat's dodgy sickie makes truancy into Great American Triumph.
Key line: 'Incredible. One of the worst performances of my career and they never doubted it for a second.'

A friend of mine recently made an excellent observation about this most hardy perennial of teen comedies. We were talking about the book – and incidentally, in almost every conversation I've had about *Stranded.* . . the first movies mentioned are either *Grease* (see p. 165), *The Breakfast Club* (see p. 263) or good old *Ferris* – and my mate observed that one's attitude to the character of Ferris Bueller gradu-ally altered as one got more wrinkly. 'When I was a kid I thought he was a cool hero,' he said. 'But now I'm in my forties I see the guy as an obnoxious arsehole.'

There was always an obnoxious arsehole element to Ferris Bueller, but this is why the choice to cast Matthew Broderick in the title role was absolutely key. There is something so easy-going and sincerely pleasant about Broderick that he is almost impossible to dislike, even when playing a craven hypocrite like Jim McAllister in *Election* (see p. 374). Apparently, the only other actor strongly considered for Ferris was John Cusack. Anyone who has sat through the preening self-regard and relentless puppy-dog ain't-I-cuteness of, say, Cusack's turns in *Say Anything.* . . and *High Fidelity* will surely agree that we would not be talking about this film if Hughes had gone for pin-up over actor. A huge part of what makes Ferris both funny and bearable is that Broderick is just a little too wimpy, girly and unsexy to be a teen superhero. There's an if-he-can-do-it-so-can-I, nerd's revenge element to his entire performance.

But, if a spoiled and smug middle-class boy who is good at every-thing, delights in humiliating those around him, and bullies and manipulates people into doing things that momentarily keep him entertained does lose his appeal as one has kids of one's own and sees the effect that type of force of nature can have on an impressionable mind, then the balance provided by *FBDO*'s second banana becomes the thing that keeps you loyal to the movie. Alan Ruck, as Ferris's neurotic and deeply unhappy sidekick Cameron Frye, is one of the most disturbing, haunted performances in this book, taking a daft slapstick picture about cool kids sticking it to bumbling adults into realms both more real and far more dark. There is something broken and near-insane about the depths of Cameron's pessimism and pain in *FBDO*, something poignant and authentic enough to make one believe that sending a car crashing through a plate glass window to die a violent and ignominious death will either save this boy's life, or end it. Thankfully, John Hughes wasn't too interested in sequels (save *Home Alone*; let's not, eh?), which allows you to direct your own. In mine, Cameron stands up to his authoritarian father (an all the more frightening character for never appearing onscreen), uses all that darkness as fuel to do something extraordinary with his life (while Ferris becomes Jim McAllister, the boy who peaked too soon) and eventually marries Mia Sara's Sloane, who finally understands that she was only banging Ferris for shallow, school-status-related reasons, and that all her real connections in this movie are actually with Cameron, who, like her, is just being dragged along as cheerleader witness to the desperate acts of an empty narcissist.

Ruck, extraordinarily, was already in his late twenties by the time he played Cameron, which makes the uncanny way he taps into shared memories of teenage fear and self-loathing even more admirable.

In even more bizarre John Hughes-potential-miscasting-disaster shenanigans, Hughes originally cast Ruck in *The Breakfast Club* when he was intending to shoot the film independently. If you're figuring that must have been for the Anthony Michael Hall part, then get this: both Hall and Emilio Estevez turned down the part of Cameron before Ruck was cast. That's right ... *Emilio Estevez*. How the fuck would that natural macho jock dumbass have played the most vulnerable and deeply wounded teen in mainstream movie history? Even with Hughes pictures, you can't help feeling that this Making Great Movies lark is more down to luck than judgement.

As you've probably worked out, I'm assuming that everyone who has bought an entire book about teen movies has seen *FBDO*, and doesn't need a big plot rundown. This stupidly popular Chicago kid throws a fake sickie from school with his girlfriend and best mate. They have unlikely triumphs and disasters. The school's dean Ed Rooney (Jones) tries to catch them and expose Ferris to his doting and gullible parents. The kid's jealous sister (the wonderful Grey) has an opportunity to dob him in, but decides that she cares for her smug git sibling after all. The adult world is gratuitously humiliated by one brilliant boy. The end.

The movie's most loved moments lie in brilliant comic and tragic set-pieces, a memorable ensemble cast, and use of dodgy 'new wave' instrumental pop that worms its way into your brain and has become so recognisable that anyone wanting a handy shorthand for taking the piss out of '80s teen movies just puts on The Beat's 'March Of The Swivel Heads' or Yello's 'Oh Yeah' under a montage of someone running through gardens.

So the question becomes: why is *Ferris Bueller's Day Off* so much more lovable than other similar teen movies?

One thing that is striking is its love of the modern world. In the majority of teen movies, what the writer(s) and director want to say, more than anything, is that the world today is going to the dogs. To this end, they use teen issues as a jumping-off point for their own angst about class, race, technology, modern people's crap taste in music and film, suburbia, small towns, big cities, their own rubbish childhoods or that general disillusion about once believing they could change the world, and now knowing they can't. Hughes seems entirely uninterested in any of this. Whatever angst turns up in *FBDO* – mainly from Cameron and Jeannie – is actual, honest-to-goodness, adults-don't-understand-because-the-past-never-happened teen angst.

One fascinating little thing about the Making Of documentaries on the current UK DVD of *FBDO* is meeting Hughes himself. He is a middle-aged man, not far from his tragically early death from a heart attack in 2009 ... yet he is very self-consciously trying to look like an '80s teen. He has a jet-black feather-cut mullet and is wearing shades. You then see pictures of him during the filming of *FBDO*, and see that he looks exactly the same. Perhaps Hughes wrote so cogently for and about '80s teenagers because, in his mind, he was one, and remained one for many years afterwards.

Because *FBDO* is shamelessly in love with tacky, synthetic '80s music and MTV; with gadgets that you don't have to touch to make work; with expensive cars and expansive gardens and kids who are up to their eyeballs in smartarse pop-culture references; with clean streets and Reagan-era money for the few. Hughes's characters always date less badly than other '80s movie teens, because he even seemed to actually understand the kids' fashions of the time, rather than surreptitiously mocking them.

It's this guilt-free embrace of its times that I suspect makes *FBDO* feel box-fresh every time you watch it. It simply refuses to inject a single note of real cynicism. Don't get me wrong ... the movie's characters are cynical as hell. But the film isn't. Take the constant, recurring, breaking of 'the fourth wall'. *FBDO*'s characters play so relentlessly to camera that the clever-cleverness should strangle the life out of the movie. But it does exactly the opposite, succeeding in its aims to make the viewer feel like a co-conspirator. And I reckon this is because Hughes wasn't trying to employ the device to appear smart. He actually, truly wanted to make the viewer feel like a part of the movie. The more guile Hughes displays, the more guileless *FBDO* feels.

Another factor in the movie's enduring popularity is its surgically precise encapsulation of a universal principle: all of us hated school. Or, more precisely, all of us hated school in our mid to late teens. Even if we went to a good school, even if we were a popular kid, even if we jumped all of our academic hurdles with qualifications coming out of our arse ... none of us quite escapes that moment, some time in adolescence, when we truly understand that school isn't a boring thing we're made to go through to earn the right to be adult and free. It's preparation for an endless, horrifying future of being forced, every day, to go to a place we don't want to be, to do things we don't want to do, for people we don't like or respect. From that moment on, whether we conform or rebel, every minute drags, every order from a teacher feels like another humiliating nail in the coffin, every exam or piece of homework feels like a traumatising battle between your parents' expectations and a barely containable desire to burn every book in existence and escape to a fairyland of everlasting childhood where no one expects you to earn a living and a nice woman puts three meals a day in front of you anyway. Tell me – are you one of those who, around once every two or three months, has a vivid nightmare about classrooms, exams and the ever-present feeling that, from the moment you first walked into your first school, you had been fooled into walking into prison? Of course you are. School is a nightmare we never get over. That's why the friendships we make then are so intense. They're the only hope we have to cling on to.

FBDO taps into this with such a committed empathy and feather-light touch that it grants us 98 minutes where we can embrace the repressed fury at the indignities we suffered at the hands of adults we can now clearly see as mediocrities (I know we all had great teachers too – apologies to mine, but you weren't enough to make up for your idiot colleagues) and laugh the anger out. Poor old Rooney becomes a symbolic Everyteacher, suffering each indignity as part of our revenge fantasy, while Ben Stein's robotic economics teacher is the epitome of the murderous boredom of the classroom. Incidentally, despite being most famous for saying the word 'Bueller' repeatedly in a stunningly annoying monotone, Ben Stein is actually a real-life right-wing Republican economist who wrote speeches for Presidents Ford and Nixon, and has remained one of Nixon's staunchest apologists. Weird.

The rest is the joy of small details – the teen ephemera of Ferris's bedroom, the hilarious Edie McClurg as Rooney's secretary, pulling stockpiled pencils out of her giant perm, the moving connection between Cameron and Sloane, attempting to locate some substance in the shadow of Ferris's grandstanding, Jennifer Grey's kung-fu kicks, just about every Jeffery Jones gurn – that earn the set-piece triumphs of the giant Twist 'N' Shout dance routine and the necessary demise of Mr Frye's car. There is something so shamelessly right about this movie that, when one of my friends gets in touch to tempt me into an occasional boozy truancy from another hard day at the laptop, she always calls our attempts at carefree hedonism 'a Ferris Bueller'. I suppose Ferris does seem more of an arsehole than he did when I was 23. But he's still an arsehole I love spending a day with.

* *

PRETTY IN PINK

1986
Starring: Molly Ringwald, Andrew McCarthy, Jon Cryer, Harry
Dean Stanton, Annie Potts, James Spader
Dir.: Howard Deutsch

Plot: The new wave Cinderella.
**Key line: 'I just wanna let them know that they didn't break
me.'**

Rock boys hated this movie. Not only was it a multi-coloured teen
romance told from a girl's point of view. Not only did it take its name
from a great post-punk song and then force the band to re-record it
with the guitars turned down and the sneer removed. Not only did
it star a girl whose entire demeanour seemed to scream, 'Men are so
fucking *boring*', and who was really plain but completely irresistible.
Not only was it obsessed with all those school rules and norms and
codes that made any unreconstructed geek shudder at the memory
of endless humiliations suffered at the hands of girls who barely
noticed you existed. Not only was it light and bright and peppy
and sentimental at the core. None of these was the worst thing. The
worst thing – the most blatant Hollywood subversion of everything
an indie boy holds dear – was the record shop. A record shop . . . run
by girls.

The post-punk record shop was, in reality, a male-only haven; the
nearest a right-on young man could get to a female-free environment
without joining a gentleman's club and therefore becoming a Tory
or, worse, your father. Worker boys oversaw consumer boys poring
through racks of records made by boys in environments made hip by
large posters of boys with guitars, who were usually The Clash. One
could have earnest conversation about the B-sides of Smiths and
Sonic Youth records, and conspire with the Masters Of The Universe
(the boys who stood behind the counter) to sneer at people – especially women, especially *older* women – who came and asked for chart
records, because chart records are stoopid. The shops were dirty,
musty and kind of smelly, which ensured that women didn't want to

hang around these palaces of geek testosterone, and became home from home for men whose women didn't understand why the presence of a drum-machine on the latest Fall single should make you sulk for a week, or why you would want to spend precious shagging time cross-referencing your albums by bands from Athens, Georgia with your albums by bands from Akron, Ohio. No style, fashion, fun, dancing, sex or pastel shades entered therein, and everything was fine, emotionally repressed, safe.

So the record shop in *Pretty In Pink* was an abomination and a blasphemous affront to our Lord Captain Beefheart. Two women who look like the punk rock girls who would never shag you run the place. One of them looks exactly like Siouxsie Sioux and talks about sex in a loud voice and shoots male thieves with a stapler. The other quietly flirts with flash prick Andrew McCarthy, bringing the entirely unwelcome taint of sex, romance and upward mobility into the previously monk-like, dressed down confines of the holy Vinyl church. The shop is dressed beautifully – especially the vinyl stapled to the ceiling and the plants and thrift-shop lamps – and you can almost smell that spicy, pine-fresh scent that women seem to make everything smell like when they spread their dastardly standards of hygiene and décor. The whole shop is a sadistic visual reminder that, (1) punk had been co-opted by Hollywood, (2) that actually punk was the idea of fashion designers rather than urban street fighters, (3) that most of the best punk was made by women, (4) that all your indie heroes wanted to sell out and have big hits but just weren't good enough at writing melodies, (5) that your hair looked like the hair of the poser blokes hanging round this shop, ergo, your hair sucked, and (6) – and worst of all – that punk and indie and art-rock and whatever was just ... pop music. No morally worse or better than Madonna or Milli Vanilli. Just less catchy. And more worthy. The whole set-up seems to be laughing at the rockbloke notion of cool. The Smiths are just another poster of pretty boys here. It is the music scene according to John Hughes. And it's evil because it's true.

Which reminds me ... did you have any idea that some geezer called Howard Deutsch directed this film? How could this be anything but a John Hughes movie? Deutsch also directed the Hughes screenplay *Some Kind Of Wonderful*, which, in case you've forgotten, is *Pretty In Pink* with the genders switched, before graduating to future classics like *Grumpier Old Men* and Lea Thompson's *Caroline*

In The City sitcom. If there's some kind of definitive opposite to 'stamping your own identity' on a movie, I reckon old Howard might be that definition.

Pretty In Pink is about a poor girl who fancies a rich, popular boy but is fancied by another, nastier rich boy, and her goofy best friend. But it's not. It's about Molly Ringwald. Her small, exhausted, heart-broken eyes. Her huge bee-stung mouth. Her bush of red hair. Her thrift-shop threads. And the way an infinite sadness engulfs her so completely that, when something happens in the story that makes a slow, reluctant smile creep around the edges of her Grand Canyon gob, it feels like Hosannas and World Peace and a preview peak through the gates of Heaven. Sarah Michelle Gellar's entire portrayal of Buffy Summers is based upon the Ringwald oeuvre, and it is here, rather than *The Breakfast Club* (see p. 263) or *Sixteen Candles*, where she reached her peak of adorableness before inevitably plummeting into obscurity by way of growing up. A thousand-yard sulk is just not an attractive thing on a grown woman. It isn't fair. But neither is high school, so, like, get over it.

Pretty In Pink is one of those movies that comes down to favourite scenes, because Hughes (and, OK, this Deutsch guy) were great at showing you funny, memorable things that didn't need much dialogue to make 'em stick. There is, for example, the bit where Blane (McCarthy) walks out of a door at school, in his yuppie casuals, and is surrounded, on all sides, by self-conscious and hostile fashion victims, sporting every take on the punk/new wave/mod/new romantic/goth/psychobilly explosion of tribal dressing-up that we Brits had managed to brainwash Yank kids into copying in the '80s, usually around five years late. Blane is our representative here, a little wary of the obvious antipathy towards his rich boy look, but also allowing our amusement at the heroic pretension of '80s youth dress codes. It's a couple of seconds that carries all of Hughes' wry affection for the peacock teens of the era.

And then there's the sheer hatred and agony on Ducky's face when he realises that Andie has a date with Blane. Jon Cryer's Ducky is a fascinating character, designed to polarise viewers. His dress style is ridiculous. His hyperactive class-clown schtick is not funny. He doesn't love and support Andie . . . he stalks her. He's a control freak in geek clothing, and the obvious inspiration for *Buffy*'s Zander Harris.

But Ducky works for *Pretty In Pink* because he is real. I'm not alone in having had hopeless crushes on female friends who just weren't attracted to me as a kid, and Ducky makes me shudder because I now realise that the self-image I built at the time – that I was cool, basically – was entirely deluded. When I attached myself like a limpet to an object of desire who wanted my love, but not my *love* . . . I looked as big a twat as Ducky. We boys all did, because we don't deal with female friendship as well as girls deal with male friendship.

So when Ducky sees Blane at the door of the record shop and his face becomes a mask of sick shock . . . let's just say I relate. We repress so much of our teenage pain because, at that time we feel so deeply about stuff that is, in the big scheme of things, utterly irrelevant. But we are so vulnerable then that small slights leave lifelong scars. Hughes is the absolute master of universally understood teenage angst, and watching his best movies is sometimes a trip down the more traumatic side streets off Memory Lane.

And, of course, there is the entire disaster of Blane and Andie's first date. *Pretty In Pink* presents a strange vision of class conflict. Here, money or aspirations aren't the problem. Blane's friends are appalling because they're hedonists. Andie's rock club milieu is terrifying because people wear punk clothes. Apart from the fact that lots of working-class kids fuck and take drugs, and lots of middle-class kids dress up . . . actually, there is no apart from that. The drama and the tension works because of the hostility to the couple generated by Ducky and Blane's slimy muckers Benny (Vernon) and Steff (Spader, a man seemingly born to ooze unfathomable depths of elegantly sociopathic perversion). But, if *Pretty In Pink* has any basis in the facts of youth social division in America in the '80s, then it's an unfamiliar kind of class war to us Brits. You just come out of the scene feeling that these two people should pick nicer friends. Thankfully, Ringwald swings the scene round with her visceral shame about showing Blane where she lives . . . again, a scene that takes me back to feelings best forgotten.

By the end, Hughes's inherent conservatism about women rears its ugly head. Andie's older punk friend Iona finds love and therefore, in an echo of Allison's makeover in *The Breakfast Club*, she must conform and embrace her inner Soccer Mom in order to enter polite society and keep a man. But, lest we forget, *Pretty In Pink* is Cinderella recast for nice kids who dig the alternative sounds of New Order because it's naughty, where Cryer is Buttons, Spader and Vernon are the ugly sisters, and Harry Dean Stanton gets to be the anti-Dennis Hopper and play the most sympathetic Bad Dad in movie history. Subversion is not here. But Molly Ringwald in a horrible pink dress at the prom is. It makes me feel like I'm eating popcorn in fluffy pyjamas with the girls. And I don't even like popcorn.

★ ★

LUCAS

1986

Starring: Corey Haim, Kerri Green, Charlie Sheen, Winona Ryder
Dir.: David Seltzer

Plot: Teen cinema's first Heroic Nerd.
Key line: 'I think it's superficial. You know . . . football heroes, cheerleaders, parties. I'd be willing to play football if all that other junk didn't go along with it.'

In March 2010, an almost-forgotten actor called Corey Haim died of what appeared to be an accidental overdose of prescription drugs. He was 38 years old. He'd been taking drugs since the age of 15 when he was, briefly, the most popular child actor in America. His biggest success, *The Lost Boys*, was a 1987 teen vampire movie that paired him with Corey Feldman, and the two starred in seven movies together. Haim couldn't escape his fellow Corey, nor find a place in entertainment as an adult. He died broke, disturbed and living with his mother, who had breast cancer.

Haim's death became international news, a typical Hollywood case of too much too soon. Eulogies from more successful stars poured out. His ex-girlfriend and *Baywatch* star Nicole Eggert commented: 'It's a little late. If people realised, he would have liked to have heard that when he was here with us, it could have maybe made a difference in his life.' She's right, right? So I'm not going to eulogise too much, especially as I'm no fan of *The Lost Boys* and didn't see this, his finest moment, until months after his death, after it came strongly recommended in *Entertainment Weekly*'s handy 50 Best High School

Movies list. Except to say that the 15-year-old Haim's portrayal of an eccentric prodigy called Lucas Blye is one of my favourite performances in this book. So it's sad that someone so talented never got to show it as an adult. That's all.

Lucas is a rare thing in teen movies: a mix of high school comedy, unrequited love story and character study. Haim and Lucas screenwriter-director David Seltzer present Blye as a motor-mouthed cross between Holden Caulfield and a baby Woody Allen. From the opening scenes, he is utterly adorable in his big glasses, battered safari hat and ragged shorts, his legs so skinny you wonder how they hold him up. For once, the teen we're watching is a little boy. And it's this that is a key part of the Lucas appeal, because not all of us were wannabe adults as teens, as teen movies would have us believe. Haim's performance strikes an authentic balance between verbal confidence and physical gawkiness, his open-mouthed, fly-catching gawp a recurring motif, reminding us how bewildering life, love and sex are in adolescence.

You're in an unusual teen movie place from the get-go, watching Lucas prowling around the countryside with a butterfly net, searching for the insects he studies with obsessive fascination, before chancing upon new-girl-in-town Maggie (Green) practising shots on a tennis court. The wire fence is the sexual line the boy can't cross, and Haim's awestruck stare is as funny and accurate a representation of hopeless first love as you could wish for. As a special eccentricity bonus, it turns out that our young hero carries a cassette recorder in his backpack. He hits play, and awards himself and us, of all things, Tchaikovsky's The Nutcracker Suite as a soundtrack for the ballet of a slender, fresh-faced redhead hitting a ball against a fence. Five minutes in and we've got our first classic scene.

We've already seen cheerleaders by this time; Lucas is not trying to ignore high school movie convention. It simply contrasts the familiar with the quiet strangeness of its central character, a boy who stalks bugs and feels that leading your dream girl through sewer tunnels in order to hear a classical music recital for free is perfectly good date material.

Lucas may be an unlikely Casanova, but he's persistent. He walks Maggie to her car – yep, this is one of those perennially sunny, white and wealthy neighbourhoods where even the toddlers drive convertibles – and boasts about how many friends he has at Park

High in Illinois, the school she's just about to start attending. When he calls over to the footballers and cheerleaders and gets no response, we think he's a fantasist. And he is . . . but not in that petty kind of way. Lucas does have cool friends. He's hiding something far more important.

This is where Seltzer's narrative scores high. You keep thinking you know exactly where this is all heading . . . and the film confounds you at every turn. Admittedly, you do work out Lucas's guilty secret long before the 'twist', but, apart from that, this is a tale that keeps you guessing. Lucas really does make good his seduction boast and introduce Maggie to the cool kids. Unfortunately, that's where his heartbreak begins.

Seltzer's character study revolves around a couple of key elements. First, Lucas has been 'accelerated' into high school by virtue of his academic prowess. He is therefore physically and emotionally younger than his immediate peers, even though he's far smarter. Second, he's a tough little bastard, and nobody's victim, even when someone sets out to make him one. Third, he's a real 14-year-old boy; that is, an utter wanker from time to time. And finally, he is having to deal with a variety of attitudes towards him, because the cool kids at Park High don't act like a mindless mob. Some want to bully him, while others see him as a kind of plucky school mascot. Lucas meets all of these responses with the same mixture of inner strength and utter bemusement.

Of course, Seltzer had no way of knowing, when he cast Haim along with Charlie Sheen as college football star Cappie, what kind of car-crash resonance these two would lend his teen classic in 2011. Haim is a revelation, but watching Sheen be the kind of stand-up guy who risks exclusion from the cool group in order to hang out with and protect Lucas and fall in love with Maggie, just at the very moment in early 2011 when the square-jawed nutter became the planet's byword for sociopathic hedonism, is very weird indeed. He just seems so sweet here. Even if, looks-wise, he isn't your particular pipe-full of crack, you'll entirely understand why Maggie swoons in the face of his jock-with-a-human-face schtick. It's also just about the only role I've seen him in where he isn't some kind of distressing parody of his father Martin's talent, as if Seltzer caught him before cynicism and drugs forced him to play shallow bad boy so regularly that fact and fiction inevitably fused. Charlie Sheen is actually good in this movie, which makes it a unique experience in itself. You can't help wondering what he and Haim got up to on set, though.

But Seltzer's winningest ticket is his dialogue. Astonishingly, these teen characters don't talk like ciphers, plot devices or self-conscious postmodern parodies of stereotypes. They talk like real kids, veering off the subject, expressing vulnerabilities in self-protective ways, pretending to be wiser than their years. This allows scenes between key characters to go beyond the usual wham-bam of comedy, tragedy and exposition, and develop into the slow and subtle dance we do when trying to find out just how far we can go with each other.

Take the scene where Maggie and Cappie find themselves alone in a laundry room, with its undertones of adult domesticity. Rather than the standard lunge 'n' snog, the pair circle each other warmly and warily, gently moving closer through humour, winsome stares, loaded questions and shared chewing gum, using their feelings about Lucas and Cappie's girlfriend Alise as a coded way of discussing their feelings for each other, getting their attack of conscience, gently moving apart in a way that lets us and each other know that their coming together is inevitable. It's charming and sexy and genuinely romantic, and, although the scene only lasts seven minutes, seven minutes is, in low-attention-span teen movie terms, the equivalent of an epic staring match between Eric Rohmer and John Cassevetes.

The one credulity-straining element surrounds Rina, played by Winona Ryder in her film debut. Rina has a big old crush on Lucas, and the obvious observation is that Ryder's far too beautiful to be the rejected girl-geek. I mean, that girl saunters onscreen and you forget where you live, never mind what Kerri Green looks like. But then again, you also remember what strange ideas teens have about what's cool or sexy or good-looking, and, in my case, how many great girls I blew off in favour of some whey-faced thing who denoted status and acceptance at school; the girl who would make me cool if I could pull her . . . which I never did. So Seltzer's probably got that about right, too. There are few things stupider in this world than an adolescent boy.

So the lovely Winona is just part of the pleasure and intrigue within *Lucas*'s pre-*Juno* (see p. 458) world. There are groovy details like Lucas's obsessive bitching about the 'superficial', which is his desperate attempt to degrade everything he can't have and everyone attractive or rich enough to have it. The strange sub-plots about locusts and a dead music teacher. A scene where Lucas is humiliated at a school assembly, yet somehow turns the moment on its head. More insect symbolism – 'cos the superficial world doesn't appreciate the beauty and intelligence of insects, right? – as the whole school hang out at a creature-feature cinema night featuring the original and brilliant version of *The Fly* with Vincent Price. Jeremy Pivens as a muscle-bound jock looking exactly the same as she does as Ari in the *Entourage* TV show. Plus the film also answers the question of why American kids are so obsessed with gridiron and cheerleading. Buses to away games. Driver too busy to worry about what's going on behind him. Parent-free canoodling and boozing opportunities legitimised by school and society in general! And finally, I get it.

Lucas also boasts one of the cleverest endings of any movie in the 1980s. Basically, poor Lucas suffers that universal rite of passage . . . the moment when one first hears, from the eternal object of desire, that they only see you as a friend. His response is a futile and heroic gesture that gains him the respect and admiration of the entire school. If I say that it involves The Big Football Game and remind you that this film was made in the air-punching, 'YEAH!!!'-hollering Reagan '80s, then you can fill in the dots. Except . . . you'd be wrong. Seltzer puts his hero in genuine peril, and takes the viewer's assumption that Hollywood can somehow make this tiny boy into the school sports hero right to hospital.

Lucas Blye's triumph is not about becoming an all-American winner. It's actually about the extraordinary kindness children are capable of when they realise that they were wrong. Seltzer manages to give his producers the inspirational ending all '80s youth movies required while keeping the movie's integrity intact *and* subverting American notions of what winning actually means. It's the icing on the cake of one of the great neglected films of its era.

★ ★

RIVER'S EDGE

1986

Starring: Crispin Glover, Keanu Reeves, Ione Skye, Daniel
Roebuck, Joshua Miller, Dennis Hopper
Dir.: Tim Hunter

Plot: The first true 'indie' teen movie.
Key line: 'I hear you're all gonna go see a dead girl.'

River's Edge is one of those movies where the central protagonist is
already dead. We learn nothing about her except that her name was
Jamie, she was skinny and blonde, that she might have talked shit
about somebody's dead mother, and that this testimony is somewhat
unreliable because it comes from the boy who murdered her. But,
without Jamie, and the haunting shots of her pale naked body and
dead blue eyes, there wouldn't be a movie. Her death gives the teens
of this godforsaken part of Sacramento, California a life, for a few
short days.

This ahead-of-its-time masterpiece was, like *Badlands* (see p.
138) and *Heavenly Creatures* (see p. 315), inspired by a real-life
murder. In 1981, a hulking 16-year-old called Anthony Jacques
Broussard raped and strangled 14-year-old Marcy Renee Conrad
to death in Miliptas, California. It was reported that the boy had
been mentally disturbed since discovering his dead mother in the
shower at age 7, and, crucially, that the murder of Marcy had
been unreported for two days despite the fact that he had shown
several friends the body. Broussard is still serving time in Folsom
Prison, of all places.

English student Neal Jimenez read the press story and was inspired
to write a screenplay. But, unlike the writers of *Badlands* and *Heavenly
Creatures*, Jimenez didn't attempt to reconstruct or fictionalise the
real story. He simply used the bare facts as foundation for a tale
about his generation: an aimless group of American teens that would
come to be media-defined as 'Generation X' or 'Slackers', who had
zoned out completely from their elders' debates about '60s liberalism
versus '80s conservatism, had no moral or ethical viewpoints, and

who saw the world through the fantasies of television and film. The result was a movie that came on like trailer-trash Brett Easton Ellis, was directed by Tim Hunter with a pungent, grungy elegance that stood in direct opposition to the plasticising of rival American teen movies, and invented the 'indie' style that defined the best American teen movies of the post-Richard Linklater (see *Dazed And Confused*, p. 307) '90s and beyond.

The plot is simple, self-contained, pulpy and full of tragic inevitability. By the banks of the river, 12-year-old Tim (Miller) discovers the monstrous John 'Samson' Tollet (Roebuck) sitting next to the frozen corpse of his girlfriend. Rather than attempting to hide the crime, Samson spills all to his school friends and brings them down to the river to show them the evidence. The group's delusional, loud-mouthed leader Layne (Glover) not only wants to cover up the crime, but sees himself as the star of his own *noir* drama, while Tim's big brother Matt (Reeves) wants to turn Samson in. Layne eventually persuades Samson to hide out at the home of Feck (Hopper), a middle-aged, one-legged dope dealer who may or may not have murdered his own girlfriend many years before. While Matt goes to the police and sets off a manhunt and a media scandal, Feck finds his own solution to the problem of a boy whose madness outstrips his own.

The weird thing about all this? It's actually a comedy.

Aesthetically, much of the movie's power comes from Tim Hunter's ability to find a sinister beauty in an ugly, poverty-stricken part of California Hollywood doesn't think we want to look at, and Jurgen Knieper's score, which dumps '80s synth new wave in favour of Bernard Herrmann-esque orchestral motifs, which juxtapose cinematic melodrama with the movie's ugly wasteland of rough scrub, dilapidated housing, battered cars and hardcore punk from the likes of Slayer and Wipers.

But the movie's greatest coups are the cast and the lead characters. *River's Edge* pulls off something that its bleak offspring largely don't. It's one thing to put blank, emotionless, amoral teens on celluloid and set out to shock. It's another to make them fun to hang out with. Crispin Glover's performance is a comic gem, allowing a potentially grim and disturbing tale to be fun. The bulky Roebuck is as believably threatening as any teen killer on celluloid. And even though Miller's tiny, androgynous Tim is every parent's pet-killing gun-stealing nightmare, you can't help but grin along with his sardonic precociousness.

And Keanu? This is the film that explains why the man became a megastar. Reeves has the thankless role: the solid nice guy amidst four male characters who get to say and do thrilling outlandish things every time they're onscreen. But he is beautiful, admirable and utterly compelling ... the perfect audience representative amongst the crazies. It's Reeves who makes the unlikely bromance between decent Matt and deluded Layne feel entirely natural.

And then there's the late Dennis Hopper. In exactly the same year that he reinvented himself as *Blue Velvet*'s Frank, the old wife-beater – Oh yeah ... he's dead and we're supposed to skip all that and be all sentimental and call him a lovable reprobate. I forgot, sorry – plays exactly the same guy here, except that the prop has changed from oxygen mask to inflatable doll. And ... he's brilliant. The old reprobate.

He gets one fuck of an entrance. Feck announces himself by playing one rude note on a saxophone while the inflatable doll looks on, open-mouthed with admiration. He hops to the front door on his one leg with a gun, opens the door, points the gun at Crispin Glover's head and growls, 'The cheque's in the mail.' Hopper and Glover mug the rest of the scene so furiously that they both burst into laughter. It could have been scripted. I prefer to think not.

Just in case you're missing the esteem in which Hopper is held around here, the dialogue references *Easy Rider* around three minutes later. How many iconic, over-the-top character actors can give a teen movie a direct link to *Rebel Without A Cause* (see p. 28)?

There are scenes that are pure black comedy genius. Samson is holed up with Feck, ragging the ruggedly handsome but confused drug casualty about his inflatable girlfriend. 'Hey Feck,' Samson asks, aggressively. 'Are you a psycho or something?' Hopper sits up straight and answers, deadpan: 'No. I'm normal. She's a doll. I know *that* ... right, Ellie?' A few minutes later he reminisces, 'I ate so much pussy in those days my beard looked like a glazed doughnut.' I hope I'm doing this stuff justice. Dennis Hopper's a great Dennis Hopper in a fair few things. But this, pound-for-pound, for me, is his best performance.

But even Hopper is outgunned by Crispin Glover. This is one of those rare and beautiful performances: a full-on scenery-chewing method camp-fest, in the tradition of Al Pacino in *Scarface* and Joe Pesci in *Goodfellas*, locating manic slapstick comedy in villainy yet somehow convincing you of some inner truth, and being so obviously enjoyed by the actor that you can almost see the peals of on-set laughter as soon as Hunter yells, 'Cut.' His Layne is a fabulous creation, somehow combining the macho, the gay, the feminine, the Valley Dude, the flamboyant glam-punk and the teen psycho in one compelling package of twitching, writhing, pop-eyed perpetual motion.

But *River's Edge* is also packed with plenty of understated and quietly moving moments. At one point, Ione Skye's Clarissa and Reeves's Matt are walking home, and the gallant Matt offers her his jacket to keep off the cold. She dismisses the need and carries on talking. The film jumps forward to them reaching their destination, and you notice that she's now wearing the jacket. In a movie where the shallow and self-absorbed reactions to a murder have subverted all the connections between people, Clarissa's acceptance of Matt's gallantry is an oasis of simple humanity, and a sure, subtle sign that these two are made of different and redeemable stuff from Layne, Samson and Tim.

River's Edge might be the ultimate generation-gap movie. The adults here, whether weak, childish mother, bullying stepdad and cops, sanctimonious ex-hippie teacher Mr Burkewaite or his '60s casualty mirror image Feck, do not share a language with these children. They don't understand them and the kids do not want to be understood. When Clarissa confesses that she admires Mr Burkewaite, an amused Matt replies, 'You respect an adult? I really do need to get stoned.'

And although he's joking, he's not joking. *River's Edge* mocks not just adult America and its misty-eyed view of itself, but everything that previous generations of writers and film-makers have said about teenagers. These kids are as alien to the grown-up inhabitants of their town as *The Blob* (see p. 44).

In the context of this movie, every reference to a 'better', more innocent American past feels like nihilistic satire. Take the scene in the tacky '50s-themed fast-food diner. As Layne and his waiter friend talk, a great Hank Ballard rhythm 'n' blues ballad is playing over the sound system, and you cannot stop yourself thinking about *American*

Graffiti (see p. 135) and how romantic and innocent the scenes played out to this kind of soundtrack were. The tune keeps playing as a now ever-increasing gang of bored teens go to look at a corpse, and you're not sure if the *American Graffiti* reference is deliberate, but it sure as hell feels like it is, and that *River's Edge* is, in a dark way, agreeing with George Lucas that kids were just nicer before '60s liberals insisted that they were old enough to know and see and experience everything – through television, through being left to their own devices by useless parents – before the girls needed sanitary towels and the boys needed razors. 'I'm here to turn back time,' dead-eyed killer Samson announces, holding a gun to a shopkeeper's head.

But conversely, *River's Edge* is so ahead of its time in look, feel and attitude that it feels like a post-internet movie; you keep expecting one of these aimless nihilists to whip out a mobile, take a snap of their decomposing friend and post it on www.cadaverblog.com.

The movie connects the '50s movie youth with their post-punk counterparts by reviving the juvenile delinquent habit of mocking media clichés about troubled teens. At one point a kid even critiques the movie itself. 'This entire episode is in bad taste. You young people are a disgrace to the human race ... to all living things ... to plants even.' But, while girlie-boy Layne comparing himself to Chuck Norris is a cultural reference made to make us guffaw, there is a serious point. When Samson explains his feelings about killing to Feck, he chooses his words carefully. 'She couldn't move, she couldn't scream. I had total control of her. Total control of her. It felt so real. It felt so ... *real*!' Which leaves you with the disturbing thought that, for the modern teen, the only action that doesn't feel like Chuck Norris or reality TV, that doesn't feel like one is hovering above oneself, watching a drama called your life unfold, unwilling to direct the action, is having the power to end life. That something this haunting can emerge from a film that's so entertaining and funny – that's why I said masterpiece earlier, and that's why I meant it.

★ ★

DIRTY DANCING

1987

Starring: Jennifer Grey, Patrick Swayze, Jerry Orbach
Dir.: Emile Ardolino

Plot: The dance-card-carrying *Communist Manifesto*
Key line: 'Baby. Corner. Don't make me say it.'

You know those montage scenes in old movies where a writer hammers out a few lines, rips the paper out of the typewriter, throws it into a wastepaper basket in sheer frustration . . . and then starts again? Well, whatever the laptop computer equivalent of that is, *Dirty Dancing*'s got me doing it.

At first, it was going to be kicked off by an essay on why women like this movie so much. Then I realised that this was based on a great many sexist assumptions about women, so . . . wastebasket.

Once I'd reminded myself that I own a penis, I thought I might try writing about the entire movie from a male perspective. I mean, I'm a relatively heterosexual man – married, kid, love football, The Clash, gangsta rap and movies in which short Italian-American men ask you to say 'ello to their leedle friends – and I *adore* this *über*-chick flick, so that seems sensible. We could start with the post-coital scene where Baby (Grey) asks Johnny (Swayze) about his sexual conquests, and the guy takes the oldest seduction trick in the book to the kind of virtuoso extreme which would win first-prize and air-punching approval at the annual Iron John Man's Man Beaver Hunt dinner and dance. He unloads a bunch of stuff about how rich, hot older women just throw themselves at him, and how no red-blooded male could possibly turn it all down. And when the girl looks all hurt and says it's OK, she understands, because he's using them, he . . . now get this, lads, 'cos this is priceless . . . opens his eyes wide in panic, looks all abused and misunderstood, and says: 'No. *They* used *me*.' And then he actually moistens his eyes at the painful memory of having to fuck all those women. What can any girl do? She gives him a look that says, 'I really am the only woman who understands you, aren't I?' and jumps the guy's bones. And the Beaver Hunt Lifetime Achievement Award goes to . . .

But taking that tack implies that the *Dirty Dancing* phenomenon is entirely bound up with tiresome gender war. And, while many of us might occasionally disconnect our occipital lobes completely and marvel at the oeuvres of Sandra Bullock and Danny Dyer, no one is going to make them iconic. *Dirty Dancing* has grossed $222 million and counting on an initial production budget of $4 million. It was the first film to sell a million copies on video. It spawned two multi-platinum soundtrack albums, a successful prequel and a stage show. It's such a universal cult among Western women that it is occasionally referred to as 'the chick *Star Wars*'. It did all this despite being shot by a choreographer who had never directed a movie before and the fact that its romantic leads hated each other's guts in real life.

You know the 'Hungry Eyes' bit, where Swayze keeps stroking Grey's arm and waist and she keeps bursting into laughter, and Swayze looks angry and glances off-camera in exasperation? That wasn't carefully scripted spontaneity. He kept stroking, she kept giggling because it tickled, and he wanted to strangle her because the two had taken an instant dislike to each other on the set of *Red Dawn* (see p. 245) and Grey had nearly quit the movie when she'd learned that Swayze had been cast. She wanted Billy Zane. But the boy couldn't dance.

And yeah . . . both the number-crunchings and the gossip about Swayze and Grey were potential starting points, too. Wastebasket.

And then I went off on one about Jennifer Grey's nose. It deserves a loving tribute, because, like poor Patrick Swayze and Emile Ardolino, it's dead. The biggest shock on the DVD of *Ferris Bueller's Day Off* (see p. 270) involves watching the Making Of doc, and this moderately attractive but unremarkable woman starts talking who you figure made the tea or gripped the key, whatever a key grip is, and the name Jennifer Grey flashes up. The weirdness isn't the plastic surgery. In Hollywood? Say it ain't so! It's the fact that this is *really good* plastic surgery, whereby the woman's face looks so natural that you wonder why Joan Rivers or Pete Burns ever had to exist. It's not some horrible butcher job. But Jennifer Grey now bears no resemblance, at all, to the girl in those '80s films. None. Totally different person.

But that's the point. She was once Barbra Streisand's obvious heiress, the world's favourite Jewish princess. She now looks like any pleasant WASP in the street.

The temptation here is to conclude that killing her USP was some kind of self-hating Jewish thing. But projecting that upon someone I've never met feels kinda racist. Besides, she's the daughter of the great Joel Grey, who became a sort of proxy anti-Nazi legend with his astonishing performance in Bob Fosse's *Cabaret* (he also has a great Bad Guy cameo in Season Five of *Buffy*, but I digress). Whatever Grey Jr's reasons, she admitted that her appearance changed so radically that it was 'like being in a witness protection programme or being invisible'. Invisible girls aren't stars. Her acting career evaporated and she was last seen, with something approaching irony, winning the 2010 season of America's *Dancing With The Stars* celeb dancing contest.

Generations of women don't fall in love with a movie *en masse* unless they strongly relate to its female protagonist. The nose was crucial because, even though Grey is luminously beautiful in *Dirty Dancing*, it's a beauty that looks natural, unforced, unthreatening . . . and attainable. Anyone can look at her one obvious imperfection, and imagine that, in the right circumstance, in the perfect moment . . . they too can be luminously beautiful and pull Patrick Swayze (or insert your own stud-muffin; I realise he wasn't everyone's cup of beef) too. How can anyone so fail to see that their 'worst' feature was the thing that every fan adored? As career suicides go, that rhinoplasty rates pretty high.

I like the nose. Hell, I *love* the nose. But I finally decided to start with something else. It comes from a scene that won't rate too high among DD fan faves, but will resonate among fans of the *Mad Men* TV show. Because these two very different screen winners share one crucial thing in common. It's a book called *The Fountainhead*.

Baby has discovered that working-class dance instructor Penny has been knocked up by middle-class Robby, who is only waiting tables at the Kellerman's dance holiday camp in the Catskills to make some spare money before going to an Ivy League college. Baby, being kind of a busybody, goes to Robby to try and persuade him that a rich brat like him could at least give the devastated Penny the money for an abortion. The cad is not playing. 'Some people count, and some people don't', he smirks. He then gives Baby a battered copy of *The Fountainhead* by Ayn Rand by way of explanation.

The Fountainhead was a huge American cult best-seller in the late '50s and early '60s, and was one of the key texts that the beats and hippies were rebelling against. It is a novel about an architect named Howard Roark who lives his life with an uncompromising adherence to the principle of individualism over collectivism. Roark wants to pursue his architectural vision of gleaming modernist buildings, and would rather starve than give financiers or ordinary people what they want ... or, rather, what they think they want, because, compared to his intellect and will, the masses are mere ants who actually have no idea what they want until men like him give it to them. Roark is a Nietzschean *Übermensch* who bends society to his skyscraper will, and also the reason why evil architects start popping up in '60s movies like *Beat Girl* (see p. 66).

The most controversial passages of *The Fountainhead* concern Roark's rape of Dominique, and the powerfully eroticised vision of a strong man conquering a woman in the same way that he conquers everything else ... and the woman loving it. The book was made into a film starring Gary Cooper, and it has a startling final shot, as Cooper/Roark poses, hands on hips, on the roof of his enormous phallic building, and we shoot up an elevator to meet him, literally shooting up his colossal penis and into the sky to worship a man who proudly straddles the entire world. Hitler would have loved it.

Incidentally, Ayn Rand was a woman.

From the moment screenwriter Eleanor Bergstein opted to put that book in the hands of the movie's Bad Guy, she was not simply writing about getting off with the cute boy at the holiday disco. She is taking Rand's hotch-potch conservative philosophical theory of Objectivism to task, and trying to gently inform the viewer about why America was not better before 1963, the year in which *Dirty Dancing* is set. One interesting little factlet about teen movies is that the four most commercially profitable films in this book are set between 1955 and 1963, the semi-mythical era when kids in their teens became teenagers, rock 'n' roll was invented, whites learned to dance like blacks, the clothes and hairstyles were deathlessly cool and everyone had a thrilling and rebellious time without need of booze and drugs, because digging those jungle rhythms in the pre-civil rights era was more rebellious than felching a crack dealer on the living-room rug while Mum and Dad are watching *Heartbeat*.

But *American Graffiti* and *Back To The Future* both insist that life was better before the onset of '60s radicalism and liberalism, and *Grease* is too busy dancing and laughing to really care. *Dirty Dancing* loves the '50s music, but, otherwise, it depicts a world, in the shape of the ludicrous Kellerman's resort, riddled with class and race divisions, hypocrisy, exploitation and back-street abortions, which is all sorted out, in the end, by a Jewish liberal idealist who teaches everyone who comes near her the value of social mobility, sexual freedom, personal sacrifice, racially mixed physical expression through dancing, and, as everyone dances together at the movie's end, and she and Johnny are simply absorbed into the group, the triumph of collectivism over the individual. When Johnny gets up onstage and announces his love for Baby, he doesn't evoke anything so shallow as her beauty or as wishy-washy as her loving nature. He's pulled her out of the corner – and her father's well-meaning but overly patriarchal influence – because she 'taught me that there are people willing to stand up for other people no matter what it costs them. Someone who's taught me about the kind of person I wanna be.' The girl isn't a hot babe who dances a bit. She's fucking Gandhi!

So maybe that iconic shot, when Johnny raises Baby high above his head on the dance floor, and the lights hit her, and the room cheers and whoops, and it delivers a great little metaphor about how a woman can only trust a man with her heart if she can trust him with her body ... you could also look at it as the union between working-class authenticity and middle-class liberal idealism, sup-porting each other as they stride purposefully into the 1960s establishing civil rights, gay rights, human rights ... and a woman's right to choose. You could. Or maybe just I could. I really like this movie.

But if we go back to that 'what women want' thing, I don't think it's too much of a leap to suggest that *Dirty Dancing* is a winning rarity ... a female wish-fulfilment romance with a founda-tion in populist feminism. In fact, it's *Where The Boys Are* (see p. 57) for the 'women can have it all' generation. Apart from the obvious pro-choice anger of the abortion sub-plot, there is a wonderfully sly moment among the all-dancing joys of the final act. Baby says, at the beginning of the movie, that it's impossible to find a man who matches up to her own father (Orbach). And the bond is so strong it has the unhealthy side effect of sidelining her mother from vital decisions. Dad lends Baby money without consulting Mom. Dad jumps to conclusions without even talking to Mom. And Baby colludes in the patriarchy by being completely uninterested in Mom, to the point where she is a bit-part character. Moreover, Baby's sister is a both a rival to Baby and a comic character, doing terrible songs onstage, competing with Baby for her father's affections.

So we get to the end, and, even as Johnny is making his impassioned speech about Baby's qualities and whisking her onto the dance floor, Dad is still all glowery and pondering whether to go a bit *Fountainhead* and take back ownership of his prize possession. But Mom, finally, intervenes, and gently insists he butt out. And, as Baby dances and Dad sees her as the young woman she is rather than the baby he thought she was, Mom turns to him, smiles, and says, 'I think she gets this from me.' It's such a clever line, undercutting Dad's chauvinism with knowing humour, and suggesting a back-story between the Housemans that implies that there's more to this trad-itional relationship than we've seen.

So these are some of the reasons why I love *Dirty Dancing*. Yes ... the music's cheesy. The romantic plot is corny. The film-making simplistic and the dancing probably not as good as it thinks it is. But then, that last point is probably why it kicked off a new wave of mass enthusiasm for learning to dance. (*Strictly Ballroom*? Great movie. But it's a remake of *Dirty Dancing* with the irony turned on.) Unlike those old Astaire and Kelly moves, you watch these dances and believe, with a little training and some laying off the junk food, that you could do it too.

Okay ... the *Communist Manifesto* crack was overdoing it a bit. But ... made you look. Because I really want the haters to watch *Dirty Dancing* again. Go with it. And if you really don't feel *anything* when Baby gets her man, you're just trying too hard not to.

★ ★

HEATHERS

1989

Starring: Winona Ryder, Christian Slater, Shannen Doherty, Lisanne Falk
Dir.: Michael Lehmann

Plot: The film that wanted to take out John Hughes.
Key line: 'I love my dead gay son!'

Dear Diary,

My teen angst bullshit has a body count.

Betty Finn was a true friend. But I sold her out for a bunch of Swatch dogs and Diet Cokeheads. There were three of them, and their names were Heather, and they made me play croquet, for deeply symbolic reasons I never understood. Then I saw Him in the school cafeteria. He had the beauty of James Dean, the voice of Jack Nicholson and the mannerisms of that old guy in the flasher mac out of *Columbo*. Who does that guy in the coat think he is anyways ... Bo Diddley?

Anyways, the boy's name was J.D. and he gave me shower nozzle masturbation material for weeks.

So we got freaky on the crocquet pitch and I told him my teen angst bullshit about the Heathers. Heather One ruled the school and was a primo beeyatch. I once asked her why we can't speak to different kinds of people at school and she replied, 'Fuck me gently with a chainsaw! Do I look like Mother Teresa?'

Now, it's one thing to want somebody out of your life. It's another thing to serve them a wake-up cup full of liquid drainer. But that's what J.D. (J.D. – I've just realised that stands for juvenile delinquent! If only I'd picked up on that!) did. Heather One went down face-first through the glass coffee table. I said, 'Oh my God! I can't believe it. I just killed my best friend!' J.D. said, 'And your worst enemy.' I said, 'Same difference'. I'm sardonic, even in a crisis.

You're wondering why I didn't talk to my parents. I tried and all my Dad could say was, 'I don't patronise bunny rabbits.' He's such a pillow case. 'Great pâté', I said to Mom, 'but I gotta motor if I'm gonna be ready for that funeral.'

But before I'd had time to process that mindfuck J.D. was shooting these two dumbass jocks who push cows over in their spare time and planting mineral water on their bodies to prove they were homos. We live in Ohio.

Next day at school, it's all, 'Did you hear? School's cancelled today because Kurt and Ram killed themselves in a repressed homosexual suicide pact.' I mean, sure ... Kurt and Ram had nothing to offer the school but date rapes and AIDS jokes. But before we know it that idiot hippie teacher Pauline has encouraged the school and the local media to group-hug over the tragedy of teen suicide, and offing yourself has become school's coolest fashion statement. Mother of shit!

By now, Heather Two has become Heather One by default and is regaling me with shit like, 'Veronica, why are you pulling my dick?' Yeah ... call me when the shuttle lands. J.D. figures she has to go. But then he figures we all have to go. He's, like, waiting 'til I burn my hand with the in-car lighter and sparking his cigarettes off my molten flesh. What's your damage? Are we going to prom or to hell?

Now I tell you: I've seen a lotta bullshit. Angel dust. Switchblades. Sexually perverse photography exhibitions involving tennis rackets. We live in Ohio. But J.D. planting a bomb in the high school basement was like bulimia ... just *so* '87. So I shot him and he strapped the bomb to himself, which allowed me a cute pay-off where I lit my cigarette off his incinerated remains. So kiss my aerobicised ass.

I blame not Heather. But rather a society that tells its youth that the answers can be found in the MTV video games. The name of that righteous dude that *can* solve their problems? It's Jesus Christ. And he's in the book. After all, the only place where different social types can genuinely get along with each other is in heaven. It'll be very.

* *

SOCIETY

1989

Starring: Billy Warlock, Devin Devasquez, Ben Slack, Evan Richards, Patrice Jennings, Ben Mayerson
Dir.: Brian Yuzna

Plot: So *this* is why Margaret Thatcher kept insisting that there's no such thing as society . . .
Key line: 'We're one big happy family. Apart from a little incest and psychosis.'

We've watched a typically dumb-looking '80s kid have two nightmares, and seen something, running underneath the credits, that could well be either utterly disgusting or pure porn if we could only make out exactly what it is, before we are introduced to the Perfect Life Of Bill Whitney. Bill, played by Billy Warlock, is rich, clever, sporty, popular and even shorter and squatter than Emilio Estevez. He wasn't just born with a silver spoon in his pouty mouth, but the entire 38-piece dining set. So why does he feel so out of place among his peers that even his family give him nightmares?

The answer given to us in Brian Yuzna's teen-body-horror satire was so what '80s America didn't want to laugh at that it took three years of European success before anyone would even release *Society* in its own home country. It is, if you will, the anti-*Back To The Future*: an anti-Reagan class-war low-budget gore-fest based on a thought that the majority of people have allowed to pass through the dark recesses of their minds from time to time, like, maybe, just after we hear of a huge bonus payment to a corporate banker while we struggle to survive a recession entirely caused by the short-term greed of corporate bankers. To paraphrase: as flies to wanton boys are we to The Rich. They kill us for their sport and then have freaky sex orgies in the blood of our entrails.

Society leers at us through an initial gauze of typical teen movieisms thrown slightly off-kilter. Rich kid Billy, despite being both short and white, is the basketball hero of Beverly Hills Academy, which of course means that he wipes the floor with his nerdy class president rival in debate just by turning up . . . even when distracted by a mean girl flashing her skimpy briefs at him while he's on the podium. Nevertheless, his parents don't seem to like him, even when he throws a meathead who appears to be trying to rape his sister out of the house, and his sister, who they seem to like way too much, has big lumps throbbing away in her back when Billy helps zip up her dress. The only place Billy can take his increasing feelings of spooked alienation is the office of his therapist Dr Cleveland (Slack), who puts it all down to typical adolescent angst. And one might buy that, if Billy wasn't catching sister Jenny (Jennings) wanking in the shower while wearing her arse and her tits on the same side of her body.

Soon, Jenny's apparent stalker Blanchard (Tim Bartell) has accosted Billy and played him an audio tape of what seems to be his entire family taking part in an orgy at Jenny's 'coming out' party. When Billy leaves the tape with Doc Cleveland, he returns to find the tape doctored and Blanchard conveniently killed in a car accident. *Society* then goes on to make you snigger and puke at Billy's quest for the 'orrible truth while simultaneously bamboozling you with exactly what gorgeous pervert Clarissa (classic seduction line: 'How do you like your tea? Milk? Sugar? Or would you like me to pee in it?') and her monstrous, moronic, furball-regurgitating mother have to do with it, in a brilliant B-movie that melds the bad taste aesthetics of John Waters and David Cronenberg into a messy mutant bleurgh-fest.

In fact, Act One has the sun-drenched, pretty-pretty and camply over-acted aesthetic of *Beverly Hills 90210* if John Waters had ever decided that his future lay in TV soap, before Act Two becomes a three-way wrestling bout between *Scooby-Doo*, *Invasion Of The Bodysnatchers* and *Twin Peaks*. Perfect preparation for an Act Three, where we learn that Billy has not been looking for anything. He's been the star of a sick interactive theatre-piece where an alternative human race called The Upper Classes have been watching him attempt to fit in with their bizarre customs for 17 years until judging him ready to eat, along with Blanchard, who is not dead. Yet. Cue the scene that proves there's something more repulsive than the blood and guts of most splatter movies.

The good folk of Beverly Hills don't so much eat Blanchard as absorb him while turning him inside out while he is still alive. Their faces attach to his body and stretch into alien pig snouts. They ooze into him, and the disfigured gourmets bathe in his body fat. I wasn't sure what to expect when I first saw the movie, but it's a hell of a lot more original and genuinely nauseating than the cannibal feast one has been expecting for an hour or so. It's the sex angle that really fucks you up, that young girls are gleefully writhing in human goo with fat, ugly old men. The spectacle reaches its peak when the old Judge who leads the society gives poor Blanchard a fist-fuck you'll never forget. *Eewww!* really doesn't cover it.

As Billy tries to escape, the Whitney family home becomes a house of horrors where every sight is worse than the last. The effects are so disgusting and maniacal that they can only have been devised by a man called Screaming Mad George. The man is a genius. But one who I never want to meet alone in a dark room without witnesses.

Billy, aided by Clarissa, her monster mom and his friend Milo, has to escape by way of what seems to be a futile, sado-masochistic fistfight. The way he turns it round has to be seen to be believed and I ain't even going to try and describe the levels of sick and wrong.

Pamela Matheson almost steals the show as the lovably grotesque Mrs Carlyn. But the stars are undoubtedly Screaming Mad George's make-up bag of horrors and Yuzna's surreal switch from camp teen thriller spoof to, arguably, the most repulsive 30 minutes ever put on celluloid. Watch. But don't eat beforehand.

1990s

EDWARD SCISSORHANDS

1990
Starring: Johnny Depp, Winona Ryder, Dianne Wiest, Anthony Michael Hall, Vincent Price
Dir.: Tim Burton

Plot: The world was never meant for one as beautiful as Johnny Depp.
Key line: 'If he weren't up there now, I don't think it would be snowing. Sometimes you can still catch me dancing in it.'

I actually had to have a heated debate with myself about whether Tim Burton's greatest work was a teen movie. Then The Missus interrupted before me and I came to blows, pointed out the whole angst/alienation/doomed first love metaphor, reasoned that the story is told from a teenage girl's viewpoint, and rested her case. This made me very happy, because *Edward Scissorhands* is one of my favourite films, and one that repeatedly accesses my inner tortured goth and shows it pictures of abandoned puppies in black eyeliner until it blubs like a little bitty baby.

First off: I realise I've pulled this gambit already – way back in the *West Side Story* entry (see p. 76) – but the list of actors that could have played everyone's favourite Punkenstein monster is just too weird to ignore. Let's get the probably apocryphal one out of the way first: rumours, unsubstantiated by Burton, have always persisted that first choice was Michael Jackson. Now, I get why this urban myth persists. Jacko was a real-life Edward: black man-turned pale-skinned alien, body and face made by surgery, permanently startled look, attempted to present himself as too innocent for this world. But a cursory watch of *The Wiz* and *Moonwalker* (see *Popcorn*) confirms that he couldn't act. And Tim Burton was fond of actors. And how much would you have had to pay the mad fucker to be anything other than the ludicrous 'King Of Pop' figure he was by 1990? And I'm getting out of here before I say something I regret about the sickening, sentimental reaction to his death from people who wouldn't have let the guy within 10 miles of their own kids.

Nope, the confirmed ones are interesting enough without fant-asising about the fanciful. Take Robert Downey Jr. Now, the guy definitely has the acting chops and the built-in bizarro. But one suspects that the possibility of the now cleaned-up superstar taking enough drugs to wander into one of the houses in Lutz, Florida (where much of *Edward Scissorhands* was shot) and clamber into bed with the kids might have made him difficult to insure.

Tom Hanks was mooted, and was obviously the safest bet. But he turned it down for ... *Bonfire Of The Vanities*! HAHAHA!!! The greatest compliment you can pay everyone's fave nice-guy thesp is that his career hardly missed a beat over that comically bad decision.

Next up is ... William Hurt. Yes ... William Hurt. The same William Hurt who was 40 years old in 1990. One can only imagine that having done a gay cross-dresser in *Kiss Of The Spider-Woman* had immediately qualified the annoying ham for anything involving heavy make-up and being abnormal in middle-American terms. I'm actually genuinely disturbed by my mental image of Hurt as *Edward Scissorhands*. Maybe *Family Guy* should give that skit a go.

Which leaves only one. You've guessed who it is, haven't you? Burton talked to Tom Cruise about the role and, to be absolutely fair to California's most admired Robert Smith clone, did so reluctantly at the behest of his paymasters, what with Cruise being The Hottest Actor In The World Right Now right then. Apparently the col-laboration was brought to an abrupt and propitious halt when the grinny Scientologist asked if the film could be rewritten to have a happy ending. I'll leave it there.

So Burton took a chance on a pretty 27-year-old failed rock star who had risen to fame in a truly dodgy-sounding US 'teen cop' show called *21 Jump Street* and whose movie experience largely consisted of being sucked into a bed and blown back out as a fountain of blood (see *A Nightmare On Elm Street*, p. 238). And what a chance, eh? Johnny Depp made himself into everyone's favourite actor *and* studly sex-muffin while wearing a costume and make-up that took two hours a day to put on (and around 30 seconds for Winona Ryder to tear off, one assumes, pruriently).

If you haven't seen this movie – well, actually, don't sit around reading, for goodness sake! Go watch it. Now, dammit!!! – then *Edward Scissorhands* is a modern fairy-tale, told by an old lady to her grandchildren, and set in a bland suburb based on Burton's childhood home of Santa Clarita Valley, California. Edward is a boy who has been made by a crazy inventor, played by Vincent Price in his final movie role. Edward has scissory appendages because his 'father' died suddenly of a heart attack before he could give his creation human hands, leaving the boy, who looks like an extreme gothic teen, permanently incomplete.

He lives alone in a spooky castle overlooking the town until Peg Boggs (Wiest, wonderful as the nicest Mom in teen movie history) discovers him while doing her Avon-selling rounds. Heartbroken by the idea of a boy living alone, she brings him home. He and her teen daughter, Kim (Ryder), fall in love. But the path of that stuff runs even less smoothly when holding hands involves unwanted amputation and many blood transfusions.

Meanwhile, the neighbours, who, like all small-towners, cannot accept anyone or anything different, react to Edward with horror, then curiosity, and then a willingness to use the boy for his extraordinary hedge and hair-clipping skills, and even, in the very funny shape of Kathy Baker's Joyce Monroe, as a sexual exotic.

Edward's nemesis is Kim's ex, boorish jock Jim (Hall), who cons his ghostly rival into crime and ends up dead. The good neighbours become an angry mob. Edward has no choice but to leave Kim for ever and return to his isolated castle, before a society that doesn't understand converts him into kitchenware. By the tale's end, we realise that the teller is Kim, now an old lady and still broken-hearted over her immortal first love, who must spend his eternity alone, sculpting ice with his scissorhands, giving the town snow. As Ryder, in outrageous senior citizen make-up, delivers the last beautiful, bereft line of dialogue, you realise that the film hasn't just been a perfectly realised metaphor for outsider teen angst and doomed teen romance taken to a poetic extreme; Edward Scissorhands is also about the sad inevitability of ageing, and the film's afterburn isn't Edward eternally alone in his tower, but Kim Boggs, living and soon dying, with the memory of a perfect lover she could never keep, too ashamed of her appearance now to contemplate seeing him again.

This compelling idea of the woman who grows old and the man who stays young – a subconscious acknowledgement of humanity's completely different treatment of ageing in men and women – recurs repeatedly in romantic teen fiction, and Twilight (see p. 468) is just as much Son of Edward Scissorhands as Daughter of Buffy. Like

Edward Cullen, this Edward is an exaggeration of the weird, cool, pale boy at the back of the class, a dangerous alien sex object who only one girl – that would be you – understands. The love is doomed from the start, and, like Angel in *Buffy* and Edward in *Twilight*, there are fundamental reasons why your love can't be consummated, and those reasons are entwined with death, making the boy both safe and frightening all at the same time; a perfect metaphor for the raging war between hormonal desire and fear of sex that every young girl must overcome. At least, so I'm guessing. I'm a boy, in case you were wondering by this time.

Most of the movies in this book are flawed. That's one of the things that makes teen movies so lovable, the way film writers and directors have to use the tension between personal stories and exploiting a market, serving an audience who are both cynical and easily bored, often on small budgets or under pressure from producers who always think a lighter, happier tone makes more money.

But *Edward Scissorhands* is an exception. I'm not sure if a perfect movie exists, but I know this one doesn't hit one false note. The cast are excellent. The production design and visual palette are extraordinary, with suburban settings cleverly made more comically grotesque than alien creature or spooky castle. The dialogue is funny and gloriously camp without veering into smartarsery. The film moves effortlessly from a modern take on Charlie Chaplin and '50s sitcom and soap, into darkness, violence and haunting sadness without leaving the viewer disoriented. And Danny Elfman's beautiful and instantly recognisable score manipulates your emotions utterly but forgivably, finding a singular sound made from equal parts Prokofiev, nursery rhyme, Disney cartoon standards and the theme from the first series of *Star Trek*.

But, in the end . . . it's Johnny Depp. I mean, really. How does he give a grotesque and comic creation so much emotion, particularly as he has to play the whole movie with his eyes in permanent shock mode and his mouth pouting like a duck's asshole? The whole performance is like some kind of physical miracle, with so few words needed that you begin to question all those cultural quips about how awful mime is.

No wonder Burton and Depp went on to form a creative partnership lasting eight movies over 21 years and counting. *Edward Scissorhands* was Burton's own teen angst made into the stuff of myth and legend. A gothic youth misfit in wealthy WASP California, Burton felt that he was so unpopular and alienated that he couldn't reach out and touch people as a kid. He came up with the metaphor to match his miserable memories, and urged screenwriter Caroline Thompson to take his look and experiences and come up with an allegory that blended Burton's resentment of jocks and babes with *Frankenstein, Beauty And The Beast,* vampire lore and Edgar Allan Poe ... and then watched as something that pretentious was given substance and soul by this unlikely genius who had spent his twenties thus far doing dumbass teen fodder. Hell ... I would have married him.

And, actually, if you nip now into Google Images and take a quick look at a picture of Depp as Edward Scissorhands right next to Helena Bonham-Carter ... maybe he did.

★ ★

DAZED AND CONFUSED

1993
Starring: Jason London, Sasha Jenson, Rory Cochrane, Wiley Wiggins, Milla Jovavich, Matthew McConaughey, Ben Affleck
Dir.: Richard Linklater

Plot: The post-grunge *American Graffiti*.
Key line: 'It's like the every-other-decade theory: The '50s were boring; the '60s rocked; and the '70s, oh God, they obviously suck, right? Maybe the '80s will be radical. I figure we'll be in our twenties ... Hey, it can't get any worse.'

Richard Linklater's second film marks a sea-change in teen movies. But it is also a fascinating bundle of contradictions. It looks and behaves like an independent film, but was financed by Universal studios. It was hugely influential but resolutely bombed at the box office. And it is, at one and the same time, a virtual remake of *American Graffiti* (see p. 135) while negating everything *American Graffiti* stands for.

In George Lucas's 1973 hit, the director revisits his own teenage years to tell a story about one night in the lives of four school-leaving teen boys. The tale is played out to a soundtrack of 1962 hits; period clothes, cars, architecture and slang are scrupulously revived and revivified; and the movie effortlessly evoked nostalgia for Americans of his own age while also entertaining '70s teens with plenty of sex, swearing, comedy, romance and neat stuff with flashy motors. Rather than following one linear plot, the movie flits around from one tale to another, presenting life more accurately as a series of vignettes. Because the budget was small, the film was dependent on strong, funny dialogue and the excellence of a virtually unknown ensemble cast.

But the Lucas agenda was full of regret and suppressed anger, because the film made an argument that life was more innocent, and therefore better, before the advent of the youth-driven cultural rebellions of the 1960s. While the meat of the movie was all fun without consequences, the revelation of the main characters' destinies provided a dark postscript that insisted that this moment in their lives was as good as it got.

In Richard Linklater's 1993 miss, the director revisits his own teenage years to tell a story of one night in the lives of a group of teen boys and girls who have just split high school for the summer holidays. The tale is played out to a soundtrack of 1976 heavy rock hits; period clothes, cars, architecture and slang are scrupulously revived and revivified, and the movie sought to evoke nostalgia for Americans of his own age while also entertaining '90s teens with plenty of sex, swearing, comedy, romance, violence and neat stuff with less flashy motors. Because the budget was small, the film was dependent on strong, funny dialogue and the excellence of a virtually unknown ensemble cast.

But the Linklater agenda contained no regret or suppressed anger because the film made an argument that life was more cynical, and therefore better, after the advent of the youth-driven cultural rebellions of the 1960s. The meat of the movie insists that all teen fun has consequences, and that some of it is really no fun at all, because being a teenager involves being around teenagers who are far nastier than you. And the movie gives no clues at all to the destinies of its characters, because it doesn't care. When you're young, you live in the moment, and the future is largely unthinkable, and if you knew it, it probably wouldn't make any difference to your immediate priorities: sex, booze, drugs and trying to avoid getting the shit kicked out of you while retaining your dignity in front of boys you look up to and girls you want to look up at.

Moreover, while any kid seeing *American Graffiti* in 1973 couldn't help but notice just how different pre-Beatles kids looked to them, and inevitably felt they were watching their parents, any kid seeing *Dazed And Confused* couldn't help but be struck by how little difference there was between a teen of '76 and their own long-haired, baggily jeaned, rock-loving and dope-smoking selves. Linklater uses his own childhood to talk to contemporary Cobain kids about theirs, and, with a central story that revolves around one pretty, strictly non-meathead jock's refusal to be bullied into temperance by his football coach, gives a big thumbs-up to the '60s most enduring achievement: the empowerment of the young to make their own choices and refuse to follow the diktats of authoritarian elders. In literal terms, Randy Floyd's refusal to sign 'the pledge' may not quite carry the risk of burning your Vietnam draft card. But, once you've followed *Dazed And Confused*'s low-key conflict between easy-going long-haired bohemians and short-haired, hierarchy-obsessed buffoons for 97 minutes – it comes close.

This, I suspect, is why *Dazed And Confused* was a box office bomb and a slow-burning video and DVD cult: the lack of a kids-today-suck theme alienated potential adult filmgoers, and a movie that has no serial killers, gratuitous tit jokes, big dance numbers, contemporary soundtrack or anything resembling a plot wasn't going to have the kids queuing at the cinema on pre-publicity alone. But once people saw it on video, word-of-mouth did its job. Because there are few more real teenagers in film than those in *Dazed And Confused*, and even fewer films that dare to show teens doing what they love doing best: nothing.

Linklater's classic is a break with tradition in more purely cinematic terms. Gone is MTV-style relentless action, rock video montage, frames crowded with colourful detritus, jock–bitch–nerd stereotypes, Hughesian wish-fulfilment, staccato editing and characters who only speak to move the plot along, crack a gag or confess their desperate angst. Instead, we have European-style long, slow takes, serene camera movement which forces our eye to wander away from central protagonists, kids who are well-rounded and basically decent except for a few arch bad guys, enough characters to confuse the casting director of *Spartacus*, and conversation that leads nowhere. These kids may like their booze and drugs, but they are also masters of cultural studies, deconstructing trash TV shows and rock records, discussing sex dreams where they were doing it with a girl who has the head of Abraham Lincoln, talking the exact aimless and beautiful bollocks that teens who are cleverer than adults think but nowhere near as smart as they think they are inevitably talk. It's the conversation that is much of the joy of *Dazed And Confused*, a quotable, random-generated dialogue that takes a cue from *Reservoir Dogs* and invents the entire *oeuvre* of Kevin Smith, for better or for worse. Maybe Linklater didn't pick up the success he deserved for doing it first. But other directors copped the feel and aped Linklater's ideas about allowing his actors to improvise around the script to make his own digressions feel more natural. The result mixed a haphazard, rambling structure with tight, taut and technically brilliant direction, as Linklater choreographs his small army of actors with the kind of unobtrusive aplomb that feels touched by genius.

But obviously I've got a little too into Linklater's languid sprawl and resolutely refused to tell you what *Dazed And Confused* is actually about. Here's the basics. It is the last day at a high school in Austin, Texas and kids put upcoming freshman kids from the neighbouring junior high school through sadistic 'hazing' rituals, talk bollocks, smoke some dope, plan a party that never happens, talk bollocks, have a drink, smoke some dope, play baseball by driving by mailboxes and smashing them, get shot at, hang out at a cool pool hall, have a drink, talk bollocks, assemble for a party in a field near one of Austin's Moonlight Towers, fight, flirt, smoke dope, talk bollocks. The movie ends with Randy 'Pink' Floyd's no to the coach, a freshman pondering his night out with The Big Kids while listening to a groovy '70s rock band called Foghat on his headphones, and a bunch of teens taking a road trip to buy Aerosmith tickets.

The film is defined by two longish episodes. The hazing rituals are bizarre and fascinating to anyone who hasn't gone to an American high school (or a British public school), and also play up a gender difference that feels rich with truth and subtext. For Mitch (played by Wiley Wiggins, a wide-eyed, long-faced girlie-boy with a winning smirk) and his fellow junior high kids, the ritual is perilous but spectacularly unimaginative. The high school bullies, led by Ben Affleck's Fred O'Bannion, run after you with big wooden paddles, and, when they catch you, they hit you on the arse with them until you can barely walk. Affleck, in an early role that serves as a bit of a red herring in his career as a leading man, is the one major character in the movie who is entirely one-dimensional, a boorish meathead who gives the movie its main stand-up-and-cheer moment when a vengeful Mitch devises a cunning plan to soak him in paint.

Meanwhile, the senior girls, led by the reliably great Parker Posey as the repellent Darla, put the juniors through a complex obstacle course of vaguely sexual sado-masochistic rituals so designed as public humiliation that every senior boy not chasing kids around with paddles gets to enjoy the spectacle as entertainment. They make the juniors suck dummies. They cover them in mustard, ketchup, eggs and flour. They call them bitches and sluts. They then force them to propose to the watching senior boys, who now resemble Kings watching slave girls degrade themselves at their majesty's pleasure. But the strangest thing is that, while the boys attempt to escape their paddling (one kid's mom even pulls a gun on O'Bannion), the girls willingly surrender to their humiliation. There is something very disturbing here about gender roles, as well as an implication that American schools tacitly encourage the abuse.

But the scene that everyone takes from *Dazed*. . . is the stoned rave in a field, a long, rambling pleasure involving kids in great clothes flirting, fighting, falling over, occasionally shuffling to some prime metal or funk and talking excellent stoner nonsense about how George Washington was part of an alien-worshipping cult. The amusingly heroic moment arrives when neurotic Jewish nerd Mike (Goldberg) works himself into enough of a humiliation frenzy to punch 'dominant male monkey motherfucker' Clint. The fight is broken up, and we know that, if it wasn't, tough boy Clint would kick poor Mike's ass into accident and emergency. But one universal male rite of passage involves understanding that you don't lose face by losing a fight . . . only by running away from one. You take your pop, hope the guy isn't so hard that you literally lose your face . . . and then write your own myth, comparing yourself to Jackson Pollock and Ernest Hemingway. And pray you don't bump into him when you're alone.

Pink (the slightly-too-pretty Jason London) is forced to make his crucial 'no' choice when he and friends, including a never-better Matthew McConaughey as David, the older kid who just can't quite break away from high school life, are caught having a ceremonial joint on the school playing field. The decision isn't just throwing a piece of paper into the face of the football coach who represents authoritarianism. It isn't even just a rejection of all-American priorities and the national obsession with college sports and their win-at-all-costs mentality. It's a break from childhood into young adulthood, because the decision will alienate him from friends as well as the adult world. It's a corny but neat summation of a film about choosing fun and friends and hedonism over duty and bullies and tradition, given poignancy by our knowledge of a coming decade which will do its level best to turn back the clock and pretend the 1960s never happened.

★ ★

TOTALLY FUCKED UP

1993

Starring: James Duval, Gilbert Luna, Lance May, Roko Belic, Susan Beshid, Jenee Gill, Alan Boyce
Dir.: Gregg Araki

Plot: To live and die gay in LA.
Key line: 'I wanna enjoy life while I'm still young enough to appreciate it. I mean, that's what it's all about. Right?'

The film begins with a shot of a small one-paragraph clip from a newspaper. It notes that, according to America's National Institute of Mental Health, 30 per cent of teenagers who commit suicide are gay, and cites a double suicide in Milwaukee. And then, after we quickly meet star James Duval, Gregg Araki spells out his intentions in crudely fonted captions: 'More teen angst.' 'Another homo movie by Gregg Araki.' 'In 15 random celluloid fragments.' 'Lifestyles of the bored and disenfranchised.'

Totally Fucked Up (or *Totally F***ed Up*, for marketing purposes) is the fourth lower-than-low-budget film by Californian early '90s 'New Queer Cinema' pioneer Gregg Araki, and the first in a 'Teenage Apocalypse Trilogy' completed by the more conventional but less engaging *The Doom Generation* and *Nowhere*. One of Araki's production tags is Muscle + Hate, a reference to a line from a cultishly influential '80s dance-industrial record called 'Join In The Chant' by British electronic band Nitzer Ebb. The more knowledge you have of alternative rock in the post-punk era, the more *Totally Fucked Up* will make sense.

The movie is dominated by fuzzy camcorder shots, a technique which has become familiar and mainstream following the success of movies like *The Blair Witch Project*, *Cloverfield* and *Paranormal Activity*, but was still relatively new in 1993. And the movie is definitely lent an added frisson by using anti-Hollywood techniques to shoot a movie which is all about teenagers who live in Hollywood. Araki is not interested in movie industry brats, the Hollywood Hills or Sunset Strip. His milieu is the rock 'n' roll *demi-monde* of West Hollywood, where young gay men and women find some refuge among artists, druggies and bohemians.

Totally Fucked Up uses a film-within-a-film structure. Steven (Luna) is filming his friends on a camcorder, mainly being interviewed by him and talking to camera. This serves as a background narrative for the plot, which is shot more conventionally. Araki also splices in short, grainy clips of other films taken from television in true guerrilla art style. Add the captions, and this should all be a mess. But it isn't. It takes 15 minutes or so to adjust to Araki's rejection of mainstream storytelling, and then you are drawn into the kids' world so completely you feel like you are hanging out with them.

Early in the movie, one of the girls mentions that there is a teen suicide cult in Yugoslavia which has led the state to ban records by Joy Division, The Cure and The Smiths. It must be true, 'cos it's in the *Los Angeles Weekly*. Along with its examinations of being young, gay and angst-ridden, *Totally Fucked Up* is also about the way the cool pose of teen misery can serve to obscure the real thing. Are all of these kids just playing at being attractively nihilistic? You can't really work out the answer to that until the end of the movie.

Despite the declaration about fragments, *Totally Fucked Up* does have a linear plot. Rejected by their parents because of their sexuality, our six teen buddies have formed an alternative family. While the boys cruise, fuck, bitch and moan, the two lesbians Michelle (Beshid) and Patricia (Gill) have formed a happy, solid relationship and want a child, possibly from sperm donated by one of their four best friends.

Meanwhile, Andy (the impossibly pretty Jimmy Dean-alike Duval, an Araki regular) is sick of being promiscuous and lonely, and envies the settled coupling of Steven (Luna) and Deric (May). Student Ian (Boyce) seems to provide the solution, just as Steven and Deric begin to unravel. But the course of true love does not run smooth in this definitively excluded netherworld of self-inflicted poverty, unsafe sex and drugs, and dark aimlessness.

Much of *Totally Fucked Up* consists of conversation, held with an endearing mix of self-conscious over-emphasis and clumsy naturalism by the amateur cast. It's this that makes it one of the best movies about how teens talk to each other; constantly attempting to mask their insecurity and vulnerability with cool poses, pop culture references and the kind of blasé sex talk that implies that fucking is just so *passé*. The witty one-liners and poetic pronouncements that screenwriters are inclined to put into the mouths of babes are eschewed in favour of a blend of angsty confessional and pretentious shite that we really say to each other when we're kidults, especially when we're from a big city and therefore feel that an elegantly wasted, been-there-done-that jadedness is the least vulnerable course to take in all matters interpersonal.

But obviously, this is not a film for the faint-hearted. We watch our heroes masturbate to gay porn; endure depressing one-night stands; get queer-bashed; express their lack of regret over the passing of the pre-AIDS 'good old days' and its fist-fucking, piss-drinking legends while also defining HIV as a government conspiracy, 'a Nazi Republican wet dream-come-true'. They say things that you simply don't expect gay men to say, like: 'I guess I haven't worked out exactly what it is I like to do yet. But I do think butt-fucking is totally gross. I mean – how can anyone put their dick where shit comes out?' And Araki and his actors make it feel like something far more true than shock tactics.

The more in tune you get with Araki's restless crash edits and digressions, the more elegant, accomplished and truly tragic the movie becomes, easily overcoming its own insistence that it is just 'more teen angst'. The inevitable suicide is finally provoked by infidelity, and *Totally Fucked Up* could be interpreted as an argument for more monogamous practice between gay men, especially as the chaotically miserable love lives of the guys are constantly contrasted with the domestic bliss enjoyed by Patricia and Michelle. But I don't think that is entirely Araki's point. *Totally Fucked Up* is less an encouragement to copy the rules and mores of straight society, and more a warning about trampling on the emotions of the vulnerable by refusing to see their 'angst' as real, and putting the alternative rules of a promiscuous lifestyle before the brittle emotions of someone who you are supposed to love, and who needs your comfort and support. And I think that's a simple sentiment about being human that you don't have to be young or gay to get behind.

Totally Fucked Up is a key work from a brave, uncompromising no-budget film-maker at the top of his game, taking a *mise en scène* that would be an unwatchable mess from a less talented writer-director, and making it sing with wonderful camera-work and virtuosity in the editing suite. It leaves you feeling that you've spent sad but rewarding times in a place in a major city that shouldn't exist, among people that America doesn't want to acknowledge, let alone embrace. It finds great beauty in ugliness, and, despite all the excellently chosen goth and indie and punk and industrial on its soundtrack, leaves you playing an old Who song in your head. That big, loud one with the synths and violins that roars about a 'Teenage wasteland', and makes you feel the double meaning of its pay-off line: 'They're all wasted!' *Totally Fucked Up* is the 'Baba O'Riley' of teen movies.

★ ★

HEAVENLY CREATURES

1994
Starring: Kate Winslet, Melanie Lynskey, Sarah Pierse, Clive Merrison, Diana Kent
Dir.: Peter Jackson

Plot: Worried about what your daughter and her BFF get up to in her bedroom? You should be . . .
Key line: 'All the best people have bad chests and bone diseases. It's all *frightfully* romantic.'

I'm writing about *Heavenly Creatures* bang in the middle of immersing myself in most of the entries from the 1950s to the 1970s. And really, I couldn't have chosen a film that better exemplified the radical shift in attitude by film-makers towards teen screen fiction from the 1990s onwards.

Heavenly Creatures is based upon real events: the murder of a woman called Honora Parker in Christchurch, New Zealand in 1954. She was murdered by her 15-year-old daughter Pauline and Pauline's best friend, 16-year-old Juliet Hulme.

This was a notorious crime in New Zealand, whipping up emotions in a similar fashion to the Moors murders or the Jamie Bulger case in the UK. So, rather than make up an exploitation script from media cuttings, co-writers Peter Jackson and Fran Walsh researched like historians. They interviewed dozens of people who knew the teen killers, and gained access to the incriminating diaries of Pauline Parker, which went into detail about the dark fantasy world she and Juliet conjured out of the intensity of their friendship. They used Pauline's diary entries word-for-word as the film's voiceover narration, and even went so far as to shoot the film in the locations where the events took place. They then auditioned hundreds of girls for the two leads, and discovered one who is acknowledged as one of the great actresses of her generation, and another who should be. The resulting film was so extraordinary that it not only invented Kate Winslet, but also gave Peter Jackson the opportunity to shoot overnight from admired maker of cult comedy splatter movies to director of the three most perfectly realised fantasy spectaculars ever made . . . that would be the *The Lord Of The Rings* trilogy, in case you were in any doubt. And no wonder, because watching *Heavenly Creatures* is one of those film experiences which leaves you in a state of shock, so effectively does it cleave the power of imagination onto the horror of true events. Its only teen movie antecedent is *Badlands* (see p. 138), which is also about true-life young killers, and also eschews docu-drama for an expressionist view of the fantasy world the murderers inhabited. But *Badlands* is all irony and iconic poses, while *Heavenly Creatures* is profoundly upsetting.

In short, it ain't *I Was A Teenage Werewolf*.

The film begins with scene setting. New Zealand in the early 1950s, a society that ran roughly 20–30 years behind its Brit or American equivalent. An opening contrasting a BBC voice narrating a tourism documentary of Christchurch in the 1950s with the hysterical screams and frantic running of two girls covered in blood.

Christchurch has upper-class Brit pretensions and the girls' school where our two murderers meet is a case in point. Uniforms and bonnets and bicycles and teachers who call a girl a 'gel'. Juliet Hulme is the new gel at Christchurch Girls High School, the English daughter of the rector of nearby Canterbury College; a pedigree so charmed that even the obnoxious teachers genuflect in her general direction. The scene establishes two crucial themes: one is the overbearingly snobbish worship of everything English and upper middle class; the other is the blackly comic contrast between the two girls. Juliet Hulme is beautiful, aristocratic, fragrant, smug, arrogant, glamorous. Pauline looks like the kind of girl who keeps spiders in her hair and eats bogies.

Winslet is great. But Lynskey is immediately astonishing, communicating everything about her secretive, alienated misfit persona without saying a single word. Her face is a picture of internal mischief and eternal discomfort, like a neurotic Denise The Menace. If she was a 21st-century teen she'd be studying emo and considering options in death metal, suicide and automatic weaponry.

We know, immediately, that she thinks she is as above her surroundings as Juliet. They've come at the same conclusion from different perspectives; one from beauty, breeding and entitlement; the other from somewhere private, dark, amused and smelly. When Ms Hulme corrects and humiliates the French teacher with immaculate superciliousness, it's love at first sight for the misanthropic Ms Parker.

The pair bond through their eroticised desire for escape from reality into fevered fantasy. Juliet's parents – her mother is a marriage guidance counsellor whose technique for keeping couples spliced involves shagging the better-looking husbands – leave her alone to go travelling at every available opportunity, even when she is hospitalised with tuberculosis (the film occasionally implies that they murdered the wrong mother). Both girls suffered from life-threatening childhood diseases that have left scars, physical and otherwise. And Pauline, like any normal teen, is just hideously embarrassed by her normal parents, poor enough to have to take in lodgers to get by, but not poor enough to be exciting.

Their escape from the repressed confines of a New Zealand childhood involve fantasising about podgy pre-rock popera legend Mario Lanza, movie stars including James Mason, Mel Ferrer and Orson Welles, and the creation of entire parallel universes called Borovnia and The Fourth World. The greatest moment in the picture comes immediately after Juliet learns that her parents are leaving her again. Bereft, Juliet begins to escape to her safe place. But, by sheer effort of will and telepathic bond, she takes Pauline with her. The girls' faces glow, the sun opens up a wound in the sky, and a magical land of ornate gardens, unicorns and supersized butterflies literally erupts from the rugged New Zealand landscape, and if you don't well up at the sheer beauty and virtuosity of this image, then you should probably stick with your Guy Ritchie flicks and give up on life's wonders entirely.

It's the enforced separation caused by Juliet's TB that spins the girls' world into madness. The pair write to each other as imaginary prince and princess Charles and Deborah, and fantasise about having a son who is a serial killer. Honora's fate is sealed when she slaps Pauline and call her a tart after one of the male boarders sneaks into her bed. Again, the normality hits you … murdered for being a typical, decent mother. Pauline loses her virginity to the boarder, still aged just 14, and hates it so much she slips off to the altogether sexier Borovnia, with its constant Lanza soundtrack and man-sized plasticine-sculpture people who look and sound a bit like James Mason. Juliet's fantasy has become Pauline's has become Juliet's. The real consequences of actions have begun to cease to matter.

Finally, both sets of parents panic about teen lesbianism and force Pauline to go into therapy. The shrink is ridiculous and grotesque, like all the adults here … except Honora Parker, significantly and respectfully. He assures her that there's an answer coming from 'medical science' for Pauline's disease of homosexuality any second now. Suddenly, Pauline is out of school and into the typing pool.

Each part of the tale – Dr Hulme's sacking from his college, the infidelity of Mrs Hulme and the resulting divorce, the heartless decision to send Juliet to South Africa with an aunt – leads inexorably to the inexorable. *Heavenly Creatures* wears its class war lightly, but it's impossible to avoid seeing that each amoral act of the upper-class Hulmes hammers another nail in the coffin of the *petit bourgeois* Honora Parker. Pauline Parker is the sicker girl and she falls in love with the Hulmes, for their class, their worldliness, their touch of bohemian glamour. They can have extraordinary fantasies projected upon them. Poor Mother simply can't.

So it is that Mrs Hulme comes up with the wizard wheeze of

allowing Pauline and Juliet to spend three weeks together before Juliet leaves, and that the intimidated and battered Parkers can't assert common sense. Just enough time for two lost girls to plan a killing.

The murder is one of the most horrible of all cinematic crime scenes. The banal conversation in the build-up, the familiarity of the walk in the woods, the brutality of the deed, how much you want to warn the victim, the plain injustice of it all ... and the bravura contrast with a monochrome depiction of what their crime means to the lives and futures of the girls, shot in the style of the movie melodrama they've been living in for too long. It breaks your heart.

Jackson really did justice to the truth here, which is, no matter how visually sumptuous or dramatically entertaining you make a killer's story ... killing itself is just ugly and barbaric. I don't really want to describe it: if you've seen *Heavenly Creatures* you'll know exactly what I mean, and if you haven't ... well ... it's pretty weird to say that I don't want to spoil it. What I *mean* is ... the shock should stand. That's what Jackson wanted you to feel – shock – and therefore, in this case, I reckon you should. It's up there with the murders in *Man Bites Dog* and *A Short Film About Killing*, in the forcing-you-to-face-your-own-love-of-screen-death department, if that's any help.

Back to the film's minor but important pleasures. There is a tiny Hitchcockian cameo from Jackson as the wino Winslet kisses after seeing Mario Lanza on the big screen. And big-ups and shout-outs to the reliably marvellous comedy actor Clive Merrison as Juliet's submissive father Dr Henry Hulme, suffering a life of being routinely humiliated by two spoiled princesses in typically quiet English desperation. In real life, Dr Hulme apparently went on to head Britain's hydrogen bomb programme. You couldn't make this stuff up.

I had a vaguely prepared thing in my head about an impassioned rant on behalf of Ms Lynskey, and how she's much better than Ms Winslet here, and how their different career trajectories are entirely about Ms Winslet's looks, and how this is another terrible example of the patriarchy at work, blahblahblah. But, after watching *Heavenly Creatures* for the third time, I've binned it. Simply because Ms Winslet is every bit as extraordinary and convincing here as Ms Lynskey, and is also luminously charismatic, which is what makes film stars film stars, when all is said and done. What I will say is that Lynskey's performance is generous as well as memorable, because, as the girls head towards the murder, Juliet, who is emotional and extrovert, is made even more beautiful by her extremes of feeling, while Pauline, who is insular and sociopathic, becomes increasingly like a screen killer: dead of eye, broody of brow, sallow, sickly pale and devoid of feeling, frightening and ugly in her single-minded pursuit of an irrational solution. The pair's performances represent the real girls' telepathy so chillingly that it should, in fact, be seen as one performance with two heads. That good.

But the major thing about *Heavenly Creatures* is its surgical examination of what I think is a secret universal fear: that there is something too intense, too potentially dangerous, too just plain fucking weird, about one-to-one friendships between teenage girls. We've all been on the receiving end of the manic laughter at some private joke, the shared language no one seems to understand, and the sexual threat of teen girls high on hormones and moments without consequences. It's a powerful, threatening, intimidating connection that Julie Burchill has written about so well, particularly in *Sugar Rush*. And, in *Heavenly Creatures*, it is taken, by Winslet and Lynskey and Jackson and Walsh, to its (il)logical extreme, until you are willing to believe that the crime is not some act of madness but the inevitable outcome of any teen female friendship that manages to successfully exclude the outside world. It is this, even more than the horror of the murder, that stays with you long after the credits roll.

And now, the creepy postscript. Both girls only spent five years in prison before making a life in Britain. When the crime was being investigated, one of the side-effect revelations was that Honora had never married Pauline's father Herbert Rieper. Which is why the film refers to both women as Rieper, but Pauline was tried under her mother's maiden name of Parker. Pauline Parker later ran a children's riding school in Kent, and was last heard of living in the Orkney Islands, off the coast of Scotland.

When the film was released the intrepid New Zealand media took it upon themselves to track down the real Juliet Hulme. She is now Anne Perry, a successful writer of crime fiction, also living in Scotland. When tracked down and questioned she said she had no opinion of Winslet's portrayal of her, because she would never watch the film.

Bizarrely, she appeared on British television in 2005, talking about the murder on daytime talk show *Trisha*. She denied that she and Pauline were ever lesbians. So that's all right, then.

But it's been 17 years since *Heavenly Creatures* was made. Has Anne Perry really not watched it at all? If she has, what did she make of being portrayed for all time as an insane, obnoxious princess who goaded a weaker person into killing her own mother? Did she and Pauline really never make contact after prison, as the courts ordered as a condition of their release, despite living in the same part of the world? What would two women who had done this as children … I mean … what would they … what could you … *say* to each other?

I suppose *Heavenly Creatures*, like most fiction, does raise more questions than it answers. But what an amazing, *amazing* puzzle.

★ ★

SPANKING THE MONKEY

1994
Starring: Jeremy Davies, Alberta Watson, Benjamin Hendrickson, Carla Gallo
Dir.: David O. Russell

Plot: The parentified teen's worst nightmare.
Key line: 'I can never get your father to do these things for me any more.'

One Christmas my mother fell down the stairs and broke her arm. I was 18 and working in my first job at a record shop, but I still lived at home. She was single and I was an only child so I had to look after her because there was no one else. I lost a job opportunity and a girlfriend. She even had a massively annoying dog that I had to walk. And, like every teenage boy, I liked to wank a lot. So there is no character anywhere in this book whose situation I relate to as easily that of Raymond Aibelli, the teen protagonist of the debut feature film by David O. Russell, master writer-director of *Three Kings* and *The Fighter*.

But, thankfully, I never had to carry my mum to the toilet. And – let me make this clear – I didn't do the thing that provides this movie's major plot-point and controversy. Let me make that very, *very* clear.

Made in low-budget, none-more-indie style with unknown actors, *Spanking The Monkey* follows the tale of Raymond (Davies) who, a couple of days before taking a prestigious pre-med internship in Washington, is called home by his obnoxious father (Hendrickson) to look after his mother (Watson), who has broken her leg, while he heads off on a sales trip. Dad has put his career before his son's future and expects Raymond to miss out on his internship to do what his father should be staying at home to do. Susan Aibelli is a needy depressive who resolutely refuses to be independent, pokes around in Raymond's private life and undermines his academic talents. The family dog intervenes every time he wants to masturbate. With his balls rapidly turning a nasty shade of angry blue, Raymond starts a relationship with a neighbouring high school girl Toni (Gallo), but is blowing it because he's taking his repressed rage at his parents out on her. Meanwhile, all this physical contact with domineering Mom is leading him directly into *Le Souffle Au Coeur* (see p. 122) territory. None of the cast plays this as a comedy, yet, somehow, Russell makes a film about boredom, the parentified child, lost opportunities, raging hormones and incest funny, as well as frightening and sad.

Russell's scenario is driven by a bracing cynicism about people and the nuclear family. Hendrickson's Tom is a memorably boo-worthy Bad Dad, the kind of guy who rings his son up to nag him about responsibilities and boast about his sales figures while ignoring the naked woman preparing herself for imminent shag action in his tacky hotel room.

But Tom has nothing on Susan in the nightmare-parent stakes. Castrating, controlling, inappropriate, nagging and in constant need of attention, she pushes every button that her son possesses and makes the viewer cover their eyes and hide behind the sofa as readily as if they were watching *Paranormal Activity* alone, in the dark, with a device that goes 'BONK!!!' at irregular intervals and a neighbour in a Michael Myers mask hammering at the window and cackling. She is an Oedipal nightmare, and enables Davies to find a performance that embodies every child who is driven to unbearable rage by their parents but can't bring themselves to say what needs to be said and break the pattern. The three are so seethingly real that you can feel years of familial tension oozing out of every pore of their suburban home.

The film's comedy comes out of that, because Russell knows exactly how uncomfortable we feel when a visibly aroused Raymond slips his oily hand underneath Mom's cast to massage her smooth, soft, tanned thighs. We can't help but get into the spirit, shouting, 'NOOOO!!! DON'T DO IT!!! RUN AWAY!!!' at the screen, enjoying our own squirming embarrassment. And we know where Raymond's going when he scuttles out of the room. And we know that the dog will find a way to stop it.

Except that it's not the dog this time. It's Raymond's old party-hearty friend Nicky (Matthew Puckett) who wants him to come out to play. By this time, Raymond sure could do with some healthy company his own age. 'I'm kinda busy,' Raymond explains. 'Busy?' Nicky responds. 'Doing what? Spanking the monkey?' Well, now that you mention it . . .

So Raymond skips out with the boys. But the reason that poor Raymond wasn't keen to get the old gang together is that they are old-fashioned rough 'n' tumble boys who prefer pussy, drugs and risky outdoor pursuits to studying, and, despite Nicky's protests, some of the other lads in the gang have a bitter anti-Raymond bug up their ass of the 'You think you're too good for us? Or are you a fag?' variety. Somebody mentions Raymond's yummy mummy and the night ends in disaster, and our flawed hero is even more alienated from everything than before.

And Mommie Dearest just won't let up. Soon she's making him wash her back in the shower and banging on about the erections he used to get as they played with a boat in the bath when he was a toddler: 'We called it the boner boat,' she cajoles, before she slips, and he catches her, and she giggles flirtily. Call social services! I don't care if he's 18!

But Susan is not a clichéd villain. She's a miserable woman whose marriage is a disaster and who is incredibly lonely, and loneliness makes more people do more terrible things than anything. And Watson is good enough to make you feel the truth of that, too.

Meanwhile, Raymond is so disconnected that a tryst with young Toni goes from so tentative she asks if he's gay to near-rape within seconds. Russell cuts between Toni's distress and the dog ravaging the picnic food. This disaster is used by Susan to move things a little closer to the inevitable.

The incest scene is suffused with discomfort and all sorts of creepy wrong. Russell's camera is suddenly tilting at queasy angles as two drunk and unhappy people slowly replace bonding by throwing food at the TV with tense touching. Russell shoots Raymond as if he was a killer, his face pale, sweaty and kind of angry, looking down at us, up to no good. The responsibility is very deliberately taken away from Susan and placed on Raymond's already overburdened shoulders, although Susan eventually meets him all the way. The scene has none of the easy pleasure of Malle's mother–son incest in *Le Souffle Au Coeur*, but Russell does replicate Malle's sparing of our blushes, and cuts away to black screen, and then to the following morning and two eggs boiling in a pan.

But, unlike Malle's jaunty memoir, *Spanking The Monkey* holds the incestuous act as the beginning of the drama, rather than the end. The film becomes a tense arm-wrestle between tragic farce and a dark study of a family where everyone is too royally screwed up to do or say the right thing, and whose dysfunction either abuses or manipulates everyone who touches them.

Raymond tells his father about him and Susan in the most fitting manner: on the phone, while Tom is waiting to go into a sales meeting. It's a sadist's revenge ... the worst thing a father could possibly hear, and miles away from where he can do anything about it. Raymond is a chip off the old block after all. But he's still no match for Susan's ability to lie under duress.

I said that *Spanking The Monkey* is funny. You must be wondering exactly where the joke is in all this. But Russell's expertise lies in his ability to show us terrible things without ever completely destroying the comic tone. He is laughing at the underlying darkness at the heart of the family unit, and encouraging us to laugh at the less bearable facts about our own.

Spanking The Monkey ends with a symbolic act of cleansing. But we never learn if the Aibelli family wash away their sins. This is as it should be. Families can't make the past go away. We just have to live with it.

★ ★

BEFORE SUNRISE

1995
Starring: Ethan Hawke, Julie Delpy
Dir.: Richard Linklater

Plot: We'll always have Paris. Except it was Vienna.
Key line: 'Love is a complex issue, you know?'

When *Dazed And Confused* director Linklater and co-writer Kim Krizan conceived a teenage *Brief Encounter*, they set out to write a teen movie as unconventional, in its understated way, as *Dogtooth* (see p. 473) or *Le Souffle Au Coeur* (p. 122). *Before Sunrise* flies in the face of everything we know about teensploitation. There is no plot. There is no action. The protagonists are not gender stereotypes. People talk a lot instead of doing stuff. There is little conflict. Pop music is replaced by highbrow classical music and the teen lovers discourse like self-consciously intellectual student travellers rather than kids because that is what they are. If your idea of screen teens is the oafish laddishness of *The Inbetweeners*, then *Before Sunrise* might make you feel physically ill, so concerned is it with politically correct maturity and comparing itself to the European tradition of intellectually charged romance exemplified by the films of Eric Rohmer, Ingmar Bergman and every acclaimed French director that isn't Jean-Luc Godard. Add earnest Ethan Hawke to the equation and *Before Sunrise* should be so suffocated by its own *Guardian* reader moral superiority and good taste that you want to slap it around and force-feed it Big Macs and alcopops until it pukes. But you don't because it is, against all odds, mesmerising, dramatic and entirely beautiful. It's less explicable than a busload of David Blaines catching bullets in their teeth.

Two students travelling alone, Jesse (Hawke) and Celine (Delpy), meet on a train from Budapest to Vienna. They are immediately attracted and Jesse persuades Celine, who is supposed to be going straight on to Paris, to get off the train with him and spend the night in Vienna before he boards a plane back to America. They can't afford a room so they stroll around the city, staying awake with each other, sketching in back-story, confessing hopes, dreams and their love for each other. They part at a station the next morning, promising that they'll meet at the same place in six months time. According to Linklater, who based the story on his own one-off meeting with an unforgettable woman in Philadelphia in the '80s, the whole film was shot and played as if the pair would definitely keep their promise. But the equally wonderful sequel, *Before Sunset*, set nine years later, reveals that one of them did not. And ... that's that. Except that it, really, really isn't.

Because Jesse and Celine are rich and real and true. They complain about having nice parents who wanted the best for them. They claim superior knowledge which they can't back up, as self-regarding kids with a wee bit of book learning are wont to do. They say ludicrous things about even death being ambiguous, because they are too young to accept their own mortality. They say trite things about war and reincarnation and media mind control that make you laugh because you've heard yourself saying them and recall that, bizarrely, you've also used this specious crap as a seduction tool, and that it worked. Perhaps that's really what falling in love is: finding someone who will find our narrative endlessly fascinating, and be the one person who won't constantly take issue or switch off and watch paint dry instead. Thanks Linsay. *Before Sunrise* makes me understand the sacrifices you make every day.

The couple encounter equally pretentious people: Viennese alternative types putting on a surrealist play; homeless men who write poetry in exchange for money. The day gradually becomes a night that gradually becomes a dream about the possibility of a utopian ideal ... where one doesn't work or care about earning money or domestic mundanities, but spends one's time wandering through faraway places, connecting with strangers and falling in a kind of love that is about something more transcendent than sex, and is especially fulfilling and intense because it is temporary. The pair reveal more about themselves because time is pressing and they need to confess, to imprint themselves upon each other's lives, to express the inexpressible, to grasp the moment and abolish tomorrow.

The fact that this is a specifically student kind of dream love is punched home by the record shop scene. This store is a vinyl paradise; the kind of place where discs hang from the ceiling in round black tribute to *Pretty In Pink* (see p. 275) and you flick through a rack and clock mint condition copies of records by Frank Zappa and The Searchers and Ella Fitzgerald and The Kinks and Gordon Lightfoot ... although someone really should have a word about their display system because the records don't seem to be sorted into genre or arranged alphabetically, so obviously this scene makes me hyper-ventilate a little. But this store makes up for it by having a proper listening booth where you can put the needle on the record yourself. Celine has picked out a tamponic folk record by Kath Bloom, and Delpy and Hawke perform a beautiful dance while standing stock still in front of a static camera in a tiny room. Slight embarrassment and amusement when the record turns out to be so folky and earnest, then slow realisation that the romantic lyrics and pure voice do pretty much sum up how they both feel. The couple stop smiling, but are still too vulnerable to each other and too shell-shocked by this whole experience to entirely connect. So they look at each other, but only, with endlessly perfect timing, when the other is looking away. At one point Hawke begins to tentatively do the leaning-in-for-a-kiss thing ... but, nope, all glory is fleeting. And the way Delpy looks at him – which he never sees, but we do – is with the kind of awe and adoration that every man wants from a woman as naturally beautiful as Delpy. The pair move, in the space of a few seconds, from two slightly annoying people thinking about shagging to two angels in whom the viewer's belief in a perfect, eternal, transcendent love is entirely invested. This is virtuoso stuff.

One of the movie's great triumphs is Vienna as a supporting character. Done badly and this film looks like a banal travelogue. But the couple journey through both its most grand buildings and most dilapidated and faded streets, and Vienna comes alive and seems to watch over them, sometimes distantly curious, sometimes richly amused, occasionally darkly threatening.

The ending is, like the rest of the movie, understated and beau-tifully true. The pair part, as they have to, and make their somewhat ludicrous six-month pact. There is no swelling music nor scenery chewing because Linklater still respects us in the morning. We cut to the places they've been in Vienna, bathed in a sad morning glow, and feel the presence of the memory of thousands of stories like this one in places that remain alive long after we die, yet, maybe, carry some imprint of our presence. We cut back to their respective trains, and two tired, lonely people, at first wistful, and then smiling, gently, at some memory of their night.

Just to undercut the romance with some reality here: the basic premise of *Before Sunrise* probably wouldn't work if made now. I mean ... the pair would be Facebook friends, and then chat thanks to Skype and a webcam, and then get bored after a month or so because long-distance relationships are just too frustrating, and some youth-cool-hunting hack director would make him wank to internet porn and her text him a sex message meant for someone else by mistake and God I'm getting depressed even thinking about what passes for romance in these increasingly cynical times, as well as what we're inevitably losing by allowing technology to make every gratification immediate.

I'm just glad that Linklater had the idea and filmed it before *Sleepless In Seattle* became *You've Got Mail*. Because *Before Sunrise* is one of the great cinematic love stories, driven by a unique absence of sentimentality and written to celebrate its viewers rather than its stars. Julie Delpy is every boy's perfect girlfriend and Ethan Hawke is a revelation, and it's their absolute integrity, commitment and absence of vanity that ultimately makes this both a teen movie and a love story unlike any other.

★ ★

KIDS

1995
Starring: Leo Fitzpatrick, Chloë Sevigny, Justin Pierce, Rosario Dawson
Dir.: Larry Clark

Plot: At last, after 40 years, every parent's worst nightmare: the children who won't learn a valuable lesson.
Key line: 'You hear disease this, disease that. Fuckin' everyone's dying an' shit. That shit is made up, Man! I don't know no kid who's dying of AIDS!'

The most controversial teen movie of the 1990s begins with a one-minute snog. Nothing that shocking about that, except that the snoggers look like children, and are eating each others faces like teens really do, all open-mouth and tongue and no attempt to be subtle. It really does point out that one minute of screen-time can feel like an hour.

Before you've got used to sitting uncomfortably, the ugly boy has talked the pretty girl into fucking. You realise that this girl may not even be a teen yet. The overhead shot of the boy's pale, skinny back and the girls' face points out how difficult it really is to tell the difference between ecstatic pleasure and agonising pain on a girl's face during sex. A voiceover provides some distraction from the image: 'Virgins – I love 'em. No diseases. No loose-as-a-goose pussy. No skank. No nuthin'. Just pure pleasure.' The punk rock of The Folk Implosion's 'Daddy Never Understood' sends a shot of pure adrenalin into your brain. None of this is right. But it's certainly something you know you have to put yourself through.

Director Larry Clark and writer Harmony Korine's notorious docu-drama about the sex, drugs and violence habits of a group of alienated New York teens has not lost its power to shock over the last sixteen years. The film revolves around a quest. Jenny (Sevigny) learns that she is HIV-positive. She insists that her only sexual partner has been Telly (Fitzpatrick), a promiscuous scumbag who is obsessed with deflowering under-age virgins. As Jenny searches for Telly to tell him the terrible news, we watch the amoral New York kids they hang with talk wigger ebonics, take drugs, have under-age sex, steal, racially abuse, rape, beat a man senseless and expose each other and everyone to the risk of infection. If you're expecting another crack here about this not being a Disney film, the joke's too near-the-knuckle. The film was funded by Bob and Harvey Weinstein of Miramax fame. Miramax is part-owned by the Walt Disney corporation. Once the paymasters had freaked out at the film's explicit content, the Weinsteins were forced to buy out Disney in order to get the film released. Good move. The pair made millions, largely from the controversy surrounding a film that appeared to encourage very young actors to have sex with each other onscreen. They didn't, incidentally. But the film was so well shot, written and acted that people almost believed that the film-makers just paid a bunch of kids to behave badly and pointed the camera at them.

There's a keen understanding of gender difference here, defined in early cutting between separate groups of boys and girls discussing sex. Both environments are living-rooms in shared houses. Both discussions are explicit and performed with such naturalism by an extraordinary young cast that they feel entirely improvised, which they weren't. But there, the similarities end. The girls' discussion is funny, light-hearted, optimistic. Although all complain about the pain and blood of losing their virginity, they appear eager to own their own stories, and entirely unwilling to compete with each other.

But the boys' discussion is brutal and contemptuous of women, and obsessed with the idea that emotions within sex are for the weak. While the girls seem informed and eager to share real experiences, the boys just want to impress each other with tales of numbers fucked and dumbass generalisations about what 'bitches' want. Everything the boys do in *Kids* is informed by the misogynist, homophobic and violent end of the multi-faceted artform that is rap music, implying that hip hop gave young American men of all races and backgrounds an excuse to indulge their worst instincts and wear them as a badge of honour. Speaking as a hip hop fan, this is just one of the uncomfortable assertions made by *Kids*, the kind of harsh truth that we anti-censorship liberals prefer to avoid.

The girls use exactly the same post-hip hop linguistic flow and parlance as the boys. But the boys use second-hand cool-speak as a weapon, largely wielded against women. Korine and Clark never halt things in order to make this point clear. You judge for yourself, and I'm sure every individual viewer might have an entirely different take on these exchanges.

But the discussions gradually move on to the film's major preoccupation. I mean, even the title of this movie is fiendishly clever: change the first letter and you have the thing that truly scares Korine and Clark. By the mid '90s, AIDS was no longer front-page news and a new generation of kids were entering the sexual arena believing that HIV was something their parents invented to stop them having fun. *Kids* is about those kids, and the potential they carry as serial killers by default.

In that sense, the teen movie it reaches out to most directly is Gregg Araki's haunting *vérité* study of gay promiscuity, *Totally Fucked Up* (see p. 312). *Kids* is the heterosexual, sensationalist version of Araki's vision of a lost tribe of inner-city children, too young to fully grasp the consequences of their cynicism and nihilism but too old to allow themselves to accept that they are children, utterly disconnected from parents, family and the parts of society that offer potential for a more civilised and civil way of life. Call it Generation X or Y or Z or whatever. These movies are indictments of an adult world which refuses to engage with children as soon as they refuse to do as they are told and obediently follow the school–college–work–breed–die life journey society maps out for all of us. As a middle ground between conformity and exclusion doesn't exist, the centre plainly cannot hold.

The film ends with a slow, quiet, reflective sadness at odds with the frantic action. The wild party – at which a drugged Jenny has finally found Telly, fucking a 13-year-old girl, potentially killing her – is over. Telly's equally amoral friend Casper (Pierce) rapes her while she sleeps. We see shots of the human debris around Washington Square Park, and watch junkies stagger and nod towards oblivion. We see Telly in bed with his conquest, and hear his voiceover justifying his actions, insisting that, 'Sometimes when you're young, the only place to go is inside', and that, if we take sex away from him, he 'really got nuthin'. We've heard much punk rock from Lou Barlow's Sebadoh and The Folk Implosion bands, but now we're listening to a gentler, sadder side of Barlow's art. Suddenly, we're looking at Casper looking at us. He looks surprised. 'Jesus Christ,' he asks us. 'What happened?' The credits roll.

What's to become of these kids, of this generation? Casper is asking the only question on your mind. And if there wasn't enough darkness here, there's a cruel punch-line. Despite Kids having taken him from Washington Square Park skateboard bum to successful actor overnight, Justin Pierce hanged himself in a Las Vegas hotel room just five years later. He was 25.

Other members of this extraordinary cast fared better. Chloë Sevigny has become a renowned actress and model, gaining an Oscar nomination for her work in 1999's Boys Don't Cry. Leo Fitzpatrick is probably best known for playing doomed junkie Johnny Weeks in the The Wire TV show. I hope the guy gets some more parts as, I dunno, a computer programmer or a puppy whisperer before he's finished, because all that self-inflicted degradation can't be good for the soul.

The cast of Kids are definitely some of the reasons why it remains a much better film than anything in the teen bleaksploitation genre it spawned, including many of Clark (see Bully, p. 409) and Korine's later works. Others include veteran photographer Clark's brilliant camera-work, which successfully lends documentary-style shooting a compositional skill and artistry that is simply beyond most directors, and Korine's characters, who may be largely appalling, but still possess dimensions, vitality and authenticity.

But really, the reason why *Kids* is here is because it is unique. All 99 other films in this book make me relate to the teenage protagonists. They reinforce my own preferred self-image of a teenager at heart and remind of me of things I used to be, and make me feel pretty good about lessons learned. *Kids* doesn't. *Kids* reminds me that I'm a parent of a 24-year-old man who got through his teenage years intact and, although he did plenty of terrible things which he'll never share with me, and rightly so, has turned out to be a decent, civilised, kind-hearted adult. *Kids* shows me that it could have been very different, and as I find myself horrified by its characters' actions, I feel hugely grateful that my son wasn't that boy.

Despite all the bare young flesh and shocking imagery, I've never felt that *Kids* was lying or exploiting children for exploitation's sake. It feels true, not just about the mid 1990s, but about the here and the now. If Clark and Korine have conned me, fair enough. A con this perfectly executed is a lesson in itself.

* *

CLUELESS

1995
Starring: Alicia Silverstone, Brittany Murphy, Paul Rudd, Stacey Dash, Dan Hedaya, Breckin Meyer
Dir.: Amy Heckerling

Plot: Jane Austen is a Valley Girl.
Key line(s): *Cher*: **'I'm captain of the Pismo Beach Disaster Relief.'**
Daddy: **'I don't think they need your skis.'**
Cher: **'Daddy! Some people lost all their belongings! Don't you think that includes athletic equipment?'**

Cher Horowitz (Silverstone) is selfish, shallow, manipulative, elitist, spoiled ... and entirely adorable. The Mean Girl memo must have got lost in the Beverly Hills post. She lives in a giant white mansion with her irascible but wildly successful lawyer dad (Hedaya), but, tragically, her mom died in a freak liposuction accident. Her best friend is an equally superficial yet adorable black girl called Dionne (Dash) and together they go to the mall, interfere in people's lives, speak in an obscure, sparky, mutant patois called Valley Speak or Valspeak, manipulate the entire school, go to the mall, compare fashion extravagances, go to the mall, enjoy their wealth and popularity, and go to the mall. Cher's life is exactly like a book by Jane Austen called *Emma* which she probably hasn't read because her favourite book is *Cliffs Notes*.

Out of this potentially aggravating concept Amy Heckerling, as both writer and director, shapes one of the greatest joys in the teen movie canon. A movie so effortlessly funny, inventive, good-natured and brilliantly performed that almost every non-dark piece of future teen film or TV, from *Buffy The Vampire Slayer* to *Glee*, was made in its image. Feisty but flawed heroines, wealthy kids in fast cars, punky pop soundtrack, California sun and smartarse dialogue woven from a cross between a knowingly superficial slang that developed among kids in the San Fernando Valley in the early '70s, slacker-surfer dudespeak, and a small-but-crucial shot of rap-derived ebonics. The relentless ingenuity of the language took an obvious cue from *Heathers* (see p. 295) but binned the nihilism, and *Clueless*, along with the *Wayne's World* and Bill And Ted movies, charmed the world until we all became, like, totally.

The success of *Clueless* (it spawned a TV spin-off series and cash-in books) and its clever Austen concept also sparked a brief trend for teen adaptations of classic novels and plays: from the excellent *Les Liaisons Dangereuses* remix *Cruel Intentions* (see p. 363) to the not-so-great likes of *Ten Things I Hate About You* (1999 – *The Taming Of The Shrew*), *O* (2001 – *Othello*) and *She's All That* (1999 – *Pygmalion*). Baz Luhrmann's whizz-bang take on *Romeo And Juliet* (see p. 343) is a little different because its dialogue remained true to the original text. But it was given permission to exist by Heckerling's simple discovery that a proven idea can always be remade about and for the modern teenager.

Clueless follows the plot of *Emma* fairly closely. Spoiled but essentially decent girl with wealthy widowed father interferes in everyone's love lives until finally learning that love is too irrational to be based upon logic and status, and therefore finally finding love herself.

Everyone lives happily ever after, but the plot was never *Emma*'s point. It was a sly satirical comedy of the upper-middle-class manners of its time, and this is where Heckerling works her magic. She makes merry sport with the American high school mores, stereotypes, consumerist obsessions and popularity-at-all-cost values that had become the lingua franca of teenage image since the '80s impact of the classic John Hughes movies, with the added ingredient of wonderfully conceived exaggerations of the slang of the period.

Hur. Sorry. Writing the word 'period' has reminded me of the bit where Cher describes her monthlies as 'riding the crimson wave'. Hur. Brilliant.

Sorry . . . back now. But no matter how skilled Heckerling's writing and directorial comic touches are, the film would embody exactly the kind of superficial self-regard it parodies without a fabulous lead performance by Ms Silverstone. She carries almost every second of the movie with effortless aplomb and gigantic amounts of the crucial element: charm. Even those of us who have little time for vapid American blondes are forced to swoon at the sheer force of her optimism, the naivety of her relentlessly positive view of life and people, and her really good dress sense. She personifies that hugely annoying but essential person in your life who always, by smiling and flirting and flattering you with just the right balance of gaucheness and irony, gets you doing things you don't want to do for no reward, like that scene in *How I Met Your Mother* where they all find themselves helping Barney move into his new apartment on their one day off, and look at each other and say, 'How the hell did that happen?' She's the angelic mirror to Reese Witherspoon's Tracy Flick in *Election* (see p. 374): Tracy could somehow control you, too, but, afterwards, you'd hate her and yourself. Cher would use you and make you love it.

The entire ensemble cast are great, especially Dash, Breckin Meyer as slacker surf dude Travis, baby-faced comedy assassin Paul Rudd as Cher's pseudo-intellectual stepbrother, and, of course, the much-missed Brittany Murphy as Cher's very own Frankenstein's monster, Tai. When Ms Murphy died suddenly in December 2009, aged 32, in one of those drug-related celebrity deaths which never gets adequately explained, cinema lost one of those rare lead actresses whose beauty and talent were buoyed by the kind of rough edges possessed by women who live in the real world. She doesn't quite steal the show from Silverstone here, but she is quirky, and funny, and just a little sad.

So ... favourite scenes. At one point, Cher's past tense voiceover opines that she felt 'impotent and out of control, which I really hate. I needed to find sanctuary in a place where I could gather my thoughts and regain my strength.' Cue a rumble of kettle drums building to a lush, romantic orchestral theme of *Gone With The Wind* proportions – and a shot of the Westside Pavilion shopping mall.

Then there's the bit where teacher Mr Hall announces that Travis has the worst record for punctuality and, buoyed by the applause, Travis walks up to Hall's front-of-class lectern and makes an Oscar-style acceptance speech: 'This is so unexpected ... Many people have contributed to my tardiness ... I'd like to thank the LA city bus driver for taking a chance on an unknown kid ...'

And the freeway scene. You see, Americans give driving licences to rich kids as easily as British governments give control of vital national institutions to Rupert Murdoch, so, when Dionne gets into the wrong lane while driving badly around their leafy, car-less suburb and ends up in actual traffic, mayhem – marauding bikers, middle-finger-raising grannies, hilarious screaming – ensue. It's a neat way to say that these kids are institutionalised within their wealthy enclave and have not been prepared for ... well ... people. Donald Faison, who plays Turk in *Scrubs*, is very good in this bit.

But despite establishing so much of the language, the look and the tone of future teen screen comedy-drama, *Clueless* remains an unusual teen comedy. While the satire at the expense of the rich and vacuous is the whole of the point, the lampooning is affectionate and good-natured. The characters are all essentially lovable and there are no bad guy ciphers or mocked victims. The relatively high presence of black teens in this definitively Caucasian milieu seems like a little white lie told with good intentions. The sex gags are sly innuendo rather than gross-out; tongue in cheek, not penis-in-pie. There is little slapstick or clowning – the laughs all come from dialogue (particularly the brilliant narration) and wry visual jokes, like the terrible portrait of Cher's dead mom, Dionne's outrageous hats and, often and uniquely, very pretty, peppy girls smiling just a little too enthusiastically at the camera. While almost every other American teen movie snarls at the rich, the film that satirises them with the greatest enthusiasm is charmed by them. Not with any serious, pro-conservative cheerleading for greed or privilege; but more of a philosophical shrug and a wry smile and a suggestion that, when all is bought and sold, the rich are people too. An unfashionable thought, but certainly one worth considering. Watch back-to-back with *Society* (see p. 297) and the truth about the Hollywood wealthy undoubtedly lies somewhere between the two.

* *

LA HAINE

1995
Starring: Vincent Cassell, Hubert Kounde, Said Taghmaoui, Karim Belkhadra
Dir.: Mathieu Kassovitz

Plot: Why do 'they' riot? It's just not a black and white issue. Key line: 'Do you know the one about the guy falling from a 50-storey building? To reassure himself, he keeps repeating: "So far, so good. So far, so good . . . "'

La Haine is one of the most powerful, controversial and acclaimed films of the 1990s. Its shock value derived from learning that the 'Hate' – to give the film's title its English translation – of the urban young for the modern world we have made for them was exactly the same in Paris as it was in London, or Baltimore, or Palestine or Rio de Janeiro.

It was shot in black and white, making it feel timeless and movable to any city or era that the viewer chose to project upon it. It reflected the confusion that each new generation felt about race, as we met a Jewish skinhead who hung out with an Arab and an African, and it foreshadowed the sharp rise of Jean-Marie Le Pen's extreme right Le Front National party in France. It was inspired by the 1993 shooting of a young Zairean boy while in police custody in Paris, and went on to predict that the kind of anti-police riot that results from such incidents would become less politicised and more opportunistic. But it is also about the masochism of people who protest by destroying their own neighbourhoods, destroying in seconds what friends and neighbours have taken years to build. It began with real footage of Parisian riots that began in 1986 and have never entirely gone away. It won its director, a French-Hungarian Jew who admitted that he had taken part in some of those riots, the coveted Best Director prize at the 1995 Cannes Film Festival, and launched the career of a major international star in the malevolently charismatic Vincent Cassell. And its influence looms over every subsequent juvie movie, from *City Of God* to *Kidulthood* to *The Class*, because it is an object lesson in how to make a political film exciting to someone who rejects politics by way of tight, dynamic plot, snappy authentic dialogue, brilliantly shot action scenes, and the kind of profane and nihilistic humour that is the major survival mechanism of the urban underclass.

The story begins with a news report about an Arab youth called Abdel, who has been badly beaten while in police custody, and the resulting street battles and lootings. We then cut to a housing project on the outskirts of Paris, and meet three boys who have nothing useful to do. Said (Taghmaoui) is an Algerian pretty boy who likes to graffiti on police vans while they're busy looking scary and para-military. Vinz (Cassell) is a crop-headed Jewish muscle-boy who prefers pretending to blow people away as he practises Travis Bickle's 'You talkin' to me?' speech from *Taxi Driver* in the mirror. Hubert (Kounde) is a charming black boxer and dope dealer who owned a gym that has just been destroyed in the previous night's rioting and who, after being punished for attempting to do something positive for the community, now just wants to escape the conflict and poverty of his sink estate.

They amble around their dystopian environment full of riot-fucked buildings and cars and scrawled with graffiti like 'Your Mother Sucks Bears', smoking dope, talking amusing macho bollocks to each other and their fellow hooded and track-suited youths, discussing their response to the endless provocations of the tooled-up police who hang around the estate, gagging for trouble.

As the trio graffiti us a picture of one day in their aimless lives, they are interrupted by the arrival of the Mayor on a media walkabout to show his concern; cops who attempt to move any assembly of youths to somewhere else, in the hope that they will either go home or riot; TV news crews trying to get good shots of disaffected yoof; younger kids telling directionless stories about what they saw on TV last night. And a cow. Can't forget the cow.

Eventually, Vinz confesses to his two compadres that he has found the gun that a cop lost on the estate in last night's disturbances. The suspense of what Vinz intends to do with his newfound power grows organically with the rising tension on a riot-torn estate that is sitting around waiting for night to fall.

Any attempt to escape the estate just reinforces the fact that these kids are not wanted in the rest of France. A visit to the hospital to see their injured friend ends in arrest for the three musketeers. They enter a police station that has obviously been attacked in the riot, and the cops glare at them like gunslingers in a western, thirsting for their blood. They escape unscathed because of the decent Arab cop who has taken them in. But Vinz won't acknowledge this copper's attempts to build bridges. With his endless talk of 'pigs', he dehumanizes the police in the way he perceives he has been dehumanized. Hate doesn't see individuals or judge by content of character.

A shooting and arrest on the estate brings out the riot police. Vinz pulls a gun on a cop, is prevented from using it by a Hubert right hook, and the three are on the bus to the big, bad city, Vinz exhilarated by the experience, Hubert sinking further into sullen introspection. The movie becomes a kind of Pilgrim's Progress through a surreal Paris, with the three conjuring political and philosophical *bon mots* while encountering numchuck-wielding coke dealers, corrupt police sadists, the shooting of a nightclub bouncer, an old man with a story about shit, a party in a bourgie art gallery, posters telling them that the world is theirs and, on a giant TV the news that their friend Abdel is dead. The crunch comes when, after all those lectures from Hubert about Vinz's gun fantasies, Vinz uses the gleaming Magnum 44 to rescue Hubert and Said from a beating by racist skinheads – and you are watching a Jewish skinhead consider murdering a Nazi while his black and brown friends try to stop him, and your short-circuited sympathies are all over the place, and Cassell is incendiary.

As the ending says, it isn't the fall that matters, it's the landing. And *La Haine* lands in a self-perpetuating and tragic place that deliberately calls back through the years to *The 400 Blows* (see p. 47) and asks you what you are going to do to stop it. Its soundtrack ticks like a time-bomb. But the film is in black and white and there's no way to tell which colour wire to cut to defuse it.

★ ★

SCREAM

1996

Starring: Neve Campbell, Skeet Ulrich, Courtney Cox, David Arquette, Matthew Lillard, Drew Barrymore, Jamie Kennedy, Rose Macgowan
Dir.: Wes Craven

Plot: Slasher master brutally slaughters his own creation. Key line: 'They're all the same. Some stupid killer stalking some big-breasted girl who can't act who's always running up the stairs when she should be going out the front door. It's insulting.'

Scream's opening scene is a writing, directing and acting master-class. It has to be, to earn the rest of the movie's right to eat itself. If we're going to watch a horror film based entirely on wry jokes about horror films, and it's not going to just be *Airplane!* with fewer belly laughs, then Scene One has to draw us into the possibility that this film will be genuinely scary.

Drew Barrymore is alone in one of those houses that hollers 'wealthy suburb. No one can hear you scream.'

She is making popcorn. The phone rings and the guy has a wrong number, but he keeps calling back. He has one of those voices which can sound perfectly charming at one pitch, and genuinely creepy at another. He phone-flirts with her and she engages. He is asking her whether she likes scary movies. He lets slip that he's watching her.

She begins to panic and hangs up. He calls back and makes it clear that she'd better not hang up again. It's a cordless phone, and the camera follows her around this light, bright beautiful home with the huge, leafy garden and the picture windows as it begins to feel like a pretty prison. The music builds with drones and carefully placed echoey thumps when the caller tells Drew something she doesn't want to hear. Incidentally, the legend that is Ms Barrymore is playing a teenage girl called Casey Becker, but there's something about the scene that makes you feel that you're watching Drew Barrymore being terrorised. The fact, perhaps, that they don't make her change look or demeanour in order to seem teenage. We love Drew Barry-more, and we don't want her to die.

It turns out that our caller has Casey's boyfriend tied up in the garden, where she can see him. The only way she can save him from being slaughtered is by answering trivia questions about teen slasher movies. The level of terror that Barrymore generates here is extra-ordinary. Her complete meltdown is what ensures that the scene is not remotely funny.

Turns out her horror movie knowledge is poorer than she thought. She forgets that the killer in the first *Friday The 13th* is not mutant baby Jason, but Jason's mom Mrs Voorhes. Boyfriend's a goner, she's next. Home is invaded. Chase ensues.

She eventually escapes into the garden with the cordless phone and tries to make a run for it. She is chased down and caught by a man (we assume) in a black cape and a mask modelled on the anguished face in Edvard Munch's *The Scream*. At this point, we assume that someone (her parents are on the way home) will save her. This is the opening scene and this is *Drew Barrymore*. If you've shelled out the money to get Drew Barrymore in your dumbass slasher flick, you don't kill her off after ten minutes ... do you? But Ghostface has a big knife and the cavalry ain't coming. He stabs her, repeatedly, with convincing sound of sharp implement sinking into flesh.

Mom and Dad have arrived home. They see signs of struggle, panic. Mom picks up the phone. She hears the unmistakable gurgling sounds of her daughter dying. They run out into the garden. The horror registers on Dad's face. Their daughter's broken and beaten body is hanging from a tree, like those sickening pictures of lynched black men from the 1920s. The camera zooms into her mutilated face. Cut!

I still remember seeing all this for the first time at the cinema. I was as bewildered as I was horrified. All the reviews had banged on about how this was a horror spoof where director Wes Craven takes the piss out of himself with an overload of references to movies like *Halloween* (see p. 169), *A Nightmare On Elm Street* (see p. 238) and *Prom Night*. I, and the rest of the audience, was not prepared to see Drew Barrymore convincingly and sadistically butchered. In fact, nothing so seriously scary happens anywhere else in *Scream*. But the first scene leads you to believe that it will. The jokes flew thick and fast, and various characters goofed around, and you had your fun picking out which 15 movies got referenced. But you were constantly tensed for something that actually hurt. The opening scene makes the movie work.

Scream is often credited with single-handedly reviving the horror genre. It was a huge box office success and has spawned three (increasingly lame) sequels to date. Its life-imitating-film-imitating-life postmodernism fulfilled its own destiny in two very different ways.

In 2000 an *Airplane!*-style take on slasher movies called *Scary Movie* was released and became a hit. Not only was *Scream* its major source of gross-out laffs, making it a postmodern spoof of a postmodern spoof, but also *Scary Movie* had been the original title of *Scream* before producer Bob Weinstein came up with his clever one-word idea. Like *Scream*, *Scary Movie* is now a sequel-spawning franchise, complete with spin-offs like *Epic Movie*, and so on and so forth.

On an even more dispiriting note, *Scream* was accused of inspiring copycat murders. In 1998 and 1999, detectives investigating two killings involving teens found *Scream* paraphernalia – including the Ghostface mask – among the killers' possessions. The resulting moral panic got as far as members of a US Senate committee being forced to watch *Scream*'s opening scene while tutting loudly. Kevin Williamson's screenplay was initially inspired by a real-life killing spree by notorious serial killer Daniel Harold Rolling aka The Gainesville Ripper, who murdered five students in one night in 1990, killed eight people in all, and was executed by lethal injection in 2006. Is this what they mean by 'the circle of life'?

Having written the most self-referential script ever, Williamson actually had an answer prepared just in case anyone accused his horror movie of inspiring violence. He put it into the mouth of one of his Ghostface killers in *Scream* itself: 'Don't blame the movies, Sid. Movies don't create psychos. They make psychos more creative.'

Scream is dominated by this kind of dialogue, which isn't just designed to make you laugh knowingly at the lazy formulas of post-*Halloween* horror movies, but at the very notion that real-life killers are informed by screen killers. Key examples include: 'There's a formula to it! A very simple formula! Everybody's a suspect!'; 'Oh please don't kill me, Mr Ghostface. I wanna be in the sequel', and

'If it gets too complicated you lose your target audience'. The in-jokiness spreads to cameos, whereby *The Exorcist*'s Linda Blair plays a reporter and Craven himself gets to be a school janitor who looks exactly like his most famous creation, Freddie Kruger. This all reaches some kind of ultimate moment of meta-movie mindfuckery in *Scream*'s most referenced and pastiched scene, The Rules.

The teens are having a party. This is where Randy (Kennedy) runs through the basic formula of every teen slasher movie, while the party watches *Halloween*, and while the very things he's mentioning are simultaneously happening in the movie. No. 1 – You can never have sex. 2 – You can never drink or do drugs. 3 – And never, ever, under any circumstances say, 'I'll be right back.'

We then cut to bitchy TV news reporter Gale Weathers (Cox) and cameraman Kenny watching a film of the same scene on a TV in their van. 'Boring,' she sneers. This really is the most smartarse and self-deprecating meta-movie ever made, no competition.

The ending is a scream. Crazed killers Stu (the wonderful Lillard) and Billy (Ulrich, primarily chosen for his startling resemblance to Johnny Depp in ... *Elm Street*, if Depp had spent three years in a psych ward that included 'make hair unfeasibly greasy' in its list of treatments) manically stabbing each other (they're attempting to frame Neve Campbell's Final Girl heroine Sid's Dad, and this *so* doesn't matter) and riffing on the subject of movies as research for murderers before Stu reveals his motive as 'peer pressure' and is killed by a television falling on his head, in true cartoon style.

In terms of reviving the horror genre, I suspect *Scream*'s impact lies more in what it destroyed rather than what it invented. Formula teen slashers were almost a done deal, unless you were Kevin Williamson and came up with concepts as fiendish as *Final Destination* (see p. 385). Film-makers who took horror seriously reacted against *Scream*'s glossy cynicism and came up with the shaky cameras and invisible, supernatural monsters of *The Blair Witch Project* and *Paranormal Activity*, freaking us out completely by introducing neo-realism to an unrealistic genre. The flipside is the kind of sadistic gore-fest represented by *Saw*, *Hostel* and *The Human Centipede*, fake snuff movies without art, drama or point. Craven and Williamson have their part to play in this, having soaked *Scream* in so much glib irony.

And somewhere in the middle are the movies that ignored *Scream*, an extraordinary run of shockers from Japan, South Korea and Hong Kong that use a universal male fear of adolescent female sexuality as their fuel.

But you know what? *Ring* isn't in this book because it's nowhere near as entertaining as *Scream*. It's too silly to be scary but refuses to own up to it. I'm as jaded and desensitised by real-life horrors on TV as the next citizen of the Western world, and *Scream* makes me laugh at that inconvenient truth. But, at the same time, in that opening scene, it lets me know that I'm not so desensitised that watching Drew Barrymore get stalked and lynched doesn't hurt. It's the cleverest trick of a very clever film.

★ ★

WILLIAM SHAKESPEARE'S ROMEO + JULIET

1996
Starring: Leonardo DiCaprio, Claire Danes, Brian Dennehy, Paul Sorvino, Harold Perrineau, Paul Rudd, John Leguizamo, Christina Pickles, Pete Postlethwaite, Miriam Margoyles, Dash Mihok
Dir.: Baz Luhrmann

Plot: A timeless tale of doomed young lovers, guns and fish.
Key line: 'Do I have to do everything around here?'

At last. A film where I don't have to decide whether a plot rundown is necessary.

Theoretically, Baz Luhrmann's brash gang warfare modernisation of *Romeo And Juliet* should be a Marmite movie. Yet no one I've ever spoken to about the flick has either trumpeted it as the greatest thing ever, nor despised it with a purist's passion. Perhaps that's because, if you'd seen a trailer, you knew exactly what you'd be getting before you'd taken your seat: Shakespeare in the style of MTV. And if you were up for that disgustingly yoof-demographic-friendly idea, then Luhrmann delivered all the way, from the narrations delivered as news reports and gossip TV, to the guns and gangs and cool macho posing, the loud pop, rock and hip hop, the low attention span crash edit frenzy and action movie clichés, the riotous explosion of bright colours, the karaoke musical interludes, the very modern beauty of the two leads. It was exactly what it said on the pitch, with big brass buckles and enough gleaming weaponry to give Tarantino fans sloppy wet dreams.

Thing is, that should have been rubbish. But it isn't. It's thrilling.

This is the one movie in the book that I really wish I could see through a 1996 teenager's eyes. A 15-year-old, perhaps, who had ignored Shakespeare at school because it seemed boring or irrelevant or too difficult. Knew *Romeo And Juliet* was about love but didn't know the actual story. Went because there was nothing else to do, or because his/her mates were going, or because DiCaprio was in it. I'm going to assume they liked it, because over $147 million worldwide, not counting home DVD sales, is the box office result of healthy teen word-of-mouth. But what did this teen want more of afterwards? MTV? Gangster movies? Leo DiCaprio? Or did they decide they really had to read some Shakespeare, try to understand the language, maybe even go see a play at the theatre? Did Luhrmann convert hitherto uninterested kids to the delights of The Bard? I think that's what Luhrmann was trying to achieve, but it's impossible to accurately measure how well he pulled it off.

There are two big reasons why *WSR+J* (*I know* – but one *must* think of the trees) works. The biggest is the cast. It really doesn't matter how many explosions, guys doing that slow-motion firing-two-guns-while-flying-through-the-air thingy or drag act song 'n' dance routines you shovel into Shakespeare by the spade-load: if you decide to ignore the *West Side Story* route and keep the original text, then the actors have to make someone who doesn't know the language understand exactly what's happening, and feel it in the gut. This cast do, every plot point and tragic inevitability, and particularly Dennehy, Margoyles, Postlethwaite and the thrillingly physical Leguizamo as Tybalt and former *Oz* star Perrineau as Mercutio, who kinda blow everyone off the screen whenever that unalterable screenplay gives them the chance.

The other reason? The fish tank scene, of course! This is not only one of the most perfectly realised evocations of love-at-first-sight ever put onscreen; it's also the one and only time I've ever been able to see the actual point of Leonardo DiCaprio. I mean, don't get me wrong. He's a surprisingly good Romeo ... as long as you put your fingers in your ears every time he speaks.

But in the fish tank scene he doesn't have to talk, so good on yer, Baz.

So . . . our star-cross'd lovers are at the big party but haven't met, and Des'ree has just started singing 'Kissing You', the movie's very own love theme. Romeo has stepped away for some quiet time and finds himself in this grand room with a big old tank full of brightly coloured tropical fish. The song is still pelting out full volume and Leo's having a gander at the fish. But suddenly, through a hole in one of those watery bushes . . . a human eye. It moves quickly. Romeo starts, and stands up straight. And he looks at something . . . and then we switch to Claire Danes as Juliet, who is on the other side of the tank. And . . . we get the look.

It's a look that makes you wonder what this magic we call screen acting is really made of. All she's doing, in essence, is opening her eyes widely and pursing her lips a little. But that really, really isn't it at all. In this look, you get shock, awe, curiosity, vulnerability, lust, and some other less easily contained emotion which I can only describe as an understanding that her life will never again be the same, and that this probably isn't a good thing. All the time, these beautiful fish are swimming in front of her, trying to attract your attention with their other-worldly colour schemes, but all you want is for them to get out the damn way so you can see that fathomless look again.

We suddenly switch to DiCaprio. And bless me cotton knickers if he isn't matching Ms Danes all the way. In the scenes up to now, the guy has looked maybe 17 years old (he was 21 at the time). But very suddenly, the boy looks 10 years old. It's as if everything he's experienced over the recent past has been sucked out of him, and he's been taken back to the exact second before he had his first sex fantasy. It's a look of . . . bewildered innocence, as if looking at the world, properly, for the first time. Then he suddenly raises both eyebrows with a slight smile, as if to say, 'Ha! Blimey. What the fuck was *that*?'

And then we get a little cutting between the two, and the song asserts itself, and the dance begins. It's an unusual sort of dance, because the partners are separated by several feet of water and two panes of glass. They are dancing with the camera as it circles warily around them, conscious of eavesdropping on such a perfect moment. The reflections of the pair in the glass distort their faces from certain angles, and they play a kind of peek-a-boo of mutual discovery. At one point, Di Caprio looks as if he's staring at a smiling mermaid with a giant face, and then the camera moves into the tank (NO! BRING THEM BACK!) and then we see Danes clearly, and DiCaprio as the mermaid. Danes's delighted smile is now just such a beacon of pure joy that you begin to tear up. This is what love-at-first-sight should be ... no ... this is what love, full-stop, should always be. It should just stay ...

'Madam!' Miriam Margoyles's Nurse interrupts. Juliet must run. And she does ... but with one last teasing smile back ... an acknowledgement, a dare, a message that she knows that Romeo is exactly where she is, and feels exactly what she feels.

And ... we're done.

From then on, it's whizz-bang-emote-crash-tragic-misunderstanding-muscle-boys-wherefore-art-thou-thou-is-dead. But you're in all that to the death because of what happens between these two beautiful young actors in precisely one minute of screen-time, with a fish tank. Keep in mind, their first looks aren't even played to each other, but to some point just off-camera. I often wonder what Luhrmann did to get that bliss out of DiCaprio. Tell him Scorsese had just called? Hold up a mirror?

Anyway ... *William Shakespeare's Romeo + Juliet* (bloody hell) is almost as good as *West Side Story*, and maybe a little better than the 1968 Franco Zefferelli version, largely because Claire Danes is in a different acting league to Olivia Hussey (see *Black Christmas*, p. 143). If the film as a whole lacks the charm of Luhrmann's low-budget debut *Strictly Ballroom*, it still marked the Aussie out as something special until *Australia* made you realise that the guy needs to stop spending money and showing off and remember why he used to be so good. But, as next up for Baz is DiCaprio as *The Great Gatsby* in 3D, one suspects that that time may be some way off.

'Tis a pity. Because his gift is not epic settings and a fondness for smacking the viewer around with his virtuosity. It's that he gets romance. He's in love with young lovers and remembers how they feel. You couldn't give the most famous love story of all to a more fitting modern director.

★ ★

STARSHIP TROOPERS

1997

Starring: Casper Van Diem, Dina Meyer, Denise Richards, Neil
Patrick Harris, Michael Ironside
Dir.: Paul Verhoeven

Plot: *Star Wars* **rewritten as an anti-fascist teen parable. Plus
giant spiders.**
**Key line: 'It's an ugly planet. A bug planet. A planet hostile
to life. A . . .** *GGGGAAAAAAAHHHHH!!!***'**

Sometimes I truly worry about people.

Starship Troopers begins like this: A fake commercial, advertising
the pleasures of young people joining the military. As the square-
jawed soldiers beam and repeat their devotion to duty, a small boy,
no older than 8, fully dressed in military uniform, jumps out from
nowhere and yelps, 'I'm doing my part too!' The line of soldiers
laugh in a toothy, forced manner. A flag with a fascistic insignia flies
as the announcer implores you to 'Join the mobile infantry and save
the world!' The words, 'Service guarantees citizenship' are added
quickly, like 'terms and conditions apply'.

Cut to another ad. This time we are in space and being told a fear-
mongering tale about 'Bug Meteors'. A caption reads 'Why We
Fight', a reference to Frank Capra's notorious World War II propaganda movies that used footage from the enemy to persuade America's boys to sign up. The film explains why a planet called Klendathu
must be 'eliminated'. The propaganda becomes news, as we join the
Klendathu invasion live, and are shouted at by the futuristic sci-fi
equivalent of an embedded war reporter. While some kind of fight
wages around him, the reporter starts in with the colour about what
a terrible planet it is. No kidding. One of the 'bugs' that is supposedly
bombing Earth with meteor showers swings into view. Before we get
a good look, it has scooped the reporter up in its buggy jaws and
snapped him in half. Soldiers who look no older than 16 scatter and
panic. One of them tells us to get out of here. The soldiers regroup

and shoot at the bug but to no avail. The bug crushes the soldier like a, well, bug.

We then get a caption saying 'One Year Earlier' and cut to a classroom where a bald man with a stump where one of his arms should be is explaining recent history to a class of clean teens in a few brusque sentences. Democracy failed. 'The social scientists brought our world to the brink of chaos.' The 'veterans' instigated a global military coup and 'imposed a stability that has lasted for generations since'. The teacher states that society functions politically through 'force. Force is violence ... the supreme authority from which all other authorities derive.'

Why do I worry about people? When this brilliant satire was first released, some people, including actual critics, thought it was a pro-fascist movie. I don't even know where to go with this. When the teacher, Michael Ironside as Lt Jean Rasczak, mentions Hiroshima and states that 'Naked force has resolved more issues throughout history than any other factor' ... some decided that *that was the director stating a firmly held philosophical opinion*! They looked at the way the troopers' uniforms were cleverly designed around former Nazi designs, and thought that they were saying *that the Nazis were teen heroes*!!! One assumes they all thought *Team America: World Police* was a desperate plea for America to bomb more Arab countries and blow up the Eiffel Tower. I despair. But not as much as Paul Verhoeven, I would imagine.

The Dutch master had already pulled the sci-fi satire trick once, and been misunderstood because he has this habit of playing dialogue and acting for laughs, and fight sequences and subtext straight, and expecting his audience to notice the difference. His 1987 classic *Robocop* is based in exactly the same future-world where corporate fascism reigns, people are hardsold laws through television ads which always ask, 'Would you like to know more?', and power looks for simple, violent solutions to complex problems. In case anyone was still under any misunderstanding about the theme of *Starship Troopers*, Verhoeven explains it himself, with admirable brevity, on the recent DVD's director's commentary: 'War makes fascists of us all.'

A number of other things make *Starship Troopers* an unusual picture. It is essentially B-movie pulp fiction, but at epic length and cost: a budget of $105 million dollars and a running time of over two hours. At a time when everyone in American cinema was being encouraged to act naturally, Verhoeven insists his performers throw back to the kind of arch comic-book style of *Star Wars*, *Raiders Of The Lost Ark* and old *Flash Gordon* and *Buck Rogers* movies and TV shows.

And, finally . . . he makes this epic space opera-satire-throwback-splatter-film-that-makes-you-go-'*bleurgh!*' into a teen movie. Complete with aching teen romance and coming-of-age themes. And then he makes the whole mess work. I would, quite literally, genuflect, if I met the guy.

The script was loosely based upon a 1959 novel, called *Starship Troopers*, by conservative science-fiction author Robert A. Heinlein. Very loosely, I guess, as Verhoeven confesses on the directors' commentary that he started to read the novel and never finished it because it made him 'bored and depressed'. This leaves Verhoeven and screenwriter to devise a fascinating future familiar to fans of the *Alien* movies and the recent, brilliant, *Battlestar Galactica* TV serial. This is a world where humanity has spread beyond Earth and corporate fascism has successfully dispensed with geographical borders and traditional gender roles. People who are white and American come from Buenos Aires. Women work and fight alongside men as equals. Being a 'citizen' of humanity is not a right, but a privilege earned by serving in the military. If you don't fight the enemy – which, currently, is the arachnids, or bugs from outer space – then you don't get to vote or be an equal member of the species. It's a society that makes a kind of sense, which is probably why *Starship Troopers* has been misunderstood. The idea that fascism might produce some good things among the very, very bad is the kind of concept that quality science fiction has always played with because it is a genre concerned with finding metaphors for our present existence. But if sci-fi isn't your thing, that's probably all a bit morally ambiguous. We like our liberalism conservative, now don't we?

Key to the film's blend of the dreamy and the gnarly are the fresh-faced, square-jawed ensemble cast. Casper Van Diem (Johnny Rico), Dina Meyer (Dizzy Flores), Denise Richards (Carmen Ibanez), Jake Busey (Ace Levy) and the sainted Neil Patrick Harris (Carl Jenkins) are all entirely perfect as perfect American children: beautiful, strong, bright, peppy, buff and possessed of gleaming white gnashers. They handle the meat of the film brilliantly, which is that, while they are at school, being filled with propaganda about the heroism (and exceptional career prospects) of military service, the concept of war is a mixture of career move and exciting game. They are more interested in who they're going to be sleeping with, just like any other teenagers. But then basic training is over, and they face the horrifying reality: that they are risking their lives fighting an enemy that is far more ferocious and powerful than their mentors led them to believe, for reasons that are entirely obscure. They are arbitrarily sorted into infantry and officer-class, the former an expendable gaggle of working-class hard men and women, destined to be shipped home in half a dozen body bags, the latter a remote elite who are authorised to play with the former's lives. Is *any* of this starting to sound familiar?

So, stunning action sequences involving human flesh being torn apart by really fast and agile giant spiders, and giant spiders being torn into grisly yellow gooey masses by heavy artillery, are neatly interwined with Luke–Leia–Han-esque love triangles and the sadness of watching happy-go-lucky, optimistic children become cynical, soulless zombies of death in order to survive. Kind of like *Red Dawn* (see p. 245), but with big eight-legged space beasties replacing Communists, and a more despairing subtext about humanity fighting and fighting and fighting for no reason at all except that that's what it always has done.

Oh yeah . . . and seeing Barney from *How I Met Your Mother* emerge at the movie's end as a futuristic Gestapo commandant complete with long black leather coat and laconic arrogance, and not knowing whether to cheer or be very, very afraid, is just one of the many strokes of unsettling genius in one of the finest of all science-fiction films.

★ ★

THE FACULTY

1998
Starring: Josh Hartnett, Clea DuVall, Elijah Wood, Laura Harris, Shawn Hatosy, Jordana Brewster, Usher Raymond, Salma Hayek, John Stewart, Bebe Neuwirth, Piper Laurie, Robert Patrick
Dir.: Robert Rodriguez

Plot: Invasion Of The Breakfast Club At Dawn Of The Dead By The Bodysnatching Things From Another World.
Key line(s): 'Do you notice anything off today here at school?'
'I'm from The South. We're all off.'

Herrington High School's a tough school. It's a Kevin Williamson school, so, like *Scream* (see p. 339), a film about it begins with a genuinely dark and frightening prologue; a woman being chased – and caught – by a homicidal male molester-monster for reasons unknown. The action then switches to the light, bright, punk-poptastic grounds of school in the morning, where the social group-ings and status of lead characters are quickly flagged up according to whether they arrive by flash car or yellow bus, whether they are alone or surrounded by friends, how hot their girlfriend is. But this school is especially extreme. Elijah Wood gets smashed in the face by the elbow of an unknown assailant, and apologises pathetically through force of Hobbit. Girls are dragging other girls out of cars and cat-fighting in the street. Plus the gothy Stokely is played by the godlike Clea DuVall, and when that girl sneers at you your testicles turn to stone ... and whether you read that as good or bad is your call, and I'll come back to it later.

The Faculty is astonishingly like a splattercore feature-length episode of *Buffy* and, like The Greatest TV Show Ever Made, it uses a horror concept as a metaphor for a universal coming-of-age experience. In *Buffy*, the shared schooldays-are-hell experience is simply rendered by basing the first three series in a school built on the mouth of hell. In *The Faculty*, the idea is just as ingenious.

Think back to your teenage school days. You are standing in the playground at break time, and there is a lull in the conversation between you and your so-called friends. You zone out and look around you. Everywhere people scurrying aimlessly or talking aimlessly or playing aimlessly. To your right, a serial bully is beating up on a kid he knows can't fight back, and people you thought you liked are cheering, faces lit up with hysterical excitement, baying for the weak kid's blood. To your left, your favourite teacher, shuffling towards his or her next class, and for the first time you *really look* at them and see just how tired and unhappy and demoralised they are, by low wages, by repetition, by disappointment. Just in front of you the girl you are hopelessly in love with is staring in awe at a spotty kid with absurd flares and a feather cut, whose family happens to be rich ... at least, that's what he says, to every girl. And it works. Meanwhile, that girl you used to like has just seen an Asian boy walk past her and held her nose and complained about the 'Paki smell'. Just behind her, you see a group of boys who all play for the football team and you can vaguely overhear them calling various girls 'fish' and howling with laughter every time one of them says 'spunk'. There is one pale girl sitting on a wall reading a book and a fat girl with BO, who leads a gang of fat girls with BO, knocks the book out of her hand and the boy sitting next to the pale girl ... laughs. Then you remember that the next lesson is some time-wasting shite called Social Studies or somesuch, and that exams are coming, and that teachers keep telling you that you must knuckle down and pass these tests because your only hope in life is O levels and an office job and marry, breed, keep your mouth shut and die. And you feel yourself grown small and distant, as if you're suddenly outside of your body and floating above this hostile, unhappy place and you get this awful fear: You're not supposed to be here. You're not one of them. Some awful cosmic mistake has been made because you don't understand why these creatures act like they do and why you stay here. Maybe you're not human. Or maybe ... you are, and absolutely no one else is. Nobody else seems to notice how weird and terrible this place is. You're growing away from friends you thought you loved. Maybe they're not those people. Maybe aliens came and took them away and everyone here is an impostor ...

And that's *The Faculty*. Aliens really did come and take everyone at school away and replace them with evil doppelgangers. The teachers are injecting alien brainwash goo straight into your ears in the nurse's room and old ladies are invading the men's showers and stripping off ... their skin, their hair, their scalps ...

And only you realise; you and a very small group of other kids who you neither like nor trust but now you have to get past the fact that they're a jock/geek/freak/dyke/bitch/drug dealer and trust them because that's all you have. And your only weapon? Drugs! Loads and loads of homemade recreational drugs! Cool, huh? I hate Kevin Williamson. He has the ideas I wish I'd had.

The Faculty has many great, scary and funny things to recommend it. Its peril is genuinely perilous, the special effects make you gag and the gags make you laugh and there's a girl's head with octopus legs. It is slickly shot by Robert Rodriguez, the best big-budget B-movie maker of his generation, a man who has the technical skills to pay the exploitation bills and who genuinely understands the fun and the smartness of the genre movie. The ensemble cast are fabulous, successfully ensuring that the movie's deliberately stereotypical post-*Breakfast Club* (see p. 263)/*Heathers* (see p. 295) jock and nerd and Bad Boy and Goth Girl and Teen Queen become rounded characters you grow to like very quickly. Because Kevin Williamson scripts are always tributes to his favourite movies, his castings of Robert Patrick and Piper Laurie doff an affectionate cap to *The Terminator 2* and *Carrie* (see p. 150) respectively, while the plot and scenario gleefully pastiches *Invasion Of The Bodysnatchers*, John Carpenter's *The Thing* and *Assault On Precinct 13* and the George A. Romero zombie movies. There are unlikely cameos from *The Daily Show* satirist John Stewart, *Frasier*'s missus Bebe Neuwirth and Salma Hayek, and they work because it seems like the entire cast are having big fun playing at being in horror movies. It effortlessly slips into that adorable *Breakfast Club* thing where the characters all start falling in love with the person they're not supposed to, and we learn how not to bow to peer pressure and judge books by their covers and hug and grow and whatnot. The Alien Queen turns out to be the person you least suspect, until you think about it for around three seconds and realise that it was obvious the whole time. The day is saved but not without some seriously comic bad taste splatter. It's a movie I watch repeatedly and, although it's not quite as brilliant as Rodriguez's peerless *From Dusk 'Til Dawn*, it ain't too far behind.

But there are reasons, way beyond film-buff(y) stuff, that I adore this movie. Actually, reason, singular. Its name is Clea DuVall. *The Faculty* has much Clea DuVall. And I'm not even going to pretend this time that this is just about her abundant acting talent, although she has that, in abundance. Let's not beat about the bush: I heart her. So much so that I would probably stalk her if I wasn't terrified of the police and extremely lazy and could afford the flight.

If you've been reading the whole book up to this point you've probably noticed a subtextual theme. One of the reasons I love teen movies is because they fill me with nostalgic emotions about the girls I was infatuated with as an adolescent. If you'd asked me at the time, I would have insisted, with every last pretentious right-on post-punk breath in my (much skinnier ... sigh) body, that I didn't have a type. But I lied like a bad rug. The girls I fell for were all the same.

Pale of skin and dark of hair and clothes. Loners. Excited suspicion and misunderstanding among their peers who were not deep and sensitive enough to understand them because they didn't have my pure heart and beautiful soul. Listened to Crass, The Cure and The Cocteau Twins. Read Sylvia Plath, *Interview With A Vampire* and the monthly newsletter from the British Union Against Vivisection. Womanly of body shape and always wore billowy, Oxfam-shop clothes to try and hide it, unless they were tomboys, in which case they wore boys' clothes. Never tanned, even in heatwaves. Changed hair colour every three months, but never blonde. Heroically refused to shave or diet and mocked girls who did. Always smelt of Patchouli oil ... hey, gotta be a drawback somewhere.

But the clincher was ... The Sadness. Their faces were like a dying kitten in the rain at Skegness, even when laughing uproariously at the dumbest joke on Earth, which I could usually be relied upon to tell. Some mysterious thing had befallen them when very young which had given them a kind of existential despair about the world, and when they weren't looking like they were about to burst into tears for the fate of the entire human race, they looked angry. Frighteningly, I-may-turn-axe-murderer-if-you-play-that-Kid-Creole-record-one-more-time angry. And that scowl was *always* what I fell for.

Clea DuVall is that scowl in full-body form. It's like every fibre of her being has been engulfed by lofty disgust for life itself. God, she's beautiful.

As you can imagine, this appeal hasn't given Jennifer Aniston any stiff competition in the box office cheesecake stakes. Men whose idea of the perfect woman is Medusa The Teenage Witch and the women who admire that are mystifyingly thin on the ground. Someone found the perfect role for her in *But I'm A Cheerleader* (see p. 367) and when that wasn't a unit-shifter – and no one loved her in the unlovable *Girl, Interrupted* – she drifted into a world of TV bit parts and indie movies no one's seen, taking time out to take promotional photos for a feminist girl band who named themselves after a P.J. Harvey album. And if this gets any more like the ideal woman I'll faint before I've finished this entry.

So ... deep breath ... *The Faculty*. It's funny, scary and stars my imaginary girlfriend. Is that Clea?

★ ★

PLEASANTVILLE

1998

Starring: Tobey Maguire, Reese Witherspoon, Kevin Connor, Natalie Ramsey, William H. Macy, Joan Allen, Jeff Daniels, J.T. Walsh, Don Knott
Dir.: Gary Ross

Plot: What's black and white and red all over?
Key line: 'There is no right house. There is no right car.'

A TV screen flicks through channels at the speed of low attention span and finally lands upon one that specialises in nothing but vintage shows in black and white. It is plugging the Pleasantville Marathon, 24 hours of a 1950s soap from 'kinder, gentler times'. The buoyant announcer voice is drenched in upbeat irony as we see short clips that represent the show's cosy, pre-'60s vision of middle-class small-town life. One of its calling cards, according to the announcer, is, 'Of course ... safe sex', and we're looking at twin beds set feet yet miles apart.

Cut to future Spider-Man Tobey Maguire, looking cute but kinda nerdy, as he so often does. He is asking out a pretty blonde girl. The way the camera frames them separately as he talks and she smiles lets you know that this isn't really happening. And it isn't. The next shot shows the pair standing yards but miles apart, and she is talking and walking with the buffest muscle-hunk imaginable, and our boy is alone.

Cut again to high school classrooms. Teachers are delivering lectures to silent pupils about the realities of the modern world: the impossibility of finding a good job; the spread of the HIV virus; the collapse of the ozone layer. We are being dared to prefer the modern world to the clean and gentle 'family values' of the Pleasantville show. In each shot, the camera begins at the back of the room, and moves slowly towards the teacher, and then fades away before we make any connection . . . inches away but miles apart. *Pleasantville* is consumed, visually, with distance: between people, between reality and fantasy, between the '90s and the '50s, between what we could be at our best and what we are at our worst, beautifully encapsulated in the vital role played by a television that won't work without a remote control. It takes a brand new cinema technology and, instead of presenting something that is all about the gimmick, uses the gimmick to write a visual poem about teenage angst, the price of freedom, the cost of repression, the American right's relentless attempts to reject progress and reason and roll back time, the distance between our hopes and our disappointments, the pleasures of unpredictability, and, of course, love. *Pleasantville* is one of the best movies of all time that is almost never presented as such, and it has profound things to say about us, yet does so in such a way that you can lie back and watch the film as *Back To The Future*-meets-*The Truman Show* popcorn fun and gain just as much pleasure. The fact that it is not routinely hailed as a classic wins its own argument about our jaded times. It dares to be idealistic and optimistic without ever becoming about one person's struggle against the odds. It's a socialist film. It therefore remains, like socialism, underrated and loved only in secret.

Pleasantville was the first film to be entirely shot and cut on digital machinery. It's this new technology that enables the movie's central visual conceit: a contemporary world in colour and an imaginary '50s world in black and white. The movie was shot in colour and the Pleasantville scenes were made monochrome by a gizmo called a Spirit DataCine. Easy-peasy now. All new in 1998.

David (Maguire) and Jennifer (Witherspoon) are middle-class teenage twin opposites. He is shy, nerdish and lousy with girls; she is brash, horny and spoiled. So every day is Geek vs Mean Girl, and you suspect, without too much back-story, that that usually ends in the predictable way. David is immediately sympathetic and Jennifer immediately annoying, and you naturally take sides when, left on their own in the house, David wants to watch the old '50s show he has become geekily obsessed with, and she wants to watch MTV before going out with her latest hunky-but-stupid conquest.

This is also a wry comment on a truth about kids. When you meet a teenager there's a quick way to tell if they're an essentially well-adjusted and decent human, or angry kid who is already working out how best to undermine and humiliate you. Nope, its nothing to do with hoods, baseball caps, mobile phone or glottal stops. You just mention some undeniably cool old thing. Could be The Beatles or Public Enemy. Could be *Reservoir Dogs* or *Some Like It Hot*. Could be rockabilly clothes or hippie clothes. If they go, 'UHH?', and make some face like you crawled from a rock, and start texting furiously ... Ah well. If they get all excited and start asking you if you've read anything by Jack Kerouac and listen to Marvin Gaye, you're on to a winner. The more retro a kid is, the more they read, the more engaged they are with the world, the less axe they have to grind. If a kid's only interest is what's hot this very second, all hope is lost. Consumerism and peer pressure's got 'em. *Pleasantville* is about all this, too.

Anyway, the TV remote gets lost, they ring for a repairman, and this old weird guy (Knotts) who is just a little too obsessed with Pleasantville shows up. A couple of presses on a brick-like remote control later, and David and Jennifer are now called Bud and Mary Sue. They live in black and white, are wearing *Grease* cast-offs and negotiating the kind of breakfast – pancakes, bacon, sausages, eggs, all drowned in syrup – that would make any vain and health-conscious modern clean teen turn bulimic.

Despite their horror, Pleasantville does have its fringe benefits. The sexy basketball captain Skip (Connor) fancies Jennifer/Mary Sue. The monochrome sun is always shining. The fire department only rescue cats because fire does not exist.

Gradually, *Pleasantville* itself becomes a comment, not on old TV or '50s values, but middle-America 1998. When the teacher explains in a geography lesson that nothing exists outside the two main streets of the town, and the kids beam with relief, this is a modern America that still only watches local news, won't travel, is frightened of what lies outside of its own neighbourhood. And when David discovers that every basketball goes in the hoop, no matter where and how you throw it, this is an America that only loves winners.

The problem is that David and Jennifer shouldn't be there, and therefore cannot help but disturb the (un)natural order of things by having a need – to return home – that isn't part of the show's script. When David/Bud advises Skip that he shouldn't ask out Mary Sue/Jennifer, and therefore fulfil his TV destiny, Skip is immediately plunged into a kind of existential despair. He throws the basketball in anger and ... it doesn't go in the hoop. And the world begins to tip into chaos.

Eventually we come to realise David and Jennifer's purpose in this world. They are here to free the repressed, cause a revolution, paint the town red and ... invent the 1960s. How they do so is a pure joy, largely involving a symbolic court battle against McCarthyism and Creationism, and introducing the good folk of Pleasantville to the joys and agonies of sex and violence.

Pleasantville's point is way beyond the scope of complexity of the majority of sombre art movies, never mind teen comedies. Because there are many good reasons for our heroes to settle in Pleasantville and stop rocking the boat. No pain. No violence. No failure. No rejection. Parents who unquestioningly adore you and wait upon you hand and foot (well, Mom does – this *is* the '50s) but stay out of your way. A life-plan mapped out for you where AIDS and unemployment and global warming don't exist and relationships live happily ever after. David and Jennifer destroy this world by killing its innocence and, just like the new ideals of the '60s begat assassination, riot, violence between youth and state, activists becoming terrorists, suicide bombers, 9/11 ... much of what comes from their meddling will undoubtedly be very, very bad.

But freedom – true freedom – is a risk. It means accepting responsibility for your fellow man and, when we don't or won't, society fails. It means being constantly unsure of why you're here, and where you fit. This is the moral argument of every dictator, exploiting the chaos that democracy inevitably causes and reasoning that our lives would surely be better if we gave up key freedoms in return for the comfort and security of a world where our role is pre-ordained and we never have to feel like we do not fit ever again. It's what leaders mean when they tell us that we are faced with a stark choice between human rights and teenage gangs or terrorists. Of course, the dictator in question, if given enough leeway, always becomes a self-appointed genocidal God. But who else would feel qualified to design our lives?

Pleasantville, the movie, insists that freedom is essential to humanity even if it means suffering, insecurity and loss of innocence. It connects the right's vision of a clean, white, well-behaved America with fascism and declares that collective action – not a leader or a hero – is necessary to ensure that that fascism is never allowed to hold sway. And that the best thing about life is The Unknown, which is the only thing that makes us get off our arses and try to shape our own futures.

But it does this in such an entertaining, funny, pretty and elegant way that not only does the movie not preach, but it also never descends into being self-righteous. It adores *Back To The Future*, even if it doesn't share its values, and much of its look and sound is a throwback to the unashamedly escapist feel of Spielberg in his early '80s blockbuster phase which, by the time it reaches its thoughtful, surprising and elegantly adult and understated ending, has become a joyful tribute to the lush '50s women's pictures of Douglas Sirk. And it still allows its teens plenty of irresponsible scope to take their snappy, cruel dialogue cues from *Heathers* (see p. 295), like the bit early on where one of Jennifer's friends, in reference to the dorkiness of David, says: 'You guys are, like, twins, though. You must be from the cool side of the uterus.'

It presents a Dream Mother, in Joan Allen's Betty Parker, who may just be the most sympathetic and heartbreaking mom in teen movie history, and forces you to acknowledge your repressed longings for a pretty, kind woman who just looks after you, for ever ... and then shows you *exactly* why you shouldn't get it.

Oh ... and a final word about Ms Witherspoon. You don't hire the sainted Reese and make her a cardboard-cutout Mean Girl. She goes on a journey, and you think you know where it's heading, and then it multiplies itself by ten and breaks a key rule of both time-travel movies and hugging-and-learning fiction. She's just one of the many reasons why *Pleasantville* is among the most brave and beautiful of all teen movies.

★ ★

RUSHMORE

1998

Starring: Jason Schwartzman, Bill Murray, Olivia Williams, Brian Cox
Dir.: Wes Anderson

Plot: The boy who never leaves school.
Key line: 'I saved Latin. What did you ever do?'

Rushmore is a movie where an unattractive and unpleasant nerd is ashamed of his sweet old dad because he's poor, lives a deluded myth of moral and intellectual superiority, orders everyone around, stalks and attempts to molest one of his teachers, and tries to kill the man she loves. It's a delightful light comedy. Nope, I'm not being ironic. It really is.

Wes Anderson's second movie is, as the director acknowledged, hugely indebted to the dry whimsy of Hal Ashby's *Harold And Maude* (see p. 126). But Ashby's movies were all attempts to comment about America from a left-wing, counter-cultural perspective, and Anderson and his *Rushmore* co-writer Owen Wilson are well-to-do products of the apolitical '90s, so their take on the wildly eccentric geek boy and the older woman is not really about anything, except perhaps their own experiences at posh prep schools put through a surrealist, film-buff filter.

Yet *Rushmore* is a more wholly satisfying movie than *Harold And Maude*, and much of that is because it has nothing specific to say about the state of the world or teenage realities. It's probably about how much Anderson and Wilson always wanted to be feted film people. But even this is buried beneath enough whimsy, random quirkiness and technical brilliance that it doesn't really matter.

Their teen protagonist Max Fischer is a wilful rejection of every movie teen male except Harold Chasen. While movie teens all want to get out of school as soon as possible, Max wants to stay in school for ever. While screen teen boys are masters at repressing their true feelings, Max has no filter whatsoever between thought and its expression. He's a What If fantasy character, deliberately scrambling any attempt to define his movie as a coming-of-age saga with insightful things to say about kids. Which is absolutely brilliant for me because I've just watched 81 movies that try to say *something* meaningful about adolescence and, boy, it's refreshing to watch one that doesn't. It just wants you to sit back and look at strange and funny things, and laugh a little, and feel like you've watched an entertaining work of art. And it succeeds at every level.

Much of this, naturally, is down to the casting of Bill Murray. Anderson was apparently so overawed when Murray walked on set that he couldn't bring himself to give him instructions publicly. Murray responded by deferring to him as overtly as possible, working for scale and even paying 25 grand out of his own pocket for a helicopter scene which would have pushed *Rushmore* over budget.

But Murray got his karmic reward. *Rushmore* reinvented him as a subtle leading man for cool indie movies, setting him up to play Bob Harris in *Lost In Translation*, the role he had been born to play. And it reminded us that he was an all-time great comedy presence, a man who could change the entire tone of a scene by hiding behind a tree at its outset, and ending it by turning tail and running away, in that uniquely funny stiff-necked-and-Bambi-legged manner that only a true clown could conceive.

Murray's Herman Blume, the equally excellent Jason Schwartzman as Max and the modestly adorable Olivia Williams as English rose Rosemary Cross play out their bizarre love triangle around the fictional elite Rushmore school. Max is a scholarship student who runs just about every extracurricular activity on campus. He's also an appalling student who is on the verge of being expelled by Brian Cox's quietly bemused principal. Herman is a disillusioned millionaire who impresses Max with his anti-elitist speech at the school – 'Take dead aim at the rich boys. Get them in your crosshairs ... and take them down' – and, bored with his own horrible meathead sons and dissolving marriage, becomes Max's friend. The basis of most of the comedy is that no one, especially Max and Herman, notices that people generally makes friends with people their own age. The pair are mirror images of each other; Max talks like a man but reacts to everything like a child; Herman is a jaded adult who longs to feel and behave like a child again.

Problems quickly develop when Max gets an intense crush on teacher Rosemary, another adult who seems happy to see this weird boy as an equal. The crush quickly becomes inappropriate and obsessive, while Herman and Rosemary fall in love. Cuckolded Max goes mental, gets himself expelled, goes to a normal school, gets into a futile feud with Herman, gets himself arrested, forces Rosemary to leave Rushmore, and despairingly accepts a lonely future working in his dad's barbershop. Its joyously corny set of resolutions and happy endings play out like a alienated kid's fantasy of heroism, and the idea that the movie might all be a play-within-a-movie-within-a-pipedream is foreshadowed by an opening scene where Max dreams about becoming the toast of Rushmore by solving an impossible maths problem, and recurring red theatre curtains that introduce each new month of the tale.

The marvels of the film lie in its gorgeous camerawork and memorable use of '60s British pop songs to comment upon the action. At one point, we are treated to a montage of Max's extracurricular activities, played out as a series of immaculately composed but very funny tableaux, and backed by the punchy, sneering, Who-esque garage-mod of The Creation's 'Making Time'. Anderson finds as much joy in staring in wonder at an old-fashioned record player in Max's dad's barbershop as he does out of the deadpan interplay between Murray and Schwartzman.

But the comedy here is slow-burning rather than belly-laffing, as when Max gives a business card to an especially Yummy Mummy which bears the legend, 'Max Fischer, Rushmore Academy, Ext. 23'. *Rushmore* revolves around the organic humour in watching a nerdy and unattractive boy playing at being a suave man-about-town, and doing it with such deluded determination that he entirely believes his own hype. He is Ferris Bueller-meets-Tracy Flick from *Election* (see p. 374), somehow enveloping his fellow pupils (and most of the faculty) in the conspiracy of his fantasy self-image, splendidly obnoxious but too funny to dislike.

Anderson's love of New Hollywood cinema of the early '70s is hit home by the comic conceit of Max's self-written and directed student play version of *Serpico*, a 1973, Sidney Lumet-directed tough cop vehicle for Al Pacino that spawned a TV series. The joke is that Max's play is actually brilliant, with the actors in full period '70s gangster threads and a perfectly proportioned and lit model train running past the tenement windows at the back of the stage. Not that Max Fischer *is* the young Wes Anderson, or anything . . .

Co-writer Owen Wilson finds his brother Luke a role, as a good brother should. Unfortunately, it's a role that consists of being verbally humiliated by a teenage über-nerd while Bill Murray looks on, sniggering. Sibling issues, much?

How Wilson went from co-writing great left-field teen movies to playing third banana to Jennifer Aniston and a dog is probably one of those tales that will make a great episode of *Entourage* one day. And, in truth, the only film of the last few years that sucks as bad as *Marley And Me* is probably Anderson and Murray's agonisingly pointless *The Life Aquatic With Steve Zissou*. But forgive 'em all because, along with the young Schwartzman in his too-small school blazer and ridiculous red beret, they conspired to make one of the few teen movies that has nothing to declare except its genius and the teen male's fixation on hand-jobs.

* *

CRUEL INTENTIONS

1999
Starring: Sarah Michelle Gellar, Ryan Philippe, Reese Witherspoon, Selma Blair
Dir.: Roger Kumble

Plot: Les Liaisons Teenereuse.
Key line(s): *Kathryn*: **'I'll give you something you've been obsessing about ever since our parents got married.'**
Sebastian: **'Be more specific.'**
Kathryn: **'In English? I'll fuck your brains out.'**

The third best of the '90s teen versions of highbrow classics (see *Clueless*, p. 332, and *William Shakespeare's Romeo + Juliet*, p. 343) sees an A-list cast attempting to recast *fin de siècle* drawing-room drama about a diseased French upper class as a post-*Heathers* (see p. 295) orgy of bad teen faith. Set in a New York made to feel like Glyndebourne with skyscrapers, *Cruel Intentions* is funny, glossy, nasty and dirty, and presented Sarah Michelle Gellar (cue Hallelujahs and hosannas!) with an opportunity to get as far away from the self-sacrificing nobility of Buffy Summers as was (super)humanly possible. Did she pull it off? We'll get back to that.

Pierre Choderlos de Laclos' original novel had already been adapted for the screen with numerous liberties taken. The most famous version, the Oscar-nominated *Dangerous Liaisons* (1988), which starred Glenn Close, Michelle Pfieffer and John Malkovich, stayed period-faithful to the novel and blew the following year's *Valmont* (Colin Firth, Annette Bening) out of the water. There had been a Korean version in 1970 (the Koreans had another go in 2003), and a 1959 Roger Vadim version that transposed the story to the 1960s. Post-*Cruel Intentions*, there's been a 2003 French TV mini-series starring Catherine Deneuve and Rupert Everett set in the 1950s, and, helpfully, a 2005 gay porn version featuring cameos from Boy George, Graham Norton and somebody called Hedda Lettuce. It really is the gift that keeps on giving.

For Hollywood teen purposes, it goes like this. Step-siblings Kathryn (Gellar) and Sebastian (Philippe) rule the New York upper-class teen social scene by fear, sex, manipulation, blackmail and humiliation. Sebastian fancies Kathryn, and she knows it. While Kathryn sets about trying to destroy the rep of the virginal Cecile (Blair) in revenge for her nicking a previous boyfriend, the pair also make a bet over whether Sebastian can bed the militantly virginal Annette (Witherspoon).

Meanwhile, Cecile falls in love with her black cello teacher, which is obviously a no-no. Sebastian falls in love with Annette. Annette falls in love with Sebastian, despite herself. Kathryn falls in love with cocaine and fucking everyone else up, especially Sebastian. She gets her comeuppance, but not in time to avert a tragic death.

Writer/director Roger Kumble set himself a daunting task and somehow pulls it off. The bitchy and occasionally disgusting dialogue zings and he has great fun reinventing the mansions, grandiose gardens and opulent drawing-rooms of period drama in a New York setting. The plot machinations are annoying because the original's plot machinations are annoying, but you don't care because you are too busy enjoying Philippe's evident pleasure in playing the gorgeous sadist to the hilt. The boy's playing against two of the finest actresses of the day here, so it's some shock that *Cruel Intentions* is undoubtedly Philippe's movie. You wonder if his effortless skill at playing an effete pervert has something to do with his subsequent lack of success as a

Hollywood leading man. Plus ... should the boy really be prettier than the girls? Unless he's Johnny Depp who is, as always, the exception that proves every rule.

The movie has flaws, though. And Flaw Number One gives me no pleasure whatsoever to report. Its name is Sarah Michelle Gellar.

Its something I am only now admitting to myself, what with being a *Buffy* obsessive and all. But it has been brought to my attention by the news, just as I'm finishing this book, that Ms Gellar's new project is on its way to dear old Albion. It's a US TV show called *Ringer* where she plays identical twins. In other words, she appears to have given up on her attempts to become a movie leading lady and has come back to genre television, where she belongs. And watching *Cruel Intentions* again, after sitting through various disappointments and/or flops like the *Scooby Doo* movies, *The Grudge* and *Southland Tales* (I'm leaving out all the straight-to-DVD disasters), you can, sadly, see exactly why.

Because, despite being more beautiful as a brunette than a blonde, and applying all her prodigious technique to all those dirty jokes and bitchy come-ons ... Philippe, Witherspoon and even Selma Blair repeatedly blow her off screen. She is supposed to be one of the most enduringly seductive but grotesque villains in literature, and you want to go with it, but ... you can't.

Why? Because she's Buffy Summers. And Buffy Summers isn't capable of such depravity.

Over 144 episodes SMG developed one of the most fully rounded characters in TV history. And just like Buffy keeps saying about her sister Dawn, 'they made her out of me'. Buffy is all the most noble qualities and quirks of mannerism and movement of Sarah Michelle Gellar. Which means she's got nothing left over to be anything else. *Which means that*, when she leans back on a bed and implies that Ryan Philippe can fuck her up the arse ... we're just not buying it. It just looks like Buffy pretending to be bad, like when she pretended to be a robot at the end of *Buffy* Season Five. And precisely the same goes for her Karen Davis in *The Grudge* (Buffy wouldn't be so scared!) and Krysta in *Southland Tales* (Buffy wouldn't be a porn star!). To lead movies, you need to be bigger than the character. You need to be you, with different names and haircuts. And therefore, if all who watch you just see the role that made you ... you're doomed.

Still, if this really is the end of SMG's movie career, *Cruel Intentions* ensures that she's left her mark on cinema history. Because, while we'd all like to pretend that what we took from this movie was its ingenious updating of the intricacies of 18th-century French literature, we didn't. Especially us guys. When someone mentions this film to us, we nod knowingly, look a little dreamy, and bond with other men on matters other than football. Because we're thinking about The Kiss.

In case you haven't seen: Kathryn is combing Cecile's hair in Central Park. They are talking about the fact that Cecile has no sexual experience at all. Ms Gellar, who is resplendent in black Jackie Onassis chic, asks, 'Haven't you practised on a girlfriend?' She turns Cecile around, instructs her to wet her lips, removes the hat (but not the shades) she's wearing, and they kiss very slightly and tenderly. Having gained approval for her teaching technique, SMG (see how I can't even bring myself to call her Kathryn? I'm barely able to stop writing the 'B' word!) suggests that they use tongues this time. Cecile seems oddly keen. SMG removes the shades. 'Coffee & TV' by Blur is playing. And the two lean slowly forward and . . .

Worlds collide, oceans flow backwards, cars crash, men as far away as Texas topple from ladders, and you can hear the spirit of Glen Quagmire off Family Guy going 'giggedy-giggedy-giggedy' until his head explodes. It's a good kiss.

The lad-mag enthusiasm for this special movie moment spelt a final coming out into the mainstream for the male obsession with lesbian sex (or a male-controlled fantasy version of lesbian sex, anyway), and many women seemed to find the scene quite sexy too. So now no TV show is complete without a 'shocking' lesbian snog. And it invented Katy Perry. It's a bit like the karmic cost of doing magic in Buffy. Even good magic has dire consequences.

The ending is kind of a problem, though. Having delighted us with snotty profanities in sophisticated settings, we're suddenly in Central Park watching a fist-fight and a death by big yellow taxi. In truth, the film hasn't earned a Romeo And Juliet-type tragedy. It's too superficial, which is part of its shallow joy. And the humiliation of Kathryn by way of a funeral and Sebastian's journals is going just fine – SMG is fabulous at shocked tears – until Kumble doubts himself, gets all self-conscious about the teen viewers getting bored or something, and dumps The Verve's 'Bittersweet Symphony' all over the scene. Not that it's a bad record. But it has absolutely nothing to do with what we're watching and turns bad karma drama into bad pop video.

The strength of *Cruel Intentions* lies in its deft balance between retaining the original's waspish sophistication and gossipy plot while giving today's kids the swearing, filth, snappy one-liners, glossy sexiness and satire at the expense of high school hierarchies and youth amorality they require. It can't bring itself to carry the original's subtext of the end of a corrupt ruling class. But at least it doesn't embarrass itself by trying.

★ ★

BUT I'M A CHEERLEADER

1999

Starring: Natasha Lyonne, Clea DuVall, RuPaul Charles, Eddie Cibrian, Bud Cort, Melanie Lynskey, Mink Stole, Cathy Moriarty, Julie Delpy
Dir.: Jamie Babbitt

Plot: The *Citizen Kane* of lesbian feminist cheerleader comedies.
Key line: 'It's so much harder once they've been through all that liberal arts brainwashing.'

But I'm A Cheerleader is a movie that simply couldn't have been made before 1999. Directed by lesbian feminist Jamie Babbitt, who served her cinematic apprenticeship as a crew member on Martin Scorsese's *The Age Of Innocence* and David Fincher's *The Game,* but scripted by gay male *Smallville* writer Brian Wayne Peterson, it is a heavily John Waters-influenced satire at the expense of therapy camps that attempt to cure children of homosexuality. It advocates gay rights and mocks the straight world by stealing and subverting the looks and sounds of high school movies, and then turning it up to eleven. It makes its gay characters heroic and its straight characters both dishonest and ridiculous. It takes stereotypes established by John Hughes movies and manipulates them until they are actively promoting homosexuality (and feminism and multiculturalism) to young people. If there's anything that the Thatcher government's 1988 Section 28 law banning local authorities from 'portraying homosexuality in a positive light' was supposed to stop, it was the funding and showing of things like this movie. Do you really need any more recommendations?

Like Waters, Babbitt's sense of humour is of the Bad Taste variety, whereby an overdriven form of kitsch is used to mock the self-appointed Moral Majority. Her choice of cast is like a history of subtly transgressive presences in American cinema. Beautifully weird teen stars in Natasha Lyonne (*American Pie*, kinda frog-faced, booze and drug problems, once arrested for walking into a neighbour's house and shouting, 'I'm going to sexually molest your dog!'), Clea DuVall (Queen of Grumpy, see *The Faculty*, p. 351), Katherine Towne (always plays a bitchy goth – really good at it) and Melanie Lynskey (so scary she's constantly cast as a murderer; see *Heavenly Creatures*, p. 315). They are joined by veterans of benign Bad Taste including black drag queen model and pop star RuPaul Charles, Bud Cort (see *Harold And Maude*, p. 126), Cathy Moriarty (best known for *Raging Bull* but at her best in soap opera piss-take *Soapdish* and B-movie celebration *Matinee*), and Waters regular Mink Stole. Julie Delpy (see *Before Sunrise*, p. 325) is beamed in from the land of Good Taste to do a cameo simply called 'Lipstick Lesbian'. The music, largely by underground gay pop groups called things like Go Sailor, Dressy Bessy and Sissy Bar, is a subtle twist on the fresh-faced college pop that dominates mainstream teen movies.

Lyonne plays Megan, an all-American, baton-wielding good girl who is dating the school hunky jock but thinking of cheerleaders in short skirts while she endures his open-mouthed, tongue-lolling snogging technique. This lack of snog enthusiasm, coupled with her ownership of a Melissa Etheridge poster and a fondness for tofu, inspires an intervention as Mom and Dad (Stole and Cort) send the confused hottie off to True Directions; a place where boys' things are painted day-glo blue, girls' things are painted day-glo pink, and various outsiders (S&M goth girl, Jewish boy, Hispanic femme-punk with a moustache, boy who likes musical theatre) are forced to confess their homosexuality to the group and learn to be ashamed.

Megan is treated to an introductory video where a victim of 'recruitment into the homosexual lifestyle' is presented in the style of a heroin addict. Beaten, bruised and resplendent in punk-biker-ex-con wear and extravagant facial piercings, she chain smokes, sniffs sickly, and recalls that: 'Even when she'd get high and push me off the back of her bike ... I'd roll in the gutter, with broken ribs ... I just kept coming back for more!' After just two months at True Directions our masochistic Biker Bertha is a beaming '50s housewife.

The reorientation therapy comes in the shape of a five-step programme, and it is Step 2 – Rediscovering Your Gender Identity – that gives Babbit free rein to indulge both her amused disgust at received notions of masculinity and femininity and her visually flamboyant perviness. The first attempt to make girls be girls involves forcing them to embrace housework. So, in a room that looks like a giant pink and blue Barbie House with walls made of cake dumped on a gay theatre stage in Greenwich Village, Ms Brown teaches the girls to vacuum. As she and her charges – all dressed in the same pink get-up, so kitsch that it immediately looks like fetish wear – get down on their knees and push vibrating implements around, Mary intones 'In and out! In and out!', and the girls' mouths and eyes light up with ironic lust.

Meanwhile, the boys, who are in powder-blue Scout uniforms with unfeasibly tight shorts, are being taught car maintenance by RuPaul's second-in-command Mike, who is opening and closing his legs and also grunting, 'In and out! In and out' before innocently asking the group, 'So ... who wants to go down with me?' The Woodcraft Folk was never like this.

Babbit's real-life mother ran a therapy group for teens with booze and drug issues called New Directions, so the entire 12-step rehab phenomenon comes in for some good-natured lampooning, too, particularly the obsession with confession. When refusenik Graham (DuVall) is urged to disclose the 'root' of her illness, she sighs, looks awkwardly shameful, and reports: 'My mother got married in pants.' She gets a supportive round of applause for her courage. Other 'roots' of adolescent sexual perversion include 'I was born in France' and 'I like balls.' The lesson? 'Women have roles. When you learn that you'll stop objectifying them.' Heh.

Camp punishments for such things as the boys looking at Mary's hot son like a piece of prime pork are harsh. 'You'll be watching sports! The whole weekend!' If you're beginning to suspect that True Directions is actually heaven on Earth, it inevitably becomes exactly that for Megan and Graham as their initial mutual antipathy inevitably turns into Big Sexy Love.

Even a displaced high school comedy has to end with graduation. And these kids' graduation ceremony has to involve – by way of a

gay bar called Cocksucker, Delpy's lipstick lesbian and a declaration
of guerrilla war on the entire conservative edifice of masculine and
feminine – a defiant coming out and a triumph of love over hate that
can only be gained through . . . cheerleading. It's very silly and very,
very cute. The parting shot is Megan's Ma and Pa at a support group
for the parents of homosexuals. Because, in a nation where sexual
reorientation camps are allowed to exist, it's obviously adult America
that is badly in need of therapy.

So by 1999 things had moved on enough to allow *But I'm A
Cheerleader* to be made. That doesn't mean they get equal rights. In
the same year that *American Pie* featured so much hetero masturbation it occasionally resembled a porn addict watching themselves on webcam, Babbit was forced to cut tiny, pointless bits of
wank action in order to get an R rating. Critics mostly hated the
movie, damning it both for preaching to the converted and not being
angry enough, while seeming to miss the point entirely of the kitsch
settings and the deliberate overstatement of teen movie stereotypes.
Perhaps it was just too much of a shock that a lesbian feminist has
both a sense of humour and a fondness for old-fashioned love stories.

The real comedy comes out of merry things like Cathy Moriarty's
squirming, twitching face and husky voice as she's trying to get a
bewildered Megan to confess her interest in 'a woman . . . in a tight
skirt . . . and her long . . . beautiful legs . . . or perhaps she's in the
bathroom . . . putting lipstick over . . . her full lips . . . or maybe in the
locker-room . . . soaping her body . . . rubbing her breasts . . . ', and
the way that Ms Lyonne's fabulous face slips from confusion, to 'wait
a minute!' suspicion, to increasingly dreamy lust. It's the repressive
right who see filthy sex in the most innocent and natural human
activities to the point where they are actually making the lifestyles
they hate seem far more exciting than they are. This is a movie where
those of us who are morally better people get to laugh at the cruel
and bigoted, because mockery is one hell of an effective way to let
someone know they can't touch you.

To this end, our gay teen heroes and heroines happily parrot the
prejudices and stereotypes of their therapists because this crap is
even more laughable when it comes out of the mouths of teens so
overwhelmingly gay that they look like the winners of the San Francisco Gay Pride Who's The Gayest Gay? contest.

So, despite making a profit on a tiny budget, Babbit hasn't been given a mainstream movie since. She's found a place in low-budget queer cinema and, happily, mainstream American TV, producing and directing shows as diverse as *The L Word*, *Malcolm In The Middle*, *Ugly Betty* and *Nip/Tuck*, because American television has shot way ahead of Hollywood in its embrace of subversive film-makers in the wake of the success of *Buffy*, *The Sopranos* and the Home Box Office channel's iconic quality TV. Of course, Babbit isn't the only director of great work in this book who hasn't gone on to be a major player. But I don't think you need to be Right-On Ron to see that being a female director is hard enough, so being one with an unashamed lesbian feminist agenda who isn't interested in making victim films might be close to impossible.

But I'm A Cheerleader ought to be ground down by the strain and struggle of trying to get something so blatantly designed to convince children that alternative lifestyles are not just valid but desirable made at all. But it isn't. It glides by cheerily, always putting laughs before agitprop, leaving bitterness aside. It's a perfect double-bill with *Bring It On* (see p. 394) because it says precisely the same thing but with far more balls. And I like balls.

★ ★

AMERICAN PIE

1999
Starring: Jason Biggs, Chris Klein, Seann William Scott, Alyson Hannigan, Natasha Lyonne, Thomas Ian Nicholas, Chris Owen, Eugene Levy, Mena Suvari, Eddie Kaye Thomas
Dir.: Paul Weitz

Plot: What you get if you take *Where The Boys Are*, switch genders, add 40 years of plummeting moral standards and some pastry.
Key line: 'I did a fair bit of masturbating when I was a little younger. I used to call it stroking the salami . . . pounding the old pud. I never did it with baked goods . . .'

American Pie represents both the end of a teen comedy era, and the launch of a new one. Just like all those appalling gross-out films that took their cue from *National Lampoon's Animal House* (see p. 161), the Weitz Brothers' debut was frat-boy comedy which entirely hinged upon dirty jokes for dirty boys to snigger at. But the film became the biggest teen comedy hit since *American Graffiti* (see p. 135) because it laughed at its male protagonists and their belief that girls could be manipulated into sex through saying the right lines or striking the right pose. The emphasis swiftly changed in teen sex comedies – at least, teen comedies that wanted to be genuinely successful – from humiliating women to humiliating men. Each time the horny lads of this Michigan high school attempt to bond around the degradation of an unwitting female, they are immediately punished – by drinking a beer-semen cocktail, by premature ejaculation, by girls who are plainly way ahead of them in the sexual knowledge stakes – and publicly exposed as the inadequate boys they are. The only way they can get what they want is by following rules laid down by women and showing the opposite sex a little respect. And, therefore, growing up. This is further hit home by female characters who do rather than are done to, have conversations about orgasms, and are played by genuinely great (and unconventional-looking) actresses like Alyson Hannigan and Mena Suvari.

Eventually this trend would lead to rude movies as multi-layered and girl-friendly as *Superbad* (see p. 454) and *Juno* (see p. 449). And, while each sequel in this franchise did a little more damage to the original's balance of the puerile, the moral and the shamefully funny, the first *American Pie*, along with the Farrelly Brothers' 1998 classic *There's Something About Mary*, paved the way for adolescent smut that didn't insist that the only way to lure male bums onto seats was to treat them to the writers' most enthusiastic misogynist fantasies. Girls could watch and get some karmic revenge for various humiliations they had suffered at the hands of oafish boys. And the boys could laugh at the oafs and reassure themselves that they were never quite *this* oafish. Major studio teen sex comedies stopped being based on the gender war fixations of male writers and directors from the '70s fear-and-loathing years and became date movies again.

The movie is framed around two parties at the house of boorish lacrosse player Stifler (Scott). At the first, four friends, the sweet-but-dorky Jim (Biggs), sweet-but-dumb jock Oz (Klein), sweet-but-pretentious Paul (Thomas) and sweet-and-that's-it-he's-just-sweet Kevin (Nicholas) prove their ineptitude with women ... although

Kevin would have at least got a fully complete BJ from his cute girlfriend Vicky (Reid) if it wasn't for that pesky Stifler and his appetite for cum-laced lager. The situation is made more desperate by the apparent sexual success of the impossibly geeky Sherman aka The Sherminator (Owen).

The four make a pact to lose their virginities before the end of the high school year. The big speech from Kevin about their duty to fight the good fight and be men is a loving tribute to the stupidity of *Animal House*. But when guys get together and plan battle strategies to defeat a resourceful enemy – women, that is – dignity is the first casualty of war.

The main victim of sustained humiliation is Jason Biggs's Jim, and *American Pie* is Biggs's movie. His broad, friendly, none-more-Jewish face – always veering between eagerness to please and bemused panic, and framed by a haircut best described as 'late Mormon' – is the image you take away. Objectively, Jim's comic sexual activities are pretty creepy, yet Biggs successfully remains charming. It's perhaps why Biggs has never really escaped the role and made the breakthrough into adult cinema, being forced to lampoon his inability to escape being known as 'the boy who fucked the pie' in Kevin Smith's *Jay And Silent Bob Strike Back*.

Which brings us to the scene where Jason Biggs fucks a pie. Jim has been assured that getting your dick sucked feels like 'warm apple pie'. So when he comes home to an empty house, and finds a warm apple pie on the kitchen table . . . what else can a po' boy do? Porn wah-wah guitar kicks in. He fingers the pie first, just to build up the right amount of pleasurable audience disgust. Jim doesn't simply put penis in pie out of curiosity. He climbs aboard and makes sweet, sweet love to the pie in the missionary position. Only one thing could be worse than Mom catching you. And that's Dad catching you. 'It's not what it looks like,' says Jim. It is, though. It's a boy fucking a pie.

Which brings us to the other best thing about *American Pie* (apart from the way *Buffy* star Hannigan says the words, 'This one time? In band camp? . . . '), Eugene Levy as Jim's dad, Noah Levenstein. After so many Bad Dads, you'll be pleased to know that Noah is lovely . . . and that's the joke. He is a man so desperate to empathise with and support his son through his adolescent sexual traumas that he buys him porn, conspires to keep the pie incident quiet, and says and does precisely the most embarrassing thing that a teenage boy can imagine a parent saying at every available opportunity, like 'Jim ... I wanna talk to you about masturbation ... '. This scene, which goes on to feature the key lines above, is a gem, as Levy's well-meaning male bonding bounces off Biggs's skin-crawling embarrassment, and every far-too-late parental sex talk you ever received passes in front of your eyes. Still, when Noah is stuck with a kid who agrees to put his first conquest on webcam and then accidentally sends the link to everyone at school before doing a sexy dance and then popping his load before anything happens – twice – one can only forgive Dad for doing his best.

Everybody eventually gets what they want, though not necessarily with the girl or in the way that they expected. Stifler, being the main sexist tool, gets the ultimate punishment when Paul – who is a neat piss-take of Andrew McCarthy's teen yuppie in *Pretty In Pink* (see p. 275) – cops off with his mother. The boys all learn a valuable lesson. Although the owners of the franchise and the stars of the show didn't. After all those crap sequels and spin-offs, get ready in 2012 for ... *American Pie: Reunion*, from the writers of *Harold And Kumar Get The Munchies*! I wish I *was* joking.

★ ★

ELECTION

1999

Starring: Matthew Broderick, Reese Witherspoon, Chris Klein, Jessica Campbell
Dir.: Alexander Payne

Plot: The irresistible force of Blonde Ambition.
Key line: 'You can't interfere with destiny. That's why it's destiny.'

This outstanding satire on American mores is based upon a novel by Tom Perrotta, which was in turn inspired by a real-life event. In 1992, a Wisconsin high school's election for Homecoming Queen made headlines in the *New York Times* when students voted for an absent, pregnant girl and staff took it upon themselves to announce a different winner and burn the original ballots. From such petty

'The perfect metaphor for the raging war between hormonal desire and fear of sex that every young girl must overcome.' Johnny Depp's class act as *Edward Scissorhands* (Pictorial Press/Alamy).

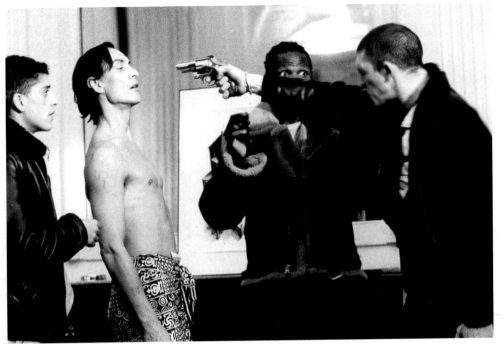

'Political and philosophical *bon mots* while encountering numchuck-wielding coke dealers.' Vincent Cassell and friends in *La Haine* (Photos 12/Alamy).

'To grasp the moment and abolish tomorrow.' Ethan Hawke and Julie Delpy get real in *Before Sunrise* (Moviestore Collection/Alamy).

'Victims of recruitment into the homosexual lifestyle.' A different kind of Pink Power in *But I'm A Cheerleader* (AF Archive/Alamy).

'"I never did it with baked goods ..."' Jason Biggs gives fatherly advice the finger in *American Pie* (Photos 12/Alamy).

'Killing each other for kicks, drugs and chump change.' The teen gang
movie grows up in *City Of God* (AF Archive/Alamy).

Left: 'Everyone dances on her estate. They make life where it doesn't exist.' Katie Jarvis steps out in *Fish Tank* (BBC Films/ The Kobal Collection).

Below left: 'Making bad taste parody into family fun.' Dame Edna Travolta offers dieting tips to Nikki Blonski in *Hairspray* (Moviestore Collection/Alamy).

Below right: 'From horrified shame to enjoying the power.' Brad Renfro turns gay stripper in *Bully* (Photos 12/Alamy).

'You'll definitely never watch *Flashdance* in quite the same way ever again.'
Dystopian dancing in *Dogtooth* (AF Archive/Alamy).

nastiness, futile rebellion and control-freakery, big ideas are born. A year after *Election* was released, American power objected to Al Gore and burned the ballots in a supposedly adult Presidential election. And if Sarah Palin purchased some bleach, she would be Tracy Flick.

But *Election* is not some self-righteous anti-right-wing rant. Alexander Payne and his co-writer Jim Taylor are far too smart for that. Although Jim McAllister (Broderick on top form) and Tracy Flick (Reese Witherspoon in one of this book's greatest performances) could be ciphers for hypocritical liberalism and quasi-fascist conservatism respectively, they are too complicated, lovable, loathable and real to be so easily labelled and contained. What is certain is that the characters and performances make a potentially parochial movie about high school politics into inflammable material that never sacrifices a pure belly laugh for the sake of the opportunity to preach.

Set in Payne's hometown of Omaha, Nebraska, *Election* deals with an on-campus war between cuddly, affable teacher McAllister and ambitious student Flick. Through voiceover, unreliable narration and brilliant use of techniques such as freeze-frame, we quickly learn that both are hiding their true selves between carefully constructed public images. While Tracy is actually hated by her fellow pupils, who give her what she wants because they are scared of her or bored with her, Jim is a frustrated victim of mid-life crisis who despises Tracy for her energy and positivity. Oh ... and he also hates her because she slept with his friend Dave, who lost both marriage and teaching job while Tracy successfully painted herself as the innocent victim.

Mr Woman-Hater and Ms Daddy Issues meet their destinies when Tracy decides to run for student body President. She is going to be elected unopposed until Jim persuades handsome, popular, injured football jock Paul Metzler (Klein) to run against her. Things are further complicated when Paul's lesbian rebel sister Tammy (Campbell), seeking revenge for Paul stealing her girlfriend, decides to throw her hat into the Presidential ring in an attempt to humiliate both Paul and the school in general.

While Jim's life dissolves over a failed attempt to have an affair with Dare's ex-wife Linda (while also dealing with his eye having been stung by a bee), Tammy sees Tracy destroying Paul's election posters. Instead of snitching, Tammy confesses to the crime, thus fulfilling her wish to be expelled and being sent to a private all-girl school full of fellow dykes.

Jim meets his Waterloo because the nice guy he chose to stop Tracy is, actually, truly nice. Paul votes for Tracy, partly because he knows she'll do a better job than him, but mainly because he thinks it's arrogant to vote for oneself. When the votes are counted, Tracy has won – by one vote. With his life in tatters, Jim refuses to accept yet more evidence that he is unable to exercise power over anything. He throws away two of Tracy's votes. And, of course, he is caught.

Having lost job, wife and home, Jim moves to New York and becomes a tour guide at the Natural History Museum. And the film ends with his last pathetic 'meeting' with Tracy. He sees her, from a distance, getting into a limousine with a renowned politician, looking rich, beautiful and successful beyond his wildest dreams at half his age. Jim throws an empty can at the limo ... and runs away like a naughty schoolboy. The last we see, he is giving a museum tour to a group of children, furiously ignoring the one girl in the group who knows the answer to all of his questions, just as he was at the beginning of the movie, still simmering with revenge fantasies and unable to move on.

Good story, eh? But *Election* is storytelling plus; a fizzing, spitting beast full of stunning performances, wry dialogue, wonderfully witty and lyrical orchestral music, hilarious sight gags, bravura directorial flourishes ... and Reese Witherspoon. The future fictional June Carter Cash is everything here that fawning critics said Nicole Kidman was in the bizarrely overrated *To Die For*, when she clearly wasn't. Her Tracy Flick is so terrifying, unstoppable, intimidating, evil ... but also sympathetic, funny, lonely, naive and full of the kind of rage that only someone who has been badly abused by the hypocritical McAllisters of this world can muster. She is the embodiment of that post-'The Greatest Love Of All' world where people believe that one will fulfil all one's dreams by just being perky, pro-active, positive and believing that God or destiny or name-your-cosmic-benefactor has chosen you to be special. While the McAllisters of this world spin in ever-decreasing circles, agonizing over the parts of themselves that are selfish and cruel, Tracy is hard, straight lines and an embrace of inner darkness forged by the belief that other people are nothing more than obstacles to be crushed by those who are plainly more deserving of success. Or: Tracy is Margaret Thatcher. Jim is Gordon Brown.

There is a wonderful freeze-frame in the first classroom scene, where Payne stops and holds on Witherspoon's face while she's talking, and catches an exact moment where all of her features are heading in different directions, rendering her comically ugly. This should be a cruel, humiliating shot, but somehow, even here, without her having any knowledge of what Payne was going to do with her face, there is a spirit, an indomitability ... and some kind of innate, instinctive understanding that this is the kind of face that this kind of person makes in an unguarded moment. It's a connection between director and actress that defies logic and heads right into magic, and makes a rule-breaking entirely static shot into one of the most memorably funny and endearing images in modern cinema.

Witherspoon is matched most of the way by Matthew Broderick. It's perhaps especially unavoidable in a book about teen movies, but you really can see Ferris Bueller (see p. 270) in Jim McAllister. I mean, it's obvious that the Ferris we meet in 1986 is a boy who has peaked too soon. And, despite the fact that Broderick is 37 years old by *Election* time, there is something of the gawky teenage boy dressing up like a man about him, like a less supernatural Tom Hanks in *Big*. You can read Jim as Ferris, heading downhill all the way from his superhero childhood, accepting a middle-ranking life as a middle-ranking teacher with a dull marriage, convincing himself he's still the populist school hero by arse-licking his way to Teacher Of The Year awards, being the all-round good egg not out of decency, but self-regard. There is something in Broderick's ever-present bland smirk and kind, gentle eyes that he understands only too well, a kind of very American, have-a-nice-day friendliness masking a deeply cynical, misanthropic bitterness about having to be nice to anyone.

Most of the comic pleasure of *Election* comes from the continuous disconnect between the voiceover narrations of Tracy and Jim, and what we see them actually doing. As such, *Election* is not just a great film about revenge, school, sex, politics, popularity and the difference between winners and losers. It's also a spectacular study of the lies we all tell ourselves in order to construct a self-image we can live with. While Jim McAllister may continue lying to himself about his usefulness through another couple of broken marriages and career failures, you come out of *Election* suspecting that Tracy's delusions will, at some point not too far away, hit her with an awful powerful showerful of truth, and she will stagger under its weight. Like Ferris, she may have won this round. But she has peaked too soon. The best testament to Payne, Taylor and Reese Witherspoon is that, even though Tracy Flick is a wholly believable right-wing monster, we know she is really a victim and hope that the truth doesn't hit her too hard. As teen comedy characters go, Tracy Flick is one unusually resonant chick.

* *

THE VIRGIN SUICIDES

1999
Starring: Kirsten Dunst, Josh Hartnett, Kathleen Turner, James Woods, Hanna R. Hall, A.J. Cook, Leslie Hayman, Chelse Swain, Scott Glenn, Danny DeVito, Giovanni Ribisi (Narrator)
Dir.: Sofia Coppola

Plot: The Girl you never get over.
Key line(s): 'What are you doing here, Honey? You're not even old enough to know how bad life gets.'
'Obviously, Doctor, you've never been a 13-year-old girl.'

In 1974 in Grosse Pointe, Michigan, five beautiful blonde sisters kill themselves. They are aged between 13 and 17, and they are popular and wealthy and loved by their parents, and no one knows why. They have great taste in romantic FM pop, too. And that shit will stick with you.

The debut feature film of Francis Ford Coppola's daughter Sofia is a faithful adaptation of Jeffery Eugenides' unconventional 1993 novel. It introduces the world to Coppola's elegant compositions, emotional distance and ability to make images sing like her favourite art-pop records. It is, from the moment a boy jumps out of a window to prove his love for another teenage girl, a film about the adolescent male's worship of budding female sexuality.

But, like the novel, it's not about the causes of suicide. The girls' parents, played with understated power by James Woods and Kathleen Turner, are Christian conservatives who, for reasons that they never go into, attempt to shelter their daughters from boys, sex and the outside world. They are part of a repressed community who are continuing to live a '50s suburban lifestyle in the '70s, like the '60s never happened. There is a backdrop of '70s recession, and many suggestions, from strikes to the closure of local industries, that Grosse Pointe is about to enter the steep decline that hit Michigan in the wake of the closures of the car factories. And one of the girls gets ill-treated by a handsome cad.

But *The Virgin Suicides* doesn't blame any of these factors. The film stops way short of accusing Christianity of destroying young lives. The Lisbons are fine for money. These girls are not afraid to disobey rules. They openly mock their parents' boundaries when a boy is invited round for dinner, and relentlessly tease the neighbourhood boys, one of whom is our excellent narrator. They have sex when their parents aren't looking. The film pokes fun at Ronald Lisbon's boring obsession with model planes, but not his and Sara Lisbon's parental grief and suffering. There is obviously something wrong with their marriage because they never talk to each other, but there is no violence or conflict. This is not a critique of religion or repressive parenting. Its blend of wry comedy and poetic elegy for doomed youth doesn't even go as far as painting the events as tragedy. We only know these girls are suicidal because they kill themselves. In *The Virgin Suicides*, teenage suicide is a beautiful romantic mystery.

The film begins with a failed suicide attempt by youngest sister Cecilia (Hall) and our introduction to the boys who worship the Lisbon sisters from afar. The parents are advised by Danny DeVito's bemused child psychiatrist to allow their girls to socialize with boys their own age. The parents throw a party, and the boys come, all togged out in their suited and booted Sunday School best.

But the gently amusing pleasures of watching junior gigolos trying to flirt with Mom Lisbon turn dark upon the arrival of Joe, a Down's Syndrome boy who is used like a performing animal by the neighbourhood children. Cecilia is so appalled by and alienated from her peers' idea of entertainment that it appears to be the last straw. She excuses herself from the party, goes upstairs, jumps out of a window and impales herself on the garden fence.

The theme of disconnection and secrecy is neatly summed up by a scene where Scott Glenn's priest Father Moody visits the bereaved family, and tries to encourage them to express their feelings, but gets absolutely nothing. Not only can none of the Lisbons talk to him but they cannot face each other either. They grieve separately, Dad watching football and being stiff upper lippy, Mom silently broken in the bedroom ... and the girls? They don't seem to care. They are arranged together in a bedroom as if posing to tease boys at a pyjama party, smiling silently, amused as always. The conspiracy they share is hidden, not just from priests and parents, but from us.

It's as if they know exactly how we'll look for clues and, like all good criminals, make sure they thoroughly clean up the crime scene. The boys get hold of Cecilia's diary. Surely the source of her agony will be there! But all they get is the aimless logging of meals and mundane family incidents, forcing the boys to play amateur psychologists, perusing the way she dots her 'i's for evidence of neurosis. But eventually they find some snippy references to Lux's crush on the garbage man, and the movie sweeps off into the sun-dappled romantic paradise that the boys project upon Lux (Dunst) and her fellow angels ... a world so much more exciting and poignant than the dull, repressed and recession-hit world that they are forced to live in. 'We felt the imprisonment of being a girl,' Ribisi's voiceover sighs, longingly ... 'We knew that the girls were really women in disguise; that they understood love, and even death, and that our job was really to create the noise that seemed to fascinate them.'

As the Grosse Pointe community become increasingly obsessed with solving the mystery of Cecilia's death wish, her remaining sisters are working on their own. They slip off the rails, led by Lux, who begins a relationship with school dreamboat Trip (Hartnett). He persuades Mr and Mrs Lisbon to allow him to take Lux to the prom using a promise to find dates for the other sisters so they can go as a group, and, after Trip and Lux are crowned Homecoming King and Queen, the pair pop Lux's cherry, in time-honoured American teen tradition, on the school football field.

But Trip breaks Lux's heart and the girls break their parents' curfew. Mrs Lisbon responds by taking the girls out of school. Despite being imprisoned by their parents' sexual paranoia, the resourceful girls stay connected to their boy worshippers by means of night-time light signals and playing each other gorgeous soft-rock love songs by Carole King, Todd Rundgren and the Bee Gees over the phone.

But Lux is a loose cannon, having sexual trysts with random men on the roof of the house, in full view of the voyeuristic boys. The exhibitionism that seems to fuel so much of the sisters' behaviour reaches its inevitable extreme, when, as the Lisbon parents' sleep, they invite the boys round. The boys believe they are there to aid a daring, romantic, midnight escape from Prison Lisbon. They are there to bear witness to a suicide pact.

The distraught Lisbons sell the house and move away from Grosse Pointe. But the town – and especially our hapless boys – never get over a tragedy that is never adequately explained. They are now men in suits, but, when they meet, all they do is go back over the events, trying to rationalise the irrational.

The Virgin Suicides is truly unlike any other teen movie, before or since. There is an obvious undercurrent of 'Suburban America eats its young' that looks back to disparate teen films by everyone from Nicholas Ray (see *Rebel Without A Cause*, p. 28) to Brian De Palma (see *Carrie*, p. 150) to Jonathan Kaplan (see *Over The Edge*, p. 184), and informs future teen classics like *Donnie Darko* (see p. 405), *Elephant* (see p. 418) and *Teeth* (see p. 458). But the film it most resembles is Robert Mulligan's 1962 adaptation of Harper Lee's tale of children and injustice in The Deep South, *To Kill A Mockingbird*. Like the earlier film, Coppola's debut masterpiece endeavours to stay faithful to a classic novel, lifting parts of the text in voiceover form, while using a dreamlike magical realism to create a truly cinematic experience which delves deeply and credibly into the mindset of children attempting to come of age in a small, incestuous place that is trying to halt the tide of progress and change.

But *The Virgin Suicides* is about sex and death, not race and justice. It is cinema's most poetic ode to adolescent female sexuality. Its use of music – the '70s hits and the aesthetically similar romantic ambience of Air and Sloan – anticipates *Donnie Darko*'s rejection of pop as mere nostalgia or backdrop for party scenes, and elegantly dramatizes the passion and warmth of teen love.

This film is the antidote to all those frat comedies about teenage boys who just want to get laid. That stuff is just what we say to each other to protect ourselves, to impress each other, to conspire in each other's need to look invulnerable. When we are alone or honest, *The Virgin Suicides* is how teenage boys really feel about girls; that they are the universe's most beautiful and awe-inspiring mystery, torturing us with their secret knowledge of love and sex and sensuality and smelling good, laughing conspiratorially at our dumb attempts to behave like equals. We worship you because, if we didn't, the human race would cease to exist. And we pretend that we don't because we have to preserve *some* dignity and self-esteem with which to do that hunting and gathering thing you don't actually need us for any more.

And the deaths? A big fat red herring. There is no reason why, because the '70s Grosse Pointe world, though repressive, is not brutal. The Lisbon sisters' death wish is an insoluble mystery because teenage girls are insoluble mysteries, and because insoluble mysteries haunt us long after a tale is told. Closure enables you to move on. Loose ends keep us trapped in the past. Therein lies the tragic beauty of this perfect film.

2000s

FINAL DESTINATION

2000

Starring: Devon Sawa, Ali Larter, Seann William Scott
Dir.: James Wong

Plot: We're all going to die. Amusingly.
Key line: 'I don't have a narcissistic deity complex. I'm not going Dahmer on you guys. This just *is*. There is a pattern for us all.'

The most commercially successful of our run of millennial teen shockers is unloved by critics. Horror fans disagree, investing money and love in a franchise that has so far produced five movies, nine books and a series of comic books. Not bad for an idea that began life as a rejected script for an episode of *The X Files*.

Writer Jeffery Reddick's original premise is dastardly in its simplicity. Fascinated by the horror of and conspiracy theories surrounding the 1996 mid-air explosion of TWA Flight 800, Reddick wondered if this unexplained tragedy that killed 230 people could only be explained by predestination: the victims were meant to die, so they did. When various psychics insisted that they had had premonitions about the explosion, the plot of *Final Destination* was complete. What if you had a premonition of a disaster, and saved your own life and those of a few other people? But if your death is part of a carefully constructed plan, then death itself could not let you walk away from your fate, lest the entire pattern be destroyed. It would track down you and your fellow survivors and kill you. So . . . how could you possibly escape and live long enough to build up crippling debts and complain about young people and their music?

Fellow *X Files* writer James Wong got it and pursued his debut directorial project as modernised teen Alfred Hitchcock, complete with crazy camera angles, suspenseful close-ups on faces and objects, scary orchestral score and black, black humour. With *Scream* (see p. 339) having reset the teen slasher genre as a postmodern form of meta-film-making, he and screenwriters Reddick and Glen Morgan named the characters of the film after horror movie legends: Alex Browning (Sawa) after *Freaks* director Tod Browning; teacher Valerie Lewton after B-movie producer Val Lewton; Terry Chaney after movie monster actor Lon Chaney; and, of course, Billy Hitchcock, played by doofus *du jour* Seann William Scott. Heavyweight legends to compare yourself to. But Wong and co. earned the right, because *Final Destination* is spectacularly great film-making. And if you don't believe me, clock the opening scenes.

So we meet Alex and find out that his high school class are flying to Paris for a study trip. Cue an orgy of fatal foreshadowing at the airport. A Hare Krishna type saying, 'Death is not the end.' Numerological omens and flight signs saying, 'Terminal'. A girl looking at pictures of Princess Diana's death in a magazine.

The brilliance of the opening sequence lies in how much creeping unease Wong and soundtrack composer Shirley Walker inject into the slowly revealed, familiar details of air travel . . . the bland suspension of the waiting areas; the luggage cart blinking beneath your feet as you walk over the boardwalk to the plane; the crying baby and the disabled man, the straight, plasticky lines of the overhead baggage cabins. The dread is cut with the dumb banter of excited teens pretending to be cool . . . boorish plans to cop off with the hot girls, bickering about money, snogging jocks. All are rendered scary by the sombre portent of Walker's score and sudden close-ups on Devon Sawa's increasingly drawn, terrified face.

We take off, things are fine, and we settle down for an airplane thriller which will play out at the same, suspenseful pace. But . . . nah. We're suddenly thrust into turbulence, chaos, shrieking and the collective nightmare of those oxygen masks we hope will never pop out of their hidey-holes while we are in a plane. We're going down. The plane disintegrates. Balls of fire and people sucked, weightless, into the night sky. The obvious only begins to dawn when a really big ball of fire rolls through what's left of the plane and incinerates our hero – yep, all a bad dream. Dream sequences are always perfectly fair game – unless you do it at the end of your movie, in which case you are the storytelling equivalent of a 12-year-old and should seek alternative employment in the growing field of fast food. But here, it's not a dream. It's a premonition. As we discussed, everyone's death is pre-ordained. Young Alex has got The Sight, and escapes death with a handful of classmates and a teacher. But just 'cos you got death sussed doesn't mean that you can cheat it. Remember how good it is at chess?

The sequels get increasingly silly. But the strength of the first movie is that it plays its scenario straight. It is respectful to the tragedy that inspired it and expertly balances laughing at death while taking grief quite seriously. Its early high school funeral scenes have a post-Columbine feel. It also has a believable take on how someone truly psychic might be treated by those around them, implying that the modern world hasn't moved on too far from the desire to burn witches at the stake.

But you don't wanna know about all that. You want the *Final Destination* franchise's perennially popular USP. You want funny deaths. You want the Rube Goldberg machine.

Rube Goldberg was an American artist, inventor and cartoonist whose work in newspapers made him hugely popular in the States from around 1915 and onwards. His specialty was comic contraptions that accomplished simple tasks by ludicrously complex means. Familiar versions on this theme might be, for example, the complex series of mechanical tools to feed the dog and make coffee triggered by clocks in the brilliantly shot opening scene of *Back To The Future* (see p. 259); or the fiendish but ultimately not-as-efficient-as-shooting-him-in-the-head killing machines utilised by Bond villains; or, my personal favourite, the bizarre series of pulleys, anvils and fake mountain pathways Wile E. Coyote would buy from capitalist running dogs Acme in his futile attempts to kill and eat Roadrunner.

This last is most pertinent to the cartoon ingenuity of *Final Destination*'s mortal coil shufflings, which are introduced to the cinematic lexicon by the unfortunate demise of Alex's best friend Tod (*Tod* is German for 'death'). The kid goes into his bathroom to do his normal ablutions. While he's taking a dump, water begins to drip out of the lavatory faucet and on to the tiled bathroom floor. Tod picks up a standard razor while the water seeps towards him, but immediately cuts himself. He sees a shadow pass behind him in the mirror, but there's nothing there. He starts to cut his nose hairs. Just as the water is snaking towards his bare feet, he decides to plug a radio into the wall socket. A neat music critic joke: John Denver's 'Rocky Mountain High' plays, and he hurriedly pulls the plug just before the water barbecues him. He walks from the mirror and the water magically turns after him. All this, incidentally, is cut with an obsessed Alex in his bedroom, surrounded by air disaster books, trying to distract himself with a copy of *Penthouse*, being freaked out by an owl at his window and ending up with a bit of paper stuck to his trousers that says, 'Tod'.

Cut back to the doomed Tod in question. He finally slips on the water and falls face first into the bathtub, pausing only to let the metal cord from the bath plug whiplash around his neck. He chokes in Hitchockian tribute style, and his eyes turn a stylish shade of red and his skin an equally striking shade of blue, and he eventually hangs himself while sitting down in his own bath. Job done, the water slides gracefully back underneath the toilet. Heh.

Although the romance between the excellently intense Alex and tough loner artist Clear Rivers (Larter) generates some proper chemistry and rooting-for-'em feelings, from then on the movie is really all about your favourite surrealist slaughter as the survivors of the air tragedy are picked off one by one by an invisible but unstoppable enemy. In opposition to old Rube, one of the best deaths belongs to ditzy jock girlfriend Terry, who says 'drop fucking dead' and then gets hit by a bus with a shock hyper-speed effect that has been ripped off so many times it deserves its own blue plaque outside Graumann's.

The quintuple death of teacher Valerie Lewton – throat slit by shard of exploding computer monitor, then chased into kitchen by ring of fire, then stabbed by falling kitchen knife, which is then hammered into her chest by a falling chair, before her house blows up – is sick genius. But I am especially fond of Seann William Scott's decapitation by railway chain.

Those who sniff about the absence of art within *Final Destination* must be mental, or plain blind. Wong modernises Hitchcock here with both a dark humour and a technical virtuosity way beyond more 'serious' directors like De Palma (see *Carrie*, p. 150) and Van Sant (see *Elephant*, p. 418). His use of deep focus, elliptical angles and Walker's music to suffuse the most innocent household object with layer upon layer of dread is so strong that the movie becomes a satire on both labour saving devices and all the futile things we've invented to see off the one inevitable fact of life. That would be death, in case you were wondering, and Wong thinks it's very, very funny that humanity believes that its technological wonders will, eventually, stop us from dying, and that that would be anything but an utter disaster. Seat belts come in for an especially hard time so, if you are a health and safety control freak, this is not the movie for you. Or maybe it is. You need to start accepting the inevitable, Buddy.

Final Destination is probably the only mainstream popcorn hit which forcibly puts the point that it's best if we all go, sooner rather than later, because the longer we stick around, the more of our planet we kill. It doesn't put it that baldly, because it's too busy tying an anvil around our necks and dropping us off a cliff to go all Al Gore on us guys.

★ ★

BATTLE ROYALE

2000
Starring: Tatsuya Fujiwara, Aki Maeda, Taro Yamamoto, Takeshi Kitano, Masanobu Ando, Kou Shibasaki
Dir.: Kinji Fukasaku

Plot: Juvenile delinquency's Final Solution.
Key line: 'If you hate someone, you take the consequences.'

If you are one of those who watched the August 2011 riots in England and, outraged by the violence and greed, felt that the best solution was to send all these 'mindless', 'feral' 'kids' off to some remote island where they could happily set fire to and steal from each other . . . then this is the movie for you.

In Fukasaku's controversial and internationally successful adaptation of Koshun Takami's novel, a class of disobedient schoolchildren are sent to an island to slaughter each other. They are victims of the Battle Royale Act, a desperate attempt by Japanese society to force its children to behave in a society in which the economic and social fabric has completely disintegrated. The film is extraordinary . . . a virtuoso mix of science fiction cautionary tale, post-apocalypse scaremongering, teen soap opera, black comedy, *grand guignol* slasher movie, surreal art film, twist-laden thriller, juvenile war movie and pure edge-of-the-seat action. Quentin Tarantino recently named it the best movie made since he began his directing career, which only goes to show that he's a much better film critic than film-maker.

Class B of the Kanagawa high school are drugged and taken to an island where their old teacher is primed and ready to let them loose upon each other. The rules of the game are set out in a horrifying and darkly comic twist on all the classroom scenes we've previously looked at, as the children are informed that they will be cast adrift on the island and forced to murder one another until only one survives.

The Battle Royale info video Class B are then shown is deeply influenced by the military propaganda ads in *Starship Troopers* (see p. 347). *Battle Royale* laughs at consumerism, at the hyper-positivity of ads aimed at children, and at the idea that the designer goods and status symbols that modern teens fetishise could – and perhaps should – be used against them. Violence and consumerism are one and the same thing here: and survival is the best product on offer, and only available to one young savage.

'Beat' Takeshi Kitano is perfect as the children's deadpan, mocking torturer-in-chief, Kitano. When we meet him at the beginning of the movie he is an embattled teacher in a suit, tired and defeated, getting accidentally stabbed by one of the wild boys and apparently seeking no reprisals. Once the Class B kids have been drugged and despatched to the Battle Royale island – with the new teacher who had apparently protested about their fate now a bloody corpse, paraded in front of them – Takeshi is now a thug in a track-suit, taking out whispering school kids with knives thrown right between the eyes, and taking laconic pleasure in the prospect of his ex-pupils ripping each other new arseholes for the kicks and thrills of an angry nation. There are few actors in existence who could embody every right-winger who has ever loved the idea of all rebellious young people being physically attacked until they break and conform without cackling maniacally and twirling a metaphorical moustache. But Kitano, who, in movies directed by himself and others, has specialised in the ... sorry, but there really is no other word ... inscrutable existential killer, was born to be this Kitano, murdering kids for fun, making you enjoy watching him do it ... and being one scary motherfucker.

This is also very much post-*Alien, Starship Troopers* and Lara Croft in its attitude to women. There is no sign here that men have any natural advantage in the violence of either the state or the teens. The winner of the previous Battle Royale, whom we see at the beginning of the film, is an increasingly familiar sight for fans of Asian extreme cinema: a small cute girl rendered hideous by long, dark feral hair, blood-splattered skin, and a smile pitched somewhere between the Mona Lisa, Carrie White and Nosferatu. Female soldiers in gas masks hand out beatings, and our ironically enthusiastic video is presented by the stereotype of the peppy, Hello Kitty, Japanese teen girl pop fan.

The music plays a key role; a constant soundtrack of exclamation mark orchestral flourishes and fanfares, smothering every image with a postmodern irony that enables the viewer to laugh at and with what is, when all is said and done, a movie about the sadistic abuse of children by an out-of-control police state. And numbers play a key role, too. Every time a kid buys the farm, a caption flashes up telling you how many players are left alive. The obvious allusion is to shoot-'em-up video games, and we can't help but wonder whether we're doing the killing using the fingers and joysticks of the film-makers. The movie wants to help us out, so it keeps score.

Oh yeah . . . a pretty vital *deus-ex-machina*. The children are forced to play the game by way of unremovable neckbands that track the kids' movements and blow the throat out if they're not following the rules. Many of the reviews of *Battle Royale* compare the movie to William Golding's classic kids-turn-feral-on-desert-island novel *Lord Of The Flies*. But Golding was examining theories of what children – and, by implication, adults – would be if left to their own devices without authority. The kids in *Battle Royale* are forced – by authority, by surveillance, by technology – to turn savage, or die. The only similarity to Golding's vision is the remote island.

What's that? Where are the parents? Glad you asked. They've been 'notified'. That's it. Ha!

As the movie is in the Japanese tradition, only a total rock star like Takeshi gets to be understated. These kids are mad-eyed screamers or born ninjas, with dimensions only allowed for Fujiwara, Maeda and Yamamoto as principal heroes Shuya, Noriko and Kawada. But these performances and characters are absolutely vital, because, without them, we're into *Human Centipede/Saw* pointless sadism territory. You have to care about these kids to care about how this all turns out. The morality of the piece begins to surface early and needs strong characterisation to hit it home: which of these kids immediately conform to the rules of the game and think only of their own survival, and which are made redeemable by their reluctance to kill and willingness to rebel?

This is an awesome action thriller high concept, and Fukasaku doesn't waste any of its possibilities and potential intrigues. Will more than one kid survive? If so, who and how? Can a bunch of bewildered children somehow fight back, kill the bad guys, and repeal the BR Law? Will anyone find true love while they're at it? Who are these two mysterious, sexy male model-looking boys who none of Class B have ever seen before? And who is gonna wipe that smirk off the face of ultimate Bad Dad Beat Takeshi? It's this simple thriller stuff that keeps you enthralled, rather than the subtexts about youth crime and punishment and the inevitable collapse of capitalism. And without great teen acting, the movie would just be exploitation without anything for a viewer to root for ... which is always failed exploitation.

As the mayhem progresses, *Battle Royale* sketches in the reasons why some form of united front among the combatants is problematic. We see flashbacks of the usual high school nastiness and name-calling, but here standard teen angst has become charged with something far more deadly. School, as we all know, is already a teen war zone, and mutual trust is unlikely when these kids are locked into patterns of cliques, bullying, romantic rivalries and humiliations. It's these short flashbacks that lend the movie poignancy, and keep it tethered to somewhere the viewer understands in an otherwise ridiculous sci-fi situation. *Battle Royale* pulls this off more convincingly than *A Clockwork Orange* (see p. 111) and *Starship Troopers* because, in spite of the high body count, it has a big heart and an extraordinary sympathy for the pressure put upon ordinary teens. Most of these scenes are unashamedly corny. But *Battle Royale* isn't trying to be *Kids* (see p. 328) More than anything, it wants you to have fun. And much of the fun comes from Fukasaku's's ability to cut from teen soap to horror nightmare at the flick of an emotional switch.

The setting is also spectacular. An island of rugged splendour that allows many gorgeous shots of unhappy children set against enormous skies, it is made evocative of harsher places by the cruel ironies of the gamekeepers. Rousing classical music by Verdi, Strauss, Bach and Schubert is played over booming loudspeakers (bringing *Apocalypse Now* to mind) as Kitano cheerily announces the names of the dead. The island increasingly resembles a mix of human zoo and concentration camp. Intimations of fascism drench *Battle Royale*, and you can feel the movie's accusatory anger at Japan's past as a member of the mid-20th century's true Axis Of Evil.

But politics is overwhelmed by pathos, as the film's most poignant theme slowly emerges. The teen romance is heartrending and made more powerful by the complete absence of sex. These kids are too busy surviving – and distrusting – to fuck. There isn't even a kiss. So the most beautiful declarations of everlasting devotion are made as children die, leaving their love untainted by mundane reality. The film becomes, first and foremost, a tale about trust and friendship, and how hard those things are to find, and how human life is worthless without them.

But *Battle Royale* is also a film about watching extraordinary and violent images and going, '*OOOooo!!!*' Chigusa (Chiaki Kuriyama) chasing a terrified potential teen rapist and then stabbing him repeatedly in the crotch. A severed head with a live grenade in its mouth. The computer geek revolutionary, using tactics taken from his '60s activist uncle, hatching a plot that evokes everything from *WarGames* (see p. 233) to suicide bombers. A girl telling her father that 'your bad breath even stinks over the phone'. The scene where a happy camp of girls cooking dinner and planning mutual survival switches, by way of the arrival of a boy and an ill-advised poisoning, into thrilling shoot-out mayhem involving all-time great images of cute young schoolgirls wielding big fucking guns.

And five main teen characters that stand for beauty among the chaos, whether they are our three aforementioned noble heroes, or two excellent bad guys in psycho Mean Girl Mitsuko (Shibasaki) and Ando's hot teen version of the existentialist hit man in a black suit, Kiriyama.

But Kitano can't help stealing the show. A face so full of the stoical acceptance of utter despair, and, in this movie, the beneficiary of what is, surely, the funniest, weirdest death in movie history. Because the film's final revelation is disturbing: a man's obsession with a girl that could be about nothing more than wanting an ideal daughter . . . but feels like something much sicker. Takeshi Kitano's power as an actor stems from his refusal to give us an easy look at his motivations, and the pleasure he takes in his own mystery. *Battle Royale* would still have been a fine movie without him. But not such a sad, disturbing or meaningful one. Because his disillusioned teacher feels like nihilism in solid form, and reminds us that, when we lose all faith in our young, it's we who become feral.

* *

BRING IT ON

2000
Starring: Kirsten Dunst, Eliza Dushku, Jesse Bradford, Gabrielle Union
Dir.: Peyton Reed

Plot: Replace NATO with cheerleaders and we *can* find a solution to the Middle East. Yes we can!
Key line: 'Courtney . . . it's not a democracy. It's a *cheer*ocracy.'

I may be completely wrong. But I harbour a strong suspicion that, when readers decide to take issue with me over the movies chosen for *Stranded*, the film I'm going to get the hardest time about is this one.

Of course, any mainstream Hollywood hit feel-good movie made for and about young girls where no one dies, joins a gang, gets tortured by a corrupt policeman, has sex with a parent or spends valuable screen-time staring soulfully out to sea, and then compounds the felony by having a happy ending, is ripe for a good, hard kicking. But *Dirty Dancing* (see p. 289) and *Footloose* (p. 251) are old enough to get both nostalgia and kitsch let-off points whereas *Bring It On* is spankingly recent and quite patently the film that invented *Glee*'s perpetually sunny high school world where teens of all colours, sexualities and disabilities are part of its Rainbow Coalition liberal utopia, and teen angst is largely confined to worries about whether we really can put the show on right here in the barn. So it's understandable that Coen Brothers fans aren't bright enough to get it.

Many critics reckoned that *Bring It On*'s story was too formulaic and that it wasn't critical enough of that peculiarly despised American minority, cheerleaders. You've got to worry about someone who watches a movie where the heroine makes impassioned rebellious speeches to her mother about her right to pursue a future of twirling batons rather than studying, and then points at a boy's Clash t-shirt and asks, 'Is that your band?', and, because there isn't a laugh-track and the girl isn't humiliated by the boy in question, doesn't pick up that this is a piss-take of the air-headed world of middle-class girls who see cheerleading as both status symbol and route to minor celebrity. The satire is gentle and affectionate, sure, but smart people – girls, teens, me – got it, so accept that those dire Michael Haneke movies are deskilling you and pay attention.

Bring It On is a perky, peppy comedy about the arcane world that is competitive cheerleading. It stars Kirsten Dunst as our adorable but somewhat shallow cheerleading captain Torrance, who is going to learn valuable lessons about race, class and the win-at-all-costs mentality. This all happens when she finds out that the routines that her school have constantly been winning the State Championship with have been stolen from a black cheerleading team from East Compton by departing captain Big Red (Lindsay Sloane), who got away with it because the East Compton school is too poor to afford the Championship's entry fee.

After various attempts to right this wrong, while still encouraging her team to be the best they can be, it all ends cheerily when her Toros come second to the East Compton Clovers in the genuinely spectacular orgy of cheerleading that is the State final. She and Clovers leader Isis (Union) bond, the various girls get the various boys of their choice, and everybody dances for joy. It's lovely, suggesting we could make poverty history and bring about World Peace if we all just balanced on each other's shoulders a lot and learned the words of 'Mickey' by Toni Basil.

On the way, we get whip-smart dialogue spat out at *The Social Network* tempo, a subplot about male cheerleaders and homophobia, Torrance's most amusing smartarse little brother Justin (Cody McMains) and top sight gags like the cheerleader auditions where various wannabes bring their personal angst with them or insist on trying out in the style of gangsta rapper, Broadway hoofer, stripper and '80s robot dancer.

And then – *Buffy*, *Tru Calling* and *Dollhouse* fans still your beating hearts – there is the one and only Eliza Dushku. Obviously, political correctness prevents me from stating my true feelings about Ms Dushku in an entry concerning a movie about high school cheer-leaders, even though she was actually 19 by the time she played punk rock gymnast Missy Pantone here. She's the kind of woman who can make creepy older men even creepier, as she revealed in a 2003 interview when she was best known as dark slayer Faith in *Buffy* and its spin-off, *Angel*. It turns out that *Buffy* was a big hit in prisons, and Ms Dushku was getting disturbing fanmail including ... 'disgusting things you don't wanna know about. ... Way more creepy than *Buffy*.'

So you can see why I don't want to add to her personal nightmares about the fantasies of old geezers 'with a bottle of beer and a moustache and a big gut' (I don't have a moustache). Let's just say I empathise with my homies on lockdown and leave it at that.

What I can tell you is that Ms Dushku is Albanian on her father's side and was recently made an honorary Albanian ambassador by the Mayor of Tirana. Which is nice. And those who believe that her *Bring It On* flips and somersaults are the work of a stunt double are sadly mistaken. Eliza – I feel I know her well enough now to call her Eliza – spent a year as part of the Romanian Olympic gymnastics team in preparation for the part. *And* I hear she plays the bassoon to concert standard and is an accomplished tree surgeon.

Back to *Bring It On* – pausing only to mention that Clare Kramer, who plays Hell-God Glory in *Buffy*, is also on board as well as *Buffy*'s composer Christophe Beck on soundtrack duties – and its wildly optimistic but benign worldview. It's subversive in a way that only cuddly pop movies can pull off. Not only does it go out of its way to deny every teen movie stereotype it can – the tattooed tough girl who likes cheerleading, the male cheerleader who isn't gay or a joke, the poor black teen who isn't a thug or a victim, the male love object (Bradford as Missy's brother Cliff) who isn't a total knob – it ends with a line that amounts to a complete rejection of American values.

After the competition is over, Cliff asks Torrance: 'So ... second place. How does it feel?' Ms Dunst smiles an adorable smile and answers, 'It feels like first.' In the context of a film that you know has been watched by a generation of American children, that line feels as useful and rebellious a sentiment as any in this book. And that, in the end, is why I love this movie.

★ ★

GINGER SNAPS

2000

Starring: Emily Perkins, Katharine Isabelle, Kris Lemche, Mimi Rogers
Dir.: John Fawcett

Plot: The period drama that Merchant–Ivory will never make. Key line: 'A bear will come after a girl on the rag. 'Cos of the smell.'

Ginger Snaps is not a movie whose motives are open to interpretation. John Fawcett and his co-screenwriter Karen Walton set out to make a feminist teen horror picture that used 'the curse' of being bitten by a werewolf as a metaphor for 'the curse' of menstruation. Mindful of male repulsion about periods, teen horror starlets who were routinely punished for having sex, and the bloody legacy of *Carrie* (see p. 150), the pair fashioned something satirical, subversive, viscerally gore-splattered and perfectly in sync with the post-*Buffy* teen fantasy landscape. The result was a film that became a cult popular enough on DVD to spawn two (sadly inferior) sequels, and introduce us to a young actress who provides one of the finest performances in screen teen history.

Emily Perkins, who plays goth sibling Brigitte Fitzgerald, takes the threatening androgyny of Melanie Lynskey in *Heavenly Creatures* (see p. 315) and Kristy McNichol in *Little Darlings* to an extreme. Draped in shapeless hoodies, t-shirts and cardigans, her very French-looking face a gaunt, sallow mask shrouded by long, lifeless, shaggy brown hair, she is an asexual creature of the night who portends dread and horror long before the action truly gets under way. She is the heroic polar opposite to every female teen character who has ever craved popularity, prettiness, fashion status symbols and male attention. Katherine Isabelle is very, *very* good as Brigitte's sexy sister Ginger, who, you know, snaps, in both a mental breakdown way and a slavering jaws way. But it's Perkins who rivets you to the screen, her hunched and ghostly sadness a visual message that, when things hit bottom, the only way to go is down. It's a performance so powerful yet layered that it ensures that *Ginger Snaps*, despite its verbal and visual humour, remains palpably frightening.

Set in a Canadian suburb, *Ginger Snaps* concerns two goth-metal sisters who have had a mutual death pact since they were 8 years old. This makes them even keener fakers of their own glorious destructions than Harold Chasen from *Harold And Maude* (see p. 126). The montage of theatrically fraudulent fatalities, made by the girls for a school project and back-dropping the opening credits, makes Ginger and Brigitte the innovative directors and stars of their own horror movie-within-a-horror-movie.

But, while Ginger is still dedicated to dying young and leaving that good-looking corpse, Brigitte is beginning to consider life as a career option. By way of contrast, their parallel pact that boys is rubbish and sex unthinkable is adhered rigidly to by plain Brigitte ... but gorgeous Ginger is beginning to visibly waver. Their mother, played by the excellent Mimi Rogers, is curious to know why her girls of 16 and 15 haven't had their periods. But it's almost like an act of will on the part of the Fitzgerald sisters, who see menstruation as the death of childhood and the inevitable harbinger of tedious adult preoccupations like bumping uglies. Sadly, nature wins every time. Ginger's backache is a portent of menstrual mayhem.

Meanwhile, as we've already seen pre-credits, something called The Beast Of Bailey Downs is turning the neighbourhood dogs into mutilated piles of squelchy entrails. Brigitte finds herself getting more intimate with one than she would care to when school Mean Girl Trina pushes her into doggy remains on the school playing field during a game of hockey, in revenge for Brigitte having called her 'Standard cumbucket-ty date-bait'. I should mention, at this point, that Ginger Snaps has enough bad (meaning good) language to make a cinema full of Scorsese gangsters blush and write a stiff letter to their local MP bemoaning falling standards among young people today.

The Ginger's-attack-by-werewolf scene is a mini-masterpiece. The sisters go to a children's playground at night, hoping to find a dead dog in order to exact darkly prankish revenge on Trina. As they attempt to move the mutilated pooch, Brigitte thinks Ginger has splashed herself with canine blood. No such luck: the blood running down her thigh is 'the curse'. A child's sprung horse begins to rock, and, before the two can process the spooky atmosphere and scarper, an unseen monster attacks with an animal roar. Brigitte is thrown to the floor. Ginger is gone. Brigitte hears her scream from the woods and runs towards her. And the pair have to battle a huge, flesh-ripping man-beast-thing with nothing but fists and a stick.

The whole memorable scene is a deft blend of whiplash camera movement and low-angle composition, Steadicam shakiness, precise sound design and bravura editing, lent real menace by Perkins's wild, terrified eyes and panicked breathing. Fawcett cheats a little monster-wise, whirling the camera around and cutting so quickly that you only occasionally fix on teeth, snout, muscular hairy body. But it does make you feel the fear and chaos, and it's a helluva lot better than the vapid animations of standard CGI, which Fawcett rejected in favour of prosthetics and real fake blood.

From there on in, it's all about being the wittiest female-coming-of-age-werewolf movie it can be. The blackly comic view of periods gives us a scene in a supermarket where Brigitte is helping Ginger buy sanitary towels. Brigitte looks up at the huge shelves piled with boxes of many colours, dwarfed by the reality of imminent woman-hood. She chooses one. 'This one has a free calendar,' she suggests, weakly, as Ginger, in the early stages of her transition into werewolf, grips her gut and bends double in agony. The film also mercilessly rips the piss out of the self-obsessed angst of teen goths while sim-ultaneously playing tribute by making Ginger and Brigitte so much better company than their peers.

While Brigitte begins to understand the fate that lies in store for Sis, Sis is shagging the school's cute but sexist dickhead Jason and becoming a predatory dominatrix. Brigitte turns to gorgeous hunk Sam (the Christian Slater-esque Lemche) for help: Sam is that rare cinematic treat, the really nice drug-dealer. The possibility that Bri-gitte and Sam will find a cure for Ginger and ensure a happy ending disappears permanently when Ginger accidentally kills Trina in a fight and the sisters hide her in the family freezer.

Drug expert Sam does discover a cure, though: a herb called Monkshood. It stops Jason – who has been infected by having unsafe sex with Ginger, therefore introducing a handy AIDS metaphor – in his tracks when he attacks Brigitte. It's all a bit late for Ginger, though. She's killed the school's guidance counsellor and janitor ... plus she has a tail.

By the time Ginger transforms completely, the film has gradually and completely abandoned black comedy for claustrophobic, gross-out horror, and an inevitable denouement where only the brave and brilliant Brigitte can save the world from the rampant Ginger-Wolf.

Despite the movie's success, *Ginger Snaps* is currently unavailable on DVD in the UK and has remained relatively obscure to all except horror devotees. One reason perhaps lies in the initial controversy surrounding its production. The April 1999 Columbine High School shootings in Colorado that inspired Gus Van Sant's extraordinary *Elephant* (see p. 418) were followed immediately by similar events at the W.R. Myers High School in Alberta, Canada. And no one would have noticed or cared that this little horror movie was just being cast and prepared for initial shooting at exactly the same time as Canada was freaking out about teenage violence and its causes, except that Ginger Snaps was being financed by Telefilm, the Canadian government's own movie-funding organisation. Tragedies surrounding children have a way of blotting out aesthetic arguments about satirical intent, so you've got to admire Telefilm for standing their ground and allowing this gem to get made at all.

By combining the kind of comically repulsive body horror favoured by David Cronenberg with a twisted take on typical high school movie conventions, Fawcett and Dalton have given us one of the best secret masterpieces of the teen genre. But it's the performance of Emily Perkins that lingers; a truly modern heroine for troubled and turbulent teenage times.

* *

GHOST WORLD

2001
Starring: Thora Birch, Scarlett Johansson, Steve Buscemi, Brad Renfro, Ileana Douglas, Bob Balaban
Dir.: Terry Zwigoff

Plot: Growing up, and why it sucks.
Key line: 'I don't want to meet someone who shares my interests. I hate my interests.'

Ghost World is a movie designed to be a cult. It is packed with exciting counter-culture nerd ephemera, from gorgeous vintage clothing to obscure pre-war jazz and blues, from retro Bollywood to jokes about Fellini's 8½, from Robert Crumb cartoons to a hatred of everything associated with contemporary globalisation. When Steve Buscemi's Seymour says, after a depressing night at a blues theme pub, 'It's simple for everybody else. You give 'em a Big Mac and a pair of Nikes and they're happy. I can't relate to 99 per cent of humanity,' you will either nod in resigned agreement or wonder why anyone would complain, and that reaction will determine whether *Ghost World* is for you. Needless to say, as a confirmed teenage snob who never grew out of it, it is *so* for me that I clasp it to my bosom like a bitchy best friend in hairgrips and Doc Martens.

Based on a funny and haunting graphic novel by Daniel Clowes, adapted for the screen by Clowes and director Terry Zwigoff, *Ghost World* introduces us to two Heavenly Creatures called Enid (Birch) and Rebecca (Johansson) who live in an unnamed alternative wonderland which they sneer at like Dorothy Parker and Virginia Woolf in day-glo pop socks. They have just graduated from high school, and *Ghost World*'s difference from other teen movies is immediately established by the fact that their graduation party is a pathetic, quickly dismissed affair where neither finds true love nor destroys the student body with telekinesis. There is a lovely, funny shot of the two girls, shot from the back, straight armed and straight-backed, swaying gently in tandem to the terrible cabaret band.

The pair live for things that are rubbish, like '50s themed diners with little jukeboxes that play hip hop, and to torment an outside world they treat with immaculate contempt. Their riot grrrl/twee-indie style is vital. The thrift-shop clothes and retro hairstyles establish the importance of never looking modern; to rebel naturally, one must dress like a toddler or a senior citizen, and preferably one from somewhere between the Second World War and 1964.

Their idea of fun is perusing lonely hearts columns and arranging meetings where they just arrive and stare at the disappointed loser. They are Mean Girls, but an even scarier brand of Mean Girl that is intellectually acute, eclectic of taste and reference, and desperate to be *un*popular.

While Enid is forced to attend a Summer School remedial class taught by a woman (the wonderful Ilieana Douglas as Roberta) who begins lessons by showing her own black and white art movie short called 'Mirror. Father. Mirror.', she and Becky also amuse themselves by stalking the lonely heart, Seymour (Buscemi), who somehow finds himself the only person, besides Becky, that Enid can bear.

Because Rebecca and Enid are slowly growing apart. Rebecca wants to move on from their private war on humanity and take her first steps to adulthood. Enid's haughty sarcasm stems from sheer terror of growing up.

So it's funny when Rebecca mentions that, to get an apartment together in the city, the pair need to buy some yuppie clothes and play the game, and Enid's immediate reaction is to dye her hair green and adopt a studiously observed '70s punk look. But it becomes sadder and sadder as Rebecca's contempt for her best friend's contrived shock tactics grows. Is sex with a funny-looking middle-aged geek who collects obscure blues 78s *really* Enid's rite of passage?

Enid's fascination with Seymour, which has been sparked by her love of a Skip James blues song she has bought from him at his record stall in a garage, even leads to her and Becky spending Saturday night in the arcane purgatory that is A Gathering Of Middle-Aged Male Record Collectors, a strange breed who I have had reason to spend time with and who really do get unnecessary over the jargon of vinyl condition and ten-band graphic equalisers.

The town has no name because it is a parallel universe; a state of mind between innocence and experience which features an old man at a bus stop always waiting for a bus that doesn't exist, and which, despite how boring the girls keep saying it is, is actually a 'hood made up of monstrously cool things like record shops, video shops, comic book shops and '50s-themed diners that don't quite see the theme through. It's like walking round the North Lanes in Brighton, actually, although the weird old men in my home town aren't waiting for non-existent buses, but their 22-year-old boyfriend who is currently having his hair done in Queen Of Cuts. I like it here and will not be seeking a mystical bus.

But one of the many fascinating points of *Ghost World* is that even cult weirdo student punk paradise becomes unbearable when you are growing but your world is shrinking. *Ghost World* bigs up vintage jazz and blues music but then undercuts that by introducing us to the kind of boring bastards who like it. It celebrates retro clothes styles and America's rich alternative cultural heritage while simultaneously critiquing retro as an empty postmodern 'take' on the past.

But Enid's kitsch is growing darker. No sooner has she dismissed her put-upon shop assistant friend Josh (Renfro) as 'this guy Becky and I like to torture', than she tortures Seymour by dragging him into the local sex shop, forcing him to buy her a leather fetish Catwoman mask. Neither Seymour nor Becky are laughing. Enid's irony is becoming forced.

Bizarre eccentrics wander through their lives, like Mulleted Convenience Store Topless Guy With Numchucks, and the crazy old hippy man in a wheelchair who takes a laptop into the coffee shop where Becky works so he can answer the obscure trivia question that wins a free coffee. And Enid's remedial art class is a 'mare, as Roberta sniffily dismisses Enid's accomplished art – which looks like Robert Crumb cartoons because some of them are by Crumb and his daughter Sophie – in favour of the girl who puts a tampon in a teacup. Enid tries to solve this problem while teaching the *Ghost World* viewer an extraordinary lesson about the racism of America's past and a real Ohio restaurant chain called Coon's Chicken. But her attempts to con the world just make things worse.

Enid has also taken it upon herself to find Seymour a girlfriend in order to deny her own attraction to someone so wildly inappropriate, and this cues a horribly, hilariously accurate scene in a dodgy blues bar where Seymour can't resist responding to a woman's friendly 'I like blues' conversational gambit with a long, dull lecture about the differences between blues and ragtime. Buscemi is brilliant here, because Seymour is a smart guy who knows this stuff does to chatting up what Napalm does to dandelions, but ... he ... just ... can't ... stop ... talking, because that geek is just who he is. His horror at Blueshammer, the white boys who play pub rock and call it 'authentic Delta blues', finishes the job.

Ghost World is neither a celebration of outsiders or riot grrls or alternative culture or rebellion, nor a movie that urges you to put away childish things and 'grow up', meaning 'conform'. It's a movie that suggests that some people simply don't fit that easily, and that, rather than conform, they must find their own path and accept the painful truth that they will be lonely and unpopular most of the time, but better that than compromise themselves to make the rest of us feel comfortable. It has one of the few strong teen characters who actually doesn't want to 'come of age'. She understands that much of what we consider 'mature' is actually deeply stupid and deeply lazy. She may not like sex enough with Seymour to be his teenage lover. But she tells him, truthfully, that he is her hero because, no matter how inadequate or dull or weak we may see him as, he is at least truly himself.

Clowes' original graphic novel was great, but the movie is even better, developing Seymour's minor character into a goofy kind of romantic lead (Zwigoff is a collector of ancient jazz and blues records) and making the extraordinary Thora Birch into the focal point of the story. Johansson is, at just 16, the star she will become, her deep voice and sneering bee-stung lips the perfect foil for Birch's pale fury.

But Birch, coming off her biggest triumph as Jane Burnham in *American Beauty*, is almost unbearably poignant and charismatic; the very essence of the bitchy outsider beauty who any nerdy boy would fall in love with if she wasn't such a ball-busting bitch, even though you know it's all for show.

And, as with all the best American post-John Hughes teen comedies, the dialogue crackles and burns. Particular favourite quotes include the note Enid leaves at Josh's house when they call and he isn't in ('Dear Josh: We came by to fuck you but you were not home. Therefore, you are gay. Signed Tiffany and Amber.'); and Enid's rude epilogue to Seymour's failed attempt to sell a record to an especially fussy collector ('So what was all that about enlarged holes and tight cracks?').

The movie ends with two journeys on a bus that shouldn't exist, the last of which is along an empty bridge; a lovely metaphor for the lonely journey a kid takes when they realise that their confused and singular nature means they have to search for their adult self alone. It's the price you pay for refusing to conform in order to belong. Because, for some of us, teenage rebellion never quite goes away. *Ghost World* is a tribute to the creative possibilities of lifelong immaturity.

★ ★

DONNIE DARKO

2001

Starring: Jake Gyllenhaal, Jena Malone, Drew Barrymore, Mary McDonell, Holmes Osborne, Katherine Ross, Patrick Swayze, Noah Wyle, Maggie Gyllenhaal
Dir.: Richard Kelly

Plot: Well . . . there's this miserable kid and a rabbit-man and a jet engine and The Apocalypse and . . . *wait a minute*! Nearly had me there. HA! Good one.
Key line: 'They just want to see what happens when they tear the world apart. They want to change things.'

Richard Kelly once stated that his unfathomable teen cult masterpiece is 'a black comedy foreshadowing the impact of the 1988 Presidential election'. That was the one where, despite the Iran-Contra scandal and hitherto unimaginable social divisions and economic chaos, the American public gave the Reagan administration a thumbs-up and elected his former CIA spook Vice-President, George Bush Snr. I guess that would explain all the wry stuff at the outset of this movie about losing Democratic candidate Michael Dukakis and the Stars And Stripes hanging over Donnie's head and 'The Star-Spangled Banner' playing on the TV as he takes his first sleepwalk, but . . . I'm getting ahead of myself.

Thank the Lord for a movie writer called Dan Kois. On the salon.com website, Mr Kois gives the world a step-by-step rundown of the *Donnie Darko* plot *and* a credible stab at the movie's meaning, having watched both the original theatrical version and the currently available 133-minute Director's Cut, and all the extras on the DVD, and Kelly's director's commentary, and even negotiated the painfully slow and oblique revelations on the *Donnie Darko* official website. You can find Kois's painstakingly assembled theorem at www.salon.com/entertainment/movies/feature/2004/07/23/darko, and you definitely should, 'cos there is no way I'm rewriting his detective work and passing it off as my own.

But Kois writes as if everyone who has ever loved this teen angst

Twin Peaks has been inspired to take the nerd's route ... spending hours on the web and talking with friends and rewatching the movie with a laptop and a Klingon dictionary to satisfy their need to know *exactly* what it all means. I think geek *Donnie Darko* fans are a minority. I reckon that most of the people who have made an initial theatrical flop into a much-loved, money-spinning DVD hit sit in front of it with friends, booze and weed, loving every second of being bamboozled and claiming it as one of the great progenitors of the kind of post-MTV surrealism we now call 'random' because the best thing about *Donnie Darko* is that it looks and sounds amazing and makes your brain work without having to come to any form of conclusion whatsoever. Except some vague idea about an angry suburban teen who gets Chosen by God or another higher power to fix a potentially catastrophic hole in time, and succeeds, and dies. And catches a kiddy-fiddler along the way, which is always cheering, especially when the director is crazy and inspired enough to cast Patrick Swayze as the bad guy. Giggle. Munch. Puzzle. Toke. Glug. Giggle. Cheer. Toke. Munch. Putitonagainitsmental!

So, for this entry and this entry only, I decided to reject my normal methodology and get into the spirit of how the movie is watched. I'm going to switch off the laptop, resist making any notes, lie back with my drugs of choice (I smoked all my crack while watching *Bring It On*, so its sugary tea and nicotine all the way) and bliss out. And then come back and write about what hits me. We'll be right back after these arcane messages.

Right. Well ... that was bracing. The first time I've watched *Donnie Darko* and felt so emotionally, as well as aesthetically, engaged. The bit where chubby Oriental outsider Cherita reveals her love for Donnie by running away from him in sheer romantic terror almost made me cry.

The reason, I think, that *Donnie Darko* is much more affecting than the similarly complex sci-fi/time-travel jiggery-pokeries of Lynch, M. Night Shyamalan and Christopher Nolan is because it is about a teenage boy. It taps into something primal and universal about that moment, in adolescence, when you've worked out how you feel about the adult world and realised that it doesn't share your sense of right and wrong. You've read certain books (perhaps provided by a favourite teacher who reminds you of Drew Barrymore) and listened to certain records (maybe British '80s songs by Tears For Fears and

Joy Division and Echo And The Bunnymen) that derive a dreamy beauty from an intellectualized form of doomed romantic angst and you've watched the government on TV and made connections between what you hate about them and school and your parents, and you are suddenly fuelled with a self-righteous idealism and an existential despair about the compromised, philistine adult world that you are expected to fit into. But you still love comic books and sci-fi and you fantasise, occasionally, about being a superhero who saves the world from all of its evil, because this is both less daunting than the prospect of political action and more noble than accepting that you just want things to be how *you* want them to be.

There is so much detail in Donnie's story that I can't help concluding that Donnie *is* Richard Kelly. That, at the age of 25, he was still haunted – and fascinated – by the teen years that made him but, instead of the usual thinly veiled semi-autobiographical rites-of-passage tale, he used his fertile imagination to concoct an entire parallel universe around his love of Graham Greene's *The Destructors* and Richard Adams' *Watership Down*; his experiences at a private school, which at various points tried to brainwash pupils into bland self-help conservatism, ban books and fire liberal teachers; his love for the perfect girl who never knew he existed; his apoplectic rage at the Reagan/Bush years; his childhood affection for *E.T.* and *Back To The Future*; his regret at disconnecting from his parents; his favourite miserabalist pop records; and, perhaps, a period when he committed petty crimes, and was sent to therapy and put on anti-depression medication. I mean, I could be way off beam here, but the major reason that *Donnie Darko* works so well lies less in the parallel universe and more in the detail about teenage life, from ridiculous conversations about the sexual organs of The Smurfs, to the vital importance a bookish teen might attach to the distinctions between being an atheist and an agnostic, to the texts you use to justify the intellectual rebel mantra that you must destroy to create. Kelly absolutely hits aspects of my own teenage angst so firmly on the noggin that I can't believe that this is just good writing. *Donnie Darko* is the most multi-dimensional movie teen of all time because he's plucked from deep within the writer's memories.

But none of this would work without the performance of Jake Gyllenhaal. His ability to switch between the obnoxious and the adorable, the malevolent and the vulnerable, the strident young rebel and the regressed child in hypnotherapy, the gibbering madman and the only sane boy on Earth, makes for one of the most complete characters in teen fiction. He has to carry a conceit so convoluted and implausible that it makes *Mulholland Drive* look like *Coronation Street*, and he neither trips over his feet nor misses a beat. Gyllenhaal glares back with hooded eyes and dark pleasure at the Jim Starks and Ferris Buellers and Alex Droogs, amused at their two dimensions, an amalgam of them all. As for how the guy's acted since ... it's been ten years since he played Donnie; shouldn't he have cured the sleepwalking by now?

And as for Kelly, I reckon the reason that his two subsequent movies *Southland Tales* and *The Box* just didn't work for people is that they possess all of his geeky imagination, but none of the heart. They have no Donnie/Gyllenhaal at their centre. They're just about fictional characters. There is nothing universal about coming of age and our idealised selves at stake. Donnie is a real boy and torn, piece by piece, from Kelly's soul.

I love *Donnie Darko*. I love its desperation to rip the world up and start again. I love its righteous fury at the fundamentalist right and their exploitation of frightened people's desperate need for easy answers. I love its teen boy wish-fulfilment, not just because Donnie saves the world, but because of that bit where Ms Barrymore tells the new girl in class to just sit next to the boy she thinks is cutest, because hot teacher and crush object conspiring to announce to the world that you're the cutest thing ever is even more thrilling to the teen narcissist than saving the planet from Republicans and rips in the time-space continuum.

But most of all, I love the idea of this alienated kid in a classroom sometime around the dawn of the '90s, being blown away by a Graham Greene short story, storing the moment away like a rabbit stores food, and, ten years of dreaming and hard work later, growing a towering work of art out of that anonymous moment. That's teenage rebellion at its best.

* *

BULLY

2001

Starring: Brad Renfro, Nick Stahl, Rachel Miner, Bijou Phillips, Michael Pitt, Leo Fitzpatrick, Kelli Garner, Daniel Franzese
Dir.: Paul Weitz

Plot: *River's Edge* **meets** *Kids*. **In hell!**
Key line(s): 'Listen: I gotta go down to Fort Lauderdale to help my friend Lisa to kill this asshole named Bobby. But if you want I can come pick you up ...'
'Er ... OK.'

I hold my hands up straight away. My love of this movie is less a guilty pleasure and more of an indefensible one. It is gratuitous, sensationalist, and pornographic in a barely legal way. It's only justification? It's all true.

Bully is based on a Florida murder trial known as the Broward County Seven case. In July 1993, seven teenagers conspired to murder another teen, Bobby Kent. One of the killers was Kent's best friend, Marty Puccio. The script for *Bully* was co-written by *American History X* writer David McKenna (under the pseudonym Zachary Long) and Roger Pullis, and based on a book called *Bully: A True Story Of High School Revenge*, a factual account of the case by Jim Schutze. No one even changed the names to protect the ... well ... guilty as fuck, actually.

But if the evidence of this movie is to be believed, Bobby Kent (the excellent Stahl) was something a little more hardcore than a common-or-garden bully. He pimps his male friends out at gay clubs. He has a Jones for homemade gay porn which he especially likes to watch while raping girls. He's a memorable monster. He's like Peter Stegman from *Class Of 1984* (see p. 205), but with the irony unplugged. I wouldn't mind if he was the usual thick-necked, mountain-sized jock (the real-life Bobby was a steroid junkie) or Latino leather-jacketed knife-boy thug. But he's a skinny, pretty, white middle-class kid. Why doesn't anyone just punch him or call the police?

Well, actually, Marty does punch him. But it makes no difference. Bobby takes the punch and then does what any good pimp does: apologises, makes all the right, loving noises, makes a victim feel empowered by having forced his tormentor to pretend to make nice for a change. And then he just continues fucking you because he knows you hate yourself enough to believe you deserve it.

One of the most striking early scenes takes place in the gay club, where Bobby pushes Marty into dancing onstage with other jailbait for cash stuffed down briefs, and the music pumps and thrusts, and Marty goes from horrified shame to enjoying the power of knowing that men will pay to watch him shake his money-maker.

This is as good a place as any to deal with the biggest criticism thrown at Larry Clark films ... gratuitous under-age sex. And my defence is ... in tatters, actually. Objection sustained. At one point in *Bully*, Clark tosses in a completely pointless close-up shot of a girl's crotch, even though it has nothing whatsoever to do with, well, anything. It's almost as if the guy is trying to make us feel implicated by giving us a boner while we watch kids do the very worst things we can imagine them doing. No idea what his problem is. You have to try and watch his movies around his attempts to turn you on with adolescent flesh.

Bobby's bullying tendencies derive, of course, from a Bad Dad. Mr Kent, blissfully unaware of how depraved his son is, doesn't approve of his friendship with Marty because he is a surfer slacker and leads a life 'of complete aimlessness', even though he was once 'a good kid'. The double irony being that it is Bobby who has beaten the 'ambition and fire in his gut' out of Marty, and that, while Marty is begging his parents to move away from Bobby, Bad Dad is now threatening to move house to get Bobby away from Marty. Sadly, they all stayed.

The biggest shock of *Bully* doesn't derive from flesh or rape scenes or even the murder itself. It stems from the possibility that there are these real kids out there who were as entirely stupid as the kids in this movie. Once the brutalized and pregnant Lisa (Miner) comes up with the murder idea, and the suggestible Marty agrees, her next course of action is to tell just about everybody – including friends like the chubby but timid Derek (Franzese), plus the perpetually stoned Donny (Pitt) and Heather (Garner) who have never even met Bobby – until it becomes some kind of open invite to a murder party.

And then discuss it in public places in loud voices, even letting the waitress at Pizza Hut know what they're up to. And then fuck up their first attempt. And then hire the world's dumbest hitman.

In this world, where teens party like dissolute adults but think like small children, they believe rumours that a tough-talking kid called Derek Kaufman (Fitzpatrick, even better here than he is *Kids*, see p. 328) is actually a hardened professional killer. After meeting initial reluctance, they eventually convince him to help them do the deed when they lure Bobby to a remote canal by the swamps.

Clark comes into his own with the tense build-up to the poorly planned killing, as we increasingly realise that the 'hitman' is as out of his depth as the six conspirators, and that only he, Marty and Lisa are truly determined to go through with it because the others believed it was some kind of stoner game. The droning guitar of Sonic Youth's Thurston Moore ratchets up the tension and the excellent ensemble cast – including Bijou Phillips as another Bobby rape victim Ali – make you feel the stress and the dire consequences of the moment.

The murder is chaotic, almost comically inept. But murder is murder. Bobby dies partly because the prospect of sex blocks out all other thoughts, and partly because he has no idea that punching someone unconscious while they're fucking and then raping their girlfriend might cause any lingering resentment.

The *River's Edge* (see p. 284) element goes into overdrive as the seven brag, snitch, lie and confess their way into arrest and court. As they sit in the courtroom, they descend into a shouting match about who did what to whom, as if the adults in the court can't hear them. But they can. The movie ends with the sentences they received in 1995. Three of them – Marty, Lisa and Donny – are still serving time in Florida correctional facilities. Lisa's child, who, according to the movie, could be Marty's or Bobby's, was born in jail.

It's hard not to conclude that Clark – who first came to prominence as a photographer of drug-taking youth – is a right-wing film-maker in disguise. *Kids*, *Bully* and the enervatingly glum *Ken Park* are diametrically opposed to a left-wing teen movie like *But I'm A Cheerleader* (see p. 367). In Jamie Babbitt's upbeat satire, teen sexuality and polymorphous perversity leads to a fully realised self, romantic fulfilment, and a violence-free happy ever after packed with tofu casseroles and lipstick lesbians.

In Clark's films, his teens have appeared to go from their first snog to rape, prostitution, babies making babies, drug addiction, ultra-violence and merrily spreading AIDS like someone taking their first sip of coffee in the morning and becoming a crack addict by teatime. What's more, these mainly white kids all play out their Sodom And Gomorrah lives to a constant hip hop soundtrack, and talk exclusively in ebonic wiggerisms. In short, black culture is destroying our nice white kids. Frog-march 'em at gunpoint to a racial reorientation camp . . . now!

So why do I like *Bully*? Well, for a start, for a movie where you know the ending before it begins, it is incredibly suspenseful. The cast are superb. And . . . I admit it . . . I like its gleeful 'Think that was bad? Watch this shit!' embrace of liberal-baiting cinematic irresponsibility. It's a thrill-ride, with an ironic ending that sticks in your throat and dares you to laugh at such tragic idiocy. What it tells you about kids of today, I don't know. But it does remind you that jails are full of some seriously dumb motherfuckers.

★ ★

CITY OF GOD

2002
Starring: Alexandre Rodrigues, Leandro Firmino de Hora, Alice Braga, Phellipe Haagensen, Seu Jorge, Graziella Moretto
Dir.: Fernando Meirelles and Kátia Lund

Plot: Good Favelas.
Key line: 'Why remain in the City Of God, where God has forgotten you?'

City Of God was one of the great shock films of the early 21st century. The surprise wasn't that it wasn't American, or that two little-known directors had made something so hugely accomplished well outside the Hollywood machine, or that life was so tough in the slums of Brazil. The shock was that someone had finally stopped connecting the global reality that is teenage gangs to the sexy kitsch of '50s juvenile delinquency, and pointed out the obvious: that kids with guns are more frightening and disturbing than men with guns.

City Of God takes young gangsters and the mayhem they cause deadly seriously, carries the full horror of youth nihilism caused by extreme poverty and state neglect, and still tells an epic tale that is fun to watch for action movie fans. It has beautiful stars, sexy moments, a stunningly conceived look, great gags, cinematic flamboyance, iconic compositions, scenes of ultra-violence that would make many a '100 Coolest Shoot-'em-up Moments' list, elegant storyboarding and a novelistic ending both uplifting and grimly ironic. But, somehow, none of this obscures the point, which is that in poor parts of the world children are killing each other for kicks, drugs and chump change, and that, as long as those children keep their slaughters away from polite society, we turn a blind eye because the poor are less than human.

The movie is based upon the novel *Cidade de Deus* by Paulo Lins, which fictionalised real gangsters, victims and events in the titular favela (shanty town) that was built by Brazil's military government to house homeless families from Rio de Janeiro in 1960. Its three acts deal with the late '60s, the mid '70s and the early '80s, and the escalation of youth crime from petty theft with menaces to organised armies fighting wars to control the drugs that flooded the slums of the world in the 1980s. The denizens of the City Of God are almost all dark-skinned Brazilians, reminding us that it's not just the northern hemisphere that distributes wealth according to pigmentation.

The plot is as labyrinthine as the City Of God's rabbit-warren sprawl, but it focuses on two boys who pursue opposing paths to surviving the harshness of their environment, but are inextricably linked by the favela's insularity.

Our hero and narrator is Buscapé, aka Rocket, a gentle, studious black boy and budding photographer whose brother Goose is in a Robin Hood-type criminal gang called The Tender Trio. When the three hoods decide to up their ante and progress from knocking over petrol trucks to robbing a rich family in the city, their big mistake is allowing Rocket's mirror image, Li'l Dice, to tag along. While the three older boys simply want to hold up the family and get out, their scary young protégé hangs around to murder the family, giggling merrily like a kid watching a cartoon.

Fast forward to the '60s and, while Rocket (now played by Rodrigues) is discovering his love of photography and hanging out with a bunch of proto-hippies who call themselves The Groovies, Li'l Dice has changed his name to Li'l Ze (the excellent, chilling de

Hora) and is taking control of the burgeoning drug trade by way of shooting everyone in sight and loving every second of it. The police approve because he is happy to pay them off and wipe out any loose-cannon criminals to keep the crime figures down.

Ze's inexorable rise begins to turn into an equally inexorable fall when his smarter and calmer second-in-command, Benny (Haagensen) decides to leave the gang life and throws a party. As the funk blares and the dirty dancing commences, Ze's status as the Alpha Male is undermined by his inability to get with the girlies. This is another of *City Of God*'s strengths, incidentally: the cliché of the hot girl who is attracted to any man with money and power is constantly avoided, and, while the story is about young men, the subsidiary female characters are strong women with dimensions who make their own decisions. This doesn't mean that things end well for them. But that's part and parcel of being trapped with reckless men with big weapons.

Anyway, Ze deals with his humiliation by humiliating a handsome ladies' man called Knockout Ned (Jorge). The party spins out of control and Benny is killed. Despite Ned having nothing to do with Benny's death, Ze has identified him as all-purpose scapegoat. He rapes Ned's girlfriend and kills his uncle and brother. The formerly passive Ned is transformed into a nihilistic vengeance machine. He hooks up with Ze's one surviving drug gang rival, Carrot, and launches a war that forces the police to intervene.

We are now in the '80s. The war between Ze's and Carrot's gangs has become protracted and notorious. The problem for Ze is that Knockout Ned is getting all the newspaper publicity. Like all under-class gangsters, Ze wants his name to 'ring out', to become an iconic figure by being known to everyone yet seemingly immune to both death and arrest. He wants to be a celebrity. He's also dumb enough to rip off an arms dealer, without wondering where his bag of state-of-the-art weaponry comes from. If he'd watched more gangster movies he would've known that the shadowy Mr Big is always a bent cop.

Cue Rocket's role in Ze's manic plans. Hearing that he is a photographer, Ze orders his lieutenants to bring him to his lair and demands he takes photos of his tooled-up gang and sell them to the newspapers. Rocket uses the photos to get his break at a newspaper but fears what will happen to him if Ze's face is actually published.

When an experienced reporter prints the shots without his knowledge, Rocket fears for his life. The reporter, Marina (Moretto), calms him down by taking his virginity. Despite Rodrigues' winning smile, this older woman tangent isn't the most believable part of the story, and does feel like wish-fulfilment for teen male viewers. But nobody's perfect.

We are now back at a familiar place and recognising how cleverly the story has been constructed. In the movie's opening scene, before we've met any of the characters, we've seen a gang chasing a chicken through chaotic passageways, a boy with a winning smile chatting to a friend about how to get a good photo without being killed, and a darkly comic climax where the boy suddenly finds himself in a no man's land between a big gang of heavily armed kids and a smaller gang of heavily armed coppers. We are now back there, fully informed of how the boy got himself in this situation by the previous two hours of action. Beautifully staged mayhem ensues.

Now, before I go on, I should apologise to those who haven't seen *City Of God* for being a big old spoiler. Because this movie is impossible to talk about without its magnificent ending; a climax that expertly balances a tying up of the two central tales and the realities of a situation which plainly has no resolution, and won't get one, anywhere, until the world ends its phoney, bloody 'war on drugs' and deals with the planet's need for a redistribution, not just of wealth, but of opportunity, education and hope.

The cops are outnumbered and back off. Rocket is ordered to take a picture of Ze and his triumphant army. They are too busy posing to notice that Ned and Carrot's gang have outflanked them on their blind side. The dirty street is now a warzone.

Knockout Ned meets his maker courtesy of a young kid who infiltrated his gang because Ned murdered his father. We have no idea of the reasons behind this boy's presence until now.

Rocket has managed to photograph the entire battle from a safe vantage point. He snaps the arrest of Carrot and Li'l Ze. The gangs have destroyed each other but the police arrive to pick off the stragglers and claim control of the streets. Rocket follows the story and sprints through the labyrinth, knowing every shortcut to catch up with the police van carrying the rival gang leaders.

Carrot is taken off to parade in front of the media, but the cops have other plans for Ze, and Rocket arrives in time to capture them for posterity. In an alley behind the cop shop, the policeman who supplies guns to the ghetto shakes Ze down for the money he owes for the weapons he stole. They let Ze go.

Ze is immediately approached by children we recognise. They are members of The Runts, a baby gang Ze terrorised earlier in the saga. They execute him, looking like toddlers firing water pistols. Rocket waits until The Runts leave and takes pictures of Ze's bullet-riddled body.

We cut to Rocket examining the products of his day's work. He looks at the shots of Ze and the gangs, and his voiceover tells us that these shots will get him magazine covers and his big break as a photo-journalist. 'But the cops . . .' he says, and his magnifying glass moves over to the snaps that prove the Brazilian police's connection to organised crime. His own question remains unanswered. The next shot is his photo of Ze's body on the front of the newspaper. The boy may be brave. But he's not stupid.

Another cut. It is a sunny day and Rocket is walking with his friend, talking about the photos he didn't print and his forthcoming internship at the paper. His friend asks him if Marina was any good in bed. 'I don't think journalists know how to screw', he replies.

His amusingly macho boast is the last we hear from our hero, because a gang of small children have taken his place in front of the camera. It is The Runts. They are carrying guns in the open, like toys, and excitedly discussing exactly who they are going to kill to take over the drug trade. We know, from earlier in the movie, that the favela is awash with myths and legends about various left-wing terrorist groups. One of The Runts asks, 'Have you heard of the Red Brigade?' Another answers, 'No. But if they come, we'll kill them.' We watch them walk away, and a tiny boy, no older than four, runs to join them. A caption reminds us that this is based on real events, and Rocket's voiceover tells us, with pride, that he is no longer Rocket, but Wilson Rodrigues, professional photographer. Cut to black.

The ending's juggling of pessimism and optimism, and the ironies of fame and infamy and truth and myth, are so satisfying that even when you're watching the movie alone on DVD, you want to give it a standing ovation. But it also flags up some of the darker life-imitating-art potential of the movie itself.

City Of God was a big global hit and attracted deserved critical acclaim, including four Oscar nominations. One of the reasons critics gave for admiring the film was that it didn't glamorize violence. Don't know what movie they were watching, but just because the teenage killers here aren't wearing Armani suits and talking in repetitive catchphrases doesn't mean the violence isn't glamorous. There are enough shots of pretty young men dying thrilling cartoon deaths over evocative music in *City Of God* to satisfy the most desensitised Jason Statham fan. And Meirelles and Lund love their images of charismatic tough guys pointing their weapons right at us and blowing us away.

So while the movie has a far bigger social conscience than most American and British gangster flicks, it still took real characters from a previously invisible area and made their names ring out around the world. One can imagine a teenage drug dealer in Cidade de Deus 2011 watching *City Of God* not as a cautionary tale about staying in school and getting out of the ghetto through hard work, but inspirational fare about how gunplay doesn't just get you cash, drugs and immediate gratification, but could make you as famous as Al Capone, John Gotti . . . or Li'l Ze. It's a sobering thought.

Not that I'm having a pop at *City Of God*'s talented makers. You shoot one of the all-time great true-crime movies and that's the risk you take. Because *City Of God*'s genius lies in tangents – the horrifying shooting of a small child's foot, a woman murdered for wanting better orgasms, the heat and funk and eroticism of Benny's party, the police killing an innocent boy while the real perpetrator walks right through the bullets and into a church – that all tie in, eventually and wonderfully, to the twin spines of the main storyline, and make you feel like you're watching a politicised black *Good Fellas* without the tips about cooking pasta sauce. *Slumdog Millionaire* borrowed its claustrophobic, heat-blasted, staccato style but left out *City Of God*'s genuinely uplifting truth that you don't have to win a million on a game show to escape hell . . . hard work and talent and a refusal to conform can be your ticket. *City Of God* doesn't make a song and dance out of Rocket's hard won triumph. Compare the two movies and you have a definition of the difference between the ironic and the glib.

* *

ELEPHANT

2003

Starring: Alex Frost, Eric Duelen, John Robinson, Elias McConnell, Jordan Taylor, Carrie Finklea, Nicole George, Brittany Mountain, Timothy Bottoms
Dir.: Gus Van Sant

Plot: Grieving for Columbine.
Key line: 'You *know* there's others like us out there, too.'

While researching this movie I ran across this one line blurb for *Elephant* on a website: 'Several ordinary high school students go through their daily routine as two others prepare for something more malevolent.' This is so pithily and elegantly put that it almost renders me redundant. The key word isn't 'malevolent'. It is 'routine'.

Elephant chooses to look at a notorious real-life mass murder by concentrating on the routine in a typical high school full of typical kids. What hits you – what makes a film so formally cold and bereft of the usual cinematic tricks employed to manipulate our emotions – is that, one day, a group of people turned up to a place they felt safe in, and set about their normal tasks, sleepwalking through the killing of time, as all of us do, everyday, unknowing that these were their last moments on Earth.

Elephant is 'about' the Columbine High School Massacre and the senseless killing of children. But it says something simple and profound that can apply to any random killing. In June 2010, a taxi driver called Derrick Bird picked up a shotgun one morning, murdered his twin brother, and then drove around rural West Cumbria in the north of England, killing eleven passers-by. When I heard about the incident I immediately found myself thinking about *Elephant*, and people, dead, after going about their daily routine in the wrong place at the wrong time. Because in this film, no one is ironically foreshadowing their oblivion with the words, 'I'll be right back' (see *Scream*, p. 339). They are alive and anonymous and unknowing, and then they are gone.

Elephant is not a fictionalisation of Columbine. At least, not exactly.

It is set in the fictional Watt High School in Portland, Oregon. Its killers are called Alex (Frost) and Eric (Duelen), not Dylan and Eric. It doesn't attempt to use the facts of the case to present the true story of the crime. But its shots of boys in combat gear toting guns are clearly inspired by the chilling closed-circuit footage of the real thing, and Gus Van Sant made it after originally setting out to make a documentary about Columbine, and then changing his mind.

It is called *Elephant* because Van Sant is a fan of a short 1989 TV film of the same name by Brit director Alan Clarke (see *Made In Britain*, p. 210). Clarke's *Elephant* is a depiction of 18 murders committed in Northern Ireland in the name of 'The Troubles'. There is no explanation or build-up or stories told about the murders. Clarke simply trains a camera on a selection of anonymous killers and follows them with long, uncut tracking shots, watching until they take a life. Then he goes on to the next. And the next, and the next, until you *just want it to stop*, which is exactly what Clarke (and his producer at BBC Northern Ireland, Danny Boyle) was trying to say.

Van Sant replicates Clarke's shooting style but misunderstood the point of the title. Clarke was referring to the phrase, 'the elephant in the room', the overriding concern that everyone in Northern Ireland was living with but no one wanted to talk about. Van Sant thought it referred to an ancient Indian parable concerning a group of blind men who try to learn what an elephant looks like by touching it. All of them touch a different part of the elephant's enormous body, and therefore come away with wildly differing ideas of what an elephant looks like. In short, no one viewpoint amounts to the complete truth. Both interpretations work equally well for Van Sant's bleakly beautiful film.

Van Sant shot in an abandoned high school building and used non-professional actors who were encouraged to improvise and co-write scenes based on their own everyday high school experiences. There is therefore very little in way of acting or dialogue in the conventional cinematic sense. There is little music, and what there is so quiet it's almost subliminal. Many of the actors use their real first names. While the characters behave as if they are in a documentary, Van Sant applies his cinematic skills in the form of looking at the same events from multiple perspectives (those blind men attempting to 'see' an elephant), a lighting scheme that adds a dream-like quality to the school without attracting attention to itself, and those long, elegant tracking shots that follow students through tasks both mundane and malevolent, all of which build up an almost unbearable tension.

The 'story' is also minimal. We meet a boy, John (Robinson), who, with his near-Albino androgyny, is the movie's most charismatic figure. He has a father, played by *The Last Picture Show* (see p. 117) star Timothy Bottoms, who is an alcoholic and has obviously made the boy into his carer rather than his responsibility. We meet a nerdy girl, Michelle (Hicks), who is obviously awkward and ashamed of her appearance. We meet Elias (McConnell), a photography student taking pictures of other kids for his portfolio.

And we get flashbacks of two ordinary-looking boys getting homo-phobically bullied by jock-types, ordering guns from a website, having breakfast with one set of perfectly normal parents, watching documentaries about Hitler, planning their crime, sharing a kiss in a shower because one of them points out that they've never kissed anyone, arriving tooled-up at the school, sparing John's life by warning him as they approach . . . and then indiscriminately killing the children we've met, plus pupils and adults that we haven't.

The panic and slaughter feels so much more real and terrifying than any violence in any movie you care to name. The pleasure the two boys are taking is a shock, to the point where you realise that you really have forgotten that they are just boys pretending.

There is one moment that stands out: a black boy called Benny (Bennie Dixon) who we haven't met before declines to run away from the carnage. He helps a girl who has frozen with fear to escape out of a window. He then circles round to creep up behind Eric and try and stop him killing the Principal Mr Luce (Malloy), who is lying before Eric, pleading for his life. Benny is handsome, athletic, cool and brave. For a few seconds . . . we are in 'a movie'. He is the essence of the young action hero and we imagine he is going to approach unheard and karate chop Eric in the head, knocking him cinematically unconscious, saving the day. But Eric has heard him coming, and turns, and shoots him dead. Bang. This isn't 'a movie'. We are back in the real world. Heroes exist. But they don't save a day designed by sick boys with guns.

Elephant ends when Alex kills Eric, and looks for more trouble, and finds it in a meat locker with two students called Nathan and Carrie. 'Eeeny meany miny moe,' he sneers, drunk on power, torturing them. The camera backs out of the meat locker, keeping an eye on the scene in case Alex decides to switch his attentions. We can't help. Cut to a cloudy blue sky. Van Sant has had enough. And so have you.

* *

THIRTEEN

2003

Starring: Evan Rachel Wood, Holly Hunter, Nikki Reed, Brady Corbet
Dir.: Catherine Hardwicke

Plot: The sneakiest teensploitation movie ever made.
Key line: 'Tracy was playing Barbies before she met Evie!'

One conclusion you may have come to, as you've watched the social message hysteria and metaphor madness of the '50s teen movie gradually mature into one of the most serious and multi-dimensional genres of the 21st century, is that the old-fashioned juvenile delinquent teensploitation flick is dead. But it isn't. Not one bit. Filmmakers still know that adult movie-goers adore being horrified by the prospect of crazed children behaving badly and coming to kill us all in our sleep. But dressing some stage-school brat in a leather jacket and calling him Buzz or Batman isn't enough to put the fear of God into right-thinking parents in these post-9/11 times. To give us back the fear, one had to extract the kitsch.

So ... take the kind of true-life scare story one finds on daytime TV or one of those insane women's magazines that scream 'My Toddler Gave Birth To Triplets!!!' at you and you only find in supermarkets. Take away the portentous opening voiceover and made-up stats about rampaging youth and exchange melodramatic music for cool indie and rap. Add shaky hand-held cameras because that means, 'This isn't a movie really. It's a documentary!' Get a really top-class, award-winning actress to play Mom, and have her be the sort of character who is both the portal through which the audience experiences the nightmare of adolescent sex and drug abuse, and the individual we can conveniently blame for everything we see, because she's *a sexually active recovering alcoholic working-class single mother*! From ... *The South*!!! For shame, yer big trailer-trash slut!

And, as what teenage boys get up to can't shock anyone after Columbine (see *Elephant*, p. 418), make it about girls; very, *very* bad girls. This has the added value of enabling you to shoot hot jailbait doing rude stuff while insisting that you are only doing it to show us the unpalatable truth, rather than to titillate male viewers, 'cos that would be wrong.

And how to make sure that no one can accuse your exploitation pic of ... well ... exploitation? A female director is a great start. But how about this: one of the barely legal stars of your movie co-wrote it, and assures us that it's based on *the facts of her own life aged 12 and 13*! Ker-ching!!! How can anyone accuse you of scaremongering and bad taste when the proof of your good intentions is right there, on set and on screen? I've been told I use the term cake-and-eat-it *way* too much. But, really, there is no other applicable epithet. So here it is, one last time: *Thirteen* is one of the great cake-and-eat-it teen movies of the last 20 years.

Meet Tracy, a beautiful blonde 13-year-old Los Angeles schoolgirl (played by 14-year-old Evan Rachel Wood), who is a meek, mild-mannered nerd adrift in a school full of wannabe Tupacs until, after just one afternoon with wildly popular Mean Girl psychopath Evie (co-writer Nikki Reed), she becomes a shop-liftin', bitch-slappin', self-harmin', girl-shaggin', boy-shaggin', drug-snortin', tongue-piercin', Mom-assaultin', lip-smackin' stowaway on the Whore Train To Oblivion. You think the boys from *The Cool And The Crazy* (see p. 39) were weird for becoming homicidal/suicidal acid casualties after just one pull on a joint? They have nothing on Tracy, who is to independent thought what Lady Gaga is to slipping into something more comfortable. Ms Reed and director/co-writer Hardwicke reckon that the cautionary drama of *Thirteen* was originally meant as a comedy. Ladies, I have some bad news for you ...

The acting is what makes the movie something more than something to laugh at. Brady Corbet, unrecognisable from his role as haunted abuse victim Brian in *Mysterious Skin* (see p. 428), is very good as Tracy's big brother Mason, attempting to survive in a house full of poisoned oestrogen. Wood kind of coasts on her looks, as many a 14-year-old would have, but Reed is a great, evil-eyed villain, who also scuppers any possibility of the movie being serious by being someone we'd all have jolly good fun following on a teenage rampage. Hunter actually got a Best Supporting Actress Oscar nomination for her reliably committed turn as Melanie Freeland, which was a bit over the top. But she does establish some sort of truth about parents who can't discipline their children effectively because they're still children at heart. She chews the scenery wildly in the movie's hilarious ... sorry ... poignant ending, as she and Wood emote all over the kitchen in a domesticated remix of an especially noisy Jerry Springer show. But there's no other way such a questionable exercise could end. Mommy's love must eventually conquer all, and the characters must hug and learn and grow, but not before much weeping and wailing and gnashing of teeth, 'cos, you know, women are emotional, and all that.

Ms Hardwicke obviously captured a kind of teen movie that the legitimate world wanted ... something that behaved like the real agony at the heart of *Mysterious Skin* or *Precious* (see p. 477) or *La Haine* (see p. 336) but didn't actually hurt. She got to direct *Twilight* (see p. 468) and had thankfully cured her most annoying directorial tic, where she puts a wobbly camera on a slightly out-of-focus face, and then SLAMS it violently into focus, as if every facial gesture of her leads is a huge emotional revelation.

I know it sounds like I don't like *Thirteen*. But I really, really do. It is a brilliant juggling of modern tabloid news stereotypes and rollercoaster plot dynamics, and it entertains because you find yourself shouting at the screen, reeling in comical horror and enjoying the fact that a teen tragedy that is playing out in real life, somewhere, everywhere, at the very moment you are watching it, has been made into an irresponsibly thrilling black comedy that has convinced itself that it's a searing exposé of the perils of peer pressure, urban hardship and liberal parenting. It's a surprise 21st-century throwback to the innocent *and* cynical joys of watching *The Blackboard Jungle* (see p. 20) and *I Was A Teenage Werewolf* (see p. 35), and laughing at adult hysteria about age-old problems of adolescence while consoling yourself with the fact that the real nightmares are always somebody else's fault, and never ours.

★ ★

MEAN GIRLS

2004

Starring: Lindsay Lohan, Rachel McAdams, Tina Fey, Tim Meadows, Lizzy Caplan, Daniel Franzese, Ana Gasteyer, Lacey Chabert, Jonathan Bennett
Dir.: Mark Waters

Plot: Why girls just can't get along.
Key line: 'Evil takes a human form in Regina George. Don't be fooled, 'cos she may seem like your typical selfish, backstabbing, slut-based ho-bag, but in reality, she is so much more than that.'

The film that made *Saturday Night Live* comedian, writer and producer Tina Fey a star is one of the most laugh-out-loud funny of all high school comedies. But beneath the dirty jokes, feelgood final act and bright and breezy filmatism, it's a movie that is pleading for some genuine social change. Adapted from a 2002 self-help manual for teenage girls and their parents called *Queen Bees And Wannabes: Helping Your Daughter Survive Cliques, Gossip, Boyfriends, And Other Realities Of Adolescence* by American educator Rosalind Wiseman, it's a movie that despairs at the way women treat each other in the modern world, but chooses to spread its sly feminist message through the medium of satire and gags about sex with hot dogs.

Lindsay Lohan plays Cady Heron, a 16-year-old who has been home-schooled because her parents are zoologists who have raised her in Africa. As Ms Lohan's narration points out, the world makes odd assumptions about home-schooled kids, before we meet some baby southern rednecks, one of whom has important knowledge to share with us: 'And on the third day, God created the Remington Bull Action Rifle. So that Man could fight the dinosaurs. And the homosexuals.' I wish I could do justice to this kid's accent in print. But I truly can't.

Photos of Cady's African experiences give us some nice visual contrast between the pleasures of a childhood in the jungle and the nightmare of a first day in the real jungle that is a high school in

Chicago. And then there's a near-miss with a speeding bus. You should keep that bit in mind.

Freaked-out Cady bonds with goth-with-attitude Janis Ian (Caplan, whose character is named in tribute to the singer-songwriter who had a folky 1975 coming-of-age hit called 'At Seventeen') and 'so gay he can't function' chubster Damian (Franzese), who immediately peer pressure Cady into missing health class. Good move, as it consists of a big meathead in a shell-suit saying, 'Don't have sex. 'Cos you will get pregnant – and die! Don't have sex in the missionary position; don't have sex standing up . . . just don't do it. Promise? OK . . . everybody take some rubbers.'

The smartass outsiders introduce Cady (and us) to The Plastics, the three young, dumb and full of mean girls who rule the school through intimidation, fear and careful accessorising. Their leader is Regina George (McAdams), a blonde hottie who, in true *Heathers* (see p. 295) style, appears to grow more popular in direct correlation to how stupendously nasty she is ('One time, she punched me in the face. It was awesome.').

Janis goes further, providing Cady with a cafeteria floor plan that sets out the school's arcane subcultural tribes. 'Asian Nerds. Cool Asians. Varsity Jocks. Unfriendly Black Hotties. Girls Who Eat Their Feelings. Girls Who Don't Eat Anything. Desperate Wannabes. Burnouts. Sexually Active Band Geeks . . .' All human life is here.

But maybe the outsiders have judged The Plastics too harshly. When some neanderthal attempts to sexually humiliate Cady in the cafeteria for the benefit of his watching mates, she is rescued by the emasculating tongue of Regina. As Janis has already observed, Cady is 'a regulation hottie' and therefore deemed worthy of Plastic acceptance.

But being elected a Queen Bee comes with a price. Cady is already being forced to choose between the cruel and superficial Plastics and the witty and decent outsiders. Janis deflects the defeat she fears is inevitable by convincing Cady that she's hanging with Regina so she can report back, giving the outsiders plenty of juicy gossip to entertain themselves with. But Janis has some kind of Regina-hating agenda that she won't reveal. If the plot is beginning to remind you of the labyrinthine secrets and lies of *Cruel Intentions* (see p. 363) it should. *Mean Girls* even nicks that movie's scrapbook/diary *deus ex machina*, as well as elements of *Final Destination, Clueless, Heathers, Ghost World, Lucas, Election* and absolutely everything by John Hughes. It's watched *a lot* of teen movies.

Anyway, this being Teen World, there has to be a romance. Hunky Aaron (Bennett) hits Cady 'like a big yellow school bus' (hope you're keeping a-hold of these bus references). Trouble is, he's Regina's ex. So begins a tale of betrayal, control freakery, subterfuge, double-cross, cat-fighting and the failure of 'Fetch' to become a teen buzz-word, played out to all-time classic slut-pop tunes by Kelis and Missy Elliott.

But the plot becomes less relevant with each viewing. *Mean Girls* is really a series of inspired skits fuelled by Fey's wry anger at the death of feminism, and the lengths women (because all of these teens are far too articulate and archetypal to be standard schoolgirls) will go to to undermine each other and collude in their own oppression. The way The Plastics force each other to wear pink, criticise tiny details of their own and each other's bodies, undermine each other's self-confidence and obsessively conspire against other girls is a bewildering truth to Fey, and one worthy of scabrous liberal satire. But, unlike the makers of *But I'm A Cheerleader* (see p. 367), Fey doesn't identify herself as a superior species, or believe it's all the fault of The Right. Therefore, her comedy is more subversive, more admiring of conventional female beauty, has a lighter touch ... and is much, much funnier. The feminist subtext is only there if you're looking out for it. If not, the movie's a hilarious piss-take of the whole notion of high school stereotypes.

For *Mean Girls* bravura encounter session scene, Fey pulls off a superb double bluff whereby her hitherto relatively minor character (Math teacher Ms Norbury) takes charge of the movie to push her pro-female message while simultaneously lampooning Fey's earnestness. By this time, Cady and Regina's battle to win Aaron has seen Cady take over Regina's life, manipulate her into getting fat, find out that Regina started a rumour that Janis was a lesbian, provoke Regina into striking back by distributing her 'Burn Book' in which everyone in school's reputation and self-esteem is destroyed (including Ms Norbury, who is accused of pushing drugs), which starts an uproarious girl riot, which is then blamed on Cady.

The strange self-perpetuating misogyny that runs rife in this school has taken over everything, and something has to be done.

Handsome black Principal Mr Duvall (the superbly deadpan Meadows) orders every girl to convene in the gym, but realises he's out of his depth when a student responds to his request to talk about 'lady problems' by declaring: 'Somebody wrote in that book that I'm lying about being a virgin because I use super-jumbo Tampons. But I can't help it if I have a heavy flow and a wide-set vagina!' Ms Norbury takes over and puts the girls through various therapeutic bonding exercises. It's all going well. 'I wish we could bake a cake made out of rainbows and smiles,' sobs one mousy girl we've never met. Turns out she doesn't go to this school. 'I just have a lot of feelings,' she sniffs.

Until Janis reveals the details of her and Cady's conspiracy against Regina and, instead of being punished, is raised high on the shoulders of a vengeful student body. Regina runs out into the street, Cady follows her, and, just as Regina is going into detail about where Cady can stick her apology . . . remember the bus? The truth hurts.

The final act is a whole bunch of amusing feelgoodery involving Cady's redemption, the Spring Fling dance, a math competition, reunion with the outsiders, getting the guy, the end of The Plastics, a girl who can predict the weather by feeling her boobs and even some form of peace pact with Regina. 'Finally, Girl World is at peace,' sighs Cady's voiceover. It sounds more like a wish than a pay-off line.

Mean Girls was a well-deserved major commercial and critical hit. It established Tina Fey as the funniest screenwriter of her generation and hammered another nail in the coffin of the myth that women just aren't funny, a point proved weekly on Fey's TV sitcom, *30 Rock*. The only sad thing about watching *Mean Girls* is that Lindsay Lohan, who is just so adorable and accomplished here, has become far more infamous as a celebrity wild child than a talented actress. But then, doesn't that just make Tina Fey's point, because how much of that is Lohan's fault, and how much of it is down to women's addiction to gossiping about the sexuality of other women and calling them nasty names?

At one point in the gym scene, Fey's Ms Norbury asks the girls to stop calling each other sluts and whores because it makes it easier for boys to call them sluts and whores. It's probably the least clever bit of dialogue I've quoted anywhere in this book. Don't mean the bitch ain't right, though.

★ ★

MYSTERIOUS SKIN

2004

Starring: Joseph Gordon-Levitt, Brady Corbet, Michelle Trachtenberg, Bill Sage, Chase Ellison, George Webster, Elizabeth Shue
Dir.: Gregg Araki

Plot: Live through this.
Key line(s): *Brian*: **'You were the best player on the team, weren't you?'**
Neil: **'Yeah. That's what he always told me.'**

It is 1981, and an image emerges from the frosty sonic drizzle of 'Golden Hair' by Slowdive. It is a small, blissfully happy boy. He appears to be getting showered by breakfast cereal. A narrator says: 'When I was 8 years old, five hours disappeared from my life . . .'

As the voiceover continues, the camera moves slowly down a wall to reveal a bespectacled blond boy, round blank eyes behind glasses framed by a baseball cap, blood dripping from his nose.

The boy's family don't ask the right questions to learn why their boy is bleeding and hiding in the cellar. But who thinks about the unthinkable: that your decision to send your kid off to play Little League baseball has led your baby into horrors unimaginable. Instead, the boy, his mom and his sister watch in awe as a spaceship flies over their house. A place to escape to. The beginning of a mystery.

Based on a 1996 novel by Scott Heim, *Mysterious Skin* is about two 18-year-old men who were both sexually abused by the same baseball coach when they were 8 years old. The trauma has taken their lives in opposite directions. Brian (Brady Corbet), the bespectacled blond, has become an insular, lonely nerd. He has blocked out the memory of what happened to him and replaced it with fantasies of UFO abductions. Neil has gone from gay promiscuity to rent boy. He remembers some of what happened, but his sordid life has been shaped by shame, because his experience was his introduction to the truth of his sexuality, and he was in love with his abuser.

When Brian finds a photo of his old Little League team, and spots the boy that he has dreamt about as his companion when abducted by aliens, he tracks Neil down. The two piece together the exact details of their ordeal, giving both the opportunity to move onwards and upwards.

Much of the early part of the film is taken up with the seduction of Neil (played as an 8-year-old by the excellent Chase Ellison) by the coach (Bill Sage). Sage's performance is one of the most memorably unusual depictions of a monster in cinema, and these early scenes set the terms, as he befriends Neil by inhabiting a little boy's world. His flat is full of computer games and sweet food and gadgets, like the Polaroid camera he uses to take photos of his prey. These are not pornographic photos, at least, not to anyone sane. They are innocent pictures of a kid making funny faces and larking about, made sinister by the viewer's knowledge of what Coach (he is not given a name) does with them.

One of the major points of the movie is that most paedophiles are not the hideous, mono-browed Quasimodos of our nightmares. They are handsome, wholesome charmers who work with or near children and who work hard to seduce a child and throw other adults off their scent. They can therefore convince themselves that they are not rapists.

One thing you begin to notice is that the scenes where Coach abuses or reveals his motives to young Neil and Brian (George Webster) do not involve the actors interacting. Araki uses subjective camerawork, whereby Sage, Webster and Ellison speak their dialogue straight to camera. Not only does this increase the intimacy and intensity of the scenes, but it also protected the child actors from the implications of their roles. The boys were given scripts which only included their dialogue and white lies were told to them about what their scenes were about. In the light of this, Sage's performance stands as one of the most extraordinary in this book, as he has to balance being a little boy's best friend, and then subtly shift to abuser, while often acting straight down the lens of a camera. It's a selfless, chilling portrayal of the low cunning involved in base depravity, yet the guy had no one to play against while successfully making you feel that you have regressed to childhood and that you are his next victim. There is a moment where Sage's eyes soften, and then harden, and then he says to us, 'Here we go', which sucks the air out of you.

I don't know if there's an award for that. But it should be created so
Sage can win it from a shortlist of one.

I'm sure I don't need to say this, but ... there are, of course, no
explicit scenes of child abuse in *Mysterious Skin*. Again, the actors
played their scenes separately. Apparently, a group called the Australian Family Association wanted the film banned because paedophiles might use it as porn. A perfect example, yet again, of how
conservatives see porn where normal people see life.

As more details unfold of how the boys have been affected by their
trauma – blackouts and constant fear for Brian, sado-masochistic
abuse of other children for Neil – Araki's choice of music adds to the
increasing sense of loss and heartbreak. The glistening 'shoegazing'
drones of Ride, the Cocteau Twins and an incidental score by
Cocteaus' guitarist Robin Guthrie and ambient composer Harold
Budd place every terrible thing into the context of sadness and
sympathy. When Neil abuses others – often in front of his shocked
but complicit best friend Wendy (played as a teen by *Buffy* star
Michelle Trachtenberg) – you understand that these kids are also
being abused by Coach, who doesn't need to be anywhere near these
boys to have control over their lives and the lives of those they meet.

Eventually, we meet Brian and Neil as young adults, played by
Corbet and the outstanding Gordon-Levitt. Keeping much of the
subjective camerawork, we follow Neil's life of amoral cynicism,
which seems to suit him until he is raped by a john in a brutal and
horribly believable scene.

This scene produces very different emotions to the shock-horror
teen sex scenes in Larry Clark movies (see *Kids*, p. 328, and *Bully*,
p. 409). While Clark seems fascinated by the idea of outraging the
viewer, Araki's unflinching gaze and deliberate editing puts you in
the place of the victim. You can almost feel the director crying
for everyone who has been shaped by the brutality of others, and
understanding that memories of trauma consist of objects in the
room, the smells and sounds, the details you would fixate on to
survive the moment. It's the hardest scene to watch in this book, and
I only resisted the temptation to fast-forward because it isn't part of
my current job description to look away. I will watch this movie many
times in the future but I doubt if I'll watch this scene again. It really
does have a there-but-for-the-grace-of-God power, even to a non-
believer.

It is the final straw that forces Neil to come to terms with his past. When Brian tracks him down, the pair break into Coach's now-empty house, and Neil leads Brian back into his nightmares, until all of his amnesiac fixations and fevered dreams make sense. Part of the truth and tragedy is that Neil is still fiercely protective of his status as Coach's favourite.

It is a scene that proves something about art. The triumphant ending is not getting the girl or killing the baddies or winning the big game. It's facing up to the darkest events, and coming to terms, and surviving and moving on to a life. And that this, too, is rendered superficial by sentimental TV movies or chat shows where you entertain the world with your agonies and get a whoop and a round of applause for giving the bored and nosey a cheap thrill. You have to find someone to trust who can hold these truths and feel their importance. And then you have to transcend what they did to you. And you become a hero, no matter what else it is that someone had forced you to be.

I was going to conclude with something about how wrong a world is that hard sells *The Inbetweeners Movie* but buries a movie like this. But as I cried buckets – again – at the profound truths of this film, I realised that just wasn't the point at all. You can't show this movie to a child to teach them how to stay safe – it's just too graphic and disturbing. It is a film that makes something very beautiful out of an ugly subject, but isn't a film you'd watch for fun on a Sunday afternoon. It is one of the most accomplished writing and directing achievements of recent years, but it never had a hope of being a mainstream money-spinner.

But its determination to portray the psychological survival mechanisms of the victim, and its truly uplifting solving of private psychological mystery could be useful, I suspect, to anyone who has been sexually, physically or mentally abused, at any age, by anyone. It feels like a letting go of rage, moving way past the gut reaction of wanting revenge against abusers to the far more important subject of how a victim escapes the control an abuser can exercise over the rest of their life.

Araki is one of the most high-profile and committed out gay directors, and showed great courage in facing up to the accusation that most diehard homophobes like to throw at gay men ... that their sexual preference is a perversion, and perverts are naturally paedophiles. Araki successfully destroys that myth by showing that a man who violates little boys is not a homosexual. He is something else … something that I don't feel qualified to sum up in a couple of words because using the usual insults to deny the humanity of paedophiles is so against the spirit of this movie, because it doesn't take us any closer to understanding child abuse and stopping it.

But *Mysterious Skin* is not bleak and grim and unwatchable nor dull and worthy. It is a profoundly moving piece of accomplished aesthetically gorgeous cinema. And, if you haven't seen it, I urge you to. You will feel different afterwards. Dehydration through extreme weeping may well be involved.

* *

NAPOLEON DYNAMITE

2004
Starring: Jon Heder, Jon Gries, Aaron Ruell, Efren Ramirez, Tina Majorino
Dir.: Jared Hess

Plot: Numb and number.
Key line(s): *Napoleon*: **'I don't even have any good skills!'**
Pedro: **'What do you mean?'**
Napoleon: **'You *know*, like, numchuck skills, bow-hunting skills, computer-hacking skills. Girls only want boyfriends who have great skills!'**

Attempting to describe the appeal of *Napoleon Dynamite* is like reviewing Fall records. You know this is good shit. You can't explain why. Why is a man throwing a steak at a man on a bike funny?

Napoleon Dynamite concerns the daily lives and surreal mannerisms of a dysfunctional family who live in some Godforsaken rural town somewhere in America, which *could* be Salt Lake City, Utah, because that's where husband-and-wife directing-writing team Jared and Jerusha Hess live. The Hesses are both members of the Church Of The Latter-Day Saints, whose adherents are better known as Mormons. Their first movie resolutely ignores religious references and messages, but it does resemble what might happen if you asked people who had had no contact with the modern world since The Osmonds were big to make a teen comedy. It is also the least smutty teen comedy in existence, unless you count accidental testicular injury and breast enhancement as smut, neither of which is here. At least, not exactly.

The movie essentially revolves around Jon Heder's extraordinary performance as the titular character . . . who, incidentally, the Hesses insisted was not named after a pseudonym used by Elvis Costello intermittently throughout the 1980s, because Napoleon and Dynamite are two words that any person might coincidentally pick out of a hat and slam together as a stupid name, right?

Watching Heder's Napoleon first time around, it honestly felt like some film-makers had found this weird guy with learning difficulties and just made a movie around him. Gangly but also kind of woman-shaped, with shoulders too narrow for his wide-hipped body and blonde curly hair, it was the way his hooded, drugged eyes never focused or made eye contact that convinced you the guy wasn't acting. He was, though, and thereby created one of the most unique and slightly disturbing comedy characters in movie history. Heder is also a Mormon, and a scoutmaster!

Napoleon lives with his brother Kip (Ruell) and (possibly lesbian) mother in a house by a field. Kip dresses like a mix between a scoutmaster, a member of The Famous Five, and Ron Mael from Sparks. He spends all his time on the internet and trying to learn self-defence by being beaten up by a TV self-defence guru.

Napoleon goes to high school on a yellow bus but, like most of the pupils in this school, he looks 27, which Heder was at the time. He has no social skills and is bullied and despised. *Napoleon Dynamite* is a movie where that's just funny.

New people come into Napoleon's life. Mom goes away and leaves the 'boys' in the care of Uncle Rico (Gries), who looks like an early '70s porn star, lives in a van, obsesses so much about his high school football glory years that he makes videos of himself throwing footballs to no one, and earns a living selling dodgy products to lonely house-wives. Napoleon also meets a schoolgirl, Deb (Majorino), who moon-lights as a glamour photographer. Not *that* kind of glamour photographer. And then there's Pedro (Ramirez), the new Mexican boy at school who has a moustache and a rad bike, but also looks 35, stares blankly into space and talks like a robot Speedy Gonzales. There is instant chemistry.

The *Napoleon Dynamite* world is like the rural flipside to the parallel universe of *Ghost World* (see p. 400). Nothing logical happens here. The self-defence maestro is married to a hulking transvestite. Men disappoint their wives by trying to snap Tupperware with their bare hands and failing. Thin white man-children marry beautiful black urbanites they met on the net. The film is often lumped into the geek teen comedy category, but I don't think Napoleon or any of its other characters are geeks. They are surreal comic characters in the tradition of Laurel and Hardy, The Marx Brothers and The Three Stooges. Like those ancient comedy teams, they inhabit an anarchic fourth dimension built entirely on delusions so stupid they defy any attempt to compare them to people you've met. The 21st-century update comes from the internet and the kind of viral YouTube comedy hit that consists of an idiot trying to do something they plainly can't and looking ridiculous, or that one where one boy tempts another to walk across a creek on a log, and then shakes the log, and the poor kid falls in in a way that couldn't be contrived by a comic or stuntman. It's the comedy of the everyday dumbass, magnified by brilliant comic acting and a deadpan, static camera that refuses to laugh.

These characters don't exist to say anything about teens coming of age, high school, the difficulties of being unpopular or even that, no matter how weird and funny-looking you are, you too can achieve your dreams if you just believe. They are there to run with their arms by their sides, look comical while playing swing ball and hitting each other, and make you wonder what the fuck they'll do next. If you see *Dumb And Dumber* as a work of enduring comic genius (Guilty!), then you'll love *Napoleon Dynamite*. If you think it's the most puerile waste of time you've ever seen, then milk-tasting competitions ('The defect in this one is bleach . . . Yessss!') and boys who look like crazy men electrocuting themselves in the balls with time machines they bought online ain't gonna do it for you.

The entire movie is building up to one golden moment, though. The Hesses know what they've got here, because they keep giving us teasing glimpses through Napoleon's bedroom door as he practices.

Pedro has run for the school election and had no idea that he had to do a 'skit'. His popular girl rival Summer Wheatley has just done a rubbish but game choreographed dance routine with her posse of girlfriends. It's left to Napoleon to rescue Pedro's honour. He runs onstage and dances to 'Canned Heat' by Jamiroquai.

Where do I begin with this towering scene of heartbreaking heartbreak? The joke is that everything Napoleon has done up to this point has been comically inept. So, as the music begins, we, like the watching audience, are expecting a car crash. And then Napoleon dances so beautifully it's almost moving. It's a bravura mix of hip hop street dance, *Saturday Night Fever* disco, acrobatics, '80s *Footloose* style, and something uniquely Jon Heder, because, as well as taking his dance completely seriously, and despite the brilliance of the steps, Napoleon *still* doesn't look quite right. The idea of the hapless goofball finding the one thing that makes him special, and it being the last thing one could possibly expect, gives the scene both comedy and poignancy, and is matched in inspired dance weirdness only by the *Flashdance* scene in *Dogtooth* (see p. 473)

The standing ovation Napoleon receives from his schoolmates probably explains why it is often said that this movie has an 'uplifting' ending. This would imply that logical stuff happens, to, like, be uplifted from. It doesn't. It's just stupid.

Don't switch off at the credits, though, or you'll miss Kip's wedding to African-American Goddess Lafawnduh, which includes the greatest love song ever written *and* Napoleon riding in on a wild honeymoon stallion he has tamed especially for the occasion. *Lucky!*

★ ★

HARD CANDY

2005
Starring: Patrick Wilson, Ellen Page
Dir.: David Slade

Plot: Juno The Paedophile Slayer.
Key line: 'I am every little girl you ever watched, touched, hurt, screwed, killed.'

Low-budget American thriller *Hard Candy* is both a two-hander and a two-parter. Although other actors do appear onscreen, this is essentially a 96-minute acting face-off between future *Juno* (see p. 449) and *Inception* star Ellen Page and the underrated Patrick Wilson. But it also deals with its controversial subject matter by taking the unsuspecting viewer down two diametrically opposed paths.

In the first act of the movie, we watch a man groom a 14-year-old for sex. He is better looking and more charming than our natural image of the child molester. She is pretty and smart, but ingenuous and impressed, as we know teenage girls can be by worldly men who appear to take an adolescent girl's opinions and tastes seriously; our skin crawls at the revelation of how easy it can be for a monster to destroy innocence, and for 20 minutes we're screaming for her to understand that she's out of her depth, playing with a sexuality she isn't old enough to understand yet, and to make a break for it, now, like the wind, for the nearest policeman, or chainsaw.

But, as we're told early on, faces can lie. And in Act Two, male viewers are suddenly enduring their worst nightmare. Because we have been watching a predator at work. But we've been looking at the wrong face.

Budding director David Slade was searching for the kind of idea that could be largely shot in one interior space to save money. He had come up with a few, but the one that stuck with him derived, as they so often do, from a newspaper. It was a report on a new Japanese phenomenon, whereby teenage girls track down paedophiles online, virtually flirt, allow themselves to be groomed, invite the sucker round. When he arrives he finds himself ambushed by a mob of girls who assault, batter and mug him.

You can see why the idea stuck. On the simple level, you get the 'what if the victim is really the predator?' real-life plot twist. But on the deeper, more disturbing level: are these girls amoral thugs or crusaders for justice? Do we cheer the karmic retribution or worry for the mental health of children who can conspire in such an act? Is this righteous revenge or just crime?

Slade approached playwright Brian Nelson who, being a huge fan of *Buffy The Vampire Slayer*, turned out to be the ideal choice. Nelson nails a story that could, potentially, be a nasty post-*Saw* trivialisation of a crime that destroys lives daily. It's full of tricksy plot twists, violence and thriller dynamics. But, through strong characterisation and a firm grip on the politics of crime and punishment, it remains serious and thought-provoking. *And* gives us one of those post-Ripley, post-Buffy, ass-kicking heroines that is believable enough to exist outside of the fevered fantasies of sci-fi-flavoured porn geeks.

Wilson is excellent. His Jeff Kohlver is a selfless portrayal of the man none of us wants to be. In the early scenes, he is a deft mix of easy-going charm and patronising sleaze. When not concentrating on manipulating his prey, his face relaxes, ever-so-slightly, into a face made cruel by depravity, but so briefly and subtly that his character never tips over into cinematic evil. For the film to work Jeff has to be the truth: that is, a guy you've met, not a hideously ugly, sweaty perv with CHILD MOLESTER stamped on his neanderthal brow. Later, when he's in peril, you feel every fibre of his terror, and this is vital too, because *Hard Candy* constantly questions our attitude to retribution. It asks: 'How many times have you felt that child abuse is the one area where you suspend your liberal values? How many times have you thought, "Just lock them up for ever. Or kill them. Or chop their balls off. They deserve it." Well ... here it is. The rough justice you want. So now you're actually seeing what you wish for, how do you feel?'

Wilson's performance is nuanced enough that you lurch in and out of sympathy with his situation. At crucial points of the movie you start to doubt that Jeff is what Hayley insists that he is. This would be just one of the problems with both vigilante action and state-sponsored violence, especially in a world where an angry mob of the linguistically challenged gathers to attack a *paediatrician*, as actually happened, in the UK, back in 2000.

But Page is on some awesome next-level shit. She's an 18-year-old actress pretending to be a 14-year-old avenging angel *and* evil genius, pretending to be a 14-year-old jailbait intellectual. This is akin to attempting to improve health care while arguing with insane Republicans, balancing an obscene budget deficit and patting your head while rubbing your tummy. But she's faultless. I mean, *faultless*. She implicates you with her tomboy sexiness. She convinces you that she's desperate for an older lover even while the director is giving you big clues that she isn't. She then convinces you that she's capable of psychopathic levels of sadism. She makes a plot that inevitably trips into *Sleuth*-style daftness feel logical, just as Sarah Michele Geller does throughout *Buffy*, and even pulls off a *Little Red Riding Hood* metaphor and a gag about girl scouts. Her Hayley is a creation every bit as compelling as her Juno, and, although most of me wants her to go on and become the biggest movie actress of her day, another small part of me wants her to be scuppered by Hollywood sexism so she can come to TV and make seven seasons-worth of Hayley kicking paedophile ass so we don't have to. In every generation there is a Chosen One. She alone will stand against the paedos, the nonces and the forces of darkness. She is . . . Ellen motherfucking Page!

Now . . . you may have noticed that I'm kind of avoiding the details of the plot. That's because I'm troubled. A few readers of *Popcorn* put the point quite forcibly that they didn't approve of the entries where I chose not to discuss key plot-points and endings, from the not unreasonable standpoint that a film can't be analysed properly without a wee bit of spoiling. And I got their point. But *Hard Candy*, though profitable on its tiny budget and admired enough to be Page's big break, wasn't seen by millions, and I'm going to assume that most readers have never seen it. And so much of the joy (and pain) of this movie is in the twists and surprises. And I've already let slip that Hayley is not what she seems and that she doesn't die. I just really want people to see this movie and suspect that they won't if I spill every detail.

But here's what I can get away with in all conscience. Hayley has chosen Jeff because he is a photographer of under-age models who she believes has molested and killed a missing girl called Donna Mauer. When the pair meet, Hayley manipulates Jeff into taking her to his home, even though both constantly refer to the risks involved and how an observer might see the situation.

She drugs his drink and he passes out. He wakes up tied to a chair. She accuses and he protests his innocence. She searches the house and fucks with his head with brazen, bracing wit: 'Did society make me a vindictive little bitch, or was I born that way? I go back and forth on that.' The things in the house, which looks like the kind of designer yuppie mansion you see in upmarket car ads, drive the situation: an indoor rock garden, a gun, saran wrap, a stash of porn, a bag of ice. He tries to escape. He fails. The book in Hayley's bag that Jeff had spotted earlier is, as she explained, a medical book. It details a specific medical procedure. The ice is meant as anaesthetic. Hayley's smart and she thinks she's smart enough to perform a successful castration. And she wants to film it so Jeff can watch . . .

That's it. Can't say any more except that that's where the . . .

um ... fun begins. The castration scene is almost as physically painful and morbidly compelling as the final act of Takashi Miike's 1999 movie *Audition*, which shares a theme about apparently submissive girls turning the tables on the men who want to use them. But there is a black humour here that is not on *Audition*'s brutal agenda, because Hayley talks so much, and is just wickedly, cruelly, gleefully funny, with a particularly great store of choice knob gags. She says everything we've ever wanted to say to a paedophile, and so much more. She wants to break Jeff's mind more than his body.

And that's all he wrote. Watch this movie. It's the bloody birth of a star.

★ ★

KIDULTHOOD

2006
Starring: Ami Ameen, Red Madrell, Noel Clarke, Adam Deacon, Femi Oyeniran, Jamie Winstone, Cornell John
Dir.: Menhaj Huda

Plot: Liberal-baiting grime in wild Notting Hill.
Key line: 'I wouldn't want that in me. If I was you I'd rip it out with a coat-hanger.'

The opening ten minutes of this extraordinary British film are, for me, the most frightening anywhere in this book. Nothing in any of the teen horror or gangster movies – or the sensationally graphic trawls through the lives of drug-addled American youth – freaks me out as much. This isn't because it's instantly familiar either – I had a few rough times at my London schools, but nothing to write home or to you about. It's because it's brilliantly scripted, acted and shot terror about something that everyone fears. That ethnically mixed schools largely populated by working-class kids in inner-city areas have slipped entirely out of control of teachers, parents, the adult world. That they really have become blackboard jungles where the violent rule and the weak are bullied beyond the point where they can cope. That education has become entirely irrelevant here because how to survive is the only study that matters. And that, like prisons, schools spit out monsters because, to live through them, a monster is what you have to become.

The key figure here – apart from first-time director Huda – is Noel Clarke. The young black actor and screenwriter, best known before *Kidulthood* as the cutely inept Mickey in the revived *Dr Who* sci-fi TV series, was a shock as soon as he swaggered onscreen here. Clarke's Sam is the nightmare hoodie, handsome face a mask of sheer fury, each word a weapon of guttural motor-mouth abuse, essaying a character which matches anything by De Niro, Pesci or Gandolfini for believable unfathomable violence. There is a movie bad guy that really sticks with you, that makes you move back away from the screen and feel genuinely threatened, and it's the one that mixes an authentic portrayal of people you've met with a face and demeanour that suggests that this being has no fear whatsoever of death. He's entirely psychologically prepared to be Pacino at the end of *Scarface*, getting riddled with bullets and still shooting back and screaming, 'Fuck You!' Or, at least, he is until he actually has to look death right in the eye, because a large part of his persona is based entirely on what he's seen in movies like *Scarface*. But until that reality finally hits, he'll never back down. He'll never be scared into stopping. He can't be reasoned with because there is no reason for his actions. He has no moral compass. He lives for the thrill of the power created by fear.

Clarke captures this guy brilliantly in a few short scenes ... and, crucially, he is not some distant monster from the Mafia or a part of America that most of us have no reason to enter. He's a kid who lives round the corner from you in London, a city which is unique for putting people from extreme ends of the social, economic and cultural scale slap-bang next to each other. You remember that movie *Notting Hill*? Its sunny, wealthy, escapist vision of this uniquely confused area of West London is accurate too. Walk down one street in London W10 or W11 and it's Hugh Grant and Julia Roberts sipping skinny lattes with the Prime Minister and discussing how many seats they want for Centre Court at Wimbledon and whether they fancy Ascot and Henley this year. Walk down the next and Sam is demanding your wallet and mobile at knife-point. Or, in the context of *Kidulthood*, two under-age girls walk right out of their sink estate and right into the posh bachelor flat of an actor who gives them money in return for sex and drugs. He doesn't exactly look or sound like Hugh Grant, but . . .

As we get our opening whistle-stop guided tour through the playground (and, boy, how inappropriate does anything as childlike as playing seem here) of this new kind of high school hell, Huda gives us everything we need to know in short scenes that scramble conventional narrative. The good-looking black boy doing something with a drill and then hiding a package in a skip; the two pleasant-looking white boys inviting everyone to a party while their parents are away; the bullied white girl and her friend being targeted by Sam, and the Catch 22 of trying to escape without a beating when looking at him is provocation and not looking at him is disrespect, and how easily he goads a chubby white girl into doing his dirty work for him; the pretty black and white girl chatting about clothes and boys and the mysterious drilling boy in particular; the sudden appearance of one teacher calling the mob into class, and your knowledge – you can almost hear the laughter of recognition among the film's prime target audience – that this overweight, middle-aged white man with the put-upon look and the awful cardigan and the weak voice is no match for any of these kids. He dares to hurry one black boy along, gets a mean, silent glare, and shrinks and looks away in fear.

So there is no help for Katie (Rebecca Martin). No adults at all anywhere near the classroom where Shaneek (Stephanie Di Rubbo), who has white skin but is all head and hand movements stolen from gangsta rap videos, and her black friend beat the pasty middle-class girl down for absolutely no reason. This is undercut with Sam's gang facing down the group in which our drilling boy (Ameen as Trevor aka Trife) dwells, stealing a Gameboy, punching Trife in the gut, loving the power. No adults here either.

Back to Shaneek and the rank, gynaecological verbal abuse she and her mate hand out to Katie. Huda has them showing out straight to camera, right into our faces, knowing that, for male viewers, the only thing worse than having your arse kicked by a Sam is having your arse kicked by these girls. Shaneek is definitely harder than me. I won't lie. I know that because of . . . the punch. One of the best punches ever thrown in a movie.

Huda is making you think that the worst thing that can happen in the scene is the humiliation. The abuse about Katie's sexual experience (she's both 'virgin' and 'slag', reinforcing this world where, once picked upon, you can't win), the slaps, the powerlessness. Teachers are absent and none of the kids has the courage to come to her aid. And then ... it just comes so suddenly. Part of the shock and power lies in the sound effect: it's neither the standard cinematic 'Thwack!' nor a realistic dull thud. It's a kind of crack meets crunch and it really fucking hurts. Shaneek is standing out of shot while Katie is against a wall, and you can see a slight jump-cut. An arm delivers a straight right and whoever has thrown it has maybe done a bit of boxing. The film is slightly speeded up. The punch looks entirely like it makes full contact on bridge of nose and forehead, and Katie's head snaps back, her reactions brilliantly real. She throws her hands up to her face, lets out a quiet 'uh' ... and her body seems to give in, exactly as it does when you've been hit hard, and weren't expecting it, and know instantly that you are not capable of fighting back. She slides down the wall into a foetal position, a broken doll. Fuck.

All this has to be as utterly convincing as it is. Because *Kidulthood*'s day-in-the-life plot is shamelessly contrived and could just look like shoved-together bits of newspaper headlines and shock confessions from daytime TV. It doesn't because this opening six minutes drags you kicking and screaming into a world where you don't want to be but can't help staring at with appalled voyeurism. It's a stunning piece of film-making and one wonders if Huda and Clarke will ever match it.

Because within minutes of the start of the film, Katie has hanged herself from her bedroom ceiling and the teens we're being asked to pal around with for the next 85 minutes *don't care* – except that they've been given the day off from school. It's a bit much, storyline-wise. But you're on the rollercoaster now and the nasty-looking dude who took your money ain't letting you off. Tough. Live with it and don't look down.

Fifteen-year-olds getting pregnant and exchanging sex for coke from posh drug dealers. Wiggers stealing beer with menaces from the Asian corner shop. It pulls you in to your safe liberal zone with a recurring gag about taxis not stopping for young black men; and then undercuts it completely by implying that they shouldn't. The plot coalesces neatly around a spiral of revenge, a real gangster uncle, West End nicking sprees, the extremes of economy and environment between wealthy white and poor black, the conscience of the potentially absent black father, a series of brutally real punch-ups, a comic sneer at the desperation of the white middle classes to impress and co-opt black working-class cool; and all of this heads towards a convergence of differing, dangerous agendas at the party and a death you don't see coming.

All the girls are materialist slappers ... until some are not. All the boys are thieving wannabe gangstas ... until a few are not. The worst words you can think of – and some you don't even understand and don't want to – are put into their mouths. Everything is played out to a soundtrack of dark, pessimistic hip hop and grime. Yet ... *Kidulthood* is funny.

The film has a raw sense of humour that constantly dares you to get into the nihilistic spirit or retreat to your liberal corner. The scene where Jay (Deacon) is successfully seducing Sam's girlfriend while we know the baddest bwoy in da hood is on his way home is like a docudrama spin on the 'look out ... the monster's coming!' schtick that provides one of cinema's most enduring pleasures by making you laugh at fear once-removed. But ... the conflict point is a 15-year-old girl who took about three minutes to agree to sex with someone she barely knows. It's really not funny, at the core. Huda and Clarke know that. They make you laugh and scream 'Behind You!!!' anyway.

Kidulthood is arguably the most irresponsible movie in this book and its gleeful rubbing of our noses in our worst assumptions about working-class teens is one of its greatest strengths. The movie has none of the self-serving get-out clause moralising and sentimentalities of those awful American teen/hip hop/gangsta movies like *Boys N the Hood*, *Juice* and *Menace II Society*. It doesn't stop to wring its hands and cry, 'Oh Lord, what can we do about the yoof? Stay in school! Families need fathers! Oh ... and now I've pretended that I'm really trying to stop black-on-black crime rather than exploiting it, can I have a bit in *Ebony* magazine and a Martin Lawrence movie please?' None of that bollocks. It walks up to your face with that stag-fight/head-butt stance that footballers have become fond of, and says, 'You're right. We're exactly what you think we are. And no, we don't know how to stop it. We're not role models just because we're black. And if you don't get this film it's not for you – it's for us. So fuck you.' And by doing so, it credits you with the intelligence to decide for yourself whether to care about the fall of England or just be a sick bastard and get off on the bit where Sam's getting his head kicked in to the strains of 'Jus' A Rascal' by Dizzee Rascal.

That's why I really, *really* love this movie. Watch it in one mood and it's a searing indictment of the moral and spiritual void at the heart of an England – young and old, rich and poor, black and white – which would increasingly and merrily sell its own granny for a blow job and a new pair of trainers. Watch it in another and its pure, malevolent fun and dumb thrills.

The sequel, *Adulthood*, is good enough, but not great. Clarke directs instead of Huda, and makes his Sam into a tough-guy hero, like a grimy *Terminator 2*. It's a good action thriller, but doesn't resonate with wider truths, partly because it's not about children. You don't feel implicated by watching and enjoying it. It's just a film.

Kidulthood isn't. It has a disturbing glee and a baleful prescience. I know it's a term that has become popularly connected to liking cheesy power ballads. But I never felt too ashamed about that. *Kidulthood* is, like Eminem records, dog racing and staring at your best mate's wife's tits, a true guilty pleasure.

★ ★

HAIRSPRAY

2007

Starring: Nikki Blonsky, John Travolta, Michelle Pfeiffer, Christopher Walken, Zac Efron, Alison Janney, Queen Latifah
Dir.: Adam Shankman

Plot: *Grease* remixed by Martin Luther King.
Key line: 'Get that chubby communist off the show!'

This is wrong. So very, very wrong. I'm an alternative boy, reared on punk rock, cult movies and that whole thing about being gay even when you're not. I hate modern musicals, especially anything staged with any similarity to *Chicago*. I don't even know who Adam bloody Shankman is. So ... why do I like this *Hairspray* even more than I love the John Waters original?

I dunno. Maybe I don't. But I do love a film that manages to be funny about racism, and especially one that includes the lines: 'I wish every day were Negro Day!' and 'This is just so Afrotastic!' That reveals that John Travolta is the most adorably funny tranny in Hollywood. And that, while obviously aimed at children on some level, somehow finds a way to smuggle John Waters himself in ... as a flasher. You've got to admire people – in this case Shankman, screenwriter Leslie Dixon and Mark O'Donnell and Thomas Meehan, who turned a cult rock movie into a hit stage musical – who can make bad taste parody into family fun while simultaneously keeping the sleaze and amping up the politics. *Hairspray* is one of those rare films that makes good and worthy intentions into irreverent entertainment.

If you are not familiar with either version, *Hairspray* is set in Baltimore in 1962, and concerns Tracy Turnblad (Blonsky), an overweight, working-class teen who wants to be the star of the local rock 'n' roll TV show, get hottest boy in school Link (Efron) and end American segregation. She does all three, and sings and dances along the way. The original Tracy was played by Ricki Lake, and the only reason the adorable Ms Blonsky isn't better is because it is actually mathematically impossible to be a better Tracy Turnblad than Ricki Lake. Don't bother getting out a calculator. I've tried it. *Mathematically impossible.*

The original established the fact that Tracy's even porkier mom Edna is played by a man. In 1988 it was Waters' mascot and symbol of porcine transsexuality Divine. It was his last role, and he was entirely wonderful. But some bright spark decided that the man to match the unmatchable was ... John Travolta. And in the history of 'It's crazy ... but it just might work!' cinematic ideas, it's among the champions, because Travolta, with his fat suit and brilliantly over-the-top Baltimore accent, is even better than Divine.

For those of us who thought a mainstream Hollywood version of a beloved Waters cult had to be a whitewash, the opening number is vital and gets us onside by establishing the wryness of the entire stage musical scenario. In 'Good Morning Baltimore', Tracy hits you with gung-ho optimism about a new day in B-More while negotiating rats, drunks and flashing John Waters. It's a fantastic opener, giving you the main themes – how early '60s kids stayed positive enough to change the world for the better in the face of poverty and class and race divisions – while establishing a fat girl heroine, a bright palette of Disney colours and a sharp eye for the hypocrisies of the American dream.

'The Nicest Kids In Town' then tips the film fully into subversive genius territory. Tracy and a friend run home to watch local sock hop TV show *The Corny Collins Show*, and 'The Nicest Kids ...' is the opening song and it's going *so well*, all Ultrabrite smiles from the dancers and teen-positive sentiments in the lyrics. Then Collins hits a new verse and his clean-cut enthusiasm curdles into something Klan-cut sinister: 'Nice white kids who like to lead the way/And once a month we have our ... Negro Day!!!'

It doesn't stop there. Class agendas have to be revealed with a bounce and a grin, too. 'Who cares about sleep when you can snooze in school/You'll never get to college but you'll sure look cool.'

From there it's all snotty gags, fun songs about how great it is to be black, or pro-black, or fat, or just plain liberal, mingled in with the sheer joy of the idea of Christopher Walken being married to John Travolta, and Michelle Pfeiffer having a ball as the pushy racist TV producer Velma Von Tussle, a kind of glam-Nazi, Catwomanesque template for Sue Sylvester out of *Glee*. Pfeiffer gets most of the best lines, what with being evil and all, particular favourites being her response to being asked how to sack Corny Collins from his own show – 'They do it all the time on *Lassie*' – and the elegant revelation of her sinister televisual agenda: 'They're kids, Corny. That's why we have to steer them in the white direction.'

You want more? There's a fabulous, poignant moment when three white girls are singing a cute, banal, Tracy-referencing number called 'The New Girl In Town' with rubbish dancing, and we suddenly switch to three sassily beautiful black girls singing the same song, which is now, funky, slinky and almost like a real Supremes-lite pop hit ... with a genuinely black pay-off line.

And while we're on fabulous and poignant ... how does one do a 'The '60s is coming. Wasn't it swinging?' song and major theme without annoying the fuck out of us all with both the familiarity and the unavoidable smugness? One smart way is to quickly turn Travolta's Edna from broad comic tranny into a gently tragic figure; a woman so ashamed of her weight that she hasn't been out of the house in over a decade, locked into that comfort-food obesity loop where she eats to make her shame bearable. Tracy's song 'Welcome To The Sixties' becomes an embrace of *everyone* different, including the black, the freaky, the (by implication) gay ... and the fat. The song and its staging insists that everyone has a chance to, literally, come out and be visible in this brave new world.

It's beautiful. And naive, sure. The absence of romantic lead roles for big women outside of movies that begin with H and end with Y proves that. But don't you love movies that give you a glimpse of a world better than the one we have to live in? Don't those glimpses encourage us to make our world better? Especially when they're aimed at the young, who have the time and the energy to change things for the better? If you're answering 'No' I honestly feel sorry for you and your Radiohead box sets. What have relentless default pessimism, cynicism and resignation ever actually achieved?

And if you can't buy that, then maybe you can buy a wobbly John Travolta dancing in the street in a pink dress and high heels . . . a big old wink to lovers of pop film and iconic dance sequences.

Among all this wish-fulfilment there's a running joke that has a real resonance for me. Every time a kid in this movie is sent to detention, they are essentially being sent to a classroom full of black kids having a party. Way back in The Dark Ages, I went to a primary school in North London that had a dustbin class called Class 3. The school had given up on these 30 kids. It was taken by an elderly male teacher who was quite obviously senile. And if you entered it to give the guy a note from your teacher, you quickly realised that all the children were black, and that, because senile Mr N couldn't control them, they were essentially having a party instead of an education. I'd love to think things have entirely changed in the ensuing 38 years. But I suspect that *would* be naive.

Is this *Hairspray really* better than the original? Well . . . the acting is different class, but then, part of Waters's aesthetic was deliberate bad acting. It's more adamant about its place as an anti-racist story, and its love of fat women is even more pronounced and, in the anorexic 21st century, this seems oddly transgressive, in a much-needed, pro-feminist, anti-health and safety way. It's more witty, but less laugh-out-loud funny. And the fact that it's more uplifting – and more the kind of film you'd show to your kid to make points about tolerance and liberalism – is in stark contrast to the original's tone of genuinely rebellious sleaze.

The major way it loses it out to Waters is in the music. The lyrics of the songs are great. But these typically wishy-washy, thinly produced showtunes are absolutely no match, musically, for the rock 'n' roll originals in the 1988 version. So while the enthusiastic dancing and smart words do hold your attention, the music itself gets you thinking about making cups of tea and the simple fact that, if rock 'n' roll and soul had sounded like this, we'd still be listening to Rosemary Clooney and living in unofficial apartheid. Which kind of defeats the film's entire point.

But let's be honest ... since the rise of Andrew Lloyd-Webber, talented composers don't go into musical theatre any more. The songs of *Grease* seem stupendous because they have absolutely no competition. This whole subcultural fusion between Lloyd-Webber, gay men who prefer diva melodrama to actual music, pop group tributes, people doing bad Irish dancing and a Broadway machine that makes money out of busloads of easily impressed out-of-town tourists has dispensed with the art of the musical and the compositional genius of the whole Gershwin/Porter aesthetic; ergo, all music for musicals is now utter dross. Sorry to sound like a snob, but, when it comes to pop culture I am, what with being a child of Bowie and Tamla Motown.

So, in those unavoidable dross stakes, *Hairspray*'s score isn't a total dog. Maybe half a dachshund, or a small labradoodle.

Oh yeah ... nearly forgot this *Hairspray*'s biggest mistake. Zac Efron. Yeuch.

But any movie that unleashes John Travolta's feminine side, let's the sainted Chris Walken and Alison Hanney be funny, and makes a connection between the great civil rights marches and musical teen comedy is doing something very, very right. The *Hairspray* remake is a funny, morally crusading celebration of fatness, blackness, rock 'n' roll style, teenage romance, integration, cross-dressing, the working class and the world-changing potential of boundless youth optimism, which, give or take Tottenham Hotspur and Thornton's Caramel Shortbreads, may be the very best things on Earth. Try doing as I did and watch it straight *after* Lee Daniels's extraordinary *Precious* (see p. 477). The themes – skin colour, body shape, food, race, class, a plump girl's fantasies about celebrity – are strangely interchangeable. *Precious* shows you the pain. *Hairspray* gives you the pleasure.

★ ★

JUNO

2007

Starring: Ellen Page, Michael Cera, Jennifer Garner, Jason Bateman, Alison Janney, JK Simmons, Olivia Thirlby
Dir.: Jason Reitman

Plot: The best teen screenplay ever written.
Key line: 'At school people are grabbing on my belly all the time . . . it's crazy. I'm a legend. They call me The Cautionary Whale.'

I've just been writing about multiple perspectives in the entry for *Elephant*, so, if it's OK with you, I'm going to stick with that for a minute. *Juno* is obviously an enormous movie in recent teen cinema, and, like most every smart, sophisticated work of art, parts of it may look very different to different people.

I've just watched *Juno* for the umpteenth time with my wife Linsay, and as soon as it was over, she expressed her surprise at how she felt about a specific scene. It's the one where Juno visits Mark Loring, the thirtysomething prospective adoptive father of her unborn baby, having bonded with him for months over shared tastes in classic guitars, alternative rock, slasher movies and ironic sarcasm. His wife Vanessa is out.

Mark has just shown Juno an obscure Japanese comic about a pregnant superhero, which makes her feel 'way less of a fat dork'. She is educating the older man in her music tastes, and instructs him to put on 'All The Young Dudes' by Mott The Hoople. It was written by David Bowie and it's kind of a power ballad. They begin to slow-dance, awkwardly, jokily. He looks down at his hands around her huge belly and cracks the 'Does it feel like there's something between us?' gag. She keeps looking vulnerably into his eyes. She holds him closer and rests her head on his chest, and she looks peaceful, and so does he, and they look like a couple. The scene is charged with sexual tension . . . which will be entirely broken seconds later, but we'll come back to that.

For me, having seen the film before, this scene is now about the one character in the movie who I don't like, and his deluded, sleazy, mid-life crisis imaginings of starting over with a barely legal shag bunny. I think that the first time I watched it, and had no idea where the scene or the characters were headed, I was just covering my eyes and silently screaming, 'NOOOOOO!!!'

But Linsay, even after knowing exactly where Mark is heading in just a few seconds, is in a very different place in the scene. She is remembering being around 16, and the first times older men showed an interest in her, and how exciting that was when you were practising to be a woman. She finds the scene sexy.

This says something important about why *Juno* is such an extraordinary movie, and the part talented collaborators from different places play in that process. Director Jason Reitman (son of *Ghostbusters* director Ivan) did the relatively unusual thing of insisting that screenwriter Diablo Cody was on set throughout the entire making of the movie. At every turn he would consult Cody and star Ellen Page about the tone of each scene. His reasoning was simple: 'I've never been a 16-year-old girl.'

It also perhaps explains why *Juno* became a hot topic in abortion-obsessed America. Pro-lifers were quick to claim it as a pro-life movie, because Juno MacGuff initially intends to terminate her pregnancy, goes to the clinic, hates the place and decides to go through with the pregnancy but give her child up for adoption. I'm going to assume that these were similar people to those who claimed that the documentary *March Of The Penguins* was actually a pro-family values polemic because people and penguins have so much in common, and therefore didn't notice that this movie's only anti-abortion activist is a comedy teen Asian on anti-depression meds holding a sign that says, 'No Babies Like Murdering', and that when Juno walks into the clinic, the bored girl at the desk is required to say: 'Welcome to Women Now where women are trusted friends. Please put your hands where I can see them and surrender any bombs.'

The controversy became more serious when a story broke in June 2008 that, in Gloucester High School in Massachusetts, 18 girls had fallen pregnant within one school year amidst allegations of a 'pregnancy pact'. Despite none of the girls going on record about having watched *Juno*, and their denial of a pact, the media attached the phrase 'The *Juno* Effect' to the story. New soundbite, old problem.

So, while accepting that there is definitely something about *Juno* that encourages people to see crucial themes from their own subjective viewpoint, I'm going to ignore everyone else and decide what is objectively true, because I'm just that kind of patriarchal oppressor. The key scene, for me, is where Juno's Christian stepmother Bren (Janney) roasts the ultrasound technician who dares to make a judgemental comment to Juno about 'poisonous' teenage mothers. Pro-life and pro-choice are not the issue here. The issue is that the pregnant teen can't win. Dehumanised as bone-thick benefit scroungers if they choose to give birth, as amoral sluts if they don't, its no surprise that people with obsessive agendas believe they have the right to project their neuroses on to people they don't see as people, but 'problems'. Juno MacGuff makes that most disrespected and unwanted of sub-species, the single teenage bearer of an 'unwanted' child, into a living, breathing, human being. No wonder we're confused.

Because *Juno* obliterates almost every archetype established by even the most complex and satisfying of our previous teen movies. A Christian stepmother who is not a witch. A working-class father (Simmons) who is happy in his life and a naturally progressive and supportive father. A teen romantic lead (the wonderful Cera) who is both a geek and athletic, and neither emotionally crippled nor a total sap. A middle-class couple who are neither role models nor snobs. A best friend (the fabulous Thirlby) who is kinda bitchy but not a bitch, sexually active (heh – Juno would hate me for using that phrase) but not a slut, and not interested in whether she's popular or not. A story where what you think you know about a character is constantly turned on its head, because people are rarely predictable. And, of course, the most rootin'est-tootin'est, classless and issue-free, ballsy yet vulnerable, fearless but scared of what any woman is scared of, teen character in movie history who also made the dumbest mistake that any 16-year-old girl could make. *Juno* bluntly refuses to accept that anything in this world is exactly as it seems, or that any character – and especially a pregnant teenage girl – is tied to any one viewpoint or form of behaviour.

The last thing Juno MacGuff is is a symbol of all teen mothers, not because teenage girls aren't like her, but because *nobody*'s like her. She is an entirely singular character – as unlikely, in her authentic way, as Napoleon Dynamite (see p. 432) or *Rushmore*'s Max Fischer (see p. 360) – through which Cody gets to present a set of What Ifs about unplanned youth pregnancy. As Cody says on one of the documentary shorts on the *Juno* DVD, she didn't talk like Juno MacGuff when she was 16. Juno is how we would all love to think we would deal with teenage with the knowledge – and sparkling wit – we have acquired since. Cody even calls Juno 'my hero', with a neat bit of unconscious double meaning.

Adults loved *Juno* as much as teens, and, for us, the characters who *are* poignantly real are Vanessa and Mark Loring (Garner and Bateman). Not only have we met them hundreds of times, but we see ourselves in them when we're being honest with ourselves. Vanessa is the successful but not outstanding career woman whose biological clock has struck 'BONG!!!' like an H-bomb and, in preparation for the moment that she believes will give her life meaning, has already allowed herself to become the all-purpose party-pooping neurotic mom she never set out to be. Mark is the man-child who plays the role of her pussy-whipped child with enthusiasm because it provides him with the psychological get-out clause for the moment when his disappointment with life and resentment of adult commitment will finally force him to fully embrace his clichéd mid-life crisis while blaming 'er indoors. Their funny but ultimately very sad journey from fake perfect marriage to inevitable dissolution is the real cautionary tale about marrying substitutes for parents and children. Their arc is brilliantly written, as we are encouraged to fall in love with Mark, for his bluff sense of humour, childlike sensibilities, cool taste in music and film and comics, and ability to relate to Juno without being intimidated or nonplussed by her apparent refusal to take any situation seriously. And we hate Vanessa because she is the essence of our view of the neurotic, needy, controlling and humourless middle-class woman who makes everyone uncomfortable. But Vanessa's need to be a mother is real, and her respect for what Juno is doing utterly genuine, while Mark is faking his way through arrested development to hide the fact that he is a passive-aggressive bully, reluctant to be a father because he is still living a fantasy of rock bands, bachelor pads and 16-year-old girlfriends who can't see him for the fraud that he is. Mark is too deluded about his youthfulness and flattered by Juno's attention to understand that her flirting is just the mix of the bored playing-at-adulthood that 16-year-olds do and a need for some comfort in the situation she is in. Bateman's face when Juno simply says, 'But you're old!' is a revelatory mirror for any guy who has fallen for a fantasy of being a boy again.

The way Cody and Reitman turn our understanding of Mark and Vanessa on its head with two set pieces is superb. A scene where Mark is coldly mocking Vanessa's need to decorate the baby's room, and the pivotal moment where Juno and Vanessa bump into each other in the mall and Vanessa finally feels the baby kick, are moments so entirely adult and so far out of the normal remit of teen comedies they are beamed in from another world entirely.

Other great *Juno* things: The lo-fi indie-punk sound world featuring Kimya Dawson and her band Moldy Peaches, Belle And Sebastian and even Buddy Holly, where love songs completely disconnect from sex and embody a childlike view of perfect romantic and innocent love; a knowing aesthetic invented by Mo Tucker's 'I'm Sticking With You', as performed by The Velvet Underground in direct opposition to their songs of heroin addiction and sado-masochistic sex, and also featured in *Juno* (the soundtrack album was an unlikely American No. 1).

The line-drawing animation in the opening credits, which firmly places the film in the same left-field graphic novel universe as *Ghost World*.

The way Reitman makes us follow Juno, tight to her shoulder from behind, as she always seems to be walking against a crowd.

The sheer genius of Paulie Bleeker emerging from his home, resplendent in his too-small, too-geeky athletics gear, to find Juno sitting in an armchair fake-smoking a pipe on his front lawn where she has arranged an impromptu living room including a tiger rug from someone's discarded furniture.

The genius of Michael Cera, a man who exists to disprove the theory that you can't trust a guy who eyes are too close together, and the slight worry that he is destined to be forever playing adorable man-children.

And, of course, Ellen Page. No matter how extraordinary Cody's screenplay is – and especially as a debut screenwriter whose previous experience was writing a blog about her experiences as a former stripper – *Juno* could not have worked without Page's intelligence, charisma and uncanny ability to tone down every emotion so that a potentially unbelievable and obnoxious character becomes utterly real and utterly admirable in every possible way. Page has taken the playing of a teenager to a whole new level in *Juno*, and every subsequent attempt is going to have to deal with Juno MacGuff looking over their shoulder, whispering, 'Hey, yeah ... I'm just calling to procure a hasty abortion.'

* *

SUPERBAD

2007
Starring: Jonah Hill, Michael Cera, Christopher Mintz-Plasse, Seth Rogan, Bill Hader, Emma Stone, Martha MacIsaac
Dir.: Greg Mottola

Plot: Teen cinema's funniest Bromantic comedy.
Key line: 'I mean, just imagine that girls weren't weirded out by our boners and stuff and just, like, wanted to see them. That's the world I one day wanna live in.'

The story goes that Evan Goldberg and Seth Rogan wrote the screenplay for *Superbad* between the ages of 13 and 15. I can't help feeling slightly intimidated and disturbed that real boys talked to each other like this. But then, this is perhaps why *Superbad* is America's most commercially successful teen comedy ever; perhaps teenage boys of today really do talk to each other about the intricacies of their taste in pornography before confessing how much they love each other. Man ... if things had been that open between boys when I was a nipper, how much less fucked up would I be?

Superbad is the high watermark of this thing we now call 'Bromance'; movies that suggest that a man really can be deeply and sincerely in love with his best friend without it meaning he is a latent homosexual. Despite the Olympian smut, slapstick humour and overload of pure belly laughs, at its heart, *Superbad* is a teen break-up movie. But the unhappy couple are a loud, chubby boy with a Jew-fro and his odd skinny friend with the strangely angelic face and a shapeless hoodie.

Superbad steals a basic structure from the winning formulas of

American Graffiti (see p. 135) and *Dazed And Confused* (see p. 307) and blends it with the male quest to lose virginity that drives *American Pie* (see p. 371). The action takes place over one day and night, and revolves around what the principals see as the last chance to party before the end of their high school years. Despite being nerdish outsiders, Seth (Hill) and Evan (Cera) have wangled an invite to the house party being thrown by the very cute Jules (Stone), who Seth would dearly love to cop off with. Evan's equally adorable crush object Becca (MacIsaac) is also going to be there. But Seth is a self-loathing product of the rules of teen hierarchy whereby a fat kid can't possibly hook up with a princess unless she is so drunk she doesn't know what she's doing. The problem of how to buy booze when you're under-age is theoretically solved by über-nerd Fogell (Mintz-Plasse), who has got himself a fake ID. The problem is that, for reasons known only to himself, he has made himself 25 years old and renamed himself McLovin. Not Something McLovin. Just McLovin. The film then becomes a quest to get alcohol in the face of over-whelming odds, which splits the three of them up and casts them adrift in a drunk and violent adult world they are not equipped to deal with.

The backdrop to all this gunplay, getting run over, thuggish party hosts in Brazilian football shirts, drunk women without sanitary towels and insane comedy policemen is that Evan has successfully applied to Dartmouth College and is about to leave the academically challenged Seth behind. And what makes it worse is that Fogell has got into Dartmouth too and he and Evan are going to room together. Seth is consumed by jealousy and fear of a future without the crutch he has been leaning on throughout his high school years, hence his sexual panic.

The title comes from a James Brown record and the comedy is played out to a soundtrack packed with blaxploitation-era funk classics mixed with classic rock and underground hip hop. The juxtaposition with these three sloppily-dressed whiter-than-white geeks and their wiggerisms is perfect.

The sight gags are great, particularly Fogell/McLovin's attempt to buy booze in the middle of a hold-up, Seth's flashback to a boyhood obsession with drawing male genitalia and the most inept police chase in movie history. But all the biggest laughs come from dialogue about sex that breaks right through the puerile and into the surreal. Particular favourites are:

Seth: 'Mama's making a pubie salad! I need some Seth's Own dressing ... I'll be the Iron Chef of pounding vadge!'

Seth again: 'What, do you think Becca's gonna be psyched that you brought a bottle of lube? Oh Evan! Thank you for bringing that lube for my pussy! I never would've been able to handle your fucking four-inch dick inside my pussy without that gigantic bottle of *loooobe*!'

Crazy cop Officer Michaels, played by Rogan himself: 'This job isn't how shows like *CSI* make it out to be. When I first joined the force, I assumed there was semen on everything, and there was some, like, huge semen database that had every bad guy's semen in it. There isn't. That doesn't exist. I dream of a world where everything is covered in semen.'

And his partner Officer Slater, played by the Jim Carrey-esque Hader: 'On my wedding night we had group sex. I wasn't involved in it. But I could hear it through the wall.'

The only joke that jars is the bit where a woman dirty-dances with Seth at a party and leaves him with a menstrual blood stain on his trousers. This feels beamed in from all those misogynist frat-boy comedies that hide their fear of women behind sexist abuse. The big strength of Rogan, Goldberg and producer Judd Apatow's best Bromances – *Knocked Up*, *The 40-Year-Old Virgin* – is that honesty about buddy love doesn't come at the expense of womankind. For a few unfortunate minutes they are remaking *Porky's* here, and it doesn't sit well with the basic decency at *Superbad*'s heart.

After 70 minutes of inspired stoopidity, *Superbad* changes tack entirely and becomes poignant. The boys get to the party, and in various states of drunkenness and anger with each other, couple up with their various objects of desire. And what they find is that the girls, unknown to them or us, are going through exactly the same insecurities and booze-related coping mechanisms.

Our two heroes have total disasters involving vomit and headbutts. It's Fogell that's getting along just fine until our doofus cops bust in. ('We just cock-blocked McLovin! We're supposed to be guiding his cock, not blocking it.') We get the only moment ever where a policeman brutalises a teen and you want to cheer, and our dumbass cops even make time to set fire to a cop car, for no good reason except that every boy wants to do it.

Time for the audacious scene. Seth and Evan get into bed with each other – OK, two sleeping bags on the floor – and tell each other that they love each other, and hold each other. There is no *Friends*-style undercutting, where our boys suddenly realise what this looks like, and jump apart, coughing and faking deeper voices. In fact, the scene goes further as they wake up the next morning and react to each other in the way any of us might if we'd had drunken sex and weren't sure how our bedmate felt about it in the cold light of day. A debate rages as to whether Seth and Evan had some kind of sex ... but I prefer to think not. They love each other and the idea that that has to be consummated undercuts the entire point of the movie. Besides, the best kind of sexual tension is the unresolved kind.

The pair go to the mall. There is a gently funny scene – playing on the gay subtext – where Seth tries on trousers and asks Evan to pass judgement on how they look, posing away ludicrously and flagging up the delights of 'male cameltoe'. They bump into Becca and Jules, and the four discuss and apologise for the drunken disasters of the previous night. Evan and Seth pair up with the girls, trying to appear casual about saying goodbye to each other. It's here that it starts to hit you that every display of neediness you've seen has come from Seth, and that Evan has been trying to cut the cord and move away from Seth from the outset of the movie. He immediately turns his attention towards Becca, and it's Seth who is looking back, his face a memorable mask of longing and fear. You do start to gather the evidence: the meat-and-two-veg drawing obsession; the constant insistence that he's the most hetero man in the world; Seth carrying Evan out of the party like Richard Gere carrying Debra Winger in *An Officer And A Gentleman*. Seth and Jules disappear into the crowd at the mall as Curtis Mayfield sings the words 'Love is strange'. Blub.

Which suggests that, even as a budding teenage writer, Seth Rogan was showing extraordinary amounts of vulnerability to his friend Evan. The poignancy is genuine, and Hill's loss and terror sticks with you after the credits roll.

But, in the final analysis, comedies are judged by how much they make you laugh, rather than how honestly they shine a light on the pain of coming of age. And, for me, *Superbad* is, pound-for-pound, the funniest teen comedy of all.

★ ★

TEETH

2007

Starring: Jess Weixler, John Hensley, Hale Appleman, Josh Pais,
Lenny Von Dohlen
Dir.: Mitchell Lichtenstein

Plot: The Vagina Dentata Monologues.
Key line: 'We found this imbedded in the penile stump.'

There is, apparently, a dark legend about female sexuality that dates
back thousands of years. It concerns 'Vagina Dentata' ... the presence of teeth inside female genitalia. Writer/director Mitchell Lichtenstein takes this ancient terror of the womb and runs with it, all
the way to the recent American phenomenon of abstinence groups,
whereby children are encouraged, by the usual means of bullying-
by-shame familiar to anyone who has been touched by the sickness
that is organised religion, to promise not to have sex before marriage.
Utilising an aesthetic that mingles the whimsical artfulness of current
'indie' film with the body horror of David Cronenberg and the 'dark
underbelly of the suburbs' surrealism of David Lynch, *Teeth* is a
modern feminist classic and a social satire to make you squirm.
Especially if you're a guy, obviously. Hell ... if you're a man crazy
enough to watch this and *Hard Candy* (see p. 435) in quick succession
you'll be going to your bed that night in a chastity belt and pants
made of Kevlar.

Teeth clamps its jaws around Dawn O'Keefe (Weixler), a fresh-
faced blonde clean teen who is local spokesperson for The Promise,
an abstinence group who aim to stop all teens having healthy hormonal release and symbolise their agenda with – ha! – a red ring. She
has a few immediate problems, though. Mom is sick. Everyone at
school hates her, understandably, except perhaps her teachers who
are so fucked up by conservative school boards and female sexuality
that they cover up the photos of pussies in text books and can't say
the word 'vulva', and one apparently normal boy, Bill (Von Dohlen),
who has the perfectly normal hots for Dawn, despite the fact that she

draws pictures of wedding dresses during Sex Ed, and who has no problems whatsoever saying vulva in class.

Plus Dawn is getting unwanted gooey thoughts and feelings about Tobey (Appleman), a boy in The Promise group. And her mirror-image stepbrother Brad (Hensley) is a mutton-chopped, tattooed, misogynist sex punk waving his satanic music and kinky sex life right in poor Dawn's face, even when she is doing chaste embroidery in her fluffy pink bedroom. He is also, when not fucking girls up the arse and trying to make them eat dog biscuits, madly in semi-incestuous love/lust with Dawn and is already missing the top of a finger from an inappropriate attempt to play house when the two were small children and their parents first got together. As I said, all this secret perversity amidst the blue skies and freshly sprinkled lawns of this suburban milieu is totally Lynchy. Dennis Hopper was presumably busy, so trouble in paradise is represented by two huge chimney stacks that loom over the town belching black smoke into the otherwise fragrant air.

The Promise land involves much self-sacrifice. When these teens go to the movies, they can't even go into a PG-13 picture because of the 'heavy making out'. So cultural life is entirely comprised of family-oriented cartoons. *Teeth* is about lots of anti-Bible Belt stuff, but one of its themes is the belief, among the reactionary, that temptations to be 'bad' will not occur if you don't look or listen to anything, what with things like sex, violence and hedonism being unnatural in some way, and only planted in us by a debased liberal culture. Unfortunately, Tobey must have missed this psychological memo because, as the cartoons honk away, he is looking at Dawn as if she is food. In fact, it becomes increasingly obvious that The Promise kids and adults talk about absolutely nothing *but* sex, under the guise of pretending to avoid it.

As we journey towards the gory inevitable, Lichtenstein has much fun with phallic belching chimneys, vaginal holes in trees and creationist heckling during science lessons about creatures who suddenly evolve nasty mutations for protection. Meanwhile, Dawn is having rule-breaking wedding-themed wank fantasies that feature slobbering monster mouths where her orgasms ought to be. Everyone who saw *Teeth* knew what the USP was before entering, so Lichtenstein has to make the build-up suspenseful, poignant and very, very funny, without letting his cast get all slapstick or ironic, thereby both depoliticising the movie and undercutting the scary. He does so, quite brilliantly.

In keeping with the beauty/beast thematic contrasts, the horror kicks off in the most beautiful setting possible. Dawn and Tobey give in to temptation and meet for a swim-date in a sun-dappled woodland lake complete with caves and waterfalls. 'This does not feel wrong at all,' Tobey whispers as they kiss, and how could it, immersed in water, blessed by warmth, alone in paradise? Teen romance really is great, isn't it? Teen sex, though: *that* can be more problematic. The pair move out of the warmth and light of the lake and into the cold darkness of a cave. Bad move. Tobey makes a smooth transition from gambolling innocent to rapist to man looking at his own detached penis lying in a pool of blood on a rock, like a big stillborn slug. He screams a lot. So does she. And who can blame them?

From there, *Teeth* is an absorbing trip through the extraordinary performance of Ms Weixler, who plays the horror for laughs and the feminism straight as she journeys from peppy *ingénue* to shocked victim to horny slut to cynical castrator without missing a beat; a scene at a gynaecologist's surgery (a memorable turn from Josh Pais as the Doctor From Hell) which manages to encompass both every male and female nightmare imaginable, self-mocking *Buffy*esque supernaturalisms; a wonderfully inappropriate seduction complete with comedy sex toy, much post-*But I'm A Cheerleader* (see p. 367) savaging of conservative American values; the usual Bad Dad replaced by one motherfucker of a Bad Son; the ultimate revenge for every one of those we-made-a-bet-I-could-shag-you plot clichés; and awe-inspiring grossness involving cocks being fucked by crabs and eaten by dogs.

Yet, somehow, *Teeth* finds a way to be a celebration of budding female sexuality and, thanks to the luminously beautiful Weixler, a genuinely erotic one. Lichtenstein's ability to lurch from one mood to its extreme opposite is unique, and probably only possible for directors who are shooting their own scripts. He knows exactly what he's trying to say, and how to say it, and there isn't a moment of bad faith or throwaway flippancy here.

Basically . . . if you repress natural things in young women in order to feed your own hypocritical and perverted misanthropy, you are going to lose something precious in a very painful way. Having made its point, *Teeth* ends exactly as it should: with a wave goodbye to those phallic chimneys, a young woman transformed into a mean motherfucking angel of penis death, and a dirty old man who's bitten off way more than he can chew. One last gleeful chuckle from the most original teen slasher movie of its day.

★ ★

THE CLASS

2008

Starring: François Bégaudeau, Franck Keita, Esmeralda Ouertani, Rachel Regulier, Boubacar Toure
Dir.: Laurent Cantet

Plot: The Parisian *Blackboard Jungle*.
Key line: 'Young people now have no shame.'

The Class is a very different kind of high school movie. Shot in stripped-down documentary style, it follows one school year in a rough, ethnically mixed school in Paris through the eyes of one French teacher and one class that he teaches. It is based on a semi-autobiographical novel by teacher François Bégaudeau, who also stars in the movie and co-wrote the screenplay. Its unknown cast and shaky, voyeuristic camerawork make the film feel entirely improvised, although it isn't. But the principal teens are ordinary high school kids, mainly using their own names and asked to improvise around specific characters from Bégaudeau's novel *Entre les murs* (which is also the French title of the movie and translates as 'Between These Walls'). It gained a Best Foreign Language Film Oscar nomination and won the Palme d'Or at Cannes; the first French film to do so since 1987. It blows away everyone who sees it but not enough people have, due to its absence of superheroes, icebergs and boys jumping into pits of shit. You come out of the film feeling like someone sent you back to school for a week, so accurately does it capture the tensions of the inner-city classroom.

The opening scenes point out that teachers are more similar to pupils than we imagine. The new ones are welcomed to the school by the old ones in an encounter meeting. They are nervous and shy when making their introductions. They assemble in a classroom and chatter amongst themselves as the head hands them folders with their classes for the new year. There is something childlike in their attempts to bond happily before being sent off to struggle, alone, with the unknown. An old hand goes through a list of a new boy's students saying, simply: 'Nice. Nice. Not nice. Nice … She's not nice at all,' and you recall being the new boy in school and having some older kid say exactly the same thing about your list of teachers.

An early exchange in the classroom defines the movie's agenda by pointing out something true and universal and extremely important about teenagers that no other film in this book either notices or cares about in quite the same way. That is, that when we are aged somewhere between 13 and 17, we are much smarter than adults take us for, but in a petty, misguided and massively irritating way.

The class enter the classroom and embark upon a time-honoured first-day-of-school tradition. They chat excitedly to each other in noisy cliques and ignore the teacher François Marin, played by Bégaudeau. He finally gets them to quieten down and launches into a typical teacher gambit about how many minutes of teaching time are lost to pupils refusing to just shut up and focus, and how many minutes of how many hours are lost in a year, and that other schools do a full hour on each lesson and therefore you will end up miles behind. A black girl called Khoumba (Regulier) starts to say something. Marin insists she put her hand up. She does and then points out that each timetabled lesson is actually 55 minutes long and therefore there are no other schools doing hour-long lessons, and Mr Marin is a liar. Marin is temporarily nonplussed, because she is, of course, right, but utterly and deliberately missing the point as only a teenager can. He regains composure and moves on. The camera is positioned throughout as if you are seated at a desk bang in the middle of the order and chaos, and, occasionally, a kid catches your eye and wonders what you're looking at before deciding you are not worth bothering with.

It's this drip-drip-drip of teenage one-upmanship that makes this class memorably real, provides the comic and traumatic moments, makes you like or dislike various characters, gives you a bracing glimpse into the pains of the teaching profession and drives the tale towards its inevitable points of conflict in an organic, anti-cinema way. Plenty of contemporary youth docu-dramas insist that ordinary people are more interesting than sexy film stars pretending to be ordinary people, but then undercut this worthy premise by finding dull people to play dislikeable characters in tales that find no space for hope or optimism. *The Class* is just better film-making driven by a man working from life experience rather than a perverse desire to establish indie credentials by drowning in bleakness. I'm thinking about the worst recent teen movies by Ken Loach (see *Kes*, p. 101), Larry Clark (see *Kids* and *Bully*, pp. 328 and 409) and Shane Meadows, as well as those by professional misery guts like Peter Mullan, Hal Hartley and Michael Haneke.

The story develops around Marin, charismatic Tunisian tough girl Esmeralda (Ouertani), Khoumba, classic back-of-the-class hip hop-informed bad boy Souleymane (Keita) and his waggish mate Boubacar (Toure). Bégaudeau's Marin is a great, real, noble but flawed character. He is trying to do the right thing but is often defeated by both the weight of colonial history and inner-city social exclusion, as well as his own ego. Like his students, he's not quite as bright as he thinks he is. The kids amuse themselves by drawing him into pointless debates, pretending that they don't understand basic phrases (shades of *The Blackboard Jungle*, see p. 20) or taking issue with his choice of words for contrived racial reasons, and they 'wipe him out' constantly because he just can't resist trying to be the biggest smartarse in the room. Bégaudeau deliberately messes with the viewer's sympathy for him, contrasting the admiration you feel for a man trying to teach French to an ethnically mixed class of kids who happily profess their hatred of France, with scenes in the staff room where he actively discourages other teachers from asking them to study Voltaire because he has no respect for their potential. He swings between the determined and positive and the dangerously jaded and cynical, something which you imagine every teacher must inevitably feel when confronted daily by children who feel that knowledge is somehow irrelevant or even uncool, and who live to be distracted.

But sometimes these kids are genuinely sly and funny, and Marin can't help but be amused. Just like the viewer; although one imagines that enjoyment of the wind-up humour of the kids is dependent on how much you remember being that kid, and whether you enjoyed it at the time, and if part of you has never stopped finding the mocking of authority funny. Despite being an obviously adult film, I still suspect that the young and young-at-heart will derive the most pleasure from *The Class*, and that those who immediately tense up and become irritated by loud teens on the bus will find this movie as grating as nails raked down a blackboard.

This is one of the many reasons why the August 2011 riots in England were so upsetting. The selfish, greedy, mocking nature of the looting and vandalism, the absence of anything amounting to real protest or political engagement, and the news media's constant insistence that the perpetrators were all teenagers (the resulting arrests and court cases proved this was not true), reinforced the ever-widening chasm in Britain between middle-class adults and working-class youth by seeming to prove that the nation's contempt for and fear of 'chavs' (white) and 'hoodies' (black) was entirely justified. Inflicting swingeing economic cuts upon youth services that are desperately needed in key problem areas is going to be easy to justify because conservative adults in those areas will support those cuts. They want revenge. They see the youth underclass as unworthy of help. They insist that they are all the same. The young and the poor are always the first to be hit by the consequences of the economic fuck-ups of the wealthy because voters hate them and it's a no-risk strategy – at least until they start setting fire to things, which is never our fault. We are never culpable. You do it to yourself, you do, and that's what really hurts . . .

Sorry. I should be paying attention at the back of *The Class* and not quoting from Radiohead songs to make hand-wringing liberal points. I see that now. Please continue.

So . . . the kids wind Marin up in class. But sometimes it's not to mock or distract, but to make important points. One of the best scenes in *The Class* involves Marin attempting to teach the kids 'the imperfect subjunctive'. Suddenly, *The Class* is talking directly to those '50s teen movies where other groups of juvenile delinquents were zoning out while Teach attempts to explain 'the subjunctive mood'. There is a conversation that explains why old screenwriters were fond of that joke. Because Marin is standing in front of a group of children whose parents come from other countries and speak different languages, trying to establish the relevance of learning the 'proper' way to speak French when, as Boubacar points out, 'We're not gonna start talking this way in the street. We'll get called stupid!'

We know the relevance, of course. You learn to talk and write the native tongue in the correct way, and all doors to social mobility are open. You might get into college. You will be able to apply and interview well for better jobs. Plus, a world of art and literature will become accessible to you and broaden your horizons, and get you out of a ghetto you didn't ask to be trapped in in the first place. But this is the nub of the crux of social exclusion: if a child's expectations have been set low, and if survival in their area is dependent on taking on the moral codes, dress styles and language of those around them, then the idea that education means movement and movement means choice and choice means fulfilment is as distant as the notion of becoming an astronaut or marrying Bill Gates. The only lessons that seem useful are ones that you can apply right now to get you through the next few days without falling off the edge of the world. The only rewards worth pursuing are immediate and material and symbolic of status, not deferred and dependent on following the agenda of those in power, who speak a different language and are not interested in yours until it pops up in a rap record or an episode of *The Wire*, in which case they'll co-opt it in order to look cool. Without any grandstand speeches or actorly emotings, this modest and strikingly spontaneous scene illuminates the failures of post-imperialist capitalism, the political nature of language, and the reasons a section of our children have no interest in our agenda.

But the downside of a teacher allowing his pupils to express themselves is immediate. Souleymane and Boubacar attempt to humiliate Marin by questioning his sexuality. They do this with low teen cunning, making it sound like an innocent enquiry rather than a challenge to his authority. Marin has to handle the homophobic taunting while remaining a good liberal, and without losing his temper or driving a wedge between himself and his class by just sending Souleymane off to the head. And he does, expertly. But can you imagine dealing with that crap every day when all you want to do is make children's lives a little better? No wonder Bégaudeau felt compelled to write a novel and make a film about his experiences. Someone has to stand up for the teachers as well as the kids. *The Class* does, so deftly that you will leave the film with assumptions about teens and teachers significantly altered.

Despite the heckling, Marin actually does successfully engage most of his students most of the time, although his biggest battle is not with outright hostility, but their inability to concentrate. But war eventually breaks out – in a way familiar to anyone who went to an inner-city state school – in a scene suffused with tension.

The whole class have failed to read a passage from *The Diary Of Anne Frank* for homework. Marin asks one black girl, the usually talkative Khoumba, to read the passage out to the class. She refuses. In seconds this has turned to an accusation of singling her out which is impossible to argue against because, if you ask one kid to do something that none of the classmates has done, you have, in effect, singled them out. If you choose any child, you've 'singled them out', if they're in the mood to take offence. The scene becomes racially charged without anyone having to say the 'R' word. All Marin can do is admit defeat and ask Esmeralda instead. Thankfully, she assents. But you understand how every perfectly reasonable teaching instruction could be the match that lights the blue touch-paper, and how much the children hold the balance of power in this unspoken agreement of education by mutual consent.

Taking his cue from ... *Anne Frank*, Marin asks the class to write their own self-portraits. This is doubly smart screenwriting because the movie never leaves the school, and we're not going to see what's happening at home to make these children so alienated from learning; they are going to have to tell us in their own words.

Of course, the movie's title is a double-edged pun. The class don't believe that Marin – or anyone of his class – is really interested in their lives, or understands what it's like to feel ashamed of where you come from or how you look. One Arab kid, Rabah (Rabah Nait Oufella), memorably dismisses the entire French middle class as 'camemberters' – people who stink of expensive cheese. But then he confesses that he believes, when all is said and done, that they are better than him and he doesn't deserve to be in their company. This is said and shot without sentimentality – this is a movie with no incidental music and no cinematic tricks employed to tell you how to feel – and is quietly devastating while still acknowledging the comic stoicism of working-class youth. Marin asks him if his exclusion from this party thrown by camemberters was 'a race thing'. 'I dunno,' the boy replies, smiling sourly, 'but the crisps were bacon-flavoured.'

The big problem in class is Souleymane, who refuses to express himself on the printed page. He likes photography, though, so Marin encourages him to produce a diary in pictures. And it's all going so well, in an encouraging-alienated-kid's-potential sort of way ... until it isn't. Because *The Class* isn't *Dangerous Minds* or *Freedom Writers* – or *To Sir, With Love* (see p. 90), for that matter – and a nice middle-class person isn't going to tame the savages with some peppy attitude and high-fives. Souleymane's rage is a done deal. And it has to find a release eventually. Meanwhile, a new kid arrives, Marin allows himself to be goaded into an insult that threatens his career, a child's mother is threatened with deportation, kids really do learn stuff and it ends with a football match ... a game in the no man's land of the playground to signal a temporary ceasefire between school and children.

The Class is a wonderful, important film. So, when the inevitable happens, and *Stranded At The Drive-In* becomes the most celebrated and discussed international best-seller of its day, and I am suddenly thrust into the media spotlight as an expert on youth, and David Cameron invites me on to the government anti-looter task force, and, at the first meeting, I'm asked for my opinions about youth and social exclusion, I shall, of course, be humble. I'll decline to make a speech and instead whip out a laptop and show them a DVD of this film. And when it's finished and they look at me, and say, 'Well ... thank you, Garry. That was a most enjoyable contemporary update on the French tradition of neo-realist classroom movies with many haunting and credible things to say about schools and ethnic minorities. But you've surely missed the point. We need answers. This film doesn't have any. At least, no easy ones ...'

Then I will smile sagely, pack my laptop away in my spiffy retro Gola bag, sigh, say, 'Thank you for your time,' and walk out of the room, swishing the tails of my long black coat behind me glamorously but tastefully, leaving them to ponder my meaning. Which will be that you can't wave a magic wand and save us from marauding gangs of feral youth if your only agenda is sticking your pasty tongue up the back passage of anyone stupid enough to vote for your worthless public school arse, you cunt. You have to do the hard and thankless work of beginning to get to grips with generations of capitalism's fuck-ups concerning imperialism, colonialism, social inequality and an obsession with state education as nothing more than a mechanised production line spitting out obedient and terrified wage slaves. And it won't be solved in your lifetime, never mind in time to win you the next election and a post-politics advisory seat on the board of News Corp, but if you start now then maybe our great-grandchildren might live in a better world than this one.

And that, of all the movies in this book that have something to say about the not-at-all-new phenomenon of juvenile delinquency, *The Class* is the truest. Because no one really wins the day. It's not a game.

★ ★

TWILIGHT

2008

Starring: Kristen Stewart, Robert Pattinson, Billy Burke
Dir.: Catherine Hardwicke

Plot: 'About three things I was absolutely positive. First, Edward was a vampire. Second, there was a part of him, and I didn't know how dominant that part might be, that thirsted for my blood. And third, I was unconditionally and irrevocably in love with him.'
Key line: 'What if I'm not the hero? What if I'm the bad guy?'

Twilight is a nigh-on perfect example of the teen movie genre. On the surface, it is about a teenage girl who falls in love with a vampire. But it's really about how teenage girls cope (or don't cope) with sexual awakening, divorced parents, distant fathers, moving to a new area, small towns, settling in at intimidating new schools – and the irresistible allure of the weird but beautiful outsider boy that your parents warned you against.

It also, like much contemporary teen fiction and all contemporary teen horror, owes much of its scenario to the *Buffy The Vampire Slayer* TV show. As with *Buffy*, we are immediately introduced to a pretty, witty but slightly strange teenage girl – Kristen Stewart as Bella Swan – who has moved to a small town with a single parent, appears to be suspicious of her new schoolmates, and seems to be guarding some kind of dark secret. Admittedly, there is no (in)convenient 'hellmouth' in the wet Washington State community of Forks and, this time around, the vampires are sitting next to our heroine in class and treating her at the local hospital rather than hanging out in the local cemetery. This allows screenwriter Melissa Rosenberg, director Catherine Hardwicke and the author of the *Twilight* novel Stephanie Meyer to play so successfully with the universally understood phenomenon of the deathlessly pale goth/emo boy who fills every girl at his school with either fascination or repulsion that *Twilight* became a global teen obsession and its star, the improbably cheekbone-alicious Robert Pattinson, an international pin-up.

But, unlike *Buffy*, *Twilight* is not interested in many of the stereotypes – jock, nerd, rich bitch, bully – that have defined the teen fiction genre since *Carrie* (see p. 150). In *Twilight*, the key conflicts are within the wan and colourless Bella, rather than inflicted upon her by Bad Kids or Nasty Authority. And the key conflict is: when gripped by first pangs of uncontrollable lust for someone obviously dangerous – does a nice girl do it or not? It's the dilemma that dominates every young woman's growing pains, way beyond the loss of virginity. *Twilight* goes all out to make the dilemma as exotic, erotic, terrifying and beautiful as it can.

So who cares if all the boys at school fancy Bella despite her sickly demeanour and obvious shyness, and the girls are too sweet and friendly to mind? The movie wastes less than ten minutes on this irrelevant stuff before Bella and Edward are being hit by tidal waves of metaphorical sexual desire masquerading as supernatural bloodlust. Their first class together involves Edward holding his nose and glaring at poor Bella while she wonders if she smells – and if that isn't a universal teen nightmare, I don't know what is.

But it isn't long before Edward is saving Bella by stopping a skidding van with his bare hands, and now *Twilight* is making a strong fist of being the ultimate teen girl wish-fulfilment fantasy. The boy is tall, thin, beautiful, mysterious, deep, slightly threatening, seemingly obsessed with you ... and he's a superhero to boot!

The direction is delightfully composed and elegant. The script and story spare and strong. The special effects occasionally magical. But *Twilight*'s success as a benchmark youth phenomenon is all about Stewart and Pattinson and a sexual chemistry that stands comparison with the old-school romantic leads of the Golden Age. As potential predator and willing potential victim, the pair have to get the tone exactly right to avoid questionable taste in paranoid times, and they do so, effortlessly, through finding an entirely recognisable kind of teenage awkwardness – an adorable fumbling towards the inevitable.

I mean, forget being a teen; when the object of your irrational lust pulls you aside and mumbles into your ear, 'If you were smart, you'd stay away from me', isn't that just red rag plus bull to the power of

ten? Edward Cullen is a very wry post-occult obsession update of
Brando in *The Wild One* (see p. 13) and Dean in *Rebel Without A
Cause* (see p. 28) – the hot rebel boy who knows exactly how to make
himself vulnerable enough to get the nice girl to fall for him.

The most unusual thing about *Twilight* is its very deliberate, almost
satirical contempt for conventional teen life. Whereas *Buffy* and
movies like *Clueless* (see p. 332) and *Cruel Intentions* (see p. 363) use
their high concepts to submerge themselves in the detail of real teen
life, taking the warp and weft of everyday adolescence into the realms
of heady metaphor, *Twilight* treats the predictable dating and prom
concerns of Bella's friends as annoying distraction from the supernatural life she has accidentally stumbled upon. When two of her
friends go to buy dresses for the prom, Bella goes along so she can
go to an occult bookshop and research the possible origins of her
weirdo lust object. She barely manages to even feign interest in
what, to her friends, is a clothing choice they'll remember well into
adulthood ... a vital rite of passage. Edward makes a very knowing
reference to the rite-of-passage thing in a prom scene that goes
through every prom night cliché at hyperspeed before our altogether
superior couple take one last look around at normality – and
skedaddle.

We never truly find out why Bella is so odd and distracted even
before Edward appears, and it seems as if she has been waiting
around her whole life for something undead to come along. While
most teen fiction elevates teen obsessions to fall in with the preoccupations of its audience, *Twilight* sneers at high school life and
normality, just like your average gothic youth. The fact that it struck
a chord with so many suggests that we're finally getting bored with
high school stereotypes – and that many more of us want to identify
with the left-field outsider than one might have imagined. It's telling,
at a time when assaults on goth and emo kids have begun to creep
into Western culture again, that the first threat Bella has to deal with
isn't from vampires or from the equally supernatural native American
friends of her father, but from pissed white male lads – the American
equivalent of chavs. No surprise that she's saved by Edward ...
although it is a little disappointing that he rescues the damsel in
distress in something as mundane as a flashy mass market car. At
least Angel from the *Buffy* show would have swooped out of the sky,
overcoat a-flailing.

In fact, *Twilight* turns back many of the feminist advances that inspired *Buffy*. It's men (or male creatures) that do the fighting here, and Bella is bashed about by blokes as much as she is buffeted around by her love for Edward. The heroine here spends much of the film literally clinging to her vampire boyfriend. The boys ask the girls to the prom and the girls talk about nothing except boys and clothes. *Twilight* may have some cool bands (and Muse) on the soundtrack and a whole goth-tattoos-and-piercing vibe going on, but its sexual politics is surprisingly old-fashioned when you consider that it was entirely shaped by women.

But all quibbles get swept aside when, around 50 minutes in, the pair finally talk about what Edward is, and he suddenly grabs Bella, and runs with her at impossible speed through imperious trees. *Twilight* gets past the whole vampires-can't-do-daylight thing by almost ignoring it (Edward just glistens, like an angel), and, when the gothic orchestral music rises up and pounds like blood, and Bella clings to her impossible man and leaves the rational world behind, it is one of the most beautiful wish-fulfilment moments in recent film. When Edward says, 'I'm the world's most dangerous predator. Every-thing about me invites you in. My voice, my face, even my smell,' you wonder if he's talking about vampires or pale and beautiful teenage boys.

Twilight doesn't go for laughs *à la Buffy*, but the scene where Edward takes Bella home to meet the vampire folks is the film's subversively witty high point. It's a rich twist on the I'm-so-embar-rassed-by-my-family gag, as Edward grimaces through the awk-wardness of his folks' struggle to not eat his girlfriend, and takes Bella upstairs for a little Debussy and a quick leap through the surrounding treetops. Sex really would be a disappointment at this point and Hardwicke refuses to ruin the literal sweeping of Bella off her feet by having the pair do the soft-focus grab 'n' groan.

But Edward and Bella do attempt sex eventually, only to be thwarted by Edward's symbolic impotence. This is a development nicked from the *Buffy* character Angel. Angel can't have sex because he is cursed to lose his soul every time he experiences 'a moment of perfect happiness' – an orgasm, to you and me. Edward's problem is that the intensity of his bloodlust for Bella means that he can't 'lose control'. Different *deus ex machina*, same metaphor: these perfect tall, dark, handsome and alien lovers can't fuck ... making them even more perfect idol material for young girls who are still frightened of sex ... or frightened that doing it is the end of innocent, emotional love.

And, like Angel, Edward is noble and self-sacrificing and doesn't drink human blood. He fights 'bad' vampires. He listens to classical music and is cultured and somewhat taciturn. But Angel didn't play superhero baseball with his family, mainly because he'd eaten them all in the 18th century. And, of course, Angel and Buffy were equally in debt to earlier teen horror classics, especially *The Lost Boys* and Anne Rice's definitive *Interview With The Vampire*.

Eventually there has to be some proper peril in *Twilight*, and the flight from and battle with psycho vamp James is exciting enough. But not as interesting perhaps, as the only part of normal teen life that *Twilight* does concern itself with. Bella's struggle to connect with her cop dad Charlie (the quietly excellent Billy Burke) forms a moving parallel sub-plot, and the film is revealed as a metaphor about the young female's struggle to understand men, especially men whose strength derives from a macho inability to show their feelings and expose their vulnerabilities.

Charlie is also teen girl wish-fulfilment, a strong, silent man who adores his daughter so much he can't express it, and is only vulnerable to his daughter and her fly-by-night mom, who is travelling America as a baseball groupie. He stays out of Bella's life, but is handsome and adorable and generous and *there*. The perfect father.

But even Dad and an unlikely dream prom can't entirely save Bella. Stewart gives a memorable portrayal of a girl who is just too much in love. Murderous vamps are nowhere near as terrifying to her as the prospect of Edward leaving her. The sequel, *New Moon*, is on its way, and if it's not about the true horror of losing yourself in impossible love, then it will be the most disappointing thing about a movie series that is going to inspire endless rip-offs, many of which will probably not be as good as the *True Blood* TV show.

Twilight is a massively important movie, not least because its two female creators have found a form of highly sexualised teen fiction that doesn't carry a hint of porn or bad faith. It treads a rare line between high school horror flick and art movie, and makes you remember how glorious, and terrible, your first love felt.

★ ★

DOGTOOTH

2009

Starring: Aggeliki Papoulia, Mary Tsoni, Christos Passalis,
Christos Stergioglou, Michelle Valley, Anna Kalaitzidou
Dir.: Yorgos Lanthimos

Plot: An isolated incident.
**Key line: (said by girl after sex with own brother) 'Do that
again, bitch, and I'll rip your guts out. I swear on my
daughter's life that you and your clan won't last long in this
neighbourhood.'**

I should confess off the bat that I have no firm evidence that the
young protagonists/victims of this extraordinary film are actually
teenagers. The family in *Dogtooth* are not given names, nor a back-
story, nor are there any details about age. At least one of the actors,
Aggeliki Papoulia, is well into her thirties but, as we've seen, this has
never been a barrier to playing celluloid teens. The kids look like
young adults, but dress like children from Enid Blyton novels. They
could be in their teens or their twenties.

But *Dogtooth* is so explicitly concerned with the darker dimensions
of 'coming of age' that, for me, it will always be a teen movie. And
no entry in the latter part of this book so exemplifies how far the teen
movie sub-genre has travelled from its roots in trashy exploitation
cinema.

In a leafy suburb in what we assume is contemporary Greece,
three 'teens' live with their parents in a home inside a walled compound. Older Daughter (Papoulia), Younger Daughter (Tsoni) and
Son (Passalis) have never seen the outside world. Father (Stergioglou)
and Mother (Valley) have created an entire alternative universe for
reasons that are never entirely clear, except that Father hates 'bad
influences'. The children are schooled at home and they and their
mother stay within their all mod cons prison while Father goes to
work. They have been raised to believe that they have an older brother
living just outside the compound walls, in grave danger because he

left. And that they will only be able to leave the compound once they have lost a 'dogtooth'.

The parents – or rather, Father, because this is a patriarchal world and Stergioglou is quietly terrifying – have convinced their children that this life is natural using various devious means. The most successful is their subversion of language. Any word that refers to the outside world has its meaning changed to refer to something domestic. 'Phone' becomes 'salt'. 'Sea' becomes 'chair'. And, just for surrealism's sake, 'zombie' becomes 'small yellow flower'. This is largely programmed into the kids using tapes recorded by Father and Mother.

There are two things that Father cannot stop from entering his children's world. One is planes flying overhead; he and Mother have got past this by convincing the children that they are toys. They then leave toy planes around the grounds and whoever finds them gets to keep them as a prize. The children are constantly forced to compete with each other at banal tasks, and the winner gets to do things like choose the evening's entertainment, like watching TV. Of course, standard programming is a no-no; watching TV means watching home videos of the family being happy in the compound. Allowing video is Father's first mistake.

The second involves the other thing Father and Mother can't prevent . . . sexual urges. At least, not in a boy, according to this family. Father deals with this by paying Christina (Kalaitzidou), a security guard at his factory, to come to the compound and have sex with Son. Christina may be so blankly amoral that she's happy to be blindfolded on the journeys there and back and have the worst sex in cinematic history for money. But she has a name, and is from the outside world, and we know early on that she will be the maverick element upon which Father's carefully constructed repression will founder.

But then, this is *Dogtooth*'s speciality. The film is staged with a deliberate, documentary blankness that foreshadows horror and dread at every turn. The actors do not act at all. They move stiffly and deliver their dialogue, which was perfectly described by Roger Ebert in the *Chicago Sun-Times* as 'composed entirely of sentences memorised from tourist phrase books', like robots. When they do move, Lanthimos uses his camera like a still photographer, finding an angle and a distance that looks beautiful but confounds the logic of conventional cinematic storytelling. There is no music at all. The film stock is as grainy you might expect from a movie that cost just €250,000 to make, and the bland interiors contrast sharply with the colourful splendours of the garden and its swimming pool.

Amidst this, the actors are stunning, and especially our three young 'uns. All three seem to ooze a sadness that doesn't know why it's there. The bizarreness of their characters' upbringing forces them to switch between being masochistically passive and sudden bursts of feral violence. And Papoulia's doleful presence is so powerful and androgynous and strangely noble that you know that she will be the one to lead the revolution. But not in any way that one might have predicted.

As I mentioned, the collapse of DadWorld is all that dastardly Christina's fault. Sexually unsatisfied by the functional porkings of Son, Christina persuades Older Daughter to give her head in exchange for a headband. When she tries this trick again, Christina refuses ... unless the dirty girl gives her the videos she has tucked in her bag. When Father and Mother aren't looking, Older Daughter gets her first information about the outside world ... from *Jaws*, *Flashdance* and *Rocky IV*.

Father goes mental, beats Older Daughter over the head with the videos, and even goes round Christina's house and gives her a somewhat physical severance package. So ... who is going to take care of Son's urges now? Who else is there? Father offers both of his daughters to Son, who, after fondling them both in the bath, chooses Older. By now, your skin is crawling right off of your body, and I haven't even mentioned the weird recurring pet motifs, including a brutally slaughtered cat, the kids being forced to get on all fours and bark like dogs, and the moment when the parents inform their offspring that Mother will be giving birth imminently to two children and a pooch. It makes a kind of sense. Trust me.

As you might imagine, being forced to fuck her brother finally sends Older Daughter round the bend. She starts blankly threatening her brother in gangsta-speak. And then comes the Mother And Father's Wedding Anniversary Dance Performance. Oh. My. God.

It begins with the daughters dancing together to Son's Spanish acoustic guitar. And ... it's really hard to paint pictures with words that adequately express why this is so desperately funny and desperately sad. Two thin girls in knee-length pastel dresses shuffle from

side to side while fluttering around with their hands and – and a lot
of this is down to that static camera and the way it feels as if it's
standing slightly too far away because it's horribly embarrassed on
our behalf – it hits home the fact that these young people know
nothing about what young people do, or how they move, or what
they listen to, or even the basic connection between dance and sex.
It's like silent comedy with music, and Papoulia, even from a distance,
has some kind of mournful comic genius Buster Keaton mojo going
on.

But it gets better. She banishes Younger Daughter and takes a
solo, to the same bit of endlessly repeating 'Manuel's Music Of The
Mountains'-type guitar. And where could she possibly have learned
solo dance moves from? Award yourself several gold stars and choose
tonight's entertainment.

Papoulia's tragic-spazztastic interpretation of *Flashdance* will,
eventually, once all those cult movie fans have word-of-mouthed it
all over the planet, become one of the most loved so-wrong-it's-
bloody-brilliant dance scenes, right up there with the line-dance from
Godard's *Bande à Part*, Travolta and Thurman in *Pulp Fiction*, the
warehouse scene from *Footloose* (see p. 251) and Jon Heder's moment
of deathless glory in *Napoleon Dynamite* (p. 432). No description can
do justice to Papoulia's perfect meld of slapstick comedy and pure
heartbreak. Treat yourself and watch it. And if you have, treat yourself
and watch it again.

But the difference between this scene and those other terp-
sichorean delights is that there's nothing much at stake in the movies
they come from. *Dogtooth*'s freaked-out flash dance comes at a point
when you are aching for these three physically and mentally battered
children to escape this parallel universe Bad Dad. Plus, none of them
is followed by a girl battering herself in the mouth with a dumbbell
to remove a dogtooth.

The movie ends with a girl in the trunk of a car and a big, pulsating
question mark. Well, two, actually. The immediate one is whether
our heroine has escaped hell alive. The other, even more haunting
one is: what the motherfuck was *that* all about?

I'm going to go with esteemed *Guardian* film critic Peter Bradshaw
on this one. In his review of *Dogtooth*, he suggested that this dystopian
art masterpiece was really about 'the essential strangeness of something society insists is the benchmark of normality: the family, a

walled city state with its own autocratic rule and untellable secrets'. I reckon he's spot on. Many wondered if the story was inspired by the horror of the 2008 Fritzl case, when a 42-year-old Austrian woman revealed that she had been kept prisoner by her father for 24 years and forced to bear seven of his children. It turned out that the screenplay had been written before the case emerged. But it's impossible to ignore the twisted synchronicity.

What *Dogtooth* undoubtedly is is one of those movies that hypnotises you with extraordinary visual technique and dark imagination, until you come out the other end, blinking in the sunlight of what we like to call 'the real world' and wondering why you've just been so compelled by something that didn't happen and you hope never has and never will. It has something vital to say about how hard every human has to strive to escape the influence of our parents, even when we were lucky enough to have nice ones, and something sneakily uplifting to say about how the free expression of cinema can defeat the best efforts of an oppressive regime to suppress information and desire. And you'll definitely never watch *Flashdance* in quite the same way ever again.

★ ★

PRECIOUS

2009

Starring: Gabourey Sidibe, Mo'Nique, Paula Patton, Mariah Carey, Lenny Kravitz
Dir.: Lee Daniels

Plot: The ultimate 'there but for the grace of God' teen movie. Key line: 'Please don't lie to me, Ms Rain. Love ain't done nothin' for me. Love beat me. Raped me. Called me an animal. Make me feel worthless. Make me sick.'

I use my emotional, visceral reactions to a song or a film in order to write. Not coming from an academic background, it's pretty much the only way I know. But that method of writing creates serious problems for me when it comes to *Precious*. It's difficult to write anything coherent at all when what you're watching makes you cry helplessly, from beginning to end, and when you come out of the experience having so much admiration for everyone involved that all you want to do is genuflect. *Precious* pushes every emotional and aesthetic button I enjoy having pushed.

So let me start by saying that I've taken on board some of the criticism of my previous books about my tendency towards hyperbole. This time around, I've been trying to avoid statements of the 'this is the bestest bestest thing ever ever ever!!!' variety. But I think I can venture this much towards this movie, hyperbolically speaking. It is the one teen movie that everyone should see.

It may be specifically about the African-American underclass. Its fictional scenario might be extreme. But it is, on some universal level, about the abuse of children, and about the reasons why children grow into teenagers who do things we fear and hate. It's all also about why the overwhelming majority of those wretched victims overcome the worst start in life and find a decency within themselves despite everything. It's an extraordinary film to watch when you feel bleak about the values of young people today. And its happy ending does not involve winning a million bucks on a game show. It's about something worth far more than that. It's about winning the strength to say no.

Based upon the novel *Push* by poet and former teacher Sapphire, *Precious* concerns a 16-year-old black girl called Claireece Precious Jones (Sidibe) living in Harlem in 1987. Precious is obese. She can barely read and write. She has been sexually abused by her father since the age of 3 and has been bequeathed two of his children and the HIV virus which will kill him. She is sexually, physically and verbally abused by her mother Mary (Mo'Nique), who despises her for taking her man, and who only sees her daughter as an unpaid housekeeper and passport to the welfare cheque that enable her to sit and watch TV all day.

When her second pregnancy (her first child is a Down's Syndrome girl she has called Mongo, short for Mongoloid, who lives with Precious's grandmother) gets her suspended from school, it is a blessing in disguise. She is sent to an alternative school for troubled girls, where the classes are smaller and the teacher is a beautiful lesbian angel called Blu Rain (Patton), who begins the long process of giving Precious both self-esteem and basic learning. At the same time, a social worker, Ms Weiss (Carey), begins to unravel the horror of Precious's home life. Finally, after the birth of her second child, the escape to a halfway house, and the HIV diagnosis, Precious finds something that could be called a life.

The Dickensian overload of *Precious* divides audiences in two. To many, it's a shock-horror daytime TV story made into Hollywood self-help therapy, which also depicts blacks on welfare as scum, all fathers as absent, and all teachers, social workers and members of the black middle class as saintly fixers of peasant lives. To the rest of us, who have had some glimpse of exactly what the poor are capable of doing to ourselves, it's a brave and inspirational film that makes a traumatic emotional climax out of three women talking in a room, and where the uplifting ending is nothing more or less than not letting the fuckers break you, no matter what.

Because *Precious* is not just about one woman's struggle. It is about a horror at the heart of black people in the richest nation on the planet. This is defined by a scene where Precious looks in the mirror and sees a white blonde looking back, and about her fantasies about light-skinned boyfriends and her white teacher who she'd love to marry her and take her to Westchester, a white, wealthy New York suburb. For anyone who has seen *Good Hair*, Chris Rock's extraordinary documentary about the price – economically, psychologically, politically – of hair weaves for black women, this is as key to *Precious* as the sexual abuse and lack of education. This is a courageous film for African-Americans to make: a story entirely inspired by the self-loathing of black people in America. Director Lee Daniels even confessed his reluctance to show the movie at the Cannes Film Festival ... should he really be showing white Europeans this view of what African-Americans are? He did, and it took some big brass testes.

Sapphire and screenwriter Geoffrey S. Fletcher's language is visceral on the subject: allowing Precious to describe herself as an animal, and her race as 'ugly black grease'. Even the food – the pig's feet and greasy chicken – that dominates so much of the interaction between Precious and Mary is presented as so repulsive that it represents a sordid masochism. With the likes of Oprah Winfrey, much-criticised black film-maker Tyler Perry, Mariah Carey, Lenny Kravitz and Mary J. Blige involved, this is the elite of black America – the role models and aspirational icons of *Ebony* magazine and the Black Entertainment Channel – collaborating to confess that black

America despises itself. It's the politics and social-historical subtexts of *Precious* that make it such a powerful and crucial film. For once, the private horror of one individual's bad life is placed in an honest political context, and then delivered with the vision of an art piece and the skill of pure entertainment.

Because the most remarkable thing about *Precious* is that it's at all watchable. It shows us, in relatively graphic detail, one of the bleakest worlds that a movie has ever depicted. Yet it is never a film that you want to just switch off. Much of this is down to Daniels's deftness as a storyteller, constantly following something dark and horrific with an image or a phrase or a joke or a song that shines a light into the abyss, using the fantasy survival mechanisms of Precious as relief. Even the voiceover – usually the first cinematic refuge of the hack scoundrel – is wonderful here, dropping short, sharp, first-person thoughts into the action that illuminate Precious's constant swings between pessimism and defiance, and occasionally breaking your heart with understated and universal truths ('I wish I could sit at the back of the class again', is, in the context of our heroine's attempt to integrate into a small classroom full of prettier and more confident strangers, an especially acute line to anyone who has ever been presented with a real opportunity but felt too terrified of failure to grasp it).

But most of it is down to Ms Sidibe … a debut film actress who enthusiastically allows herself to look like a monster, but still, somehow, through some kind of magic that I don't pretend to understand, emerges as someone not pitiable, but fully lovable. She is the antidote to every pointlessly blank and amoral teen of post-*Kids* (see p. 328) cinema I've had the misfortune of having to meet on this journey through teen cinema. It's a performance beyond great acting. It embodies the very best qualities of the human spirit. The day this girl walked into an audition is the day that Daniels had a movie, rather than an ordeal.

There are a few minutes, early in the movie, where Precious has to attend to her mother's sexual needs (offscreen, incidentally, and this is crucial; an ugly mother raping her obese daughter is just too much to show in any detail, and Daniels knows it, and constantly gives us new and shocking information and then has the good grace to move away before we just up and leave the cinema), then steal a bucket of ten chicken pieces from a local black business, then stuff herself, and then, made sick by her own greed, vomit into a bin.

Somehow, Sidibe and Daniels make this haunting and . . . compelling. Precious never feels like exploitation when every second of it could. Because Sidibe possesses a light that never goes out.

But she is matched all the way by Mo'Nique. I rarely think about actors as people who sacrifice for their job, but this vivacious and pretty comedienne's performance as Mary Lee Johnston is among the bravest things anyone has put on screen. Because Mary is scum. Abusive, bullying, sick scum, with no saving graces lent to her by circumstances or mental health problems or even the glamour that the bad guy role usually lends to any character. She is as repulsively ugly as she is bereft of morality or humanity, and, again, she could be just too nasty to be remotely believable. But Mo'Nique makes her real, and this is where the courage comes in, because I don't think anyone will look at Mo'Nique, the real person, in the same way ever again. She dredged something terrible up from inside her to give Mary truth. Something that is hers and hers alone. No one wants people to see the worst that they can be, so to do this in a film seen by millions takes an absence of fear and vanity that I can barely comprehend.

When Mo'Nique speaks to Precious, she conjures the legacy of slavery. Because this 'mother' *is* a slave-master, and a reminder that black people were and are every bit as capable of utter fascism as those who ripped Africans from their lives and homes and forced them to build America at gunpoint. Black people are not lent nobility by racism in *Precious*. Goodness is something earned, and victim status is not enough to justify evil. Again, Mary is not given a back-story that justifies her sexual, physical and verbal abuse of her own daughter. This is deliberate, because nothing could justify her actions.

So Mo'Nique has to work within a vacuum of morality, and, again, be watchable. The scenes within the dark, claustrophobic home are so filled with a tension entirely created by the depths of Mary's depravity that you feel, when we get back to the comparative safety of the street, hospital or classroom, as relieved to escape Mary as Precious does. She is a monster way beyond anything dreamed up for a horror flick, because she makes you believe that she exists, and that, right at this very moment, a child somewhere on the planet is having to live with her and attempt to survive. She is the embodiment of every one of those true-life crimes involving mothers killing their children through violence or neglect . . . plus all those Myra Hindleys and Rose Wests who behave in ways that we don't want to believe women are capable of, and therefore attract our outrage far more readily than the male equivalent. Her self-justifying speech in the scene in Ms Weiss's office is worse than her violence, because it insists that this woman has learned nothing, possesses no remorse, is nothing more than an overgrown child entirely driven by her own wants at any given second, and bemused, even hurt, that anyone would question her for that. You imagine that she will go to her grave convinced that a father's repeated rape of her daughter was her daughter's fault, and cursing the world for not seeing it from her point of view. Mary is a character beyond the pale; every human's worst nightmare. What a fucking *star* Mo'Nique is.

So I watch *Precious* and I cry a lot. I buy into the idea that any child feeling ill-treated at home or suffering from chronic lack of self-esteem might watch this movie and use it as fuel for the inner-strength to survive and move on. I love the film because it sets itself against the dominant cultural theory of the day that political film-making must be emotionally cold, or the other dominant theory that art film must be bereft of a desire to say something, hiding behind the 'audiences can make their own minds up' all-purpose get-out clause. The makers of *Precious* are as angry at the black poor as they are at the society that creates their petri dish. They want us to know. And they don't care how that makes them look. Fair fucking play.

* *

FISH TANK

2009

Starring: Katie Jarvis, Kierston Wareing, Michael Fassbender, Rebecca Griffiths
Dir.: Andrea Arnold

Plot: *Meantime* meets *Le Haine* meets *A Taste Of Honey* in the London that isn't London.
Key line: 'I like you. I'll kill you last.'

Fifteen-year-old Mia Williams always seems to move with a purpose. This is unusual, when she appears not to go to school, and doesn't work, and is in a place which could be defined by its aimlessness. But we often have to run to keep up with her, as she tries to free a horse, or wades into a river, or headbutts a girl in the face. She is almost always alone, and says little, and when she does it's usually abuse, so you have to watch her. You have to watch her because you want to know what she's thinking. You have to watch her because you know she's extraordinary, but she doesn't, so you know she's going to do something very, very wrong.

A casting director working for British docu-drama director Andrea Arnold spotted Mia – or, rather, the girl who plays her, Katie Jarvis – on a platform at Tilbury railway station. She was shouting, arguing with her boyfriend. Arnold, who had already won acclaim for her equally excellent debut film *Red Road*, made the angry girl the star of her second movie. She had never acted before. Had no idea she wanted to. Hasn't since, despite being nominated for awards and signing to a hotshot agency.

Katie – or rather, Mia, the girl she plays – lives in a shitty flat in a bleak council estate in East London. Except this isn't real East London. This is the no man's land between city and suburb that is Havering, or something like it. She only wears vests and grey track-suit bottoms, and she's wire-thin. She dances to classic hip hop . . . it's the only thing she likes to do, and she thinks she could maybe do it professionally. Her favourite seems to be 'Juice (Know The Ledge)' by Rakim, which was the theme to a teen movie called *Juice* starring Tupac Shakur. Everyone dances on her estate. They make life where it doesn't exist.

Mia sees horses and tries to free them. The travellers who have this particular horse tied up catch her and try to molest her. But a third boy with a dog rescues her.

Mia lives with her mother Joanna (Wareing) and her little sister Tyler (Griffiths). We don't know where Dad is. Her mother looks barely old enough to have a teenage daughter. She has parties where everyone gets drunk and women get fingered in the kitchen and no one cares that Mia and her funny, foul-mouthed sister are there.

Joanna has a boyfriend. He's a handsome Irish rogue who has loud sex with Joanna. But, while Joanna can't wait to get rid of Mia at every opportunity, Connor (Fassbender) seems to like Mia's company. When she tells him he's a dick he just laughs. He takes liberties, like spanking her. He invites Mia and Tyler out on a drive to a river, and Mia feels the sun in her eyes and the wind in her hair, and he plays Bobby Womack's version of 'California Dreamin'' at top volume. He shows Mia how to catch fish without a rod. He dances with her to James Brown in a pub car park. But Joanna ruins it. And Mia walks away, with purpose, to who knows where.

Mia begins to turn up at Wickes, the DIY warehouse where Connor works. But she also hangs out with Billy, the boy who rescued her. She hangs around while he scavenges through car scrapyards. He's a friend but Connor makes her want to compete with her mother. He asks her to smell his cologne and time moves slowly.

She practises her dancing. She posts a letter.

One night, Connor can't sleep after sex with Joanna. Mia joins him in the lounge and tells him that the letter was an application for a dancing job. She wants to show him her audition piece, a dance to 'California Dreamin''. For once, the stark light outside the window is romantic. The dance is not great, but it is poignant, and vulnerable, and it does what it sets out to do. Connor breaks laws – the official one about the age of consent, and the bigger, unofficial one about not fucking your girlfriend's daughter. The next morning he dumps Joanna. 'Did I tell you I almost had you aborted,' Joanna mumbles. 'I even made the appointment.'

Now Mia has a real purpose. She finds Connor's address. She marches down a dual carriageway. Billy tries to attract her attention but you can't interrupt Mia once she gets something into her head. She walks all the way to an altogether different kind of housing estate. Here, there are new houses and grass verges and birds sing. Connor is home. He won't let her in. He drives her to Tilbury station where her alter-ego accidentally shouted herself into a new life months before. But she doesn't get on the train. It isn't over. She walks back in the rain to Connor's house.

There is no answer so she breaks into the garden. She has a purpose. She breaks into the house. She finds a digital camcorder. She pushes a button and there is a little girl singing, and a woman kneeling proudly next to her. For a second, Mia is lost for a purpose. But it doesn't take long. She pisses on the lounge carpet. She is almost caught by the singing girl and the proud woman, but leaps over the garden fence.

But she can't leave. It isn't over. She spies on the loving nuclear family from a few doors down. The little girl rides past Mia on a scooter. Mia has a purpose again. When the little girl rides by again, she calls her name, 'Keira!' The little girl talks to the nice lady who wants to play a game. And of course she goes with her. The nice lady has a purpose . . .

The way Arnold suddenly switches a slice of life into every parent's worst nightmare, and trusts that you will not completely despise the battered Mia, is one of the most brave, shocking, heart-stopping things I've ever felt in a cinema. It isn't over, of course. There is worse to come . . . and then something that struggles towards better, and the possibility of new life. And that dance audition is exactly what you thought it would be. But Arnold still manages to use women dancing together as an image of reconciliation between people who can't talk about their feelings.

Mia Williams, even though she is flawed beyond belief, even though she has no smartarse high school dialogue or trend-setting hipster slang, is one of the most complete and sympathetic characters in teen fiction. Andrea Arnold's casting director found a real girl that day at Tibury station, and Arnold built something around her that contained elements of so many stars of this book . . . the accusatory ball of chaos Antoine Doinel (see *The 400 Blows*, p. 47); the parentified dreamer Jo (*A Taste Of Honey*, p. 70); the broken child who sees wild life as freedom, Billy Casper (*Kes*, p. 101); the relentless precocious loner Juno MacGuff (see *Juno*, p. 449); the hip hop-informed lost sink estate boys of *Le Haine* (see, p. 336); the endless running towards nothing of Colin Smith (*The Loneliness Of The Long-Distance Runner*, see p. 87).

While the majority of *verité* directors seem content to find dull people, make them do terrible things, and then expect us to watch them instead of whipping ourselves with sticks, Arnold keeps her *Fish Tank* swimming with ideas and strangeness and beauty and grimy comedy, as well as scenes that go beyond 'reality' into horror, and are filmed with a horror master's touch.

Most of all, though, *Fish Tank* discovered someone, in Katie Jarvis, who seemed to symbolise much of what we fear is wrong with working-class Western youth without creating a stereotype, or leaving the viewer with an absence of hope.

Ms Jarvis was much praised for her performance, but has not appeared in anything else yet. She did become a mother in 2009, a little before her eighteenth birthday.

★ ★

THE SOCIAL NETWORK

2010
Starring: Jesse Eisenberg, Andrew Garfield, Justin Timberlake, Brenda Song
Dir.: David Fincher

Plot: The geek shall inherit the Earth.
Key line: 'You are probably going to be a very successful computer person. But you're going to go through life thinking that girls don't like you because you're a nerd. And I want you to know from the bottom of my heart that that won't be true. It'll be because you're an asshole.'

I think most of us who love film fantasise, occasionally, about doing it. No, not directing; that looks like really hard work. And screenwriting ... well, yeah, I suppose, if you can write. But it doesn't have that Top Of The World, Ma buzz. How many screenwriters can you name? They're the bit at the Oscars where we go for a piss.

By doing it, I mean acting. Sixty-foot-high face on a huge screen. Immortality by default. Lots of dinner party stories about spending three months in Guantanamo Bay to research my motivation and how much fun it was to work with Marty, Quenty and Chow Yun Fatty. Groovy. I mean, I was the lead in the school play a couple of times – my Selfish Giant was very highly regarded – and Russell Brand can do it, so how hard can it be?

But there's one aspect of acting that terrifies me. Not fight scenes or hanging off buildings engulfed by fireballs ... that's what stunt doubles are for, right? Getting me kit off? No problem. I fix Clea DuVall with my best seducto eyes, rip my shirt off ... and they CGI in the body of David Boreanaz and everyone's a winner. No, there's just one recurring acting dream that wakes me up with cold sweats and the sneering taunts of Martin Sheen still ringing in my ears.

I walk on to a set for my first big break. Someone hands me my lines. Alison Janney and Matthew Perry and Jesse Eisenberg wish me luck, but exchange knowing looks. I look down at the script, and it says, at the top, in fancy lettering that looks like it's been written by way of quill dipped in the blood of failed actors: 'Written by Aaron Sorkin'. High-pitched violins shriek. But only I can hear them.

Suddenly, the director yells action and Janney, Eisenberg and Perry are all talking really quickly, without pausing. Every word I can make out sounds like an especially high-falutin' newspaper column, complete with relevant stats, 18-syllable words, obscure acronyms and a final gag that allows each of them to smile wryly for exactly 0.0047 seconds before the next speaker finds the perfect riposte, without blinking or breathing. I think they're talking about the Middle East or quantum physics or Dick Chaney's poll ratings, but it could be about which of Haydn's 104 symphonies has the most sophisticated harmonic counterpoint. And it goes on. And on. And on, and suddenly . . . they all stop. And look at me. It's my cue. Time stops, turns inside out, expands to the size of John Goodman before contracting to one-millionth of the circumference of Paris Hilton's single brain cell. I sweat, and giggle, and then wet myself. A stain spreads across the crotch of my white trousers (I'm playing a sailor). A Japanese girl with unfeasibly long, straw-like black hair climbs out of a camera and crawls towards me, grinning. And Russell Brand is standing behind the director, laughing manically and stroking a white cat . . .

I'll stop now. What I'm saying is that Aaron Sorkin writes scripts comprising lots of very clever words which, no matter which director is in charge, are required to be said very quickly in endlessly overlapping conversations, and where the actor in question is still required to be charming and funny. It's like Howard Hawks directing the thoughts of Groucho Marx, Gore Vidal and Stephen Hawking simultaneously. *The West Wing* was entirely made up of this, as if Sorkin was attempting to give the viewer a complete history of every US Presidential dilemma since Lincoln while looking impatiently at his watch and juggling apples. It's heady, intimidating stuff.

When it doesn't work – see Sorkin's awful TV exec drama *Studio 60 On Sunset Strip* – it makes for smug, alienating viewing. But when it does – the glory of *The West Wing* – it is a profoundly inspiring celebration of intelligence and reason and their part in any admirable moral compass. *The West Wing* restores your faith in politics. But *The Social Network* does . . . something else.

The presence of Fincher's modern classic at the very end of this book is a happy accident. *Submarine* came out after this, but turned out to be shit. But that was a lucky break because *The Social Network* really is the perfect finish.

We began, 57 years ago, with a boy in sexy clothes riding a motorcycle around America and causing trouble. His life is entirely exterior. Girls adore him. He is rebelling against everything, including language, as he is barely able to mumble anything beyond 'fire bad, tree pretty'. He has no money, no home, no future, and he is thrilling and shaggable for those very reasons. The film he is in gave a name to the biggest musical group of all time, changed fashion, transformed acting styles, invented teensploitation and gave a prescient face and shape to the 'children's crusade' that was the 1960s. But critics hated it and still do, unable to look past its exploitation agenda and camp melodrama, unable to relate to a hero who is all action and no words – except, of course, for the two words (is 'Whaddya' one word or three?) that shook the whole of Western culture.

Fifty-seven years later, and the hero of the most commercially successful and critically acclaimed teen movie of his day has no interest in style. He sits in a small dark room in a university, stares at a computer screen and taps away on a keyboard. His life is entirely interior. Girls reject him. He is so articulate that one can barely keep up with what he is saying, yet he is socially inept. He is every bit as arrogant and contemptuous as Wild Johnny, but Johnny's inner confidence is based on knowledge of his sex appeal and capacity for violence, whereas Mark Zuckerberg's inner confidence derives entirely from his IQ and his understanding of what young people really want.

The major thing the two have in common is independence. Parents don't appear in their story. They're an irrelevance. They are lone frontiersmen with no use for adult mentoring or intervention.

But Johnny is, in economic and political terms, a born loser. A trophy for second place in a race taunts him ... and he had to steal that. There is no place for him in the real America. You can imagine a future for him where he gets used by various women for sex before they marry someone with prospects. Spends a few months here and there in jail. When his looks and energy finally go, he'll be a school janitor or a fat, drunk mechanic, reminiscing about his glory days when he led a gang and people who now own his ass once trembled in fear.

Mark is the proof that all the people who tried to lecture Johnny about staying in school and getting off his bike and looking for work were right. He is the physically weak and aesthetically challenged nerd that every teen movie that Johnny inspired insisted was a loser, for no other reason than young people wouldn't want to watch him, or be him, or fuck him. But, after 50-plus years of the corporate world hard-selling youth, endlessly questing for the next big (young) thing, inventing technologies that only kids truly understand, the nerd is now The Master Of The Universe. The modern world has been created for him to exploit. Our terror of the young is contrasted with our awe of them, and no one asks if the kid has enough experience any more, or makes him make the tea, doff his cap and pay his dues. So he sits in his dark and lonely room, and invents the modern world by pushing buttons (we used to think he would destroy the world by pushing buttons; see *WarGames*, p. 233), and acquires the kind of money, power and glory that people three times his age can only dream of. So much so that Aaron Sorkin and David Fincher make films about him, and millions watch them, and wish they were him, even though he's a wanker.

It's a teenager's world now, whether they're inventing the way we communicate or firebombing our house. They just allow us to live in it.

So Fincher applies his art of darkness to a true-life get-rich-quick story that should not push our thrill buttons. A boy (Eisenberg) invents a misogynist website as revenge for being dumped. It's a hit. Twin Harvard rich boys employ the boy as a programmer for their Harvard-only dating website. The boy accepts, but develops the idea into something called Thefacebook and persuades his friend (Garfield) to invest money and partner up. Thefacebook is a hit. While the twins decide whether to sue the boy for stealing their idea, the boy is introduced to the flash git (Timberlake) who invented illegal music file-sharing site Napster. He suggests dropping the 'the' and they expand Facebook's reach. It's a hit. But Napster Git is slyly manoeuvring the boy's mate out of the picture and spending the money on drugs and loose women, and everything collapses into lawsuits and home truths about greed and ambition.

This doesn't stop social networking on computers becoming the biggest cultural hit since rock 'n' roll. And everyone goes home with big bags of money. So why the fuck should we care?

Well, Sorkin's corking screenplay, Fincher's sepia tones and coolly detached camera, and an extraordinary young ensemble cast led by Eisenberg, Garfield and the big happy shock of the annoyingly talented Trousersnake have plenty to do with it. But once you cut through the film's terribly modern sense of ironic distance, visual integrity and lack of traditional melodrama, it plays one of the oldest Hollywood tricks in the book: the capitalist comfort-food trick.

You know the one. You've spent your last pennies entering the cinema. All you can think about is your shit job and whether you can afford the mortgage and your kids' new shoes this month. And the next couple of hours of pictures puts an arm around you and tells you what you need to hear in order to just keep going until someone finally pays you a pitiful pension and consigns you to final years of visiting stately homes and being horrible to your family. It tells you that The Rich aren't happy. That they're not as nice as you. That the reason that they have everything and you have nothing is actually *because* they're not as nice as you. And this one has real legs, because it's about real millionaires who are still alive and didn't sue anyone when they were portrayed as bitter, greedy, elitist, misogynist asswipes. So it must be true. Ergo, the reason you must accept your lot and play the game is because people don't get money and power in this world unless they are soulless monsters. So accept your place, and like it. Because you're *nice*.

It's pretty funny that the teen movie, of all genres, has finally come to this. The settings and the characters' attitudes to class, money, ambition and gender in *The Social Network* are almost identical to the comically fascistic WASPs in *National Lampoon's Animal House* (see p. 161), way back in the punk era. Hell, the Winkelvoss twins (both played by Armie Hammer with the assistance of CGI and body double Josh Pence) even look, dress, talk and glare down their noses like all-rowing versions of Marmalard and Neidermeyer. What was revenge comedy exaggeration is now presented as serious docudrama. Rather than contesting their lawsuit, Zuckerberg should have just thrown a toga party and attacked the twins with golf balls.

I'm not knocking; 100 Best is what the cover says and *The Social Network* enters that list with ease. It's by some way the most mature and unlikely thriller made out of teenagers coming of age. It's just amusing that it is seen as a more substantial film than, say, *Teeth* or *Kidulthood* because there are long shots of skies and buildings, because everyone talks really quickly, because its colours are muted, because it's not 'genre', because there's no physical action and because its lead protagonist doesn't show emotions. Some things have not changed in 57 years and movie critics are among them.

And what about this whole Faction thing that has become increasingly popular and accepted? When did it become OK to fictionalise the lives of people when they are still alive? Is this a good or bad thing? Why don't these people sue? Is it because being portrayed for all eternity as an utter tosspot is still better than being ignored? When asked about the film by Oprah Winfrey, the real Zuckerberg said, 'This is my life. So I know it's not so dramatic.' But once they make a Hollywood blockbuster about you, is it really your life any more? Complete strangers believe they know you and your darkest secrets. Is that the final irony, that the big winners of today get to own everything – except themselves?

All of these questions and more will almost certainly be answered by future cinematic images of teens. Now *The Social Network* has been a success, one expects that movie execs are trawling the sewers of pulp fiction and reality TV, looking for true teens to fictionalise. Some of them will be Zuckerbergs. Others will, I suspect, be real-life versions of Claireece Precious Jones (see *Precious*, p. 477), parading their most degrading dirty linen in front of us in order to keep hope alive and make themselves immortal. The thing that will affect the teen movie most in the future will be the abolition of privacy, something that the protagonists of *The Social Network* have done much to establish. After all these visions, in the films in this book, of incest and paedophilia, parental violence and rampant bullying, extreme violence and sexual nihilism ... what stories will film need to tell to satiate our jaded palates? Can't be sure. But I think the strange success of *The Social Network* may offer clues. More talking than sex or violence. Wildly fictionalised accounts of recent events. People you can't love, but you do recognise. A comforting message hiding behind a cool disregard for hugging and learning. And a pale young man, sitting at a computer, hitting the refresh button, waiting for a message that never comes, isolated by a method of communication that is killing human interaction and that he invented himself. 'I can't connect,' Zuckerberg says, at the beginning of his journey to riches.

The kids used to go to the drive-in and watch themselves with others. Now they watch themselves at home, in the dark, alone. We've come a long way in 57 years. From the Atomic Age to atomised. But we've still washed up in the same place. Stranded.

★ ★

MOVIES THAT DIDN'T MAKE IT

So . . . you've invested in this here weighty tome. And cheers, by the way. But you've done what most people do in these situations and rifled through the index to find your favourite teen movie . . . and it isn't there. Because you love this film so much, you can only imagine that I've failed to do my research and completely forgotten it, and you're now preparing that stiff letter to Orion evoking the Trades Descriptions Act. Let me save you the bother. I did see your favourite teen movie. I don't like it. Or, at least, I don't like it enough to put it in my Top 100 list. Hence this here epilogue, where I briefly explain my reasons for omitting what I suspect are the best known and loved teen movies that didn't make the cut.

I figured I'd kick off with the movie which, if conversations I've had about the book over the last 18 months are anything to go by, is the absence which will upset most readers of an '80s vintage. Alan Parker's *Fame* (1980) spawned hit records, a wildly popular spin-off TV series and a craze for leg warmers. But, really, don't be taken in by your nostalgia. Its an awful, *awful* movie, packed with scenery-chewing bad acting, gags that aren't funny, rubbish songs, terrible dancing and, in Leroy, the least convincing Angry Black Boy From The Projects in cinematic history. Plus its stage school setting is the beginning of the whole thing about masses of young people believing that they are entitled to be famous just 'cos they really, really want it. Which they're not. So I hate it. While we're on the subject of the erratic Parker, his *Birdy* (1984) has enough adolescent flashback in it to count as a teen movie, but it's also a laughable hippy throwback whereby Matthew Modine escapes his Vietnam experiences by imagining he's a bird, which involves him crouching a lot and occasionally making a bird noise, while Nicholas Cage keeps wailing 'Birdeee!!!' at him through broken teeth. Why didn't they just call a Viet vet? *Viet vet!* No? Tough crowd.

The '80s is the decade most associated with the American teen movie. But the deluge of films made, blended with Reagan-era politics, ensured there were plenty of mediocrities and utter dogs. Even The Teen Master John Hughes was not unaffected. *Sixteen Candles*

(1984) nearly got in because it *is* Hughes's first directorial stab at the high school movie and stars the sainted Molly Ringwald (see *The Breakfast Club*, p. 263, *Pretty In Pink*, p. 275), but later and better Hughes movies render it redundant. *Some Kind Of Wonderful* (1987) is just a lame-ass gender-switch *Pretty In Pink*. And *Weird Science* (1985), in which two high school losers make a 'perfect' woman with, like, weird science, is Hughes's sterling attempt to win the Most Sexist Feminist Backlash Teen Movie Of The Reagan Era award, but isn't vile enough to match up to *Porky's* (1982), *Revenge Of The Nerds* (1984) or bizarre pre-Reagan Israeli entry *Lemon Popsicle* (1978).

Still, in the gratuitous offence stakes, even that set of bitch-baiting bottom-feeders have to genuflect in the general direction of the extraordinary *Soul Man* (1986), in which a blacked-up C. Thomas Howell (see *The Outsiders*, p. 226) takes pills to make himself African-American so he can get a scholarship to Harvard. I know. I barely know where to start, but I'll finish by pointing out that Leslie Nielsen, Julia Louis-Dreyfus and – Gawd help us – James Earl Jones were somehow dragged into this black and white minstrel revival attempt. Rumours of a remake with Justin Bieber and Morgan Freeman were unconfirmed at press time.

Sticking with the '80s, Cameron Crowe's two stabs at high school movies, *Fast Times At Ridgemont High* (1982, written by Crowe, directed by Amy Heckerling) and *Say Anything* (1989) are star-studded and often cited as 'intelligent' and 'adult' takes on the teen movie genre. But, like all Crowe movies, they are actually bland exercises in self-regarding middlebrow cool. *Pump Up The Volume* (1990) is in a similar vein, undercutting a great performance by Christian Slater (see *Heathers*, p. 295) as a rebel pirate DJ with its ludicrous fight-the-power plot.

The enduring appeal of the *I Was A Teenage Werewolf* (see p. 35) idea sired a couple of hugely popular '80s remixes. *The Lost Boys* (1987) is stylish and influential but ultimately soulless, while *Teen Wolf* (1985) is an embarrassment. Mystifyingly, the latter remained cultish enough to justify a current TV series revival.

At least *Teen Wolf* wasn't meant to be scary. But I remain consistently baffled by the continuing success of Sean S. Cunningham's teen slasher megahit *Friday The 13th* (1980). A slew of sequels, Jason merchandise and spin-offs, an awful recent remake, and *still* the cheap and nasty original is so clunky and badly shot that not even a young Kevin Bacon (see *Footloose*, p. 251) can save it. Similarly, the presence of Scream Queen Jamie Lee Curtis (see *Halloween*, p. 169) isn't enough to make 1980 Canadian teen horrors *Terror Train* and *Prom Night* any less predictable than their titles suggest. Far closer to sneaking in, slasher-wise, was *I Know What You Did Last Summer* (1997), but its ingeniously daft crime-and-punishment plotting just doesn't have the savage wit of even the worst of the *Final Destination* (see p. 385) movies.

I Know What's star Freddie Prinze Jr – probably better known these days as Mr Sarah Michelle Gellar – popped up again in *She's All That* (1999), an attempt to give George Bernard Shaw's *Pygmalion* (aka *My Fair Lady*) a high school makeover. He needn't have bothered. The same year's *10 Things I Hate About You*, which tried the same trick on Shakespeare's *The Taming Of The Shrew*, has a few choice moments due to a strong cast, including Julia Stiles, Heath Ledger and Joseph Gordon-Levitt (see *Mysterious Skin*, p. 428), but just isn't a tale designed to survive these post-feminist times. But the worst of the teened-up literary classics comes courtesy of one of those serious and respected American art directors. *My Own Private Idaho* (1991) sees Gus Van Sant (see *Elephant*, p. 418) update Shakespeare's *Henry IV* plays by way of a book about gay hustlers, a B.52's song, River Phoenix and Keanu Reeves and make a godawful mess that somehow bestowed cool upon everybody involved. The early '90s was just trying so hard not to be the '80s that any old pretentious cack seemed preferable to *Police Academy 5*.

While we're on the subject of Keanu, I, like, totally get how influential *Bill & Ted's Excellent Adventure* (1989) and *Bill & Ted's Bogus Journey* (1991) are. But the only actual funny thing is when they grin moronically and play air guitar and a guitar screeches, and I don't think you can really base two movies on one gag. *Wayne's World* (1992) and its sequel are much, *much* funnier, but Wayne and Garth aren't teens. It's the same joke as *Harold And Kumar Get The Munchies* (2004); that is, the main characters are much too old to be behaving like this.

From the other side of that spectrum, *Confessions Of A Teenage Drama Queen* (2004) and *The Karate Kid* (1984) are both cute enough enterprises. But, despite featuring teen protagonists, they are both clearly aimed at pre-teen children.

There are two good reasons why *Dead Poet's Society* (1989) isn't here. One is Robin. The other is Williams. If I were commissioned to write books on The Top 100 Movies About Enchanted Board Games, The Top 100 Movies About Rebellious DJs in Vietnam Army Bases and The Top 100 Happy Days Spin-Offs Involving An Alien, I would still find a way to not include Robin Williams. O Captain, my Captain, my big hairy arse.

Dead Poet's Society is part of a tradition of movies about inspiring teachers who triumph against the overwhelming odds of not being Sidney Poitier (see *To Sir, With Love*, p. 90). The most infamously awful was *Dangerous Minds* (1995) which reckoned we'd buy ethnic savages being tamed by Michele Pfeiffer, but did give the world 'Gangsta's Paradise' by Coolio so fair play. Not quite as patronising (but almost) was *Freedom Writers* (2007), where Hilary Swank played another real-life white teacher who apparently gets ghetto sainthood for, you know, *doing her job.*

There were a few movies I expected to include and was surprised how disappointed I was when seeing them for the first time in many years. I loved *Big Wednesday* back in 1978, but obviously surfing and post-Vietnam hand-wringing doesn't do it for me any more, so macho screenwriting legend John Milius is represented solely by *Red Dawn* (see p. 245). Neither Richard Linklater's *subUrbia* (1996) nor Penelope Spheeris's *Suburbia* (1984) are dramatic or insightful enough to hold the attention, despite the track records of their directors and the authenticity of their settings.

The biggest surprise omission, from my perspective anyway, was Alan Clarke's *Scum* (1979), the controversial punk-era borstal exposé from the director of *Made In Britain* (see p. 210). The movie made Ray Winstone a star and induced a generation or two of geezers to shout 'OO's The Daddy Now?' at each other after one too many lagers. But *fuck me* has it dated, with its Chim Chim Cheree accents and hysterical, depressing tone which seemed to suggest that every petty crim was just an oppressed anti-establishment revolutionary-in-waiting. It had an evil sister too, called *Scrubbers* (1983), which almost crept into the book on account of starring the most comically butch women ever featured in a movie. But, Kathy Burke aside, the acting was just too appalling, and most of the prisoners looked 40.

Other Brit rejects included *Bronco Bullfrog* (1970), a London-based docu-drama which has a cult following derived from its documenting of the mod-meets-skinhead subculture known as suedehead.

All very worthy, all very dull, much like Richard Ayoade's *Submarine* (2010), apart from the worthy bit. Another surprise for me was just how awful Bill Forsyth's hit Scottish school comedy *Gregory's Girl* (1981) is 30 years after seeming revolutionary. My generation just hadn't seen ourselves depicted onscreen unless we were in borstal, rioting in Brighton or training a kestrel. So we ignored the lousy direction, awful acting, terrible incidental music . . . things you can't ignore three decades later. Not guilty of any of the above is tough Brixton reggae drama *Babylon* (1980). It just didn't *quite* make the Top 100, and this was partly because I'd written about it in my rock movies book *Popcorn*, and had little else to say.

The same goes for high school movie spoof *Rock 'n' Roll High School* (1979), which, while being lovable cult entertainment, is in the end made by the presence of the Ramones, Mary Woronov (see *Night Of The Comet*, p. 241) and P.J. Soles (see *Carrie*, p. 150 and *Halloween*, p. 169), rather than the gags. The post-*Scary Movie* teen spoof *Not Another Teen Movie* (2001) has its moments, but the cynicism is wearing.

African-American teen cinema is notable only by its absence. John Singleton's *Boyz N The Hood* felt like a major movie in 1991, again, because no one had seen the lives of ordinary black American kids in a mainstream movie before. But two decades later the sentimentality and one-dimensional preachiness is dated and cloying, and has been put firmly in its place by the extraordinary achievement that was Season Four of TV cop show *The Wire*. The same goes for fellow teen gangsta dramas *Juice* (1992) and *Menace II Society* (1993). African-American teen comedies *Cooley High* (1975) and *House Party* (1990) are worth a look for the lurid depictions of the fashions and dance styles of their time. You'll wait a long time for a laugh, though.

It's not all about Hollywood, of course. I was very excited about seeing critically acclaimed Mexican teen movie *Y Tu Mama Tambien* (2001), but then it turned out to be puerile male wish-fulfilment after all. *Mon Père, Ce Héros* (1991), with its sly take on a semi-incestuous father–daughter relationship, was a contender, but, like the same year's *Flirting*, the Australian teen drama that introduced Nicole Kidman to the world, it was just a little slow and cosy. Also from Australia and presenting a future superstar, *Romper Stomper* (1992) went all out to give us some Alan Clarke-style shock-horror about fascist skinheads but would have been comically bad without the intensity and authority of Russell Crowe. Michael Haneke is a taste I'm increasingly chuffed not to have acquired, and his *Benny's Video* (1992) is just a duller and nastier take on the themes of *Elephant*.

And it's back to The States for the home straight. *High School Confidential* (1958) and *Gidget* (1959) made an early teen movie case for inclusion but *The Cool And The Crazy* (see p. 39) and *Where The Boys Are* (see p. 57), respectively, make better fists of similar themes. More recently, teen madness drama *Girl, Interrupted* (1999) under-cuts a great cast with rather too much hugging and learning, Hal Hartley's *Trust* (1991) starts in the middle of nowhere and decides to stay there, and Coppola's *Peggy Sue Got Married* (1986) is *Back To The Future* (see p. 259) on valium. One oddity worth tracking down is *The Little Girl Who Lives Down The Lane* (1976), a novelistic forerunner of *Hard Candy* (see p. 435) starring Martin Sheen (see *Badlands*, p. 138) as the paedophile and Jodie Foster as the lone teen heroine. A little too self-conscious and disjointed to merit inclusion, but great acting.

The teen movie has, as I've argued elsewhere, reached its peak as a sub-genre since the beginning of the new century. Cue seven movies that only failed to make the list because there were just too many recent crackers to include them all. *Freaky Friday* (2003) updated a lightweight Disney body swap comedy from 1976 (which also starred Jodie Foster) to charming effect by teaming Lindsay Lohan (see *Mean Girls*, p. 424) and Jamie Lee Curtis (see *Halloween*, p. 169); *Winter's Bone* (2010) was a gritty American gothic thriller with a teen protagonist; and *Kick Ass* was a neat subversion of the superhero genre sadly scuppered by a jarring, over-violent last act.

Our last near-misses all feature talents struggling to match the excellence of *Juno* (see p. 449). Diablo Cody's follow-up screenplay to *Juno*, *Jennifer's Body* (2009), couldn't quite pull off its teen *femme* serial killer conceit. *Nick And Norah's Infinite Playlist* (2008) and *Youth In Revolt* (2009) make you worry for Michael Cera's prospects of playing anything else but gentle teen misfits well into his sixties. Final nod goes to the greatest young acting talent of her generation, Ellen Page. Roller derby comedy *Whip It* (2009) is probably Number 101 when it comes right down to it, not least because it's the first movie directed by Drew Barrymore (see *Scream*, p. 339 and *Donnie Darko*, p. 405).

INDEX